Law | Book | Culture in the Middle Ages

Explorations in Medieval Culture

VOLUME 14

The titles published in this series are listed at *brill.com/emc*

Law | Book | Culture in the Middle Ages

Edited by

Thom Gobbitt

BRILL

LEIDEN | BOSTON

Cover illustration: Detail of fol. 148v. of Madrid, BNE, MS 413, Codex legum longobardorum. With kind permission of the Biblioteca Nacional de España, Madrid.

FWF (Austrian Science Fund), Project No. P-29968 "Lombard Law-Books and Book Culture, 850–1025", (May 01, 2017 to April 30, 2020)

Library of Congress Cataloging-in-Publication Data

Names: Gobbitt, Thom, editor, author.
Title: Law | book | culture in the Middle Ages / edited by Thom Gobbitt.
Description: Leiden,The Netherlands : Koninklijke Brill NV, [2021] | Series: Explorations in medieval culture, 2352-0299 ; volume 14 | Includes bibliographical references and index.
Identifiers: LCCN 2020052235 (print) | LCCN 2020052236 (ebook) | ISBN 9789004448346 (hardback) | ISBN 9789004448650 (ebook)
Subjects: LCSH: Law, Medieval–Europe. | Law–Europe–History–To 1500. | Law, Medieval.
Classification: LCC KJ147 .L386 2021 (print) | LCC KJ147 (ebook) | DDC 349.409/02–dc23
LC record available at https://lccn.loc.gov/2020052235
LC ebook record available at https://lccn.loc.gov/2020052236

Typeface for the Latin, Greek, and Cyrillic scripts: "Brill". See and download: brill.com/brill-typeface.

ISSN 2352-0299
ISBN 978-90-04-44834-6 (hardback)
ISBN 978-90-04-44865-0 (e-book)

This book is printed on acid-free paper and produced in a sustainable manner.

Printed by Printforce, United Kingdom

For Matt, Alex and Ellie

Contents

Acknowledgements

First and foremost, I would like to thank the contributors to this collection, both those whose chapters are included here, as well as those who for various personal reasons had to withdraw along the way. Work on this edited collection ran in parallel to my Austrian Science Fund (FWF) postdoctoral research project, "Lombard Law-Books and Book Cultures, 850 to 1025" (Project Number P-29968), and the various perspectives on medieval laws and book cultures it contains enriched that study beyond measure.

Thanks must also go to all those who have helped and advised. While there is not space to name everybody here, Marcella Mulder's patience, hard work and direction are highly appreciated. Likewise, Dr. Larissa Tracy's motivation, and for inviting me to assemble this collection. The considered and beneficial suggestions from the anonymous reviewers are also greatly appreciated and highly valued. Particular thanks must also go to Dr. Bojana Radovanovic, for her dedicated review of the stylesheet—any errors remain my own!

Thank you also to Dr. Jaqueline Bemmer for many fruitful discussions about medieval legal cultures, and particularly for insight and advice relating especially to Irish and Roman law; to Dr. Clemens Gantner, Dr. Rutger Kramer and Dr. Shazia Juna, for conversations and suggestions that have helped me to further contextualize laws and law-books in their historical settings, as well as motivation, encouragement and constructive critique along the way. Finally, thanks go to my family, and especially my mum, who was a great source of enthusiasm in the earlier phases but, sadly, did not live to see the volume completed.

Thom Gobbitt
Vienna, 2020

Figures and Tables

Figures

Tables

Abbreviations

CISAM	Centro Italiano di Studi sull'alto Medioevo
MGH	Monumenta Germaniae Historica
MGH Conc.	Concilia
MGH Epp.	Epistolae (in Quart)
MGH LL	Leges (in Folio)
MGH SS rer.Lang.	Scriptores rerum Langobardicarum et Italicarum
MGH SSRG	Scriptores rerum Germanicarum in usum scholarum separatim editi
PL	Patrologiae Cursus Completus, Series Latina

Notes on Contributors

Rolf H. Bremmer, Jr., Leiden University
Hannah Burrows, University of Aberdeen
Sonia Colafrancesco, Università degli Studi G.D'Annunzio Chieti
Jan van Doren, Princeton University
Stefan Drechsler, University of Bergen
Daniela Fruscione Pistoresi, Frankfurt University
Thom Gobbitt, Austrian Academy of Sciences
Katherine J. Har, Independent scholar
Lucy Hennings, Oxford Internet Institute
Petar Parvanov, Central European University
Fangzhe Dimurjan Qiu, University College Dublin
Ben Reinhard, Christendom College
Sara Elin Roberts, University of Chester
Francesco Sangriso, University of Genoa
Chiara Simbolotti, Università degli Studi di Torino

INTRODUCTION

Law | Book | Culture in the Middle Ages

Thom Gobbitt

Medieval laws, regulatory texts and legal/normative structures have left their trace in the historical record in numerous forms. The following collection brings together a range of chapters looking closely at approaches to law and legal cultures spanning much of the Middle Ages, from the seventh to the fifteenth centuries and beyond. The scope covers much of Western Europe and into Central Europe, examining regions from Norway to Italy, and from Ireland to Bulgaria. Across this broad expanse of time and space, law and legal culture were continuously and significantly reproduced, innovated and developed. A major aim of this collection is to synthesize the approaches of the history of law and the history of the book, and thereby open up further avenues for new interpretations of medieval legal literacy and culture. This collection aims to present a selection of materially and literately engaged readings of laws and legal cultures spanning the Middle Ages.

Much work, of course, has already been done on medieval laws in their manuscript, literate and literary contexts, and the contributors to this volume engage with and expand this well-established tradition. The augmented readings produced by associating multiple texts, legal and otherwise, within a specific manuscript, has been widely discussed in the scholarship of medieval law,[1] and forms a fundamental starting point underlying this collection. The consideration of law as literature is a field of growing significance,[2] as are rep-

1 Mary P. Richards, "The Manuscript Contexts of the Old English Law: Tradition and Innovation," in *Studies in Earlier Old English Prose*, ed. Paul E. Szarmach (New York: SUNY Press, 1986); Stephanie Hollis, "Old English 'Cattle-Theft Charms': Manuscript Contexts and Social Uses," *Anglia: Zeitschrift für Englische Philologie* 115 (1997): 139–64; Patrick Wormald, "Chapter 4. The Manuscripts of Legislation," in *The Making of English Law: King Alfred to the Twelfth Century* (Oxford: Blackwell, 1999), 162–263; Walter Pohl, "Memory, Identity and Power in Lombard Italy," in *The Uses of the Past in the Early Middle Ages*, ed. Yitzhak Hen and Matthew Innes (Cambridge: University Press, 2000); Thom Gobbitt, "Materiality, Stratigraphy and Artefact Biography: Codicological Features of a Late-Eleventh-Century Manuscript of the Lombard Laws," *Studia Neophilologica* 86 (2014): 48–67; Thom Gobbitt, "Palaeographic Preferences and Manuscript Contexts of a Mid-Eleventh-Century English Legal Collection: London, British Library, Cotton MS Nero A. I (Part A)," *Scriptorium* 69 (2015): 61–77.

2 Patrick Wormald, Chapter 6. "Legislation as Literature," in *Making of English Law*, 416–76; Nick Everett, "Literacy and the Law in Lombard Government," *Early Medieval Europe* 9 (2000):

 | DOI:10.1163/9789004448650_002

resentations of law in literature.[3] Contributors to this collection address both of these themes. The direct evidence of manuscripts have also been considered in the development of law, particularly in relation to Carolingian legal culture,[4] and the legal studies leading to the juristic revival.[5] These studies lay the foundations for a manuscript-led history of medieval law, which may be expanded significantly through the specific application of the theoretical and methodological approaches developed in the recent scholarship of history of the book.[6]

93–127; Nick Everett, *Literacy in Lombard Italy, c. 568–774* (Cambridge: Cambridge University Press, 2003).

3 Catherine Cubitt, "'As the Lawbook Teaches': Reeves, Lawbooks and Urban Life in the Anonymous Old English Legend of the Seven Sleepers," *English Historical Review* 124 (2009): 1021–49.

4 Rosamond McKitterick, "Some Carolingian Law Books and their Function," in *Authority and Power. Studies on Mediaeval Law and Government presented to Walter Ullmann on his 70th birthday*, ed. Peter Linehan and Brian Tierney (Cambridge: Cambridge University Press, 1980); Rosamond McKitterick, *Carolingians and the Written Word* (Cambridge: Cambridge University Press, 1989); Rosamond McKitterick, "Script and Book Production," in *Carolingian Culture: Emulation and Innovation* (Cambridge: Cambridge University Press, 1994), 221–47; Thomas Faulkner, "Carolingian Kings and the *Leges Barbarorum*," in *Early Medieval Law in Context*, ed. Jenny Benham, *Historical Research* 86 (2013): 443–64; Thomas Faulkner, *Law and Authority in the Early Middle Ages* (Cambridge: Cambridge University Press, 2016); Hayley LaVoy, "Hirmindrut Sculdarissa: A Ninth-Century Woman's Original Letter and its Implications," *Journal of Medieval Latin* 25 (2015): 29–50.

5 Charles M. Radding, *The Origins of Medieval Jurisprudence: Pavia and Bologna, 850–1150* (New Haven, CT: Yale University Press, 1988); Charles M. Radding, "Legal Theory and Practice in Eleventh-Century Italy," *Law and History Review* 21 (2003): 377–81; Charles M. Radding and Antonio Ciaralli, *The Corpus Iuris Civilis in the Middle Ages: Manuscripts and Transmissions from the Sixth Century to the Juristic Revival* (Leiden: Brill, 2007).

6 Peter Ganz, ed., *The Role of the Book in Medieval Culture: Proceedings of the Oxford International Symposium 26 September–1 October 1982* (Turnhout: Brepols, 1986); Derek Pearsall, ed., *New Directions in Later Medieval Manuscript Studies: Essays from the 1998 Harvard Conference* (York: York Medieval Press, 2000); Johann Peter Gumbert, "Skins, Sheets and Quires," in *New Directions in Later Medieval Manuscript Studies. Essays from the 1998 Harvard Conference*, ed. Derek Pearsall (York: York University Press, 2000); Johann Peter Gumbert, "Codicological Units: Towards a Terminology for the Stratigraphy of the Non-Homogenous Codex," *Segno E Testo* 2 (2004): 17–42; Malcolm Parkes, *Scribes, Scripts and Readers: Studies in the Communication, Presentation and Dissemination of Medieval Texts* (London: Hambledon Press, 1991); Malcolm Parkes, *Their Hands Before Our Eyes: A Closer Look at Scribes: The Lyell Lectures Delivered in the University of Oxford, 1999* (Oxford: Ashgate, 2008); Erik Kwakkel, ed., *The European Book in the Twelfth Century* (Cambridge: Cambridge University Press, 2018); Erik Kwakkel, Rosamond McKitterick, and Rodney Thomson, *Turning Over a New Leaf: Change and Development in the Medieval Manuscript* (Chicago: University of Chicago Press, 2012); Simon Eliot and Jonathan Rose, eds., *A Companion to The History of the Book* (Oxford: Blackwell, 2007); Jonathan Wilcox, ed., *Scraped, Stroked and Bound: Materially Engaged Readings of Medieval Manuscripts* (Turnhout: Brepols, 2013).

The contextualization of legal texts within the materiality of the written word are fundamental to understanding how laws and related texts were actualized and adapted, but are often concealed from view when the legislators and the authorial, historic moment in which a new law was produced are prioritized over the agency of their subsequent implementation and development. Law and literacy extend beyond the debates and contrasts of strong and weak legal literacies, that is where law is seen as pragmatic, even black-letter legal dogmatism, or else only as ideological statement. Law as literature rejects the binary opposition of these, and sees them in interplay, with the recognition that both elements can mutually coexist, and simultaneously need investigation without one limiting the other.[7] The direction in the study of early medieval legal cultures led by Rosamond McKitterick, while still seeing pragmatism and idealism as a somewhat contrasting binary, has nevertheless lain strong foundations for integrated interpretations of the pair,[8] and provides a cognitive framework that can be extended beyond the early medieval period and, I would argue, well past the juristic revival of Roman law. Through the manuscript-led perspective of the developing book cultures in which legal texts were transmitted and developed, an even greater granularity can be revealed that moves analysis beyond sweeping questions of why, and returns focus to the equally important questions of what, where and, most intriguing of all, how.

The study of law, legal texts and legal cultures is, of course, far from new, but to date relatively little attention has been given to the later literate cultures in which legal texts were augmented and updated, except when a distinctive intellectual moment occurs in the transmission of the laws, such as when a given legal text was redacted or systemized into a new form. Studies of reception tend to focus on what might be deemed authorial interventions, while subtle augmentations and appropriations can be lost from view. This approach to laws is made explicit through the reductionist, critical editions of the nineteenth to mid-twentieth century, which have sought to reconstruct "best-texts" of the authorial form of the laws as first promulgated, redacted or systemized.[9]

7 Rosamond McKitterick, "The Uses of Literacy in Carolingian and Post-Carolingian Europe: Literate Conventions of Memory," in *Scrivere E Leggere Nell'Alto Medioevo, Settimane di Studio Della Fondazione Centro Italiano di Studi Sull'Alto Medioevo* 59, ed. CISAM (Spoletto: CISAM, 2012).

8 McKitterick, "Some Carolingian Law Books," 13–27; McKitterick, *Carolingians and the Written Word.*

9 See for example, the various critical editions of barbarian laws and capitularies published by the Monumenta Germaniae Historica, such as the series of *Leges, Leges Nationum Germanicarum, Capitularia Regum Francorum,* and so forth. For details, see http://www.dmgh.de/.

Much of the work on laws and related texts has focused on the legal content itself, underlying sources of law,[10] the legislators themselves, their motives for legislation and the historical contexts in which a given law or document was first produced,[11] the socio-legal institutions of specific *gentes*, nations, state and government, legal culture,[12] and arguments for the extent and role of pragmatic legal literacy across the medieval period and the professionalization of law.[13] This work has been tremendously influential for understanding structures of authority, power and ideology across the medieval period, but prioritizing agency in the upper echelons of society has allowed the agency of individuals adapting and implementing law at the local level to be marginalized or even erased.

Scholarship in the second half of the twentieth century and into the twenty-first has already done much to problematize approaches centered on "best-

10 Hagith Sivan, "The Appropriation of Roman Law in Barbarian Hands: 'Roman-Barbarian' Marriage in Visigothic Gaul and Spain," in *Strategies of Distinction: The Construction of Ethnic Communities, 300–800*, ed. Walter Pohl and Helmut Reimitz (Brill: Leiden, 1998); Everett, "Literacy and the Law", 93–127.

11 Christine E. Fell, "Some Questions of Layout and Legal Manuscripts," in *'Lastworda Betst' Essays in Memory of Christine E. Fell with her Unpublished Writing*, ed. Carole Hough and Kathryn Lowe (Donington: Tyas, 2002); Gerhard Dilcher and Eva-Marie Distler, eds., *Leges, Gentes, Regna: zur Rolle von germanischen Rechtsgewohnheiten und lateinischer Schrifttradition bei der Ausbildung der frühmittelalterlichen Rechtskultur* (Berlin: Erich Schmidt Verlag, 2006); Per Andersen, Mia Münster-Swendsen, and Helle Vogt, eds., *Law Before Gratian: Law in Western Europe c. 500–1100* (Copenhagen: DJØF, 2007); Stephen Baxter, Catherine E. Karkov, Janet L. Nelson, and David Pelteret, eds., *Early Medieval Studies in Memory of Patrick Wormald* (Bodmin: Ashgate, 2009); Stefan Jurasinski, Lisi Oliver, and Andrew Rabin, eds., *English Law before Magna Carta: Felix Liebermann and Die Gesetze der Angelsachsen* (Leiden: Brill, 2010); Jenny Benham, ed., *Early Medieval Law in Context, Historical Research* 86 (2013): 443–64.

12 Katherine Fischer-Drew, "Notes on Lombard Institutions / Lombard Laws and Anglo-Saxon Dooms," *Rice Institute Pamphlet* 43 (1956): i–ix, 1–125; Bruce O'Brien, "From *Morðor* to *Murdrum*: the Preconquest Origin and Norman Revival of the Murder Fine," *Speculum* 71 (1996): 321–57; Lisi Oliver, *The Body Legal in Barbarian Law* (Toronto: Toronto University Press, 2011); Patrick Wormald, "The *Leges Barbarorum*: Law and Ethnicity in the Medieval West," in *Regna and Gentes: The Relationship Between Late Antiquity and Early Medieval Peoples and Kingdoms in the Transformation of the Roman World*, ed. Hans-Werner Goetz, Jörg Jamut, and Walter Pohl (Leiden: Brill, 2003).

13 Patrick Wormald, "*Lex Scripta* and *Verbum Regis*: Legislation and Germanic Kingship, from Euric to Cnut," in *Early Medieval Kingship*, ed. Peter H. Sawyer and Ian N. Wood (Leeds: University Press, 1977); Susan Reynolds, "The Emergence of Professional Law in the Long Twelfth Century," *Law and History Review* 21 (2003): 347–66; Radding, "Legal Theory," 377–81.

text" readings of laws, but critical editions frequently remain central to the study of medieval laws. The contributors to this collection engage with edited texts in various ways, with some utilizing them to assess legal strategies in overview, or else to extract specific words or phrasings employed in the laws and legal texts, while others use the edited texts in a support role, as points of reference and comparison when engaging directly with the manuscripts themselves. Others engage more actively with the edited text, providing critical editions of individual manuscript extracts or else taking a manuscript-led approach to deconstructing and problematizing extant editions and catalogue descriptions of texts and books.

While the manuscripts and book cultures of law form the unifying thread beneath the surface of this volume, this topic is approached from numerous angles that inform on each other to produce a multifaceted interpretation of legal literacies across the span of the Middle Ages. The study of the cultures of books and documents of laws and legal texts offered here draws upon the same range of written sources, but is further augmented with other literary and historiographic items. Many of the pieces here, instead, take a manuscript-led perspective, viewing law-books and legal documents as being equally significant attestation of its content. The agency and intentions of later scribes and readers, and the legal and literate cultural contexts within which they worked, are given equal weight and validity as those of the original legislators. The transmission and reception of legal texts are of vital importance in understanding the development of law, legal literacy and legal culture in both local context and in relation to overarching power structures.

Studies on medieval legal texts have often drawn on a wide variety sources, such as law-codes, capitularies, formularies, charters and cartularies, treaties, and other regulatory texts as well as glosses, commentaries, *placita* and other items arising from or responding to medieval legal studies and legal cultures.[14] However, ideas of what constituted law and legal texts developed widely across the

14 Of particular interest are Charles M. Radding, "*Petre te appellat Martinus*: Eleventh-Century Judicial Procedure as Seen Through the Glosses of Walcausus," in *La Giustizia nell'Alto medioevo II (secoli IX–XI), 11–17 aprile 1996, Settimane di Studio del Centro Italiano di Studi sull'Alto Medioevo* 44 (1997); Alice Rio, *Legal Practice and the Written Word in the Early Middle Ages: Frankish Formulae, c. 500–1000* (Cambridge: Cambridge University Press, 2009); Laura Wangerin, "Royal Feuds and the Politics of Sanctity in Anglo-Saxon England and Ottonian Saxony," *Mirabilia*, 18 (2014): 78–94; Ben Snook, *The Anglo-Saxon Chancery: The History, Language and Production of Anglo-Saxon Charters from Alfred to Edgar* (Woodbridge, UK: Boydell & Brewer, 2015).

medieval period, meaning that a simple definition of the subject material of laws which is simultaneously applicable to the early, high and late medieval periods is complicated, if not impossible. A number of studies charting the overall development of European law have been produced,[15] favoring the overall trajectory of Roman law, and the development of the European Civil law and English Common law. In such models, the early medieval period is frequently presented as a legal Other, as often as not defined by what is seen to be missing—an age without jurists—as what is included.[16] In a recent assessment of lawbooks in the twelfth century, Charles Radding observes that across the course of the long twelfth century, the manuscript formats employed for secular law-books (specifically the systemized collection of Lombard laws and Frankish and Saxon capitularies employed in Italy), for Roman Law, and for Canon Law had all semi-independently converged into a similar format. He also notes that there has been no recent study re-evaluating what constitutes a medieval legal text,[17] and unfortunately such a comprehensive reassessment is also beyond the scope of this current collection. The edges of law and legal texts were also problematized by Janet Nelson, through her framing of law and liturgy as "misconceived alternatives", positioning them rather as comparable genres utilized to implement similar aims.[18]

The boundaries of what constitutes a law or legal text then are often blurred. In this collection the hazy lines have been accepted, quietly, and the definition of law and regulatory/normative texts has been left deliberately open. Consequently, this has drawn in a wide variety of approaches circulating around

---

15 See for example: Tamar Herzog, *A Short History of European Law: The Last Two and a Half Millennia* (Cambridge, MA: Harvard University Press, 2018), particularly Chapters 2 to 6; Manlio Bellomo, *The Common Legal Past of Europe 1000–1800*, trans. Lydia G. Cochrane (Washington DC: Catholic University of America Press, 1995, originally published as *L'Europa del diritto commune*, Rome: Il Cigno Galileo Galilei, 1988). A more specific focus on the trajectory of the Roman law from late antiquity to the High Middle Ages, can be found in Radding and Ciaralli, *The Corpus Iuris Civilis in the Middle Ages*.

16 Bellomo, *Common Legal Past of Europe*, Chapter 2, 34–54; Herzog interrogates this concept, to argue that while there may have been no jurists per se, the evidence nevertheless suggests experts who acted as legal advisors, *Short History of European Law*, Chapter 3, 47–61.

17 Charles M. Radding, "Law Books," in *The European Book in the Twelfth Century*, ed. Erik Kwakkel (Cambridge: Cambridge University Press, 2018).

18 Janet L. Nelson, "Liturgy or Law: Misconceived Alternatives," in *Early Medieval Studies in Memory of Patrick Wormald*, ed Stephen Baxter, Catherine Karkov, Janet L. Nelson, and David Pelteret (London: Routledge, 2009).

medieval responses to social regulation from institutions and communities at the more local scale or in elite positions, to the large scale through various *regna*.

Secular law forms the major thread here, of course, both from the perspective of charters and diplomatics, as well as the various codifications and promulgations of law; but other approaches are also seen, including the interplay of legal texts with other literary genres through to comparative readings of law-codes against mortuary practice in the archaeological record.

The title of this collection deliberately invites creative engagement from its contributors and readers alike, with the parts, "law", "book" and "culture" each being able to stand alone—but being open equally to combination. The contributions stand at the intersection of the cultures of books and documents, and the cultures of law and normative regulation. Where these two broad strands of law and books meet, the reader is inevitably brought to the various facets of legal literacy, and these form an underlying thread that is woven throughout the chapters. The scope of what might be considered as legal literacies is relatively broad, ranging from the pragmatic, in which we see medieval actors applying and developing what is literally the letter of the law, through to the, in which laws and other normative texts are considered as vehicles for strategies of identification and elite power within a socio-political framework. In practice, of course, there is no reason why these two extremes must be mutually exclusive, and most laws and normative texts, and the literate cultures in which they were produced and deployed may combine both elements, sometimes dynamically as the needs of the communities utilizing the legal texts varied and changed. This brings scholars to the literate cultures of books and documents, to scribes and readers, and to questions of transmission, augmentation and emendation.

A great deal of work has been done over the last several decades in the history of medieval law and this volume takes into account some of the most important trends in this research. The contributions to this collection augment their analytical approach to laws and legal texts with a range of methodologies and theories drawn from other disciplines, such as linguistics, literature and philology, but extensively from manuscript studies and the history of the book. The authors engage theoretically and methodologically with a wide range of laws and related texts, focusing on the legal and literate contexts of their production, emendation and use. This emphasis of the materiality of law and the agency of scribes and readers contributes both specific examples and wider conceptual frameworks to approaches to the history of law that prioritize immediacy and local significance over grand narratives and state structure. The authors reflect a wide range of academic experience, employing a complementary range of multidisciplinary approaches to the study of the literacy and materiality of medieval legal texts. New perspectives on the transmission and appropriation of laws and related texts are opened, and present nuanced interpretations of their interrelationship with the contexts and needs of medieval societies.

The fifteen chapters in this volume interrogate medieval literate cultures of laws and related legal texts, books and literacy, then, are broad reaching both in their disciplinary stances and their chronological and geographical focus. An astute reader will quickly note that some areas are more heavily addressed, both Italy and Scandinavia, for instance. Conversely, other areas are sadly omitted, no chapter addresses the Iberian peninsula, and only one ventures into central Europe. A collection such as this is, of course, shaped primarily by the responses to its initial call for submissions. Moreover, with a collection that has taken many years to manifest it is also inevitable that some contributors have been lost along the way. The initial collection was set to include chapters on a further range of subjects and legal themes across western Europe, including: West Roman vulgar law, early Irish peace treaties, maledictory sanction clauses, legal and colloquial phraseology in Reinhard Fuchs, *mise-en-page* and paratextual elements in Norwegian law-books, formation of a city archive in Portugal, the development of copyright from letters to law, and a study of student laws and regulatory cultures at the universities of Bologna, Paris and Oxford. Each is sadly missed, but hopefully will find its own home elsewhere with the course of time.

The chapters gathered here are arranged in four broad and somewhat overlapping themes: *Law-Books*, *Law and Society*, *Legal Practice*, and *Text and Edition*, and in so doing progresses through various aspects of the production and use of law-books and legal texts as both the subject, and the means, of historical enquiry.

1 Law-Books

The first thematic sections, *Law-Books*, gathers five chapters on book production and the selection and organization of legal texts in their manuscript context, particularly through the use—or omission—of textual associations, the use of decorative elements, paratext and framing elements, and intertextual references.

The collection opens with Stefan Drechsler's detailed analysis of the production of a Norwegian law manuscript, *Lundarbók*, in the fourteenth century, using in particular an art-historical approach to center the scribal strategies and layout of the legal materials within the broader contexts of legal studies and Roman law in the Scandinavian contexts. In *Lundarbók*, Drechsler sees the organizational foundations of later Norwegian law-books.

The second chapter, by Ben Reinhard, turns to the production of early English law books, in the eleventh century, focusing on the treatment of the *Polity* text of Archbishop Wulfstan (d. 1023) in manuscript context. Through a codicological re-assessment of a single manuscript witness, the archbishop's *vade mecum*. By re-constructing the original reading of the texts, the manuscript reveals a deeper view into Wulfstan's intellectual and legal interests, extending and confirming the view of the archbishop as homilist and statesman.

In the third chapter, Thom Gobbitt delves into Lombard Law-books of the ninth and tenth centuries. He examines how the omission and truncation of the royal prologues from the various legislative session of Liutprand (d. 744), reflect the scribal strategies develop their respective exemplars and, to direct reader's interactions with the legal texts. While the deliberate omission of prologues has usually been seen as an innovation of the eleventh century, Gobbitt argues that it is better seen as the development of a strategy and argues that these erratic approaches to omitting prologues lay the foundations for that future strategy.

The fourth chapter, by Rolf H. Bremmer Jr, turns attention to Frisian laws and law-books in the thirteenth century, and in their broader manuscript contexts. The law-books are read through the framework of textual communities and intertextual connections, particularly through reference to historiographical and biblical materials. In so doing, Bremmer explores and demonstrates how they were deployed in the construction of a discrete Frisian identity, and the reception and construction of authority within these law-books.

In the fifth and final chapter of the *Law-Books* section, Fangzhe Qiu also considers the deliberate construction of intertextual connections in the Irish law-books of the later medieval period. Through analysis of the Irish learned tradition of *senchas*, literary cross-referencing through provision, narration and exposition, in relation to history, literature and grammar, and in turn let legal references permeate into other intellectual fields. The intertextual connections not only augmented the legal content, but situated them in historical and intellectual contexts, which Qiu argues form strategies for constructing the authority and validity of the laws.

2 Law and Society

The interconnecting themes explored in the previous section, already lay the foundations for the next section, *Law and Society*, which includes a further four chapters.

The sixth chapter of the volume, by Lucy Hennings, begins with its feet firmly in the book contexts of administration, examining the book cultures and, particularly, ownership of books by the Royal Wardrobe in England in the thirty-third to thirty-sixth regnal years (1248–61) of King Henry III (1207–72). While the materials for English administrative libraries are enigmatic, dispersed and fragmentary, Hennings considers the interrelationship of private ownership of books with administrative cultures. Thereby, *mise-en-page*, paratext and book production, are investigated for their insight into the private learning of royal administrators within a textual and intellectual context.

The seventh chapter takes us back into the early medieval period, with Jan van Doren examining the interweaving of legal culture and literacy, and the jurisprudential process and thought through Lothar II's (835–69) divorce case against Queen Theutberga (d. 875). He examines the texts arising in the contexts of the divorce, as responses to legal precedents underlying the texts where they are rarely made explicit. Van Doren argues for a greater legal significance underlying the construction, elaboration and organization of principles of law and jurisprudence in the texts, that are overshadowed by their relatively short lifespan as the divorce was rapidly overtaken by continuing socio-political developments.

In the eighth chapter Katherine J. Har considers the manuscript contexts of the *Leges Anglorum Londonis Collectae*, in thirteenth-century England. She takes a manuscript led approach to investigate the association of texts within the collection as a critique of contemporary kingship in contrast to the historical *regnum Anglorum*, from the laws of Ine and Arthurian legend, to the time of Henry II. Har argues that the compiler presents the kingdom as a whole through the lens of *imperium*, while at the time selects and augments texts to reinforce the customary rights of London and set the city simultaneously as both independent from and integral to the *regnum*.

The section on *Law and Society* concludes in the ninth chapter with Francesco Sangriso turning attention to Scandinavia and the terminology of inheritance rights, *óðal*, across the thirteenth century. He explores the development of this term through a wide selection of legal, historiographic and literary texts from the period, examining it within the conflict of royal power and landed elites. Ultimately, Sangriso argues for the royal appropriation of the institution, and the deployment of *óðal* in poetic texts as a symbol of absolute lordship reflecting the ancestral lands where the king had full and unconditional power. The shift in emphasis to terminology in this chapter prepares the readers attention for the third thematic section, *Legal Practice*, exploring both the pragmatic literate activities of legal practitioners and evidence for their changing roles, as well as the interpretation of archaeological evidence through comparison with contemporary written law.

3 Legal Practice

Here we begin in tenth-century southern Italy, with the volumes tenth chapter being Sonia Colafrancesco's examination of legal practitioners working in both Roman and Lombard law. She investigates evidence from the *Codex Diplomaticus Cavensis*, with focus on documents that reveal the simultaneous use of both laws, and in so doing illuminates the historical strategies and legal motivations of their respective scribes. Colafrancesco argues through this for the active creation of new legal practices and through that a new society, through the continued influence of Lombard law modifying and in turn modified by Roman law, in response to specific social circumstances.

In the eleventh chapter, Petar Parvanov brings attention to mortuary practices and deviant burials as material evidence of the enactment of law in the Bulgarian legal context, and in comparative contrast with the Balkans as a whole and through theoretical approaches developed for early medieval England. He examines developing practices across multiple sites from the tenth to thirteenth centuries in particular, and problematises the interpretation of deviant burials within interpretative contexts of vampirism. Parvanov positions the burials instead as the outcome of legal practice within the developing legal contexts evinced in the spread of Christianity and consolidation of central authority and social strata,

In the twelfth chapter, Hannah Burrows focuses on the depiction of legal practitioners in the Icelandic sagas, with particular emphasis on the naming strategies underlying the terminology used to define them. Particular emphasis comes to the distinctive terminology for those who were trained in the law, those who were good at winning law-suits, and where they might overlap. Burrows further nuances these terminologies, considering the narrative and historicizing contexts in which they were deployed and the extent to which they were informed by the developing "real life" legal contexts.

The thirteenth chapter rounds out the section on *Legal Practice*, with Daniella Fruscione bringing attention back to Lombard laws and notaries, once more, but now within the period when they still ruled over the Lombard regnum. She undertakes a close reading of two very different charters, to investigate and contrast the ways in which law was deployed by both trained legal practitioners and informed individuals to shape and construct legal rights and social position. Fruscione sees in these charters immediate legal concerns and the foundations of long-term family strategies, through the agency of their respective authors.

4 Texts and Editions

In the final thematic section, the attention of the concluding two chapters turns to *Texts and Editions*, and with the emphasis on the production of modern editions of medieval laws and legal collections. In the fourteenth chapter, Chiara Simbolotti presents a critical discussion and edition of a manuscript fragment of a Lombard law-book, now surviving as only a single bifolium, in the Biblioteca Nazionale Universitaria, Turin. In addition to the critical edition, she presents the bifolium in the historical contexts of the production of the laws and law-books as well as its ongoing provenance through to its incorporation into the modern library collections. Simbolotti argues on palaeographic grounds for a production date of the later eleventh century, and through critical comparison with other Lombard law-books identifies the textual variant of the laws as the *Lombarda*.

In the fifteenth and final chapter of the collection, Sara Elin Roberts brings focus to Welsh law and law-books, and the engaging and dramatic circumstances surrounding the production of their first modern critical edition. She presents a detailed biographical analysis of their editor, Anuerin Owen, and his access to and use of manuscripts, and concludes with an appendix gathering together the relevant manuscripts, arrange according to the main textual variants of the manuscripts and the identifying sigla which still remain in use. While Roberts problematises some of the decisions made in categorizing the manuscripts to produce the edition, she argues that understanding of these limitations in turn permits critical usage of the now dated edition.

This optimistic and informed stance, I would argue, rounds out the collection as a whole, arguing that extant if problematic and older editions of the legal materials nevertheless inform and guide the reader and researcher. Rather than "throwing the baby out with the bath water", the theoretical stances underpinning the production of a critical edition position it as a further variant of the laws, provides a further in-route into a manuscript-led study. While modern editions may smooth over manuscript variations, they nevertheless provide a guide and an augmented reading of our various law-books and legal texts, and may help unravel the manuscript contexts as well as the literate and legal cultures in which they were produced and used.

PART 1

Law-Books

CHAPTER 1

Production and Content of the Fourteenth-Century Norwegian Law Manuscript *Lundarbók*

Stefan Drechsler

In Old Norse research, a considerable number of studies have grouped Norwegian manuscripts according to their scribes and textual content.[1] By comparison, the illuminations of these codices have been scarcely researched. The law codex *Lundarbók* (Lund, Universitetsbiblioteket, MS Medaltidahandskrift 15; previously known as Hist. Litt. 12 fol.), probably produced in Bergen in the early fourteenth century, is one such manuscript.[2] As the oldest Norwegian codex featuring legal iconography, *Lundarbók* provides crucial information about the establishment of an iconographic catalogue for younger law manuscripts from the North, since Scandinavian law manuscripts prior to ca. 1320 do not feature historiated book painting.[3]

The aim of this chapter is to shed light on a largely understudied field of illuminated vernacular European law cultures—the book painting of medieval legal manuscripts in Norway.[4] In the spirit of Material Philology, the article will

1 I would like to thank Universitetsbiblioteket, Lund, the Kongelige Bibliotek, Copenhagen, and Stofnun Árna Magnússonar á Íslandi, Reykjavík, for providing me with images for the present chapter. Furthermore, I would like to thank Thom Gobbitt for invaluable comments on an earlier version of this chapter. For a short overview of medieval Norwegian scribes, see Magnus Rindal, "The History of Old Nordic Manuscripts II: Old Norwegian (incl. Faroese)," in *The Nordic Languages: An International Handbook of the History of the North Germanic Languages*, ed. Oskar Bandle et al. (Berlin: De Gruyter, 2002), 802–03, and Odd Einar Haugen, "The Development of Latin Script I: In Norway," in *The Nordic Languages: An International Handbook of the History of the North Germanic Languages*, ed. Oskar Bandle et al. (Berlin: De Gruyter, 2002), 830–31.

2 For the dating of *Lundarbók*, see Vilhelm Gödel, *Fornnorsk-isländsk litteratur i Sverige*, I (Stockholm: Hæggström boktrykkeri, 1897), 28; and Stefán Karlsson, "Lítið eitt um Lundarbók," in *Eivindarmál. Heiðursrit til Eivind Weyhe á seksti ára degi hansara 25. apríl 2002*, ed. Anfinnur Johansen (Tórshavn: Føroya Fróðskaparfelag, 2002), 224, 227.

3 For illuminations in some of the earliest of these manuscripts, see Stefan Drechsler, "Illuminated Manuscript Production in Western Iceland in the Thirteenth and Early Fourteenth Centuries," *Gripla* XXVIII (2017): 169–96.

4 For book painting of the only other fourteenth-century Norwegian law manuscript containing historiated illuminations, *Codex Hardenbergianus* (Det Kongelige Bibliotek, Copen-

 | DOI:10.1163/9789004448650_003

discuss important textual and iconographic features of *Lundarbók* in relation to distinct stages of the production of the manuscript. Finally, influences from iconographic programs from collections of canon and civil law texts, such as *Decretum Gratiani* or *Corpus iuris civilis* will be investigated. Due to the mass-produced nature of these Latin texts by the early fourteenth century,[5] one might assume that they had an influence on the book painting of law codices in Scandinavia. As will be shown, however, *Lundarbók* provides evidence for a unique Scandinavian legal iconographic catalogue with a particular focus on royal power, dependent on the textual content of the codex. In addition, the previous claim that *Lundarbók* was produced for the intended use of the diocese of Kirkjubær is confirmed, primarily due to the distinctive Faroese scribe, as well as a text and an iconographic reference specific to the Faroe Islands.

Lundarbók includes the renewed *Gulaþingslǫg Landslaganna*, a west Norwegian law-code belonging to the regional variants of the national law of Norway, the *Landslǫg*, the maritime law *Farmannalǫg* and *Bæjarbók Bjǫrgvinjar*, the vernacular city law of Bergen; all three were established by King Magnús *lagabœtir* (the "Law-Mender") Hákonarson (1238–80) and accepted at the west Norwegian law assemblies on June 24, 1274, and January 22, 1276, and sometime in 1276, respectively. *Landslǫg* is a national law-code built on the revision of a number of regional laws promulgated at the legal assemblies of Norway in ca. 1267–74 under the auspices of King Magnús. The establishment of *Landslǫg* has been suggested to be of international rather than national provenance,[6] primarily due to three international advocates of King Magnús: the Norwegian law man and ambassador Lóðinn leppr (d. 1288), chancellor Þórir Hákonarson (d. 1317) and Auðunn Hugleiksson (1240–1302), *stallari* (equerry) and *féhirði* (treasurer) to the king and (later) baron, had great

---

hagen, MS GKS 1154 fol.), see Knut Berg, "The Illuminations in No. 1154 Folio in the Old Royal Collection, Copenhagen," in *King Magnus Håkonsson's Laws of Norway and other legal texts*, ed. Knut Berg and Magnus Rindal (Oslo: Selskapet til Utgivelse av gamle Norse håndskrifter, 1983).

5 For a short introduction to the establishment and circulation of canonical and secular law manuscripts in the twelfth and the thirteenth centuries, see Peter Clarke, "The Growth of Canon and Civil Law Studies, 1070–1535," in *Illuminating the Law: Legal Manuscripts in Cambridge Collections*, ed. Susan L'Engle and Robert Gibbs (London: Harvey Miller, 2001), 22–23.

6 For international influence on the establishment of *Landslǫg*, see Jørn Øyrehagen Sunde, "Daughters of God and Counsellors of the Judges of Men: Changes in the Legal Culture of the Norwegian Realm in the High Middle Ages," in *New Approaches to Early Law in Scandinavia*, ed. Stefan Brink and Lisa Collinson (Turnhout: Brepols, 2014), 133, 160–61.

influence on the establishment of the *Landslǫg*. Auðunn likely studied canon law in Paris and Bologna,[7] travelled widely around medieval Europe,[8] and plausibly brought international standards of ecclesiastical and civil legal administration to Norway in the 1260s and 1270s.[9]

In the decades and centuries following its establishment, *Landslǫg* was widely copied: a total of 39 (almost) complete manuscripts and a further 55 fragmented manuscripts are known to belong to the medieval transmission of *Landslǫg* up to 1550.[10] *Gulaþingslǫg Landslaganna* (named *Landslǫg* [G] in the following), the regional version of *Landslǫg* featured in *Lundarbók*,[11] was established in 1274 for the west Norwegian coastlines of Agder in the south and Sunnmøre in the north, the Faroe Islands, Shetland Islands, Orkney Islands, (possibly) Greenland and later the Norwegian inland counties of Hallingdal and Valdres. In addition to *Landslǫg*, King Magnús also established local assembly city laws in the major cities of Norway: Bergen in the west, Oslo and Tønsberg in the east and Niðaróss (now Trondheim) in the north.

Lundarbók features sections of the late thirteenth-century, ecclesiastical Norwegian law *Gulaþingsgerð Kristinréttar yngri*, as well as *Hirðskrá*, a secular work commissioned by King Magnús contemporaneously with *Landslǫg* in the 1270s. *Hirðskrá* comprises a number of laws concerning the regulation of

7 For a summary of the life of Auðunn Hugleiksson see Knut Helle, *Kong og gode men i norsk riksstyring ca. 1150–1319* (Bergen: Universitetsforlaget, 1972), 41, 486–87, 581.

8 For an overview of primary sources mentioning the travels of Auðunn Hugleiksson see Yngve Nedrebø et al, *Audun Hugleiksson, Frå Kongens råd til galgen* (Førde: Selja Forlag, 2002), 17–20.

9 For the medieval transmission of *Landslǫg*, see Gustav Storm, *Om Haandskrifter og Oversættelser af Magnus Lagabøters Love* (Christiania: I Commission hos Jacob Dybwad, 1878), 11, and Magnus Rindal, "Dei norske mellomalderloverne. Alder, overlevering, utgåver," in *Skriftlege kjelder til kunnskap om nordisk mellomalder* (Oslo: Noregs forskningsråd, 1995), 13; for the city laws of medieval Norway, see Knut Helle, *Norge blir en stat 1130–1319, Handbok i Norges historie* (Bergen: Universitetsforlaget, 1974), 182.

10 For a list of the medieval manuscripts and fragments of *Landslǫg*, see Magnus Rindal and Bjørg Dale Spørck, eds. *Kong Magnus Håkonsson Lagabøtes landslog* (Norrøn tekst med fullstendig variantapparat, del 1) (Oslo: Arkivverket, 2018), 18–38; In addition, see Anna Catharina Horn, *Lov og tekst i middelalderen. Produksjon og resepsjon av Magnus lagabøtes landslov* (Gothenburg: Institutionen för svenska språket, 2016), 5.

11 The regional laws of *Landslǫg* comprise of law sides at Gulaþing in the west, Borgarþing in the south-east, Eiðsívaþing in the east and Frostaþing north near to Niðaróss (now Trondheim). For a concise introduction to the establishment of these regional Norwegian lawcodes, see Dieter Strauch, *Mittelalterliches Nordisches Recht bis 1500. Eine Quellenkunde* (Berlin: de Gruyter, 2011), 114–48.

the royal guards and courtly households.[12] Finally, a large number of ecclesiastical and royal amendments are added to the main texts of *Lundarbók*, some of which appear here for the first time, as well as an (incomplete) ecclesiastical *calendarium*. Divided into eighteen gatherings and two loosely attached folio leaves, the textual content comprises five distinctive production units.[13] In *Lundarbók*, production units are separated by empty verso sides of the final folio leaves. Accordingly, these empty folio leaves are found at fol. 23^{v}, fol. 51^{v}, and the completely empty leaf, fol. 60. The production units IV and V are incomplete. Each comprising a set of fairly similar gatherings, as shown in Table 1.1. Apart from distinctive breaks between the production units as indicated in the sets of gatherings, the main texts in these production units have also been written individually in these sections. This is particularly seen in the space left at the last recto leaves of the last gatherings, which features a similar ruling pattern as previous leaves, but no further added text (see Figure 1.1).[14] One can therefore conclude that all five production units were written independently, but by a single scribe at approximately the same time, and, as will be shown, clearly at the same place of work.

The respective royal amendments in the second production unit are commissioned by King Eiríkr Magnússon (1268–99) on March 9, 1295 (dealing with local affairs in Bergen) and September 16, 1282 (on trade and taxes in Bergen), by King Hákon Magnússon on August 8, 1299 (on land exchange), February 9, 1302 (on the loading and sale of goods and treatments of the poor), June 11, 1302 (on the trade of goods in northern Norway and the tributary lands of Norway), March 5, 1304 (on weapon liability in trading cities), November 1, 1311 (on the prohibition of coins currently in circulation), April 29, 1314 (on goldsmiths in Bergen), on October 21, 1314 (on dress codes in Bergen), July 30, 1316 (on customs for foreigners) and on November 14–15, 1316 (on gatherings of merchants in Bergen). Finally, an incomplete amendment decreed by King Magnús Eiríksson (1316–74) on July 19, 1320 is featured, describing the privileges of the city of Bergen.[15]

In *Lundarbók*, only the sections 1, 3, 9–27, 29–32 of *Gulaþingsgerð Kristinréttar yngri* are featured. The following texts consist of a (from Latin to Old Norse

12 For a concise introduction to the establishment of these Norwegian laws, see Strauch, *Mittelalterliches Nordisches Recht bis 1500*, 109–82.

13 The term "manuscript production unit" is borrowed from Erik Kwakkel, "Towards a Terminology for the Analysis of Composite Manuscripts," *Gazette du livre médiéval* 41 (2002): 12–19.

14 On the ruling pattern in *Lundarbók*, see Horn, *Lov og tekst i middelalderen*, 146–47.

15 For these royal amendments, see Rudolph Keyser and Peter A. Munch, *Norges Gamle Love indtil 1387. Tredie Bind* (Christiania: Gröndahl, 1849), 12–16, 23–26, 41–44, 68–69, 91–93, 108–10, 118–24, 134–35, 149–50.

TABLE 1.1 The textual content and codicological structure of Lund, MS Mh 15 *Lundarbók*

Production unit	Gathering	Extent	Content
I	1 (8 folios)	Fol. 1–8	*Hirðskrá* (fol. 1ra–23ra)
	2 (9 folios)	Fol. 9–17	
	3 (6 folios)	Fol. 18–23	
II	4 (8 folios)	Fol. 24–31	*Bæjarbók Bjǫrgvinjar* (fol. 24ra–38^{ra22}),
	5 (8 folios)	Fol. 32–39	*Farmannalǫg* (fol. 38^{rb1}–44^{va8}),
	6 (8 folios)	Fol. 40–47	*Réttarbót Eiríks Magnússonar* (fol. $44^{va11-26}$),
	7 (4 folios)	Fol. 48–51	Royal amendments (fol. 44vb–51rb)
III	8 (9 folios)	Fol. 52–60	*Gulaþingsgerð Kristinréttar yngri* (sections 1–24),
			A section on Eden and perjury,
			Ecclesiastical amendments
IV	9 (8 folios)	Fol. 61–68	*Gulaþingslǫg Landslaganna* (fol. 61va–126^{rb10}),
	10 (8 folios)	Fol. 69–76	*Mannhelgisbálkr* (section 26; fol. 126^{rb11}–128^{rb3}) with
	11 (8 folios)	Fol. 77–84	accompanying royal amendments (fol. 128^{rb6}–128^{vb7};
	12 (8 folios)	Fol. 85–92	fol. 128^{v10}–130ra),
	13 (8 folios)	Fol. 93–100	Royal amendments (fol. 130rb–139vb)
	14 (8 folios)	Fol. 101–8	
	15 (8 folios)	Fol. 109–16	
	16 (8 folios)	Fol. 117–24	
	17 (8 folios)	Fol. 125–32	
	18 (7 folios)	Fol. 133–39	
V	Glued in	Fol. 140–41	*Calendarium*

translated) letter by Cardinal Vilhelm of Sabina (on holy days and the property of the Church) from 1247, a text on oaths, followed by Pope Innocent IV's permission of Cardinal Vilhelm's letter from September 7, 1248. Finally, parts of Archbishop Jón rauði's laws are featured (on dead people's property).[16]

16 For these ecclesiastical letters and amendments, see Rudolph Kayser and Peter A. Munch,

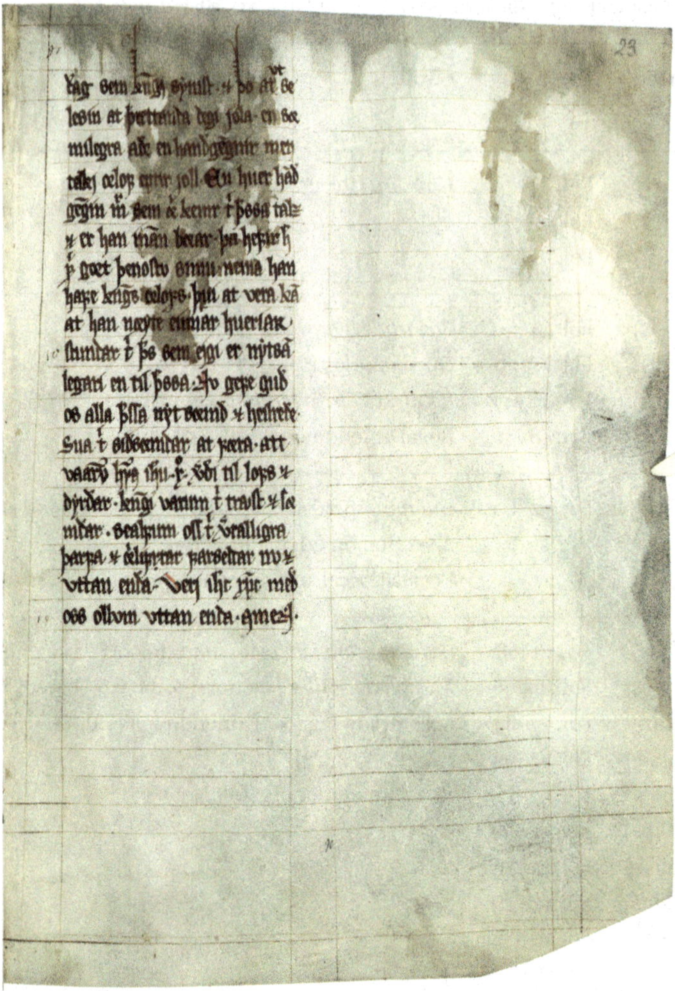

FIGURE 1.1 Lund, MS Mh 15 *Lundarbók*, fol. 23r: *Hirðskrá*. 1305–20
PHOTO: LUND, UNIVERSITETSBIBLIOTEKET

The royal amendments found in the fourth production unit were decreed by King Eiríkr Magnússon in 1280 (on general amendments), King Hákon Magnússon on June 28, 1298 (on amendments for the people of the Faroe Islands), October 11, 1303 (on the duties of retainers), ca. 1306 (on the kinship of married people), ca. 1308–09 (an incomplete amendment on the rights and obligations

Norges Gamle Love indtil 1387. Andet Bind (Christiania: Gröndahl, 1848), 337, 379–81, 454–58.

of clerics), December 26, 1309 (on the selfishness of royal officers), May 2, 1313 (on general amendments), June 23, 1310 (on the presence of royal officials at the law assemblies) and on May 15, 1311 (on the rights of the retainers as regards the public levy).[17]

Lundarbók was written in a regular, highly skilled yet partly outdated *Northern Textualis* hand in ca. 1305–20.[18] An example for the outdated script style may be seen in the use of *litterae elongatae* on the top lines (see Figure 1.3); a typographic emphasis which outside of Norway is mostly common in Carolingian and Pre-Gothic documentary script.[19]

The provenance of *Lundarbók* is unknown up until the seventeenth century:[20] The earliest owner was the Franciscan monastery of Stockholm in the seventeenth century, as indicated by the fact that a strawberry vine bordure, the mark of the monastery, was painted to the lower marginalia on fol. 1r. Later on, the codex was transferred to the Benedictine nunnery at Vadstena in southern Sweden. In 1682, it came into the possession of the scholar and aristocrat Jacob Reenhielm (to whom an alternative name of *Lundarbók* refers: *Codex Reenhielmianus*). After Reenhielm died in 1691, the manuscript was bequeathed to the University of Lund.

The manuscript was most likely written in Bergen, since, among other things, a local character of most of the texts and orthographic peculiarities of the scribe indicate a workshop at or nearby the important Norwegian city. Previously, Mikjel Sørlie argued that the scribe was the priest Þrondr *færøyski*, who probably has written manuscripts for the Faroese bishop Erlendr (d. 1308) in Bergen in the latter part of the thirteenth century.[21] This remains, however, an unproven hypothesis, as no evidence exists to link the codex with Bishop Erlendr directly. More convincingly, Gustav Storm and Stefán Karlsson have suggested that *Lundarbók* was produced for Árni Sigurðarson (d. 1314), bishop

---

17 For these amendments, see Kayser and Munch, *Norges Gamle Love indtil 1387. Andet Bind*, 174–178, and Keyser and Munch, *Norges Gamle Love indtil 1387. Tredie Bind*, 3–11, 59–62, 66–67, 63, 86–91, 99–102, 138–41.

18 For the dating of *Lundarbók*, see n. 3; for the orthography of the single scribe and other medieval Faroese documents, see Guðvarður Már Gunnlaugsson, "Færeyskar málheimildir," *Frændafundur* 3 (2000): 91–105, with further references. For the *Northern Textualis* script, see Albert Derolez, *The Palaeography of Gothic Manuscript Books: From the Twelfth to the Early Sixteenth Century* (Cambridge: Cambridge University Press, 2003), 72–101.

19 See Derolez, *Palaeography of Gothic Manuscript Books*, 59.

20 For the provenance of *Lundarbók*, see Gödel, *Fornnorsk-isländsk litteratur*, 29. A number of theories about the earliest ownership have been suggested; for discussion, see Karlsson, "Lítið eitt um Lundarbók," 220 and 223, with further references.

21 See Mikjel Sørlie, *En færøysk-norsk lovbok fra omkring 1310* (Bergen: Universitetsforlaget, 1964), 64, 73.

of Bergen, and was intended to be transferred to the Faroe Islands after completion by the Norwegian Signar *munkr*, who became Bishop of Kirkjubær in 1321.[22] Bishop Árni took care of a number of errands in the Faroe diocese after the previous bishop of Kirkjubær died in 1308.[23] Due to the dating of several of the royal amendments featured in *Lundarbók*, it is likely that all main texts were written during the lifetime of Bishop Árni, and probably at the Cathedral of Bergen: most royal amendments were written later than the main texts, which is indicated by a smaller script (though written by the same hand) and a different *mise-en-page*.[24] Since these royal amendments are dated to 1313 (production unit IV) and 1320 (production unit II) at the latest, it must be assumed that they were added once the main texts of *Lundarbók* were finished. As for the dating of production units I, III and V, it is less clear when they were written, yet they seem to have been produced contemporaneously with production units II and IV, since the orthography of the scribe and the *mise-en-page* of the folio leaves is the same throughout (apart from for the later added legal supplements).

The Bergen-specific focus of the royal amendments does not contradict the claim that *Lundarbók* was produced for the Faroese diocese. Both *Landslǫg* and previous, regional versions of the *Gulaþingslǫg* were in force in the Faroe Islands from 1271 onwards, similar to all royal amendments featured in *Lundarbók*. The clearest indication of the Faroese connection is, however, the *Réttarbót Hákonar Magnússonar* (*Sauðabréfit*) featured in *Lundarbók*, a royal amendment mentioned above by King Hákon Magnússon (1270–1319), which includes administrative instructions specific to the Faroe Islands. As will be shown below, the illumination of *Sauðabréfit* is also extraordinary in relation to other historiated initials in the same codex.

The folios of *Lundarbók* are considerably large, with a total size of 295 × 210 mm. Apart from two missing folio leaves at the beginning of the production unit V, the *calendarium*, and two missing leaves at the end of the royal amendments in production unit IV, *Lundarbók* is complete.[25] The manuscript features an unusually clear and well-organized *mise-en-page*, with a ruling pattern of two columns of 26 lines each (see Figure 1.1). The codex is neatly and

22 For this, see Karlsson, "Lítið eitt um Lundarbók," 223, and Gustav Storm, *Norges Gamle Love indtil 1387. Fjerde Bind* (Christiania: Grøndal & Søn, 1885), 698–700. Sørlie, *En færøysk-norsk lovbok*, 67–68, argued for a similar connection to Bishop Árni but did not investigate a direct use of *Lundarbók* in the diocese of Kirkjubær.

23 Karlsson, "Lítið eitt um Lundarbók," 220.

24 Storm, *Norges Gamle Love indtil 1387*, 699. A *mis-en-page* of a codex generally refers to the compositional principles of page layout.

25 Gödel, *Fornnorsk-isländsk litteratur*, 29.

consistently executed, ruled on both sides with the lines drawn in lead, which indicates an efficient workshop at the time of production. Empty verso leaves following incomplete recto sides feature no rulings, however. The missing ruling pattern here indicates the working mode of the scribe, who may have added the rulings directly before the writing process.

On the basis of the professional layout, Anna Catharina Horn has argued that an established workshop was responsible for the production of *Lundarbók*.[26] According to Horn, *Landslǫg* (G) in *Lundarbók* shared a common exemplar with two other codices from the early fourteenth century (although they probably do not originate from the same workshop or milieu): Copenhagen, Den Arnamagnæanske Samling, MSS AM 60 4to, AM 304 fol. and AM 322 fol.[27] Similar to *Lundarbók*, all of these manuscripts also feature the city law of Bergen, but no further similarities between *Lundarbók* and these legal codices are visible with respect to textual content or book painting.

The well-preserved state and the limited comments added to the margins suggest that *Lundarbók* was not only handled with great care by its later owners; it might also never have been used intensively by its original client. Despite its well-preserved state, however, the arrangement of the different production units of *Lundarbók* is puzzling. Overall, the current codicological structure of *Lundarbók* does not seem to represent the original one. In contemporaneously produced medieval Norwegian manuscripts containing *Landslǫg*, this law-code is always placed first in the codices. Through liaison with Stefán Karlsson, who has argued that *Landslǫg* was initially placed before *Bæjarbók Bjǫrgvinjar* due to an empty recto leaf at the beginning of the former and which was likely used as a cover for the codex,[28] I argue that a similar structure was initially intended for *Lundarbók*: at the beginning of a supplement decreed by the Norwegian King Eiríkr Magnússon, fol. 44va, it is mentioned that "z ganga sua allar utt sem standa j lanðz bokinni" [and so all (sections) as they are stated in *Landslǫg*].[29] In *Lundarbók*, these are found in the fourth production unit only, which would originally have been placed first, if this reference is taken at face value. A similar situation appears at the beginning of *Bæjarbók Bjǫrgvinjar*, where on f. 24^{v}, b26–27 not only is a similar wording found, but also the majority of chapters of the *Bæjarbók Bjǫrgvinjar* are only listed with their first sentence up to the end of the text on f. 26^{v}, a1.

---

26 Horn, *Lov og tekst i middelalderen*, 146–47, 218.

27 See Horn, *Lov og tekst i middelalderen*, 218, as well as 106–20. For the textual content of the listed manuscripts, see Storm, *Norges Gamle Love indtil 1387*, 476–77, 502–14, 547–49.

28 See Karlsson, "Lítið eitt um Lundarbók", 220.

29 All translations and transcriptions are made by the author.

Vernacular law manuscripts from Iceland, such as the splendid *Skarðsbók* (Reykjavík, Stofnun Árna Magnússonar í íslenskum fræðum, MS AM 350 fol.) from 1363, first feature the *Landslǫg*-influenced Icelandic law *Jónsbók*, followed by a number of royal amendments. *Jónsbók* was ratified and posthumously introduced in Iceland in 1281 by King Hákon Magnússon of Norway. A few decades before, in 1262–64, Iceland had become part of the Norwegian kingdom. Soon after its introduction and similar to *Landslǫg*, *Jónsbók* became one of the most widely copied vernacular laws in medieval and Early Modern Scandinavia, with about 100 known complete copies and 40 fragments prior to the sixteenth century.[30]

Next to *Jónsbók* in *Skarðsbók* is *Hirðskrá* and the Icelandic ecclesiastical laws named *Kristinréttr Árna biskups*.[31] It is likely, then, that *Lundarbók* also once had a similar textual arrangement: first, *Landslǫg* (IV) is featured, followed by *Bæjarbók Bjǫrgvinjar* (II), *Hirðskrá* (I), and, finally, *Gulaþingsgerð Kristinréttar yngri* (III). As will be discussed below, the hierarchical structure of the (historiated) illuminations indicate a similar textual structure for *Lundarbók*. The incomplete, now glued-in and worn *calendarium* (V) may have been placed in the beginning (as is often the case in medieval psalters),[32] but the worn state of its folio leaves, in combination with it being glued-in only (and not bound), make it equally likely to have never been part of the original manuscript. Nevertheless, the *calendarium* was undoubtedly written and illuminated by the same scribe and illuminator that was or were responsible for the other parts of the manuscript.

Lundarbók comprises book painting which, for the time of production, represents a then outdated mixture of Romanesque and early Gothic styles with a limited catalogue of ornamental models:[33] Romanesque mirrored volute spirals of floral palmettes at extended initial bands in red and blue, combined

---

30 For the establishment of *Jónsbók* and its medieval transmission, see Már Jónsson, Introduction to *Jónsbók. Lögbók Íslendinga hver samþykkt var á alþingi árið 1578* (Reykjavík: Háskólaútgáfan, 2004), 1–17.

31 For the dating of Reykjavík, MS AM 350 fol., see Kristian Kålund, *Katalog over den Arnamagnæanske håndskriftsamling*, I (Copenhagen: Gyldendalske Boghandel, 1889), 284–285; for the textual structure, see Jakob Benediktsson, *Skarðsbók: Jónsbók and Other Laws and Precepts: MS. No. 350 fol. in The Arna-Magnæan Collection at the University Library of Copenhagen* (Copenhagen: Munksgaard, 1942), 11–15.

32 For medieval Icelandic examples, see Lena Liepe, *Studies in Icelandic Fourteenth Century Book Painting* (Reykholt: Snorrastofa, 2009), 183–202.

33 For an introduction to Romanesque and early Gothic book painting, see Jonathan J.G. Alexander, *Medieval Illuminators and Their Methods of Work* (New Haven, CT: Yale University Press, 1992), 95–120.

with early Gothic *fleuronné* pen-flourishing, are painted throughout, together with frequent *fleur-de-lis*. Despite their international character, *fleur-de-lis* are barely used for the ornamentation of western Scandinavian law manuscripts. It therefore is not entirely unlikely that the numerous use of *fleur-de-lis* in *Lundarbók* may hint towards a potential, maryological indication for the Cathedral of Kirkjubær as being the place of initial use of the manuscript, since this church was dedicated to the Mother of God from the late thirteenth century onwards.[34]

A consistent use of the same ornamental catalogue, style and same color palette indicate the illuminator to be the same throughout. It is tempting to assume, though unverifiable, that the single scribe and rubricator was also the same individual who illuminated the codex: however, the ink of the rubrics has a slightly lighter red color than the red color palettes used for the illuminations. Nevertheless, further research is needed to verify potential significant differences between the inks used. Despite its vivid execution, the ornamentation style of *Lundarbók* had fallen out of use in other parts of Europe about 100 years prior to the production of the manuscript. This very late use of Romanesque ornamentation is exemplified by a particular ornamental model, the head of a beast blowing two-folded volute spirals embellished with palmette flowers (see Figure 1.4). To my knowledge, in the Scandinavian context this ornamentation is exclusive to *Lundarbók*, and at an international level, such outdated Romanesque models rarely appear in book painting of the early fourteenth century; similar models are however found in English and French manuscripts from the early-twelfth century. One such example is the *Gallican Psalter* with *Glossa Ordinaria*, MS McClean 33 (now at Cambridge, Fitzwilliam Museum). It was produced in ca. 1125 in the Maine or central Loire region of France, but no exact parallels for the ornamentation have been found to date.[35] Otherwise, the style of the ornamentation of *Lundarbók* is typical for contemporaneously produced Norwegian manuscripts, although direct influences are less easily traceable. Horn suggested a stylistic affinity with the somewhat contemporaneously-produced *Landslǫg* manuscript, Stockholm, Kungliga Biblioteket, MS Holm perg 29 4to,[36] which indeed features related Romanesque

34 See Karlsson, "Lítið eitt um Lundarbók," 220.

35 For Cambridge, MS McClean 33, see Deirdre Jackson, Nigel Morgan, and Stella Panayotova, *A Catalogue of Illuminated Western Books in the Fitzwilliam Museum and the Cambridge Colleges, Part Three: France* (London: Harvey Miller, 2014), 63–64.

36 Stockholm, MS Holm perg 29 4to consists of several production units. It has been dated to ca. 1300–1400 (with a further, later addition from the fifteenth century). For the dating of MS Holm perg 29 4to, see Vilhelm Gödel, *Katalog öfver Kongl. bibliotekets fornisländska och*

ornamentation and similar yellow backgrounds of the initials and letter shapes.[37] The *Landslǫg* redaction of Stockholm, MS Holm perg 29 4to, however, is not closely related to the same law text in *Lundarbók* as mentioned above, and a closer stylistic comparison between these two law manuscripts can only be made on the assumption of shared ornamental models.

Non-figural book painting, such as in *Lundarbók*, is not exclusively limited to Norwegian manuscripts; another example of similar floral ornamentation is found in the Icelandic fragment Oslo, Riksarkivet, MS NRA 71, which was produced as early as ca. 1250–75.[38] Major initials in *Lundarbók* are painted with filled-in ornamentation in red, blue and partially green, with interlaced, repetitive patterns of steeped gables, as well as stylized wine or acanthus frieze, filled in with rectangular white dots. The outer parts of major initials are further embellished with external floral motifs in the counters, such as stylized, threefold acanthus leaves, as well as *œfs-de-grenouille*. In addition, connected to major initials, trumpet-formed volute tendrils with palmette endings are found in connection to the whorled-patterned grylli head ornamentation mentioned above.

Contemporaneously with *Lundarbók*, Norwegian *Landslǫg* manuscripts such as Copenhagen, MSS AM 56 4to and AM 304 fol. feature similar ornamentation of major initials too, namely Romanesque zig-zag patterns with elongated shafts painted in blue and red. Originally, this ornamentation derives from French or English manuscript painting of the late twelfth and early thirteenth centuries,[39] but Copenhagen, MSS AM 56 4to and AM 304 fol., together with *Lundarbók*, suggest that the embellishment of legal manuscripts in western Norway was somewhat uniform during the first two decades of the fourteenth century. Historiated book painting, however, is particular for *Lundarbók*, since, save MS Holm perg 29 4to, no other Norwegian law manuscript from that time features text-related illuminations. In line with Romanesque ornamentation, the early

---

fornnorska handskrifter (Stockholm: Kongelige Biblioteket, 1897–1900), 80–84, Keyser and Munch, *Norges Gamle Love indtil 1387. Andet Bind*, 182, Storm, *Norges Gamle Love indtil 1387*, 655; and Didrik Arup Seip, *Norsk språkhistorie til omkring 1370* (Oslo: Aschehoug, 1955), 229, 232.

37 See Horn, *Lov og tekst i middelalderen*, 160, 162.

38 For the dating of Oslo, MS NRA 71, see Hreinn Benediktsson, *The Life of St. Gregory and his Dialogues: Fragments of an Icelandic Manuscript from the 13th Century* (Copenhagen: Munksgaard, 1963), 15–16, 45.

39 For an overview of French and English twelfth-century and early thirteenth-century ornamentation see Walter Cahn, *Romanesque Manuscripts: The Twelfth Century, Volume One: Texts and Illustrations* (London: Harvey Miller, 1994); Nigel Morgan, *Early Gothic Manuscripts 1190–1250*, I (London: Harvey Miller, 1986–88).

Gothic figural style of *Lundarbók* is internationally outdated. For example, the style of the drapery is identified as the *Muldenfaltenstil*, which is employed in ecclesiastical English and French manuscripts dated to ca. 1200–60. A distant similarity with the style of the drapery in *Lundarbók* might be seen in the mid-thirteenth century "de Brailes group" from Oxford. Most comparable are the *De Brailes Hours* from ca. 1240, where similar linear, sharp outlines and energetic angular poses are shown. This is not to say that a close similarity between the figural style of *Lundarbók* and the *De Brailes Hours* exists. On the contrary, the temporal distance and the textual nature of the two manuscripts make it impossible to find closer stylistic similarities.[40] Generally in England, such drapery folds vanish in the later decades of the thirteenth century, while in Norway, this style remained in use and is still found in seals, stone sculptures and altar frontals until ca. 1300.[41] In the wider context of contemporary Norwegian art, therefore, the figural style of *Lundarbók* is considerably out of date.

Iconographic images in *Lundarbók* generally provide text-related meanings. Some initials feature zoomorphic content, while others are embellished with vegetal ornamentation. Major initials are painted between four and six lines high, in black, red and blue colours before a golden-interlaced terminal background. The major initials are given in Table 1.2.

TABLE 1.2 The major initials of Lund, MS Mh 15 *Lundarbók*

Production unit	Position and size	Text	Chapter	Iconography
I	Fol. $1^{ra3–8}$	*Hirðskrá*		King with sword
II	Fol. $24^{ra2–5}$	*Bæjarbók*	*Bréf Magnúss konungs*	King with book
	Fol. $24^{ra9–12}$	*Bjǫrgvinjar*	*Þingfararbálkr*	Hand blessing
	Fol. $26^{va5–10}$		*Kristindómsbálkr*	*Unhistoriated*
	Fol. $32^{va22–25}$		*Kaupabálkr*	*Unhistoriated*
	Fol. $38^{rb1–5}$	*Farmannalǫg*		*Unhistoriated*
	Fol. $44^{va11–13}$	*Réttarbót Magnúsar Eiríkssonar*		King blessing
III	Fol. $52^{ra2–6}$	*Gulaþingsgerð Kristinréttar yngri*		Head of Christ

40 For the *De Brailes Hours* and the British *Muldenfaltenstil* see Morgan, *Early Gothic Manuscripts 1190–1250*, I, 28, 118–23.

41 Nigel Morgan, "Dating, Style and Groupings," in *Painted Altar Frontals of Norway*, ed. Unn Plahter, Erla B. Hohler, Nigel Morgan, and Anne Wichstrøm, 3 vols. (London: Archtype, 2004), 1:25–28.

TABLE 1.2 The major initials of Lund, MS Mh 15 *Lundarbók* (*cont.*)

Production unit	Position and size	Text	Chapter	Iconography
IV	Fol. 61^{va4-9}	*Gulaþingsgerð Landslaganna*	*Bréf Magnúss konungs*	King and Queen
	Fol. $62^{va12-15}$		*Þingfararbálkr*	Head of Christ
	Fol. 66^{ra4-8}		*Kristindómsbálkr*	*Christ in Majesty*
	Fol. $70^{ra16-21}$		*Landavarnarbálkr*	Knight armed
	Fol. 76^{ra1-6}		*Mannhelgisbálkr*	2 figures arguing
	Fol. 86^{ra1-6}		*Erfðabálkr*, Kvennagiptingar	2 figures swearing
	Fol. $88^{va18-23}$		*Erfðabálkr*	1 figure above, 3 figures below
	Fol. 94^{vb6-10}		*Landabrigðabálkr*, Óðalsskiptum	2 figures swearing
	Fol. 96^{va9-13}		*Landabrigðabálkr*, Landsleigu ok varnar	1 figure swearing
	Fol. 99^{rb7-11}		*Landsleigubálkr*	2 human heads above, 1 gryllus below
	Fol. 118^{rb3-8}		*Kaupabálkr*	2 figures swearing
	Fol. $125^{rb17-21}$		*Þjófabálkr*	1 hanged figure
	Fol. 128^{rb6-9}		*Réttarbót Hákonar Hákonarsonar*	King blessing
	Fol. $128^{vb10-13}$		*Réttarbót Magnúsar Hákonarsonar*	Head of King
	Fol. 130^{rb2-5}	*Réttarbót Eiríks Magnússonar*		Head of King
	Fol. $132^{va16-20}$	*Réttarbót Hákonar Magnússonar* (*Sauðabréfit*)		2 rams
V	Fol. 140–141	*Calendarium*		Hunting with falcon (May), pulling weeds (June), ploughing (July), harvesting grain (August) and fruits (September), sowing (October), butchering (November), brewing (December)

FIGURE 1.2 Lund, MS Mh 15 *Lundarbók*, fol. 1r: *Hirðskrá*. 1305–20
PHOTO: LUND, UNIVERSITETSBIBLIOTEKET

In its present state, *Lundarbók* starts with *Hirðskrá* on fol. 1r and depicts a seated king, holding a sword on his lap in one hand; the other is shown with a demanding gesture (see Figure 1.2).[42] The gesture of the king is clearly described in the introduced text. On fol. 11v, introduced by a minor initial depicting a grotesque human head, the gesture of the king is identified as provisions made for the appointment of Old Norse earls:

> Þan tima s*ka*l k*onun*gr hirð man | gera er æ*igi* standa borð fy*rir* | k*onu*ngi. k*onun*gr s*ka*l haua sverd um || kne ser vigslu suerd þat sem *hann var* | koranaðr með *ok* venda aptr dogsko | num vndir hond ser *ok* leggia meðal | kæfla fram yf*ir* hægra kne. sidan | s*ka*l han sueipa fetil sylgiunni up yf*ir* | meðal kaflan *ok* gripa sua hægri he*n* | di upp yfir alt saman.

42 In the present chapter, it is not possible to provide images of all major initials of *Lundarbók*. However, a digital facsimile of the manuscript is available at "Miscellany: Law," in *Alvin: Platform for Digital Collections and Digitized Cultural Heritage*, Universitetsbiblioteket, Lund, accessed October 15, 2019, https://www.alvin-portal.org/alvin/view.jsf?pid=alvin-record:14709.

> [Around the time when the king wants to appoint *hirðmenn* (to the court), a table must not stand before the king. The king shall have his coronation sword on his knee, if he is crowned. He shall turn the strap-buckle around the hilt and grip everything with his right hand from above].

The humorous character of the minor initial in the subchapter that introduces the text above remains mysterious; it might refer to the social challenges a king has to face when appointing various earls in his kingdom. The demanding gesture of the king, at least, is found in various major initials of *Lundarbók*, among others in the following production unit II starting on fol. 24ʳ *Bréf Magnúss konungs* of *Bœjarbók Bjǫrgvinjar*, an introductory section written by King Magnús Hákonarson for the medieval city law of Bergen. Accordingly, the major initial depicts a similarly clad king, holding a book in his right hand (see Figure 1.3). Both the presence of the book and the left hand of the king pointing towards the introduced text indicate the initial as a reduced version of an author portrait. Such portraits became increasingly common in legal iconography in the thirteenth century.[43] In this regard, the image in *Lundarbók* may be seen as following a standard opening of medieval law texts. Only three lines below on fol. 24ʳ, a second major initial introduces *Þingfararbálkr*, which is the first major section of *Bœjarbók Bjǫrgvinjar*. In the initial, a blessing hand is shown. The introduced text signifies the blessing hand as a symbolic depiction of the Christian belief of local judges: "Friðr *ok* blezan uars | h*er*ra ih*es*u x*ris*ti arnaðar | orð uarar fru sancte | marie *ok* hinnar helgv | sunnifo se með ollum biorg | viniar þings monnv*m* bæði | nu *ok* iafnan." [May the peace and blessing of Our Lord Jesus Christ, the intercession of the holy lady Mary and St. Sunniva be with us who are members of the General Assembly now and forever].

The depicted hand, therefore, might be interpreted as a visual hint towards Christ, Mary, Sunniva of Selje, saint of the diocese of Bergen, or, more likely, a bishop of Bergen or Kirkjubær, to give blessing for the assembled law men. All following major initials in *Bœjarbók Bjǫrgvinjar* feature grylli figures only, without any reference to the introduced sections of the city law. Overall, the presence of such grylli figures in major initials suggests that *Bœjarbók Bjǫrgvinjar* may have been considered less important for the visual content of *Lundarbók* than the main law-code in the codex, *Landslǫg* (G). Furthermore, it

43 Andreas Bauer, "Das Recht im Bild. Bildquellen des Mittelalters als Informationsträger für die Rechtsgeschichte," in *Kloster und Bildung im Mittelalter*, ed. Nathalie Kruppa and Jürgen Wilke (Göttingen: Vandenhoeck und Ruprecht, 2006), 268.

FIGURE 1.3
Lund, MS Mh 15 *Lundarbók*, fol. 24[r]: *Bæjarbók Bjǫrgvinjar*. 1305–20
PHOTO: LUND, UNIVERSITETS-BIBLIOTEKET

is likely that by the time that *Lundarbók* was illuminated, *Bæjarbók Bjǫrgvinjar* had no, or a much less strict, iconographic program than *Landslǫg* (G), which will be discussed below. Prior to *Landslǫg* (G), a royal amendment by King Magnús Hákonarson is added at fol. 44[v], depicting a crowned king with a blessing hand. The royal gesture and overall iconographic content closely resemble the first major initial of *Bæjarbók Bjǫrgvinjar* above, which is probably due to the origin of the two texts: the author of the two texts was the same person, King Magnús Hákonarson.

The following production unit III features selected chapters of *Gulaþingsgerð Kristinréttar yngri*. The first main initial on fol. 52[r] depicts a human face only, which is likely a depiction of Christ, due to the appearance of the same image in a later part of the manuscript. In addition, similar to the previously described *Þingfararbálkr* in *Bæjarbók Bjǫrgvinjar*, the rubric of the text refers to the importance of the Christian faith for the people of the Gulaþing, thus suggesting that the face depicts a divine rather than a human figure; Accordingly, the rubric reads "her hefur kristin dom ok | kristiliga trv til guds" (here begins [the section on] Christendom and the Christian belief in God). Later initials in *Gulaþingsgerð Kristinréttar yngri* depict grylli faces similar to the ones in *Hirðskrá*. Most of these sections describe moral restrictions against having an affair, or orders to observe church feast days. It is clear that the humorous character of these minor initials again refers to the potentially less educated nature of the general public and (lower) aristocracy, in contrast to the royal elite.

The most intensely illuminated part of *Lundarbók* is without doubt the next production unit, *Landslǫg* (G). The introductory *Bréf Magnúss konungs* on fol. 61^v, here written in its entirety, and in subsequent sections, features a major initial with historiated content. Both the number and the variety of iconographic images used for this production unit of *Lundarbók* suggest that by the time that *Lundarbók* was illuminated, an iconographic program for *Landslǫg* existed. *Bréf Magnúss konungs* depicts King Magnús Hákonarson and Queen Ingibjǫrg Eiríksdóttir (1244–87) in the initial (see Figure 1.4).[44] It remains obscure why Queen Ingibjǫrg is given such a prominent place in the book painting of *Lundarbók*, since she is not known to have played a significant political role in the law making during her lifetime. The gesture of the two crowned royal figures, however, clearly indicates the act of a vow. Queen Ingibjǫrg and King Magnús were crowned in Bergen by Archbishop Einar Gunnarsson on September 14, 1261, and, in addition to it, Ingibjǫrg was the first queen to be crowned in Norwegian history. It is likely that the initial refers symbolically to the coronation ceremony, since the introduced text also refers to the coronation of the king. The book in King Magnús' hand might represent the *Landslǫg* law itself. However, the iconographic content of this initial is no standard reference to his political role in the modernization and nationalization of the Norwegian laws. Thus, probably not surprising, the iconography is unparalleled in medieval legal imagery. The gesture of the two royal figures, however, is related, with the exception that King Magnús holds a book in his hand, presumably the

---

44 The identification of the two royal figures has been suggested by Stefka Georgieva Eriksen, "Litterær kultur i Norge i Eufemias tid," in *Eufemias. Oslos Midelalderdronning*, ed. Bjørn Bandlien (Oslo: Dreyers Forlag, 2012), 162.

FIGURE 1.4 Lund, MS Mh 15 *Lundarbók*, fol. 61^{v}: *Bréf Magnúss konungs*. 1305–20
PHOTO: LUND, UNIVERSITETSBIBLIOTEKET

introduced law similar to the initial on fol. 24^{r}. The rubric and introductory text, however, is less detailed and only refer to King Magnús as author of the law and two of the districts in which it is in use:

> Her hefr lavgbok þa er virðulegr h*er*ra | Magnus *konungr* hin koronadi skipadr *ok* gaf | ollum gula þings mo*nnu*m. | MAGNVS | konungr son | hakonar k*on*ungs | sendir urdu | legum h*er*ra jone | erkib*isku*pe *ok* oll*um*. | odrum guds uinum *ok* sa m*onnum* j frostu | eða gula þings laugum.
>
> [Here begins the law book which the venerable lord King Magnus the Crowned and Anointed gave to all people of the Gulaþing. King Magnus, son of King Hákon, sends regards to Lord John the Archbishop and all other ecclesiastical people and the people of the Frosta or Gulaþing districts].

The iconography of the following *Þingfararbálkr* on fol. 62va refers both iconographically and textually to the previously mentioned Head of Christ at the beginning of *Gulaþingsgerð Kristinréttar yngri*: apart from some minor differences, the two laws generally refer to similar ecclesiastical subjects. It is obvious that they were intended to be remembered mnemonically.[45] This is also similar to the following section of *Landslǫg, Kristindómsbálkr*, which sets out the fundamental Christian faith on which Norwegian society is based. It is therefore not surprising that the initial depicts a standard of Christian iconography, Christ in Majesty.

According to Gudmund Sandvik, the initial three sections of *Landslǫg, Bréf Magnúss konungs, Þingfararbálkr* and *Kristindómsbálkr* should all be understood as a unit, since they each give the king the legitimacy to rule in their own ways. Furthermore, the following *Landavarnarbálkr* and *Mannhelgisbálkr* are combined too as they share the inner and outer law justification and peace of medieval Norway.[46] The following sections, on the contrary, deal exclusively with domestic regulations. Concerning the book painting of *Lundarbók*, Sandvik's theory can be adopted to some extent, since the iconographic content of the first four initials of *Landslǫg* all indicate a royal focus. The Christian iconographic content of *Kristindómsbálkr* is no exception in Sandvik's categorization, since it similarly relates to the religious basis of medieval Norwegian sovereignty. Accordingly, the following initial introduces the section *Landavarnarbálkr*, the regulations of the levy in times of war. The illumination depicts a fully armed knight in chain mail, wearing a kettle helmet and holding a sword on his shoulders (see Figure 1.5). In his right hand, the soldier holds a shield with an unusual cover. It is not entirely clear if the shield is to be understood in a heraldic way, but the general layout is somewhat similar to the coat of arms of Auðunn Hugleiksson, the previously mentioned *stallari* (equerry) and *féhirði* (treasurer) to King Magnús and his son, King Eiríkr Magnússon. Similar to the (potentially) heraldic symbol in *Lundarbók*, the seal of Auðunn from ca. 1290 depicts a riding knight with framing *fleur-de-lis*, though the seal does not feature the added six dots in the initial in *Lundarbók* but a stylized rose.[47] In either way, it remains a mystery as to where the illuminator received the iconographic model from, but the general content of this

---

45 On the study of memory techniques in medieval manuscript design and book painting, see Mary Carruthers, *The Book of Memory. A Study of Memory in Medieval Culture* (Cambridge: Cambridge University Press, 2008), 274–337.

46 See Gudmund Sandvik, "Sættargjerda i Tunsberg og kongens jurisdiksjon," in *Samfunn, rett ok rettferdighet. Festskrift til Torstein Eckhoffs 70-årsdag*, ed. Anders Bratholm, Torkel Opsahl, and Magnus Aarbakke (Oslo: Tano, 1986), 566–69.

47 For the seal of Auðunn Hugleiksson, see Henrik J. Huitfeldt-Kaas, Christopher Brinchmann, and Oluv Kolsrud, eds., *Norske Sigiller fra Middelalderen, Første Bind: Verdslige Sigiller indtil aar 1400*, (Oslo: Kristiana Lithografiske Aktiebolag og Det Mallingske Boktrykkeri, 1899–1950), 95, nos. 1341b and 1342b.

FIGURE 1.5 Lund, MS Mh 15 *Lundarbók*, fol. 70^{r}: *Landavarnarbálkr*. 1305–20
PHOTO: LUND, UNIVERSITETSBIBLIOTEKET

initial clearly refers to a royal setting, the depicted knight representing the army of the king directly.

As indicated above, all of the following major initials in *Landslǫg* involve a switch from a royal to domestic setting: the next initial at the beginning of *Mannhelgisbálkr*, the section about personal rights and the maintenance of peace, depicts two seemingly arguing figures, holding each other's shoulders with one hand and pointing towards the ground with the other. It is likely that the two figures freely represent the text, as quarrelling figures with crossed arms are known to represent struggle in secular legal iconography.[48] In contrast, the

48 For a late twelfth-century example of quarrelling figures with crossed hands from southern Germany, see Christine Jakobi-Mirwald, "Gratian in Schäftlarn," in *AusBILDung des Rechts. Systematisierung und Vermittlung von Wissen in mittelalterlichen Rechtshandschriften*, ed. Kristin Böse and Susanne Wittekind (Frankfurt: Peter Lang, 2009), 83. For the iconography in illuminated legal manuscripts in general, see Gernot Kocher, *Zeichen und Symbole des Rechts. Eine historische Ikonographie* (Berlin: De Gruyter, 1992).

FIGURE 1.6 Lund, MS Mh 15 *Lundarbók*, fol. 88^{v}: *Erfðabálkr*. 1305–20
PHOTO: LUND, UNIVERSITETSBIBLIOTEKET

following major initial depicts concord and serves to introduce *Kvennagiptingar*, a subsection to *Erfðabálkr*. This and the following section of *Landslǫg* discusses inheritance while *Kvennagiptingar* specifies various legal aspects on marriage. In the initial the two depicted figures have a raised hand in a gesture of agreement. According to the subsection of *Erfðabálkr* the initial introduces, the two figures either depict family members of the persons to be married, or bride and broom directly. A similar gesture is also found in the following initial at the start of chapter seven of *Erfðabálkr* (see Figure 1.6). It is a lively depiction of the content of this section: the upper part depicts a seemingly sleeping figure, who, without doubt, represents the deceased from whom the inheritance is conveyed. The lower part of the initial depicts three figures, two of whom are shown swearing towards the text to the right (a gesture which is found again in the following major initial). A third figure on the left acts as witness, which, according to the text, is required to make such an agreement lawful.[49] Almost similar to *Kvennagiptingar*, the following initial at the start of a large section

49 For a related example from the German *Sachsenspiegel* corpus, see Kocher, *Zeichen und Symbole des Rechts*, 51.

on inheritance, *Landabrigðabálkr*, depicts two figures with their hands aloft, swearing towards the introduced rubric and text. It identifies the two figures as heirs:

> Her hefr hin v. hluth | gula þings bokar með oðals skiptu*m* | *ok* heiti þessi landa brigði. cap*itulu*m. Nu skipta bræðe .ij. eða | fleiri oðolum sin a | millim æða komir þ*at* | er oðollum eigv at fyl | gia. þ*at* er dottir *ok* sonar | dottir fauðe systir *ok* brodvr | dottir *ok* s*ka*l i þa kuils odol hver | fa sem lottin erv.
>
> [Here begins the fifth section of *Gulaþingbók* about the change of inheritance. And this is called *Landsbrigða*[bálkr]. *Capitulum*. Now if two brothers or more want to divide their inheritance between them, the inheritance is not further divided. But if a daughter, and the son of a daughter, has a sister and a brother, everyone shall get their share of the inheritance].

Although the following initial of *Landabrigðabálkr*, still at the same major location of the same section, only depicts a single figure, the action of that figure remains the same as in the previous major initial. Finally, the following section on the lease of land, *Landsleigubálkr*, depicts two heads in the upper part of the initial (E), looking at one another. The part below features a grylli figure with no relation to the text, but the text it introduces identifies the two depicted human heads not as heirs but as either a landlord and a tenant of land, or two witnesses for a lease of land: "Ef maðr vill annars | mans iorð leiga undir | but sit þa s*ka*l han taka | ser boli vel *ok* uanlega | m*enn* .ij. vatta skilrika." [If a man wants to rent the land on which he lives from another man, then he shall take a good property and two witnesses to make the agreement lawful].

The following section, *Kaupabálkr*, about domestic and foreign trade, again relates to the iconographic model used for the previous *Mannhelgisbálkr* and depicts two figures shaking hands with one another and directing their other hand towards the ground below (see Figure 1.7). As this chapter describes trade regulations, the meaning of this scene is twofold: while the handshake references the agreement between the two figures,[50] the pointing hands possibly indicate the measured goods to be traded. The final major initial of *Landslǫg* introduces *Þjófabálkr*, the treatment and punishments of thieves. It differs from previous patterns. According to the text, the initial depicts a hanged figure in

50 Kocher, *Zeichen und Symbole des Rechts*, 50.

FIGURE 1.7 Lund, MS Mh 15 *Lundarbók*, fol. 118r: *Kaupabálkr*. 1305–20
PHOTO: LUND, UNIVERSITETSBIBLIOTEKET

the inner field, with his hands bound behind his back and a noose around his neck. Unfortunately, *Landslǫg* does not refer very detailed to the killing of thieves, but numerous references in earlier vernacular laws and the vernacular literature of western Scandinavia indicate that handing was indeed a common execution procedure for thieves.[51]

Following the core text of *Landslǫg* (G), a royal amendment from King Hákon Hákonarson at fol. 128rb switches the iconographic content of the book painting again to the royal program: the iconography depicts a seated king with a gesture, clothing and overall appearance similar to the same iconographic model as the previous *Bréf Magnúss konungs* of the law-code: the depicted kin, however, is not King Magnús but rather his father, King Hákon Hákonarson. The next major initial is found on the following folio leaf—at the beginning of the royal amendment—and depicts a bearded face, which the text indicates is likely to be King Magnús. The next initial starts an additional royal amend-

51 For references, see Kari Ellen Gade, "Hanging in Northern Law and Literature," *Maal og Minne* (1986): 159–83.

FIGURE 1.8 Lund, MS Mh 15, *Lundarbók*, fol. 132v: *Sauðabréfit*. 1305–20
PHOTO: LUND, UNIVERSITETSBIBLIOTEKET

ment from King Eiríkr Magnússon. Both the rubric and the upper part of the initial identify the crowned figure as King Eiríkr (the lower part is filled with a mirrored acanthus leaf only).

The final major initial, again a royal amendment, is found on fol. 132va and focusses on a different iconographic topic, depicting two rams (see Figure 1.8). According to the text *Sauðabréfit*—a royal amendment specifically written for the people of the Faroe Islands—the two rams have a historiated function, in that they symbolically represent the Faroe Islands (the "Sheep Islands"). Within *Lundarbók*, this initial is the only major initial containing animals (or grylli figures) which refer to the textual content. Due to their self-referentiality, it is likely that the two animals are indeed intended to symbolize the Faroe Islands, but it is unknown if by the time of production of *Lundarbók*, they were used as heraldic symbol. On the Faroe Islands, a ram depicted as part of an Escutcheon appears first on one of the famous pew gables from the St. Olav's Church of Kirkjubær, dated to 1405–10.[52] Nevertheless, the unusual yet clearly historiated content of the initial—in combination with the textual content of *Sauðabréfit*

52 Knud J. Krogh, *Kirkjubøarstólarnir og Kirkjubøur, Brot úr søgu føroyska biskupssøtisins* (Tórshavn: Emil Thomsen, 1988), 34.

and the Faroese orthography of the scribe—may be a further indication that Kirkjubær was the initial place of use of *Lundarbók*.

The fifth and final production unit of current *Lundarbók* features a fragmentary liturgical *calendarium*. It was without doubt written by the same scribe as the other parts, and also illuminated by the same craftsman, although the variety of colors deviates from the previous pattern, with a stronger use of green and less blue. As mentioned above, the darker color of the parchment might indicate the *calendarium* as a manuscript "block" of *Lundarbók*, rather than an actual production unit.[53] But due to the same scribe and illuminator, it may be argued that the *calendarium* was either always part of *Lundarbók*, but placed first in the original manuscript (this would explain its used condition), or that it was originally independent from the other sections of *Lundarbók*, but always used in a similar historical setting (due to the same craftsmen responsible for the two productions). Only two leaves of the original four of the *calendarium* remain. The iconographic models of the remaining months (May–December), however, offer similarities with calendars used in England in the second half of the thirteenth century. Famous examples including similar iconographic circles of the calendar in *Lundarbók* are the *Rutland Psalter*, London, British Library, MS Add. 62925 from ca. 1260 (the calendar is found on fol. 1^{r}–6^{v}) and the *Grandison Psalter*, London, British Library, MS Add. 21926 from ca. 1270–80 (the calendar is here on fol. 3^{r}–8^{v}).[54]

According to Stefán Karlsson, several entries in the calendar of *Lundarbók* suggest a degree of contact with the British Isles: saints including St. Dunstanus (May 19), St. Columba (June 9) and St. Branden (May 16) are mentioned, all of whom are rather uncommon in western Scandinavian calendars. An Icelandic Psalter from the first decades of the fourteenth century, however, mentions Bishop Erlendr in a *calendarium*, as well as St. Columba and St. Þórlákr. The lavishly illuminated codex, Copenhagen, Den Arnamagnæanske Samling, MS AM 241 a fol., has been suggested to be product of a scriptorium in western Iceland. Similar to *Lundarbók*, Copenhagen, AM 241 a fol. features figural paintings in the *Muldenfaltenstil*. Since the two codices were produced contemporaneously, they demonstrate that the (English-style) *Muldenfaltenstil* was used in

53 Manuscript "blocks" indicate texts of originally independent manuscripts which were subsequently joined together in a composite book. For this term, see Johann P. Gumbert, "One Book with Many Texts: The Latin Tradition," in *Codices Miscellanearum*, ed. Ria Jansen-Sieben and Hans van Dijk (Brussels: Archives et Bibliothèques de Belgique, 1999).

54 For the *Rutland* and *Grandison Psalters*, see Morgan, *Early Gothic Manuscripts*, II, nr 112 and 165.

Norway and Iceland at roughly the same time.[55] Nevertheless, St. Dunstanus was worshipped in the Archdiocese of Niðaróss (now Trondheim), and a veneration of St. Branden existed in the Faroe Islands in the fifteenth century.[56] Finally, mention of the mass of St Þorlákr Þórhallsson (December 23) indicates that Icelandic ecclesiastical dates were also known to the scribe of *Lundarbók*.[57] In conclusion, despite the somewhat unusual addition to the otherwise mainly secular content of *Lundarbók*, the text and image of the *calendarium* show several influences from northern Atlantic cultures.

Influences from abroad are also seen in the iconographic images of *Lundarbók*. Generally, initials in law manuscripts depicting single figures are known from the whole European Continent, particular from codices dated to the late-twelfth and early thirteenth centuries. At the same time, few images of established iconographic catalogues from popular legal codes, such as *Corpus iuris civilis* or fictional cases as in *Decretum Gratiani*, relate to the iconographic program of *Lundarbók* directly. On the contrary, the legal content of the initials in the Norwegian manuscript exemplify an individual catalogue of legal topics, and indicate the need for a close reading of the gestures of the depicted figures, and how they relate to the sections initiated. An early example from the *Decretum Gratiani* corpus dated to ca. 1165–70, which includes an unusual iconographic program, is the southern German manuscript, Munich, Bayrische Staatsbibliothek, MS Ms. Clm. 17161.[58] Similar to *Lundarbók*, this codex features a variety of iconographic topics, all of which are closely related to the didactic character of the text and additional glosses, but less closely to the otherwise already generalized catalogues of the same canon law.[59] Similar to *Lundarbók*, the number of figures in Munich, MS Clm. 17161 consists of a maximum of three, which are schematized according to important figures described

55 For the dating and content of Copenhagen, AM 241 fol., see Merete Geert Andersen, *Katalog over AM Accessoria 7. De latinske fragmenter* (Copenhagen: C.A. Reitzels Forlag, 2008), 94–95, with further references, and Lilli Gjerløw, *Liturgica Islandica*, vol. 1 (Copenhagen: C.A. Reitzels Forlag, 1980), 125; for the illuminations see Liepe, *Studies in Icelandic Fourteenth Century Book Painting*, 185–98.

56 See Karlsson, "Lítið eitt um Lundarbók," 219.

57 See Karlsson, "Lítið eitt um Lundarbók," 219–20, with further references.

58 For the textual content of Munich, MS Clm. 17161, see Elisabeth Klemm, *Die romanischen Handschriften der Bayrischen Staatsbibliothek* (Wiesbaden: Reichert, 1980), 2:99–100. For an overview of the iconographic content, see Jakobi-Mirwald, "Gratian in Schäftlarn," 82–97.

59 For the schematization of iconographic catalogues in medieval legal manuscripts, see Susan L'Engle, "Layout and Decoration," in *Illuminating the Law: Legal Manuscripts in Cambridge Collections*, ed. Susan L'Engle and Robert Gibbs (London: Harvey Miller, 2001), 75.

in the introduced fictional *Causae*. The exemplary character of the figures in *Lundarbók* is indeed comparable to the illuminated *Causae* in the *Decretum Gratiani* codex in Munich, and others of the same textual type, but no direct iconographic influence is visible. As shown above, initials in *Lundarbók* instead often follow (parts of) the introduced (often common law) texts rather closely or lead towards a central textual element. General iconographic influences are detectable in a number of ways, but no direct iconographic models are found. For example, the iconographic approach taken in *Lundarbók* for *Erfðabálkr* is similar to that used for inheritance in the *Decretum Gratiani*, as this iconographic model is depicted at the start of *Causa VIII* and *Causa XXXV* in illuminated manuscripts of the late twelfth, thirteenth and early fourteenth centuries.[60] Furthermore, the hanged thief in *Þjófabálkr* resembles a hanged man who is often shown at the start of *Causa XV* in *Decretum Gratiani* codices, although the *Decretum* illuminations display an example of a sinful priest only.[61] Hanged men are featured in Roman law manuscripts too, mainly at the beginning of *Institutiones* 4.1,1, in which the treatment of thieves is discussed, similar to *Þjófabálkr* in *Landslǫg* (and *Jónsbók*).[62] Nevertheless, apart from this example, few iconographic models in *Lundarbók* seem to have been taken directly from the illuminated Roman law manuscripts. Rather, they stem from an otherwise unknown legal iconographic Norwegian program in the early fourteenth century, which however was undoubtedly inspired by *Decretum Gratiani* or *Corpus iuris civilis* manuscripts.

The historiated book painting of *Codex Hardenbergianus* (Copenhagen, Det Kongelige Bibliotek, MS GKS 1154 fol.), a legal manuscript from (possibly) Bergen and produced ca. 1350–60, refers in a number of ways to the illuminations of *Lundarbók*.[63] Though painted in a more elaborate way, the text-related

60 For an overview over the iconography of *Decretum Gratiani* manuscripts, see Anthony Melnikas, *The Corpus of the Miniatures in the Manuscripts of Decretum Gratiani*, I–III (Rome: Libreria Ateneo Salesiano, 1975).

61 For an iconographic example, see Melnikas, *Miniatures in the Manuscripts of Decretum Gratiani*, 500.

62 For explanations and an iconographic example for the *Institutiones* 4.1,1 chapter, see Friedrich Ebel, Andreas Fijal, and Gernot Kocher, *Römisches Rechtsleben im Mittelalter. Miniaturen aus den Handschriften des Corpus iuris civilis* (Heidelberg: C.F. Müller, 1988), 162–63.

63 For the production history and dating of *Codex Hardenbergianus*, see Stefán Karlsson, "Lovskriver i to lande: Codex Hardenbergianus og Codex Belgsdalensis," in *Festskrift til Alfred Jakobsen*, ed. Jan Ragnar Hagland, Jan Terje Faarland and Jarle Rønhovd (Trondheim: Tapir, 1987); For an alternative dating see Magnus Rindal, "No. 1154 Folio in the Old Royal Collection, Copenhagen," in *King Magnus Håkonsson's Laws of Norway and other legal texts*, ed. Knut Berg and Magnus Rindal (Oslo: Selskapet til Utgivelse av gamle Norse

FIGURE 1.9 Copenhagen, Kongelige Bibliotek, MS GKS 1154 fol. *Codex Hardenbergianus*, fol. 9v: *Landavarnarbálkr*. 1350–60
PHOTO: OSLO, NASJONALBIBLIOTEKET

iconographic content is found here again. This is exemplified by the major initial at the beginning of *Landavarnarbálkr*, and also in *Codex Hardenbergianus*, where soldiers are depicted with kettle helmets, shields and chain mail (see Figure 1.9). The overall design of the initial in this younger *Landslǫg* (G) codex, however, stems from other sources, depicting several heavily armed soldiers at the stern of a seafaring vessel.

Contemporaneously produced with *Codex Hardenbergianus*, *Jónsbók* manuscripts from Iceland provide a number of references to the iconographic catalogue of *Lundarbók*. These law manuscripts suggest that an influence coming from Norway to Iceland existed in the decades of the fourteenth century following the production of *Lundarbók*. This is exemplified in *Svalbarðsbók* (Reykjavík, Stofnun Árna Magnússonar í íslenskum fræðum, MS AM 343 fol.) from ca. 1330–40, one of the earliest Icelandic *Jónsbók* codices embellished with historiated initials:[64] Similar to *Lundarbók* (and other *Jónsbók* codices),

håndskrifter, 1983), 21–23; for its iconographic content, see Berg, "The Illuminations in No. 1154 Folio."

64 For the dating of *Svalbarðsbók*, see Kålund, *Katalog* I, 279.

FIGURE 1.10 Reykjavík, MS AM 350 fol. *Skarðsbók*, fol. 91r: *Hirðskrá*. 1363
PHOTO: JÓHANNA ÓLAFSDÓTTIR

Svalbarðsbók features a Christ in Majesty initial at the beginning of *Kristindómsbálkr*, which might indicate a standard iconography for this section of *Landslǫg* and *Jónsbók* too.

Probably the most obvious example of a similar use of iconographic images in Icelandic *Jónsbók* codices to the historiated major initials in *Lundarbók*, however, is found in the superb *Skarðsbók*. Besides *Jónsbók*, ecclesiastical laws, statues and royal amendments, *Skarðsbók* also features a major initial at the beginning of *Hirðskrá* (see Figure 1.10). In comparison with the initial in *Lundarbók*, the seated king with a sword on his knees appears to be related to a number of images in *Lundarbók*, as indeed is his demanding gesture. As with the example in *Codex Hardenbergianus*, *Skarðsbók* features an elaborated form of the same textual reference (see above). A second reference from fourteenth-century Iceland is the *Jónsbók* Reykjavík, Stofnun Árna Magnússonar í íslenskum fræðum, MS GKS 3269a 4to, which was written and illuminated in ca. 1350.[65] At the beginning of *Erfðabálkr*, an arrangement comparable to the same text in *Lundarbók* is shown (see Figure 1.11): in Reykjavik, MS

65 For the dating of Reykjavík, MS GKS 3269a 4to, see Alfred Jakobsen, *Studier i Clarus saga: Til spørsmålet om sagaens norske proveniens* (Bergen: Årbok for Universitetet i Bergen, 1964), 46, 12.

FIGURE 1.11 Reykjavík, MS GKS 3269a 4to, fol. 30r: *Erfðabálkr*. 1350
PHOTO: JÓHANNA ÓLAFSDÓTTIR

GKS 3269a 4to, the deceased is depicted in the part below, together with the heir on the right. Nevertheless, as with the other examples from Iceland, Reykjavík, MS GKS 3269a 4to adds a further artistic dimension to the historiated content of the iconographic model, as it depicts in the upper part of the initial the objects to be (potentially) inherited: livestock. In western Scandinavia, the depiction of a hanged thief in a major initial of *Þjófabálkr* is rather unusual. Although fourteenth-century Icelandic manuscripts depict numerous hanged thieves, the act of hanging is generally not depicted within the initial. More commonly, the conviction of the thief is depicted, followed by the execution, which is either found in the margin on the left or in the *bas-de-page*. The earliest example from Iceland has been dated to ca. 1400: the codex Copenhagen, Det Kongelige Bibliotek, MS Thott 1280 fol., a *Jónsbók* codex which, on textual and iconographic terms, is less closely related to other Icelandic *Jónsbók* manuscripts from the same century. The example from Copenhagen, Thott 1280 fol. suggests, however, that in terms of fourteenth-century Icelandic book painting, the iconographic model used in *Lundarbók* was less commonly used than other iconographic images. Other contemporaneously produced Icelandic manuscripts from the later decades of the fourteenth century relate rather generally to the legal iconographic program of *Lundarbók*.[66] Further

66 For *Þjófabálkr* in Thott 1280 fol and other Icelandic manuscripts, see Stefan Drechsler, "The

examples such as the act of swearing an oath, as in the beginning of *Kvennagiptingar* and the two initials in the first major section of *Landsleigubálkr*, are only generally reflected in the Icelandic *Jónsbók* codices. At the same time, however, they provide evidence for a program of legal iconography in Scandinavia, for which *Lundarbók* might well be seen to be an initial attempt.

With the arrival of legal iconography in Iceland in ca. 1330–40, several often workshop-related iconographic programs were used and copied, some of which indicate a similar approach to the individual sections of *Jónsbók*, which itself is textually related to the Norwegian *Landslǫg*, as mentioned above.[67] The first half of the fourteenth century gave rise to the illumination of a large amount of legal manuscripts illuminated in Norway. This ceased abruptly with the arrival of the Black Death in 1349, after which fewer legal manuscripts were produced in the second half of the fourteenth century.[68] Further indication of the lack of illuminated Norwegian law manuscripts following the arrival of the Black Death may be a change of royal interest in vernacular Scandinavian laws: under the rule of King Magnús Eiríksson, *Landslǫg* ("Code of the Realm") was established in Sweden, and it is likely that the Norwegian book production was affected by these royal instructions.[69]

During and after the plague years, a number of Icelandic scribes worked in Bergen.[70] By that time, the Norwegian iconographic program seems to have been more strongly affected by the established Icelandic program, as indicated in *Codex Hardenbergianus*, the only known historiated legal manuscript which was produced after the Great Plague. It was written by an Icelandic scribe in Norway, most likely in Bergen, and it is fairly likely that it was also illuminated there.[71] Similar to *Lundarbók*, the figural illuminations of *Codex Hardenbergianus* often feature only two to three figures. Yet not all images are comparable

---

Illuminated Þjófabálkr in Fourteenth-Century Icelandic Jónsbók Manuscripts," *Viking and Medieval Scandinavia* 12 (2016): 1–40.

67 For an overview of medieval Icelandic manuscript groups, see Sverrir Tómasson, "The History of Old Nordic Manuscripts I: Old Icelandic," in *The Nordic Languages: An International Handbook of the History of the North Germanic Languages*, ed. Oskar Bandle et al. (Berlin: De Gruyter, 2002), 796–99, and Guðvarður Már Gunnlaugsson, "Voru scriptoria í íslenskum klaustrum?" in *Íslensk klausturmenning á miðöldum*, ed. Haraldur Bernharðsson (Reykjavík: Háskólaútgáfan, 2014), 186–94.

68 Storm, *Om håndskrifter og Oversættelser*, 12–13.

69 Horn, *Lov og tekst i middelalderen*, 41.

70 For some examples from the second half of the fourteenth century, see Karlsson, "Lovskriver i to lande," and Stefán Karlsson, "Helgafellsbók í Noregi," *Opuscula* IV (1970): 279–303.

71 Karl Gunnar Johansson and Lena Liepe, "Text and Images in Norwegian and Icelandic Fourteenth-Century Legal Manuscripts," in *The Power of Book: Medial Approaches to*

to the older Norwegian codex, such as the illumination of *Landavarnarbálkr* discussed above. Furthermore, some initials in *Codex Hardenbergianus* refer to initials known otherwise only from Icelandic *Jónsbók* manuscripts, or to lost iconographic models. Nevertheless, it is likely that *Lundarbók* and *Codex Hardenbergianus* are productions of a loose network of scribes and illuminators working in western Norway, if not from a scriptorium based in Bergen itself, with some contact to Icelandic workshops producing *Jónsbók* manuscripts. Through such networks, iconographic models were exchanged and further developed in the early decades of the fourteenth century.

In conclusion, the textual and iconographic content of *Lundarbók* is exceptional in many ways: first and foremost, it is the earliest Scandinavian law manuscript to include iconographic images. As was shown, a number of these images suggest influences from European law manuscripts, which might have come to Norway during the time at which the regional Norwegian law texts were redefined and re-written in the early 1270s under the auspices of the often-depicted King Magnús Hákonarson. The influence on the contemporaneously altered *Járnsíða* codex for Iceland, which is partly based on the renewed *Landslǫg* but was later incorporated into *Jónsbók*, is not visible until twenty years after *Lundarbók* was finished in ca. 1320. Influences from legal manuscripts produced elsewhere in Europe are not directly visible in the major initials of *Lundarbók*, which is probably due to the focus on the textual content by the scribe, the rubricator and the illuminator in the same codex.

The division of historiated major initials in the five production units suggests that the initial arrangement of these codicological sections must have been different to that found today. Apart from the badly worn *calendarium*, the most important laws (*Landslǫg* [G] and *Bæjarbók Bjǫrgvinjar*) were likely added first, followed by the less illuminated production units *Hirðskrá* and *Gulaþingsgerð Kristinréttar yngri*. The difference in quality and quantity of the illuminations in the different sections in *Lundarbók* are possibly due to a less well established legal iconographic program in some of the texts, such as *Hirðskrá* and *Gulaþingsgerð Kristinréttar yngri*. I argue, therefore, that for the less illuminated texts in *Lundarbók*, the artist had less resources ready to be used by the time of production. The lack of historiated images in these sections, however, is certainly not due to a lack of motivation, since the quality of the illuminations is of a similarly high quality throughout the manuscript. As discussed above, similar textual and iconographic content is found in the Icelandic *Jóns-*

Medieval Nordic Legal Manuscripts, ed. Lena Rohrbach (Berlin: Nordeuropa-Institut der Humboldt-Universität, 2014), 133–34, with further references.

bók manuscript *Skarðsbók*, and it is likely that the text and image of *Lundarbók* were once arranged in a similar way.

The focus on royal and other secular topics of most of the historiated initials may suggest a secular use of *Lundarbók*. Nevertheless, the text and image of the ecclesiastical calendar at the end of the manuscript may well point towards a continuous ecclesiastical usage, despite its unclear relation to the other production units, as well as the Christological focus exhibited in some of the main initials. This is not only indicated in the earliest known provenance of *Lundarbók*; it may also strengthen the previous assumption that *Lundarbók* was exclusively produced for the diocese of Kirkjubær. Both the Faroese-written text and the vivid secular as well as Christian iconographic images of the codex indeed suggest that the manuscript was intended to be used by a well-read cleric dealing on a daily basis with the secular and ecclesiastical matters of the Faroese people.

CHAPTER 2

Wulfstan and the Reordered *Polity* of Cotton Nero A.i

Ben Reinhard

Few Anglo-Saxon legal texts have received as much praise or as little study as Wulfstan's (d. 1023) *Institutes of Polity*. The text has been hailed as Wulfstan's "greatest achievement in the fields of law and politics;"[1] Wulfstan himself, "homilist and statesman," is universally recognized as the most prolific legislator of Anglo-Saxon England and is credited by Patrick Wormald as the most important architect of the early English state.[2] With good reason: as the author of the latter laws of Æthelred (ca. 966–1016) and the long-enduring codes of Cnut (ca. 990–1035), Wulfstan's political thought helped to govern England for nearly a century; *Polity* is perhaps the purest expression of that thought.[3] *Polity* is in its own right a "remarkable document in Old English literature" that "defines the duties of all classes of men, and in the process defines also the limits of power and therefore the interrelation of the church and the secular arm."[4] The greatest achievement of Anglo-Saxon England's greatest law-giver, and an early exploration of the relationship of ecclesiastical and secular power to boot: it would seem *Polity* should be one of the most-studied texts in the early English corpus. But this is not the case. *Polity* has been largely neglected by the scholarly community—there is still no book-length study of the text, and those few studies that do exist rely on an out-of-date and out-of-print edition.[5] The state

1 Stanley Greenfield, *A Critical History of Old English Literature* (New York: New York University Press, 1965), 53.

2 See Dorothy Whitelock, "Archbishop Wulfstan, Homilist and Statesman," *Transactions of the Royal Historical Society* 24 (1942): 25–45. See also Patrick Wormald, "Archbishop Wulfstan: Eleventh-Century State Builder," in *Wulfstan, Archbishop of York: The Proceedings of the Second Alcuin Conference*, ed. Matthew Townend, Studies in the Early Middle Ages 10 (Turnhout: Brepols, 2004).

3 See Wormald, "Archbishop Wulfstan: State-Builder," 22.

4 Dorothy Bethurum, *The Homilies of Wulfstan* (Oxford: Clarendon Press, 1957), 76–78.

5 *Polity* was last edited six decades ago as *I Polity* and *II Polity* by Karl Jost, in *Die "Institutes of Polity, Civil and Ecclesiastical": Ein Werk erzbischof Wulfstans von York*, Swiss Studies in English 47 (Bern: Francke, 1959). Andrew Rabin's new English translation of *Polity*, in his *The Political Writings of Archbishop Wulfstan of York* (Manchester: University Press, 2015), 101–124, is a welcome sign that *Polity* may soon receive the attention it is due.

 | DOI:10.1163/9789004448650_004

of *Polity* scholarship encourages us to return to the manuscripts that contain it; when we do, we gain new insights into the genesis of *Polity* and the development of Wulfstan's political thought. This return to Wulfstan's manuscripts reveals *Polity*—and, with it, Wulfstan's larger social project—as a product of a specifically Gregorian understanding of episcopal duty and pastoral care.

A brief consideration of *Polity*'s editorial history makes it clear how necessary this return to the manuscripts is. The text was last edited by Karl Jost in 1959, who recognized two recensions of the text: a simpler and shorter *I Polity* and an expanded *II Polity*, both of which are reflected in the edition. Unfortunately, Jost worked well before the late-20th-century revolution in editing[6]—a fact made clear by even a brief glance at his table of contents. In his edition, *Polity*'s chapters are presented with a shocking insensitivity to manuscript order: some are rearranged, others exiled to appendices. Even those chapters presented in the proper sequence are scattered throughout the edition, so that chapters contiguous in manuscript appears dozens of pages apart in print. The result is an edition that fails to be a reasonably accurate representation of any of its manuscript witnesses. To make matters worse, Jost's edition was published before N.R. Ker's seminal article[7] identifying the handwriting of Archbishop Wulfstan. Because of this Jost, like others before him, suppressed the interventions of meddling scribes without realizing that one of those scribes was the author himself! All of this points to one unavoidable conclusion: if we are to

6 The attitude of the new, manuscript-centric school of editors is aptly summed up by Patrick Wormald's observation that "the key to a rounded appreciation of the archbishop is to read him not in our editions but in his own." See Wormald, "Archbishop Wulfstan and the Holiness of Society," in *Anglo-Saxon History: Basic Readings*, ed. David A.E. Pelteret, Basic Readings in Anglo-Saxon England 6 (New York: Garland, 2000), 192. Other examples of this attitude could be multiplied; for the purposes of the current study, the most relevant are Andy Orchard, "On Editing Wulfstan," in *Early Medieval English Texts and Interpretations: Studies Presented to Donald G. Scragg*, ed. Elaine Treharne and Susan Rosser, Medieval and Renaissance Texts and Studies 252 (Tempe, AZ: Arizona Center for Medieval and Renaissance Studies, 2002), and "Re-editing Wulfstan: Where's the Point?" in *Wulfstan, Archbishop of York: The Proceedings of the Second Alcuin Conference*, ed. Matthew Townend, Studies in the Early Middle Ages 10 (Turnhout: Brepols, 2004); Joyce Tally Lionarons, *The Homiletic Writings of Archbishop Wulfstan* (Woodbridge: D.S. Brewer, 2010), 24; and Joyce Hill, "Ælfric, Authorial Identity, and the Changing Text," in *The Editing of Old English*, ed. Donald G. Scragg and Paul E. Szarmach (Cambridge: D.S. Brewer, 1994), 183. A particularly good example of what can be gained by such manuscript-contextual reading can be found in Katie Har, "Discussing London and the *Regnum Anglorum* after the 1204 Loss of Normandy," Chapter 8 in this volume.

7 Neil R. Ker, "The Handwriting of Archbishop Wulfstan," in *England Before the Conquest: Studies in Primary Sources Presented to Dorothy Whitelock*, ed. Peter Clemoes and Kathleen Hughes (Cambridge: University Press, 1971).

understand the nature and meaning of this "remarkable document," we must return to the manuscripts that originally contained it.

There are three primary manuscript witnesses to the text: Cambridge, Corpus Christi College, MS 201; Oxford, Bodleian Library, MS Junius 121, and London, British Library, MS Cotton Nero A.i.[8] Since the publication of Jost's edition, it has been widely accepted that Cambridge, MS 201 preserves the earliest version of the text and Oxford, MS Junius 121 the final, with London, MS Cotton Nero A.i serving as something of an intermediary between the two[9]—though there are some indications to the contrary.[10] As Andrew Rabin reminds us, "the extent to which any of the different manuscript versions represent a complete, fully realized draft remain[s] a mystery."[11] But whichever version of *Polity*'s text is the earliest, it cannot be doubted that London, MS Cotton Nero A.i provides the earliest manuscript witness to *Polity* as a whole,[12] and, granting the importance of the other manuscripts, arguably the most important insight into Wulfstan's thought.

It seems at first blush unlikely that this should be so: Cambridge, MS 201 and Oxford, MS Junius 121 are usually treated as the most important manuscripts, and with good reason. Both manuscripts preserve essentially complete and unified versions of the text. Cambridge, MS 201 gives us *I Polity*, even if a few chapters of *II Polity* occur dozens of pages later; Oxford, MS Junius 121 gives *II Polity*, even if non-*Polity* material is interspersed among its chapters. By comparison, Nero's text appears to be disordered, disjointed, and repetitive. It provides chapters from *II Polity* mixed, seemingly at random, with related homilies

8 Helmut Gneuss and Michael Lapidge, *Anglo-Saxon Manuscripts: A Bibliographical Handlist of Manuscripts and Manuscript Fragments Written or Owned in England up to 1100*, Toronto Anglo-Saxon Series 15 (Toronto: University of Toronto Press, 2015), 65.5 (s. xi^{1} or xi med., Winchester NM?); 644 (s. xi$^{3/4}$, Worcester); 341 (1003x1023, Worcester). Scattered chapters also occur in London, British Library, MS Cotton Tiberius A.iii (Gneuss and Lapidge, *Anglo-Saxon Manuscripts*, 363, s. xi med. Canterbury CC) and Cambridge University Library, MS Additional 3206 (Gneuss and Lapidge, *Anglo-Saxon Manuscripts*, 30, s. xi^{2}).

9 For Jost's original arguments, see his "*Institutes of Polity*," 16 ff. Jost's arrangement has become an assumed foundation for subsequent studies, for instance, Renee Trilling, "Sovereignty and Social Order," in *The Bishop Reformed: Studies of Episcopal Power and Culture in the Central Middle Ages*, ed. John S. Ott and Anna Trumbore Jones (Aldershot: Ashgate, 2007).

10 See Ben Reinhard, "Cotton Nero A.i and the Origins of Wulfstan's *Polity*," *Journal of English and Germanic Philology* 119.2 (2020), 175–89.

11 Rabin, *Political Writings*, 100.

12 Though it is a composite manuscript (see below), the relevant section of London, MS Nero A.i is dated by Gneuss and Lapidge to 1003x1023. Oxford, MS Junius 121 is dated to s. xi$^{3/4}$; Cambridge, MS 201 to s. xi^{1} or xi^{med}.

and chapters of the earlier version. Chapters labeled *II Polity* by Jost occur on fols. 102^{r}–105^{r} and again at fol. 120^{r};[13] chapters from *I Polity* at 70^{r}–98^{v}. Notably, four of these chapters seem redundant, with alternate versions appearing elsewhere in the manuscript: the chapter "Be cynge" appears in its *I Polity* incarnation at 70^{r}; and its *II Polity* version at 120^{r}; first and second versions of "Be sacerdan" occur at fols. 72^{r} and 102^{r}; of "Be abbodum" at fols. 73^{r} and 103^{v}; of "Be munecan" at fols. 73^{r} and 103^{v}. The decision to use London, MS Cotton Nero A.i primarily as a source for variant readings seems justified.

Despite all this apparent chaos, however, one critical fact remains: London, MS Cotton Nero A.i is the only surviving *Polity* manuscript that Wulfstan ever handled. More than that, the manuscript's *Polity* preserves additions, annotations, and corrections in Wulfstan's own hand. It is true that Nero A.i will never offer the "polished" final text of the other manuscripts. But it may give us something even more valuable: a witness to Wulfstan's habits of revision and a guide to how he read, interpreted, and developed his own works. Viewed in this way, the apparent chaos of the manuscript offers something like a fossilized record of the text's development, at precisely the stage that that development was being made.

Before it can serve as a reliable witness to Wulfstan's developing thought, however, we must be sure that we are dealing with a manuscript that Wulfstan would actually have recognized, as the manuscript now known as London, MS Cotton Nero A.i did not exist in the eleventh century. The first layer of reconstructions is relatively easy. As it exists today, the manuscript is clearly composite, containing a late eleventh-century manuscript in Old English (fols. 3–57), an early eleventh-century manuscript in Old English and Latin (fols. 70–177), and various early modern additions assembled by chance in the late-sixteenth century; there is no evidence for the two halves of the manuscript being united before then.[14] As *Polity* is contained only in the early eleventh-century portion, the others can be safely excluded from the study. Once the later additions have been excluded, the real work begins: not even fols. 70–177 are identical to Wulfstan's eleventh-century *vade mecum*. In the first place, it is clear that the manuscript has lost leaves and content in the long course of the centuries—the third quire in particular is nothing more than a stub of its former self. All other quires in the manuscript have at least ten folios today; it has only three, and is heavily worn on its final folio. As many as eleven folios might have been lost, and it is impossible to guess what they might have originally contained. We are

13 Jost, "*Institutes of Polity*," 10–11.

14 See Patrick Wormald, *The Making of English Law: King Alfred to the Twelfth Century*, Vol. I: *Legislation and its Limits* (Oxford: Blackwell, 1999), 226.

on much firmer ground in other, less dramatic cases of folio loss such as quire 6, which lost a bifolium between 126^r and 127^v.[15] Fortunately, as J.E. Cross points out, we are able to make a good guess at the original contents of the lost pages: both the opening material on 126^v and the concluding material on 127^r can be matched to tracts held in other Wulfstan manuscripts. The section that ends on f. 127^r shares an identical ending with the excerpt *De electione sacerdotalium ordinum* found on pp. 100–101 of Cambridge, Corpus Christi College, MS 190 (Gneuss-Lapidge 59, s. xi^1 Worcester); *De pastore et predicatore* breaks off where other manuscripts—Oxford, Bodleian Library, MS Barlow 37 and Cambridge, Corpus Christi College, MS 265 (Gneuss-Lapidge 73, s. xi med.–xi$^{3/4}$) continue.[16] Though these tracts are not quite long enough to account for all the material in the lost bifolium, we can reasonably conclude that the original manuscript contained two tracts (an expanded version of *De Pastore et Predicatore* and a *De electione sacerdotalium ordinum*) where today there is only one.

Restoring the original order of the manuscript is perhaps even more important than reconstructing folios lost to wear and tear. In its current form, the manuscript begins—as most Anglo-Saxonists have done since the sixteenth century—with the Old English; the Latin occurs towards the end, as an appendix or afterthought. But even a cursory examination makes it clear that the layout of the manuscript was once very different from what it is today. Quires 1–3 (fols. 70^r–96^v; Wormald's section a) form an internally unified, self-contained block of text: they make a distinct start at quire 1, run continuously with each other, share a single scribe, and are codicologically uniform.[17] These quires have obviously always traveled together. Quires 6–9 (fols. 122^r–67^v; Wormald's section d) make another such block. The remaining three quires—4 (fols. 97^r–108^v; Wormald's section b), 5 (fols. 109^r–21^v; Wormald's section c), and 10 (fols. 168^r–77^v, Wormald's section e)—have no clear and incontrovertible connection to either block of text or to each other, though 4 was partially written, and 10 entirely, by the scribe of 6–9. The final folios of quire 3 are badly worn, suggesting that at some point they made up the end of the manuscript; similarly, the first folio of quire 6 is worn, suggesting it was once at the begin-

15 For this and similar cases of folio loss found in quire 2, quire 4, and quire 5, see Henry R. Loyn, *A Wulfstan Manuscript* (*British Museum Cotton Nero A.i*), *Early English Manuscripts in Facsimile* 17 (Copenhagen: Rosenkilde and Bagger, 1971), 48.

16 See James E. Cross, "Missing Folios in Cotton MS. Nero A.I," *British Library Journal* 16 (1990): 99–100. For the purposes of this article, I assume that the fragmentary *De electione* was substantially the same as the tract in Cambridge, MS 190; I make no such assumptions about the conclusion of *De pastore*.

17 Here I borrow the section titles adopted by Wormald, in *Making of English Law*, 199.

ning.[18] Quires 5 and 10 are, from a codicological perspective, distinct outliers: where all the others are relatively uniform, 5 and 10 both have noticeably larger written space and more lines per page. Finally, at some point or another, Wulfstan annotated every section of the manuscript *except* quire 10. It seems reasonable to conclude that the quire did not join the manuscript until sometime after it had left Wulfstan's possession.

From all of this, it is clear enough that the current form of London, MS Cotton Nero A.i(B) bears little resemblance to the original, early-eleventh-century version of the manuscript. If this is true, the text of *Polity* currently in the manuscript is a far cry from what it originally contained as well. It is seriously out of order and contains some chapters that it should not contain. What today is the cardinal manuscript witness for the development of *Polity* did not exist until, probably, the sixteenth century;[19] in other words, all scholarship on Nero's *Polity* has been based on an early modern chimera. But even though some scholars have recognized the manuscript's fractured form, they have shied away from its implications. Loyn recognized that the manuscript might have gone through multiple stages of evolution but had no interest in reconstructing its original order.[20] Wormald was more optimistic and attempted to untie this tangled knot of information, arguing:

> The evidence is compatible with, perhaps best explained by, the following propositions: the manuscript once began with section d) before proceeding to b) and then a); b) was subsequently supplemented by Wulfstan and his *amanuensis*, and a)'s place was at the same time taken by c); then or soon afterwards e) was added to d); it was not until the sixteenth century that section a) re-established contact with the rest of the volume, and only then was the Old English put before the Latin.[21]

One can quibble with certain parts of this reconstruction—the account the intermediate stages of the manuscript's development seems to me particularly difficult to prove—but it is hard to argue with its first and last stages. If these are correct, the original Nero version of *Polity* would be almost nothing like

18 These codicological data are discussed in greater detail by Wormald, *Making of English Law*, 198. A full description of the features of the various quires is available in *Making of English Law*, 200–1.

19 For the early modern "origin" of London, MS Cotton Nero A.i, see Wormald, *Making of English Law*, 198 ff.

20 See Loyn, *Wulfstan Manuscript*, 23.

21 Wormald, *Making of English Law*, 199.

the version presented by modern editors. In spite of this, even Wormald, in his discussions of *Polity*, treated the modern manuscript (and Jost's edition based upon it) as the received text.[22]

But what if we were to follow Wormald's argument to its logical conclusion? The codicological evidence strongly suggests that the manuscript known and used by Wulfstan proceeded as follows:

Section I (modern quires 6–9; Wormald's section d)
  De ueneratione sacerdotum
  Uerba ezechielis prophete de pastoribus non recte agentibus
  De pastore et predicatore [fragmentary]
  De electione sacerdotalium ordinum [fragmentary]
  De clericis siue eclesiasticis gradis
  Canons[23]
Section II (modern quire 4; Wormald's section b)
  Item de episcopis
  Item (Biscopas scylan bocum)
  Incipit de synodo
  Biscpas scoldan symle
  Be sacerdan
  Be munecum
  Be gerefa
Section III (modern quires 1–3; Wormald's section a)
  Institutes of Polity[24]
  Be cristendome
  Be godcundre warnunge
  Laws[25]

---

22 See Wormald, "Archbishop Wulfstan and the Holiness of Society", and *Making of English Law*, 354.

23 These canons include the portions of the text formerly known as the *Excerptiones Pseudo-Ecgberti* and now called *Wulfstan's Canon Law Collection*, as well as an assorted variety of penitential texts. The latter group includes portions of the *Penitential of Pseudo-Theodore* and the *Penitential of Pseudo-Ecgbert*. Most of these canons are printed in Bernard Fehr, *Die Hirtenbriefe Ælfrics*, Bibliothek der angelsächsischen Prosa IX (Hamburg: Henri Grand, 1914) and Benjamin Thorpe, *Ancient Laws and Institutes of England*, Vol. II (London: Eyre and Spottiswode, 1840); a select number are included in James E. Cross and Andrew Hamer, *Wulfstan's Canon Law Collection* (Cambridge: D.S. Brewer, 1999).

24 While the chapters in the preceding quire are a part of *Polity* as well, quire 6 presents the most easily recognizable version of the text, beginning with the king and ending with all Christian men.

25 This portion of the manuscript includes the following law codes: Æthelstan I, Edmund I, Edgar III, Ethelred V, *Be griðe and be munde*, and the *Norðhymbra cyricgrið*.

At some point relatively early in the manuscript's development—and possibly while Wulfstan still had it in his possession—section Ia (quire 10, concerned entirely with canons on Lenten penance) was added between sections I and II. Whether or not we admit this quire, the reorganization allows us to make a few preliminary observations. In the first place, we see that the original manuscript gave pride of place to its Latin texts. This of course should not surprise us, as the Anglo-Saxons themselves did not share Anglo-Saxonists' preference for Old English over Latin, and Wulfstan was famously dependent on Latin models in his writings.[26] More important is the parallel structure revealed by the reorganization: the original manuscript was divided into two parts of four quires each. The Latin section begins with a series of exhortations to those in high clerical office and then proceeds to a series of canons for all members of society; the Old English begins with *Polity* texts on bishops, and then proceeds to the chapters on the rest of society.

The pride of place accorded the Latin tracts encourages us to give them a closer look. In its original form, the manuscript began with a series of six Latin tracts; the five that survive are listed above.[27] The texts are united by their proximity to each other and similarity in focus: all five treat on the responsibility of the bishop and his clergy to admonish the sinner, govern rightly, and advise the king—and detail the striking penalties incurred by negligence. The shared location and content encourages us to read them as a unit, which for convenience's sake I will call "the Pastoral Group." Taken together, these texts can be read as the theoretical mandate for the rest of the manuscript—and for the legislative and homiletic projects that dominated Wulfstan's career.

Despite their prominence in London, MS Cotton Nero A.i, the texts of this Pastoral Group have never been treated as particularly important. Only one of them has ever been edited, and that more through chance than actual editorial interest: Wulfstan translated the *Uerba Ezechielis* into Old English, and therefore Bethurum included it in her collection.[28] The neglect is even more shocking when we consider that such texts are not unique to London, MS Cotton Nero A.i, but are scattered throughout the rest of Wulfstan's manuscript corpus

26 Eight of the twenty-one homilies edited by Bethurum are presented alongside a substantial Latin source, and almost all of them depend directly on some Latin source or other. Wormald, *Making of English Law*, 202 suggests that "the Latin sections of the manuscript provide the raw material for the Old English." This is certainly true—with the caveat that the Latin sections ought not be reduced simply to sources.

27 A sixth—which originally occupied f. 122r of the manuscript—has been lost to wear and tear.

28 See Bethurum, *Homilies of Wulfstan*, Homily XVIa.

as well. Similar blocks of texts are found in Oxford, MS Barlow 37 and Cambridge, Corpus Christi College, MS 190;[29] another related text block is inserted towards the end of the canons in London, MS Cotton Nero A.i. Most significantly, one other Wulfstan manuscript begins in almost exactly the same way: a strikingly similar group of texts is found at the beginning of Cambridge, Corpus Christi College, MS 265, another manuscript witness to Wulfstan's handbook. That manuscript begins with a sermon entitled *Incipit ammonitio spiritalis doctrine*, a text closely related to Nero's *De ueneratione*; the second text, the *Admonitio episcopalis vitae*, has a strong resemblance to several of the Pastoral Group texts.[30] Together, these texts make up a more substantial body of episcopal and sacerdotal theology than we find anywhere else in the Wulfstan's corpus.

These works deserve careful study. They are, in the first place, valuable in their own right as witnesses to the development of pastoral theology and practice in late Anglo-Saxon England. Even more importantly, they can provide a unifying motivation for the entirety of Wulfstan's Old English corpus. It has long been recognized that a great number of Wulfstan's works were inspired by—and perhaps demanded by—his views about his role as archbishop: his eschatological homilies, the laws, and the great *Sermo Lupi* have all been attributed to this impulse.[31] However, previous study has focused almost entirely on Wulfstan's Old English corpus, and so emerged with an unnecessarily limited idea of Wulfstan's ideas on the subject. Surveying Bethurum XVI and XVIII, *Polity*, the *Sermo Lupi*, and *I Cnut*, Jonathan Wilcox argued:

> The complex of writing Wulfstan addressed to bishops can be distilled to a fairly small number of specific injunctions. Foremost are the injunctions to preach and pray … the most insistent charge made by the archbishop is to cry out, heedless of the perils of the world.[32]

29 Because of its late date, Oxford, MS Barlow 37 lacks a Gneuss and Lapidge entry; for Cambridge, MS 190, see Gneuss and Lapidge, *Anglo-Saxon Manuscripts*, 59 (s. xi^{1}).

30 For Cambridge, MS 265, see the excellent online facsimile available through Stanford University: "Cambridge, Corpus Christi College, MS 265: Wulfstan's Handbook and other Ecclesiastical Extracts," *Parker Library on the Web*, accessed July 16, 2018, https://parker.stanford.edu/parker/catalog/nh277tk2537. Thomas N. Hall edits the *Admonitio episcoporum utilis* in his "Wulfstan's Latin Sermons," in *Wulfstan, Archbishop of York: The Proceedings of the Second Alcuin Conference*, ed. Matthew Townend, Studies in the Early Middle Ages 10 (Turnhout: Brepols, 2004).

31 The foundational study on the subject, as on so many others, is Whitelock's "Homilist and Statesman." See also Lionarons, *Archbishop Wulfstam*, 108–16 and Wormald, "Archbishop Wulfstan and the Holiness of Society".

32 Jonathan Wilcox, "The Wolf on the Shepherds," in *Wulfstan, Archbishop of York:*

These three injunctions certainly do show up regularly in Wulfstan's Old English writings, and they provide an accurate picture of Wulfstan's pastoral preoccupations. But they do not exhaust the subject: the Old English writings tell us relatively little about where Wulfstan's pastoral ideals originated, or why he felt them to be so important.

This should give us pause, as there can be no doubt that he did find these ideals important, and he certainly did his best to put them into practice. After all, of all the educated and solicitous Anglo-Saxon bishops of the seventh through eleventh centuries, very few match Wulfstan's demonstrated zeal for pastoral care, and none match his program for comprehensive societal renewal. Wormald points out that Wulfstan's pastoral program should not seem strange to us: he was only fulfilling standard expectations of episcopal duty. He notes:

> Wulfstan's conjunction of homily and law was not a bastard progeny of a union of moral and jural genres better kept well apart. It was a wholly logical response to the position of Carolingian and sub-Carolingian bishops as God's good servants and the king's too. *The surprise is only that Wulfstan was the one European bishop of his time to adopt this approach.*[33]

That is, while it may have been perfectly logical for other sub-Carolingian bishops to do what Wulfstan did, the fact remains that they did *not* do it; Wulfstan remains a massive outlier. On their own, the Old English texts are insufficient to explain this; indeed, they are part of the puzzle. Nor do they provide a particularly full or nuanced view of Wulfstan's thought on the matter: they simply do not provide sufficient material to make a balanced judgment. If it is true that we cannot understand Wulfstan's corpus without properly understanding his views of the bishop's pastoral vocation, then the texts of the Pastoral Group are the first place to start.

The texts in question are composed of a variety of sources—biblical, patristic, papal, and canonical—cobbled together more or less gracefully. While it is of course difficult to identify an author for such composite texts,[34] circumstantial evidence connects them rather closely to the archbishop: they were

The Proceedings of the Second Alcuin Conference, ed. Matthew Townend, Studies in the Early Middle Ages 10 (Turnhout: Brepols, 2004), 406–07.

33 Wormald, "Archbishop Wulfstan: State-Builder," 21. Emphasis mine.

34 Though of course it has been attempted. Bethurum adopted the practice of editing Wulfstan's Latin sources as his own homilies—so the *Uerba Ezechielis* becomes Bethurum, *Homilies of Wulfstan*, Homily XVIa; Thomas Hall attributed others to Wulfstan based on similar rhetorical technique. See Hall, "Wulfstan's Latin Sermons," 93–140.

owned, annotated, and used by Wulfstan. Subject matter makes the connection even stronger. The texts of the Pastoral Group presume to instruct, counsel, and rebuke priests and even bishops; Jost saw this as evidence that the compiler likely was a bishop or (more likely still) an archbishop himself.[35]

When we examine the sources of the Pastoral Group, even stronger ties to Wulfstanian Worcester emerge. In his discussion of the group, Loyn had noted that the texts were mostly composed of "material from the scriptures, mostly Ezekiel and Isaiah, the letter of St. Boniface to Cuthbert and the legatine synod of 787."[36] This is, on the face of it, odd, as neither the letter nor the synod are particular favorites of Wulfstan. But Loyn's analysis may not tell the full story: given Cross's reconstruction of the two incomplete homilies and advances in Anglo-Saxon source-hunting, it is time to take a second look. A quick glance at the texts seems to corroborate Loyn's assessment. Boniface's letter to Cuthbert is certainly a critical source: it provides the bulk of the text of the *Uerba Ezechielis* and all but two of the biblical citations contained in it. Echoes of the legatine synod can also be detected in the texts—even if they are a less important source than suggested by Loyn. But many more sources lie behind the rest of the works: *De ueneratione* draws on a number of sources well known to Wulfstan, including Benedict of Anian and his own canon law collection; *De pastore* quotes Alcuin's letter to Æthelhard and the *Canones Hibernensis*.[37] Karl Jost points to a range of scattered sources that make up the rest of the text block, several of which were known to Wulfstan in other circumstances.[38]

For all this, neither Jost nor Loyn recognized the most important source-text of all, and the one that ties the group most closely to Wulfstan's workshop at Worcester: the *Regula Pastoralis* of Pope Gregory the Great (ca. 540–604).[39] The text was long known in Anglo-Saxon England. St. Boniface cites it approvingly

35 Karl Jost, *Wulfstanstudien*, Swiss Studies in English 23 (Bern: Francke, 1950), 69. Speaking of Napier XLI/Bethurum, *Homilies of Wulfstan*, Homily XVIa, Jost argues that only a bishop or archbishop could have spoken so strongly to priests and bishops; Hall, "Wulfstan's Latin Sermons," 108 agrees. Jost is probably correct about the Old English homily, and the Latin extracts speak even more forcefully than the Old English distillation does.

36 Loyn, *Wulfstan Manuscript*, 49. Consciously or not, Loyn here echoes Jost's earlier claim that the texts are "eine Sammlung von Exzerpten aus der Vulgata und den Kirchenvätern mit verbindendem Text." See Jost, *Wulfstanstudien*, 63.

37 Dorothy Bethurum Loomis noted that Alcuin was one of Wulfstan's favourite sources, used in numerous homilies and in *Polity*. See Dorothy Bethurum, "A Letter of Protest from the English Bishops to the Pope," in *Philologica: the Malone Anniversary Studies*, ed. Thomas A. Kirby and Henry Bosley Woolf (Baltimore: Johns Hopkins Press, 1949), 98.

38 Jost, *Wulfstanstudien*, 53–62.

39 For the purposes of this study, all citations will be drawn from Gregory the Great, *Regula Pastoralis*, ed. Floribert Rommel (Turin: Città Nuova, 2008).

in his letter to Cuthbert—a letter that Wulfstan certainly knew, as it provided the bulk of his *Uerba ezechielis*—and Alfred famously translated it among the other books "þe nidbeðyrfesta sien eallum monnum to witanne" [that are most needful for all men to know].[40] Even more importantly, the *Regula Pastoralis* was a text known to Wulfstan, in both its Old English and Latin versions. Wulfstan owned and annotated the translation contained in the manuscript now known as Oxford, Bodleian Library, MS Hatton 20,[41] and his library at Worcester housed at least one copy of the Latin original.[42] Its influence throughout the group of texts makes a strong argument for their origin in Wulfstanian Worcester.

Gregory's impact on the Pastoral Group can be seen in a number of ways. In one instance, the dependence is obvious: *De electione sacerdotum* is a freewheeling adaptation of *RP* I.11. Both the chapter and the sermon begin with a paraphrase of God's instruction to Moses and Aaron on choosing priests (in the case of *De electione*, "Eligatur sacerdos sine macula")[43] and proceed with an extended allegorical explanation of the physical requirements of the Old Testament priests. There are, however, noticeable differences in the allegorical interpretations, in wording if not in overall sense: for instance, both texts agree that the fat man is the one who is too attached to worldly pleasures, but they disagree on why this matters. Gregory had focused on the sin of luxury and its attendant shame: the *ponderosus* is the one who "eius animus voluptate luxuriae sine ullo repugnationis stimulo delectatur" [delights his soul in the delight of luxury without any twinge of disgust]. By contrast, *De electione* is particularly concerned with the consistency of the preacher's witness to his flock; the fat man is the one "qui carnalibus desideriis pressus . munditiam corporis quam subditis predicare debuerat . ipse non seruat." [who, oppressed by carnal desires, does not himself preserve the cleanness of body which he ought to preach to his subordinates].[44] Similarly, both texts agree that the man with a broken nose signifies one lacking in discretion, but they disagree slightly

---

40 See Henry Sweet, ed., *King Alfred's West-Saxon Version of Gregory's Pastoral Care, Early English Text Society* 45 (London: Oxford University Press, 1871), 6.7.

41 See Neil R. Ker, ed. *The Pastoral Care*, Early English Manuscripts in Facsimile 6 (Copenhagen: Rosenkilde and Bagger, 1956) and Ker, "Handwriting of Archbishop Wulfstam."

42 The Worcester Cathedral Chapter Library contains one eighth-century fragment of the text (MS Add. 3). Glasgow, University Library, MS Hunter 431 (s. x–xi) is a Worcester manuscript produced, in all likelihood, in or around Wulfstan's episcopacy. See Richard W. Clement, "A Handlist of Manuscripts Containing Gregory's *Regula Pastoralis*," *Manuscripta* 28 (1984): 33–44.

43 Cambridge, MS 190, p. 100, ll. 7–8.

44 Cambridge, MS 190, p. 100, ll. 24–6.

on what discretion means: for Gregory, a moderately sized nose signified the ability to discriminate appropriately, avoiding both too gross generalizations and too subtle distinctions. Once again, *De electione* begins with the same general allegorical reading and, once again, takes a more moralizing note, referring directly to the preacher's relationship with his subordinates:

> Grandi . uel paruo . aut torto naso est quem discretionis penitus ignorans . nunc nimis asper . nunc nimis remissus ; Ubi misericors esse debuerat . crudelis est ; Ubi seuerus . ibi laborat uideri pius
>
> [Having a great, or a little, or a crooked nose is the one who, inwardly ignorant of discernment is sometimes too harsh; others, too lax. Where he ought to be merciful, he is cruel; where he ought to be stern, he labors to appear merciful].[45]

In both cases, the adaptation is close enough to prove clear dependence, but different enough to demand explanation. It looks almost as though the allegorical exposition had been reconstructed by memory, perhaps by someone with particular anxiety about a bishop's relationship with his clergy and the laity under his supervision.

While the dependence of *De electione* on *RP* I.11 is obvious and undeniable, other connections between the Pastoral Group and Gregory are less obvious—but still perceptible. Such is the case with *De ueneratione* and book II of the *Regula Pastoralis*, in which Gregory writes of Eli who, *falsa pietate superatus* [overcome by false tenderness], neglected to chastise his evil sons. The Alfredian translation provides a nearly literal reading: *falsa pietate* becomes *leasre mildheortnesse*.[46] *De ueneratione* departs from both, constructing a warning exemplum out of his *stultam indulgentiam* [foolish leniency].[47] Neither Alfred nor Gregory can serve as an immediate source for this construction, as *De ueneratione*'s words are found directly in several early medieval sources, including a papal letters and a canon collection.[48] In spite of this, given the reliance on the *Regula Pastoralis* elsewhere, it is difficult to escape the notion that Wulf-

45 Cambridge, MS 190, p. 100, ll. 19–21.

46 Compare *RP* 2.6 and Sweet, *Gregory's Pastoral Care*, 122.4.

47 London, British Library, MS Cotton Nero A.i, 125r, ll. 1–2.

48 It is found first in Pope Hormisdas, *Epistola per Universas Provincias*. Edited by Jacques-Paul Migne, PL 63, col. 529C. Perhaps a more likely source, given Wulfstan's canonical interests, is Pope John II, *Canones Joanni Ascripti*, PL 66, col. 31C.

TABLE 2.1 Scriptural citations in the *Regula Pastoralis* and the Pastoral Group. Texts in bold are contained in the *Regula Pastoralis*. Texts *italicized* are shared with other members of the Pastoral Group.

Regula Past. I.11, II.3–4	*De uener. sacerdotum*	*Uerba ezechielis*	*De pastore et predicatore*	*De electione sacerdotum*
Lev. 21:18–20	*Jer. 1:7*	Ez. 3:17	**Is. 40:9**	**Lev. 21:18–20**
Is. 40:9	Ex. 22:8	Ez. 34:2	*Jer. 1:17*	Matt. 25:23
Is. 56:10	**Mal. 2:7**	**Is. 56:10**	***Is. 58:1***	
Is. 58:1	Rom. 13:1–2	Ez. 34:9–10	***II Tim. 4:2***	
Mal. 2:7	I Tim. 6:17	Hos. 4:8	John 10:11–12	
II Tim. 4:2	***II Tim. 4:2***		Matt. 5:10	
	Luke 10:16		*Luke 10:16*	
	Is. 58:1		Num. 16:31–34	
			Ps. 33:20	

stan's knowledge of Gregory's text did not in some way encourage the inclusion of the Eli exemplum.

For all this, the most important parallels between Gregory's *Regula Pastoralis* and the texts of the Pastoral Group come in the biblical passages they both cite. While it is true that the Pastoral Group texts are composed largely of a pastiche of favorite biblical citations, the passages were not chosen at random: they follow, almost directly, the passages cited in the second book of the *Regula Pastoralis*. Table 2.1 makes the reliance of the Pastoral Group on Gregory clear.

While the *Regula Pastoralis* (*RP*) does not provide every biblical citation in the Pastoral Group, every member of the group that cites scripture shares a citation with Gregory.[49] The bulk of these come from *RP* 2.4, which quotes Isaiah 56:10 and 58:1, II Tim. 4:2, and Mal. 2:7; one chapter earlier, Gregory quotes Isaiah 40:9. Naturally enough, *Regula Pastoralis* I.11 supplies the quotation from Mosaic law on choosing a priest. Together, these three chapters provide a sizeable chunk of the biblical quotations in the Pastoral Group: this alone would be sufficient to suggest at least some relationship. Even more strikingly, *every* biblical citation from the three chapters of the *Regula Pastoralis* is represented,

49 It is important to note that the *Uerba ezechielis* citation of Isaiah 56:10 is, like the other scriptural citations in the tract, all but certainly derived directly from the letter of St. Boniface, and not directly from the *Regula pastoralis* itself.

in some form, in the Pastoral Group. The importance of this should not be overlooked: Loyn is certainly right that "material from the scriptures, mostly Ezekiel and Isaiah"[50] forms the backbone of the Pastoral Group. But the bulk of that scriptural material is supplied directly from Gregory's own exegetical writings. Gregory, and not the Vulgate *per se*, is the governing influence here.

If the texts of the Pastoral Group are rooted in the *Regula Pastoralis*, then *Polity*—or at least its clerical chapters—is rooted in the Pastoral Group. This fact is suggested by the structure of London, MS Cotton Nero A.i: just as the texts of the Pastoral Group begin the Latin section of the manuscript, *Polity*'s chapters on clergy begin the Old English section. On its own, this symmetry would be enough to argue for some relationship between the two text blocks—but the similarities go beyond manuscript order. The text groups are united in their message, too: and, as suggested above, this message provides the theoretical mandate for Wulfstan's larger project of societal renewal.

Two distinct themes unite the five tracts with each other and with the introduction to *Polity* as contained in London, MS Cotton Nero A.i. First, in both the Pastoral Group and Nero's *Polity*, Wulfstan's view of the higher degrees of clerics is heavily conditioned, and perhaps determined, by biblical models. The Christian *sacerdos* and *episcopus* carry on the mission of Old Testament priest and prophet, and of the apostles after them, and of Jesus Christ as the archetypical *pastor bonus*. The archbishop holds the place of the apostles in his diocese and is entitled to the respect due them: "Archiepiscopus princeps episcoporum dicitur. Tenet uicem apostolicam" [The archbishop is called the chief of bishops. He stands in the place of the apostles].[51] The dignity and respect accorded them is the same: as *De pastore et predicatore* has it, "Qui enim despicit preconem . timeat iudicem ... Ipse enim dicit, *Qui uos audit . me audit . et qui uos spernit . me spernit*" [If anyone should despise the messenger, let him fear the judge. He himself says, "He that heareth you, heareth me; and he that despiseth you, despiseth me"].[52] But for all that Christ and the apostles provide the most

50 See above, n. 36.

51 See *De clericis*, London, MS Cotton Nero A.i. fol. 127^{r}, ll. 18–9. An interesting analog to this view comes in the tenth-century Blickling Homily, *Dominica Tertia in Quadregesima* (IV.45): "Hwæne monaþ God maran gafoles þonne þone biscop? Forþon þe se biscop biþ Godes gingra, and he biþ efenhalig his apostolum, and efenhlete his witgum" [From whom does God ask more tribute than from the bishop? For the bishop is God's servant, and he is just as holy as his apostles, and of the same rank as his prophets], contained in Richard Morris, ed., *The Blickling Homilies of the Tenth Century, Early English Texts Society* 58, 63, 73 (London: 1874–80). Similarly, Wulfstan homily XVII.31–2, *Lectio Secundum Lucam*, makes bishops the *gespelian* of Peter.

52 London, MS Cotton Nero A.i, fol. 126^{v}, ll. 4–8.

elevated and dignified models for eleventh-century *pastores*, their Old Testament forbears provide the most vivid. The preacher is called to ascend on a high mountain and raise his voice like a trumpet, like Isaiah, and like Jeremiah to cry out before the powerful.[53] According to *De ueneratione sacerdotum*, canon law is the particular domain of the ordained, who, like the Old Testament priests, deserve to be called angels, or even gods.[54] By contrast, lay people who presume to challenge clerical authority have as their model the sons of Core, who presumed to challenge Moses and Aaron, and were swallowed whole by the earth and descended alive into hell.[55]

The revised *Polity* chapters reinforce this biblical modeling. In fact, just as the Pastoral Group can be connected to Gregory's *Regula Pastoralis* on the basis of shared biblical quotations, the opening chapters of Nero's *Polity* can be linked to the Pastoral Group. The chapter rubricated simply *Item*[56] quotes Luke 10:16 ("Qui uos audit, me audit"), which is quoted in both *De ueneratione sacerdotum* and *De pastore et predicatore*. The same chapter also includes an Old English paraphrase of the parable of the hireling and the good shepherd of John 10:11–12, which is also referenced directly by both Latin chapters. The overarching message is the same, too: the good shepherd must follow the biblical example of Christ and the apostles. It is the pastors' duty to preach faithfully and without remission, and it is the laity's duty to obey.

Understandably enough, some scholars have interpreted this vigorous defense and exaltation of the priesthood as a simple attempt to increase clerical power and prestige. There is something to this, and few would deny that Wulfstan had a high view of sacerdotal dignity. Even so, however, it is not enough to read these texts merely as "praise of the priestly vocation".[57] What praise there is does not come free of charge. If the priest or bishop shares in the dignity of the faithful Old Testament preacher, he risks incurring the damnation of the false prophet. Indeed, the tracts insist on the dangers of the priesthood even more than they champion the honor of it; wherever reward is offered, punishment is threatened.[58] This thread, implicit in all five texts, is made explicit in *De electione*: if the priest neglects his duties, "indubitanter non premia sed

53 Per *De pastore*, London, MS Cotton Nero A.i, fol. 126^{r}, ll. 2–8.

54 *De ueneratione*, London, MS Cotton Nero A.i, fol. 123^{v} l. 22–fol. 124^{r}, l. 5.

55 *De pastore*, London, MS Cotton Nero A.i, fol. 126^{v}, ll. 12–24.

56 "Item de episcopis," ed. Jost, *II Polity*, in *Institutes of Polity*, 58–81.

57 This is Jost's term for this genre of literature: "Lob des Priesterberufs." See Jost, *Wulfstanstudien*, 82.

58 The same is true of the Blickling homily, which places the negligent bishop in hell and makes reward contingent upon faithful service. See above, n. 51.

penas percipiet" [He will doubtless receive not reward, but punishment].[59] The bishop has under his charge many souls, and will have to give an account for each one and receive punishment or reward as a result:[60] The principle has its roots in Benedict's *Rule*, II.37–38, which makes precisely the same point regarding the abbot:

> Sciatque quia qui suscipit animas regendas paret se ad rationem reddendam. Et quantum sub cura sua fratrum se habere scieret numerum, agnoscat pro certo quia in die judicii ipsarum omnium animarum redditurus est Domino rationem, sine dubio addita et suae animae.
>
> [The abbot must know that anyone undertaking the charge of souls must be ready to account for them. Whatever the number of brothers he has in his care, let him realize that on judgment day he will surely have to submit a reckoning for all their souls—and indeed for his own as well].[61]

The application of the monastic standard to an episcopal context is alarming, even audacious. After all, the abbot is responsible for a (relatively) small monastic community vowed to poverty, chastity, and obedience; the bishop for an entire diocese. One gets the sense that the compiler was aware of this fact: where the *Rule* stated that the abbot must give an account for "however many" souls were in his care, *De electione* warns the bishop that he will give an account for each of the 100,000 souls of his diocese. The personal stakes could not be much higher.

This principle is made graphically evident in the Eli exemplum in *De pastore*. The foolish priest Eli neglected to punish his wicked sons; as a result, both sons were killed on the same day along with 30,000 of their countrymen, and the Ark of the Testament was captured. But a worse fate still awaited Eli: "ipse retro cadens. fractis ceruicibus mortuus est . et nomen ipsius de libro uite deletum est" [he, falling backwards, died with a broken neck, and his name was removed from the Book of Life].[62] The strongest warnings of all are found in the *Uerba ezechielis*. The Lord speaks *terribiliter* to the misbehaving shepherds:

---

59 *De electione*, Cambridge, MS 190, p. 101, ll. 7–8.

60 *De electione*, Cambridge, MS 190, p. 101, ll. 11–3.

61 Translation taken from: Timothy Fry, ed., *RB 1980: The Rule of St. Benedict in Latin and English with Notes* (Collegeville: The Liturgical Press, 1981), II.37–38.

62 *De ueneratione*, London, MS Cotton Nero A.i, fol. 125r, ll. 8–11. While the bulk of the Eli exemplum has thematic parallels in Gregory's *Regula* and direct word-for-word parallels papal canon collections (see above), the last clause—on the removal of Eli's name from the Book of Life—seems to be an addition original to Wulfstan's manuscripts.

the blood of the sheep will be required at their hands. As the compiler notes, only those who do not believe would not tremble at this: "Ad hec igitur quis non tremescat? Nisi qui uerbis diuinis non credit" [Who therefore will not grow afraid at this, except for the one who does not believe the divine words?].[63]

Polity's chapters on priests and bishops likewise reflect these concerns. This is most explicit in the chapter *Be sacerdon*. The chapter warns priests with the words of an unspecified prophet: "Be þam spæc se witega and þus cwæð: 'Ue sacerdotibus qui comedunt peccata populi'." [The prophet spoke concerning them, and thus said, 'Woe to you priests, who eat the sins of the people'].[64] This is especially telling, as the Latin quotation does not occur in that precise form in any book of the Bible: it is, in fact, a paraphrase of Hosea 4:8. But while the quote is not found in that precise form in the Vulgate, it *is* mirrored exactly in the *Uerba ezechielis* of the Pastoral Group.[65] *De electione* had warned bishops that they would have to render an account for each of the thousands of souls in their diocese. *Be sacerdan* makes the same point—*mutatis mutandis*, in very similar words. We have a priest for a bishop, and a *scriftscire* for a diocese—but otherwise, the argument is identical:

> Sacerd sceal on his scriftscire wislice and wærlice lædan and læran þa godcundan heorde, þe he healdan sceal.
>
> And ægðer he sceal ge wel bodian ge wel bysnian oðrum mannum.
>
> and ægðer he sceal æt Godes dome gescead agyldan, ge his sylfes dæda ge ealles þæs folces þe he to godes handa healdan sceal.[66]
>
> [A priest should wisely and carefully lead and teach the spiritual flock which he must guard in his confessional district. He should both teach well and give a good example to other men. At the judgment of God, he will have to give an account both for his own deeds, and for the deeds of those people he must keep on God's behalf.]

---

63 *Uerba ezechielis*, London, MS Cotton Nero A.i, fol. 125v, ll. 8–9.

64 "Be Sacerdan," ed. Jost, *II Polity*, in *Institutes of Polity*, 121.

65 For all this, the certain *immediate* source for *Polity* is the *Penitential Ps. Egbert*, which includes both the pseudo-quotation and the subsequent exegesis. See Joseph Raith, ed., *Die Altenglischen Version des Halitgar'schen Bussbuches. Bibliothek der angelsächsischen Prosa XIII* (Hamburg: Henri Grand, 1933).

66 "Be Sacerdan," ed. Jost, *II Polity*, in *Institutes of Polity*, 102–4, with abbreviations silently expanded and MS *sceal* restored for Jost's *scolde*. The passage above also betrays strong influence of Benedict's *Rule* II.37–38; see above, n. 61. It looks very much as though Wulfstan is extending the responsibilities of the abbot to the local parish priest.

In addition to all the thematic similarities, one crucial structural similarity unites *Polity* and the Pastoral Group: as mentioned before, the Pastoral Group begins the Latin section of the manuscript; *Polity*'s chapters on bishops and priests begin the Old English. The purpose in either section seems to be the same: to establish the role of the preacher—to correct sinners, admonish the powerful, and protect his flock. Once these duties have been established, we can proceed to the practical application of those duties: canons in the Latin section; *Polity* and the laws in the Old English.

The implications of all this are clear: here, in Wulfstan's *vade mecum*, we find a key to his understanding of himself and his project for the renewal of the English church and people. Together, the texts of *Polity* and the Pastoral Group serve as a kind of personal manifesto rooted in the pastoral theology of Gregory the Great. In these tracts, Wulfstan is revealed as the shepherd of souls; it is his duty to preach, instruct, and rebuke. He will be judged harshly if he fails to do so. The whole of this theory is encapsulated in the *II Polity* chapter "Be ðeodwitan," a text with its own echoes of the Pastoral Group. The chapter concludes with a strikingly personal reflection on his own vocation as bishop—a confession all the more striking because such first-person reflection is almost unknown in Wulfstan's writings. He writes:

> Ic wat swyðe georne me sylfne forworhtne
> wordes and dæde ealles to swyðe,
> ne dear þeah for Godes ege forwygian mid ealle
> fela þara þinga þe dereð þisse þeode.[67]
>
> [I know full well myself to be guilty, in word and in deed, all too much. Nevertheless, I do not dare, for the fear of God, to keep silent about all the things that harm this nation.]

The bishop's entire career—laws, homilies, penitential edicts, and statecraft—should be read in light of these convictions. Indeed, even those elements of Wulfstan's project found most unsettling by modern readers—for instance, his promotion of grotesque mutilation in place of capital punishment[68]—become

67 Ed. Jost, *II Polity*, in *Institutes of Polity*, 57. The same words appear at the conclusion of Bethurum, *Homilies of Wulfstan*, Homily XVII.

68 See, for instance, Katherine O'Brien O'Keeffe, "Body and Law in Late Anglo-Saxon England," *Anglo Saxon England* 27 (1998): 209–32. O'Brien O'Keeffe notes a tendency to "extend the reach of the law inward to the soul" in Wulfstanian legislation (230). She is certainly right to observe this development. It is my hope that this article has demonstrated that

intelligible in this light. As bishop, Wulfstan understood his duty to be the salvation of as many souls as possible. All other concerns—including the codification of English law and the salvation of the English state—were secondary to this pastoral mission and, indeed, byproducts of it. To put the matter another way: Wulfstan was, in Whitelock's famous formulation, the homilist and statesman[69]—but only because he was a bishop first.

such developments were a natural outgrowth of his understanding of his pastoral vocation.

69 Whitelock, "Homilist and Statesman," 25–45.

CHAPTER 3

Liutprand's Prologues in the *Edictus Langobardorum*

Thom Gobbitt

The prologues to the laws of the early medieval Lombard king, Liutprand (king from 712, d. 744), each introduce new sets of legislation that were issued across the course of the first twenty-three years of his reign, in fifteen separate sessions dating from February 28, 713 to March 1, 735. These laws form a part of the collection now known as the *Edictus Langobardorum*,[1] the collected legislation of the Lombards, beginning with Rothari (ca. 606–52) on November 22, 643 through to Aistulf (d. 756) on March 1, 755. These laws continued to be used following the Carolingian conquest of what is now northern Italy in 774 (and with further legislation issued in the south).[2] The legal content of Liutprand's laws and, especially, their framing in the prologues outlining the underlying motivations and contexts for issuing new legislation, position the laws within the legal imagination of the law-givers. They construct the political, socio-legal and religious rhetoric of Lombard royal ideology, reflecting what the law-givers considered to be "the model of an ideal state."[3] More than just suggesting the idealized society imagined by Liutprand and his advisors in the early-eighth century, however, the ongoing treatment of the prologues and laws in their subsequent manuscript transmission informs on how scribes and readers of law-books responded to these legal materials, and anticipated their use. Moreover, variant approaches taken within the scope of a single law-book can underscore the existence of multiple strategies to transmit and update the legal and rhetorical contents, and are suggestive of the broader book cultures both in them and their now-lost exemplars.

1 The critical editions of the *Edictus Langobardorum* remain: Friedrich Bluhme, ed., *Edictus Langobardorum*, MGH LL 4 ed. Georg Henry Pertz (Hannover: Hahn, 1868); Claudio Azzara and Stefano Gasparri, ed. and trans., *La Leggi dei Longobardi: Storia, Memoria e Diritto di un Popolo Germanico* (Rome: Viella, 2005).

2 Paulo Delogu, "Lombard and Carolingian Italy," in *The New Cambridge Medieval History*, vol. 2, *c. 700–c. 900*, ed. Rosamond McKitterick (Cambridge: Cambridge University Press, 1995), 301, 306–07.

3 Delogu, "Lombard and Carolingian Italy," 290.

The complete removal of the prologues from Liutprand's laws (and other legislation issued by single ruler in multiple phases) has been seen in modern scholarship as the result of an early-eleventh-century intervention into the Lombard laws to produce the text edited in the modern day as the *Liber Papiensis*.[4] This new variant of the legal text, once treated as a single authorial redaction of the legal content, has since the late nineteenth century been considered more as an idea of how the laws (alongside a selection of later Carolingian and Ottonian capitularies specifically relating to Italy) could be used, that instead might be re-compiled on demand.[5] This re-invention focused the legal content to its "practical essentials," in particular removing all trace of the prologues to the various law-givers and, especially, legislative phases.[6] However, in the oldest surviving manuscripts of Liutprand's laws (from the eighth and ninth centuries), strategies in which some of the prologues were either selectively truncated or even were completely removed can already be seen. This approach then becomes even more widely attested in the Lombard law-books of the tenth century, see Table 3.1.

Rather than truncation and, particularly, removal being revolutionary approaches to the prologues taken by producers of Lombard law-books in the eleventh century, it will instead be shown here that their removal marked the completion of an underlying, if erratically deployed strategy which was already heavily developed in the manuscript contexts of the laws. While modern, critical editions of the Lombard laws have obscured these varied scribal strategies, returning focus to the manuscripts themselves reveals how widespread they were. The principle focus here is on the interplay between book cultures and the framing of the laws as exhibited in the prologues, but to understand the implications of strategies of omission and truncation it will first

4 Alfred Boretius, ed., *Liber Legis Langobardorum Papiensis Dictus*, MGH LL 4 (Hannover: Hahn, 1868); Johannes Merkel, *Die Geschichte des Langobardenrechts* (Berlin: Verlag von Wilhelm Hertz, 1850); Antonio Azara and Ernesto Eula "*Liber Papiensis*," in *Novissimo Digesto Italiano*, 9 ("Inve-L"), 3rd ed. (Turin: Unione Tipografico-Editrice, 1957), 829; Thom Gobbitt, *The Liber Papiensis in the Long Eleventh Century: Manuscripts, Materiality and Mise-en-Page* (Leeds: Kismet Press, 2021).

5 Robert von Nostitz-Rieneck, "Zur Frage der Existenz eines "Liber Papiensis"," *Historisches Jahrbuch* 11 (1890): 687–708; Charles M. Radding, *The Origins of Medieval Jurisprudence, Pavia and Bologna, 850–1150* (New Haven, CT: Yale University Press, 1988), 82; Gobbitt, *Liber Papiensis*.

6 Charles M. Radding and Antonio Ciaralli, *The Corpus Iuris Civilis in the Middle Ages: Manuscripts and Transmission from the Sixth Century to the Juristic Revival* (Leiden: Brill, 2007), 141; Charles M. Radding, "Reviving Justinian's *Corpus*: The Case of the Code," in *Law Before Gratian: Law in Western Europe c. 500–1100*, ed. Per Andersen, Mia Münster-Swendsen, and Helle Vogt (Copenhagen: DJØF Publishing, 2007), 41–42.

TABLE 3.1 Treatment of Liutprand's prologues from the mid-eighth to mid-eleventh centuries

Reg. year	Vercelli 188	Ivrea 34	Vatican Lat. 5359	Wolfenbüttel Cod. 130	Madrid 413	Paris Lat. 4614	Paris Lat. 4613	Gotha Memb. I 84	Cava 4	Milan O 53 sup
1	full	full	full	full	full	full	full	truncated	full	–
5	full	truncated	full	–	full	full	truncated	–	full	–
8	full	truncated	full	–	–	full	truncated	–	full	–
9	partial[a]	truncated	full	–	full	full	truncated	–	truncated & full[b]	–
11	truncated	truncated	full	–	truncated & full[c]	full	truncated	full	full	–
12	–	truncated	full	–	full	full	truncated	full	full	–
13	full	truncated	full	–	full	full	full	–	full	–
14	full	truncated	full	–	–	full	–	full	full	truncated
15	full	truncated	–	–	–	full	n/a[a]	–	–	–
16	–	truncated	–	–	–	full	n/a[a]	–	–	–
17	–	truncated	n/a	–	full	full	full	–	full	–
19	–	truncated	–	–	full	full	full	–	full	full
21	[no prol.]	[no prol.]	[no prol.]	[no prol.]	[no prol.]	[no prol.]	[no prol.]	[no prol.]	[no prol.]	–
22	n/a[a]	full	full	–	full	full	full	full	full	–
23	n/a[a]	full	full	–	full	full	full	full	full	–

a Missing folio(s).

b Truncated version on fol. 88^{v}, ll. 14–18, and a full version on fol. 91^{r}, l. 19–fol. 91^{v}, l. 16.

c Full version on fol. 89^{r}, ll. 4–16, and a truncated version on fol. 92^{r}, ll. 6–11.

be useful to consider the rhetorical roles that the full prologues actually took as literary and legal texts.

The prologue to Liutprand's legislation of the first year (713) addresses several points. In a discussion of Lombard law-giving, Piergiusseppe Scardigli begins by arguing that "Der König hat das Gesetzgebesrecht" [the king has the right to issue law], but adding that Rothari was the first to actually dare to do so.[7] In Liutprand's prologues, however, as with Rothari's, we rather see that this right was being actively constructed on numerous rhetorical grounds, rather than simply being taken as a passively accepted socio-legal norm. That is to say, the prologues underscore (and create) the legitimacy to issue and emend law for the Lombards, rather than simply expressing an unproblematically established norm. This rhetorical framework needs to be considered in light of Patrick Wormald's assessment of early medieval law-giving as a whole, and his fundamental observation that the question was less a matter of what kings did for the laws, and more of what issuing a law-code did for the legitimacy of the king.[8] Although Wormald recognizes a relatively greater degree of pragmatic legal literacy in the areas south of the Alps, partially in response to the overt legislative mentalities of Liutprand and his advisors evident in the prologues, Rosamond McKitterick's critique of the assumption of a stark north-south division across the Alps is of significance here. She argues that in practice the two sides were more closely matched, with a greater degree of pragmatic legal literacy in the regions to the north of the Alp, while at the same time suspects the pragmatic use of law-books in the south may have been over-emphasized in the scholarship.[9] In addition to the legislative tone of the prologues, the rhetorical

7 Piergiusseppe Scardagli, "Von Langobardischen Königen und Herzögen: Möglichkeiten und Grenzen der Namenkundlichen Betrachtungsweise," in *Die Langobarden: Herrschaft und Identität*, ed. Walter Pohl and Peter Erhart (Vienna: Verlag der Österreichischen Akademie der Wissneshcaften, 2005), 464.

8 Patrick Wormald, "The *Leges Barbarorum*: Law and Ethnicity in the Medieval West," in *Regna and Gentes: The Relationship Between Late Antiquity and Early Medieval Peoples and Kingdoms in the Transformation of the Roman World*, ed. Hans-Werner Goetz, Jörg Jamut, and Walter Pohl (Leiden: Brill, 2003); Patrick Wormald, "*Lex Scripta* and *Verbum Regis*: Legislation and Germanic Kingship from Euric to Cnut," in *Early Medieval Kingship*, ed. Peter H. Sawyer and Ian N. Wood (Leeds, Leeds University Press, 1977).

9 Rosamond McKitterick, "Some Carolingian Law Books and their Function," in *Authority and Power: Studies on Mediaeval Law and Government Presented to Walter Ullmann on his 70th birthday*, ed. Peter Linehan and Brian Tierney (Cambridge: Cambridge University Press, 1980); Rosamond McKitterick, *Carolingians and the Written Word* (Cambridge: Cambridge University Press, 1989); Rosamond McKitterick, "Script and Book Production," in *Carolingian Culture: Emulation and Innovation* (Cambridge: Cambridge University Press, 1994), 221–47.

construction of a king's right to legislate, alongside legitimacy to be king, must then be at the forefront when reading the prologues.

Written in the first-person from Liutprand's perspective, the prologue to the laws of Liutprand's first year (713) begins by emphasizing that he, a "christianus catholicus princeps" [Christian catholic prince], has been influenced to judge wisely, trusting in God rather than to his own wisdom. Divine inspiration and the protection of God occur repeatedly throughout the remainder of the prologue, and in many of those which follow. While we may take this as a heartfelt attestation of how law should be implemented by a Christian law-giver with an eye on the good of his soul, at the same time it also serves to legitimize the giving of laws within a framework of biblical kingship, with a direct reference to Soloman and Proverbs 21:1, as well as a citation of the Apostle James attestation, reflecting on the giving of good law, that "omnum donum optimum et omnum datum perfectum desursum est" [every good gift and every perfect gift is from above] (James 1:17).[10]

Many of the later prologues continue to embed Liutprand's law-giving within a religious framework of seeking divine approval and sometimes salvation. In an overview of Lombard political rhetoric, Dick Harrison argues that the extent of piety expressed in Liutprand's prologues increases steadily as the years go by, and particularly so in the fifteenth and sixteenth years (727 and 728).[11] I would suggest that this overall interpretation needs to be re-assessed, although there is a dramatic increase in the religious framing in the prologue to the sixteenth year. Otherwise, I would argue that the general trend in the prologues is in fact towards a decrease in religious framing, with a counterpoint increase in expressions of socio-legal motivations and legal practice. These latter elements become steadily more prevalent from the thirteenth and fourteenth years onwards, so the shift in emphasis should be seen as interdependent threads, rather than being inversely related to each other.

One partial exception to the decrease in religious framing of the laws is in the formulas accompanying the naming of the law-giver ("in deo nomini" [in the name of God] and in particular variations of "deo dilecte" [favored of God]), as well as when giving the year of Liutprand's reign ("deo protogente" [with

10 Liutprand, prologue to year one: Bluhme, *Edictus Langobardorum*, 107–08; translation emended from Katherine Fischer-Drew, trans., *The Lombard Laws* (Cinnaminson, NJ: University of Pennsylvania Press, 1996), 144.

11 Dick Harrison, "Political Rhetoric and Political Ideology in Lombard Italy," in *Strategies of Distinction: The Construction of Ethnic Communities, 300–800*, ed. Walter Pohl and Helmut Reimitz (Leiden: Brill, 1998), 243–44, 248–49; Dick Harrison, *The Early State and the Towns: Forms of Integration in Lombard Italy AD568–774* (Lund: Lund University Press, 1993), 108.

God's protection] or related expressions). Even these decrease somewhat, as in the prologues for the fourteenth to nineteenth years inclusive Liutprand is not normally identified by name, so there is no reason to include the accompanying formula, although as will be seen, these were retroactively introduced into these prologues in an early ninth-century manuscript, Ivrea, Biblioteca Capitolare, MS 34,[12] as part of a broader strategy of emendation and truncation. This insertion of Liutprand's name, however, was not continued in the other, later manuscripts. Outside of the formulaic framing of title and year, many of the later prologues then have few expressions of pious motivation in them, and there are none at all in fact in the prologues for the eighth, thirteenth, nineteenth and twenty-second years.

The second major theme used to legitimize the laws in the prologue is a direct call back to the legislation of the preceding Lombard kings, Rothari and Grimwald in the law-book. Here Liutprand argues, similar to how Grimwald had previously done in the prologue to his laws issued in July 668, through an inventive re-writing of Rothari's prologue (643), that should any "[…] langobardorum princeps eus successor superfluum quid inibi reperit, ex eo sapienter aufferit, et quod minus invenerit" [[…] prince of the Lombards, one of his successors, discover anything superfluous there, he should remove it, and that which he finds lacking, he should add].[13] In this, both Liutprand and Grimwald twisted the specific words of Rothari to suit their own ends, for in Rothari's prologue it only outlines that he and his councilors had themselves engaged in these activities of emendation, but no injunction was made to his successors.[14]

This strategy of referring back to the previous law-givers, however, is not continued in Liutprand's later prologues, and no further mention is made there of the previous Lombard kings. Instead Liutprand only refers back to his own earlier legislative phases, this occurs in nearly all his legislative phases from the fifth through to the nineteenth years, with the exception only of thirteenth year. In the thirteenth year, as well as in the twenty-second and twenty-third, the previous legislative phases are not mentioned directly in the prologue, but the absence at that time of laws in the law-book addressing the subject of the

---

12 "Ivrea, Biblioteca Capitolare, XXXIV (5)," in *Bibliotheca Legum: A Database on Carolingian Secular Law Texts*, ed. Karl Ubl, accessed November 06, 2019, http://www.leges.uni-koeln.de/en/mss/codices/ivrea-bc-xxxiv-5/; "Ivrea, Biblioteca Capitolare, XXXIV," in *Capitularia: Edition der fränkischen Herrschererlasse*, ed. Karl Ubl, accessed November 06, 2019, https://capitularia.uni-koeln.de/en/mss/ivrea-bc-xxxiv/.

13 Liutprand, Prologue to year one: Bluhme, *Edictus Langobardorum*, 107–08; Fischer-Drew, *Lombard Laws*, 144–45.

14 Rothari, Prologue, Nos. 386 and 388; Grimwald, Prologue: Bluhme, *Edictus Langobardorum*, 1–3, 89–90, 91.

promulgation is noted instead.[15] For Liutprand, then, the legitimacy to issue further legislation arose from the fact that he had already legislated previously, and perhaps by the final legislative phases of his reign even that reminder was not necessary.

The third thread in the legitimization of Liutprand's laws from the prologue to his first year identifies the groups of people who were present at the session where the law was promulgated. Specifically named are judges from Austria, Neustria and Tuscany, the *reliquis fideles meis langobardis* [remainder of my sworn Lombard followers],[16] and the other people who were present. Unlike in the epilogue to the *Edictus Rothari*, No. 386, no explicit mention is made of the *gairethinx* here, that is the legal gathering of (free, male) Lombards in the confirmation of the new laws.[17] Nevertheless, the referral to the people gathered at the assembly parallels the somewhat public confirmation of the law in Rothari No. 386,[18] just as the specific mentions of the *iudices* [judges] in Rothari's epilogue and Grimwald's prologue are echoed again in the prologue to Liutprand's first year.[19] Again, these threads are continued to varying extents in later prologues. While the *iudices* [judges] are mentioned in almost every prologue, except for the eighth, eleventh and twenty-second years, the specific reference to them having come from Austria, Neustria and Tuscany is dropped from the ninth year onwards. The two exceptions to this are the fourteenth year, where locations are reintroduced, but only Austria and Neustria are mentioned, and then the seventeenth year when Tuscany is also included once more. Presumably usual patterns of attendance stopped drawing attention, and notice was only made when things changed. Other social groups who are named in the later prologues vary, in the eighth year the veris optimatibus [major nobles] are mentioned instead of the *iudices*, alongside the nobilibus langobardis [noble Lombards]. As "iudices" is better understood in the Lombard laws as a collective term for the dukes and *gastalds*, and related judicial functionaries, the various noble Lombards referred to here may be synonymous.[20] Otherwise the

---

15 Liutprand, Prologues to years thirteen, twenty-two and twenty-three: Bluhme, *Edictus Langobardorum*, 133–34, 169, and 171–72.

16 Liutprand, Prologue to year one: Bluhme, *Edictus Langobardorum*, 107–08; Fischer-Drew, *Lombard Laws*, 144–45.

17 Stefano Gasparri, "Kingship Rituals and Ideology in Lombard Italy," in *Rituals of Power: From Late Antiquity to the Early Middle Ages*, ed. Frans Theuws and Janet L. Nelson (Leiden: Brill, 2000), 98–101.

18 Rothari, No. 386: Bluhme, *Edictus Langobardorum*, 89–90.

19 Rothari, Nos. 386, Grimwald, Prologue, and Liutprand, Prologue to year one: Bluhme, *Edictus Langobardorum*, 89–90, 91, 107–108; Delogu, "Lombard and Carolingian Italy," 293.

20 Delogu, "Lombard and Carolingian Italy," 293; François Bougard, *La Justice Dans le Roy-*

main group mentioned is again the Lombard *fideles* [faithful followers] of Liutprand,[21] who appear in about half of the prologues.

Socio-legal motivations for issuing the new sets of laws are scattered throughout the prologues, although are omitted from the ninth to twelfth years then return from their onwards. Coupled with the falling away, overall, of religious framing, the socio-legal motivations appear to become more prominent. The prologue to Liutprand's laws of the thirteenth year is particularly informative, as it reflects on the historical contexts preceding the promulgation, and the process by which the new legal content was established. It specifically notes that cases have been brought before Liutprand that were the subject of some controversy, and that an immediate judgement was postponed in favor of discussion—with the *iudices*, not just in their presence—and the establishment of the new laws addressing a response to the situations.[22] This desire for consistency becomes apparent once more in the prologue to the fourteenth year, where it is observed that, in cases not covered clearly in the law-book, some *iudices* judge "according to unwritten custom and others according to judicial discretion" [alii per consuitutinem, alii per erbitrium iudicare estimabant].[23] Here an attempt is made to smooth over the multiple approaches to situations arising from such approach, by clarifying the law in a range of situations. The same issue of judges varying between unwritten custom and their own discretion arises again in the prologue to the fifteenth year,[24] suggesting perhaps that the previous years' investigations into judicial malpractice had continued to yield situations that needed addressing. By the prologue to the twenty-second year, and indirectly in that of the twenty-third year, there is mention of situations that caused some doubt for the judges [erat iudicibus nostris dubium ad iudicandum],[25] which might again be taken to suggest that the events of those previous years had left judges wary of judging by local custom or their own discretion, and felt it more prudent to first check with Liutprand and the Lombard court instead.

Further reference to controversies that needed addressing, but without specific statement of a delay in judgement or inconsistent approaches taken by

---

aume d'Italie: De la Fin du VIIIe Siècle au Debut du XIe Siècle (Rome: École Française de Rome, Palais Farnèse, 1995), 141.

21 Delogu, "Lombard and Carolingian Italy," 293.

22 Liutprand, Prologue to year thirteen: Bluhme, *Edictus Langobardorum*, 133–34.

23 Liutprand, Prologue to year fourteen: Bluhme, *Edictus Langobardorum*, 135; Fischer-Drew, *Lombard Laws*, 173–74.

24 Liutprand, Prologue to year fifteen: Bluhme, *Edictus Langobardorum*, 141.

25 Liutprand, Prologue to year twenty-two: Bluhme, *Edictus Langobardorum*, 169.

judges arise in the prologue to the seventeenth year. At the same time, the prologue to the seventeenth year, and also that for the nineteenth, explicitly sets the date of promulgation (March 1, 729 and March 1, 731, respectively) as the point for which the new law was to be implemented, with cases that are already completed not to be re-opened, while new cases or those still in progress to be judged according to the new legislation. The prologues, then, also mark legal time, and reflect the continued intellectual development of the legal system. Throughout the prologues to Liutprand's legislation a sense of continual reflection and iteration is presented, and the relationship between law-givers and the broader Lombard populace seems to be both close and flowing frequently in both directions. At times the weight of this input appears apparent, as can be seen in the opening words to the prologue of the nineteenth year: "Superstitiosae et vanae contentiones assidue nostrum impulsare clementiam non cessant" [Our clemency is constantly beseeched by the unceasing controversies of the superstitious and vain].[26] While sounding a little weary, it nonetheless appears to have been taken as motivation rather than burden by Liutprand and his councilors.

Against this backdrop of literary and rhetorical framing, then, scribes producing variants of the law-books—already from the eighth century—selected which prologues, or parts thereof, to retain. As the complete removal of all prologues is considered one of the defining features of the *Liber Papiensis*, it is probably most useful to begin with comparable removal strategies attested in the earlier manuscripts of the *Edictus Langobardorum*, before considering the strategies of selective truncation.

Some of the prologues are in fact already omitted from the oldest surviving manuscript of the *Edictus Langobardorum* to include the laws of Liutprand, Vercelli, Biblioteca Capitolare Eusebiana, MS 188.[27] The laws of Liutprand run from fol. 109^v, l. 11, to their now-abrupt ending partway through those of the twenty-first year, on fol. 169^v, l. 24. Moreover, with its mid-eighth century dating, this is the only surviving Lombard law-book with Liutprand's legislation, which was produced prior to the Carolingian conquest of the Lombard *regnum*. As the end of the capitula list includes the laws of the twenty-second and twenty-third years, with some parts just visible on the remains of the badly damaged

26 Liutprand, prologue to year nineteen: Bluhme, *Edictus Langobardorum*, 155; Fischer-Drew, *Lombard Laws*, 194–95.

27 "Vercelli, Biblioteca Capitolare Eusebiana, CLXXXVIII," in *Bibliotheca Legum: A Database on Carolingian Secular Law Texts*, ed. Karl Ubl, accessed November 06, 2019, http://www.leges.uni-koeln.de/en/mss/codices/vercelli-bce-clxxxviii/.

fol. 16^{v}, as well as on fols. 17^{r}–18^{r},[28] it must post-date the last of these, 735. If not necessarily contemporary with the final years of Liutprand's reign, before his death in 744, the law-book is unlikely to postdate them by more than a quarter of a century at most. Consequently, it might be expected that the treatment of the contents would more-closely reflect Lombard—or even Liutprandic—royal interests and rhetoric, especially considering its north Italian point of origin where royal control was stronger than in the south.[29]

Despite the early date of the Vercelli manuscript, there is already some disruption identifiable in the prologues. The full prologues are given for years 1 to 11 and 14 and 15, while that for the thirteenth year (fol. 134^{v}, l. 21–fol. 135^{r}, l. 18) omits only a single word, March, in the second version of the dating clause. The original form of the prologue for year twelve cannot be judged, as it was one of the now lost folios, but in the later supply folios the prologue was omitted, with the section beginning instead directly with Liutprand, No. 54,[30] at the top of fol. 129^{r}. The remaining years in the law-code, that is sixteen (fol. 149^{v}), seventeen (fol. 152^{v}), nineteen (fol. 157^{r}) and twenty-one (fol. 163^{v}) all omit prologues. Those of the twenty-second and twenty-third years cannot be assessed, as these also have also been lost from the manuscript.

The motivations for omitting the prologues for the sixteenth to twenty-first years from Vercelli, MS 188 are not immediately apparent. It cannot be that these are the years in which Liutprand does not identify himself as the law-giver for the *gentis langobardorum* [people of the Lombards], as that pattern had already begun in earlier legislative phases, comprising the prologues for the fourteenth to nineteenth years, inclusive. There is some emphasis on what might be considered socio-legal motivations for issuing new laws in these prologues, but with the exception of the prologues for the ninth to twelfth years this pattern can be found throughout the laws. Religious motivations for issuing new laws are completely absent from the prologue to the nineteenth year (and also those of the eighth and thirteenth years, nor that of the twenty-second year, not included in the Vercelli manuscript), and barely mentioned in the prologue to the seventeenth year (nor the fourteenth or twenty-third years), where it is hoped that the new additions will be pleasing to God.[31]

This certainly contrasts with the greater emphasis on divine approval seen in the earlier prologues (especially for the first, fifth and twelfth years which all make multiple reference to the divine), but the sixteenth year has one of

28 Liutprand, Capitula list: Bluhme, *Edictus Langobardorum*, 96–106.
29 Delogu, "Lombard and Carolingian Italy," 296.
30 Liutprand No. 54: Bluhme, *Edictus Langobardorum*, 128–29.
31 Liutprand, Prologue, seventeenth year: Bluhme, *Edictus Langobardorum*, 150.

the most intensive appeals to the divine found across all the prologues, with hopes that the laws will contribute to the salvation of the nation, be beneficial for Liutprand's soul, and they directly call on God's witness that the motivations are not for personal gain but are intended to please God.[32] That these laws were issued in 728, the same year that the fortress of Sutri, that Liutprand had captured in the previous year (727), was returned to Rome, may also be of relevance.[33] Diplomatic circumstances may have required a greater display of piety on Liutprand's behalf than had been more usual in his more recent legislation, and the public proclamation of new law would have provided an ideal circumstance for making such a statement. What matters here, is that the grounds for excluding the group of prologues for the sixteenth to twenty-first years from the Vercelli manuscript, then, cannot have been due to the lessening of religious sentiments being expressed. No absolute and cohesive pattern to explain the omission of these prologues based on their contents, then, presents itself. Perhaps the Vercelli manuscript (or its exemplar) had itself been compiled from a number of exemplars, in turn corresponding to different groups of the legislation, if not necessarily that of individual years, and those from the sixteenth year onwards were already without their prologues.

The omission of one or more entire prologues to Liuptrand's laws from the later manuscripts is also widely attested, and in fact only one of the seven manuscripts from the long tenth century includes the full collection of prologues: Paris, Bibliothèque Nationale de France, MS Lat. 4614.[34] Even here, however there is some disruption in their layout as the prologues to the laws from the first to eleventh years (with capitula lists) are written continuously before the main body of the laws begin (fol. 27v, l. a3 to fol. 28v, l. b16). The later legislative phases, from fol. 35r, l. a10 to fol. 50v, l. b35, then have their prologues at the outset of each set of laws, (here mostly without capitula lists, with the exception of the seventeenth year, fol. 42r, l. b31–fol. 42v, l. a21 and the twentieth year, fol. 46v, ll. a22–b16). This intriguing organizational structure is beyond the scope of this current study, save for noting that, with some allowances for the confusion in the use of capitula numbering, it may imply the unification of (at least) two disparate and self-contained versions of Liutprand's laws, that had clearly been organized according to fundamentally different strategies.

---

32 Liutprand, Prologue, sixteenth year: Bluhme, *Edictus Langobardorum*, 146–47.

33 See, Neil Christie, *The Lombards* (Oxford: Blackwell, 1995), 102; Delogu, "Lombard and Carolingian Italy," 294.

34 "Paris, Bibliothèque Nationale, Lat. 4614," in *Bibliotheca Legum: A Database on Carolingian Secular Law Texts*, ed. Karl Ubl, accessed November 06, 2019, http://www.leges.uni-koeln.de/en/mss/codices/paris-bn-lat-4614/.

The scribes of the other six manuscripts of Liutprand's laws from the ninth and tenth centuries deliberately omitted one or, usually, more prologues—or else copied directly from manuscripts where that was already the case. Paris, Bibliothèque Nationale de France, MS Lat. 4613 is almost complete, omitting only a single prologue, that of the fourteenth year, fol. 33v.[35] However, as the folios with the onset of the laws for the fifteenth and sixteenth years are now both lost, even here at least two more could theoretically have been omitted. Moreover, as will be seen shortly, a sizeable number of prologues from Paris, MS Lat. 4613 have also been truncated. In the early eleventh-century, Cava de'Tirreni, Biblitoeca della Badia, MS 4,[36] produced in southern Italy, probably Benevento, two of Liutprand's prologues are omitted: those of the fifteenth year (fol. 116r) and the sixteenth year (fol. 121r). There are at least three prologues omitted from Vatican, Biblioteca Apostolica Vaticana, MS Vat. Lat. 5359,[37] a palimpsest produced, probably in Verona, in the later ninth or tenth centuries. The omitted prologues comprise those for the fifteenth (fol. 109r), sixteenth (fol. 113r) and nineteenth (fol. 118v) years, while the folio with the onset of the seventeenth year is now lost. Four of Liutprand's prologues are omitted from the tenth-century Madrid, Biblioteca Nacional, MS 413,[38] produced in southern

35 "Paris, Bibliothèque Nationale, Lat. 4613," in *Bibliotheca Legum: A Database on Carolingian Secular Law Texts*, ed. Karl Ubl, accessed November 06, 2019, http://www.leges.uni-koeln.de/en/mss/codices/paris-bn-lat-4613/; "Paris, Bibliothèque Nationale, Lat. 4613," in *Capitularia: Edition der fränkischen Herrschererlasse*, ed. Karl Ubl, accessed November 06, 2019, https://capitularia.uni-koeln.de/en/mss/paris-bn-lat-4613/; "Paris, Bibliothèque Nationale de France, MS Lat. 4613," in *Early Medieval Laws and Law-Books*, ed. Thom Gobbitt, last modified February 06, 2020, https://thomgobbitt.files.wordpress.com/2020/02/paris-bnf-ms-lat-4613.pdf.

36 "Cava de'Tirreni, Biblioteca della Badia, 4," in *Bibliotheca Legum: A Database on Carolingian Secular Law Texts*, ed. Karl Ubl, accessed November 06, 2019, http://www.leges.uni-koeln.de/en/mss/codices/cava-dei-tirreni-bdb-4/; "Cava de'Tirreni, Biblioteca della Badia, 4," in *Capitularia: Edition der fränkischen Herrschererlasse*, ed. Karl Ubl, accessed November 06, 2019, https://capitularia.uni-koeln.de/en/mss/cava-dei-tirreni-bdb-4/.

37 "Vatican, Biblioteca Apostolica Vaticana, Vat. Lat. 5359," in *Bibliotheca Legum: A Database on Carolingian Secular Law Texts*, ed. Karl Ubl, accessed November 06, 2019, http://www.leges.uni-koeln.de/en/mss/codices/vatikan-bav-vat-lat-5359/; "Vatican, Biblioteca Apostolica Vaticana, Vat. Lat. 5359," in *Capitularia: Edition der fränkischen Herrschererlasse*, ed. Karl Ubl, accessed November 06, 2019, https://capitularia.uni-koeln.de/en/mss/vatikan-bav-vat-lat-5359/.

38 "Madrid, Biblioteca Nacional, 413," in *Bibliotheca Legum: A Database on Carolingian Secular Law Texts*, ed. Karl Ubl, accessed November 06, 2019, http://www.leges.uni-koeln.de/en/mss/codices/madrid-bn-413/; "Madrid, Biblioteca Nacional, MS 413," in *Early Medieval Laws and Law-Books*, ed. Thom Gobbitt, last modified 01 April 2018, https://thomgobbitt.files.wordpress.com/2018/04/madrid_bn_ms413_april2018.pdf.

Italy, probably in Benevento or Salerno. Here the prologue and all laws for the eight year are omitted, as well as Liutprand's prologues for the fourteenth to sixteenth years (fols. 104^{v}, 110^{r} and 114^{v}, respectively). The copy of Liutprand's laws from the *Edictus Langobardorum* (rather than its copy of the *Liber Legum* which is beyond the scope of this study) in Gotha, Forschungsbibliothek, MS Memb. I. 84, produced in Mainz in the tenth century,[39] omits as many as eight of the prologues, that is to say more than half, and comprising those for the fifth to ninth years, the thirteenth year, and then the fifteenth to nineteenth years, inclusive.[40] While this is a significantly large number, it does not match that of Wolfenbüttel, Herzog August Bibliothek, MS Cod. Guelf. 130. Blank.,[41] which was also produced in the tenth-century in northern Italy, although had moved north of the Alps to be in the possession of the cathedral of Augsberg by the eleventh or twelfth century. Here all of the prologues except for that of the first year are omitted.

In the near-complete omission of prologues, then, the Wolfenbüttel manuscript is already therefore very much a complete precursor of the *Liber Papiensis*. This in fact becomes even more apparent as the prologue to Liutprand's first year is retained also in four of the seven manuscripts of the *Liber Papiensis*.[42] The reason that it is not usually treated as a version of the *Liber Papiensis* in its own right, is that while it does have an extensive capitulary collection

39 The manuscript is now composite, comprising four independent, codicological units, with the *Liber Legum* and *Edictus Langobardorum* having been produced in originally separate parts: "Gotha, Forschungsbibliothek, Memb. I 84," in *Bibliotheca Legum: A Database on Carolingian Secular Law Texts*, ed. Karl Ubl, accessed November 06, 2019, http://www.leges.uni-koeln.de/en/mss/codices/gotha-flb-memb-i-84/; "Gotha, Forschungsbibliothek, Memb. I 84," in *Capitularia: Edition der fränkischen Herrschererlasse*, ed. Karl Ubl, accessed November 06, 2019, https://capitularia.uni-koeln.de/en/mss/gotha-flb-memb-i-84/.

40 The omitted prologues in Gotha, Forschungsbibliothek, MS, Memb. I. 84 are respectively from fols. 360^{r} (year five), 360^{v} (year eight), 361^{r} (year nine), 365^{r} (year thirteen), 366^{v} (year fifteen), 367^{v} (year sixteen), 368^{r} (year seventeen), and 369^{v} (year nineteen).

41 "Wolfenbüttel, Herzog August Bibliothek, Cod. Guelf. 130 Blank.," in *Bibliotheca Legum: A Database on Carolingian Secular Law Texts*, ed. Karl Ubl, accessed November 06, 2019, http://www.leges.uni-koeln.de/en/mss/codices/wolfenbuettel-hab-blankenb-130/; "Wolfenbüttel, Herzog August Bibliothek, Cod. Guelf. 130 Blank.," in *Capitularia: Edition der fränkischen Herrschererlasse*, ed. Karl Ubl, accessed November 06, 2019, https://capitularia.uni-koeln.de/en/mss/wolfenbuettel-hab-blankenb-130/.

42 That is, Liutprand's prologue for the first year is retained in: Vienna, Österreichische Nationalbibliothek, MS Cod. 471 (third quarter of the eleventh century, in or around Pavia), fol. 48^{r}, l. 33–fol. 48^{v}, l. 28; Paris, Bibliothèque Nationale de France, MS Lat. 9656 (third quarter of the eleventh century, in or around Pavia), fol. 37^{r}, l. 30–fol. 37^{v}, l. 17; London, British Library, MS Add. 5411 (second half of the eleventh century, northern Italy), fol. 53^{v},

of its own (fols. 73ʳ–136ᵛ), like Cava, MS 4 and Paris, MS Lat. 4613, these have not been through the editorial filter limiting them only to legislation of relevance to Italy.[43] Nor does it have the integrated glosses, cross-references and other scholarly apparatus of the Lombardist legal studies that began to flourish in the eleventh-century. However, with increasing evidence that the laws and capitularies in the *Liber Papiensis* comprise two related but materially independent volumes, that developing ideas were transferred back and forth between, rather than being conceived and implemented simultaneously,[44] the different set of capitularies being included should not then impact on assessment of the treatment of the laws. If the laws in the Wolfenbüttel manuscript, and those of Liutprand in particular, are considered in their own right, then the streamlining of the laws to bring the focus down only to that which was required for interpretation of the legal content, and the exclusion of the narrative framings of royal ideology is clearly apparent. While this could allow the Wolfenbüttel manuscript, from this perspective at least, to be seen as something of a halfway mark between the *Edictus Langobardorum* and the *Liber Papiensis*, the question becomes what is to be made of the manuscripts where only some prologues have been removed.

The argument that some prologues are being focused down to only that content relevant for interpreting the laws loses some strength, when considered alongside the other legislative phases where their full prologue had been retained. In these latter, the laws were seemingly transmitted within the underlying framework of royal authority and Lombard political ideology. It is worth noting which of the prologues are omitted the most: that is to say, excluding Paris, MS Lat. 4613 which is missing the relevant folios, the prologues to the fifteenth and sixteenth years are consistently omitted, that is from five of the remaining six manuscripts of the long-tenth century, while those of the fourteenth year are omitted from three (Wolfenbüttel, MS Cod. Guelf. 130 Blank, Madrid, MS 413, and Paris, MS 4613), while those of the nineteenth year are also

l. 22–54ᵛ, l. 13; and Venice, Biblioteca Nazionale Marciana, MS Lat. v. 81 (2751) (late-eleventh century, northern Italy), fol. 31ʳ, l. 24–fol. 31ᵛ, l. 27. See, Gobbitt, *Liber Papiensis*.

43 Charles M. Radding, "Legal Manuscripts in Eleventh-Century Italy: From Royal Edict to Scholarly Compilation," in *Organizing the Written Word: Scripts, Manuscripts and Texts. Proceedings of the First Utrecht Symposium on Medieval Literacy, Utrecht 5–7 June 1997*, ed. Marco Mostert, *Utrecht Studies in Medieval Literacy*, 2 (Turnhout: Brepols, forthcoming) (I would like to thank Prof. Radding for allowing me access to a copy of this chapter preceding its unfortunately much-delayed publication).

44 Nostitz-Rieneck, "Zur Frage der Existenz eines "Liber Papiensis"," 708; Thom Gobbitt, "Codicological Features of a Late-Eleventh-Century Manuscript of the Lombard Laws," *Studia Neophilologica* 86 (2014): 48–67; Gobbitt, *Liber Papiensis*.

omitted from three (Vatican, MS Vat. Lat. 5359, and Gotha, MS Memb. I. 84 this time, along with Wolfenbüttel, MS Cod. Guelf. 130 Blank, of course). The prologue to the seventeenth year is omitted from two of the manuscripts, again Wolfenbüttel, MS Cod. Guelf. 130 Blank. and Gotha, MS Memb. I. 84, and cannot be assessed in Vatican, MS Vat. Lat. 5359 due to the missing folio.

There is a definite focus in the prologues selected for removal, then, comprising various overlaps of the run of laws from the fourteenth to nineteenth (or twenty-first) years. This coincides somewhat with the pattern already seen in the Vercelli manuscript, where it was the laws from the sixteenth to nineteenth (or twenty-first) year that were omitted. As with the Vercelli manuscript, this comprises many of the prologues in which Liutprand did not identify himself by name, and it is interesting that prologues are once again included in the manuscripts for the twenty-second and twenty-third years, (present in all but Wolfenbüttel, MS Cod. Guelf. 130 Blank.) when identification of the lawgiver was re-introduced. The omission of prologues in which Liutprand does not name himself would make sense as an explanation, but again no single manuscript excludes all of these prologues only.

The contradictions seen in the other possible motivations discussed for the selection of prologues for omission in the Vercelli manuscript are again of relevance here. Firstly, many but again not all of the prologues with minimal religious reference to divine motivations and with focus only on the secular, socio-legal motivations having been removed. Likewise the counterpart view, wherein the prologue for the sixteenth year, which has the most overt religious framing in all of Liutprand's collected prologues, perhaps equaled only by that of the very first year, is also one of the ones which is most consistently removed, while other prologues with overtly expressed religious motivations are likewise retained.

Again, it seems unlikely that all of these manuscripts, or their respective exemplars, could have been compiled from multiple sources that had each treated the laws and prologues differently. But no other clear explanation presents itself, that explains the entire picture, even within the scope of a single manuscript. Rather, it seems, that each of the phases of Liutprand's legislation laws was being treated semi-independently, which may suggest scattered exemplars, but certainly suggests scattered, individual and potentially isolated (conceptually if not materially) engagement with the component parts of the texts. There may therefore have been ongoing interests in focusing the laws down to their legal essentials, already from the eighth century, and certainly prevalent across the long tenth century, and these interests could feed into the broader book cultures and contexts where the law-books were produced with prologues retained—at least when immediately available.

The deliberate truncation of some of the prologues would appear to echo a similar piecemeal approach to the laws. With the exception of the omission of a single word, "martiarum" [March], from the prologue to the thirteenth year in Vercelli, MS 188, fol. 135r, l. 12, which could simply have been a copying error, the compiler of the oldest manuscript of Liutprand's laws does not employ a truncation strategy. The next surviving manuscript, Ivrea, MS 34,[45] however, most certainly does, and in fact has the most pronounced set of intentional truncations to the prologues surviving in any of the law-books.

Ivrea, MS 34 is a composite collection of three maybe four parts, dating to around 830, so well within the period of Carolingian rule in Italy. The manuscript now comprises 1) a capitulary collection (fols. 1–56, Quires 1–8)), having been joined to 2) a self-contained copy of the *Edictus Rothari* (fols. 57–104, Quires 9–14), and with 3) the laws of the later Lombard kings then running from fols. 105–66 (Quires 15–22). Further capitularies having been added in additional half-sheet at the end of Quire 22 (fol. 107), which may form a fourth production block. The Laws of Liutprand begin on fol. 108v, l. 5 (following on immediately from the *Memoratorium de mercedibus commanicorum*,[46] fol. 107v, l. 1–fol. 108v, l. 4), and conclude on fol. 159v, l. 6. Prologues to each of the various phases of Liutprand's legislation, barring that of the twenty-first, are included, but only those of the first, twenty-second and twenty-third are in their full form. Each of the others has been truncated and sometimes also emended heavily.

The truncation of the items is generally quite consistent in approach, focusing the content down to, firstly, naming Liutprand as the law-giver, and identifying who the laws are for, that is the "gentis langobardorum" [people of the Lombards], and, secondly, giving the date, regnal year and indiction for when the law was promulgated. Where formulaic references to the divine are included as parts of these, they are usually retained—although in the fifth year the "omnipotentis" [almighty] adjective is dropped from the usual "Ego in dei [omnipotentis] nomine Liutprand" [I, in the name of [almighty] God, Liutprand] opening to the prologue, fol. 115r, l. 10. A further point of intervention can be found in variations between whether the royal plural is used for

45 "Ivrea, Biblioteca Capitolare, XXXIV (5)," in *Bibliotheca Legum: A Database on Carolingian Secular Law Texts*, ed. Karl Ubl, accessed May 04, 2020, http://www.leges.uni-koeln.de/mss/handschrift/ivrea-bc-xxxiv-5/; "Ivrea, Biblioteca Capitolare, XXXIV," in *Capitularia: Edition der fränkischen Herrschererlasse*, ed. Karl Ubl, accessed May 04, 2020, https://capitularia.uni-koeln.de/en/mss/ivrea-bc-xxxiv/.

46 Bluhme, ed., *Capitula Extra Edictum Vagantia: I. Grimoaldi Sive Liutprandi Memoratorium de Mercedibus Commacinorum*, in Bluhme, *Edictus Langobardorum*, 176–80.

Liutprand or else the singular voice, although these variations are more widely spread across the surviving manuscripts of the ninth and tenth centuries, and would probably benefit from a dedicated study in their own right.

Some of the truncated and emended versions of the prologues have seemingly been produced from the prologues for other years, rather than from the underlying text itself. One clear example of this is for the fifteenth year, where the "deo largiente" [with God's generosity] formulaic addition to the year of Liutprand's reign, seems to have been drawn from the prologue for the preceding year, rather than drawing on the prologue of the fifteenth year's more usual "deo protegente" [with God's protection] form. Further, even more explicit examples of intervention in the prologues can be seen in those of the fourteenth (fol. 133^{v}, ll. 10–14), fifteenth (fol. 137^{v}, ll. 15–17), sixteenth (fol. 141^{v}, ll. 7–9), seventeenth (fol. 143^{v}, ll. 15–18) and nineteenth (fol. 146^{v}, ll. 17–19) years. In these, the underlying prologues do not usually include explicit identification of Liutprand as the law-giver, but this has then been inserted into the truncated text, immediately preceding the dating clause.

Barring a few minor differences in how case abbreviations are employed between the different versions, four of these five re-constructed prologues frame Liutprand's name and title in similar terms: "Ego liutprand excellentissimus gentis langobardorum rex" [I Liutprand most excellent king of the Lombard people], with the primary variation being that the fifteenth year inserts an additional "rex" [king] immediately after *exellentissimus* [most excellent], while the sixteenth year inserts the additional *rex* before it. None of the prologues in the preceding years had (fully) omitted the formulaic reference to the divine, so the simpler form here of "ego liutprand" [I Liutprand] must have been deliberately reduced by the scribe of the Ivrea manuscript themselves, or at least the redactor of a previous exemplar. The prologue for the twelfth year has the "langobardorum rex" arrangement, although the scribe or exemplar would also have had to redact out the religious framing of the paired adjectives "xpiane 7 catholice" [Christian and Catholic] which there preceded and modified the naming of the "gentis langobardorum". The earlier positioning in the phrasing of *rex* immediately after *excellentissimus* (per the variant for the fifteenth year) can be found in the prologues for the fifth, ninth and eleventh years, while similar to the variant for the seventeenth year, it immediately precedes "gentis" in the prologue of the thirteenth year. None of this, then, gives a satisfactory explanation for a single source for these emended versions of the prologue, and perhaps suggest rather that the scribe (or that of an underlying exemplar) drew primarily on that of the twelfth year, but had the various phrasings of the others in mind at least, and that those sometimes slipped into their formulation and copying.

The biggest variation in the augmented emendations of the prologues is to be found in the seventeenth year, however, and it will be useful to undertake a close investigation of the entire prologue, from fol. 143[v]:

l. 15 Ego in dei omnipotentis nomine excell*entissimus*
l. 16 d*e*o dilecte gentis langobarum rex. hoc adiungere
l. 17 p*re*vidimus anno regni mei xpo protegente xvii die
l. 18 Kalendarum martiarum indictione xi

> [I in the name of almighty God, Liutprand, most excellent and favoured by God, king of the people of the Lombards. We provide these additions in the seventeenth year, Christ protecting, of my reign, on the first (kalends) of March in the eleventh indiction].[47]

The first point to note here, is that it bears almost no resemblance to the more regular version of the prologue usually transmitted with the laws of the seventeenth year.[48] Unlike the preceding prologues where the title naming Liutprand and the Lombards has been introduced, this variant also inserts the formulaic "in God's name". Moreover, the adjective *omnipotentis* [almighty] has also been added, whereas in the prologue to the fifth year it had had been deliberately excised even when the other parts of this formula were retained. Considering the similarities between the re-constructed forms for the title used in the previous four prologues in the Ivrea manuscript, it seems unlikely that the scribe simply produced this fuller version from the top of the head, and the closest version in the previous laws is that of the eleventh year, followed by the prologues for the eighth and ninth years. The greatest variation is that the formulaic "deo dilecte" [favoured by God] element has also been re-inserted into the prologue to follow and augment *excellentisimus* [most excellent], which most closely echoes the form in the prologue for the ninth year, although with redacting or emending other associated elements, such as reference to the catholicity and fortune of the Lombards in the fifth year, could have been taken from another prologue.

Keeping a direct reference to the new volume of laws, here the phrasing "adiungere previdimus" [we provide (these) additions] is not otherwise attested in the truncated prologues of the Ivrea manuscript, but is to be found in the full prologue for the twenty-third year, fol. 157[r], l. 9. As the laws have been copied in

47 Translation emended from Fischer-Drew, *Lombard Laws*, 150–51, 153, 158.

48 Liutprand, Prologue to the seventeenth year: Bluhme, *Edictus Langobardorum*, 150.

reading order, and assuming it was the Ivrea scribe who undertook the redaction, the scribe would not yet have copied this item, but presumably the exemplar would already have been available. Alternatively, the phrasing could have been drawn from the un-emended versions of the prologues for any of the three preceding years. The one source it could not have been taken from is a full version of the prologue for the seventeenth year itself, as that did not otherwise include such a statement, at least in the versions of the prologue that have survived to the modern day.

A further point of variation here in the prologue to the seventeenth year, is that the year of the reign is given with the formulaic phrasing "xpo protegente" [with Christ's protection]. The more usual form in the underlying versions of this prologue is for it to be the seventeenth year "deo protegente" [with God's protection]. Christ's protection for the years of Liutprand's reign is, however, specifically named in the prologue to the laws of the preceding year, fol. 141v, l. 8. It therefore seems quite possible that the phrasing may have been taken directly from the last prologue that the scribe had redacted, instead of being derived directly from an exemplar for the seventeenth year itself. The only variations between the phrasing of this part of the prologue given in the Ivrea manuscript is the word ordering, with "xpi protogente" following "regni mei" [of my reign] in the seventeenth year, but preceding it for the seventeenth year. Such a re-ordering could easily happen if the scribe had identified and read the phrase they wanted to use, and then written it down from memory as a sentence, rather than copying it word by word.

Finally, the indiction given in the prologue is "xi". However, technically this is a year out, and 729 should instead be the twelfth indiction. As all the other indications given in the manuscript are correct, it seems likely that this was copied along with the phrasing and that the scribe forgot to update it. Taking these points together, the most logical explanation seems to be that the exemplar was lacking a prologue for the seventeenth year, and the scribe produced a new one. In light of the extensive truncation and augmentation already seen across the prologues this is perhaps not a surprising occurrence. What it is perhaps more unexpected here, is that they did not undertake a similar intervention several folios later, when they copied the laws of the twenty-first year and chose to leave them still without a prologue rather than constructing a new one (fol. 151r).

Where prologues in the later manuscripts have also been truncated, it is almost always with the same strategy of selection, reducing content to the same features of the underlying text. The closest comparable manuscript is Paris, MS Lat. 4613, which has truncated versions for the prologues to the laws of the fifth to twelfth years, inclusive. Again, with the exception of the formulaic phrasing in Liutprand's naming of himself and the Lombard people, and again in the dating clause, it is the broader motivations, both divine and socio-legal, and the identification of who had been involved in deciding the contents of the laws which have been removed.

There is still enough variation in some of the later truncated prologues to suggest that they were derived from multiple sources, perhaps re-compiled from an idea of what elements should be retained, rather than having being drawn from a root that shared the specific truncated texts of the versions in the Ivrea manuscript. This can be made apparent with a comparison of the truncated prologues to the fifth year, giving that of the Ivrea manuscript (fol. 115^{r}, ll. 10–15) as the base, and with shared elements from Paris, MS Lat. 4613, (fol. 19^{v}, ll. 13–15), given in bold, and with elements only in the Paris manuscript given in square brackets:

> **Ego in dei** [ominipotentis] **nomine Liutprand excell*entissimus* rex gentis** feliicissime hac catholice deo quie dilecte **langobardorum** . nunc iterum annuente dei omnipotentis […]i mis*ericordi*a di*a*e **kalendarum martiarum anno regni** [mei] n*ost*ri deo p*ro*pitio quinto **indictione** [xiiii] quarta decima.

> **[I, in the name of** [Almighty] **God, Liutprand, most excellent king** favoured by God **of the** most happy and catholic **people of the Lombards,** now therefore with the compassion of almighty God, **on the 1st of March in the** fifth **year**, with God's favour, **of** [my] our **reign, in the fourteenth indiction].**[49]

In addition to the change from spelling out the indiction year in words to simply using roman numerals, a number of further changes have been made. Further elements have been removed, many of which expand the formulae used to frame Liutprand, the Lombards and the year of his reign in relation to divine favor. Liutprand is no longer "favored of God", the Lombards are neither "most happy," nor "catholic," and the promulgation is not made "with the compassion of almighty God." While these are nevertheless coherent truncations, in what is perhaps a fit of overzealousness the detail that it was the fifth year of Liutprand's reign has also been removed. None of these changes would preclude the Paris version having been derived from that in the Ivrea manuscript, as a further phase of truncation could easily be imagined. A few minor variations

49 Liutprand, prologue to year five: Ivrea, MS 34, fol. 115^{r}, ll. 10–15; Paris, MS Lat. 4613, fol. 19^{v}, ll. 13–15; Bluhme, *Edictus Langobardorum*, 109–10; translation emended from Fischer-Drew, *Lombard Laws*, 146–47.

could be scribal, the change from royal plural to a singular voice, and the reordering of the kalends date and the year of reign, neither of which directly reflects on whether the two had a common source. Whether the addition of "almighty" before God was done by the scribe from what might be considered gut feeling is uncertain; while a feasible ad hoc addition, it is also enough of a return to the original form of the prologue to speculate whether the scribe (or their exemplar) had produced this truncation anew, rather than by further truncating the already shortened variant of a variant derived from somewhere in the same stem as the Ivrea manuscript.

The three further truncated prologues copied throughout the Paris manuscript from the eighth to eleventh years, again all echo the truncated versions seen in the Ivrea manuscript, but with subtle variations. There are no instances as apparent as that in the fifth year, where a further layer of formulaic expressions of divine favor have also been removed, but that is more because they were never a part of the version as seen in the Ivrea manuscript, rather than that they were retained into the tenth century. Two of these prologues also have comparable versions in other manuscripts, both from southern Italy, with the truncated prologue for the ninth year also being present in Cava, MS 4, fol. 88^{v}, ll. 14–18, while that for the eleventh year is included in Madrid, MS 413, fol. 92^{r}, ll. 6–11. Interestingly, full copies of these prologues are also included in both the Cava (fol. 91^{r}, l. 19–fol. 91^{v}, l. 16) and Madrid (fol. 89^{r}, ll. 4–16) manuscripts. The inclusion of two versions in each manuscript but of different prologues in each case, is intriguing. At the very least, it suggests that the approach that had been developed in the early-ninth century had spread widely in Italy, and that there were multiple versions circulating simultaneously to each other. Their compilers were clearly able to draw selectively on multiple parts. Furthermore, the disordering of some sets of laws from their usual chronological arrangement in the Cava manuscript, and the total omission of the laws for the eighth year from the Madrid manuscript, again suggests that their respective compilers were drawing on multiple exemplars that related to smaller sections of the *Edictus Langobardorum*, that could be individually consulted and arranged at will.

The question that must be raised even if it cannot be answered here, is to what extent does the relatively close similarity in the specific variants of the prologues in the manuscripts of the long-tenth century, and the close similarity in their strategies for selection and truncation suggest an underlying common source. That is, do the tenth-century manuscripts owe a direct debt to the specific book contexts of the Ivrea manuscript, or at least its now-lost exemplars and close siblings, or rather do we have a conceptual approach to the prologues and laws that was itself spread and implemented on multiple occasions from fuller exemplars. The presence of both truncated and full prologues in the Cava and Madrid manuscripts suggest that, if this is the case, it must have happened further back in the transmission of the laws, and certainly that neither of the truncated versions were actively produced for these new law-books.

The larger collection of truncated prologues, and the lack of corresponding full versions in the earlier parts of Paris, MS 4613 may conversely indicate that these prologues had been produced anew, if not by the scribe themselves, then in their exemplar. While there is close overlap with the strategies of truncation employed in the Paris manuscript and that seen in the Ivrea manuscript overall, there are still variations. The prologues to the eighth, ninth and twelfth years in the Paris manuscript, each add at the end variants on "feliciter" [happily], to the dating clause, that are present in neither the Ivrea manuscript nor the underlying full prologue itself, as transmitted in other law-books. Other variations are more subtle, but attention should be drawn to the fact that where the Ivrea manuscript had created prologues identifying Liutprand as law-giver by name for the laws of the later years. Conversely, in Paris, MS 4613, with the exception of the complete omission of the prologue for the fourteenth year, the others were kept in full. Even if the truncated variants were drawn from the Ivrea manuscript, directly or indirectly, then a separate, more full source must have been available for the latter parts, or else the scribe for reason that are unclear abandoned the strategy of truncating prologues partway through copying. On codicological grounds it is clear that this division is not due to the manuscript having been composited from two independent blocks, it is written throughout by the same scribal hand, and the transition to full prologues from truncated versions occurs within the material contexts of a single quire, (Quire 5).

A related strategy for truncating the prologues can also be seen in one further manuscript, Gotha, MS Memb. I. 84., however here it is applied only to the prologue of the first year of Liutprand's reign, which runs from fol. 358^{r}, ll. b22–b33. Although, as already discussed, eight of the other fourteen prologues are omitted entirely from this manuscript. The Gotha manuscript stands out, though, as this is the only surviving version of the *Edictus Langobardorum* in which the prologue to Liutprand's first year has been deliberately truncated. That this truncation is not due to later loss of materials is confirmed by it beginning and ending within the material contexts of a single page, and the scribe (or that of their exemplar) therefore, here again, as in the other manuscripts with truncated prologues, made this alteration deliberately.

At the outset of this discussion, three broad elements in the prologue to Liutprand's first year were identified: firstly, the religious framing with biblical quotes; secondly, the restating of the previous Lombard law-givers; and thirdly,

Liutprand's identification of himself, the date of issue and the other people involved in the law-giving. In the Gotha manuscript the truncation omits the first two of these, and begins "Ego in dei nomine liutprandi" [I in God's name Liutprand] (fol. 358ʳ, l. b22). What is particularly interesting here is that the first four lines of the prologue, corresponding to the part which identifies Liutprand and the *gentis langobardorum*, have been written as a rubric in red ink, fol. 358ʳ, ll. b22–25. It has also been made into an (almost) self-contained text, as the usual opening two words of this third section, "ob hoc" [thus], which normally serves to link the reflection on law-giving by the preceding kings with that of Liuptrand's own, has also been removed. Grammatically the rubric cannot be considered to be completely self-contained, as the verb does not in fact come until the end of the entire prologue itself (fol. 358ʳ, l. b33). The abrupt onset and lack of a verb seen in many of the other heavily truncated prologues are again echoed here then.

The augmentations following in the rubricated part of the Gotha manuscript variant of the prologue, reiterate some of the religious justifications for law-giving and related associations in brief form. Liutprand (or whoever drafted the prologue) still frames himself and his reign "in the name of God" [IN DEI NOMINE] (fol. 358ʳ, l. b22), as "beloved by God" [DEO QVE DILECTE] (fol. 358ʳ, l. b24), as being "protected by God" [deo protogente] (fol. 358ʳ, l. b25), and promulgating "in fear and love of God" [deo timore & amore] (fol. 358ʳ, l. b32). Moreover, two of these have not just been retained from the prologue as more usually transmitted, but are deliberate insertions either by the scribe of the Gotha manuscript or its exemplar. Firstly, "et catholicus" [and catholic] is added to make an alliterative pairing following on from "christianus" [Christian] on l. b23. This wording may have been drawn from the otherwise truncated opening lines of the prologue, but could as easily also have been taken from the prologue to the twenty-third year where the pairing is also made explicitly,[50] or perhaps from the fifth or ninth years where the Catholicism of the Lombard *gens* [people] is specifically stressed.[51] While this may have been a concern in Liutprand's own time, these laws were issued only a few decades after the Lombard conversion from arianism,[52] the choice to insert emphasis of the specifically catholic beliefs of the law-giver in the tenth-century Gotha manuscript is intriguing.

50 Liutprand, Prologue to the twenty-third year: Bluhme, *Edictus Langobardorum*, 171–72.

51 Liutprand, Prologues to the fifth and ninth years: Bluhme, *Edictus Langobardorum*, 109–10, 116.

52 I would like to thank Herwig Wolfram for reminding me of how short a distance it was between the official, as it were, conversion of the Lombards to Catholicism and the first year of Liutprand's reign and law-giving (Pers. Com. November 2019).

Secondly, the addition of "deo qui dilecte" [beloved of God] as a modifier to Liutprand (fol. 358r, l. b24), again make sure that while many of the detailed religious elements included in the prologue were removed, they are still stressed. The removal of divine references form the first section of the underlying prologue, then, cannot be taken as an unproblematically deployed strategy here, with the insertions into the naming formula countering somewhat those which had been quietly removed.

A further point of some significance in the rubricated part, is that after these insertions, the more usual "Langobardorum rex" [king of the Lombards] of the prologue is changed to "rex gentis langobardorum" [king of the people of the Lombards] (fol. 358r, ll. b24–25). Even the retention of the prologues direct reference to the Lombards, especially in light of its considered truncation, would be of interest, but the deliberate expansion of the phrasing brings closer attention to it. Ethnogenesis of the Lombards and reproduction of that identity as a group may clearly still have been of interest, even into the tenth century—long after the Carolingian conquest in 774. Here, though, it must be remembered that the Gotha manuscript was almost certainly not produced in Italy, but more likely north of the Alps in Mainz or perhaps Fulda.[53] As such, this approach in the Gotha manuscript may be less a matter of ethnogenesis of a group from the inside, but more the recognition from people outside the group, identifying the laws as belonging to a specific people or territory.[54]

It must again be remembered, however, that the constructed prologues in the ninth century Ivrea, MS 34 (those from the fourteenth to the nineteenth years) identifying Liutprand by name, also bring deliberate emphasis back to the *gentis langobardorum*. Within the Carolingian contexts of production in the 830s, the tantalizing question becomes whether that represented the identification of the people to whom the law applied, within the broader contexts of Carolingian legal pluralism and the personality of law, or if it represented post-conquest Lombard resistance, ethnogenesis and constructions of identity. While either interpretation may predominate in a given manuscript, neither is necessarily mutually exclusive.

53 "Gotha, Forschungsbibliothek, Memb. I 84," in *Bibliotheca Legum: A Database on Carolingian Secular Law Texts*, ed. Karl Ubl, accessed November 06, 2019, http://www.leges.uni-koeln.de/en/mss/codices/gotha-flb-memb-i-84/; "Gotha, Forschungsbibliothek, Memb. I 84," in *Capitularia: Edition der fränkischen Herrschererlasse*, ed. Karl Ubl, accessed November 06, 2019, https://capitularia.uni-koeln.de/en/mss/gotha-flb-memb-i-84/.

54 Nick Everett, "How Territorial was Lombard Law?," in *Die Langobarden: Die Herrschaft und Identität*, ed. Walter Pohl and Peter Erhart (Vienna: Verlag der Österreichischen der Wissenschaften, 2005).

Overall, it can be seen from the manuscript evidence that the transmission of the prologues to Liutprand's laws from the eighth to the eleventh centuries, is far more complicated than the two-phase approach corresponding to the main versions of the laws as edited: from the *Edictus Langobardorum* to the *Liber Papiensis*. While the near-total removal of the prologues to Liutprand's legislation, especially the later phases after that of the first year, is certainly a wide-spread feature in the *Liber Papiensis*, it was clearly an approach that was already under development. Wolfenbüttel, MS Cod. Guelf. 130, distinctly not an early variant of the *Liber Papiensis* when assessed in terms of its treatment of the capitularies already demonstrated the total removal of three prologues except for that of the first year. In that it had already focused the laws down to only the "practical essentials" and thereby omitting everything "that was not necessary for interpreting the law,"[55] and at the expense of the Lombard royal and political rhetoric the prologues had previously transmitted. Taken alone, the Wolfenbüttel manuscript could easily be seen as a precursor to the *Liber Papiensis*, a halfway mark as it were in the development of the laws as a text; innovations leading into the developments of the eleventh century. But, as has been shown, removal of some prologues already dates back to the middle of the eighth century, almost contemporary to Liutprand himself. The removal of prologues, therefore, is a practice that was already underway in the Lombard period.

The selective truncation of prologues could easily be understood as a transitory point in the path from the inclusion of full prologue to its total removal. Such a simple linear model however seems to convenient, and the manuscript evidence, however, suggests otherwise, positioning it as an approach developed in the Carolingian period, and then erratically employed into the tenth century. The focus in these truncated prologues to information that would have been of interest to a person working with the law in a practical setting seems apparent: who issued the law, for whom, and when. Presumably this became less relevant in the later tenth century and into the eleventh as legal collections focused on the laws and capitularies that were only in force in Italy came into being. And it is worth noting that, while the notably large collection of capitularies included in Paris, MS Lat. 4613 is not the same as those in the *Liber Papiensis*, the compiler of the manuscript nevertheless reveals a strong Italian focus.[56] Overall, it seems that there are two individual strategies of alteration being employed, truncation and removal, along with the retention of full prologues. Not only

55 Radding and Ciaralli, *Corpus Iuris Civilis in the Middle Ages*, 141; Radding, "Reviving Justinian's *Corpus*," 41–42.

56 Radding, "Legal Manuscripts."

does the use of these overlap chronologically, but in some manuscripts two or all three approaches are taken.

While some patterns can be loosely drawn for where a given strategy is deployed in the production of a given manuscript, most do not seem compelling explanations when looking at the treatment of Liutprand's laws collectively. Multiple approaches are clearly in play within the tenth-century manuscripts, but the manuscript evidence clearly indicates a range of approaches, including those strongly suggestive of legal professionals, already being in place. With a few exceptions the approach seems piecemeal, at best, and this is made particularly apparent in Madrid, MS 413 and Cava, MS 4, where in each a truncated prologue was also supplemented with its full version. This in itself implies compilation from multiple exemplars, and consequently those having been drawn from a collection of disrupted materials. The disordering (in Cava, MS 4) or even total omission (in Madrid, MS 413) of the full sets of laws from the eighth year, both points at a likely shared set of exemplars, and further confirms their disparate nature. Perhaps only a series of books which had once been full copies of the *Edictus Langobardorum* and were now severely truncated were available to the scribes, and they overlapped them as best they could. More likely, different legislative phases had been circulating in different versions and, the approaches to the contents had varied between them. As both the Cava and Madrid manuscripts originated in the south of Italy, this could of course simply represent the library and archive conditions in that region. But the overlap in approaches, and the erratic treatments of prologues, with the manuscripts produced in the north, even without apparent attempts to supply full copies of the prologues where an exemplar may have supplied only a truncated one, suggest a similar range of manuscript contexts for the laws. That is to say, the larger and fuller collections of the *Edictus Langobardorum* that have survived may well have been produced and used in cathedral and monastic contexts, as has been argued in the scholarship.[57] But that may simply a be a matter of which manuscripts have survived. When these books were produced they were already being compiled from a range of contexts, some of which were prioritizing readings of the text that focused and facilitated access on the legal content and what was necessary to interpret the law. Where it has been argued that the compilers of the eleventh century *Liber Papiensis* had reached beyond the contemporary book contexts of the *Edictus Langobardorum*, to draw instead on laws on loose leaves and fragmentary texts held in

57 Radding and Ciaralli, *Corpus Iuris Civilis in the Middle Ages*, 141; Radding, "Reviving Justinian's *Corpus*," 41–42; Radding, "Legal Manuscripts;" Charles M. Radding, "Legal Theory and Practice in Eleventh-Century Italy," *Law and History Review* 21 (2003): 377–78.

older archives and book chests,[58] the composite and variable nature seen here in many of the manuscripts of the *Edictus Langobardorum* suggests that these scribes had also behaved in this manner.

The transition into the eleventh century manuscript contexts for the production and use of the Lombard laws, then, was not simply an abrupt change from monasteries and cathedrals to legal professionals, or "from royal edict to scholarly compilation." While scholarly focus on the Lombard laws was clearly something which continued to grow and flourish, indeed well into the twelfth century and beyond, in the transition from the tenth to the eleventh century, it was less a revolutionary change in hands, and rather a focusing down to one approach amongst many. The cultures of legal literacy surrounding these law-books in the tenth century at the least lay the direct foundations for the development of the *Liber Papiensis*. However, those roots also go back much further. The specific interests of the Lombardist legal scholars in how the laws might be used were already present in nascent form, even within the Lombard period, an intertwined thread throughout the transmission and reception of the laws, where rhetorical constructions of royal ideology and prestige were already sometimes elided to clarify the written cultures of pragmatically focused legal interest.

58 Thom Gobbitt "Scribal Communities and Lombard Law-Books: Charlemagne's Herstal Capitulary within the Eleventh-Century *Liber Papiensis*," in *Creating Communities and Others in Early Medieval Europe*, ed. Richard Broome (Leeds: Kismet Press, forthcoming).

CHAPTER 4

More than Language: Law and Textual Communities in Medieval Frisia

Rolf H. Bremmer Jr

For linguists, there is no doubt: language united the Frisian part of the North Sea littoral in the Middle Ages above anything else.[1] The Frisian language, though closely related, differed significantly from that of the neighboring Saxons and Franks. While they went *ter kerke*, the Frisians went *to there tsierke* "to (the) church"; what was a *dag* "day" for their neighbors, was a *dei* in Frisia. A chest was opened with a *slotel/slötel* "key" by Frank and Saxon, the Frisian used her *kei*.[2]

Not only did the language of the Frisians distinguish itself from those of their neighbors, even within the Frisian language space some remarkable varieties may also be discerned. For the High Middle Ages, Frisia can be roughly divided into three dialect regions: the districts between the rivers Vlie and Lauwers to the west, covering about the same area as the modern Dutch province of Friesland; the region in the middle, between the Lauwers and what was for a long time an almost impenetrable stretch of marshland, north of Aurich; and the lands east of this marshland up to the Weser estuary.[3] These three regions probably had very ancient roots. Such a supposition follows not merely from the fact that the groups that lived within them had developed different varieties of Frisian; other indications support it. In the course of the eighth century, each of the three regions became the target of a different missionary project.

---

1 This paper is a translated, adapted and extended version of my valedictory lecture as Professor (by special appointment for the Fryske Akademy) of Frisian Language and Literature, entitled "Meer dan taal: tekstgemeenschappen in het middeleeuwse Friesland," delivered at Leiden University on 16 June 2017. An English version was presented as a guest-lecture at St Andrews University, Institute of Medieval Studies, 7 October 2019. I would like to thank Oebele Vries and Jenneka Janzen for their valuable comments on drafts of this paper.

2 For a detailed physiognomy of Old Frisian in relation to its immediately neighboring languages, see Rolf H. Bremmer Jr, *Introduction to Old Frisian. History, Grammar, Reader, Glossary* (Amsterdam: John Benjamins, 2009), § 204.

3 For further information on the dialectal differences, see Bremmer, *Introduction to Old Frisian*, §§ 205–13.

 | DOI:10.1163/9789004448650_006

Apparently, they differed not just in dialect, but probably also formed slightly differing social and political unities. Consequently, each of these three regions came to resort under a different episcopal see, namely Utrecht, founded by Willibrord in 690; Münster, with Liudger consecrated as its first bishop in 805; and Bremen, chosen by Willehad in 787. Utrecht and Münster belonged to the archbishopric of Cologne, Bremen fell under that of Hamburg. As a result, Frisia was not overarched by one pastoral supervisor and hence intrinsically lacked a unifying ecclesiastical superstructure.

Admittedly, medieval Frisia was a shrinking territory. From the Scheldt estuary in the south, Frisian had been forced to retreat from the late seventh century before the steadily expanding Frankish tongue, more or less the precursor of Modern Dutch. The disappearance of Frisian from the county of Holland was caused by changing political circumstances. Because the ruling elite, that is the count and his entourage, directed themselves to the Frankish conquerors, they also adopted their language. How exactly this shift of language took place is difficult to establish, because it was already almost complete when the production of vernacular documents started to accelerate in Holland in the thirteenth century. Nevertheless, especially in personal names and place-names the Frisian residue remained visible for a long time, although by 1300 Frisian had well-nigh been given up west of the mouth of the former Zuyder Zea (now IJsselmeer).[4]

The districts situated between the Vlie and the Weser, on which this contribution will focus, remained Frisophone for a long time. Originally, they were divided over some four counties, which had been granted by the Holy Roman Emperor to feudal counts who lived far away from their Frisian fiefs. As a result of various circumstances, the Frisians had managed to pull out of this comital system in the course of the eleventh and twelfth centuries and became virtually independent. Government was decentralized and the area fell apart into some twenty factually independent lands (called *terrae* or *universitates* in contemporaneous Latin documents), each of which organized their own judicial system.

Even though these lands differed in the details of how each was organized, in general they had in common that their administration was entrusted to the allodial landowners, who each in turn held office on a board of judge-administrators. Such boards also functioned as the government of the land in

4 Cf. Michiel de Vaan, *The Dawn of Dutch. Language Contact in the Western Low Countries before 1200* (Amsterdam: John Benjamins, 2017), chapter 6; for traces of Frisian in former Frisian territory in particular, see chapter 6.5.

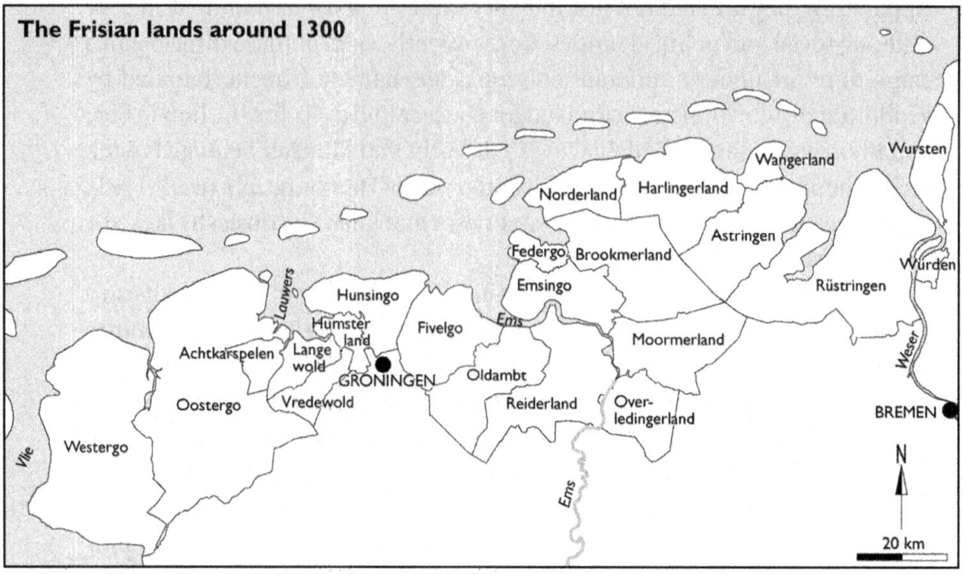

FIGURE 4.1 The Frisian lands around 1300. Groningen and Bremen lie outside Frisian territory, but are given for orientation.
DESIGN © ARJEN VERSLOOT

their dealings with the outside world.[5] While on the one hand the Frisians were united in having the same language, on the other their fragmented governmental administration did not contribute well to fostering an organic Frisian unity. It is true, efforts had been staged to create a kind of supra-Frisian federation, but the desired effect had been limited. In the thirteenth century, representatives of all the Frisian lands convened at regular intervals at the *Upstallesbam*, a tree on a natural elevation near Aurich in Brokmerland, not far from the present-day border between the Netherlands and Ostfriesland, Germany. Here complaints could be presented concerning cases that had proved too difficult to be solved by judges of a regional assembly. However, more concrete information about the activities and efficacy of this supra-regional assembly are almost completely absent.[6] Accordingly, there was hardly a question of an intra-Frisian judicial community either.

5 Oebele Vries, *Het Heilige Roomse Rijk en de Friese vrijheid* (Leeuwarden: De Tille, 1986), 14–21.
6 Hendrik D. Meijering, *De Willekeuren van de Opstalsboom (1323). Een filologisch-historische monografie* (Groningen: V. R. B.-Offsetdrukkerij, 1974), 288–97; cf. Wolfgang Schwarz, "Die Stätte des Upstalsbooms; die archäologische Wahrnehmung des Upstalsbooms," in *Die Friesische Freiheit des Mittelalters—Leben und Legende*, ed. Hajo van Lengen (Aurich: Ostfriesische Landschaft, 2003).

Given the apparent disunity in ecclesiastical, administrative, and judicial arenas, was there anything more than language that united the medieval Frisians? My answer is brief and clear: yes. From the quantity of Frisian texts that have come down to us it can indeed be concluded that a number of them constitute the beginning of a pan-Frisian canon. By reference to these texts I shall argue that, in addition to a Frisian language community, there was also a Frisian textual community. I shall first explain what I mean with the latter term.

The concept of the "textual community" was developed in the 1980s by the Canadian historian Brian Stock in his study of the rise of heterodox movements at the end of the twelfth century.[7] Since then, the notion underlying this concept has greatly gained popularity and, sometimes with further adaptations and modifications, it has been applied with much success. According to Stock, a textual community concerns the identity of a group, usually sectarian, which is determined by subscribing to and studying a well-defined corpus of texts. Literacy was a dominant feature of such groups, and it was precisely the exponential growth of the level of literacy in the twelfth century that enabled the rise of such communities.[8]

Textual communities often sprang up around a charismatic person. Brian Stock actually developed his theory on the occasion of an investigation into Peter Waldo, who in Lyons around 1175 started a movement that later was to be named after him: the Waldensians. The young merchant Waldo was taken in by Christ's appeal in the Gospels to the rich young man to give all his possessions away to the poor (Matthew 19, Mark 10, Luke 18). He therefore encouraged that the New Testament be translated into Occitan/Provençal, the vernacular of southern France. In the writings of the Evangelists and Apostles he and his followers found plenty of matter for their criticisms of Church and society alike. Waldo proclaimed and divulged his tenets in a brief profession of faith, including his conviction that the text of the Bible should be strictly adhered to and that its interpretation was not necessarily depending on what the Church Fathers had expounded.[9] This profession became central to the Waldensian

7 Brian Stock, *The Implications of Literacy. Written Language and Models of Interpretation in the Eleventh and Twelfth Centuries* (Princeton: Princeton University Press, 1983).

8 Robert I. Moore, "Literacy and the Making of Heresy, c. 1000–c.1150," in *Heresy and Literacy, 1000–1530*, ed. Peter Biller and Anne Hudson (Cambridge: Cambridge University Press, 1994), 6–7.

9 On the Waldensians, see, e.g., Euan Cameron, *Waldenses: Rejections of Holy Church in Medieval Europe* (Oxford: Blackwell, 2000).

community. Briefly then, in a religious textual community the text, the written word, is the center around which their common identity revolves. The text also affects the lives of semi-literate and illiterate adherents, because the principal figures of a community spread and interpret the contents of the text both orally and in written form. The members of the community in their turn accept this interpretation, internalize it through memorization and thus "c[o]me to understand their identities."[10]

However, a textual community can also come into being in other ways, for example, around a monastic reformer like Bernard of Clairvaux, who remained within the fold of the Church,[11] or on account of kinship or solidarity with a particular district. This last possibility will prove relevant for my argument. The common denominator in this process is a group desiring to distinguish itself from the broader community of which it is a part. In their endeavor to become completely different, the members of a group are directed or driven by an appeal to a closely demarcated text corpus.[12] Therefore, deviation from society at large, for whatever reason, also presupposes a degree of literacy. A textual community is moreover characterized by a certain chain of leadership and authority that is based on an expertness in dealing with texts. In this last-named aspect philological and political skills come together, as the German Egyptologist Jan Assmann wittily remarked.[13] Leadership accrues to the person who is most knowledgeable and who has developed the skill to explain the core text most lucidly and in doing so is able to bind people to him- or herself and to one another.

By way of an exploration I will apply the concept of the textual community to thirteenth-century Frisia. Whatever literature has come down to us from that period is almost entirely confined to texts of a juridical nature. I shall try to answer a number of questions. Firstly, which group (or groups) can be detected and what are the basic texts at their core? Next, can any coherence be detected between these core texts? Finally, to what extent is the group leadership involved with the authoritative explanation of core texts?

---

10 Stock, *Implications of Literacy*, 90; quotation from C. Annette Grisé, "The Textual Community of Syon Abbey," *Florilegium* 19 (2002): 149.

11 On textual community and the Cistercians, see Constance Hoffman Berman, *The Cistercian Evolution: The Invention of a Religious Order in Twelfth-Century Europe* (Philadelphia, PA: University of Pennsylvania Press, 2000), 97–99.

12 Cf. Nikolaus Staubach, "Die *Devotio moderna* als Textgemeinschaft," in *Schnittpunkte. Deutsch-Niederländische Literaturbeziehungen im späten Mittelalter*, ed. Angelika Lehmann-Benz, Ulrike Zellmann, and Urban Küsters (Münster: Waxmann, 2003).

13 Jan Assmann, *Religion und kulturelles Gedächtnis. Zehn Studien* (Munich: Beck, 2000), 96.

Before turning to what I consider to be the core texts, some further historical context is required for a better understanding of the situation. Around the year 1200 withdrawal from the Holy Roman Empire was largely completed and the Frisian lands had become *de facto* independent, albeit not *de jure*. They no longer tolerated any territorial, feudal lord—whether duke or count—above them, and recognized only the Holy Roman Emperor as their immediate superior. Consequently, the Frisians should not be considered as seceded in a religious respect, but can be regarded as a group of political secessors. The dominant faction within this group consisted of the allodial landowners. Free from territorial lordship they governed their own territories by means of judges whom they elected from their own ranks. In fact, their liberation, and with it their position outside what was held to be a God-given political-feudal constellation, was unheard of within western Europe at the time. This position therefore urgently required justification. Indeed, vindication was found before long and depended on the quickly growing level of literacy in western Europe which had also just reached Frisia around that time.[14]

As Brian Stock has pointed out, heterodox and monastic deviant movements based themselves on their own authoritative texts, of which the leader or a leading elite had an exclusive right of interpretation. An appeal to these authoritative texts was necessary to justify the group's reasons for breaking away from the established tradition. But then it had also to be demonstrated that these texts were superior to those claimed to be truth-holding by widely respected traditions and imposing institutions. The Frisians indeed appear to have possessed such authoritative texts which I would like to dwell on now. The most important of these are undoubtedly two legal codes which, like a conjoined twin, always come inseparably, one after the other, in the manuscripts in which they were written down: the *Seventeen Statutes* and the *Twenty-four Landlaws*. The *Seventeen Statutes*, a collection of seventeen legal rules claiming to carry royal approval, sum up how the Frisians arranged their relationship with the head of the Holy Roman Empire and what rights they are entitled to concerning the ownership of long-held familial land, freedom of feudal authority structures, and the peace to live a life according to their own traditions, customs and jurisdiction. The *Twenty-four Landlaws* regard the legal rules that were in

14 On the coming of, especially pragmatic, literacy to medieval Frisia, see my *'Hir is eskriven.' Lezen en schrijven in de Friese landen rond 1300* (Hilversum: Verloren, 2004); for a succinct account, cf. Marco Mostert, "The Early History of Written Culture in the Northern Netherlands," in *Along the Oral-Written Continuum. Types of Text, Relations and Their Implications*, ed. Slavica Ranković (Turnhout: Brepols, 2010), 473–86.

force in the Frisian lands. They establish especially the mutual rights and obligations of the allodial landowners. Although we do not know where exactly, when, or by whom, these two collections of statutes and landlaws were drafted and subsequently linked together, it is striking that they are found in the entire Frisian territory, from the east to the west, and well before 1300.

The *Seventeen Statutes* and *Twenty-four Landlaws* stand out within the corpus of Old Frisian legal texts on account of their proliferation. They have been handed down integrally in six manuscripts and one incunable: R_1, E_1, H_1, H_2, U, J and D.[15] Many more manuscripts must have existed, though, because surviving copies of the linked texts of the *Seventeen Statutes* and *Twenty-four Landlaws* are based on two different redactions,[16] while the Low German translation preserved from the land of Rüstringen was made from yet another redaction.[17] Om,[18] a late fourteenth-century fragment of the *Seventeen Statutes* from the Ommelanden—the Frisian lands between the Lauwers and the Ems—also testifies to a wide dissemination, as does the "discovery" of a lost tenth Statute.[19] Further evidence is presented through early modern textual collations with redactions from now lost manuscripts, penned in the margins of E_1 and H_2 by, presumably, legal antiquaries.[20]

We may assume, because there are sufficient indications for doing so, that social life in Frisia before the arrival of, especially pragmatic, literacy was organized according to oral traditions.[21] Tradition by its very nature leads to the rise and continuation of customs, within this context of legal customs. Such common conventions should not be subjected to critical analysis by those who adhere to them, because they have become time-honored cornerstones of social life. Typically, traditions are not written down, but firmly anchored

15 For the sigla conventionally used for manuscripts in Frisian Studies, see, e.g. Bremmer, *Introduction to Old Frisian*, §14.

16 Bremmer, *'Hir is eskriven'*, 112.

17 Nicolaas E. Algra, *Zeventien Keuren en Vierentwintig Landrechten* (Doorn: Graal, 1991), 55.

18 Leeuwarden, Tresoar, MS Hs 150/g; cf. Rolf H. Bremmer Jr, "Codifying the Law: Frisian Legal Manuscripts around 1300," in *Vernacular Manuscript Culture 1000–1500*, ed. Erik Kwakkel (Leiden: Leiden University Press, 2018), 176–77.

19 Johanneke Krolis-Sytsema, "De weirekke tsiende Kêst. Oer in ûnbekende ferzy fan de 17 Kêsten," *It Beaken* 55 (1993): 83–95.

20 See Pieter Sipma, ed., *De Eerste Emsinger Codex*. Oudfriese Taal- en Rechtsbronnen 4 (The Hague: Martinus Nijhoff, 1942), 34, and Jelle Hoekstra, *De Eerste en de Tweede Hunsinger Codex*. Oudfriese Taal- en Rechtsbronnen 6 (The Hague: Martinus Nijhoff, 1950), 14–15, respectively.

21 Rolf H. Bremmer Jr, "The Orality of Medieval Frisian Law," in *Directions for Old Frisian Philology*, ed. Rolf H. Bremmer Jr, Stephen Laker, and Oebele Vries, Amsterdamer Beiträge zur älteren Germanistik 73 (Amsterdam: Rodopi, 2014).

in life and passed on by repeaters of the past.[22] However, when they are written down, the very act is indicative of a break from tradition, or at least of a crisis, according to Assmann.[23] Traditions are implicit, internalized, incarnate in the individual bearers who set the example and pass them on to the next generation. However, traditions are, above all, lived and modeled in rites and customs; the very moment traditions are fixed in writing, they become explicit, tangible, objective and what is more, they become fixed. Recording them in writing breaks the chain of living transmission. The push for writing them down, according to Assmann,[24] must come from outside and when it comes, these very traditions will start to change.

The question therefore is: which particular event occasioned the Frisians to entrust these statutes and landlaws to parchment, and with it, to give a start to their canonization? Even though the Frisian lands, as we have seen, did not at all together constitute a political unity, now, with the appropriation of these two legal texts, from the Vlie in the west to the Weser in the east, the Frisians expressed their language-transcending interconnectedness. This hypothetical sequence can also be turned around: after these two codes had been drafted at a certain time and place in one of the Frisian lands, they exercised such an attraction that by embracing them a supraregional Frisian textual community could come about. It is precisely through the acceptance of those *Seventeen Statutes* and *Twenty-four Landlaws* that a district endorsed for itself a Frisian identity. With it, a district also distinguished itself politically with reference to the Holy Roman Empire. What occasioned the adoption of these two legal codes by the individual lands must have been the Frisians' dissolving their feudal ties with the Empire. It is salient to note that while accepting and copying both texts, the numbers seventeen and twenty-four were reverently preserved. Because they were apparently so greatly respected, it makes sense to dwell a moment on these numbers.

Whether the integers seventeen and twenty-four were arbitrarily chosen or purposefully adopted because they were taken to be imbued with some deeper significance—that they form part of the canonization of the *Seventeen Statutes* and *Twenty-four Landlaws* can hardly be seen otherwise. Quite remarkably, scarcely any attention has been devoted to these two numbers in the standard scholarly literature, if at all. In his doctoral thesis on the *Seventeen Statutes* defended in 1940, Jelle Hoekstra presented an extensive survey of what ideas

22 Cf. Walter J. Ong, *Orality and Literacy. The Technologizing of the Word*, 3rd ed. (London: Routledge, 2002), 41.

23 Assmann, *Religion und kulturelles Gedächtnis*, 82.

24 Assmann, *Gedächtnis*, 82.

and interpretations had been expounded on these sources of law with respect to the place of their origin, the time when they had been conceived, their historical reliability and so on. But he did not spend a word on the number seventeen itself.[25] And when Nicolaas Algra, more than fifty years after Hoekstra's study, published a hefty tome on the subject, he broached neither the problem of the number of statutes nor of the landlaws.[26]

Seventeen and twenty-four may not be particularly meaningful integers to the average legal historian. However, the more arithmetically gifted among their ranks will certainly know that seventeen is a prime number, that is a number greater than one, divisible only by itself and by one. Those who are really at home in mathematics know that twenty-four is the factorial function of four—a phenomenon that is indicated algebraically with an exclamation mark: 4!—that is to say twenty-four is the outcome of the multiplication of the descending series $4 \times 3 \times 2 \times 1$.[27]

In the Middle Ages people looked differently at numbers; they were especially intrigued by the symbolism that might lie hidden behind the quantity they expressed. A rich scholarly tradition had evolved around the importance of number symbolism. Numbers belonged to God's creation and consequently it was held that they were charged with a deeper significance. Surely, Solomon expressed a feeling of profound awe when he addressed God in the (deuterocanonical) Book of Wisdom (10:20): "Thou hast ordered all things in measure, and number, and weight" (Douay-Rheims). The exegete was tasked with laying bare the subtle implications which the Almighty had invested in numbers, essential for gaining soul-saving truths. Perhaps the most influential theologian in this respect was Church Father St. Augustine of Hippo (354–430). In various places, in ever changing contexts and detail, he brings up the number seventeen in connection with the Miraculous Catch of Fish which five disciples experienced shortly after Christ's resurrection. According to the Evangelist John (21:11), in a pericope to be read during Holy Week, Simon Peter hauled 153 fish from the water. Why this specific number, Augustine wondered. Mathematically he knew that 153 was a triangular number: if an equilateral triangle is filled with seventeen objects on the baseline, which are decreased by one in each subsequent layer until there is only one object left at the top, they add exactly up to 153.[28]

---

25 Jelle Hoekstra, *Die gemeinfriesische siebzehn Küren* (Assen: van Gorcum, 1940), 13–26.

26 Algra, *Zeventien Keuren en Vierentwintig Landrechten*.

27 I gratefully acknowledge guidance by my son Rolf (III) in this point.

28 E.g., Aurelius Augustine, *Psalmum XLIX Enaratio. Sermo ad plebem*, in *Enarrationes in Psalmos* (001–079), ed. Jacques-Paul Migne, PL (Paris: Imprimerie Catholique, 1844–1855)

What was special too, according to Augustine, was that seventeen was the sum of ten and seven. A man cannot obtain eternal bliss without observing the Ten Commandments, but he can only keep them with the help of the Seven Gifts of the Holy Ghost. Hence, seven is the number of bliss. For that reason, God blessed the seventh day and sanctified it (Exodus 20:11). Church Father St. Gregory the Great (c. 540–604) took a somewhat different route in his exegesis of the Miraculous Catch. He, too, believed that ten and seven were perfect numbers, together amounting to seventeen. Moreover, he argued, if seventeen is multiplied by the holy number of the Trinity, the outcome is fifty-one; if this multiplication is repeated, the result is 153.[29] These and more methods of explaining 153 with the number seventeen were also put forward by other *patres*, such as Jerome, Isidore of Seville and the Venerable Bede. Later medieval theologians, too, including the famous Thomas Aquinas, joined their voices of consent to this chorus, as extensively discussed by Robert Stein in an article on the question of why the Low Countries in the Later Middle Ages counted precisely seventeen provinces. Stein also draws attention to the eleventh-century historiographer Adam of Bremen who remarked that Frisia consists of seventeen districts;[30] Stein furthermore briefly mentions the *Seventeen Statutes*.[31]

In addition to the number seventeen, twenty-four also had a deeper meaning to medieval theologians. The number was especially discussed in commentaries on the Revelation of St. John. In chapter four, John describes how around God's heavenly throne he beheld twenty-four thrones on which twenty-four elders were seated. He also saw four living creatures before God's throne, each of whom had six wings. The sum can quickly be made: $4 \times 6 = 24$. The four creatures looked as follows: the first one resembled a lion, the second appeared as a young ox, the third had a face like a man, and the fourth was similar to a flying eagle. They were taken to represent the four Evangelists. The Church

---

36:570–72, § 9; Aurelius Augustine, *Sermones Ad Populum. Classis II. De Tempore*, ed. Jacques-Paul Migne, 248.5, 249.3, PL 38: 1161a, 1163c; 250.3, PL 38:1167b, and 270.7, PL 38: 1245a.

29 Gregory the Great, *Homiliarum in Evangelia Libri Duo* 24.4, ed. Jacques-Paul Migne, PL 76: 1168c.

30 Adam of Bremen, *History of the Archbishops of Hamburg-Bremen*, trans. Francis J. Tschan, with new introduction by Timothy Reuter (New York: Columbia University Press, 1959; repr., 2002), Book IV.x Schol. 118: "Frisia is a coastal region, inaccessible because of impassable swamps, and it comprises seventeen districts."

31 Robert Stein, "Seventeen: The Multiplicity of a Unity in the Low Countries," in *The Ideology of Burgundy: The Promotion of National Consciousness 1364–1565*, ed. Jonathan D.B. D'Arcy and Jan R. Veenstra (Leiden: Brill, 2006), 255–58, 249–50, respectively.

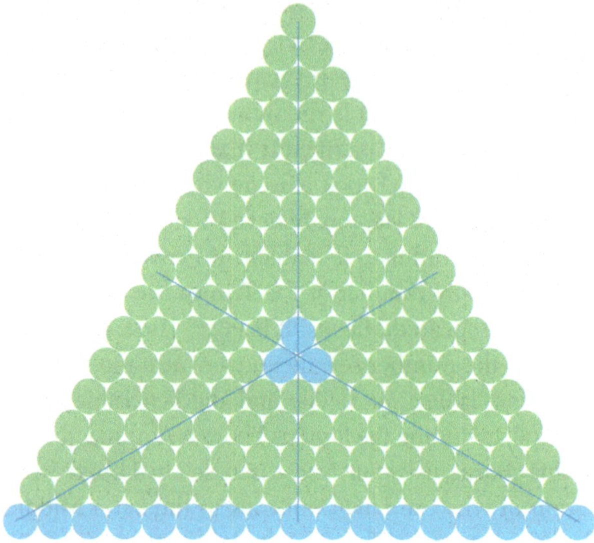

FIGURE 4.2 153 is the triangular number of 17.

Father Victorinus (d. 304) explained the number twenty-four in this vision as a reference to the twenty-four books of the Old Testament, according to the traditional Jewish count,[32] which supported the testimony of the four Evangelists. Victorinus also held that the number twenty-four referred to the twelve tribes of the Israelites and to the twelve apostles. The number was also associated with priesthood: King David appointed twenty-four families from whom the courses of priests were taken that had to serve in the temple (1 Chronicles 24 [!]). Following this interpretation, the twenty-four elders in John's vision reflected the twenty-four priests from the old dispensation. All such interpretations serve to emphasize the supposed unity of the Old and New Testaments. Similar opinions as held by Victorinus were also expressed by Caesarius of Arles (ca. 468–542) and the Venerable Bede (672–735).[33] The twelfth-century Hugh of St. Victor, one of the most influential theologians of the High Middle Ages, also concurred with this interpretation.[34] Moreover, the Hebrew and

32 Cf. Edmon L. Gallagher, *Hebrew Scripture in Patristic Biblical Theory: Canon, Language, Text* (Leiden: Brill, 2012), 52–53.

33 C. William Weinreich, ed. and trans., *Commentaries on Revelation by Victorinus of Petovium, Apringius of Beja, Caesarius of Arles, and Bede the Venerable* (Downers Grove, IL: Intervarsity Press, 2011).

34 Cornelia Linde, "Twelfth-Century Notions of the Canon of the Bible," in *Reading the Bible in the Middle Ages*, ed. Jinty Nelson and Damien Kempf (London: Bloomsbury, 2015), 11.

Greek alphabets consisted of twenty-four characters, expressing a complete fullness. Finally, and perhaps again not coincidentally, 17 + 7 (the holy number) = 24. In conclusion, then, it can be established that the *Seventeen Statutes* and *Twenty-four Landlaws* during their transmission from one manuscript to the next, rather than being extended in response to new social demands, retained their respective numbers because a deep symbolic, and probably even holy value was attached to them.[35]

What else made the *Seventeen Statutes* and *Twenty-four Landlaws* take up such a special position? This was, remarkably, the attribution of the Frisians' independence from feudal landlords and their right to establish for themselves the rules according to which their social life was to be arranged to a favor granted by Charlemagne. Time and again, for example, in the version contained in the First Rüstring Manuscript,[36] when the individual statutes of the *Seventeen Statutes* are enumerated, it is mentioned that they were King Charles's (i.e. Charlemagne's) gift. This is how the first statute begins:

> Thit is thiv forme liodkest and thes kyning Kerles ieft and londriucht allera Frisona ...[37]
>
> [This is the first people's statute and King Charles's gift and landlaw of all Frisians ...]

The historical irony, of course, is that four hundred years earlier Charlemagne had violently subjected the Frisians and annexed their territory into his ever-expanding empire, whereas here he is put down as an impressively obliging benefactor. Also, immediately following the twenty-fourth landlaw, there is a short epilogue, in which it appears that these two legal texts belong inextricably together. Their importance is once more fully expounded to the reader/listener:

> Thit send tha siuguntine liodkesta and tha fiuwer and twintich londriucht, ther alle Frisa mith hiara fia kapadon and mith riuchte bruka skilun,

35 On the role of numbers in the structure of Old Frisian texts, see also Concetta Giliberto, "Theological and Doctrinal Texts in the Old Frisian *Thet Autentica Riocht*," *Philologia Frisica anno 2014* (2015): 136–53.

36 Oldenburg, Niedersächsiches Staatsarchiv, MS Bestand 24–1, Ab. Nr. 1; c. 1300.

37 Wybren Jan Buma and Wilhelm Ebel, eds., *Das Rüstringer Recht*. Altfriesische Rechtsquellen 1 (Göttingen: Musterschmidt, 1963), R_1 III.1. All translations are mine, unless otherwise stated. Words added between square brackets are intended to make the sometimes terse legal prose more understandable.

ief se moton. Hwande thi kinig Kerl bed thet se alle riuchte thing hilde and ouonade, alsa longe sa se lifde, and hwasa hia ⟨thes riuchtes⟩ birauade, thet hi ⟨alra nethena⟩ birauad wrde fara Godis achnon and fara alle Godis heligon, ther an himulrike send and an irthrike.[38]

[These are the *Seventeen Statutes* and *Twenty-four Landlaws* which all Frisians purchased with their money and will lawfully use, when they can. For King Charles ordered them to observe and apply all legal decrees, as long as they lived, and [he declared that] whoever would rob them [i.e. the Frisians] from this law, that he [i.e. the perpetrator] himself would be robbed of all grace before God's eyes and before all God's saints, who are in heaven and on earth.]

This is quite something to claim, and it is moreover stated with great authority. It is therefore doubtless to conclude that behind these words a strategic leader can be detected, someone of the stature to whom Assmann ascribes a role in bringing about a textual community. The assertion of the epilogue's author is all inclusive, as appears from the threefold use of the word "all". By means of a material transaction King Charles had endowed *all* Frisians with these rights. Next, Charlemagne had ordered the Frisians to observe *all* their legal decrees for *all* their lives, just like God wished the Israelites would keep His commandments (Deuteronomy 5:29). Observance of this order results in bonding the group internally. So holy were these two legal codes that the outsider who dared violently deprive the Frisians from them, was not threatened with counter-violence but with a malediction, under invocation of the highest and most powerful authority there conceivably was: God and *all* his saints.[39] The addition "in heaven and on earth" lends an almost eschatological dimension to the curse and conjures up associations with Judgement Day. A contemporaneous translator into Latin interpreted this passage slightly differently, however, making Charlemagne already pronounce the verdict in the here and now:

---

38 Buma and Ebel, *Das Rüstringer Recht.*, R_1 IV. 25. I have added the words between angular brackets to indicate emendation of what I take to be a defective text. The emendation is based on the testimony of this passage in the First Emsingo Manuscript, see Wybren Jan Buma and Wilhelm Ebel, eds., *Das Emsiger Recht*, Altfriesische Rechtsquellen 3 (Göttingen: Vandenhoeck & Ruprecht, 1967), A III.18. I owe gratitude to Ton Hilhorst for helping me understand this passage and its Latin version.

39 Cf. Peter T. Leeson, "'God Damn': The Law of Economics of Monastic Malediction," *Journal of Law, Economics and Organization* 30.1 (2012): 193–216.

> ... et quicunque eos petitionibus spoliarent, illos iudicauit et condempnauit coram Deo et omnibus sanctis suis in celesti regno et terrestri. Amen.[40]
>
> [... and whoever would deprive them of these statutes, he (i.e. Charles) judged and condemned in the presence of God and of all his saints both in the celestial and the terrestrial kingdom. Amen.]

The conclusion is inescapable: this menacing imprecation against those who would wish to harm the Frisians' law, punctuated in the Latin version with a heartfelt "amen," aimed at effectuating a closing of Frisian ranks against the big, bad world out there.[41] Such an interpretation concurs with Stock's reasoning that within dissenting groups there is "a parallel use of texts, both to structure the internal behaviour of the groups' members and to provide solidarity against the outside world."[42]

Other advocates of the Frisian cause likewise seized the opportunity anonymously to provide the *Seventeen Statutes* and *Twenty-four Landlaws* with an afterword and in so doing invested them with historical remembrance and hence foregrounded their importance. The redaction contained in the two Hunsingo codices offers an appropriate example. The epilogist opens with a rather business-like summation, in prose:

> Thise riucht keren Fresa and bad him thi keneng Kerl ti hebbane and te haldane, to helpe and to nethum alle Fresum.
>
> [The Frisians chose these rights [i.e. the *Seventeen Statutes* and *Twenty-four Landlaws*] and King Charles ordered them to be preserved and observed as a help and profit for all Frisians.]

Again, the inclusive word "all" is being deployed here when the advantage of following the two legal codes is proffered. But then the author gets the spirit, nay, he becomes lyrical, and concludes with a four-line poem. Not with a threatening curse this time, as we have seen above, but by utilizing the "we" form.

40 Hoekstra, *De Eerste en Tweede Hunsinger Codex*, III.5–7.

41 On threatening with excommunicating curses elsewhere in Frisian law, see Rolf H. Bremmer Jr, "From Alien to Familiar: Christ in Language and Law of Medieval Frisia," in *Myths, Martyrs, and Modernity. Studies in the History of Religions in Honour of Jan N. Bremmer*, ed. Jitse Dijkstra, Justin Kroesen, and Yme Kuiper (Leiden: Brill, 2010), 543.

42 Stock, *Implications of Literacy*, 90.

Thus, he appeals to, and at the same time reinforces, a feeling of togetherness in combination with a presence of the sacred:

> Forth scele wi se halda
> and God scel urse walda
> thes teddera and thes stitha
> and alle vnriuchte thing scele wi formitha.[43]
>
> [From now on we shall observe them and [then] God will rule us, the weak and the strong, and we shall avoid all unlawful things.]

With some imagination one can hear resonating in these words an echo of Moses delivering God's law to the Israelites in the desert and the covenant that was concluded between God and His people, with both a promise and an obligation. The individual Frisian observing the statutes and landlaws is not the one who matters, but rather the Frisian people as a whole, both weak and strong—that is the poor and the rich, widows and housewives, orphans and parented, servants and landowners. They must carry the responsibility for upholding and abiding by the law; in return the blessing of God's rule will be bestowed upon His people.

Notwithstanding the attribution to Charlemagne to make the *Seventeen Statutes* and *Twenty-four Landlaws* radiate authority, someone in the second quarter of the thirteenth century seized the opportunity conspicuously to secure the importance of these two legal sources. To this end he (assuming the author was male) composed an extensive Prologue, thus lending a new dimension to their special character. This anonymous was a literate man and well versed in various contemporaneous works, among which there must have been versions of imperial and universal chronicles such as were gaining popularity in Germany at the time.[44] He begins his lengthy introduction with an exposition of the very beginning of Frisian law. In this way he filled as it were the time gap that preceded the days of Charlemagne. His argument opens with the following words:

43 Wybren Jan Buma and Wilhelm Ebel, eds., *Das Hunsingoer Recht*. Altfriesische Rechtsquellen 4 (Göttingen: Vandenhoeck & Ruprecht, 1969), III.26.

44 Brian Murdoch, "Authority and Authenticity: Comments on the Prologues to the Old Frisian Laws," in *Approaches to Old Frisian Philology*, ed. Rolf H. Bremmer Jr, Thomas S.B. Johnston, and Oebele Vries, Amsterdamer Beiträge zur älteren Germanistik 49 (Amsterdam: Rodopi, 1998).

> Hir is eskriuin thet wi Frisa alsek londriuht hebbe and halde, sa God selua sette and ebad, thet wi hilde alle afte thing and alle riuhte thing. Efter thes bedon hit ande bennon alle irthkiningar efter Romulo and Remo—thet weron tha tvene brother ther Rume erost stifton—Julius and Octauianus; alsa hiton tha forma fiuwer kiningar ther to Rume kiningar weron. Thit riuht skref God selua, use Hera.[45]
>
> [Here is written that we Frisians have and hold such landlaws as God himself ordained and commanded, [namely] that we observe all legal matters and all lawful matters. After this all earthly kings ordered and proclaimed it after Romulus and Remus—these were the two brothers who first founded Rome—[and] Julius [Caesar] and Octavian [Augustus]; thus were called the first four kings who were kings in Rome. This law was written by God himself, our Lord.]

In this passage Charlemagne is no longer the origin of Frisian law, but the role of prime legislator is now ascribed to God himself. It is impossible, one would think, to pride oneself on a more exclusive beginning. But no, a divine lawmaker was not yet sufficient, as it appears, for the Highest of all is given the company of mortal potentates who are here called the first Roman kings. In this way the author combines both divine authority and the dignity of the Roman past with the unquestionable authoritative tradition of the Frisian legal customs themselves. Immediately following this grand overture, the author lists the Ten Commandments, each commandment given first in Latin and then followed by a Frisian translation. The commandments are concluded by an improvisation on Christ's summary of the Law (Matthew 22:37–40; Mark 12:30–31; Luke 10:27–28), viz. that one must love God with a pure heart and one's fellow Christian like oneself. In a manner of afterword to the Ten Commandments the author reminds his audience of the journey which the people of Israel made through the desert on their winding way to the land flowing "fon melokon and fon hunige", with milk and honey, to the Holy Land, to Jerusalem. Next a tropological interpretation is given to this major episode in the history of salvation: God will lead everyone who observes the (Frisian) law to the celestial Jerusalem; however, those who fail to do so He will lock up in hell, just as He had confined the Egyptians in the Red Sea.[46] This interpretation already contains the germ

45 Buma and Ebel, *Rüstringer Recht*, I.1.

46 Cf. Murdoch, "Authority and Authenticity," 224–25.

of a conviction that was to be elaborated in later narratives: the Frisians are a chosen people, called by God—the Israelites of the new dispensation.[47]

After his moral explanation of the desert journey, the author continues with an account of all who ordered these laws to be observed: the prophets who lived before Christ's birth: "thi goda Moses and sin brother Aaron", Joshua and Samuel, Isaiah and Jeremiah. These six suffice, for there follow twenty-five Old Testament kings by name,[48] of whom only Solomon is honored with an epithet, viz. "thi wisa" (the wise). These biblical authorities are trodden on their heels after Christ's birth by a sheer endless row of named rulers—105 in all—who maintained the tradition of confirming the law. The list is a real *tour de force* and would have been pretty boring if the author had not interspersed, and thus structured, his enumeration with small pieces of information of church history, on such characters as Emperor Decius, "ther breda lit sancte Laurentius" [who ordered St. Lawrence to be roasted] or the (Eastern) Roman Emperor Archadius, "vnder sine tidon was sancte Augustinus, thi heliga biscop" [in his days lived St. Augustine, the holy bishop]. Likewise, we are informed in passing that during the reign of Emperor Phocas, St. Gregory (the Great) organized the conversion of England; we learn as well of the four bishops who in the days of the noble Charlemagne, son of Pepin, turned the Frisians into Christians: Boniface, Willibrord, Willehad, and Liudger (in this order). The enumeration ends with the Holy Roman Emperor Frederick II of Hohenstaufen (1194–1245).[49] This last name suggests that the Prologue was written during or shortly after his reign.

The number of emperors and kings varies from redaction to redaction. While the Rüstring Prologue parades the names of 105 rulers, starting from Julius Caesar, that of the Hunsingo Manuscripts mentions only forty-seven, and in manuscript Jus the tally ends at forty-three.[50] For the man who penned the Pro-

47 See Johannes A. Mol and Justine Smithuis, "De Friezen als uitverkoren volk. Religieus-patriottische geschiedschrijving in vijftiende-eeuws Friesland," *Jaarboek voor Middeleeuwse Geschiedenis* 11 (2008): 165–204; cf. Mary Garrison, "Divine Elections for Nations—A Difficult Rhetoric for Medieval Scholars?" in *The Making of Christian Myths in the Periphery of Latin Christendom (c. 1000–1300)*, ed. Lars B. Mortensen (Copenhagen: Museum Tusculanum Press, 2006).

48 Based on Jesus's genealogy as given in Matthew 1:6–17, see Murdoch, "Authority and Authenticity," 233.

49 For a detailed discussion of the kings and emperors as they appear in this listing, see Murdoch, "Authority and Authenticity," 234–40.

50 Buma and Ebel, *Rüstringer Recht*, I.14; Buma and Ebel, *Hunsingoer Recht*, I.6; and Wybren Jan Buma, Wilhelm Ebel, with Martina Tragter-Schubert, eds., *Westerlauwersches Recht I: Jus municipale Frisonum*, 2 vols. Altfriesische Rechtsquellen 6 (Göttingen: Vandenhoeck & Ruprecht, 1977), VII.2, respectively.

logue into the First Emsigo Manuscript the task of cataloguing all those names seems to have been too daunting, yet he found an ingenious solution: "Thiu fiuwer and fiuwertich kenega and othere moneghe, thera send alle soghentech, hebbet to Rome kenegar ewesen." [These forty-four kings (he actually lists forty-three names, RHB) and many others, of whom there are seventy in all, were kings in Rome.][51] No list in any of the redactions of the Prologue adds up to this sum, yet seventy can hardly have been chosen arbitrarily: the solemn number recurs time and again, both in the Bible and beyond, to define a sizeable yet limited group. For example, the Babylonian confusion of tongues resulted in the rise of seventy peoples (Genesis 10); Moses appointed seventy elders to help him rule the Israelites (Numbers 11:6); Christ dispatched seventy disciples to spread his Gospel (Luke 10:1–24);[52] in seventy days, seventy wise scribes translated the sacred books from Hebrew into Greek—hence this translation is known as Septuagint. Evidently, the Emsingo scribe-redactor applied his learning here to even more firmly tie the Frisians up into the great tradition of the Christian and Roman past.

Returning to the First Rüstring Manuscript, the Prologue finishes with a brief conclusion:

> Thesse kiningar hebbath ewesen kiningar to Rome efter Kerstes berthe. Hia vrievon alle Frison efter thes kining Kerles ieft frihalsa and fria spreka, and setton and stedgadon allera kininga ieft, thet send allera Frisona kesta and londriucht. *Hic expliciunt Reges.*[53]
>
> [These kings have been kings in Rome after Christ's birth. They granted all Frisians, in line with King Charles's privilege, freedom [from feudal obligations] and free jurisdiction, and instituted and confirmed the privileges of all kings, namely the statutes and landlaws of all Frisians. *Here end the Kings.*]

Framed between an opening in which "we Frisians" observe their law given by God himself and a conclusion in which "all Frisians" are privileged by "all kings" to live sovereignly in their own judiciary system according to the statutes and

51 Buma and Ebel, *Emsiger Recht*, II.6.

52 Seventy disciples according to some manuscript witnessess, seventy-two to others, cf. Bruce Metzger and Bart D. Ehrman, *The Text of the New Testament: Its Transmission, Corruption, and Restoration* (Oxford: Oxford University Press, 2005), 340–42.

53 Buma and Ebel, *Rüstringer Recht*, I.15. The Latin explicit is a scribal addition, only found in the Rüstring version of the Prologue.

landlaws of "all Frisians", the prologist has delivered a highly seductive narrative. Around it he rallied an audience that was all too willing to imbibe his profession of Frisian exclusiveness and to subscribe to it.

The Prologue and the *Seventeen Statutes* and *Twenty-four Landlaws* comprise the canon around which the Frisian textual community grouped itself. Even though the various Frisian lands experienced different developments as a result of adopting all kinds of local laws, this supraregional community proved coherent enough to last for a long time. For despite the often-deficient survival of medieval Frisian manuscripts, there is still sufficient evidence of a lively exchange of other legal texts between the Frisian lands. Not only did this circulation disregard natural barriers, such as ditches, canals, rivers, lakes, and marshes, it also ignored diocesan borders. A fine example in point is the *Rüstring Dike Law*, which begins as follows:

> Thet is ac londriucht, thet wi Frisa hagon ene seburch to stiftande and to sterande, enne geldene hop, ther umbe al Frislond lith.[54]
>
> [This is also landlaw, that we Frisians must found and fortify a sea stronghold, a golden hoop, which lies around all Frisia.]

Until recently, it was held that this law text ordering the Frisians to build and maintain a dike was typically drafted for Rüstringen, the easternmost of the Frisian lands, until Thomas Johnston discovered some time ago that the same text was also circulating in Humsterland, situated immediately on the east bank of the Lauwers.[55] Johnston also demonstrated that this dike law showed further—intertextual—indications of a supra-regional character, since it contained expressions and phrases that also occur in other texts from west of the Lauwers, such as the *Elder Skeltanariucht*. However, since Johnston was particularly concerned with the political-ideological implications of his discovery,[56] he seems to have overlooked its religious dimension. The dike law concludes, as it happens, with a humble statement of dependence on the Lord and, through the heavenly key-bearer, on His representative on earth, the Pope: "ief us God

54 Buma and Ebel, *Rüstringer Recht*, X.10.

55 Thomas S.B. Johnston, "*Ene zie borch tho bouwenn*': A New Look at the Pan-Frisian Dike Law of a Low German Ommeland Version," *Us Wurk* 44 (1995): 1–37.

56 Cf. Thomas S.B. Johnston, "Old Frisian Law and the Frisian Freedom Ideology: Text and Manuscript Composition as a Marketing Device," in *Approaches to Old Frisian Philology*, ed. Rolf H. Bremmer Jr, Thomas S.B. Johnston, and Oebele Vries, Amsterdamer Beiträge zur älteren Germanistik 49 (Amsterdam: Rodopi, 1998).

helpe wili and Sante Peder" [If God and Saint Peter will help us].[57] Building and maintaining dikes was clearly not just a secular, feet-in-the mud necessity for "us Frisians", but appears to have been deeply intertwined with the transcendental.

To sum up briefly, by way of an interim conclusion: a first application of the concept of textual community, as developed by Brian Stock, together with the notion of canonization advanced by Jan Assmann, has brought to light how in the thirteenth century anonymous authors exploited supra-regional Frisian laws, notably the *Seventeen Statutes* and the *Twenty-four Landlaws*, by enveloping them in historically and religiously enhanced prologues and epilogues. It was these authors' express intention to inspire and unite a select following—the land-owning elite—by providing them with a justification for a *status aparte* that vied in holiness with that of the Holy Roman Empire of which it remained officially a part.

Sometimes a legal textual community can be seen operating within a smaller geographical space, such as Frisia west of the Lauwers. I shall demonstrate this claim with the help of the *Book of Rudolf*, sometimes called the book of "keyser Rolluf" or even "keyser Rolf".[58] Briefly summarized, this book, most likely written around the middle of the thirteenth century,[59] narrates how one—not further specified—day the Frisians were summoned to appear in a place called Bordeus before Emperor Rudolf in order to receive from him a collection of legal rules of a variegating nature.[60] Between the regulations, but also into the decrees themselves, the anonymous author has managed to weave a sizeable history of the Frisians, of their liberty, their loss of it, and how they received this liberty back again from Charlemagne. The historical matter in the *Book* is usually presented in verse. This author, too, mentions the promise of heaven for abiding by the law and the threat of hell for the law-breakers, with reference to the fate suffered by the Egyptians in the Red Sea.[61] In all likelihood, therefore, he was familiar with the Prologue to the *Seventeen Statutes* and *Twenty-four Landlaws*.

57 Buma and Ebel, *Rüstringer Recht*, X.10.

58 Buma, Ebel and Tragter-Schubert, *Jus municipale Frisonum*, II, 309.

59 Pieter Gerbenzon, *Zeer voorlopige lijst van de belangrijkste middeleeuwse rechtsbronnen uit het Groot-Friese gebied tussen Vlie en Wezer*, 2nd ed. (Groningen: Juridisch Instituut, Rijksuniversiteit, 1975), no. 133, decides for the second half of the twelfth century, while Buma, Ebel, and Tragter-Schubert, *Jus municipale Frisonum*, 511–12, argue for the first half.

60 For an extensive summary, see Henny S.E. Bos-van der Heide, *Het Rudolfsboek* (Assen: van Gorcum, 1937), 11–17.

61 Buma, Ebel, and Tragter-Schubert, *Jus municipale Frisonum*, XVIII.1c (end).

Especially towards the end of his book, the author frequently refers to the Bible and he always does so in Latin. With this choice of language he impresses the reader as having enjoyed a solid clerical education. Remarkably, his quotations from the Bible tend to be rather free, sometimes consisting of parts of different verses pasted together, and they seem not always to have been taken from a current version of the Vulgate. It also looks as though the author has drawn from as yet unsourced apocryphal texts, such as his claim that the Acts of the Apostles relate how Pilate, after his perverse judgements, left his palace in order to go to hell and never return from there: "Vnde jn Actibus apostolorum: Egressus est Pilatus a pretorio suo post praua iudicia sua ad infernum ire et nunquam redire."[62] According to the current opinion about his death, based on medieval apocryphal texts, such as the anti-Jewish *Vindicta Salvatoris* and *Mors Pilati*,[63] and sustained, for example, in the famous *Aurea legenda* by Jacques de Voragine (1228–1298), Pilate committed suicide.[64] Clearly, then, the person behind the *Book of Rudolf* was not afraid to take up an independent position. He also, somewhat abruptly, finishes his book with a Latin quotation, this time with a legal maxim that enjoyed quite some popularity in his day: "Conscientes et agentes malum equali pena puniantur" [Acting and consenting parties are liable to the same punishment].[65] By the way, the word "book" in the *Book of Rudolf* should not give occasion to thoughts of a sizeable tome. In the most recent edition, it takes up only seventeen pages of spaciously printed text, and is divided by the editors into exactly twenty-four sections.[66] Coincidences happen, don't they?

---

62 Buma, Ebel, and Tragter-Schubert, *Jus municipale Frisonum*, XVIII.24, 382 (bottom).

63 J.K. Elliott, ed., *The Apocryphal New Testament. A Collection of Apocryphal Literature in an English Translation* (Oxford: Clarendon Press, 1993), 213–16 and 216–17, respectively.

64 Alexander Murray, *Suicide in the Middle Ages*, vol. 2: *The Curse on Self-Murder* (Oxford: Oxford University Press, 2000), 339–343. I would like to thank Brandon Hawk and Martin Foys for guidance in this point.

65 Buma, Ebel, and Tragter-Schubert, *Jus municipale Frisonum*, XVIII.24, 384. Cf. Peter D. Clarke, "Peter the Chanter, Innocent III and Theological Views on Collective Guilt and Punishment," *Journal of Ecclesiastical History* 52 (2000): 14: "a commonplace of late twelfth-century canonistic discourse." William Langland (ca. 1330–1387?) also used the sentence in his hugely popular *Piers Plowman* (B- and C-versions); for a helpful discussion, see Nick Gray, "Langland's Quotations from Penitential Tradition," *Modern Philology* 84 (1986): 54–55. On the role of maxims and proverbs in Old Frisian legal texts, see most recently Rolf H. Bremmer Jr, "'The Fleeing Foot is the Confessing Hand': Proverbs in the Old Frisian Laws," in *La tradizione gnomica nelle letterature germaniche medievali*, ed. Marina Cometta et al., Collana Di/Segni 13 (Milan: Ledizioni, 2018), and, briefly, Bremmer, "Orality of Medieval Frisian Law," 30–32.

66 Buma, Ebel and Tragter-Schubert, *Jus municipale Frisonum*, XVIII.

The *Book of Rudolf* enjoyed considerable esteem and, as a result, exercised its influence in Frisia west of the Lauwers and even further, to the east of that river. It survives in three manuscripts, J, U, and D,[67] and in an incomplete transcription made by the early-modern Frisian historian Bernard Furmerius (1544–1601) of what looks to have been an early-fifteenth-century manuscript.[68] The *Book* was referred to as an authoritative legal source in various later texts, one of which is the *Excerpta legum*, a fifteenth-century vernacular collection of Roman and canon law, provided with comments.[69] In a rule concerning nightly burglary—after sunset, when fire in the hearths has been covered with ashes and the doors are locked—it is stated that the burglar may be executed on the spot. The commentator first appeals to a landlaw—not one of the *Twenty-four Landlaws*, but rather a thirteenth-century tract rubricated as "Fan en schaeckraef" [About violent robbery][70]—that clearly [claerlick] implies this punishment, and next refers to the law of Emperor Rudolf [keyser Rudolphi riucht] that is even clearer [claerlicker] on this point.[71] Another collection of Roman and canon law, together with an admixture of traditional Frisian laws, is the *Jurisprudentia Frisica*, a late-fifteenth-century composition. In many respects this work can be considered an adapted version of the *Excerpta*, and like it, despite their Latin titles, it is written in Frisian, but with frequent references to or quotations from Latin sources.[72] Here, too, on several occasions, reference is made to "keyser Roleffs riucht," each time with due respect.[73] The *Book* was also received east of the Lauwers, outside the immedi-

67 On these sigils, see n. 15.

68 The text according to the three manuscripts was diplomatically edited by Bos-van der Heide, *Rudolfsboek*; the Furmerius-fragment by Pieter Gerbenzon, ed., *Rudolfsboek–materiael*, Estrikken 32 (Groningen: Frysk Ynstitút, Rijksuniversiteit Groningen, 1961), 1–39.

69 Extensively discussed in Pieter Gerbenzon, *Excerpta legum. Onderzoekingen betreffende enkele Friese rechtsboeken uit de vijftiende eeuw* (Groningen: J.B. Wolters, 1956).

70 Buma, Ebel, and Tragter-Schubert, *Jus municipale Frisonum*, XVI. On the various meanings of the word *londriucht*, see Oebele Vries, "*Thet is ac londriucht.* Landrechte und Landrecht im mittelalterlichen Friesland," in *Directions for Old Frisian Philology*, ed. Rolf H. Bremmer Jr, Stephen Laker, and Oebele Vries, Amsterdamer Beiträge zur älteren Germanistik 73 (Amsterdam: Rodopi, 2014).

71 Wybren Jan Buma, Pieter Gerbenzon, and Martina Tragter-Schubert, eds., *Codex Aysma. Die altfriesische Texte herausgegeben und übersetzt* (Assen: van Gorcum, 1993), *Excerpta legum* I.24. Other references to the *Book of Rudolf* to be found in *Excerpta* I.53 and I.260.

72 Pieter Gerbenzon, "Aantekeningen over de *Jurisprudentia Frisica*, een laat-vijftiende-eeuwse Westerlauwers-Friese bewerking van de *Exerpta legum*," *Tijdschrift voor Rechtsgeschiedenis/Legal History Review* 57 (1989): 21–67 and 339–84 (with summary in English 373–74).

73 Montanus Hettema, *Jurisprudentia Frisica, of Friesche Regtskennis*, 2 vols. (Leeuwarden: H.C. Schetsberg, 1834–35), Tituli 26.28, 50.24, 50.26.

ate political sphere of influence of the lands west of that river, as is evidenced by the Fivelgo Manuscript. In it, a fifteenth-century tract on inheritance succession closes its last regulation with a rule taken from the *Book*, a source which is duly acknowledged:

> Dat riucht bibiuth vs to halden keyser Rolf in sine boke by vs lif and bi vser sele ende bida leste ordele. Ende Spegel van Sassen sprecht ac ther destelike alsa dervan.[74]
>
> [Emperor Rudolf orders us to observe this rule [about succession] in his book on [pain of] our body and our soul and the Last Judgement. And the Saxon Mirror, too, speaks in the same manner of this rule.]

Clearly, the audience is enjoined here to not disregard the Emperor's decree with a threat of eternal, that is religious consequences. To make the full weight of its importance understood, the narrating legislator places the book on the same level as the far more famous and influential *Sachsenspiegel*. Finally, as a testimony to the high regard in which it was held by later generations, the *Book of Rudolf* survived the shift from Frisian to Low German that took place in the lands east of the Lauwers in the course of the fifteenth century. It was diligently translated into Low German, and survives in three different redactions in some thirty sixteenth-century manuscripts.[75]

Contrary to its evident medieval popularity, the *Book of Rudolf* was poorly received by scholars in modern times. One of the first to call attention to it was the late-eighteenth-century East Frisian legal historian Tilemann Dotias Wiarda (1746–1826). In his criticism he did not spare the whip. The *Book* was to him a monstrosity [Missgeburt] from the Late Middle Ages, patched together from passages lifted from other legal texts.[76] The greatest scholar of Old Frisian law from the nineteenth century, Karl Freiherr von Richthofen (1811–1888), was plainly damning in his judgement of this "fabricated" work. He deemed it a "concoction" [Machwerk], a chaotic "*Mixtum compositum*", which had been assembled "without purpose" [sinnlos] in the fifteenth century from the Bible, from Roman and canon law, as well as from a wide variety of older Frisian legal

---

74 Wybren Jan Buma and Wilhelm Ebel, eds., *Das Fivelgoer Recht*. Altfriesische Rechtsquellen 5 (Göttingen: Vandenhoeck & Ruprecht, 1972), XIX.13.

75 See Gerbenzon, *Rudolsboekmateriael*, 67.

76 Tilemann D. Wiarda, *Asega-Buch. Ein Altfriesisches Gesetz-buch der Rüstringer* (Berlin: Friedrich Nicolai, 1805), LX.

sources.[77] As a pupil of the Romantic scholar Jacob Grimm, von Richthofen would have been charmed especially by legal texts that presumably found their origin in "the people."[78] Scholarly legal compositions, on the other hand, compared most unfavorably in his eyes with the "real stuff" from popular tradition. Sometimes a positive judgement is passed, such as that by Pieter Sipma. In addition to a good deal of criticism of the author's lack of historical knowledge and critical capacity, Sipma praised the *Book of Rudolf* for its unity in structure and even called it a tiny piece of art.[79] The last to have expressed themselves critically on the *Book* were Wybren Jan Buma and Wilhelm Ebel. Seeking a middle position, they were willing to agree a little with Sipma, to the extent that they thought the legal decrees were rather well composed. Unfortunately, however, in their opinion these decrees were overgrown by the tangleweed of historical and mythical digressions. In fact, with a semblance of reluctance, Buma and Ebel echoed von Richthofen's authoritative opinion.[80] All of these scholars, with the exception perhaps of Sipma, approached the *Book* as legal historians and initially took it at face-value. When they concluded that its contents could not be verified and abounded with fictive claims and rules, they rejected it as an aimless treatise. They deplored from their positivist perspective that, in the words of Buma and Ebel, "the defense of the Frisian Freedom and the sacredness of law […], which must have been pleasing to the Frisians' tribal consciousness, to our taste were so long-windedly presented."[81]

That the *Book of Rudolf* is confronting us with a special kind of legal literature is crystal clear. First of all, there is the narrator who introduces the book. He presents Emperor Rudolf as an industrious researcher who has studied the legal books of both the Roman Emperor and the Pope.[82] In other words, Emperor Rudolf is fully at home with what we now call Roman and canon law, and with this quality attributed to him the author expects the Emperor to inspire trust in the reader/audience when he performs as a legislator. Sometimes the author stages the Emperor in the third person, sometimes, so as to increase authen-

77 Karl von Richthofen, *Untersuchungen über friesische Rechtsgeschichte*, 3 vols. (Berlin: Wilhelm Hertz, 1882–1886), 1, 327.

78 See, e.g., Kaius Tuori, *Lawyers and Savages: Ancient History and Legal Realism in the Making of Legal Anthropology* (Abingdon: Routledge, 2015), 37–39.

79 Pieter Sipma, *Bijdrage tot de kennis van Het Rudolfsboek* (The Hague: Martinus Nijhoff, 1930), 27.

80 Buma, Ebel, and Tragter-Schubert, *Jus municipale Frisonum*, 313.

81 Buma, Ebel, and Tragter-Schubert, *Jus municipale Frisonum*: "die Verteidigung der friesischen Freiheit [und] die Heiligkeit des Rechtes […] dem Stammesbewußtsein der Friesen zusagen mußten, nach unserem Geschmack so weitschweifig dargestellt werden."

82 Buma, Ebel, and Tragter-Schubert, *Jus municipale Frisonum*, XVIII.2 and 17.

ticity, he has him deliver his regulations to the gathered Frisians in the first person.[83] Towards the end of the book, Rudolf takes his leave from the Frisians in the first person and soon afterwards, according to the narrator, he dies. The narrator then continues in the first person,[84] thus, almost unnoticed, tacitly adopting Rudolf's role as legal expert. Put differently, we can also regard the author of the *Book of Rudolf* as a strategic philologist as defined by Assmann.[85] The narrator and his alias Rudolf have a well-defined audience before their mind's eye—the Free Frisians—that is constantly addressed with the plural "you". In this manner a bond is being constructed, as if between leader and followers, a typical characteristic of a textual community. Even in his first address, the narrator has Emperor Rudolf declare that his prime concern is "dae era dis Fresiska fridomes."[86] It is this honor which is the rallying point around which the audience is assembled.

Scholars, beginning with Francis Junius and Jan van Vliet in the seventeenth century,[87] have racked their brains over the historicity of an Emperor Rudolf who supposedly granted a collection of rights to the Frisians. Was it Rudolph of Swabia (1077–1080) or Rudolph of Habsburg (1273–1291)? Nor did it appear possible to trace the whereabouts of "Bordeus," the place to where Rudolf summoned the Frisians before him. Likewise, efforts to identify the author of the book have remained without generally accepted results.[88] The problem of historicity can therefore be better moved aside and replaced by the question after *auctoritas*.

In order to build credibility with readers and audience, medieval writers were expected to appeal to authoritative authors.[89] This phenomenon is also

83 For example, Buma, Ebel, and Tragter-Schubert, *Jus municipale Frisonum*, XVIII.1a and 1c, respectively.

84 Buma, Ebel, and Tragter-Schubert, *Jus municipale Frisonum*, XVIII.23.

85 See above, n. 13.

86 Buma, Ebel, and Tragter-Schubert, *Jus municipale Frisonum*, XVIII.1a; cf. Oebele Vries, "*Frisonica libertas*: Frisian Freedom as an Instance of Medieval Liberty," *Journal of Medieval History* 41 (2015): 235.

87 See Kees Dekker, "The Old Frisian Studies of Jan van Vliet (1622–1666) and Thomas Marshall (1621–1685)," in *Approaches to Old Frisian Studies*, ed. Rolf H. Bremmer Jr, Thomas S.B. Johnston, and Oebele Vries, Amsterdamer Beiträge zur älteren Germanistik 49 (Amsterdam: Rodopi, 1998), 119.

88 The arguments for the various positions are briefly discussed in Buma, Ebel, and Tragter-Schubert, *Jus municipale Frisonum*, 310–12, who decide in favor of Rudolph of Swabia and accept a date of composition between 1215 and 1217. I am not convinced by their reasoning, though.

89 Jan Ziolkowski. "Cultures of Authority in the Long Twelfth Century," *Journal of English and Germanic Philology* 108 (2009): 421–48, especially at 438–39.

found in Old Frisian literature. For example, two different descriptions of the month-by-month growth of the fetus are attributed to St. Augustine, "thi hilige biscop";[90] an account of the five keys of wisdom is put in the mouth of Solomon, "who was the wisest of all earthly men";[91] a description of the fifteen signs of Doomsday is ascribed to St Jerome "who found them written in the books of the Jews,"[92] while *Thet Freske Riim*, a fifteenth-century imaginative account of Frisian history in verse, is attributed to a "Master Alwyn."[93] Nobody in Frisian Studies today would in all seriousness credit these four authorities with these pieces; it can indeed be demonstrated that the attributions are fictive: the oldest known version of the Latin text on the growth of the fetus, of which a variant is also recorded for Old English, is found without an attribution in a St. Gall manuscript of ca. 800; the earliest mention of the five keys is included anonymously in the *Collectanea* by Sedulius Scotus, a ninth-century Irish scholar; the oldest enumeration of the Fifteen Signs of Doomsday appears in the early ninth-century *Collectanea* of Pseudo-Bede, but the text is attributed for the first time to Jerome by Peter Damian in the eleventh century; "Master Alwyn" is explained as a corruption of "Alcuin", but surely this Anglo-Saxon scholar (ca. 735–804), for all his learning, cannot be accounted for having written a fifteenth-century Old Frisian poem.[94] Staging Emperor Rudolf as the author of a number of Frisian legal regulations should therefore be seen in the light of such fictive attributions.

The suggestion that the staging of Emperor Rudolf as a legislator at Bordeus is fanciful can be further underpinned. The authorship that is being pretended for the *Book of Rudolf* strongly resembles the case in which Geoffrey Chaucer staged a certain Lollius as *auctour*, his authoritative source, for his romance *Troilus and Criseyde*. Dozens of articles and chapters have been devoted to iden-

90 Buma and Ebel, *Emsiger Recht*, A v.19 and C I.199, respectively.

91 Buma and Ebel, *Hunsigoer Recht*, IV.1.

92 Buma and Ebel, *Rüstringer Recht*, XI.1.

93 Alistair Campbell, ed., *Thet Freske Riim. Tractatus Alvini* (The Hague: Martinus Nijhoff, 1952), 2–3.

94 See, respectively, Rolf H. Bremmer Jr, "Leiden, Vossianus Lat. Q. 69 (Part 2): Schoolbook or Proto-Encyclopaedic Miscellany?" in *Practice in Learning: The Transfer of Encyclopaedic Knowledge in the Early Middle Ages*, ed. Rolf H. Bremmer Jr and Kees Dekker (Leuven: Peeters, 2010), 33–34; Vivien Law, *Wisdom, Authority and Grammar in the Seventh Century* (Cambridge: Cambridge University Press, 1995), 42 and n. 3; Martin MacNamara, "The (Fifteen) Signs of Doomsday in Irish Tradition," *Warszawskie Studia Teologiczne* 20.2 (2007): 225, and Concetta Giliberto, "The Fifteen Signs of Doomsday in the Rüstring Manuscript," in *Advances in Old Frisian Philology*, ed. Rolf H. Bremmer Jr, Stephen Laker, and Oebele Vries, Amsterdamer Beiträge zur älteren Germanistik 64 (Amsterdam: Rodopi, 2007), 130–35; for Alcuin, see previous note.

tify this so-called Roman historian, but without any trustworthy result. Today it is generally agreed that Chaucer was making fun of the conventional idea of his day that in order to be a good writer one must appeal to an established author from the past.[95] Instead, Chaucer made up his own authority. Something similar, I would argue, can be seen in action here, too. The author of the *Book of Rudolf* created a fictive Emperor Rudolph, who at a fictive place called Bordeus summoned the Frisians before him. Such a scenario enabled the author to construe a narrative through which to deliver his message, of which the basic tenor is "the honor of the Frisian freedom." This message is wrapped up in a narrative that for its form is ambitious, namely in prosimetrum—partly prose, partly verse.[96] As for its contents, the *Book of Rudolf* consists of a fabricated past, an unequally divided quantity of legal rules, and a religious discourse. The half-dozen Latin quotations from the Bible and one from canon law provided an added aura of authority, for the unlearned people as much as for the literate professionals. With this blend the author, through his narrator, intended to bring his Frisian audience/readership together in order to enhance their conviction that they, under God's guidance, were a special people, different from all others.

Looking back at the examples of textual communities grouped around a select number of Old Frisian legal texts, it is striking to observe that their strategic leaders took up a modest stance. What their names were, whereabouts they lived, what their position was in daily life—we are given no clue whatsoever. They were certainly no big shots of the calibre of a Peter Waldo or a Bernard of Clairvaux. Yet, they should be credited with the knack of seizing an opportunity when they saw it. In the situation of political ambiguity that had arisen by the *de facto* independence within the Holy Roman Empire of the Frisian lands, these men (I presume) deployed their Latinate learning to produce historical and theological arguments with which to bolster the pretentious claims of Frisian separateness. In doing so, they assumed the role of textual patrons of the free Frisians.[97] In contrast to the grandness of their assertions, their anonymity reveals an unpretentiousness that befits that of Old Frisian literature, which has to make do without big names and is lacking in smash hits

95 See the editor's introduction to Geoffrey Chaucer, *Troilus and Criseyde*, 1.395 and elsewhere. In *The Riverside Chaucer*, ed. Larry Benson, 3rd ed. (Oxford: Oxford University Press, 1988; repr., 2008), 1022, and, e.g., Bella Millet, "Chaucer, Lollius, and the Medieval Theory of Authorship," in *Studies in the Age of Chaucer*, Proceedings, No. 1: *Reconstructing Chaucer*, ed. Paul Strohm and Thomas J. Heffernan (1984): 93–103.

96 Cf. Joseph Harris and Karl Reichl, eds., *Prosimetrum: Crosscultural Perspectives on Narrative in Prose and Verse* (Cambridge: D.S. Brewer, 1997).

97 Cf. Stock, *Implications of Literacy*, 10.

such as *Beowulf* or the *Nibelungenlied*. Anyone who aspired to be a writer in medieval Frisia, it seems, had to release his creative energy in namelessly drafting laws and legal treatises and, occasionally, in imaginative national history. However, when such legal texts and historiographic narratives are scrutinized under a magnifying glass, as I hope to have demonstrated, ever new aspects of the medieval Frisian writing and reading culture jump to the eye. Not epoch making, perhaps, nor grand or compelling, but in harmony with the modest Old Frisian text corpus.

CHAPTER 5

Law, Law-Books and Tradition in Early Medieval Ireland

Fangzhe Qiu

The richness of medieval Irish law texts can be appreciated from multiple perspectives.[1] As regulations of behaviors they cover a dazzling array of topics in such detail, that historians are able to reconstruct many aspects of medieval Irish society from them. From a linguistic angle, the strata of compositions in law texts traverse a millennium from the seventh to the seventeenth century, and thus afford valuable witnesses to the development of the Irish language. The law texts refer freely to history, literature, medical theories and religious texts, sometimes even bearing unique testimony to texts that are otherwise lost. The late medieval manuscripts that record law texts are no less a kaleidoscope of learning, with texts on many other subjects copied side by side with law tracts.

How, and why, does the study of law seamlessly merge with those of other subjects, both in the selection of texts in manuscripts and in the law texts themselves? This article aims to demonstrate the organic connection between law texts and the medieval Irish learned tradition as a whole, called *senchas*[2] in Old Irish. This article firstly provides a general account of early Irish law, and secondly examines the discourses and techniques employed in early Irish law texts and law-books that creates intertextuality with other branches of *senchas*. The term "intertextuality" here denotes more than a collective description of the sharing, exchange and interdependence of words, figures, themes, story-plots and temporal-local settings between texts. It is a conscious construction, laden with the ideology of medieval European textual culture, and can be described, in the words of Neil Wright, as "the way in which early medieval writ-

1 This paper is derived from the author's unpublished PhD thesis: Fangzhe Qiu, "Narratives in Early Irish Law Tracts" (PhD thesis, University College Cork, 2015). The author wants to express gratitude to the editor for his invitation to contribute to the book, as well as to Prof. John Carey, Prof. Liam Breatnach and Dr. Kevin Murray who read earlier drafts of this work and gave many insightful comments.

2 Francis John Byrne, "Senchas: The Nature of Gaelic Historical Tradition," *Historical Studies* 9 (1974): 138, 150.

 | DOI:10.1163/9789004448650_007

ers' medium and message could be informed by and interact with other texts which they had read, text which would, for the most part, also have been familiar to their audience."[3] It is argued, that such intense intertextuality between all branches of the learned tradition established the authority of the law texts in the lack of direct royal legislation and enforcement, and at the same time continuously renewed the tradition in a dynamic process.

Ireland had never been part of the Roman Empire, and Roman Law left little influence on the vernacular Irish law of the Early Middle Ages.[4] Some institutions of early medieval Irish laws may have been in existence long before the first law-books in Ireland were even written.[5] However, judging from linguistic evidence and historical references, vernacular law texts were first written down in Ireland in the seventh and the eighth centuries in Old Irish,[6] using the Roman alphabet and an orthography that is based on a form of Latin used in Britain and brought to Ireland by British missionaries around the fifth century.[7] The seventh and eighth centuries witness an explosion in vernacular text production in Ireland, when a large number of legal, genealogical, homiletic and narrative texts were committed to letters. Among these are two substantial legal compilations. The first is called *Senchas Már* [Great tradition], which consists of 47 independent tracts, according to the extant evidence.[8] It was probably compiled in the north of Ireland under the aegis of the religious center of Armagh in the latter half of the seventh century.[9] The second was in all

3 Neil Wright, *History and Literature in Late Antiquity and the Early Medieval West: Studies in Intertextuality* (Aldershot: Ashgate Publishing Limited, 1995), vii. See also Rolf H. Bremmer Jr, "More than Language: Law and Textual Communities in Medieval Frisia," Chapter 4 in this volume.

4 Thomas M. Charles-Edwards, *The Early Mediaeval Gaelic Lawyer*, ASNC Publications 4 (Cambridge: Cambridge University Press, 1999), 3–5.

5 Fergus Kelly, *A Guide to Early Irish Law* (Dublin: Dublin Institute for Advanced Studies, 1988), 231–32.

6 Liam Breatnach, *A Companion to the Corpus Iuris Hibernici*, Early Irish Law Series 5 (Dublin: Dublin Institute for Advanced Studies, 2005), 354–55; Pamela O'Neill, "Unravelling Time in Early Irish Law," in *Language and Power in the Celtic World: Papers from the Seventh Australian Conference of Celtic Studies, University of Sydney, September 2010*, ed. Anders Ahlqvist and Pamela O'Neill (Sydney: University of Sydney, 2011).

7 Paul Russell, "'What was Best of Every Language': The Early History of the Irish Language," in *Prehistoric and Early Ireland*, ed. Dáibhí Ó Cróinín, New history of Ireland 1 (Oxford: Oxford University Press, 2005), 415–18.

8 Liam Breatnach, "On the Original Extent of the 'Senchas Már'," *Ériu* 47 (1996): 1–43; Neil McLeod, "A True Companion to the *Corpus Iuris Hibernici* [Review of: Liam Breatnach, *A Companion to the Corpus Iuris Hibernici*, Early Irish Law Series 5 (Dublin, 2005)]," *Peritia* 19 (2005): 136–63.

9 Liam Breatnach, *The Early Irish Law Text Senchas Már and The Question of Its Date*, E.C. Quig-

likelihood composed in Munster, in the southwest of Ireland, between 712 and 742 judging from internal references.[10] It has two constituent texts, titled *Bretha Nemed Toísech* [The first judgments of the privileged classes] and *Bretha Nemed Dédenach* [The last judgments of the privileged classes] respectively, and as a whole is commonly known as the *Bretha Nemed* [Judgments of the privileged classes]. Besides these two compilations, there are more than twenty Old Irish law tracts that survive in full or in fragments, and some others that leave only hints of their existence.[11] The Old Irish law tracts thus constitute a large corpus that surpasses any other Western European vernacular legal tradition in terms of size and variety, and the repercussions of this rush of textualization were lasting and profound: it seems that all aspects of the legal system had been given textual expression by that time, so that no major law tract was produced after the ninth century; and whatever form the law might have had in its pre-written life, it was thereafter fixed and more or less faithfully transmitted for the next millennium.

The vernacular Irish law tracts are quite distinct in several aspects from the Germanic law-codes on the continent and in England. The majority of early Irish law tracts are not promulgated codes made by royal legislature, but law-books composed and copied by the jurists of mixed legal, poetic and ecclesiastical backgrounds, and thus their authority and currency rely on the guardianship of a learned class.[12] They not only cover remedy and penalty for offences but also actively construct and regulate all aspects of social life, ranging from the binding of clientship, marriage arrangements, dissolution of contracts, and allocation of mill-usage, to the keeping of bees and the story repertoire of a poetic scholar. The individual tracts do not always agree with each other on the same subject matter which may reflect regional differences,[13] changes over

---

gin Memorial Lectures 13 (Cambridge: Department of Anglo-Saxon, Norse, and Celtic, University of Cambridge, 2011).

10 Liam Breatnach, "Canon Law and Secular Law in Early Ireland: The Significance of *Bretha Nemed*," *Peritia* 3 (1984): 439–59.

11 See a list of extant legal tracts in Kelly, *Guide to Early Irish Law*, 264–83, and Breatnach, *Corpus Iuris Hibernici*, chap. 5.

12 Liam Breatnach, "Lawyers in Early Ireland," in *Brehons, Serjeants and Attorneys: Studies in the History of the Irish Legal Profession*, ed. Daire Hogan and W.N. Osborough (Dublin: Irish Academic Press, 1990); Charles-Edwards, *Early Mediaeval Gaelic Lawyer*, 8–9. Compare this to the situation in Wales where the law texts were compiled as one code of law under the supervision of the royal court and its officials, see the contribution by Sarah Elin Roberts, "'A Rather Laborious and Harassing Occupation': The Creation of the Ancient Laws and Institutes of Wales," Chapter 15 in this volume.

13 e.g., Fangzhe Qiu, "The Ulster Cycle in the Law Tracts," in *Ulidia 4: Proceedings of the Fourth*

time,[14] or merely divergent opinions among the jurists.[15] Moreover, early Irish law seldom relies on a centralized authority to adjudicate or to enforce the judgment; although the king presides over the cases, either as the judge or as a supporting dignitary, if the cases are submitted to him.[16] Rather, the judicial function is shared between the judges, the lords, the poetic scholars and the clergy, while disputes are settled, and judgments are enforced, mostly by means of a highly sophisticated system of pledges, sureties, and witnesses.[17] This lack of centralized authority in law mirrors the reality of early medieval Ireland as a politically fragmented, rural society, locally controlled by petty kings and kin groups.

Promulgated laws indeed existed in early medieval Ireland. These include two types, namely *rechtgae* [edict; pl. *rechtgai*] and *cáin* [penal regulation; pl. *cánai*], though there are a few non-promulgated law texts that also bear the title of *cáin*. *Cánai* were jointly promulgated and sponsored by royal and ecclesiastical powers to assert their authority, while *rechtgai* mostly arose in response to special conditions such as invasion or famine.[18] They seem to have needed to be renewed or reissued after a certain period.[19] The most famous promulgated law is the *cáin* of Adomnán, which was promulgated in 697 to protect non-combatants, such as the clergy, children and women.[20] Ecclesi-

---

International Conference on the Ulster Cycle of Tales, ed. Mícheál Ó Mainnín and Gregory Toner (Dublin: Four Courts Press, 2017), 19–22.

14 e.g., Daniel A. Binchy, ed., *Críth Gablach* (Dublin: Dublin Institute for Advanced Studies, 1941), 2, ll. 47–51.

15 Neil McLeod, "Di Ércib Fola," *Ériu* 52 (2002): 123–216.

16 See Marilyn Gerriets, "The King as Judge in Early Ireland," *Celtica* 20 (1988): 29–52 and the description of the seating of court in Fergus Kelly, "An Old-Irish Text on Court Procedure," *Peritia* 5 (1986): 74–106.

17 A good but brief introduction to the various procedures and sureties in Irish law can be found in Richard Sharpe, "Dispute Settlement in Medieval Ireland: A Preliminary Inquiry," in *The Settlement of Disputes in Early Medieval Europe*, ed. Wendy Davies and Paul Fouracre (Cambridge: Cambridge University Press, 1986). The law tract *Cóic Conara Fuigill* [Five Paths of Litigation], which details a wide range of procedures used in binding contracts and litigations, has been edited and translated in Christophe Archan, *Les Chemins du Jugement. Procédure et Science du Droit dans l'Irlande Médiévale*, Romanité et Modernité du Droit (Paris: De Boccard, 2007).

18 Charles-Edwards, *Early Mediaeval Gaelic Lawyer*, 52–61.

19 Julianna Grigg, "Aspects of the *Cáin*: Adomnán's *Lex Innocentium*," *Journal of the Australian Early Medieval Association* 1 (2005): 41–50; Neil McLeod, "*Cáin Adomnáin* and the Lombards," in *Language and Power in the Celtic World*, ed. Anders Ahlqvist and Pamela O'Neill (Sydney: University of Sydney, 2011).

20 Kuno Meyer, ed., *Cáin Adamnáin: An Old Irish Treatise on the Law of Adamnan* (Oxford:

astical legislations, including canon laws and penitentials, are abundant and influential, culminating in the late-seventh or early-eighth century *Collectio Canonum Hibernensis* [The Irish collection of canons] which is the earliest systematic canon law collection in Europe.[21] The ecclesiastical laws and the customary laws are interlinked: some Old Irish law tracts, such as *Córus Bésgnai* [The ordering of discipline][22] or *Bretha Nemed*, derive their contents from the Scriptures or the canons,[23] while the *Collectio Canonum Hibernensis* makes references to secular legal concepts.[24]

Law tracts compiled in the Old Irish period have been subject to centuries of copying, glossing, accretion and redaction. The outcome is an accumulated body of annotated law texts consisting of diverse chronological layers. The term commonly used for the portion of the original Old Irish law tracts is "canonical texts"; words or sentences of the canonical texts are annotated by "glosses"; and continuous sections, or the subject matter as a whole, are discussed independently of the immediate wording of the canonical text in "commentaries". The commentaries are not tied to specific words and can remark on various topics at the same time; therefore, they are often collected from various sources to form a body of explications to early Irish law. A thematically organized collection of extracts from canonical tracts accompanied by commentaries forms a "digest."[25] The earliest glosses seem to have been made in the Old Irish period, not long after the compilation of the canonical texts themselves,[26] but throughout the Middle Ages and Early Modern period, fresh glosses and commentaries kept being furnished to the canonical texts. Therefore, the *mise-en-page* of a legal manuscript page varies from running canonical text with interlinear glosses in smaller script to long paragraphs of digests

Oxford Clarendon Press, 1905); Pádraig Ó Néill and David Dumville, eds., *Cáin Adomnáin and Canones Adomnani* (Cambridge: Department of Anglo-Saxon, Norse, and Celtic, University of Cambridge, 2003).

21 Hermann Wasserschleben, ed., *Die irische Kanonensammlung* (Giessen: J. Rickersche Buchhandlung, 1874). Roy Flechner, ed., *The Hibernensis*, 2 vols. (Washington, D. C.: Catholic University of America Press, 2019).

22 Liam Breatnach, ed., *Córus Bésgnai: An Old Irish Law Tract on the Church and Society*, Early Irish Law Series 7 (Dublin: Dublin Institute for Advanced Studies, 2017).

23 Breatnach, "Canon Law".

24 Donnchadh Ó Corráin, Liam Breatnach, and Aidan Breen, "The Laws of the Irish," *Peritia* 3 (1984): 382–438.

25 For a fuller description of the types of combination of textual layers see: Fergus Kelly, "Texts and Transmissions: The Law-Texts," in *Irland und Europa im früheren Mittelalteren: Texte und Überlieferung*, ed. Próinséas Ní Chatháin and Michael Richter (Dublin: Four Courts Press, 2002); Breatnach, *Corpus Iuris Hibernici*, 92–99.

26 Breatnach, *Corpus Iuris Hibernici*, 338–46.

interspersed with occasional quotations of canonical texts which are formally undistinguishable from the digests.[27]

All texts of Old Irish customary law survive only in manuscripts from the Late Middle Ages. The earliest manuscript that records vernacular Irish law texts is the twelfth-century Oxford, Bodleian Library, MS Rawlinson B 502 which, however, is predominantly non-legal in content and includes only two law tracts.[28] The majority of manuscripts which contain a substantial portion of legal materials were written between the fourteenth and the seventeenth century by scribes from the late medieval learned legal families, such as the Mac Aodhagáin who quickly emerged on the stage in the fourteenth century.[29] None of the manuscripts is purely legal in content: poetic,[30] medical,[31] historical and grammatical texts are copied side by side with law texts in the same manuscript. These manuscripts also present later compositions that are evidently designed as instructional materials in the form of pedagogical verse[32] or moot pleading,[33] which indicates the primary function of the law-books as manuals for private study. Each law-book fossilizes a moment in the fluid scholastic tradition,[34] while representing a textual unity in grammatical and legal discourse.[35]

The mixture of a broad array of genres in manuscripts that contain law tracts is mirrored at an intra-textual level. Modern scholars identify certain early Irish texts as "law tracts" as they describe rules that govern behaviour within society,

27 Kelly, *Guide to Early Irish Law*, 225–31.

28 Brian Ó Cuív, *Catalogue of Irish Language Manuscripts in the Bodleian Library at Oxford and Oxford College Libraries*, 2 vols. (Dublin: Dublin Institute for Advanced Studies, 2001), 1:163–201.

29 Katharine Simms, "The Brehons of Later Medieval Ireland," in *Brehons, Serjeants and Attorneys: Studies in the History of the Irish Legal Profession*, ed. Daire Hogan and William Osborough (Dublin: Irish Academic Press, 1990).

30 e.g. Fangzhe Qiu, "Manuscript Contexts of Early Irish Law Tracts: A Case Study on *Uraicecht Becc*," *Proceedings of the Harvard Celtic Colloquium* 35 (2015): 150–71.

31 e.g., Daniel A. Binchy, "Bretha Crólige," *Ériu* 12 (1938): 1–77; Daniel A. Binchy, "Bretha Déin Chécht," *Ériu* 20 (1966): 1–66.

32 e.g., Máirín Ní Dhonnchadha, "An Address to a Student of Law," in *Sages, Saints and Storytellers: Celtic Studies in Honour of Professor James Carney*, ed. Donnchadh Ó Corráin, Liam Breatnach, and Kim McCone (Maynooth: An Sagart, 1989).

33 e.g., Daniel A. Binchy, ed., *Corpus Iuris Hibernici*, 6 vols. (Dublin: Dublin Institute for Advanced Studies, 1978), 6:2204.1–2208.19.

34 Katharine Simms, "Charles Lynegar, the O Luinín family and the Study of Seanchas," in *A Miracle of Learning: Studies in Manuscripts and Irish Learning: Essays in Honour of William O'Sullivan*, ed. Toby C. Barnard and Dáibhí Ó Cróinín (Aldershot: Ashgate Publishing Limited, 1998).

35 Martin Irvine, *The Making of Textual Culture: "Grammatica" and Literary Theory, 350–1100* (Cambridge: Cambridge University Press, 1994), 390–91.

yet these texts are never totally legal or even regulatory in nature. Some law tracts are embedded in narratives or arcane poems.[36] Words in law texts are often subject to grammatical and exegetical analysis, and exemplified by verses and stories from the literary tradition, while saints' lives and place-name lore are adapted to explain the origins of the law tracts.[37] These extra-legal contents can be found in all layers of the law texts; in other words, they are not merely products of inquisitive glossators, but also part of the original composition in the Early Middle Ages.

The fuzzy display of discourses and contents in early Irish law texts and manuscripts stands in stark contrast to most modern laws and poses difficulty for modern editors who wish to cherry-pick the "purely legal" content. However, such variety is the quintessential characteristic of medieval Irish legal writing. The following analysis tries to reveal the form and reason of such variety in unity, by examining the discourses used in early Irish law texts and the way they bridge contents from diverse branches of learning.

In terms of mode of discourse, three types can be found in early Irish law texts, namely, provision, narration and exposition. In comparison, most modern law texts consist solely of provisions, which are either *apodictic*, making unconditional statements, or *casuistic*, comprising a hypothetical protasis of condition and an apodosis of legal consequence. These two types are also predominant in the provisions of early Irish law. For example *ni bi sena iar naititiu* [let there not be denial after recognition of right] (apodictic)[38] and *mas asa laim docuaid, is amail cetsceinm* [if it is out of his hand that it (the anvil) has come, it is regarded as the first springing] (casuistic).[39] In the Irish tradition provisions are characteristic of, but not confined to, law texts in the strict sense. Texts laying out the rights and duties of tribes and kings, such as *Lebor na Cert* [The Book of Rights][40] and "A Poem on the Airgíalla,"[41] include a large num-

36 For examples see the "Saga of Fergus mac Léti": Binchy, *Corpus Iuris Hibernici*, 2:352.26–356.38, 3:881.4–883.36, 5:1663.20–1666.28, edited in Daniel A. Binchy, "The Saga of Fergus Mac Léti," *Ériu* 16 (1952): 33–48; Daniel A. Binchy, "An Archaic Legal Poem," *Celtica* 9 (1971): 152–68.

37 e.g., Fangzhe Qiu, "Wandering Cows and Obscure Words: a Rimeless Poem from Legal Manuscripts and Beyond," *Studia Celtica Fennica* 10 (2013): 90–111; Paul Russell, "Laws, Glossaries and Legal Glossaries in Early Ireland," *Zeitschrift für celtische Philologie* 51 (1999): 85–115.

38 Binchy, *Corpus Iuris Hibernici*, 4:1361.27.

39 Binchy, *Corpus Iuris Hibernici*, 2:267.21.

40 Myles Dillon, ed., *Lebor na Cert: The Book of Rights*, Irish Texts Society 46 (London: Irish Texts Society, 1962).

41 Máirín O Daly, "A Poem on the Airgialla," *Ériu* 16 (1952): 179–88.

ber of provisions, but these are seldom regarded as laws but rather as historical documents like charters, because the undertakers of duties and rights in them are usually specific holders of titles or tribes. Penitentials and wisdom texts, the compilation of which was closely related to the production of secular law texts,[42] contain provisions or didactic injunctions that are similar to provisions; and the *geis* [prohibition, injunction] in early Irish literature, imposed on kings and heroes to avoid or perform certain ritualized deeds, generally takes the form of provision and has a social and cosmological dimension.[43] This typically legal discourse provides intertextuality between law and different types of texts. Such continuum in discourse between law texts and other branches of *senchas*, however, is even better attested in the other two modes of discourse, namely narration and exposition.

The abundance of narratives in early Irish law texts may strike not only modern jurists, but also their medieval counterparts outside Ireland, as outlandish. So far more than 110 narratives have been identified,[44] in the most extensive current edition of early Irish law texts, the six-volume *Corpus Iuris Hibernici*.[45] These range from terse passages sketching the skeleton of incidents,[46] to full-length sagas embellished with ornate verses;[47] from accounts of the mythical past,[48] to those of contemporary affairs;[49] from the exodus and Christ's Passion,[50] to conversation of countrymen.[51] They appear in almost every possible

42 Marilyn Gerriets, "Theft, Penitentials and the Compilation of the Early Irish Laws," *Celtica* 22 (1991): 18–32. Fergus Kelly, ed., *Audacht Morainn* (Dublin: Dublin Institute for Advanced Studies, 1976), xviii–xix.

43 Thomas M. Charles-Edwards, "Geis, Prophecy, Omen, and Oath," *Celtica* 23 (1999): 38–59; Tom Sjöblom, "Before *Geis* Became Magical: A Study of the Evolution of an Early Irish Religious Concept," *Studia Celtica* 32 (1998): 85–94.

44 For a preliminary list of these narratives see Fangzhe Qiu, "Narratives in Early Irish Law: A Typological Study," in *Medieval Irish Law: Texts and Contexts*, ed. Anders Ahlqvist and Pamela O'Neill (Sydney: University of Sydney, 2013).

45 Binchy, *Corpus Iuris Hibernici.*

46 e.g. the reference to John 8.7 in a commentary, Binchy, *Corpus Iuris Hibernici*, 3:847.8–11, 5:1924.1–9.

47 e.g. the "Saga of Fergus mac Léti", Binchy, "Saga of Fergus Mac Léti,".

48 e.g. the narrative concerning the first battle ever fought in Ireland, Binchy, *Corpus Iuris Hibernici*, 2:380.1–13, 5:1686.28–1687.3.

49 e.g. an anecdote attributing the Papal Bull *Laudabiliter* which purported to grant Henry II the right over Ireland to the offence of some local churls, Binchy, *Corpus Iuris Hibernici*, 6:1950.18–23.

50 e.g. a discussion of Longinus's piercing of Christ in Binchy, *Corpus Iuris Hibernici*, 4:1305 .34–37.

51 e.g. a passage that claims to record the poetic dialogue of two Connacht men, Binchy, *Cor-*

location: some serve as introduction to a law tract, some in the annotations, and some even as part of the canonical text itself. No modern or medieval Western European legal tradition uses narratives in such an extensive and systematic manner, perhaps apart from the Aggadic *halakhah* materials in the rabbinic tradition.[52] These materials may afford some comparison to the Irish legal narratives in terms of number and variety, but much further research is needed to reveal whether there are more similarities between the two apart from superficial resemblance. Yet it will seem less exotic if one keeps in mind that narration is the primary discourse of *senchas*: much of early Irish literature, historiography, onomastic lore and hagiography is written in prose or verse narrative. In stark contrast to the timeless, universal provision, narration is inherently temporal and individual, and thus particularly suitable for documenting cultural memory. When narration is employed in law texts, it affirms that the law texts are not merely collections of norms, but also the product and memory of the *longue durée* of Irish history. Moreover, narration in law texts is not isolated from the writing practice in other types of texts. Narratives originating outside the law lost none of their style and appeal when adopted into legal contexts; and many narratives of legal origin relate their stories so skillfully and dramatically that they can claim to be literature in every sense of the word. Rhetorical devices employed by literary works are ubiquitous in the legal narratives, such as the "narrative openers" identified by Proinsias Mac Cana,[53] or the use of prosimetrum to carry out various textual functions.[54] Narratives appear at the same nodal points in law texts as in genealogy, glossaries and the place-name lore (*dindṡenchas*): they arise in response to questions of origin, supply contextual information, or exemplify concepts and words.[55]

While the mode of narration renders possible the formal assimilation of law texts to other branches of the *senchas*, the contents of legal narratives construct temporal-personal relationships that are shared by non-legal narratives, and thereby locate the composition of the law tracts or the origin of the rules

---

pus Iuris Hibernici, 6:2112.36–39, edited in Calvert Watkins, ed., "Varia III," *Ériu* 29 (1978): 155–65.

52 Moshe Simon-Shoshan, *Stories of the Law: Narrative Discourse and the Construction of Authority in the Mishnah* (New York: Oxford University Press, 2012).

53 Proinsias Mac Cana, "Narrative Openers and Progress Markers in Irish," in *A Celtic Florilegium: Studies in Memory of Brendan O Hehir*, ed. Kathryn A. Clar, Eve E. Sweetser, and Claire Thomas (Lawrence, MA: Celtic Studies Publications, 1996).

54 For typological studies see Proinsias Mac Cana, "Notes on the Combination of Prose and Verse in Early Irish Narrative," in *Early Irish Literature: Media and Communication*, ed. Stephen N. Tranter and Hildegard L.C. Tristram (Tübingen: Narr, 1989).

55 Qiu, "Narratives in Early Irish law," 116–22.

in the time-space in the collective memory. A few legal narratives have direct textual precedents outside of the law tracts,[56] while some others provided for the texts or stories in sagas and bardic poetry.[57] Many legal narratives, however, do not have exact counterpart outside the law tracts, but they derive their story plots and *dramatis personae* from non-legal texts. No fewer than forty-five legal narratives, for instance, adopt the narrative universe of the Ulster Cycle, which is a large corpus of sagas that center on the martial activities of the ancient Ulster heroes.[58] A legal commentary[59] exemplifies the concept of *lúaithrind* [quick engraving] with a pattern received from a supernatural figure and engraved on Cú Chulainn's shield when he returns from his martial training in Britain. Upon reading this, medieval Irish readers would certainly recall the fearsome combats wrought by this hero, and *lúaithrind* would have been recognized as a prime craft that conveys (supernatural) valor to the shield-bearer. This connection further substantiates the main point of the law text commented on, namely that a wright must be able to perform *lúaithrinde lúathluth* [swift movement of quick engraving] to achieve a privileged status.[60] Such intertextual cohesion between the legal narrative and the Ulster Cycle stories thus invokes rich cross-references and places the law tracts into a cultural and historical coordinate grid.

However, it is worth bearing in mind the nature of *senchas* as a collective memory. Gregory Toner has argued that it is precarious to impose modern conceptions of "history" on the medieval art of handling the past.[61] Despite that the contents of *senchas* are overwhelmingly presented as knowledge from the past or about the past, *senchas*'s accounts of the past do not guarantee historicity as we understand the concept today, as *senchas* is primarily a textual tradition, and is concerned with textual authority, rather than with empirical

---

56 e.g., Binchy, *Corpus Iuris Hibernici*, 1:250.1–32, quoting from the *Dindṡenchas* of Achall, Edward John Gwynn, ed., *The Metrical Dindshenchas*, 5 vols. (Dublin: Hodges & Figgis, 1935; repr., Dublin: Dublin Institute for Advanced Studies, 1991), 1:46.

57 e.g., Binchy, *Corpus Iuris Hibernici*, 6:2230.1–2, 2232.33–37 was copied into the saga *Scéla Moṡauluim* [The Tidings of Moṡaulum], in Máirín O Daly, ed., *Cath Maige Mucrama: the Battle of Mag Mucrama*, Irish Texts Society 50 (London: Irish Texts Society, 1975), 76–77.

58 Qiu, "Ulster Cycle in the Law Tracts".

59 Binchy, *Corpus Iuris Hibernici*, 6:2114.5–24, edited in Myles Dillon, ed. "Stories from the Law-tracts," *Ériu* 11 (1932): 42–65 (54–55), translated in Richard Irvine Best, "Cuchulainn's Shield," *Ériu* 5 (1911), 72.

60 Binchy, *Corpus Iuris Hibernici*, 6:2219.37–38, which also appear in the triads, see Kuno Meyer, *The Triads of Ireland*, Todd Lecture Series, vol. 13 (Dublin: Hodges & Figgis, 1906), 16–17.

61 Gregory Toner, "The Ulster Cycle: Historiography or Fiction?" *Cambrian Medieval Celtic Studies* 40 (Winter 2000): 1–20.

verity, as remarked by Mary Carruthers, "in considering medieval views of textual authority, one needs always to keep in mind that *auctores* were, first of all, texts, not people."[62]

Two textually related legal narratives which propose to explain the situation of the making of law tracts *Cáin Ḟuithirbe* [The regulation of Fuithirbe] and *Anfuigell* [Wrong judgment?] may serve to show how, even for medieval readers, textual authority is established through intertextual links rather than through historical veracity of the account. Neither of these two tracts survives in full; only snippets from their canonical texts are preserved with extensive glosses and commentaries. Both texts appear to deal with a variety of topics and it is hard to postulate their original extents from the sporadic extracts.[63]

What survives of *Cáin Ḟuithirbe* includes a list of names of Munster kings who might have convened to promulgate the law,[64] which suggests that the time of its composition was during the reign of the King of Munster Finguine mac Cathail Chon-cen-máthair, and more specifically between 678 and 683.[65] A Middle Irish introductory narrative is appended to *Cáin Ḟuithirbe* and reaffirms this date.[66] Moreover, the Middle Irish narrative claims the author of the law tract to be Amairgen son of Amalgaid from the Déssi, a poet who was dispatched by the people of Munster to learn native law, and returned to compose it on the plain of Fuithirbe, probably the modern Muckross Demesne in Co. Kerry.[67] So far, a late seventh-century date of composition seems secure,[68] yet the appealing historical value is certainly "spoiled" by the additional assertion by the Middle Irish narrative that the tract "was afterwards shown to St. Patrick after [his] coming" in the fifth century and was subject to the saint's extensive revision.[69]

Clearly, historicity was not the concern here, as the fifth-century saint could not have any knowledge of a composition made in the seventh century. The medieval authors' purpose was rather to link their texts with significant moments in the *senchas*, and in this case the moment is no other than St.

62 Mary Carruthers, *The Book of Memory: A Study of Memory in Medieval Culture* (Cambridge: Cambridge University Press, 1990), 190.

63 Breatnach, *Corpus Iuris Hibernici*, 165, 215–16.

64 Binchy, *Corpus Iuris Hibernici*, 5:1554.1–19.

65 Daniel A. Binchy, "The Date and Provenance of *Uraicecht Becc*," *Ériu* 18 (1958): 52–54; Liam Breatnach, "The Ecclesiastical Element in the Old-Irish Legal Tract *Cáin Fhuithirbe*," *Peritia* 5 (1986): 36–52.

66 Binchy, *Corpus Iuris Hibernici*, 2:687.37–688.20.

67 Seán Ó Coileáin, "Mag Fuithirbe Revisited," *Éigse* 23 (1989): 26.

68 But see Ó Coileáin's caveat in "Mag Fuithirbe".

69 Binchy, "*Uraicecht Becc*," 52.

Patrick's censuring of the pagan laws of the Irish to ensure that they conform to Christian doctrines, a legend pervasively invoked in *Senchas Már* to explain the origin of that collection, especially in the "Pseudo-historical prologue to *Senchas Már*", a possibly ninth-century narrative prefixed to some copies of *Senchas Már* tracts.[70] Though *Cáin Ḟuithirbe* does not belong to that collection, it is deliberately linked to *Senchas Már* not only by employing the Patrician legend, but perhaps also by stating that the knowledge needed to compose this tract was obtained by learning outside of Munster. In the related prologue of *Anfuigell*, it is more explicitly pointed out that the learning necessary for composing the tract was acquired in "the North", where *Senchas Már* was compiled.[71]

Cáin Ḟuithirbe was promulgated by a number of minor kings in the late seventh century, but it portrays itself as part of the heritage from St. Patrick's Christianizing mission, and thus deserves currency throughout the whole of Ireland in the same manner as *Senchas Már*,[72] not just to be limited to the province of Munster. Moreover, the Middle Irish narrative also makes reference to the Passion of Christ to support St. Patrick's abrogation of the excessive gentile rules, and addresses the Irishmen as descendants of Míl, thus subscribing to the account regarding the origin of the Irish nation as invented by contemporary historiographers.[73] Besides showing erudition in many threads of learning, the prologue effectively provides multiple recognized cultural clues to liaise with the learned tradition and to render itself part of it,[74] and the number and prominence of such cultural clues in a text contains are far more important than their harmonious organization.

The Middle Irish introduction to *Anfuigell* [Wrong Judgement?][75] was clearly modelled upon the prologue to *Cáin Ḟuithirbe*. It gives Cummaín, who was well trained in Latin learning but did not quite qualify in native law, as the author, perhaps intending Cumméne Fota. Cumméne Fota was a renowned *sapiens* [sage, scholar], but he died in 662, more than a decade before the start

70 This legend has been edited and translated in John Carey, ed., "An Edition of the Pseudo-Historical Prologue to the Senchas Már," *Ériu* 45 (1994): 1–32.

71 Binchy, *Corpus Iuris Hibernici*, 3:979.26.

72 *Senchas Már* apparently regards itself in effect over the whole island of Ireland, as indicated by the many references in the canonical parts of its constituent texts to "this island," see Breatnach, *Early Irish Law Text*, 37–39.

73 John Carey, *The Irish National Origin-Legend: Synthetic Pseudohistory* (Cambridge: Department of Anglo-Saxon, Norse, and Celtic, Cambridge University, 1994).

74 Robin Chapman Stacey, "Law and Literature in Ireland and Wales," in *Medieval Celtic Literature and Society*, ed. Helen Fulton (Dublin: Four Courts Press, 2005), 75.

75 Binchy, *Corpus Iuris Hibernici*, 3:979.23–26.

of the reign of Finguine (678–695) which is claimed in the narrative as the time of composition.[76] Meanwhile, all other elements are identical to the *Cáin Ḟuithirbe* prologue, including the eponymous place-name *Mag Fuithirbe*. Such identity of time, place and cause in the making of two law tracts is unlikely, and any informed reader in medieval Ireland would not have hesitated to dismiss the historicity of the information in the *Anfuigell* prologue. Again, what matters to the author of the *Anfuigell* prologue is becoming part of the tradition, and *Anfuigell* indeed partakes in the authority of *Cáin Ḟuithirbe* by appropriating its narrative, as well as by attributing the authorship to the long deceased Cumméne Fota (if it is really he who is intended): a Munster figure prominent in both secular and ecclesiastical literary contexts.

Personages in legal narratives, even those who indeed lived in the historical period, always appear in connection with certain master narratives as recognized by the *senchas*. Cenn Fáelad's lineage (of the royal family of Cenél nEógain in the Northern half of Ireland) and his obituary (679) are consistently documented in the genealogies and the annals,[77] and his fame as a prime scholar (*sapiens*) and his career in the minor monasteries of Túaim Drecain and Daire Luráin is probably historically authentic.[78] However, the central theme in the longer narratives about Cenn Fáelad, which are shared by narratives appended to the law tract *Bretha Étgid* [Judgments of Inadvertence][79] and to the grammatical treatise *Auraicept na nÉces* [Scholars' primer][80] and by the longer version of the saga *Cath Maige Roth* [The battle of Mag Roth][81] is that Cenn Fáelad lost his "brain of forgetfulness" in the battle of Mag Roth and was transported to Túaim Drecain for recuperation, where he combined the teaching of three schools. This theme is not present in any annalistic record and is probably a later accretion to the tradition, using Cenn Fáelad as a prototypal learned figure and the three schools as allegory to the components of the Irish intellectualism.[82] The battle of Mag Roth (637) marked a turn in the politics

76 Binchy, "*Uraicecht Becc*," 52.

77 Seán Mac Airt and Gearóid Mac Niocaill, eds., *The Annals of Ulster (to A.D. 1131) Part I, Text and Translation* (Dublin: Dublin Institute for Advanced Studies, 1983), s. a. 679.

78 Kim McCone, "Zur Frage der Register im frühen Irischen," in *Early Irish Literature: Media and Communication*, ed. Stephen N. Tranter and Hildegard L.C. Tristram (Tübingen: Narr, 1989), 66.

79 Binchy, *Corpus Iuris Hibernici*, 1:250.33–251.3; 3:926.5–18; RIA MS. D v 2, 64ra (edited in Breatnach, *Corpus Iuris Hibernici*, 381–82).

80 George Calder, *Auraicept na n-Éces: The Scholars' Primer* (Edinburgh: J. Grant, 1917), 6–7.

81 John O'Donovan, *The Banquet of Dun na n-Gedh and the Battle of Magh Rath* (Dublin: Irish Archaeological Society, 1842), 278–84.

82 Proinsias Mac Cana, "The Three Languages and the Three Laws," *Studia Celtica* 5 (1970):

of the North of Ireland in the seventh century and forms a key nodal point of the collective memory,[83] and the prestige of both *Auraicept na nÉces* and *Cath Maige Roth* may have helped further propagate the doctrine.[84] The theme is overtly symbolic, but by the Middle Irish period when the abovementioned narratives were composed, it had acquired a canonical status and later compositions that wished to mention Cenn Fáelad had to subscribe to it.

Such is the weight of this tradition that *Bretha Étgid* presents it side by side with another narrative as alternative explanations to the origin of the tract. That Middle Irish narrative immediately precedes the Cenn Fáelad story in three copies of the tract, and attributes the composition of *Bretha Étgid* to Cormac mac Airt, a pre-historic legendary king of Ireland.[85] It reports that Cormac mac Airt lost an eye in a strife, and therefore forfeited his kingship to his son, to whom Cormac preached *Bretha Étgid* as an instruction on rightful kingship. Cormac is the central figure in numerous Irish narratives, and has been regarded as the prime example of a just and wise king to whom are attributed wisdom texts,[86] and stories on ordeals.[87] Moreover, the strife in which Cormac lost his eye is reported to have led to the expulsion of the Déissi tribes from midland, a legend featuring prominently in the *senchas*,[88] more so since the tenth century when the Déissi tribe Dál Cais played a significant role in Irish politics. The canonical text of *Bretha Étgid* does not mention Cormac mac Airt, but

62–78; McCone, "Register im frühen Irischen," 65; Hildegard L.C. Tristram, "Warum Cenn Faelad sein 'Gehirn des Vergessens' verlor—Wort und Schrift in der älteren irischen Literatur," in *Deutsche, Kelten und Iren: 150 Jahre deutsche Keltologie* (Hamburg: Buske, 1990) 207–48.

83 Francis John Byrne, *Irish Kings and High-kings* (Dublin: Four Courts Press, 1987), 113–14.

84 The latter tale is included in the "List A" of the tale-lists compiled in around the tenth century (edited in Proinsias Mac Cana, ed., *The Learned Tales of Medieval Ireland* (Dublin: Dublin Institute for Advanced Studies, 1980), 43) and presumably was well-known then, see Gregory Toner, "Reconstructing the Earliest Irish Text Tale Lists," *Éigse* 32 (2000): 88–120.

85 Binchy, *Corpus Iuris Hibernici*, 1:250.1–32; 3:925.1–926.4; RIA MS. D v 2, 64ra (edited in Breatnach, *Corpus Iuris Hibernici*, 381–82).

86 Narratives concerning Cormac and their significance have been fruitfully explored in Tomás Ó Cathasaigh, *The Heroic Biography of Cormac Mac Airt* (Dublin: Dublin Institute for Advanced Studies, 1977); see also, Kuno Meyer, ed., *Tecosca Cormaic: The Instructions of King Cormac Mac Airt*, Todd Lecture Series, vol. 15 (Dublin: Hodges & Figgis, 1909).

87 Whitley Stokes, "The Irish Ordeals, Cormac's Adventure in the Land of Promise, and the Decision as to Cormac's Sword," in *Irische Texte 3.1*, ed. Ernst Windisch and Whitley Stokes (Leipzig: Verlag von S. Hirzel, 1891).

88 e.g., Kuno Meyer, "The Expulsion of the Déssi," *Ériu* 3 (1907): 135–42; Vernam Hull, "The Later Version of the Expulsion of the Déssi," *Zeitschrift für Celtische Philologie* 27 (1959): 14–65; Whitley Stokes, "The Annals of Tigernach," *Revue Celtique* 17 (1896): 19–20.

many passages of it start with the set formula *a maic ara·feiser* [O son so that you would find out], and therefore imply a similar, if not the same, backdrop of a royal father preaching his son.

Logically, there cannot be two compositions—one in prehistory, the other in the seventh century—of the same tract. A commentator of *Bretha Étgid* tried to reconcile this by suggesting that the passages beginning with *blaí* [immunity] and *a maic ara·feiser* [O son so that you should find out] are authored by Cormac, the others by Cenn Fáelad.[89] But the canonical text of *Bretha Étgid* is obviously a unity with *blaí, a maic ara·feiser* and other types of passages interwoven together. Again, these legal narratives betray the efforts of medieval Irish jurists in connecting law texts to as many cultural and historical nodal points as possible: *Bretha Étgid* is thus both the words of a prehistorical sagacious king, and the study of a seventh-century scholar; it resulted from an offence that foreshadowed the rise of the Dál Cais, and from a battle that consolidated the hegemony of the Uí Néill dynasty over the north of Ireland in the coming centuries. By such connection, law texts join the *senchas* and in turn reassert the authority of the *senchas* in a dynamic process. This process, termed "traditionalization" by anthropologists, systematically links texts (and other cultural artifacts) to a conceived meaningful past, a collective memory acknowledged by members of the community as valid guidance for their self-recognition and their lives.[90] As Tom Mould points out, "the traditional past is evoked not merely as part of a general dialogue with the past, but as part of an attempt to provide authority for one's own narrative performance and interpretation by supporting or contributing to a community's sense of what is 'traditional'."[91]

Exposition organizes the provisions and offers critical analyses of their words and meanings, rather than directly stipulating a rule. Expository passages construct a framework in which provisions can be presented, and link general provisions to more detailed ones, or provisions to narratives. Through exposition the provisions are objectified as texts and disposed according to the ideology of *grammatica*, which embraced all arts and disciplines that were based on texts.[92] Charles-Edwards has shown that three stylistic features char-

89 Binchy, *Corpus Iuris Hibernici*, 1:250.16–18.

90 Richard Bauman and Charles Briggs, "Genre, Intertextuality, and Social Power," *Journal of Linguistic Anthropology* 2 (1992): 131–72; Richard Bauman, "Mediational Performance, Traditionalization, and the Authorization of Discourse," in *Verbal Art Across Cultures: The Aesthetics and Proto-aesthetics of Communication*, ed. Hubert Knoblauch and Helga Kotthoff (Tübingen: Gunter Narr, 2001).

91 Tom Mould, "The Paradox of Traditionalization: Negotiating the Past in Choctaw Prophetic Discourse," *Journal of Folklore Research* 42.3 (2005): 257.

92 Irvine, *Making of Textual Culture*, 6.

acteristic of Irish legal exposition are rooted in the Latin grammatical culture, namely etymology, enumeration and classroom dialogue.[93] Enumeration and classroom dialogue are ubiquitous in the law tracts. Apart from the etymological analysis by dissecting word into smaller units, illustrated with instances from *Bretha Comaithchesa* by Charles-Edwards in the aforementioned article, one finds clear signs of the so called "etymological aetiology" based on the philosophy of Isidore of Seville,[94] and on the principle of *enarratio* in medieval *grammatica*. In the canonical part of the tract *Di Chethairṡlicht Athgabálae* [On the four divisions of distraint], for instance, the period of five-day's stay in the distraint procedure is explained as originating from the name of a woman Cóicthe (literally "of five days" or "the fifth day") who was involved in the first case that demands for such a period.[95] The judge's name Sen mac Áigi [senior son of fixed period] in the same tract, and the name of the first female-slave in Ireland, Mugdorn ingen Moga [slave-fist daughter of male-slave] in a narrative found in *Bretha im·Fuillemu Gell* [Judgments on the interests of pledges], are also manifest examples of this type.

There are more terms and techniques for which the Irish legal expositions are indebted to the *grammatica* tradition. Eight introductions prefixed to law tracts employ the *accessus ad auctores* schema to provide an introductory summary of the making of the tract.[96] The supplement of an *accessus* before an authoritative text as an introduction is a salient feature in the medieval *grammatica* tradition and can be traced to the influence of Aelius Donatus, a late antique grammarian. Donatus made extensive use of Suetonius's lost work, and incorporated a *vita* of Vergil which precedes his partly lost commentary

93 Thomas M. Charles-Edwards, "Review Article: The *Corpus Iuris Hibernici*," *Studia Hibernica* 20 (1980): 147.

94 Rolf Baumgarten, "Etymological Aetiology in Irish Tradition," *Ériu* 41 (1990): 115–22; Rolf Baumgarten, "Creative Medieval Etymology and Irish Hagiography (Lasair, Columba, Senán)," *Ériu* 54 (2004): 49–78.

95 Binchy, *Corpus Iuris Hibernici*, 2:406.26–407.26.

96 1) Binchy, *Corpus Iuris Hibernici*, 1:250.1–32 (*Bretha Étgid*) and a copy in Binchy, *Corpus Iuris Hibernici*, 3:925.1–926.4; 2) Binchy, *Corpus Iuris Hibernici*, 1:250.32–35 (*Bretha Étgid*) and a copy in Binchy, *Corpus Iuris Hibernici*, 3:926.5–18; 3) Binchy, *Corpus Iuris Hibernici*, 6:2186.37–38 (*Córus Iubaile* [The Ordering of Limitation Periods]; 4) Binchy, *Corpus Iuris Hibernici*, 2:1–342.21 (Pseudo-historical Prologue to *Senchas Már*) and four copies; 4) Binchy, *Corpus Iuris Hibernici*, 2:87.37–688.20 (*Cáin Ḟuithirbe*); 5) Binchy, *Corpus Iuris Hibernici*, 6:2143.41 (*Fothae Becc* [Small Foundation]; 6) Binchy, *Corpus Iuris Hibernici*, 3:979.23–26 (*Anfuigell*); 7) Binchy, *Corpus Iuris Hibernici*, 3:1027.21–1028.12 (*Cóic Conara Fuigill* [Five Paths of Litigation]) and a copy in Binchy, *Corpus Iuris Hibernici*, 4:1280.1–21; 8) Binchy, *Corpus Iuris Hibernici*, 4:1338.5–1341.7 (*Mellbretha* [Sport Judgments]).

to Vergil's works.[97] An *accessus*, or a *materia* or an *ingressus* as it is called in different disciplines, was regarded since late antiquity as a necessary preliminary before the students could set out on quests for a text's *sententia*, the deeper, spiritual meaning.[98] This attitude echoes the fundamental role of *grammatica* in the formation of a textual culture in the Middle Ages, when aspiring students had to learn first to correctly read the letters and to understand the literal sense (*lectio*) before any inquiry of interpretation and appreciation (*enarratio, emendatio* and *iudicium*) could be undertaken.[99]

There are several types of *accessus* schema during the Middle Ages, which have been conveniently classified by R.W. Hunt.[100] The single type that all the Irish law tracts adopt is what Hunt terms "type A": this normally consists of the four topics of *locus, tempus, persona* and *causa scribendi*, or rendered into Irish *locc* [place], *aimser* [time], *persa* [person] and *tucait scríbindi* [reason of writing] or *fáth airicc* [reason of obtaining] respectively. This type is abbreviated from the *septem circumstantiae* of the classic rhetoricians, especially in Boethius's *De differentiis topicis*,[101] which include *tempus, locus et persona, res, causa, qualitas* (*modus*) and *facultas* (*materia*).[102] The schema itself was used by continental theologians of the sixth and seventh century in their commentaries on the Bible, but it was also extended to commentary on literary texts, for instance by Remigius of Auxerre,[103] and was adopted by the Irish literati, probably through acquaintance with the works of Boethius. The schema occurs not only in Irish exegetic[104] and grammatical texts such as *Auraicept na nÉces* [Scholars' Primer], but also in introductory commentaries to hagiography and other compositions about saints (e.g. *Amra Coluim Chille* [Wonder of St. Columba],[105] and *Félire Óengusso* [The Martyrology of Óen-

97 Irvine, *Making of Textual Culture*, 121–24.

98 Alastair Minnis, *Medieval Theory of Authorship: Scholastic Literary Attitudes in the Later Middle Ages* (London: Scholar Press, 1984), 13–14.

99 Irvine, *Making of Textual Culture*, 4–5.

100 Richard William Hunt, "The Introductions to the 'Artes' in the Twelfth Century," in *Studia Mediaevalia in Honorem Admodum Reverendi Patris Raymundi Josephi Martin Ordinis Praedicatorum s. theologiae magistri* LXXUM *natalem diem agentis* (Bruges: De Tempel, 1948).

101 Minnis, *Medieval Theory*, 224, n. 53.

102 Hunt, "'Artes' in the Twelfth Century," 126, n. 1.

103 Minnis, *Medieval Theory*, 16–17.

104 Including Hiberno-Latin exegetic works, see Bernhard Bischoff, "Turning Points in the History of Latin Exegesis in the Early Irish Church," trans. Colm O'Grady, in *Biblical Studies: The Medieval Irish Contribution*, ed. Martin McNamara (Dublin: Irish Biblical Association, 1976), 84–87.

105 Whitley Stokes, "The Bodleian *Amra Coluim Chille*," *Revue Celtique* 20 (1899): 36–38.

gus]),[106] heroic sagas (e.g. *Táin Bó Cúailnge* [The Cattle-raid of Cooley][107]) and legal texts. The use of the *accessus* schema to introduce a text makes the text an object of the standardized reading practice, and the various genres of Irish texts are thus united under the guiding principles of medieval *grammatica* into an integrated learned tradition.

In addition to the *accessus*, expository markers derived from the *grammatica* tradition (and often translated from Latin)[108] are staple ingredients of Irish law texts, such as *.i.* [= i.e.] and *amail* [= *quasi*, as],[109] *cair* [= *quaere*, ask] and *ní hansa* [not difficult],[110] *cid ara n-eperr* [= *unde dicitur*, why is it called], *arailiu* [= *aliter*, otherwise], *óndí* [= *ab eo quod est*, from that which is] and their variants,[111] *desimrecht* [an example], etc. These markers are frequent in legal texts, but they are also part of a shared textual culture and have been used extensively in other types of Irish texts. Besides, several law texts actually engage in meta-theoretical discussion on *grammatica* and other arts, or deploy grammatical analytic terms to illustrate their content. For instance, a commentary to the *Pseudo-historical Prologue to Senchas Már*[112] tries to explain the order of *locc*, *persa* and *aimsir* used in the *accessus* from the perspective of biblical cosmology,[113] adapted from a prose version of *Saltair na Rann* [The Psalter of Quatrains], a Middle Irish versified account of the sacred history, thereby connecting the law text with exegesis. What follows that passage[114] is an interesting description of the twelve winds and their colours. The wind-diagram is rooted in classical geography, and is present in Isidore's *Etymologiae*;[115] but

106 Whitley Stokes, *The Martyrology of Oengus the Culdee: Félire Óengusso Céli Dé* (London: Harrison and Sons, 1905), 2, 8.

107 Robin Flower, "Quidam Scotigena .i. Discipulus Boëthii or Boëthius and the Four Conditions of a Tale," *Ériu* 8 (1916): 150–54.

108 Donnchadh Ó Corráin, "Creating the Past: The Early Irish Genealogical Tradition," *Peritia* 12 (1998): 193.

109 Paul Russell, "Quasi: Bridging the Etymological Gap in Early Irish Glossaries," in *A Companion in Linguistics: A Festschrift for Anders Ahlqvist on the Occasion of His Sixtieth Birthday*, ed. Bernadette Smelik et al. (Nijmegen: De Keltische Draak, 2005).

110 Rolf Baumgarten, "Discourse Markers in Medieval Irish Texts: Cs̄, Cair, Nī and Similar Features," *Ériu* 43 (1992): 1–37.

111 Paul Russell, "The Sounds of a Silence: The Growth of Cormac's Glossary," *Cambridge Medieval Celtic Studies* 15 (Summer 1988): 1–30 (22).

112 Binchy, *Corpus Iuris Hibernici*, 2:342.40–344.11.

113 Edited in John Carey, ed., "A Tract on the Creation," *Éigse* 21 (1986): 1–9. Slightly different versions of the beginning of this passage are included in the introduction to *Cáin Ḟuithirbe* [The regulation of Fuithirbe], Binchy, *Corpus Iuris Hibernici*, 2:688.20–290, and in the Preface to *Félire Óengusso* [the Martyrology of Óengus], Stokes, *Martyrology of Oengus*, 2.

114 Binchy, *Corpus Iuris Hibernici*, 2:343.12–22.

115 Isidore of Seville, *Etymologiae*, 13.11.2–4, in *The Etymologies of Isidore of Seville*, ed. Stephen

the doctrine here is also interwoven with Christian spirituality and indigenous topography.[116] One needs not be surprised at such a richness of grammatical thoughts and materials in the law, after all, if we are to believe in the statement in the Middle Irish tract *Urchuillti Bretheman* [Injunction of judges],[117] that judges are to be learned in the details of *Auraicept na nÉces*, an instruction manual on grammatical analysis of the Irish language, as well as in law tracts.[118]

The influence of grammatical study is even more salient in the opening part of the law tract *Cóic Conara Fuigill* [Five paths of judgment],[119] which enumerates the key grammatical concepts needed for analyzing the parts of the "paths" (*conara*), such as *fid ⁊ deach, reim ⁊ forbaidh, alt ⁊ indsci ⁊ etargairi* [letter and foot, declension and accent, syllable and gender and inflection].[120] These "seven things according to which Gaelic is measured" are important grammatical tools employed extensively in *Auraicept na nÉces*. They have already been included in the oldest core of the *Auraicept*[121] and were further elaborated as to their meanings and particularities in the later "Book of Ferchertne", a constituent of the *Auraicept* as it is found today.[122] Moreover, according to a Middle Irish tract on verse craft, any student of poetry aspiring to become a *fili* [poetic scholar] has to master exactly these same elements of language,[123] as a learned *fili* is distinguished from a bard by formal education which involves such grammatical training. A copy of the law tract *Uraicecht Becc* [Small primer],[124] engages with a prolonged discussion of basic Latin and Irish grammar elements before the canonical law text itself begins; this introductory matter utilizes the

---

A. Barney, W.J. Lewis, J.A. Beach, and Oliver Berghof (Cambridge: Cambridge University Press, 2006), 275.

116 John Carey, "Cosmology in Saltair na Rann," *Celtica* 17 (1985): 33–52; Barbara Obrist, "Wind Diagrams and Medieval Cosmology," *Speculum* 72.1 (1997): 33–84; Alfred K. Siewers, "The Bluest-Greyest-Greenest Eye: Colours of Martyrdom and Colours of the Winds as Iconographic Landscape," *Cambrian Medieval Celtic Studies* 50 (Winter 2005): 31–66.

117 Binchy, *Corpus Iuris Hibernici*, 6:2103.20–22.

118 Anders Ahlqvist, "Old Irish *Airaiccecht* 'Primer, etc.'," in *Medieval Irish Law: Texts and Contexts*, ed. Anders Ahlqvist and Pamela O'Neill (Sydney: University of Sydney, 2013), 233.

119 Binchy, *Corpus Iuris Hibernici*, 3:1027.25–3.

120 Erich Poppe, "*Grammatica, Grammatic*, Augustine, and the *Táin*," in *Ildánach Ildírech: A Festschrift for Proinsias Mac Cana*, ed. John Carey, John T. Koch, and Pierre-Yves Lambert (Andover: Celtic Studies Publications, 1999), 204.

121 Anders Ahlqvist, *The Early Irish Linguist: An Edition of the Canonical Part of the Auraicept na nÉces* (Helsinki: Societas Scientiarum Fennica, 1982), 50.

122 Calder, *Auraicept na n-Éces*, 54 ff.

123 Rudolf Thurneysen, "Mittelirische Verslehren," in *Irische Texte* 3.1, ed. Whitley Stokes and Ernst Windisch (Leipzig: Verlag von S. Hirzel, 1891), 6.

124 Binchy, *Corpus Iuris Hibernici*, 6:2255.1–2256.12.

triad *bunad* ⁊ *inne* ⁊ *airbert* [basis and essence and application] to expose the meaning and usage of words. These three meta-theoretical concepts can again be found among the teachings of the *Auraicept na nÉces*;[125] and they have been applied to examination of the word *étgid* [inadvertence] in *Bretha Étgid*,[126] and of the word *senchas* in the commentary to the Introduction to *Senchas Már*[127] as well. Another paradigm of *ainm* [name], *indaithmech* [analysis] and *érchoílliud* [definition] is used in examining the word *ferb* [word] in a commentary to *Di Chethairṡlicht Athgabálae*.[128]

These features are of course not limited to law texts. Scholars have shown the fundamental role of *grammatica* in the formation of Irish textual tradition, which stretches far beyond the linguistic context.[129] By participating in the same discursive and interpretative framework with other texts, law texts not only share terms but also freely exchange information and perspectives with other constituents of the *senchas*: it is little wonder that one finds such a wide spectrum of approaches in law texts, including grammatical, historical, poetic and theological contents, and a similar opulence of legal perspective in literature, historiography and place-name lore.[130] Here, as in other parts of Western Europe, *grammatica* provides the protocol for a text to be interpreted and evaluated by other texts, genres and discourses, producing a culture that was explicitly intertextual.[131] The share of expository mode and *grammatica* protocol between law and the rest of *senchas* provides an intertextuality through which law texts are accepted as traditional and authoritative.

The discourse of provision constitutes the skeleton of the law texts and defines them as documents recording the regulatory norms of the society; the discourse of narration provide ample references, both in format and in con-

125 Calder, *Auraicept na n-Éces*, 54–55.

126 Binchy, *Corpus Iuris Hibernici*, 1:251.4–14; Russell, "Growth of Cormac's Glossary," 23.

127 Binchy, *Corpus Iuris Hibernici*, 2:344.28–31.

128 Binchy, *Corpus Iuris Hibernici*, 5:1664.5.

129 Morgan Thomas Davies, "Protocols of Reading in Early Irish Literature: Notes on Some Notes to 'Orgain Denna Ríg' and 'Amra Coluim Cille'," *Cambrian Medieval Celtic Studies* 32 (Winter 1996): 1–24; Erich Poppe, "Latinate Terminology in Auraicept na n-Éces," in *History of Linguistics 1996, Volume 1. Traditions in Linguistics Worldwide*, ed. David Cram, Andrew Robert Linn and Elke Nowak (Amsterdam: John Benjamins Publishing, 1999); Abigail Burnyeat, "The Early Irish *Grammaticus*?" *Aiste* 1 (2007): 181–217.

130 Thomas M. Charles-Edwards, "Honour and Status in Some Irish and Welsh Prose Tales," *Ériu* 29 (1978): 123–41; Tomás Ó Cathasaigh, *Táin Bó Cúailnge and Early Irish Law* (Dublin: Faculty of Celtic Studies, University College Dublin, 2005); Christophe Archan, "Les Règles de Droit dans la Prose du Dindshenchas de Rennes," *Droit et Cultures* 64.2 (2012): 91–113, Arnamagnæan Commission, *Dictionary of Old Norse Prose* online, http://onp.ku.dk/.

131 Irvine, *Making of Textual Culture*, 15.

tent, for the law texts to be located in the intertextual network of the learned tradition *senchas*; and the discourse of exposition further create a forum for the law texts and other products of the *senchas* to converse to each other, and to texts even further afield from the *grammatica* tradition. By actively participating in such an intertextual dialogue, medieval Irish law texts acquired their traditional and authoritative status and thus remained in effect without promulgation and enforcement by the sovereign.

Despite the gradual eclipse of the power of Gaelic chieftains and the decline in the use of native law in the Late Middle Ages in Ireland, the prestige of early medieval law texts lived on and intertextual links were still being constructed and strengthened: Old Irish texts are still being cited as authority in a court pleading composed perhaps in the sixteenth century,[132] which may have witnessed the final stage of native Irish legal writing. During the early seventeenth century controversy known as "the Contention of the Bards", bardic poets from all over Ireland were composing verses to support the political and genealogical precedence of each's own patron. One of these poems quotes from the canonical text of the Old Irish law tract *Ántechtae* [Splendid Appropriateness].[133] The part in *Ántechtae* cited by the bardic poet,[134] in turn, narrates in rimeless verse the story of *Cath Maige Mucrama* [The Battle of the Plain of Pig-counting], a prominent tale that relates the defeat of Art, the father of Cormac mac Airt, and the career of Lugaid mac Con.[135] The bardic poet Lughaidh Ó Cléirigh resorted to the law text, and by inference, to the whole tradition surrounding *Cath Maige Mucrama*, in order to argue that the Northern kings should take precedence over the Southern kings, because according to *Ántechtae* and *Cath Maige Mucrama*, the ancestor of Northern kings, Cormac mac Airt, was entitled to compensation by Ligairne, the murderer of Art in the battle and a Leinster adherent to Lugaid mac Con. The tradition, even at the dimming moment of the seventeenth century immediately before the vanishing of the native learned class, was still lively defining the present by referring to the textual past.

132 Binchy, *Corpus Iuris Hibernici*, 6:2204.1–2208.19.

133 Lambert McKenna, ed., *Iomarbhagh na Bhfileadh: The Contention of the Bards* (London: Irish Texts Society, 1920), 88–89.

134 Binchy, *Corpus Iuris Hibernici*, 4:1244.18–1245.16.

135 O Daly, *Cath Maige Mucrama*.

PART 2

Law and Society

CHAPTER 6

De Divortio et de Resignatione: A Case of Carolingian Legal Precedent?

Jan van Doren

In 860 Hincmar of Rheims (806–82) compiled a treatise now known as *De Divortio Lotharii Regis et Theutbergae Reginae*,[1] in response to two sets of inquiries regarding his knowledge of, and involvement in, the divorce proceedings of King Lothar II (835–69) of Lotharingia from his queen, Theutberga (d. 875), which took place at two councils at Aachen in 860.[2] *De Divortio* is a lengthy treatise by the hand of the later Carolingian Empire's most (in)famous archbishop discussing and ultimately opposing the procedures that were followed at these councils. *De Divortio* also contains a longer exposé on Hincmar's understanding of the institution of marriage and the possibilities for divorce and eventual remarriage. Hincmar updated, annotated and glossed many parts of the sole surviving manuscript with more extensive authoritative passages, even after the "original" version had become somewhat obsolete in the rapidly evolving circumstances surrounding the case.[3] As such, *De Divortio* is a work of great jurisprudence and legal, canonical thought.

---

1 This is a non-contemporary title. The standard edition is Hincmar of Rheims, *De Divortio Lotharii regis et Theutbergae reginae*, ed. Letha Böhringer, MGH Conc. 4, sup. 1 (Hannover: Hahnsche Buchhandlung, 1992), with a recent translation in: Rachel Stone and Charles West, trans., *The Divorce of King Lothar and Queen Theutberga: Hincmar of Rheims's* De Divortio (Manchester: Manchester University Press, 2016).

2 For a more extensive study of the divorce case as whole, see Karl Heidecker, *The Divorce of Lothar II: Christian Marriage and Political Power in the Carolingian World*, trans. Tanis M. Guest (Ithaca: Cornell University Press, 2010); see also: Wilfried Hartmann, *Die Synoden der Karolingerzeit im Frankenreich und in Italiën* (Paderborn: F. Schöningh, 1989), 274–85; Abigail Firey, *A Contrite Heart: Prosecution and Redemption in the Carolingian Empire* (Boston: Brill, 2009); Jean Devisse, *Hincmar, archevêque de Reims, 845–882*, 3 vols. (Genève: Droz, 1975–1976), 1:367–468; Stuart Airlie, "Private Bodies and the Body Politic in the Divorce Case of Lothar II," *Past & Present* 161 (1998): 3–38.

3 Paris, Bibliothèque Nationale de France, MS Lat. 2866; Karl Heidecker, "Gathering and Recycling Authorative Texts: The Importance of Marginalia in Hincmar of Rheims' *De Divortio*," in *Organizing the Written Word: Proceedings of the First Utrecht Symposium on Medieval Literacy, Utrecht 5–7 June 1997*, ed. Marco Mostert (Turnhout: Brepols, forthcoming); Heidecker, *Divorce of Lothar II*, 36–62; Hincmar, *De Divortio*, ed. Böhringer, 1–98.

 | DOI:10.1163/9789004448650_008

The anonymous group of Lotharingian bishops and noblemen that had sent Hincmar their inquiry suggests that there was a famous legal precedent for the procedures of Lothar and Theutberga's divorce case: the resignation, or deposition, of Archbishop Ebbo of Rheims (c. 775–851) in 835, after Louis the Pious' (778–840) restoration to the imperial throne.[4] Ebbo had resigned from his see by means of a secret confession confirmed by witnesses, a written statement, and the public acceptance of penance. Theutberga was ostensibly divorced from Lothar by means of a similar judicial process.[5] Hincmar opposed the procedures followed in the divorce case but, in order to ensure the legitimacy of his own position as archbishop of Rheims, which crucially depended on the proper, canonical deposition of Ebbo, could not do so without dismantling and weighing the procedures followed in both cases.

In what follows, Hincmar's criticism of the procedures of Theutberga's trial as well as his criticism of the use of Ebbo's trial as legal precedent will be analyzed in order to bring forth the similarities and distinctions between the two cases. On what grounds was the precedential link between the two cases based, and with what purpose? This comparison sheds light on the importance of legalistic, procedure-based reasoning in legitimizing or delegitimizing high profile legal cases during the ninth century. The way in which Hincmar presents Ebbo's case will then be used to similarly elucidate the debates surrounding Ebbo's deposition and, in particular, to highlight the problems and ambiguities that arose from Carolingian conflations of what were traditionally classified in scholarship as separate penitential, ecclesiastical, medicinal procedures, and legal, secular, punitive procedures.[6] This Carolingian legal and political experimentation became most apparent in the time of Louis the Pious and would have long-lasting repercussions.

---

4 Mayke de Jong, *The Penitential State: Authority and Atonement in the Age of Louis the Pious, 814–840* (Cambridge: Cambridge University Press, 2009); Courtney Booker, *Past Convictions: The Penance of Louis the Pious and the Decline of the Carolingians* (Philadelphia, PA: University of Pennsylvania Press, 2009). For other studies on the creation of legal precedent see the chapters on "Legal Practice" in this volume, and in particular Sonia Colafrancesco, "Juridical Dualism in Medieval Southern Italy: Studies on the *Codex Diplomaticus Cavensis*," Chapter 10.

5 Hincmar, *De Divortio*, ed. Böhringer, *interrogatio* 1, 114.

6 For an overview of both the traditional and the more recent scholarly traditions, see, Mayke de Jong, "What was Public about Public Penance? *Paenitentia publica* and Justice in the Carolingian World," in *La Giustizia Nell'Alto Medioevo (Secoli IX–XI), 11–17 aprile 1996, Settimane di Studio del Centro Italiano di Studi Sull'Alto Medioevo* 44, 2 vols. (Spoleto: Presso La Sede del Centro, 1997); Raymund Kottje, "Buße oder Strafe? Zur '*iustitia*' in den '*libri paenitentiales*'," in *La Giustizia Nell'Alto Medioevo (Secoli V–VII), 7–13 aprile 1994, Settimane di Studio del Centro Italiano di Studi Sull'Alto Medioevo* 42, 2 vols. (Spoleto: Presso La Sede del Centro, 1995).

The resulting Carolingian legal culture was pluralistic, both in the sense of possible sources of law, and in the sense of the overlapping secular and ecclesiastical spheres of law.[7] Hincmar's dismantling of both cases provides valuable information not only about the division of justice in the 860s—or lack thereof—but also about the function of written accounts of councils and assemblies in Carolingian public and legal discourses. Furthermore, the parts of the *De Divortio* dedicated to the specific precedential link between the two cases show the legitimizing and editorial strategies Hincmar used to support his claims. Unsurprisingly, similar strategies were at work on both sides of the aisle in Ebbo's case, and the joint appearance of both cases in *De Divortio* is therefore a useful point of confluence from which to examine both cases in a new light, by focusing on them as a potential example, whether justifiably or not at the time, of Carolingian case law.

As with all divorce cases, this one started with marriage. In 855, after his succession to the Lotharingian throne, Lothar II abandoned his concubine Waldrada (c. 840–post 869), in favor of Theutberga, who was a member of the powerful Bosonid family. No doubt this marriage was meant to cement political alliances which would help Lothar II have a prosperous rule and, hopefully, plentiful offspring. By 857, however, Lothar's relationship with both Theutberga and her family had soured or become obsolete, and damaging rumors regarding Theutberga's fitness as queen had begun to circulate. The charges levelled against her were dire indeed: she was said to have had incestual, sodomitical intercourse with her brother Hucbert (820–64), and to have aborted the resulting child.[8] As a result, Lothar II sought to repudiate Theutberga altogether, her crimes making her unworthy of both the crown and of marriage.

Apparently lacking the political clout to unilaterally rid himself of Theutberga, Lothar convened a trial in 858 presided over by laymen and advised by bishops.[9] The apparent lack or inadequacy of witnesses and oath swearers for both parties then resulted in the trial coming down to an ordeal of boiling water in 858. Theutberga's champion was judged to have passed the ordeal, his

7 See among others, Matthew Innes, "Charlemagne, Written Law and Justice," in *Law, Custom and Justice in Late Antiquity and the Early Middle Ages*, ed. Alice Rio (London: Centre for Hellenic Studies, 2011); Rachel Stone, *Morality and Masculinity in the Carolingian Empire* (Cambridge: Cambridge University Press, 2012), 159–73; Hartmann, *Synoden der Karolingerzeit*, 445–74; Jong, *Penitential State*, 4–5; Firey, *Prosecution and Redemption in the Carolingian Empire*, 59.

8 Hincmar, *De Divortio*, ed. Böhringer, 114, 177–96.

9 Though he was by no means powerless either, Airlie, "Private Bodies," 10; On the trial see Heidecker, *Divorce of Lothar II*, 63–72.

hand being "*incoctus*" [uncooked].[10] Theutberga was cleared of all charges and Theutberga and Lothar II were formally reunited, though the *Annales Bertiniani*, also compiled under Hincmar's direction, claim that Lothar locked up his queen.[11]

Lothar was not ready to throw in the towel quite yet however, despite what should have been a decisive divine judgement in favor of Theutberga.[12] In early 860, he instead convened a series of two councils at which he sought to push through his divorce. Originally intended to include bishops not only from the Middle Kingdom, but also from the other Frankish kingdoms, it was on a canonical stage that Lothar now sought to rid himself of Theutberga. Hincmar himself, for instance, had been expressly invited by Adventius of Metz (r. 858–75) to attend the councils, but, smelling trouble, excused himself by various means and later vehemently attested that he had neither attended the councils, nor sent a representative to assent to its decisions on his behalf.[13] In the end, only bishops from Lothar's own kingdom attended. But even within Lotharingia there was no total agreement on the propriety of the king's conduct and divorce, despite the seeming unanimity of the resulting proceedings. This is how Hincmar, despite his earlier reluctance, got involved.

After the councils' conclusion, a group of doubtful—possibly even dissenting—bishops and other magnates anonymously sent out a series of eight *interrogationes* regarding Lothar's divorce attempt.[14] In it they questioned the validity of the accusations made against Theutberga—had she not been cleared by the ordeal?—as well as the validity of the proceedings. They also wondered if it was true that Hincmar himself had assented to the divorce, and furthermore likened the case to that of Ebbo of Rheims; if he had been properly deposed from his episcopal see by means of a secret confession, could Theutberga not have been divorced from Lothar in a similar fashion?[15] Other questions regarding the proper authorities on marriage and remarriage, the possible involvement of witchcraft, and the validity of ordeals then follow. The pointed questions regarding Hincmar's involvement, especially, and the direct appellation to Ebbo, whose specter eternally haunted Hincmar's archiepisco-

---

10 Hincmar, *De Divortio*, ed. Böhringer, 114.

11 Georg Waitz, ed., *Annales Bertiniani*, MGH SSRG 5 (Hannover: Hahn, 1883), 50.

12 Hincmar, *De Divortio*, ed. Böhringer, 114; On ordeals: Heidecker, *Divorce of Lothar II*, 66–67; Robert Bartlett, *Trial by Fire and Water: The Medieval Judicial Ordeal* (Oxford: Oxford University Press, 1986), 13–33.

13 Hincmar, *De Divortio*, ed. Böhringer, 129–32.

14 Stone and West give a good overview of the questions, Stone and West, *Divorce of King Lothar*, 25.

15 Hincmar, *De Divortio*, ed. Böhringer, 114.

pacy,[16] are clear signs that Hincmar's anonymous interrogators were trying to force the archbishop's hand into writing a response. Yet, crucially, they were not just that: the severity and thoroughness of Hincmar's response show that both the claim to his assent and the assertion of the link between the divorce case and the deposition case can well be seen as part of a larger strategy to establish a stronger base of consensus, legitimacy and authority for the decisions of the Aachen councils of January and February 860, and thus for Lothar's divorce itself.

That these two questions serve as the anonymous questioners' opening salvo, is no small wonder then. They draw Hincmar out, but they also immediately targeted several of the core issues of Lothar's divorce case: the lack of support from other kingdoms, as well as its potentially dubious legal proceedings. Philip Buc has long since pointed out that it was not enough to just have a trial, or any other ritualized enactment of power, but that such enactments subsequently needed to be broadcasted effectively, their meanings and interpretations tightly controlled.[17] The questions Hincmar received, and the response he wrote to them, *De Divortio* itself, constituted both a critical analysis of Lothar and his followers' representations of the proceedings of the two Aachen councils, as well as a competing interpretation of what had happened. It's perhaps a little unfair to Lothar's side of the story that our only access to the written proceedings and *canones* of the two Aachen councils are contained within—and therefore are framed by—*De Divortio*.

Several scholars have, however, shown that *De Divortio* should not merely be seen as a partisan critique of Lothar's attempted divorce, written with the specific purpose of discrediting his personal conduct and invalidating his subsequent marriage to Waldrada so as to leave Lothar without an heir.[18] Though Hincmar was certainly a prominent member of Charles the Bald's (823–77) court, his opposition to the divorce proceedings is initially rather reserved, leaving room for the possibility that the crimes Theutberga had been accused of could be true, in which case she would have indeed been rendered unfit for marriage and queenship, provided there was a properly conducted retrial.[19] It is only after receiving a second set of questions late in the summer of 860, and possibly after having spoken with Theutberga, who by that time had fled to

16 Steffan Patzold, *Episcopus: Wissen über Bischöfe im Frankenreich des späten 8. bis frühen 10. Jahrhunderts* (Ostfildern: Jan Thorbecke Verlag, 2008), 315–60.

17 Philip Buc, *The Dangers of Ritual: Between Early Medieval Texts and Social Scientific Theory* (Princeton: Princeton University Press, 2001), 51–87.

18 Airlie, "Private Bodies," 10–12, Heidecker, *Divorce of Lothar II*, 46–48.

19 Hincmar, *De Divortio*, ed. Böhringer, 195, 219.

West Frankia, that Hincmar's interpretation of events turned decisively against Lothar and his bishops.[20] His response to these questions, as well as a dossier on a related divorce case, were later added to the original material of the first version of *De Divortio*. These additions were likely circulated on their own, like the first version of *De Divortio* had been. Today, only what is assumed to be Hincmar's composite working manuscript, Paris, Bibliothèque Nationale de France, MS Lat. 2866, in which the many alterations, emendations and additions he made to *De Divortio* are visible, remains to us today.[21] The manuscript thus contains not only *De Divortio* in what is arguably its final state, it also contains hints to Hincmar's editing methods and ways of arguing. Not only can this show when Hincmar wished to strengthen an argument by adding additional authoritative references, it can similarly show when he lacked such references.[22]

Jean Devisse had already narrowed in on the remarkable procedural focus of the first *interrogationes* and *responsiones* of *De Divortio*.[23] Hincmar's main concern in this section of *De Divortio* is with legal process, which, to be proper and correct, should correspond both with secular laws and norms, and, most importantly, not conflict with divine law either.[24] The archbishop of Rheims therefore brings to bear his vast knowledge and understanding of ecclesiastical law upon the proceedings of the councils of Aachen in January and February 860. His goal: to invalidate them on procedural—if not necessarily principal—grounds, and to disconnect them from the suggestion that

> sicut Ebo quondam Remorum episcopus per libellum secretae confessionis a sede et ordine est submotus, ita et ista per libellum secretae confessionis a maritali removeatur consortio
>
> [just as Ebbo, the former bishop of Rheims, was removed from his seat and his [episcopal] order thanks to a booklet of secret confession, so [Theutberga] could be removed from marital union through a booklet of secret confession].[25]

---

20 Waitz, *Annales Bertiniani*, 83–84.

21 Stone and West, *Divorce of King Lothar*, 16–18; Heidecker, "Gathering and Recycling Authorative Texts;" Heidecker, *Divorce of Lothar II*, 36–62; Hincmar, *De Divortio*, ed. 1–98.

22 Hincmar, *De Divortio*, ed. Böhringer, 39–40, 49–51; Heidecker, "Gathering and Recycling Authorative Texts".

23 Devisse, *Hincmar*, 1:409–28.

24 Hincmar, *De Divortio*, ed. Böhringer, 188.

25 Hincmar, *De Divortio*, ed. Böhringer, 114; Stone and West, *Divorce of King Lothar*, 96.

Hincmar's first *responsio* begins right after an account of the first council of Aachen in January 860 and concerns itself primarily with addressing the procedures followed at both Aachen councils of 860, leaving the link with Ebbo's resignation for his second *responsio*.[26] This first account of the January council, known as the *Libellus octo capitolorum* [Booklet of Eight Chapters], accompanied the list of eight questions to which Hincmar was writing in answer, and is part of the first recension of *De Divortio*.[27] Hincmar gives an extensive critique of these proceedings and then later expanded on this critique when both a different version of the proceedings of January 860, the *Libellus septem capitolorum* [Booklet of Seven Chapters] and an account of the second council in February 860, the *Tomus prolixus* [Verbose Volume] had become available to him.

The Booklet of Eight Chapters focuses in particular upon the conduct of the bishops during the first council, and purports to be a booklet directed to the episcopate at large by the bishops present (ch. 1).[28] It relates how Lothar had come to the bishops in a solemn and humble fashion, asking them for advice and for medicine for the soul in a case that greatly pained him. He claimed that Theutberga wished to withdraw from their marriage bed against his wishes, and was stalwart in her desire to do so (ch. 2–3). Subsequently the bishops were summoned by a messenger to speak with Theutberga, who also sought their council (ch. 4). The booklet does its best to portray Theutberga as a true penitent, earnestly seeking aid and spiritual betterment (ch. 4–7). The bishops explicitly warn her that she is not to give false testimony against herself, neither out of fear, persuasion or deception, nor out of any hope of gain (ch. 5). Theutberga claims that she had earnestly and voluntarily confessed her sins in secret to Gunthar of Cologne (d. 873), whom she asks to testify to her unworthiness as queen due to these sins. Gunthar first attempts to get Theutberga to confess to the other bishops present, but she refuses (ch. 6). The bishops then give her another warning that she cannot make a complaint [*querimoniam*] nor attempt some other kind of treachery [*aliquas insidias*], should she be allowed to divorce Lothar and give up the crown. Theutberga swears that she shall not (ch. 7). After Theutberga has thus implicated herself and also transferred the heavy task of testifying to her unworthiness to Gunthar, the bishops hear him out and Gunthar seems to reveal the contents of Theutberga's

26 Hincmar, *De Divortio*, ed. Böhringer, 125.

27 Stone and West, *Divorce of King Lothar*, 16–20.

28 Hincmar, *De Divortio*, ed. Böhringer, 115–16; Firey, *Prosecution and Redemption in the Carolingian Empire*, 16–17, therefore calls this the "bishop's brief."

confession. The bishops then proclaim that they shall similarly share what they know about this confession with their fellow bishops face-to-face [*viva voce*] (ch. 8).

The language of the Booklet of Eight Chapters is somewhat veiled, but as Hincmar similarly picks up on, it's aimed at making Theutberga seem to actively seek both a divorce from Lothar and to pursue a penitential solution to her crimes, overtly excluding the possibility that she was being coerced into confessing. A double surety against Theutberga fighting the decisions of the council later on is then implemented by having her swear that she will not later contest the decisions of the council. Hincmar forcefully argues against several points in this booklet. To start off, he is suspicious of the many warnings the bishops issue Theutberga, suggesting that the bishops already knew what she had confessed to Gunthar, which would undermine the secrecy of the confession and disallow it from being seen as a secret confession, as it was still portrayed here.[29] This critique cuts right to the heart of the matter of Hincmar's larger, over-arching concerns with the divorce case as a whole: the treatment of Theutberga's confession, in various stages of the two councils, as either secret or public confessions of sins—and therefore penitential deeds, fitting to an ecclesiastical arena and setting—or as confessions not of sins, but of guilt, as Hincmar deems fitting for an actual trial.[30] Not only was the status of the confession being either secret or public essential to the possible medicinal remedies that could be offered to the penitent, secret confessions were also out of place in an actual legal, potentially punitive, trial.[31] This booklet, Hincmar argues, "conventum sonat episcopalem, qui pro causa generali fieri debet, et secretam describit confessionem, quae specialem postulat medicinam" [speaks of an episcopal meeting, which should take place for a general matter, yet describes a secret confession, which demands a special medicine].[32] It does not matter to Hincmar whether Theutberga had confessed to just Gunthar or to multiple bishops at the same time, nor that she had given permission to these bishops to share her confession amongst themselves. The contents of the confession should have remained secret.[33] Furthermore, he continues, secret confessions did not provide a proper basis for a judgement to be made by a gathering of bishops, for it is forbidden to judge on the basis of hidden

29 Hincmar, *De Divortio*, ed. Böhringer, 116.

30 Stone and West, *Divorce of King Lothar*, 42–44.

31 Hincmar, *De Divortio*, ed. Böhringer, 119.

32 Hincmar, *De Divortio*, ed. Böhringer, 117; Stone and West, *Divorce of King Lothar*, 101.

33 Hincmar, *De Divortio*, ed. Böhringer, 118.

things. Here Hincmar twisted the words of Innocent I on the different prosecution of male and female adulterers to suit his own purposes.[34]

Hincmar backs up his statements with various biblical citations, canon law, and papal decrees and writings. His usual way of arguing in *De Divortio* depends very heavily on authoritative citations and references, many of which require a particular brand of Hincmarian skewing to fit his argument. Nevertheless, Hincmar builds up his critique of the Booklet of Eight Chapters rather carefully, obviously keeping an eye on his other *responsiones* to make them all line up. Broadly speaking, Hincmar criticizes the Lotharingian bishops' blending of canonical proceedings which were appropriate for the imposition of public penance, proceedings that were appropriate for the imposition of secret penance, and proceedings that would fit a less penitentiary, more punitive style of judgement. He continued this line of reasoning when he added the other two conciliar accounts.

The Booklet of Seven Chapters initially focuses less on the agency of the bishops and Theutberga: it starts off by emphasizing Lothar's authority and reframes the events of the first council in Aachen in 860 as taking place on his initiative. Hincmar dismisses this booklet as ludicrous but nonetheless included it in *De Divortio* as a further reflection on the improper, maybe even confused nature of the council's proceedings.[35] The discrepancies between its account and that of the Booklet of Eight Chapters throw further doubt on the divorce case as a whole. Especially the Booklet of Seven Chapters' rather casual treatment of the secrecy of Theutberga's confession, even more than that of the first account, seems to bother Hincmar. In this booklet, the king does not appear as a sorrowful penitent, requiring the aid and advice of the bishops, nor is Theutberga initially depicted as one. Lothar is depicted as a righteous king, who, despite having knowledge of Theutberga's sins, does not speak out against the ordeal of 858 which she supposedly passed only due to Divine leniency (ch. 1–2). After much deliberation, both secret and public, Lothar sends his bishops to Theutberga to inquire after the rumors that had begun to spread about her. She confesses to this episcopal delegation, not just to Gunthar, in full (ch. 3). According to the bishops Theutberga then asks to be allowed to take the veil and to retreat from secular life (ch. 4–7). The bishops, recognizing that she had had no willing part in the crime that was done unto her violently, suggest that the king let her retreat from the marital bed as she asks, again stressing that Theutberga had confessed willingly and without evil intent (ch. 7).

34 Hincmar, *De Divortio*, ed. Böhringer, 119.

35 Hincmar, *De Divortio*, ed. Böhringer, 119–20.

Though Hincmar only implicitly criticizes these proceedings as he advances his argument, his remarks regarding the Booklet of Eight Chapters nevertheless throw light on the strategies at play in the Booklet of Seven Chapters. Hincmar was an experienced participant in the public discourse, and a key political player at the time. He knew how to frame events in his favor, and similarly knew how others could apply such tactics. By summarily dismissing the Booklet of Seven Chapters, he both makes the Booklet of Eight Chapters the primary reference for the January 860 council of Aachen—which suits his arguments regarding the secrecy of Theutberga's confession better—and casts doubt on the competency and authority of the composers of the Booklet of Seven Chapters. The strategy of the composers of the Booklet of Seven Chapters was pretty obvious: emphasize Lothar's royal justice, de-emphasize Theutberga's initiative to seek secret penance, and de-emphasize the secrecy of Theutberga's confession. The warnings against anything but a true, sincere confession again serve the purpose of putting Theutberga in a double bind: she is made aware of the spiritual gravity of making a false confession, and bound from coming back on her word at a later time. These warnings presupposed that had she been coerced, she would have—or should have—rather admitted to that fact and faced the consequences. Should she later find herself in a position where disputing her divorce would become expedient, she would then become a perjurer twice over if she were to fight her current confession. It is no wonder that Hincmar called similar warnings in the Booklet of Eight Chapters suspect [*suspectum*][36] and later devotes some time to the difficulty of being entangled in conflicting oaths.[37]

The third account finally, as relayed in the Verbose Volume—of which we only have the few chapters in *De Divortio*—presents us with the proceedings of the February council in Aachen in 860, which is described as "in generali conventu obtimatum ex regno almi Hlotharii actum est concilium episcoporum" [a council of bishops [which] was held at a general meeting of the magnates of the propitious Lothar at the palace of Aachen].[38] The setting of the February council, as compared to the somewhat private setting described in the Booklets of Seven and Eight chapters, is decidedly more formal and public. Its proceedings, as the name Verbose Volume certainly suggest, are also more detailed and extensive than the other two accounts. Theutberga is said to have spoken honestly and truthfully about what had happened to her and, having been given no guarantees that her confession would be "celandi aut superandi" [hidden

36 Hincmar, *De Divortio*, ed. Böhringer, 117.

37 Hincmar, *De Divortio*, ed. Böhringer, 203–05.

38 Hincmar, *De Divortio*, ed. Böhringer, 121; Stone and West, *Divorce of King Lothar*, 107.

or passed over],[39] she confirmed the rumors and repeated them, first to the king then to the bishops and some laymen (ch. 15), presumably those present at the council. She subsequently handed over a small charter [*cartula*] of her confession, which, it is stressed again, she gave willingly, and then begged the king to be allowed to undertake penance and to be released from the marital bond.[40]

The text of her *cartula*, confirming that her brother had forced her into a sodomitical, incestual relationship, was then read out at the council to the horror of all listeners and it was also recorded in full within the proceedings (ch. 15–16). The bishops quickly gathered around the king to ascertain themselves that the king had not forced Theutberga to give this heinous confession (ch. 16). He proclaimed that he had not, and that he had furthermore attempted to keep the matter hidden, despite having known the truth and even having known that the outcome of her ordeal had been false. Alas, the rumor had spread far and wide, and Lothar now found himself forced to address the wickedness that had festered in his kingdom (ch. 16). Apparently satisfied with this answer the bishops turned to Theutberga once more, asking her whether or not she had confessed falsely, under pressure, or with the intent of pursuing further plots later, to which she answered, with a bitter look [*aspero intuit*],[41] that she had not (ch. 17). Many others, laymen included, came to warn her of the dangers should she confess falsely, but she remained steadfast. After a digression upon the dangers of such a novel crime as had been inflicted upon Theutberga spreading (ch. 18), a judgment is then rendered (ch. 19): "[…] lugendam incesti pollutionem in publicum exalatam 'publica poenitentiae satisfactione purgandam' decrevimus." [[…] we decreed that this lamentable pollution of incest, breathed out into the public, "should be purged by the performance of public penance"].[42]

Theutberga's trial at the Aachen council in February 860, as narrated in the Verbose Volume, is made out to be a public affair: Theutberga narrated her sins to the king, bishops and a part of the laity, they were furthermore read out loud from her written confession and, finally, rumors about them had been circulating for a long time. The crime was also of such a severity that it formed a threat to the public weal. The composers even try to safeguard the proceedings against

39 Hincmar, *De Divortio*, ed. Böhringer, 121; Stone and West, *Divorce of King Lothar*, 107.

40 Hincmar, *De Divortio*, ed. Böhringer, 121.

41 Hincmar, *De Divortio*, ed. Böhringer, 121; Stone and West, *Divorce of King Lothar*, 109.

42 Hincmar, *De Divortio*, ed. Böhringer, 122; Stone and West, *Divorce of King Lothar*, 110. The quote refers to Leo I, *Epistola* 167, ed. Jacques-Paul Migne, PL (Paris: Imprimerie Catholique, 1844–1855), 54:1207.

claims such as Hincmar's of the improper handling of Theutberga's secret confession, mentioning as they do the lack of guarantees given to Theutberga as to the secrecy of her narration of the sins perpetrated against her by Hucbert. They portray Theutberga as a dismayed and repentant penitent, yet it is not her misery that is put center stage: Lothar's tearful sighing [*lacrimosis superiis*] and his patient and noble conduct handling the secrecy of this shameful matter thus far, appear to make him the true victim, as well as the true hero, in this matter. His bishops are portrayed as stern and watchful of falsehoods during the trial and then, as they pronounce their (!) sentence of public penance, as the ones taking proper action against the spread of a terrible wickedness in Lothar's realm. Any shred of secrecy that had clung to Theutberga's confession had similarly been purged: her written confession was read out and publicized in a clear attempt to make her much rumored sins as public as possible.

Hincmar finds little to praise in the proceedings. First he refers to a different letter of Pope Leo I (c. 400–61) than the one quoted at the end of the trial's proceedings, which bans the usage of booklets of confession in this manner: instead of collecting their sins in such a booklet and making them public, the sinner should confess secretly to a priest and undergo secret penance.[43] If Theutberga had, as the Verbose Volume says, actually handed over a written confession to the king and confessed also in front of laymen, it should be them and not the bishops who should pass judgement over her and her fitness for marriage before the case could then be referred to the bishops, if needed, for a medicinal judgement [*iudicium medicinale*]. He implies that the divorce cases as a whole should have been tried by the laity, as Theutberga, even though she was queen, was still a laywoman. Karl Heidecker has already pointed out that such a neat division of responsibilities of justice did not exist yet at the time; Hincmar himself also complicates the matter by later claiming that it was still necessary for clergymen to involve themselves in divorce cases when their medicinal, i.e. penitential, severity is warranted.[44] The procedures followed according to the Verbose Volume were therefore inadequate, as they met neither the standards for a penitential procedure, nor those for a punitive procedure. No verdict had been reached by the king and the laity, in front of whom Theutberga had accused herself, so the bishops' imposition of penance had been premature.[45] Given all that had passed, Hincmar feels that the bishops

43 Hincmar, *De Divortio*, ed. Böhringer, 123, 176.

44 Hincmar, *De Divortio*, ed. Böhringer, 140–41; Heidecker, *Divorce of Lothar II*, 11–35.

45 Hincmar, *De Divortio*, ed. Böhringer, 124.

had acted rashly, and that a general council of bishops should have and could still be called to discuss this obviously grave problem.[46]

Taken together, Hincmar's critique of all three written proceedings of the Aachen councils of 860 shows a remarkable concern on his behalf with procedure, and with the proper division of, and responsibilities for, the maintenance of justice. His response offers insights into his own legal thinking, which seeks to create neater distinctions between ecclesiastical justice and secular justice than were likely observed at his time. Bishops, like most Carolingian magnates, owed allegiance not only to the church, but also to their monarch, and their positions were not necessarily politically neutral.[47] Given what we know of the rest of Hincmar's career, we cannot take such idealism entirely at face value, but, even as a partially politically inspired argument, his procedural critique shows the validity of such reasoning in Carolingian public discourse: arguments based on legal procedure mattered and could counter, or even dispel, the aura of legitimacy that ought to accompany "official" pronouncements such as the proceedings of the Aachen councils. Though the eventual involvement of the papacy made *De Divortio*'s contribution to the divorce case's difficulties potentially less potent in the end, it had originally been composed to provide ammunition to refute Lothar's divorce attempt. Furthermore, through its broader discussion of marriage, divorce and other attendant matters, *De Divortio* provides a valuable window on how legal issues such as these were discussed among the Carolingian intellectual elite. To establish proper procedure, Hincmar gathered as many authoritative statements as he could find, whereas Lothar's bishops had apparently looked to a little more recent precedent: Ebbo's resignation.

The importance of Hincmar's procedural arguments becomes even clearer when the suggestion that the manner in which Theutberga ostensibly sought to divorce from Lothar strongly resembled Ebbo's resignation is taken into account. Hincmar himself sarcastically admits that the two cases might look very similar indeed to a layman's eyes.[48] The archbishop's annoyance is understandable: from the start of Hincmar's archiepiscopacy, he had been dealing with the fall-out of Ebbo's resignation and repeated attempts to return to his see.[49] To better understand Hincmar's arguments for dismissing the validity of the link between the two cases, it's important now to take Ebbo's resignation into consideration.

46 Hincmar, *De Divortio*, ed. Böhringer, 125.

47 Heidecker, *Divorce of Lothar II e*, 130–35; Hartmann, *Synoden der Karolingerzeit*, 404–06.

48 Hincmar, *De Divortio*, ed. Böhringer, 125.

49 Devisse, *Hincmar*, 71–97; Patzold, *Episcopus*, 315–60.

After Louis the Pious regained his throne in 834 he needed to publicly and forcefully counter the charges of scandal, neglect, sacrilege, perjury, and homicide that had been brought against him in 833.[50] His son and main opponent Lothar I had retreated to Italy, taking many of his co-conspirators with him, but Louis' restoration would need to be grandiosely confirmed for proper order to be restored. At a general assembly at Metz in 835, Louis was reinvested with his imperial regalia and a new official account of what had happened in 833 was drafted by those present, attesting to the falsehoods Louis had been accused of as well as to the propriety of his return to office. History was rewritten and Louis' honor was almost fully redeemed. All that was left was to apportion the blame for his earlier deposition. It was Ebbo, archbishop of Rheims, who came to be identified as the ringleader of the conspiracy against the restored emperor.[51]

None of the conciliar texts of the proceedings survive, but brief accounts are given in the *Annales Bertiniani* as well as in the biographies of Louis' life by Thegan (pre 800–c. 850) and the Astronomer.[52] After the gathered magnates and bishops had all confirmed and publicized the new, "official" narrative of the events that had led to the imposition of public penance on Louis, Ebbo was brought forward at the council. In Metz, he was forced to publicly proclaim the iniquity of his accusations against Louis the Pious and to then reaffirm the justness of the 834 restoration. Afterwards, the council moved to the emperor's palace at Thionville and a synod was convened there. It was at this synod that Ebbo confessed to a capital sin in secret, professed his unworthiness of being an archbishop, confirmed this unworthiness through a written statement and the testimony of several witnesses, and subsequently resigned with the consent and judgment of the bishops present to undertake an act of penance.[53] Thegan and the Astronomer add their own interpretations of the account. Thegan, who all throughout his *Gesta Hludowici imperatoris* had been very hostile to Ebbo, proclaims that the matter had not yet been dealt with properly, maintaining that Ebbo had got off easily under the pretext of religious piety and ought

50 Albert Werminghoff, ed., *Episcoporum de poenitentia, quam Hludowicus imperator professus est, relatio Compendiensis*, MGH Conc. 2/2 (Hannover: Hahn, 1908), 695; Jong, *Penitential State*, 271–279.

51 Waitz, *Annales Bertiniani*, 10–11; Jong, *Penitential State*, 252–54; Booker, *Past Convictions*, 68–103, 183–210.

52 Waitz, *Annales Bertiniani*; Astronomer, *Vita Hludowici imperatoris*, ed. Ernst Tremp, MGH SSRG 64 (Hannover: Hahnsche Buchhandlung, 1995); Thegan, *Gesta Hludowici imperatoris*, ed. Ernst Tremp, MGH SSRG 64 (Hannover: Hahnsche Buchhandlung, 1995).

53 Waitz, *Annales Bertiniani*, 10–11.

to have been judged and punished more severely.[54] The Astronomer adds that Louis had originally been looking to condemn more people than just Ebbo, but Ebbo was the only one who was had been captured. Ebbo then complained that he was being singled out, to which the other bishops present quickly responded saying that they had been at the Council of Soissoins against their will. In the time between the council of Metz and the synod at Thionville, Ebbo realized his predicament and approached several other bishops who suggested that Ebbo confess in secret and undergo secret penance, which he then promptly did. He then signed and confirmed the booklet describing his secret confession and handed it over to the gathered bishops, who relayed it to the emperor afterwards.[55] Both Thegan and the Astronomer suggest, then, that Ebbo got off easily, likely due to the complicity of his fellow bishops.[56]

These narratives all suggest similarities to Theutberga's case: the public nature of the trial, the stress on Ebbo's willingness and agency, the use of a booklet confirming an earlier confession which was likewise publicized, and the actions of the bishops in imposing penance on Ebbo. They even hint at similar dealings to those that happened before the second, larger council in Aachen. Before Ebbo was officially tried in Thionville, he too was approached by bishops who beseeched him to do penance, whether out of sincerity or otherwise. Though no similar contemporary framing narrative as the Verbose Volume exists for Ebbo's case, we do have several other documents related to Ebbo's resignation that suggest, as the *Annales Bertiniani* mention, that Ebbo's booklet of confession had been publicized.[57] It was used, both by Ebbo, Ebbo's supporters and by Ebbo's opponents, to either contest or defend the status of his resignation and concomitant vacating of the see of Rheims.[58]

The most telling of these is a *libellus* compiled by Theoderich of Cambrai (r. 831/32–863) for the Council of Soissons in 853, a booklet that claims to be a continuation of a similar but earlier *libellus* composed by Jonas of Orléans (c. 760–843) after the Synod of Thionville.[59] In the introduction to Jonas' *libellus*, Theoderich is not circumspect in his opinion: the booklet would show that Ebbo had been deposed [[*Ebonem*] *manifestum est fuisse depositum*].[60] Ebbo is

54 Thegan, *Gesta Hludowici imperatoris*, 242–52; Booker, *Past Convictions*, 187–88.

55 Astronomer, *Vita Hludowici imperatoris*, 500–02; Booker, *Past Convictions*, 187–88.

56 Booker, *Past Convictions*, 189–90.

57 For a slightly longer overview, see Booker, *Past Convictions*, 188–89.

58 Patzold, *Episcopus*, 325–31.

59 Theoderich of Cambrai, *Libellus Theoderici Cameracensis*, ed. Wilfried Hartmann, MGH Conc. 3, (Hannover: Hahnsche Buchhandlung, 1984).

60 Theoderich, *Libellus*, 290.

said to have signed a confirmation of his confession at the Synod of Thionville with the following contents:

> Ego Ebo indignus episcopus recognoscens fragilitatem meam et pondera peccatorum meorum testes confessores meos Aiulfum videlicet archiepiscopum et Badaradum episcopum necnon et Modoinum episcopum constitui mihi iudices delictorum meorum et puram ipsis confessionem dedi, quaerens remedium poenitendi et salutem animae meae, ut recederem ab officio et ministerio pontificali, quo me recognosco esse indignum et alienum me reddens pro reatibus meis, in quibus peccasse secreto ipsis confessus sum, eo scilicet modo, ut ipsi sint testes alio succedendi et consecrandi subrogandique in loco meo, qui digne praeesse et prodesse possit ecclesiae, cui hactenus indignus praefui. Et ut inde ultra nullam repetitionem aut interpellationem auctoritate canonica facere valeam, manu propria mea subscribens firmavi. Ebo quondam episcopus subscripsi.
>
> [I, Ebbo, unworthy bishop, aware of my weakness and the weight of my sins, have appointed three witnesses [and] confessors, namely Archbishop Aiulf [of Bourges] and Bishop Badurad [of Paderborn] and also Bishop Modoin [of Autun], as judges of my sins, and I have given them a pure confession, asking for the remedy of penance and the well-being of my soul, that I would retire from the episcopal office and ministry, for which I recognize myself to be unworthy, and declaring myself unsuitable because of my sins, which I secretly confessed to them I had committed, in the sense that they themselves would be witnesses to the succession, consecration and election in my place of someone who, with dignity, can lead and further the bishopric that until now I headed unworthily; and so that furthermore I will not be capable of any reclamation or judicial appeal based on canonical authority, I have confirmed this, subscribing in my own hand. I Ebbo onetime bishop have subscribed.][61]

In its framing of the events the *libellus* sticks closely to narrative of the *Annales Bertiniani* but it also provides several canonical legitimizations of the trial's proceedings and the definitive nature of Ebbo's resignation.[62] The Council of Soissons was convened by Hincmar, among other reasons, to oversee the

61 Theoderich, *Libellus*, 291; translation gratefully obtained from Mayke de Jong when I was still a participant in her 2011 Research Seminar in Utrecht.

62 Theoderich, *Libellus*, 290–93.

deposition of all priests Ebbo had ordained during his brief return to the see of Rheims in 840. Affirming the definitive nature of the former archbishop's own deposition was an important step for Hincmar, both in ridding himself of his predecessor's legacy, and in fully legitimizing his own ordination as archbishop.[63] This *libellus* includes a long list of subscriptions of bishops that had attended and approved the proceedings of Thionville, and it also lists another set of three *testes* who had ostensibly witnessed Ebbo's confession to the three *testes confessores* mentioned in the confirmation: Notho of Arles (r. ca. 824–35), Theoderich himself, and Achardus of Noyon (c. 830/838). Ebbo presented these men to his *exceptis iudicibus* [chosen judges], who are not named but might be assumed to be the three *confessores* from before, to attest to his having given a confession.[64] Ebbo then accepted the verdict of these judges, and according to his own confession, withdrew from his *ministerium*. Though the exact nature of the offence Ebbo had confessed to was never revealed, Theoderich adds that the crime was so serious that had Ebbo confessed to it before he had been ordained, he would have never been ordained in the first place.[65]

Not only was Hincmar involved in the Council of Soissons in 853, Theoderich's *libellus* is also cited in *De Divortio*.[66] In his second *responsio*, Hincmar tries to establish Ebbo's trial as an exemplar of proper procedure: all standards for an ecclesiastical trial were met and there had been no unbecoming intermixing of protocols. Hincmar briefly recounts the events of 835, sticking closely to the script provided by Theoderich's *libellus*, whilst placing especial emphasis on the presence of an accusation which Ebbo received from the synod, the presence of his elected judges and the presence of his witnesses. Though, as will become clear, this is an oversimplification of the proceedings, it reveals Hincmar's wider interest in having Ebbo's resignation seem as simple and straightforward as possible. Later on he would quote from the Psuedo-Isidorian Decretals specifically on the nature of proper procedure to claim that four types of persons needed to be present at a judgement: chosen judges [*iudices electos*], accusers [*accusatores*], defenders [*defensores*] and witnesses [*testes*].[67] The way in which Ebbo's confession is framed in Theoderich's *libellus* makes it seem as if all four groups, Ebbo being the *defensor*, were present

63 Booker, *Past Convictions*, 195; Hartmann, *Synoden der Karolingerzeit*, 245–49; Patzold, *Episcopus*, 325–30.

64 Theoderich, *Libellus*, 291; Charles the Bald's already mentioned letter lists the same names, suggesting he either had access to Theoderich's *libellus* or to a different version of these proceedings stemming from the council of Thionville itself.

65 Theoderich, *Libellus*, 291.

66 Hincmar, *De Divortio*, ed. Böhringer, 128.

67 Hincmar, *De Divortio*, ed. Böhringer, 168.

to hear and judge Ebbo's crimes, lending a stronger air of officiality to the proceedings that, from the narrative accounts, appeared a lot more muddled. Ebbo himself had tried to exploit the ambiguity of what exactly had occurred at Thionville in 835 to his advantage, making similar arguments to invalidate the proceedings as Hincmar had done for the councils of 860. In his first *Apologeticum*, Ebbo would denounce the status of the synod, calling it a *tribunale palatinum* instead, to which he had been forced to show up—something a synod could not have made him do.[68] He had also not been convicted of a crime, but had rather by divine inspiration confessed his sins to three bishops, Aiulf, Badurad and Modoin, and undertaken his penance willingly.[69] In this way, Ebbo sought to reframe the words of his booklet of confirmation, which he also inserted into his *Apologeticum*, to turn his act of confession into an exemplary act, which had allowed him to purge his sins and to eventually return to his see.

Though Ebbo's counterarguments do not figure explicitly in *De Divortio*, Hincmar does certainly guard against them implicitly when arguing the differences between a divorce case and an episcopal resignation. Already in his first *responsio* Hincmar had said that it was forbidden for a woman to attempt to divorce her husband on the basis of a secret confession. This argument would return several times throughout *De Divortio*.[70] Another difference was that a man and a woman, even if divorced, could and should ideally be reconciled and brought back together, whereas a bishop who had been deposed could not be reconciled to his see.[71] This argument both thwarts Lothar's attempts at getting divorced, for Hincmar holds to one of the strictest standards for divorce and remarriage among early medieval theologians,[72] and serves as a surety against Lothar's divorce potentially succeeding: whatever the outcome, a bishop's deposition was a whole other matter than the separation of a husband and wife.[73] Husbands and their wives were simply of another order, to which separate rules applied, both in regard to legal proceedings as in regard

68 Ebbo of Rheims, *Apologetici Ebonis forma prior*, ed. Albert Werminghoff, MGH Conc.*a* 2/2 (Hannover: Hahn, 1908), 795.

69 Ebbo, *Apologetici forma prior*, 797.

70 Hincmar, *De Divortio*, ed. Böhringer, 123, 128–29, 139–40.

71 Hincmar, *De Divortio*, ed. Böhringer, 127–28.

72 Stone and West, *Divorce of King Lothar*, 45–54; Riccardo Bof and Conrad Leyser, "Divorce and Remarriage Between Late Antiquity and the Early Middle Ages: Canon Law and Conflict Resolution," in *Making Early Medieval Societies Conflict and Belonging in the Latin West, 300–1200*, ed. Kate Cooper and Conrad Leyser (Cambridge: Cambridge University Press, 2016).

73 Hincmar, *De Divortio*, ed. Böhringer, 125–29.

to the possibility of reconciliation. He bases this on the notion that a man and a woman, once joined in marriage, would become one flesh, and would therefore become inseparable as regards human actions. If a man and a woman divorced, which was only admissible in the case of adultery, they still ought to both remain celibate and ideally seek reconciliation after the guilty party had done penance.[74] Any clergyman who resigned from his see, according to both Hincmar and Theoderich's authorities, could not return to his erstwhile position.[75]

Though plenty of decretals and canons give Hincmar the possibility to show that the manner in which Ebbo had resigned from his see had been according to due process, he had a harder time proving that a husband and a wife should not be able to divorce in similar fashion. In a marginal addition to the main text Hincmar even claims that the practice of attempting to divorce or to convict one's spouse on the basis of such written confessions was widespread at the time.[76] Hincmar, in accordance with his earlier assertions that Theutberga should be accorded a proper trial, claims that a divorce is not possible without there having first been a public judgement of examination [sine public examinationis iudicio].[77] The conclusion of Hincmar's second *responsio* then goes as follows:

> Unde cautissime ac prudentissime auctoritatis ecclesiasticae disciplinalis providit discretio, ut ab officio sacri ministerii conscientia testimonium perhibente viri ecclesiastici se removere et dignis poenitentiae fructibus possint insistere, [...] Vir autem et mulier, quoniam auctoritate sacra dicente iam non sunt duo, sed una caro, secreta confessione vel porrecto libello separari non possunt [...].
>
> [Hence the disciplinary discretion of ecclesiastical authority provides very cautiously and prudently that ecclesiastical men may be able to remove themselves from the office of sacred ministry, with their conscience providing evidence, and may apply themselves to the worthy fruits of penance [...]. But a husband and wife, since holy authority says

74 Hincmar, *De Divortio*, ed. Böhringer, 125–26.

75 Ebbo, as well as Hrabanus Maurus, who was to be Ebbo's keeper for a while after Ebbo's resignation, appealed to a different, more lenient tradition that allowed clergymen who had done proper penance to return to their station. Kottje, "Buße oder Strafe?," 456–62.

76 Hincmar, *De Divortio*, ed. Böhringer, 128.

77 Hincmar, *De Divortio*, ed. Böhringer, 128.

> now they are not two but one flesh, cannot separate by secret confession or by presenting a notification[...].][78]

Hincmar therefore wanted his readers to believe that comparing the divorce proceedings to the ecclesiastical resignation proceedings was like comparing apples to oranges: they were fruits of a different order. For his argument to work, it was important that he framed the proceedings of Theutberga's divorce case as a misguided attempt at ecclesiastical procedure, which thus demanded another public judgement to set right. Here, the mixed messages sent by the three accounts of Theutberga's trial certainly helped Hincmar establish a narrative that makes it seem like Theutberga in fact made a secret confession, the secrecy of which was then improperly handled and eventually breached. This allowed Hincmar to, in effect, claim a mistrial and to demand a retrial, throwing a spanner in the works of Lothar's divorce machinations. Hincmar claimed that if the bishops had indeed received Theutberga's confession in secret, they should burden her with the proper type of penance, but no more. If they however wished to carry through with the divorce and find the truth behind the many rumors that were causing scandal all around the realm—scandal to which the proceedings of 860 might well only be contributing—they should try her publicly, and her brother Hucbert as well.[79] This furthermore allowed Hincmar to cast Ebbo's resignation as the perfect embodiment of a proper ecclesiastical procedure by which a sinful bishop might resign, with the attendant judgement of his peers, from his *ministerium*. In one fell swoop, Ebbo's trial is both distanced from the divorce proceedings and used to discredit their procedures.

Neither the divorce proceedings nor those of the resignation can be categorized so easily, however, and they both present similar problems. In both cases, suspicions or accusations of coercion and threat are raised: neither Ebbo nor Theutberga was truly free to do as they pleased. This tension could be exploited both to make the would-be penitents seem dishonest or scheming, or to make the parties that presided over their cases seem of ill or even fraudulent intent. Furthermore, the status of their confession was suspect in both cases: Theutberga's was read aloud, and in the Verbose Volume treated as a public confession for which public penance was warranted. In Ebbo's case, the nature of the crime to which he had confessed was never revealed, though many people both contemporary and modern have speculated on it. The booklet attesting to his secret confession was however publicized, as was Theutberga's full confession

78 Hincmar, *De Divortio*, ed. Böhringer, 129; Stone and West, *Divorce of King Lothar*, 120.

79 Hincmar, *De Divortio*, ed. Böhringer, 130, 184–87.

apparently, and both these measures go against the original intention of the possibility for secret confession: that penitents could repent in secret without fearing that their exact sins would become known to all.[80] In both cases, what should have been a penitential proceeding became a method to delegitimize and to defame the penitent, in effect making it impossible for Ebbo to hold ecclesiastical office or for Theutberga to serve as queen.

Mayke de Jong has pointed out that this method of ridding oneself of a political opponent remained a popular tactic after Louis the Pious' reign.[81] Louis the Pious himself had undergone a public penance which perhaps even more resembled Theutberga's trial than Ebbo's did.[82] Ebbo's own resignation and the attendant proceedings had themselves occurred as part of Louis the Pious' restoration, in which the emperor's erstwhile degradation was reversed step by step. The three cases were most certainly linked, and Hincmar even refers to Louis' penance in *De Divortio*, but for understandable reasons—Louis' public penance of 833 had been struck from the record and denounced as a false trial—it could likely no longer serve as a direct legal precedent for later cases.[83] That De Jong was certainly right about the influence of Louis' political and legal experimentations with penance as both a source of legitimization for a ruler when undertaken voluntarily, and as a means to depose, demote or otherwise neutralize a political opponent when it was imposed, is shown by the penitential narrative presented for Theutberga in *De Divortio*.

Yet such methods were by no means unchallengeable. Both the divorce case and Ebbo's resignation are testaments to the fact that establishing an authoritative narrative of a particularly important political event was paramount. Conciliar degrees were circulated, sometimes in multiple versions, and they were framed in specific ways to guide the understanding of their recipients. Hincmar was not alone in being able to see through these framing narratives and to discern the true intentions of the composers; he was similarly no stranger to compiling such framing narratives himself. The official productions stemming from councils were important tools, both of propaganda and, as Hincmar shows, of argumentation. Especially prominent trials or events from the past, like Ebbo's and Louis the Pious' could be used as precedent for later cases. Again, this was not an unchallengeable proposition. Yet as Hincmar treatment of the suggestion of legal precedent between Ebbo's resignation and Theutberga's divorce shows, it was not the principle of precedent but

80 Hincmar, *De Divortio*, ed. Böhringer, 176.

81 De Jong, *The Penitential State*, 264.

82 *Episcoporum de poenitentia*, ed. Werminghoff.

83 Hincmar, *De Divortio*, ed. Böhringer, 247; Jong, *Penitential State*, 214–59.

the actual proceedings and the applicability of these proceedings that were in question. Like nowadays, legal precedent could not simply be claimed, it had to be argued.

That not all agreed on Hincmar's neat divisions of justice is obvious: the bishops on Lothar's side thought that the procedures they had followed had been perfectly applicable. In Ebbo's case, there similarly were multiple interested parties. Hincmar's terseness and strictness in handling his predecessor's legacy had likely ensured that Ebbo's resignation would be long debated still: as late as 868 Pope Hadrian II (r. 867–72) had to intervene in the matter when Charles the Bald had Wulfad (d. 876), one of the priests ordained by Ebbo during his brief period of restoration, ordained as archbishop of Bourges.[84] Despite what amounted to a gag order issued by Hadrian, the case so haunted Hincmar, that in the 877 *Visio Bernoldi*, he could not refrain from getting a parting shot in at Ebbo, depicting him as being tormented in the afterlife. Even after being saved by Bernold's intercession, Hincmar still depicted Ebbo as merely a layman when he ascended to heaven.[85]

Theutberga's divorce case had a slightly shorter afterlife. Though *De Divortio* apparently circulated, it was swiftly overtaken by events following the councils of Aachen in 860. Lothar moved ahead with marrying Waldrada, again assisted by his loyal bishops at the Council of Metz in 863. When he sent his two most trusted bishops, Theutgaud of Trier and Gunthar of Cologne, to Rome to have the proceedings of this council confirmed, however, Pope Nicholas I (r. 858–67) turned on him, nullifying the council's decisions and deposing Theutgaud and Gunthar, subsequently making life very difficult for Lothar. Even when Lothar had managed to gain some support for his divorce from his uncle Charles the Bald, the pope remained adamant in refusing to let Lothar divorce Theutberga and marry Waldrada. With the death of Nicholas I and the ordination of Hadrian II, Lothar hoped his fortunes had changed. Yet in 869 Hadrian II only granted Lothar a much less grandiose meeting than expected, and though gifts were exchanged which could signal the pope's forgiveness of Lothar's erstwhile behaviour, all of this was done on the basis of the oath Lothar swore that he had not had contact with Waldrada after Nicholas I had excommunicated her. As the *Annales Bertiniani*, at the time kept up to date by Hincmar, relate, Lothar had sworn this falsely. On his way back from Rome, he and many of his men who

---

84 Hadrian II, *Epistola 3*, MGH *Epistola* 6, ed. Ernst Dümmler, Ernst Perels et al., (Berlin: Weidmannsche Buchhandlung, 1925), 699–700.

85 Hincmar, *Visio Bernoldi*: Maaike van der Lugt, ed., "Tradition and Revision. The textual tradition of Hincmar of Reims' *Visio Bernoldi*. With a New Critical Edition," *Archivum Latinitatis Medii Aevi* 52 (1994): 140–48.

had not spoken up about this falsehood, were struck by a plague and perished in a *iudicium dei*.[86] Lothar was not alive to argue back, and as his kingdom was being divvied up by his uncles in the absence of legitimate heirs, his erstwhile supporters had other things to worry about.

86 Waitz, *Annales Bertiniani*, 100–01.

CHAPTER 7

Reading the Law in Royal Government: *Ius Commune* Texts and Administrative Mentalities in Thirteenth-Century England

Lucy Hennings

> Et de Lx s. de magistro W. de Kilkenny pro quibusdam libris sibi venditis.
>
> [And from Master W[illiam] de Kilkenny, 60 shillings for the purchase of certain books for him].[1]

This enigmatic and nonspecific entry in the Wardrobe accounts for the period between the 33rd and 36th regnal years (1248–51) of the reign of Henry III, is one of only a handful of pieces of evidence for book ownership in English royal government during the thirteenth century, and the reign of that king in particular.[2] Before the Richmond inventory of 1535, no official record of an English royal library survives, much less any cataloguing of books that may have been in use in the offices of the administration more broadly. However, to argue that an absence of a formal inventory should imply that there was not any significant book ownership or use in royal government before the sixteenth century would clearly be misguided. Although the evidence is more dispersed and fragmentary, work done by such scholars as Susan Cavanaugh has unequivocally demonstrated the acquisition and use of books at Westminster over the thirteenth and fourteenth centuries.[3] The lack of clear evidence for the reign of Henry III in particular should not be assumed to demonstrate a break

1 Kew, The National Archives, E 372/95 *Rot.* 7 *m.* 1, printed in *The Wardrobe Accounts of Henry III*, ed. Benjamin Linley Wild, Publications of the Pipe Roll Society, n.s. 58 (London: Pipe Roll Society, 2012), 53.

2 The author would like to extend their gratitude to the AHRC, the Institute of Historical Research and the Royal Historical Society for providing funding for the DPhil studies from which this article is drawn. Particular thanks go to Professors John Watts and Chris Wickham, and Dr. Katarina Stultrajterova, who read and commented on earlier drafts of this paper.

3 Susan H. Cavanaugh, "Royal Books: King John to Richard II," *The Library: Transactions of the Bibliographical Society*, 6th series, 10:4 (1988): 304–16; Charles F. Briggs, *Giles of Rome's* De Regimine Principum. *Reading and Writing Politics at Court and University, c.1275–c.1525* (Cambridge: Cambridge University Press, 1999), 54.

 | DOI:10.1163/9789004448650_009

period in royal book culture between the reigns of his father King John and his son Edward I. In order to understand the influence of reading habits on the development of the mentalities of English government during this period, it must be situated within its broader chronological context, and within a consideration of manuscript acquisition and use in England at this time more broadly.

The study of mentalities sits at the intersection between the "real" character of people's thoughts and their textual transmission, thus to understand the mental world of thirteenth-century English government requires recognition of the textual traditions that both shaped and were shaped by its broader conceptual context.[4] To explore the full dimensions of administrative culture of thirteenth-century England, and the reign of Henry III in particular, it is necessary to reconstruct the textual milieu within which its members operated. This can be achieved through an analytical synthesis in which authorship and textual content are considered alongside their material manuscript context. These manuscripts were anything but static artefacts. Their various stages of compilation, annotation and circulation are fundamental to our understanding of the mental world of their producers, owners and readers. Certainly, various aspects of the material life cycle of the text are recognized as being of considerable importance in understanding their reception and influence, and the literature on this topic is complex and extensive.[5] For consideration of legal texts in particular, some areas of this scholarship are of especial importance. These include the development of glossing and marginalia, which were of central importance to the study and teaching of learned law in the High Middle Ages.[6] Another key element of textual culture is the organization of compilations and other miscellanies, as the intertextual relationships in any given compilation also provide important insights to reading preferences and *habitus*, as much as any individual text within a collection.[7] In considering these various

---

4 Michel Vovelle, *Ideologies and Mentalities*, trans. Eamon O'Flaherty (Cambridge: Cambridge University Press, 1990), 12.

5 A good introduction to these discussions can be found in, Stephen G. Nichols and Siegfried Wenzel, "Introduction," in *The Whole Book: Cultural Perspectives on the Medieval Miscellany*, ed. Stephen G. Nichols and Siegfried Wenzel (Ann Arbor: University of Michigan Press, 1996), 2–6. Elsewhere in this volume, Stefan Drechsler explores the importance of the text-iconography relationship in legal manuscripts, an area which has so far received little attention, "Production and Context of the Fourteenth-Century Norwegian Law Manuscript, Lundarbók," Chapter 1.

6 Stephen G. Nichols, "On the Sociology of Medieval Manuscript Annotation," in *Annotation and Its Texts*, ed. Stephen A. Barney (Oxford: Oxford University Press, 1991).

7 The most significant scholarship on this topic remains Malcolm B. Parkes, "The Influence of the Concepts of *Ordinatio* and *Compilatio* on the Development of the Book," in *Medieval*

elements in conjunction it is thus possible to provide a multi-layered commentary on the usage, reception and influence of the texts contained within various manuscript sources. Fundamentally, it is essential to recognize that individual texts were not fixed static objects, and manuscripts played a key part in the life-cycle of texts and readership interpretations.[8]

It has increasingly been recognised that the development of theories of the state and conceptions of kingship and royal government in England, particularly from the thirteenth century onwards, was influenced by the *Ius Commune*, the Roman Civil and Canon laws, even as the English Common Law asserted its academic and procedural independence. Much of the literature on this topic has tended to focus on the reign of Edward I, but his father's rule also saw the adoption of vocabularies of government which drew upon these intellectual traditions.[9] This influence was facilitated by both the circulation of manuscript material, and by the growing prominence in royal government of an internationalizing clerical elite, an increasing proportion of whom were university-trained, or experienced in diplomacy and the workings of the papal *curia* in particular. Master William of Kilkenny, whose book purchases were a lone example of textual acquisition within the royal government at this time, was a prominent member of this network. Educated at Oxford, Kilkenny first appeared in the records as a royal clerk (*clericus regis*) in 1232, and in 1234 he was appointed as one of the king's proctors at the papal curia. He went on to serve as Keeper of the Wardrobe and then Chancellor, resigning from his office in 1255, when he was elected to the bishopric of Ely, although he continued

---

Learning and Literature. Essays Presented to Richard William Hunt, ed. Jonathan James G. Alexander and Margaret T. Gibson (Oxford: Clarendon Press, 1976). On intertextual connections see also, Rolf H. Bremmer Jr, "More than Language: Law and Textual Communities in Medieval Frisia," and Fangzhe Qiu, "Law, Law-Books and Tradition in Early Medieval Ireland," Chapters 4 and 5, respectively, in this volume.

8 John G.A. Pocock, "Texts as Events," in *The Politics of Discourse: The Literature and History of Seventeenth-Century England*, ed. Kevin Sharpe and Steven N. Zwicker (London: University of California Press, 1987).

9 Gaines Post, *Studies in Medieval Legal Thought. Public Law and the State, 1100–1322* (Princeton NJ: Princeton University Press, 1964); Ernst Kantorowicz, "Kingship under the Impact of Scientific Jurisprudence," in *Selected Studies* (Locust Valley: J.J. Augstin, 1965), 151–66; Joseph P. Canning, "Ideas of the State in Thirteenth and Fourteenth-Century Commentators on the Roman Law," *Transactions of the Royal Historical Society*, 5th series, 33 (1983): 1–27; for a recent exploration of the reign of Edward I in this context, see Caroline Burt, *Edward I and the Governance of England, 1272–1307* (Cambridge: Cambridge University Press, 2013). For the reign of Henry III, see Lucy Hennings, "*Haec detestabilis adjectio*: The Clause *non obstante* and the Governance of England During the Personal Rule of Henry III, 1230–1250," *Proceedings of the Fifteenth International Congress of Medieval Canon Law* (forthcoming).

to serve the king in a diplomatic capacity.[10] Although the details of the books purchased are not included in the wardrobe accounts, given Kilkenny's training and career it is not implausible to presume that they may well have been texts of the civil and canon laws. An analysis of the circulation of these types of manuscript in thirteenth-century England can explore the kinds of material which played a role in shaping the intellectual milieu of royal government and its administrative mentalities. Added to the two laws, it is also worth considering the circulation of material related to the art of letter writing, *dictamen*, as this was crucial in the communication of these legal vocabularies, and particularly their application to questions of secular authority and rulership.

The manuscripts of canon law represent the largest proportion of manuscripts from the three categories being considered here. An earlier historiographical tradition has minimized the influence of canon law beyond the sphere of church administration in favor of a narrative of the development of the English Common law. However, more recent scholarship has emphasized the vitality of this legal tradition in England, emphasizing not only the creative contributions made by English canonists, but also the cross-fertilization with other strands of law and government.[11] The academic study of canon law flourished alongside the everyday pragmatic necessity of church law in practice. This continuation of practice meant that not only was there a diverse and growing field of academic commentary on existing texts, but there was a steady influx of new laws and texts to be commented upon. This gave canon law a vitality and applicability that went well beyond the schoolroom and framed a far broader readership and circulation of manuscripts.

Certainly, the flourishing of canon law and the profusion of manuscript material from the twelfth century onwards owed a great deal to the work of the schools and the undertakings of the preeminent law teachers of Bologna in particular.[12] Gratian's *Decretum* was by far and away the most prevalent canon

10 *Patent Rolls of the Reign of Henry III: Preserved in the Public Record Office*, 6 vols, ed. Henry C. Maxwell Lyte (London: H. M. S. O., 1901–13), 3: 64; Edward Foss, *The Judges of England, From the Time of the Conquest*, 9 vols. (London: Longman, Brown, Green and Longmans, 1948–64), 2: 375–77; Robert C. Stacey, "Kilkenny, William of (d. 1256), Administrator and Bishop of Ely," *Oxford Dictionary of National Biography*, accessed December 11, 2017, http://www.oxforddnb.com/view/10.1093/ref:odnb/9780198614128.001.0001/odnb-9780198614128-e-15527; *Patent Rolls Henry III*, ed. Henry C. Maxwell Lyte, 4: 487.

11 William Stubbs, *Seventeen Lectures on the Study of Medieval and Modern History and Kindred Subjects* (Oxford: Clarendon Press, 1886), 313; for more recent rehabilitation of the place of canon law in English legal history, cf. Paul Brand, *The Origins of the English Legal Profession* (Oxford: Blackwell, 1992), 145.

12 James A. Brundage, *Medieval Canon Law* (London: Longman, 1995), 57.

law text of this period, often surviving in multiple copies in a single collection.[13] However exceptionally popular Gratian's codification of canon law had been, in England as on the continent, it did not by any means constitute a culmination of canonist studies. Over the course of the late twelfth and thirteenth centuries, the leading canonist jurists, based primarily in Bologna, followed in two main intellectual trends—the decretists, who produced commentaries and glosses on the *decretum*, and the decretalists, who responded to the condition of canon law as a living and evolving legal system by continuing to collect, codify and comment upon the new laws, mostly issued in papal letters.[14] The works of both decretists and decretalists survive from thirteenth-century England, reflecting the responsive and reflective character of the study of canon law in England, as well as its close association with the major intellectual trends of juridical thought in Bologna.

Of the twelfth-century decretists, Huguccio had by far the most widespread reception in England, with both his *Summa* on the *Decretum* and his *Liber Derivationem* on etymologies circulating in English collections. A partial copy of Huguccio's *Summa* survives in Cambridge, Pembroke College, MS 72, formerly belonging to the Benedictine Abbey of Bury St. Edmunds, while Durham, Cathedral, MS C. 1. 20 preserves a fourteenth-century copy of the *Liber Derivationem*.[15] The existence of further copies of this text can be attested by testamentary evidence, as Abbot Robert of Sutton bequeathed a copy to Peterborough Abbey upon his death in 1274, and the bequest to St. Paul's Cathedral by Ralph Baldock, Bishop of London, found in an inventory of 1313–14 covering over five rolls, included both the *Summa* and the *Liber Derivationum*.[16] The other decretist whose works circulated widely in thirteenth-century England was Bartholomew of Brescia, whose gloss on the *Decretum* revised the *Glossa ordinaria* of Johannes Teutonicus around 1240 and was used as a standard gloss on copies of the *Decretum* after this date, such as the copy preserved in London, British Library, MS Royal 9.C.iii. The circulation of the works by these decretists indicates that reception of Gratian in England was anything but passive in the

13 Neil R. Ker, *Medieval Libraries of Great Britain: A List of Surviving Books*, 2nd ed. (London: Royal Historical Society, 1964), 60–76.

14 Oswald J. Reichel, *The Canon Law of Church Institutions*, vol. 1 (London: Society for Promoting Christian Knowledge, 1922), 28.

15 Ker, *Medieval Libraries*, 18, 69.

16 Montague R. James, ed., *List of Manuscripts Formerly in Peterborough Abbey Library*, Supplement to the Bibliographical Society's Transactions, No. 5 (Oxford: Oxford University Press, 1926), 23; Christopher M. Woolgar, ed., *Testamentary Records of the English and Welsh Episcopate, 1200–1413*, Canterbury and York Society 102 (Woodbridge, UK: Boydell & Brewer 2011), 75–81.

thirteenth century and engaged with the developments of glosses and commentaries by the circle of these scholars in Bologna.

While the decretists explored and clarified the great codification of Gratian, their work was not the whole sum of canon law scholarship in the twelfth and thirteenth centuries. The work of the decretalists, concentrating on the new compilations of papal letters and producing commentaries upon the same, formed a major strand of Bolognese juridical output in the thirteenth century and increasingly dominated the English canon law material of the same period. The most widespread of the decretal texts was the *Liber extra*, the standardized compilation of the decretals of Gregory IX, undertaken by Raymund of Peñafort and confirmed as authoritative in 1234. As with the *Decretum*, the influence of this later text can be seen in cases where there is evidence for multiple ownership by both individual collectors and within larger library collections. The surviving manuscripts from Durham Cathedral include at least six copies of the *Decretales Gregorii noni* dating from the mid to late thirteenth century, indicating the widespread circulation and popularity of this compilation during this period.[17] The popularity of the decretals also stimulated an interest in the literature of commentary which developed around them in decretalist scholarship. Perhaps the most prominent of the decretalists was Raymund of Peñafort himself; in addition to his great codification project, manuscripts of Raymund's *Summa Casuum* survive in multiple copies from thirteenth-century, originating from a diverse number of collections, including Lincoln Cathedral and Christ Church Canterbury.[18] The popularity of this work can be attested by the existence of abridgements, such as that preserved in London, Lambeth Palace, MS 404, and another included in the bequest of Abbot Robert of Sutton to Peterborough Abbey in 1274.[19] Other works by Raymund also circulated in thirteenth-century England, although not as widely. His *Summa de Poenitentia et Matrimonio* appears to survive in only one copy, now preserved in the archives of Merton College Oxford, although more copies may have existed that do not now survive, as six copies of the "Summa fratris Raimundi de poenitencia" were listed in the 1247 catalogue of the manuscripts of Gloucester abbey.[20]

17 Ker, *Medieval Libraries*, 69–70.

18 Ker, *Medieval Libraries*, 37, 87, 118.

19 Montague R. James, ed., *A Descriptive Catalogue of the Manuscripts in the Library of Lambeth Palace. The Mediaeval Manuscripts* (Cambridge: Cambridge University Press, 1932), 559–60; James, *Peterborough Abbey Manuscripts*, 23. Sutton's bequest also included a full and unabridged version of Raymund's *Summa*.

20 Rodney M. Thomson, ed., *A Descriptive Catalogue of the Medieval Manuscripts of Merton College, Oxford*, (Cambridge: Cambridge University Press, 2009), 51–52; For the Gloucester abbey catalogue, see Cambridge, Trinity College, MS 724, printed in Thomas Hearne,

The pre-eminence and authoritative character attributed to the work of Raymund of Peñafort in Gregory IX's preamble to the decretals certainly appears to have be matched by the dominance of his works in thirteenth-century English collections.

Of the earlier commentators on the decretals, most prominent in the English material are the works of Geoffrey of Trani, whose *Summa super titulis Decretalium*, composed ca. 1243 survives in multiple copies from English collections. Indeed, the speed with which Trani's work was transmitted to England should be noted, as the copy surviving in Worcester, Cathedral Chapter Library, MS F.7 was likely composed at Oxford not long after 1251, that is to say less than a decade after the composition of the work.[21] Another surviving thirteenth-century copy belonged to Reading Abbey, now Cambridge, Pembroke College, MS 274 and the *Summa Gaufridi* listed in the bequest of Robert of Sutton may be identified with this text.[22] Later in the thirteenth-century perhaps the greatest contribution of glossatorial scholarship can be seen in the establishment of the *glossa ordinaria* of Bernard Botone of Parma, which circulated from 1263 onwards.[23] Given this date of composition, Bernard's gloss has relatively little significance for the study of canon law in England during the reign of Henry III, however, it is nonetheless valuable to observe its prominence in English *decretal* manuscripts from the late thirteenth century onwards, most prominently in the so-called Smithfield *Decretals*.[24] Interest in the latest developments of the Bolognese jurists continued throughout the long thirteenth-century and was not a transitory or insignificant phenomenon.

While it is thus plain that the academic discipline of canon law played a substantial role in shaping its English reception, it is crucial to assert that the scholastic study of the canon law over the thirteenth century was anything but abstract and detached from the concerns of practice and utility. The works of both the decretists and the decretalists aimed at the creation and dissemination of standardized texts and associated commentaries, reflecting the practical and utilitarian focus of university studies in canon law during the

Johannis, confratris & monachi Glastoniensis, chronica sive historia de rebus Glastoniensibus, 2 vols. (Oxford, 1726), 2, 430.

21 Rodney M. Thomson and Michael Gullick, eds., *A Descriptive Catalogue of the Medieval Manuscripts in Worcester Cathedral Library* (Woodbridge, UK: D.S. Brewer, 2001), 8–9.

22 Alan Coates, *English Medieval Books: The Reading Abbey Collections from Foundation to Dispersal* (Oxford: Oxford University Press, 1999), 158; James, *Peterborough Abbey Manuscripts*, 23.

23 Beryl Smalley and Stephen Kuttner, "The 'Glossa Ordinaria' to the Gregorian Decretals," *English Historical Review* 60, 236 (1945): 97–105.

24 London, British Library, MS Royal 10.E.iv.

thirteenth century.[25] But of these two trends of scholarship it has been shown that the texts of the decretalists enjoyed greater circulation and popularity in thirteenth-century England than those of the decretists. This was more than academic fashion—it demonstrated a desire to remain acquainted with the latest developments and assertions of papal legal thought and its interpretation by the leading juristic thinkers of the time.[26]

Certainly, the manuscript evidence for canon law material in England demonstrates a distinct strand of pragmatic material, closely connected to the practice of canon law rather than its theoretical dimensions. Given the focus on utility that lay at the heart of the conception of canon law, making an absolute distinction between scholarly and pragmatic material is neither useful nor appropriate. It may perhaps be more useful to refer to this more pragmatic material as syncretic, as it occupied a space and served a function that was divorced from neither the scholarly nor the pragmatic fields. Even individuals who might be at first identified with university scholastic law also produced works which had a distinctly procedural flavor and focus, and these formed an important category among the canon law material received in thirteenth-century English collections. The most prominent of these authors was the unimpeachably scholastic Tancred of Bologna, whose procedural manual the *Ordo iudiciarius* circulated widely in England as well as abroad. This work, which was composed 1214–16 survives in multiple copies from this period, including two copies preserved in the archives of Worcester Cathedral.[27]

In addition to being widely read, Tancred was widely imitated, and a number of other similar *ordines* also circulated, including the *Ordo Iudiciarius "Olim"* of Otto of Pavia as well as the *Summa aurea* of the English canonist William of Drogheda. Lawrence of Somercotes, a Canon of Chichester, and possibly a kinsman to Cardinal Robert Somercotes and the king's clerk John of Somercotes, was another English ecclesiastic to have composed a procedural canon

25 Stephen Kuttner, *The History of Ideas and Doctrines of Canon Law in the Middle Ages*, 2nd ed., (Aldershot: Variorum Reprints, 1992), 1–16, originally published as "Harmony from Dissonance: An Interpretation of Medieval Canon Law," *Wimmer Lecture X, 1956, St. Vincent College* (Latrobe, PA: Archabbey Press, 1960); Edward Peters, "The Sacred Muses and the Twelve Table: Legal Education and Practice, Latin Philology and Rhetoric, and Roman History," in *Law as Profession and Practice in Medieval Europe. Essays in Honour of James A. Brundage*, ed. Kenneth Pennington and Melodie H. Eichbauer (Farnham: Ashgate, 2011), 144.

26 Giulio Silano, "Of Sleep and Sleeplessness: The Papacy and the Law, 1150–1300," in *The Religious Roles of the Papacy: Ideals and Realities 1150–1300*, ed. Christopher Ryan (Toronto: Pontifical Institute of Medieval Studies, 1989).

27 Worcester, Cathedral Library, MSS F.47 ff. 1–35 and F.159 ff. 87–98.

law treatise.[28] His treatise on ecclesiastical elections in England was composed around the year 1254 and explicitly addressed the question of harmonizing diverse forms in practice. Somercotes was direct about the practical purpose of his treatise, complaining that canon law teaching did not sufficiently engage with the procedural realities of episcopal elections, with the possibility of great danger arising from variation.[29] Multiple copies of this text survive, and while the majority date from the fourteenth century onwards, at least two can be dated to the thirteenth century, London, Lambeth Palace, MS 74 and another was recorded on the 1280 cartulary of Lincoln Cathedral.[30] That manuscripts of this relatively minor work circulated and survive in some number within a relatively short period of time after its composition indicate its popularity and the relevance of the assertion Somercotes made attempting to unify scholastic teaching with the practice and necessities of canon law.

Among such "practical" texts, perhaps the most prominent category was that of formularies, or letter collections. As a genre these functioned to provide assistance to those involved in enforcing canon law, on a day-to-day and utilitarian basis.[31] Due to their commonly private and individual nature, formularies survive in far more limited numbers than more conventional scholastic legal manuscripts.[32] They could also vary enormously in their form and content and indeed their preservation often reflected their interest or relevance on other topics, and they were frequently included in manuscript compilations with more theoretical material. One example of this is in the quite widely circulated judge-delegate formulary known as "A., B., C., iudices." Two early thirteenth-century English copies of this text survive, one in Cambridge, Gonville and Caius College, MS 150 (44) and the other in London, British

28 For the career of Laurence of Somercotes and his possible familiar connections, see C.H. Lawrence, "Somercotes [Somerton], Laurence of (fl. 1245–1258), Ecclesiastic and Canonist," *Oxford Dictionary of National Biography*, accessed December 11, 2017, http://www.oxforddnb.com/view/10.1093/ref:odnb/9780198614128.001.0001/odnb-9780198614128-e-25998.

29 Alfred von Wretschko, ed., *Der Traktat des Laurentius de Somercote Kanonikus von Chichester über die Vornahme von Bischofswahlen. Enstanden im Jahre 1254* (Weimar: H. Böhlaus, 1907), 27–28.

30 Wretschko, *Traktat des Laurentius de Somercote*, 23.

31 Peter Herde, "Papal Formularies for Letters of Justice (13th–16th Centuries): Their Development and Significance for Medieval Canon Law," in *Diplomatik, Kanonistik, Paläographie: Studien zu den historischen Grundwissenschaften* (Stuttgart: Anton Hiersemann, 2008), 123.

32 Jane Sayers, "The Procedure of the Courts of the Judges Delegate," in *Law and Records in Medieval England—Studies on the Medieval Papacy, Monasteries and Records* (London: Variorum Reprints, 1988), 47.

Library, MS Royal 15. B.iv. The Gonville and Caius manuscript largely comprises three volumes of the pre-Gregorian decretals *Quinque compilationes antiquae* dating from around 1220, with the constitutions of the 1222 Council at Oxford added in another hand. The Royal manuscript presents an even greater diversity of material in addition to the formulary, containing commentaries of Priscian and Donatus, the letters of Peter of Blois, fragments of Euclidian geometry, fragments of Boethius on the Prior Analects of Aristotle, assorted theological works as well as a number of pieces on the civil and canon laws, including the decretals of Alexander III (1159–81).[33] The aggregation of legal, logical, grammatical, theological and mathematical material in the Royal manuscript would appear to suggest an academic context, perhaps even an association with the University of Oxford, and other early formularies from Oxford survive in which scholastic and procedural material can be found alongside each other. The occurrence of such canonical formularies in manuscripts of a broader scholastic interest emphasizes the recognized association between the study and the practice of canon law.

The combination of theoretical and practical material should indeed be seen as one of the distinguishing features of legal miscellanies or compilations, and a number of these survive for the thirteenth century; analysis of these manuscripts can demonstrate a reading practice which also associated theoretical texts with practical legal notes. Oxford, Corpus Christi College, MS 154, dating from 1278 or soon after, contains a number of canon law texts, including Sicard of Cremona's *Summa Decreti*, and the *Distinctiones* of Peter of Blois. The last twenty-three folios of this manuscript contain assorted documents related to the Augustinian monastery of Llanthony (secunda) in Gloucestershire, including numerous formulae for visitations, summonses and proceedings against malefactors.[34] The absence of incipits, rubrication or capitulae from this manuscript seem to suggest the appearance of a notebook compilation rather than a scholarly textbook. This becomes increasingly clear with the documents relating to Llanthony priory, which were written in various hands and scripts with no meaningful rubrication or clear organizational principle. This somewhat disorganized and multi-stage appendage to this manuscript compares strikingly with the relatively minimal annotation on the theoretical material. Its contents form a practical appendix to the theoretical treatises and

33 F. Donald Logan, "An Early Thirteenth-Century Papal Judge-Delegate Formulary of English Origin," *Studia Gratiana* 14:4 (1967): 78.

34 Rodney M. Thomson, ed., *A Descriptive Catalogue of the Medieval Manuscripts of Corpus Christi College, Oxford* (Cambridge: Cambridge University Press, 2011), 78–80.

represent a concern to associate scholastic legal training with the legal practice and concerns of a particular monastic house.[35]

Oxford, MS 154 is by no means an isolated example of such a lawyer's notebook from the thirteenth century combining scholarly works on the canon law with material and marginalia of a more practical nature. Two manuscripts preserved in Worcester Cathedral can also be identified as legal notebooks of this type, MS F.146 and MS F.159, both of which also feature extensive marginal annotations evidencing a responsive readership. The texts included in Worcester, MS F.159 are in themselves ones which are particularly associated with practical applications of canon law, including Tancred of Bologna's eminently practical *Ordo Iudiciarius* and multiple other such ordines.[36] The manuscript is heavily annotated throughout, with extensive marginalia and frequent use of assorted manicules. Although it is not always possible to derive reading practice from the use of such finding aids, there is some suggestion in this manuscript that they were related to the content of the text, as can be seen in the addition of a pointing face depicting the head of a king in the margin of the section of Benencasa of Arezzo's *Casus Decretorum* that discussed the powers of the king within the kingdom.[37] That the manuscript may be associated with a practicing lawyer can be suggested by the marginal annotations on the partial copy of book four of the *Decretals* at the end of the manuscript. These include references to cases in church courts in Staffordshire (fol. 187^v) and Lincoln (fol. 188^v).

The interpolation of theoretical treatises with material related to cases is even more substantial in Worcester, MS F.146, which appears to be an even more informal and personal manuscript than Worcester, MS F.159.[38] The manuscript also included the *Liber Iudicum* of the Spanish canonist Johannes de Deo and the *Constitutions* of Innocent IV, both in full and abbreviated forms, as well as a number of notes and commentaries on the civil law. In addition to these more "scholarly" treatises, Worcester, MS F.146 also contains an extensive quantity of case material related to the West Midlands, including documents related to the Hospital of Holy Trinity, Northampton and the controversy between the Archbishop of Canterbury, Boniface of Savoy and the prior and chapter of Worcester. The relationship between these two categories of material within this manuscript, the procedural treatises and the case material, can be seen to be more substantive than their inclusion in the same miscellaneous legal notebook. The assorted case reports found in folios 19^r–23^v and 24^v are inter-

35 Oxford, Corpus Christi College, MS 154, ff. 105–26.

36 Thomson and Gullick, *Worcester Cathedral Manuscripts*, 107–08.

37 Worcester, MS F. 159, fol. 118^v.

38 Thomson and Gullick, *Worcester Cathedral Manuscripts*, 100–01.

spersed with notes on civil law, but it is the marginalia found on Benencasa of Arezzo's *Casus Decretorum* that are of particular interest. Notation on this text include reference to cases, including one involving the abbot of Worcester on fol. 14^r. Furthermore, the headings of this text are annotated in the same hand as that referring to the case law with mnemonic verses throughout. The use of verse mnemonics is particularly striking alongside the inclusion of material by Johannes de Deo, whose extensive writings on canon law included at least two verse treatises, most prominently his *Arbor versificata* on consanguinity, which comprised twenty-four such verses and appears to have been aimed at his students at Bologna.[39] The inclusion of mnemonics in Worcester, MS F.146 not only demonstrates a responsive reading of the texts, but also illuminates the practical legal mentalities shaping this readership. Manuscripts such as Oxford, MS 154 and Worcester, MSS F.146 and F.159 not only demonstrated an interest in practical and procedural works on canon law, but also indicate that such works could be associated with the careers of working advocates and an interest in what might properly be called case law.

Considering the long thirteenth century more broadly, it is possible to make some observations regarding the circulation of canonist materials in royal government. Inventories of book ownership by officials associated with the royal government mostly date from the first half of the fourteenth century, but would appear to support a distinctly "scholastic" flavor to this canon law material. Although the canon law books of Ralph Baldock, bishop of London, were largely left to St. Paul's Cathedral upon his death in 1313, he was also a leading counsellor to Edward I and as such these texts should also be considered with respect to his position in royal government.[40] Baldock's collection of canon law texts was certainly extensive and demonstrated a marked preference for decretal scholarship with multiple glosses, including that of Innocent IV as well as works for Geoffrey of Trani, Raymund of Peñafort and Hostiensis.[41] An even more markedly scholastic overtone can be found in the inventories of books belonging to Master Peter de Peckham, clerk of Edward I's Treasurer William Marsh, whose books were taken into the custody of the Exchequer upon his death in 1293. Peckham's collection included multiple decretals and other *summae*, including one "que vocatur innocentus," which might be identified as

39 Samuel Worby, *Law and Kinship in Thirteenth-Century England* (Woodbridge, UK: Boydell & Brewer, 2010), 34–35.

40 Tipping, H.A. "Baldock, Ralph (d. 1313), Administrator and Bishop of London." *Oxford Dictionary of National Biography*, accessed December 11, 2017, http://www.oxforddnb.com/view/10.1093/ref:odnb/9780198614128.001.0001/odnb-9780198614128-e-1154.

41 Woolgar, *Testamentary Records*, 75–81.

that of Innocent IV. Perhaps the clearest expression of the scholastic associations of Peckham's collection can be found in the entry regarding his volume of Hostiensis, which is described as being "xxj pecie" of the *Summa*. The pecia system was a characteristic feature of the university book trade, and the inclusion of this volume in Peckham's inventory supports the argument for its presence at Oxford, with which university he may be associated.[42]

The Peckham inventory, which passed on his death not into an ecclesiastical collection but into the hands of the Exchequer, raises the question of canon law book ownership not just by figures associated with the royal government but by the government and the king himself. In 1313 Edward II ordered the barons and treasurer of the Exchequer to release thirty-three books out of the Exchequer to be brought to him at Windsor Park, where he had withdrawn from the council imposed by the Ordainers in 1311. It seems unlikely that this act would have emptied the Exchequer of its book collection, and volumes in the Peckham inventory are not found in this list, which included multiple copies of several texts, among which was the more recent *Apparatus* of Innocent IV, as well as an unspecified *summa* of Tancred.[43] This book list, together with the Peckham inventories, suggests that there was a rich repository of canon law material accumulated within the Exchequer, and while this material tended towards a scholastic context, the emphasis on the decretalists indicates an interest in the utilitarian aspects of canon law, particularly in relation to contemporary papal legislation and commentaries on it. In considering the king's personal books, two wardrobe accounts from the reign of Edward I testify to the presence of ten volumes on canon law in that far more personal household office. Both of these accounts date from around 1299–1300 and each contain around twenty books, with only one item, a *legenda vetera*, appearing in both lists.[44] Thus of approximately forty books to be found in Wardrobe at this time, almost a quarter were

42 Robert J. Whitwell, "Libraries of a Civilian and Canonists and of a Common Lawyer," *Law Quarterly Review* 21 (1905): 398–99; Martha Carlin, "Fetcham [Peckham], Peter of [Pierre d'Abernon] (fl. 1267–1276), Translator and Poet." *Oxford Dictionary of National Biography*, accessed December 11, 2017, http://www.oxforddnb.com/view/10.1093/ref:odnb/9780198614128.001.0001/odnb-9780198614128-e-52678; Graham Pollard, "The *pecia* System in the Medieval Universities," in *Medieval Scribes, Manuscripts and Libraries. Essays Presented to N. R. Ker*, ed. Malcolm B. Parkes and Andrew G. Watson (London: Scolar Press, 1978), 148; Nigel Ramsay, "Law" in *the Cambridge History of the Book in Britain. Volume II: 1100–1400*, ed. Nigel Morgan and Rodney M. Thomson (Cambridge: Cambridge University Press, 2008), 264–65.

43 Cavanaugh, "Royal Books," 308; *Calendar of the Close Rolls Preserved in the Public Record Office: Edward II, 1313–18*, ed. Great Britain Public Record Office (London: H. M. S. O., 1893), 10.

44 Cavanaugh, "Royal Books," 307.

volumes of canon law. Connection with the Exchequer books can be identified in the presence of another *Summa* of Tancred, suggesting that there was not a major divergence in the character of the canon law materials received in the Wardrobe as opposed to the Exchequer, which appears to have tended towards decretal and procedural works which may have had more practical implications for royal government, particularly in its relationship to the papacy.

Turning to a consideration of the Roman civil law, a consideration of the manuscript evidence emphasizes the symbiotic relationship between the civilian and canonist traditions, both through proximity within both compiled codices and historically specific collections of multiple volumes. Where their provenance can be established, civil law manuscripts regularly appear in collections that also possessed substantial holdings of canonist material.[45] Furthermore, a sense that contemporaries recognized the connection between the two laws can be gained from consulting library catalogues. The Glastonbury Abbey catalogue of 1247 lists six books on the civil law immediately following the records of the eight canon law texts in the same collection.[46] Additionally, bequests indicate that private owners of civil law manuscripts were also likely to be owners of canonist texts. The books bequeathed by Abbot Benedict to Peterborough Abbey upon his death in 1193 included eleven legal texts, of which four were civilian texts.[47] Similarly, Ralph Baldock's Inventory included at least six civil law texts among a far larger proportion of canonist texts.[48] In cataloguing and categorization at the very least, there was not a firm division between the texts of the two laws.

This interpenetration is not only evident in coincidence within collections, but also in the compilation of manuscripts themselves. Indeed, it is not always easy to distinguish clearly between manuscripts on the basis of treating "civil" or "canon" law separately as it was not uncommon for them to occur in the same compilations or miscellanies. Worcester, MS F.7 is in the most part composed of Geoffrey of Trani's *Summa Super Titulis Decretalium*, but the manuscript also included Azo's *Brocarda* of civil law maxims (ex. 12th century), as well as Bartholomew of Brescia's canonical *Brocarda* (c. 1234). Geoffrey of Trani was a student of Azo at Bologna and this may serve to explain the linkage of these two texts; certainly the school context played an important role in the production of

45 Ker, *Medieval Libraries*, 19, 22, 44, 69, 98–99, 109, 156, 174, 176, 207, 210–12, 216.

46 Hearne, *Chronica sive historia de rebus Glastoniensibus*, 2, 430.

47 James, *Peterborough Abbey Manuscripts*, 21.

48 Woolgar, *Testamentary Records*, 76–7, cf. Neil R. Ker, "Books at St. Paul's Cathedral Before 1313," in *Books, Collectors and Libraries: Studies in the Medieval Heritage*, ed. Andrew G. Watson (London: Hambledon, 1985), 209; Tipping, "Baldock, Ralph (d. 1313)."

this manuscript, which was probably created at Oxford soon after 1251.[49] However, the inclusion of the two Brocardica specifically is suggestive of a wider methodological association between the two laws. This collection of maxims resolved in an abridged disputational format apparent legal contradictions, which were noted in complete glosses but were collected and summarized in such brocardica.[50] The inclusion of this text as an appendage to Trani's *Summa* may be said to reflect the way in which civil law maxims were expanded and transformed in canonist writings.[51]

A more direct interface between civil and canon law texts can be seen in Worcester, MS F.146, which is comprised of four separate sections bound together, incorporating both civil and canon texts. The second of the four booklets contains the *Liber Iudicum* of Johannes de Deo and assorted commentaries on the civil law. In addition to this, the first five folios comprise reports of cases from the church courts, interspersed with notes on the civil law. In their catalogue entry for this manuscript Rodney Thomson and Michael Gullick have suggested that this was a lawyer's handbook associated with Worcester from the late thirteenth century. Accepting this description of the manuscript, it would appear that lawyers practicing in the church courts in the late thirteenth century not only consulted both civil and canon law texts, but also appended to their observations of cases in the church courts notes on the civil law.[52] Comparison of these two Worcester manuscripts emphasizes the way in which the scholarly influence of civil law upon canonist learning can also be observed in the evidence of the practice of law in the church courts. Thus, both in the composition of collections and the compilation of manuscripts, the civil and canon laws were in many ways inextricably bound together.

While the church continued to create new law, the body of Roman civil law set down by Justinian was finite.[53] However, the completeness of Justinian's leg-

---

49 Worcester, Cathedral Library, MS F. 7; Thomson and Gullick, *Worcester Cathedral Manuscripts*, 8–9.

50 Harry Dorndop and Eltjo J.H. Schrage, "The Sources of Medieval Learned Law," in *The Creation of the ius commune: From Casus to Regula*, ed. John W. Cairns and Paul J. du Plessis (Edinburgh: Edinburgh University Press, 2010), 22.

51 Robert C. Figueira, "Decretalists, Medieval Papal Legislation, and the Roman Law of Offices and Jurisdiction," *Res Publica Litterarum: Studies in the Classical Tradition* 9 (1986): 119.

52 Worcester, Cathedral Library, MS F.146; Thomson and Gullick, *Worcester Cathedral Manuscripts*, 100–01.

53 Peter Clarke, "The Growth of Canon and Civil Law Studies, 1070–1535," in *Illuminating the Law: Legal Manuscripts in Cambridge Collections*, ed. Susan L'Engle and Robert Gibbs (London: Harvey Miller, 2001), 27.

islative undertaking and its textual standardization in the twelfth century did not signify an end to civilian scholarship. New laws were not propagated, but the work of the glossators stimulated the growth of a vibrant and dynamic body of scholarship, and the English collections were not cut off from this contemporary literature. The study of civil law in England required staying abreast of the major developments in Bologna. Where an English civil juridical tradition existed, it often could be found alongside the major Bolognese texts. One example of this is the twelfth century *Brocardica "Dolum,"* a treatise that survives in six manuscripts of English provenance, including Worcester, MS F.14, in which it is bound with Justinian's *Instituta*, Azo's *Brocarda*, the *Apparatus de Regulis Iuris* of Bulgarus, the *Titulus de Verborum Significatione* from the Digest and the *Ordo Iudiciarius "Olim"* of Otto of Pavia, all texts with strong Bolognese connections.[54] The civil law, as it was studied and appeared in manuscripts from thirteenth-century England was conversant with the dominant contemporary writers of the continent.

Analysis of the glossators most prominent in English civil law material indicates that English jurists were very much engaged with the contemporary developments and dominant texts standardized at Bologna in the early thirteenth century. Among the English manuscript material it is clear that the works of Azo and his pupil Accursius (c. 1182–1263) enjoyed the most widespread circulation. Manuscripts of Azo certainly enjoyed a broad geographical circulation in thirteenth century England. An Italian manuscript of Azo's Summa survives in London, Lambeth Palace, MS 16, on the closing flyleaf of which is a note that in 1273 this manuscript, belonging to a Hugh of Skeffling was pledged for the value of forty shillings to a master Stephen of Hedon, both locations in Holderness (Yorks).[55] Even more popular than Azo was the *Glossa Ordinaria* of his pupil Accursius. This popularity can be particularly well testified by the evidence of English scholars at Bologna, who in the latter half of the thirteenth century commissioned copies of Justinian specifying their desire for this apparatus. One English scholar, William "Anglige," sold his copy of the Codex with an Accursian gloss in 1268 to a Castilian scholar Pontius de Urgius for the exorbitant sum of sixty-six Bolognese pounds.[56] Italian manuscripts with Accursian apparatus certainly made their way back to

---

54 Worcester, Cathedral Library, MS F.14; Thomson and Gullick, *Worcester Cathedral Manuscripts*, 14; Matthias Schwaibold, *Brocardica. 'Dolum per subsequentia purgari'. Eine englische Sammlung von Argumenten des römischen Rechts aus dem 12. Jahrhundert* (Frankfurt: Klostermann, 1985).

55 James, *Lambeth Palace*, 28–29.

56 *Chartularium Studii Bononiensis. Documenti per la Storia Dell'Università di Bologna dalle*

England. Oxford, Corpus Christi College, MS 73 is comprised of two booklets, a term defined by Pamela Robinson to refer to "a small but structurally independent production containing a single work or a number of short works."[57] the first of which, comprising Justinian's *Institutes*, *Authentica* and *Tres Libri*, was of Italian origin, with the Accursian gloss in an English hand, likely added in Oxford—the same glossing hand also composed the second booklet of Frederick II's *Constitutiones Feodorum*, also with Accursian gloss, both booklets being in use in Oxford from ca. 1300.[58] The *Glossa Ordinaria* was largely completed by 1230 and its prominence in English civil law collections from the mid-thirteenth century onwards indicates that the study of civil law in England engaged closely with the contemporary developments in Bologna.

Certainly, the evidence of Roman law manuscript ownership and distribution reflects a far closer relationship with the universities than the more disparate canon law material. In England this particularly close association between the civil law and the universities was strengthened in the reign of Henry III by his 1234 prohibition of its teaching in London, which focused existing teaching within the two universities.[59] Indeed, this textual association could be explicitly recognized by contemporaries, as can be seen in the case of the books brought to Evesham by its Abbot Thomas of Marlborough. The titles of the *libri utriusque iuris* brought by Thomas were not named in the Evesham chronicle, but they are identified as having been used by him when teaching at Oxford and Exeter.[60] In addition to these connections of personnel, civil law manuscripts themselves can be seen to emerge from a university milieu. Further to the evidence for the purchase of civil law manuscripts by English students at Bologna demonstrated above, it is possible to identify

Origini Fino al Secolo XV. 13 vols. (Bologna: Istituto per la storia dell'Università di Bologna, 1907–40), 8, 109.

57 Pamela Robinson, "The "Booklet": a Self-Contained Unit in Composite Manuscripts," *Codicologica* 3 (1980): 46–69.

58 Thomson, *Medieval Manuscripts of Corpus Christi College Oxford*, 38–39.

59 John Selden, *Ad fletam dissertatio* historica (London, 1647), 525; *Close Rolls of the Reign of Henry III: Preserved in the Public Record Office*, 14 vols, ed. Great Britain Public Record Office (London: H. M. S. O., 1902–38), 3: 26; John L. Barton, "The Study of Civil Law before 1380," in *A History of the University of Oxford. Volume I—The Early Oxford Schools*, ed. Jeremy I. Catto, Trevor Henry Aston, and Ralph Evans (Oxford: Oxford University Press, 1984), 521.

60 William D. Macray, ed., *Chronicon Abbatiae de Evesham ad annum 1418* (London: Longman, Green, Longman, Roberts and Green, 1863), 267. Jane E. Sayers, "Marlborough, Thomas of (d. 1236), Historian, Lawyer, and Abbot of Evesham," *Oxford Dictionary of National Biography*, accessed December 11, 2017, http://www.oxforddnb.com/view/10.1093/ref:odnb/9780198614128.001.0001/odnb-9780198614128-e-18077.

manuscripts of Roman law which can be seen to have been either produced or used at the universities of Oxford and Cambridge and had subsequently migrated elsewhere. A twelfth-century French manuscript of the *Infortiatum* of Justinian now in the Vatican (Biblioteca Apostolica Vaticana, MS Lat. 1414) features Accursius's *Glossa Ordinaria* and *Additiones* to that Gloss in a thirteenth century English hand and may well have been associated with Oxford.[61] Structurally in the text, the addition of the glosses and the inclusion of a rubrication table as a finding aid for the manuscript appears to indicate a scholastic context.[62] Both the known owners of civil law manuscripts and the evidence provided by the manuscripts themselves would appear to suggest that these treatises were closely connected with the university context.

As with the circulation of canon law manuscripts, the connection between the administration of Henry III and the schools provided a meaningful channel for the communication of these ideas and texts, particularly through the recruitment of university-trained *magistri* for the offices of government. The connection between the civil and canon laws further expanded this channel of communication. When the books of Peter de Peckham, clerk of the Treasurer William March, were taken into the custody of the Exchequer in 1293, these included seven volumes of civil law; three copies of the *Code*, one with the *apparatus de verborum significatione*, the three parts of the *Digest*, *vetus*, *novum* and *infortiatum*, and one further volume containing the *Institutes* and *Authentica* along with the three extraordinary books of the *Code*. Although no direct connection has been made between Peckham and the universities, he is referred to in the treasury memorandum that records this bequest as magister and the texts listed bear a close correlation with those required for inception in Civil Law at Oxford.[63] That the volumes were deposited in the Exchequer also appears to suggest that this was considered an appropriate location for them and civil law texts continued to be found within the offices of the Exchequer. The books released to Edward II from the Exchequer in 1313 included a number of civilian as well as canonical texts.[64] While these texts may have ultimately been among those gifted by the king to his foundation of King's Hall in Cambridge in 1317, the continued association between civil law texts, the uni-

61 Stephen Kuttner and Reinhard Elze, eds., *A Catalogue of Canon and Roman Law Manuscripts in the Vatican Library*, 2 vols. (Vatican City: Biblioteca Apostolica Vaticana, 1986–87) 1: 210–11.

62 Parkes, "Influence of the Concepts of *Ordinatio* and *Compilatio*," 115–41.

63 Whitwell, "Libraries of a Civilian and Canonists," 398–99; Carlin, "Fetcham Peter."

64 *Calendar of Close Rolls: Edward II*, 2: 10.

versities and the exchequer is not to be understated.[65] Indeed, the foundation was closely connected both with the training of educated clerks for service in royal and ecclesiastical administration, as well as the extension of the household offices and Chapel Royal in particular.[66] The evidence for the book collections of the king and royal government in the reign of Henry III is extremely limited and difficult to substantiate; however, the overlap between prosopographical evidence and the deposition of books of civil law in the Exchequer in the later thirteenth and early fourteenth centuries makes a compelling case for an excepted connection between the scholarly milieu from which civil law texts originated and the government mentalité of Henry III's kingdom.

While the existing literature on the *ars dictaminis* in medieval England has tended to focus on the theoretical treatises, the manuscript evidence from thirteenth-century England depicts a far more diverse body of material.[67] In addition to the academic theory, the works of the *dictatores* were inextricably connected with practical and model material. Letter-books and formularies have as much bearing on the reception of the cursus in England as do the more didactic manuscripts, and the distinction between these categories was not always clear. Dictaminal exemplars were not necessarily defined by the purpose of their author but by their subsequent function, so that diverse sources of canon law as well as international diplomatic could enrich the theoretical literature. In this interplay between theory and practice, the English manuscript evidence reflects a distinct preference for pragmatism and functionalism, suggesting that these practices were conceived of not only in terms of literary elegance, but also in their direct utility and applicability.

The theoretical dictaminal material that circulated in thirteenth-century England was for the most part of continental origin, however it may be described as falling into two broad types, the French and the Bolognese, the poetic and the legal. Until the mid-thirteenth century the dictaminal treatises that were received into England were of French origin, rather than directly imported from Bologna, and this preference for French works allowed for a greater flexibility in the reception and practice of dictamen in England. In contrast to the rigid and schematized system set out first in Bologna by Alberic of Monte Cassino the conception of dictaminal rules in the French artes was posi-

65 For the donation to King's Hall, see Cavanaugh, "Royal Books," 308.

66 Alan B. Cobban, "Edward II, Pope John XXII and the University of Cambridge," *Bulletin of the John Rylands Library*, 47:1 (1964): 52–58.

67 Noel Denholm-Young, "The Cursus in England," in *Collected Papers* (Cardiff: University of Wales Press, 1969), 42–73; Martin Camargo, *Essays on Medieval Rhetoric* (Farnham: Ashgate, Variorum, 2012).

tioned within a wider and more broadly humanistic framework of the *ars grammatica*.[68] Martin Camargo has identified the *Flores Dictaminum* of Bernard of Meung as the most popular of the French dictaminal treatises received in England; at least two manuscript copies can be dated to the mid to late thirteenth century.[69] Certainly the thirteenth-century English authors upon the *ars dictaminis* can be seen as fitting more broadly into the poetic French dictaminal mode. The work of Geoffrey of Vinsauf, who was trained at both Paris and Bologna, was among the most widespread in thirteenth-century England, and demonstrates a marked tendency towards the French school.[70] His *Documentum* was used in Oxford schools in the early thirteenth century, alongside the works of another English *dictator* in the French tradition, Gervase of Melkley.[71] This early phase of the reception of dictamen in England explored through the theoretical treatises emphasizes the French school of dictatores, primarily concerned with the arts of poetry and literary elegance more than the intricacies of Bolognese law and administration.[72]

Despite this early flourishing of theoretical and poetical *artes dictaminis*, over the course of the thirteenth century the English manuscript evidence demonstrates an increasing desire for the more pragmatic and systematizing Bolognese *dictatores*. Of the more theoretical Bolognese authors, Guido Faba perhaps attained the greatest prominence. The dictaminal miscellany, London, British Library, MS Add. 8167, in addition to containing one of the surviving thirteenth-century copies of Bernard of Meung, also includes a number of Faba's treatises, although the precise number has been disputed.[73] Faba's recep-

68 James J. Murphy, *Rhetoric in the Middle Ages: A History of Rhetorical Theory from Saint Augustine to the Renaissance* (Berkeley, CA: University of California Press, 1974), 226–29, 239.

69 Paris, Bibliothèque Nationale de France, MS Lat.14193 and London, British Library, MS Add.8167; Martin Camargo, "The English Manuscripts of Bernard of Meung's *Flores Dictaminum*," *Viator* 12 (1981): 198, cf. Franz-Josef Schmale, "Der Briefsteller Bernhards von Meung," *Mitteilungen des Instituts für Österreichische Geschichtsforschung*, 66 (1958): 1–28.

70 Martin Camargo, "Vinsauf, Geoffrey of [called Galfridus Anglicus] (fl. 1208–1213), Poet and Teacher of Grammar and Rhetoric." *Oxford Dictionary of National Biography*, accessed December 11, 2017, http://www.oxforddnb.com/view/10.1093/ref:odnb/9780198614128.001.0001/odnb-9780198614128-e-28326.

71 Camargo, Martin, ed., *Medieval Rhetorics of Prose Composition. Five English* Artes Dictandi *and their Tradition* (Binghampton: Medieval & Renaissance Texts & Studies, 1995), 21.

72 Denholm-Young, "*Cursus* in England," 49.

73 Denholm-Young, "*Cursus* in England," 67–8; Camargo, "English Manuscripts of Bernard of Meung," 205–6; Virgilio Pini, "La "Summa de Vitiis et virtutibus" di Guido Faba," *Quadrivium* 1 (1956): 41–43.

tion in England is further testified by the appearance in Oxford, New College, MS 255 of a work of his known as the *Rota nova*. Indeed, this is the only surviving copy of this work and is a highly theoretical treatise, although its introduction has a semi-autobiographical character.[74] Other Italian authors whose works circulated in thirteenth century England included Thomas of Capua and the Roman notary Richard de Pophis, the latter of whose work particularly focused on the dictaminal style of the Roman curia.[75] This increasing proportion of Italian works reflects a growing desire for pragmatic and utilitarian approaches to dictamen, moving away from the theoretical and conceptual approach favored by the French authors.

In addition to the acquisition of particular authors and texts, the codicological evidence also points towards an increasing concern for pragmatism and utilitarian attitudes to dictaminal studies. The vast majority of medieval teaching manuscripts were bound together to form collections organized for subject matter.[76] Given this context, the tendency not only to include model letters within theoretical treatises, but also to bind them together in compilations with additional exemplars demonstrates how the teaching of dictamen in England was closely connected with considerations of letter-writing in practice. Despite the abstract nature of the *Rota nova* and the uncertain identifications of some of the "Fabian" texts in London, MS Add. 8167, what both of these compilations demonstrate is the tendency not only to consult the more function-oriented Bolognese authors, but for English dictaminal manuscripts to contain an increasing proportion of formulary material.[77] Oxford, MS 255 has been discussed only briefly by Noel Denholm-Young and Ernst Kantorowicz,[78] and studying the finding aids and presentation of the material included along with the *Rota Nova* suggests that the formatting of the manuscript reflected a particular concern with the consultation of the exemplary material.

74 Oxford, New College, MS 255.

75 A copy of Richard de Pophis's *Summa Dictaminis* survives in Oxford, Merton College, MS 194. Based on internal evidence, Thomson dated this manuscript to the latter half of the thirteenth century, rather than the fifteenth-century attribution given by Denholm-Young: Thomson, *Medieval Manuscripts of Merton College*, 141.

76 Camargo, *Essays on Medieval Rhetoric*, 167, originally published as "Beyond the *Libri Catoniani*: Models of Latin Prose Style at Oxford University ca. 1400," *Mediaeval Studies* 59 (1994): 165–87.

77 Camargo, "English Manuscripts of Bernard of Meung," 205–6; Martha Carlin and David Crouch, eds., *Lost Letters of Medieval Life. English Society, 1200–1250* (Philadelphia, PA: Penn, 2013), 5–7.

78 Denholm-Young, "*Cursus* in England," 64; Ernst Kantorowicz, "An "Autobiography" of Guido Faba," in *Selected Studies* (Locust Valley, NY: J.J. Augstin, 1965), 197.

This evidence can be seen both in the original presentation manuscript and in the subsequent addition of marginalia and capitula. On fol. 17^{v} of Oxford, MS 255, examples of forms of ecclesiastical address in model letters which, according to the *incipit*, were composed by Guido Faba are clearly arranged for ease of visibility and consultation, with well-spaced lines between each address, the use of alternating red and blue capitals, and a descending hierarchy ordered according to the different grades of recipient.[79] The relation of this model material to practice is also made visible in the presentation of the text, as can be shown in the form letters on fols. 32^{v}–33^{r}. These exempla are mostly papal and imperial in their style and the first line of each address has been composed in narrow elongated capitals, imitating the dominant charter style of the thirteenth century. Clearly these exempla were recorded by a scribe familiar with administrative scripts. Marginal additions also sought to encourage easy consultation of the exempla. In the form letters attributed to Bolognese scholars (fols. 40^{v}–49^{r}) each separate form letter is clearly marked not only by the use of red capitals, but also by the addition of pointers in the margin at the beginning of each model. Other marginalia also suggest this functionalist attitude. There is little marginal annotation on the folios of the *Rota Nova*, except for occasional pen tests on fols. 4^{r-v} and 9^{v}–10^{r}, and the one substantive marginal addition is made on fol. 7^{r}, which has been misplaced and should in fact be the first folio. At the foot of this folio, in a hand identified by Denholm-Young as being not much later than that of the main scribal hand, a table of forms for the use of polysyllabics has been presented.[80] Of all the marginal additions to this manuscript this coheres most closely to the theoretical and rhythmical strictures of the cursus, yet its clear tabulation indicates a utilitarian and pragmatic consultative readership. This would indicate that, even when there was a marked interest in the conceptual aspects dictamen, this tended to be framed in a functional fashion.

Perhaps the greatest evidence of this utilitarian attitude to dictamen can be found in the popularity of model letter collections independent from the theoretical speculations of the *dictatores*. In this respect, the works of the Imperial proto-notary Petrus de Vinea were by far the most influential in England. Copying of his letters, compiled after his death in 1249 by his pupil Nicholas de Rocca into six books without prefatory or theoretical material, was prolific in England from the late thirteenth century onwards.[81] Indeed, the rapid reception

79 Oxford, MS 255, fol. 17^{v}.

80 fols. 4^{r-v}, 9^{v}–10^{r}, 7^{r}.

81 Ernst Kantorowicz, "The Prologue to *Fleta* and the School of Petrus de Vinea," *Speculum* 32 (1957): 231–49.

of de Vinea's work can be testified by the existence of several late thirteenth-century manuscripts of English provenance. While Denholm-Young dated all the English de Vinea manuscripts he listed as of fourteenth-century origin or later, subsequent work, especially the definitive catalogue of Hans Martin Schaller, has identified thirteenth-century copies, among them manuscripts not identified by Denholm-Young.[82] Among these manuscripts the most precise provenance can be established for that now in the collection of Corpus Christi College, Cambridge. This manuscript was originally in the collection of the Benedictine Cathedral Priory of Canterbury, Christ Church, belonging to Nicholas of Sandwich, prior 1258–80.[83] In all, the extreme popularity of de Vinea in fourteenth-century manuscripts suggests that this built upon a thirteenth-century tradition.

But what does the manuscript evidence of de Vinea material suggest about the reception of dictamen in thirteenth-century England and how was this material received? In his work on the reception of de Vinea's material in England, Ernst Kantorowicz referred to the concept of recipient transmission; the copying and circulation of letters by de Vinea from the official correspondence, thus predating the composition of the "official" Epistolae.[84] The most widespread recipient transmission can be seen in the use and recording of de Vinea's official correspondence on behalf of Frederick II, which subsequently appeared in the chronicle accounts of Matthew Paris and Roger of Wendover.[85] Other isolated letters separate from the official collections appear in Oxford, Bodleian Library, MS Auct. F. 1. 8 and London, British Library, MS Hargrave 313. The Bodleian manuscript has one Vinean letter, that of Frederick II to the Roman Cardinals in 1229 appended to a copy of the *Policraticus* of John of Salisbury and the letters of Symmachus and Arnulph of Lisieux.[86] The Hargrave manuscript also contains only a single charter of Frederick II, in a manuscript containing an assortment of material relating to English legal history and the exchequer in particular.[87] This inclusion in such a manuscript of legal and administrative interest suggests that the products and style of the imperial

82 Denholm-Young, "*Cursus* in England," 68. cf. Hans Martin Schaller, ed., *Handschriftenverzeichnis zur Briefsammlung des Petrus de Vinea* (Hannover: Hahn, 2002).

83 Cambridge, Corpus Christi College, MS 288; Schaller, *Handschrifenverzeichnis*, 48.

84 Kantorowicz, "Prologue to *Fleta*," 171.

85 Kantorowicz, "Prologue to *Fleta*," 171; Ernst Kantorowicz, "Petrus de Vinea in England," *Mitteilungen des Instituts für Österreichische Geschichtsforschung* 51 (1937): 75; Otto Vehse, *Die amtliche Propaganda in der Staatskunst Friedrichs II* (Munich: Münchner Drucke, 1929), 216–36.

86 Oxford, Bodleian Library, MS Auct. F.1.8, fol. 140^{v}.

87 London, British Library, MS Hargrave 313, fol. 100^{r,b}.

chancery, including those penned by de Vinea were of interest to those actively engaged in the administration of thirteenth-century England.[88]

There is however another observation that can be made about the de Vinea manuscripts and the inclusion of dictaminal models in such compilations, from which broader conclusions about the place of the *ars dictaminis* in English manuscript culture can be drawn. The reception and use of stylistic models was far more widespread and flexible than a rigid obedience to the most rigid rules of the *ars dictaminis*. Indeed, it should be noted that this discipline was not monolithic and uniform, but rather reflected a graded hierarchy of complexity.[89] The use of formularies and model letters was far more widespread than the adoption of the most elegant forms of the *stilus supremus*, both on the Continent and in England.[90] In this respect, the use of exempla material indicates a far wider reception of letter-writing practice, a reception that was not restricted to the writings of the theoretical proponents of the *ars dictaminis*. The *ars dictaminis* was not without an English audience, but over the course of the thirteenth century the interest became increasingly pragmatic. This was reflected not only in a growing appetite for the products of the Bolognese *dictatores*, but also with an increasing move towards exempla material over theoretical treatises and the proliferation of model letter collections. This shift towards exempla over theory was not restricted to England, and has been the basis for criticism of the thirteenth-century dictamen becoming increasingly sterile and mechanistic.[91] However, it may instead be concluded that this exemplary function of *dictamen* allowed for its closer integration with the world of legal studies and administration.[92] With this close relationship between legal and dictaminal material it is possible to postulate a far broader influence of papal and imperial style and rhetoric into the governmental mentalities of thirteenth-

88 Benoit Grévin, "Writing Techniques in Thirteenth- and Fourteenth-Century England: The Role of the Sicilian and Papal Letter Collections as Practical Models for the Shaping of Royal Propaganda," in *Fourteenth-Century England VII*, ed. Mark Ormrod (Woodbridge, UK: Boydell & Brewer, 2012).

89 Peter Herde, "Literary Activities of the Imperial and Papal Chanceries during the Struggle Between Frederick II and the Papacy," in *Intellectual Life at the Court of Frederick II Hohenstaufen*, ed. William Tromzo (Washington, DC; National Gallery of Art, 1994), 227.

90 Herde, "Papal Formularies," 123, Giles Constable, *Letters and Letter-Collections* (Turnhout: Brepols, 1976), 11; Crouch and Carlin, *Lost Letters of Medieval Life*, 1–5.

91 Constable, *Letters and Letter-Collections*, 36–37; Louis J. Paetow, *The Arts Course at Medieval Universities with Special Reference to Grammar and Rhetoric* (Champaign, IL: University of Illinois Studies, 1910), 76.

92 Henry G. Richardson, "Letters of the Oxford *Dictatores*," in *Formularies Which Bear on the History of Oxford c.1204–1420*, ed. Herbert E. Salter, William A. Pantin and Henry G. Richardson, 2 vols. (Oxford: Clarendon Press, 1942) 2: 345.

century England than would appear from an analysis of dictamen based solely upon the theoretical treatises of the *ars dictaminis.*

Having considered in turn the circulation of these three distinct but interrelated categories of manuscript in thirteenth-century England, it is possible to draw some more general observations about these textual traditions in framing the administrative mentalities of this period. Three main conclusions can thus be drawn; first, that these manuscripts tended to aggregate together in increasingly specialist collections, developed both for academic study and also practical application; second, that participants in the manuscript culture of thirteenth-century England were informed and selective consumers able to make deliberate choices about their manuscript material; third and finally, that this preferential readership increasingly inclined towards pragmatic and utilitarian material over theoretical treatises. This utilitarian aspect is the most significant for the influence of this integrated body of texts upon the development of government mentalities in the reign of Henry III, as it indicates the association of this material not with pure scholarly abstraction, but with questions of practical application and administration. Even the *ars dictaminis*, which in its theoretical form presents the most restricted body of manuscript evidence, when understood in relation to the role of exemplary material in letter-writing practice possessed a far broader and pragmatic base, closely connected with the concerns of law and governance.

We cannot know for certain what the volumes purchased by William de Kilkenny were in the Wardrobe account, but it can be demonstrated that he lived and operated within a textual culture in which manuscripts of the learned law and the *ars dictaminis* circulated. The development of increasingly specialized collections indicates the existence of informed "consumers" who were not passively receptive of all material, but displayed a selective preference for certain authors and texts. The codicological evidence for the composition of compilations, including such textual features as rubrication and annotations in glosses or marginalia, further demonstrated a critically engaged and responsive readership, whose interests tended towards those off pragmatism and utility. Combined with sporadic evidence for ownership of this type of material within the royal household, it can be asserted that this textual culture formed an important aspect in developing a *mentalité* of government over the long thirteenth century, including the reign of Henry III.

CHAPTER 8

Discussing London and the *Regnum Anglorum* after the 1204 Loss of Normandy

Katherine J. Har

King John's (r. 1199–1216) loss of Normandy in 1204 and subsequent losses in Anjou, Maine, and portions of Aquitaine and Poitou represented a substantial contraction of the previously cross-Channel Angevin realm.[1] These events were then followed by costly and ambitious attempts by John to regain his continental lands in the period from 1204 to the Battle of Bouvines in 1214. Anxieties arising from circumstances precipitated by these events are reflected in the early thirteenth-century legal and historical compilation known as the *Leges Anglorum Londoniis Collectae*, in the particular care taken with its description of the *regnum Anglorum* and in its depictions of good kingship, critiquing the current state of affairs. Previous scholarship has shown how the inclusion of comparative models of good Christian kingship in Lucius of Britain, King Arthur, and Prester John[2] and the elegiac account of the death and burial of John's brother Richard I (r. 1189–1199)[3] fit within the *Leges Anglorum*'s overall apparatus of critique of John's reign, the latter particularly referencing John's loss of Normandy. Tensions between the early thirteenth-century reality of John's realm compared with the idealized and historical depictions of what the *Leges Anglorum* compiler suggests it could and ought to have been should be seen as a unifying characteristic for its component texts and deserves another look as an important aspect of both the compilation's contents and form in a more general sense than previously discussed. For the *Leges Anglorum* compiler the strength

1 I would like to thank Thom Gobbitt for his comments on earlier versions of this chapter and George Garnett and Alison Hudson for their comments on portions of my doctoral thesis from which this is partially derived. Earlier versions of this chapter were presented at IMC Leeds and Kalamazoo ICMS.

2 Walter Ullmann, "On the Influence of Geoffrey of Monmouth in English History," in *The Church and the Law in the Earlier Middle Ages: Selected Essays* (London: Variorum Reprints, 1975), 258–63; Derek Keene, "Text, Visualisation and Politics: London, 1150–1250," *Transactions of the Royal Historical Society*, 6th series 18 (2008): esp. 83–86.

3 John Gillingham, "Stupor mundi: 1204 et un obituaire de Richard Coeur de Lion depuis longtemps tombé dans l'oubli," in *Plantagenêts et Capétiens: confrontations et héritages*, ed. Martin Aurell and Noël-Yves Tonnerre (Turnhout: Brepols, 2006), 400–08.

 | DOI:10.1163/9789004448650_010

and stability of the kingdom corresponded to the personal strength of its king. The compiler accordingly emphasized a king's role in the maintenance of his kingdom and in perpetuating the laws and the just administration of the same. And of particular relevance to the Angevin realm of this time, the king ought to be careful not to alienate any rights or land belonging to the crown and consequently he also ought to restore those which have been lost.[4] As Derek Keene put it, the "message of this collection, compiled after the loss of Normandy in 1204, is that King John had much to live up to."[5]

The *Leges Anglorum* contains a variety of legal, historical, and narrative texts and is one of the chief sources for London's customs in the late twelfth and early thirteenth centuries. It was produced during the reign of King John, and its earliest extant copy (Manchester, John Rylands Library, MS Latin 155 and London, British Library, MS Add. 14252) dates from this period.[6] The compilation opens with several anonymous twelfth-century legal treatises and compilations, each with wide circulation histories of their own: the *Quadripartitus* (containing early English law-codes in Latin translation), the *Tripartita* (containing the *Articuli Willelmi*, *Leges Edwardi Confessoris*, and a genealogy of the dukes of Normandy and kings of England), the *Leges Henrici Primi*, and *Glanvill*. In the *Leges Anglorum*, these texts are organized chronologically to provide an account of the laws of the *regnum Anglorum* covering the period from Ine to Henry II.[7] These are followed by an assortment of texts which brings the period covered by this compilation up to the early thirteenth century and give an

4 *Leges Edwardi* 11.1A2, ed. Felix Liebermann, in *Die Gesetze der Angelsachsen*, 3 vols. (Halle: Max Niemeyer, 1903–1916), 1:627–70; Manchester, John Rylands Library, MS Latin 155, fol. 57r; Ullmann, "Geoffrey of Monmouth," 262–63. Citation of the *Leges Edwardi* follows subdivisions from the edition in "Leges Edwardi Confessoris," in *Gesetze der Angelsachsen*, ed. Liebermann, 1:627–70.

5 Keene, "Text, Visualisation and Politics," 85.

6 On the corpus of extant manuscripts, see, Felix Liebermann, *Über die Leges Anglorum saeculo XIII. ineunte Londoniis collectae* (Halle: Max Niemeyer, 1894), 101–04; Neil R. Ker, "Liber Custumarum, and Other Manuscripts Formerly at the Guildhall," *Guildhall Miscellany* 3 (1954): 37–45; Jeremy I. Catto, "Andrew Horn: Law and History in Fourteenth-Century England," in *The Writing of the Middle Ages: Essays Presented to Richard William Southern*, ed. Ralph Henry C. Davis and John Michael Wallace-Hadrill (Oxford: Clarendon Press, 1981), 372–74, 76–78.

On dating: Liebermann, *Über die Leges Anglorum*, 79, 91, 101; Mary Bateson, "A London Municipal Collection of the Reign of John," *English Historical Review* 17 (1902): 482; Felix Liebermann, "A Contemporary Manuscript of the 'Leges Anglorum Londoniis Collectae'," *English Historical Review* 28 (1913): 734; Ralph Hanna, *London Literature, 1300–1380* (Cambridge: Cambridge University Press, 2004), 71.

7 Patrick Wormald, "Quadripartitus," in *Legal Culture in the Early Medieval West: Law as Text, Image and Experience* (London: Hambledon Press, 1999), 239, in relation to the *Quadripartitus*; but more generally in Keene, "Text, Visualisation and Politics," 83.

account of the laws and franchises of the city of London with a special emphasis on the unique liberties enjoyed by the city.

Together, interpolations to the otherwise familiar legal texts of the first half of the *Leges Anglorum* and the choices made in the selection of texts in the municipally-focused second half of the compilation have been instrumental in establishing the compilation's status as a narrative of both London and kingdom-wide politics and political dissent.[8] In particular, the compilation's versions of the *Leges Edwardi* and the *Leges Henrici Primi* have been discussed as reflections of the political issues at stake in London's opposition to the state of royal government and in the circumstances which led to the granting of *Magna Carta*.[9] Recurrent themes in this version of the *Leges Edwardi* emphasize the rights of the crown, the unity and extent of the kingdom, and the king's tripartite responsibilities to protect Church and realm, to promote good laws and abolish bad ones, and to do justice according to council. These emendations show a particular penchant for Geoffrey of Monmouth's *Historia Regum Britanniae*[10] and a knowledge of and interest in the city of London, which manifests itself by highlighting the antiquity and pre-eminence of London and its citizens. Emulating the discussion of London in relation to the wider kingdom found in the *Leges Anglorum*'s contents and presentation, the city is depicted simultaneously as an independent entity whose carefully guarded liberties

8 On the characteristic features of the compilation more generally, see: Liebermann, *Über die Leges Anglorum*; Bateson, "London Municipal Collection," 480–511, 707–30; Liebermann, "Contemporary Manuscript," 732–45; Martin Weinbaum, *London unter Eduard I und II*, 2 vols., Beihefte zur Vierteljahrschrift für Sozial- und Wirtschaftsgeschichte 28–29 (Stuttgart: W. Kohlhammer, 1933), vol. 2.

9 F. Maurice Powicke, *Stephen Langton: Being the Ford Lectures Delivered in the University of Oxford in Hilary Term 1927* (Oxford: Clarendon Press, 1928), 114. This context has continued to be discussed in more recent work, see: Ullmann, "Geoffrey of Monmouth," 258–63; James C. Holt, *Magna Carta*, ed. George Garnett and John Hudson, 3rd ed. (Cambridge: Cambridge University Press, 2015), 102–03, 21; Christopher N.L. Brooke and Gillian Keir, *London 800–1216: The Shaping of a City* (Berkeley, CA: University of California Press, 1975), 51–53; Wormald, "Quadripartitus," 81–114; Bruce O'Brien, *God's Peace and King's Peace: The Laws of Edward the Confessor* (Philadelphia, PA: University of Pennsylvania Press, 1999), 118–19, 21; Patrick Wormald, *The Making of English Law: King Alfred to the Twelfth Century, I: Legislation and its Limits* (Oxford: Blackwell, 2001), 238; Gillingham, "Stupor mundi," 397–411; Keene, "Text, Visualisation and Politics," 69–99, esp. 87–9; Bruce O'Brien, "Forgers of Law and Their Readers: The Crafting of English Political Identities between the Norman Conquest and the Magna Carta," *PS: Political Science and Politics* 43 (2010): 467–73; Holt, *Magna Carta*, "Introduction," by George Garnett and John Hudson, 19–25.

10 Liebermann, *Über die Leges Anglorum*, 5, 29, 40, 43, 62, 94, 97; Ullmann, "Geoffrey of Monmouth," 257–76; O'Brien, "Forgers of Law," 470–72.

distinguished its citizens from the wider *regnum Anglorum* and as an integral part of the same *regnum Anglorum*, both the seat of the kingdom and its mirror.

The *Leges Anglorum*'s politically and historically tinged discussion of the *regnum Anglorum* will be explored to contribute toward a more nuanced consideration of London and the experience of its citizens within a shrinking Angevin realm. The compilation shows a particular and contemporarily pertinent interest in the extent, unity, and stability of the kingdom both past and present, interests which are particularly visible in three aspects: In an overarching form, the repetition of geographical descriptions of the kingdom are integral to the compilation's overall structure and organization, tying idealized accounts of the realm to an overarching narrative of the kingdom's durability. Additionally, both the compilation's particular use and juxtaposition of the terms "regnum Anglorum" and "regnum Britanniae" and the attentiveness shown to the breadth of the kingdom contribute to the *Leges Anglorum*'s hallmark chronological narrative of the continuity and implied stability of the kingdom's legal and administrative practices from the distant past to the early thirteenth century. After contextualizing the anxieties and sense of malaise in both London and the *regnum Anglorum* during this period more broadly, this article will take each outlined structural facet in turn to explore their contributions toward the understanding of good kingship put forward in the *Leges Anglorum* as a whole and their relevance to John's perceived shortcomings with regards to the substantial contraction of the Angevin realm.

The events from 1204 to 1214 coincided with the king's increasingly firm and active hand in the exaction of debts and collection of taxes, contributing to a general air of malaise in England. No longer regularly absent and on the Continent, King John became almost permanently resident north of the Channel. In the first part of his reign, John had spent a substantial amount of time in France and in particular Normandy, where he appears to have spent at least half his time based off his known whereabouts for the period from 1199 to what ended up being his final departure from the duchy in December 1203.[11] The revenues recorded in the pipe rolls after 1207 are substantially larger than the totals audited between 1194 and 1204 by the Exchequer.[12] The average annual rev-

11 Paul Webster, "King John and Rouen: Royal Iteration, Kingship, and the Norman 'Capital', c. 1199–c. 1204," in *Society and Culture in Medieval Rouen, 911–1300*, ed. Leonie V. Hicks and Elma Brenner (Turnhout: Brepols, 2013), 310–13.

12 Nick Barratt, "The Impact of the Loss of Normandy on the English Exchequer: the Pipe Roll Evidence," in *Foundations of Medieval Scholarship: Records edited in honour of David Crook*, ed. Paul Brand and Sean Cunningham (York: Borthwick Institute / National Archives, 2008), 136.

enue audited at the English Exchequer from 1194 to 1199, under Richard I, was just under £25,000. In 1204 the annual revenue at the Exchequer was £24,000 and by 1210 nearly double those figures at just under £48,000.[13] Following the refusal of Exchequer officials to answer writs of *Libertate* in January 1207 to pay the king's expenses while based in London, John replaced the royal treasuries at Westminster and Winchester with castle treasuries under his direct control, spread regionally across royal castles, and where money could be more easily deposited and accessed.[14] From 1204 to 1212, in total £300,000 was audited at the Exchequer, with £241,000 paid into the Exchequer of receipt and an additional £25,000 paid to castellans at regional castle treasuries and other non-Exchequer entities.[15] A new tax on income and movable goods, a levy of a shilling from every mark, resulted in a revenue of £60,046.[16] This was in addition to the establishment of import and export duties payable directly to the crown, which had started in 1202 and continued in various forms through 1210.[17] Royal administration and justice were ever more efficiently harnessed, also becoming more oppressive and arbitrary. The pipe rolls contain many examples of fines ultimately for the benevolence or goodwill of king, often set at high sums and paid in full within the same Exchequer year.[18]

The loss of Normandy and its knock-on effects had multiple layers of significance for London mercantile interests as well as for important London families which often included royal officials, such as sheriffs and Exchequer officials, like the Cornhills whose genealogy appears in the *Leges Anglorum*.[19] Londoners felt comparable effects to the rest of the kingdom from the increasingly firm royal hand exacting debts and collecting taxes. And given that they were in an important municipal and commercial center, they also experienced complications to their commercial interests which were heavily attuned to the Continent. In the genealogy of the dukes of Normandy and kings of England, the third text of the *Tripartita*, the *Leges Anglorum* concludes with what John Gillingham describes as an especially elegiac account of Richard I, whose

13 Barratt, "The Impact of the Loss of Normandy," 135–37.

14 John Edward Austin Jolliffe, "The Chamber and the Castle Treasuries under King John," in *Studies in Medieval History Presented to Frederick Maurice Powicke*, ed. Richard William Hunt, William Abel Pantin, and Richard W. Southern (Oxford: Clarendon Press, 1948), 128–32.

15 Barratt, "Impact on the English Exchequer," 137.

16 Ralph V. Turner, *King John* (London: Longman, 1994), 113; A. Mary Kirkus, ed. *Pipe Roll 9 John*, Pipe Roll Society 60 (London: J.W. Ruddock 1946), xxi.

17 Turner, *King John*, 113–14.

18 Barratt, "Impact on the English Exchequer," 137.

19 London, British Library, MS Add. 14252, fol. 127v.

death leads to a *stupor mundi*.[20] This description of Richard, whose heart was buried in Rouen Cathedral, has been interpreted as part of the *Leges Anglorum*'s critique of John's reign.[21] The emphasis on the closeness of Richard to Rouen reflects the author, a Londoner, mourning John's loss of Normandy to the Capetians, especially the loss of Rouen, an important commercial center with which Londoners had had important trading links with since the early eleventh century.[22] Rouennais merchants had long enjoyed special rights in London, including exemption from certain tolls and, since the reign of Edward the Confessor, their own wharf.[23] In particular, Rouen was a focal point in the Western European wine-trading network and functioned as a distribution center covering Normandy and the south and east of England.[24] Rouennais merchants were granted a monopoly on the exportation of wine to England via the Seine estuary in ca. 1172–78.[25]

In the *Leges Anglorum*'s account of Richard I's burial, Rouen is described as the capital (*capud*) of Neustria.[26] Rouen was the preeminent city in Normandy, a status also attributed to it by Orderic Vitalis,[27] making it the Norman parallel to London in England. Rouen's liberties, as laid out in its *Établissements*, served as a model for those of La Rochelle and other continental towns under Angevin rule, perhaps not unlike the way the liberties of other English towns were sometimes modeled on those of London.[28] These were liberties which John, shortly

20 Manchester, MS Latin 155, fol. 87r; Gillingham, "Stupor mundi," 400–08.

21 Gillingham, "Stupor mundi," 405.

22 Gillingham, "Stupor mundi," 405–06.

23 A Charter of the future King Henry II as duke of Normandy from 1150–1 (Henry W.C. Davis et al., eds., *Regesta Regum Anglo-Normannorum 1066–1154*, 4 vols. [Oxford: Clarendon Press, 1913–1969], 3:268–69 [no. 729]); David Bates, "Rouen from 900 to 1204: From Scandinavian Settlement to Angevin 'Capital'," in *Medieval Art, Architecture and Archaeology at Rouen*, ed. Jenny Stratford, British Archaeological Association Conference Transactions (London: British Archaeological Association, 1993), 5–7.

24 Brooke and Keir, *London 800–1216*, 265–66; Eleonora M. Carus-Wilson, "The Effects of the Acquisition and of the Loss of Gascony on the English Wine Trade," in *Medieval Merchant Ventures: Collected Studies* (London: Methuen, 1954); Webster, "King John and Rouen," 324; Alain Sadourny, "Les marchands normands en Angleterre au lendemain de la conquête de 1204," *Les Cahiers d'études médiévales de l'université de Rouen* 1 (1979): 133–34.

25 A Charter of Henry II from 1172/3–78 (Léopold Delisle and Élie Berger, eds., *Recueil des actes d'Henri II, roi d'Angleterre*, 3 vols. [Paris: Imprimerie Nationale, 1916–1927], 2:89–90 [no. 256]); Roger Dion, *Histoire de la vigne et du vin en France des origines au XXe siècle* (Paris: CNRS, 1959), 216–17.

26 London, MS Add. 14252, fol. 87r.

27 Orderic Vitalis, *Historia Ecclesiastica* 8.15, ed. and trans. Marjorie Chibnall (Oxford: Clarendon Press, 1989–1980), 4:224–25.

28 Adolphus Ballard, ed. *British Borough Charters 1042–1216* (Cambridge: Cambridge Univer-

after his accession as duke, both confirmed and augmented.[29] Among their various titles, the Norman and Angevin kings were usually styled first off as *rex Anglorum* and *dux Normannorum*, or as the form later became *rex Anglie* and *dux Normannie*. Of the Anglo-Norman, Angevin, and Aquitanian components of the Angevin realm, it was England and Normandy which enjoyed the longer established and broader community of shared interests. The special place of Rouen can also be seen in a writ of King John, dating from 1202, where Rouen Cathedral is said to be held in special affection on account of its role as royal and ducal burial site.[30] If for all of its importance and close connections, Rouen and the rest of the duchy of Normandy had still been lost, the events of 1204 and subsequent years may have contributed to a general sense of foreboding about the future across the Channel too.

In the *Leges Anglorum*, historical precedents were employed to emphasize the continuity and implied stability of the *regnum Anglorum* and its customs to date. They show a concern for the extent and unity of the past and present kingdom and also highlight the role of the king in their establishment and maintenance, modeled by predecessors, both legendary and historical. The use of historical context to highlight continuity and precedent in the compilation's component texts occurs both through interpolations to the individual texts and structurally through the use of framing materials and the compilation's overall organization.[31] Together with an overarching chronological organiza-

sity Press, 1913), 12–15; Carl Stephenson, *Borough and Town: A Study of Urban Origins in England* (Cambridge, MA: Mediaeval Academy of America, 1933), 134–35; Edward Miller and John Hatcher, *Medieval England: Towns, Commerce and Crafts, 1086–1348* (London: Longman, 1995), 309; John Hudson, *The Oxford History of the Laws of England. Volume II: 871–1216* (Oxford: Oxford University Press, 2012), 813–14.

29 Webster, "King John and Rouen," 317; Nicholas Vincent, "Jean sans Terre et les Normands avant 1199: le comte de Mortain à la lumière de ses chartes," in *1204. La Normandie entre Plantagenêts et Capétiens*, ed. Anne-Marie Flambard Héricher and Véronique Gazeau (Turnhout: Brepols, 2007), 54.

30 Bates, "Rouen from 900 to 1204," 5; Thomas D. Hardy, ed. *Rotuli Litterarum Patentium in Turri Londinensi asservati* (London: Eyre & Spottiswoode, 1835), 19a.

31 Some of the range of approaches to such means of establishing authority across multiple traditions can be seen in other chapters. For a discussion of the use of historical and biblical attributions to lend authority within the Frisian context of the *Seventeen Statutes* and the *Twenty-four Landlaws*, see: Rolf Bremmer, "More than Language: Law and Textual Communities in Medieval Frisia," Chapter 4 of this volume. On Irish legal compilations representing a tradition where the form and contents of the extant manuscripts indicates a more regular practice of presenting law texts within a continuous historical context, which placed an importance on "intertextual links," see: Fangzhe Qiu, "Law, Law-books and Tradition in Early Medieval Ireland," Chapter 5 of this volume.

tion and the insertion of chronicle, narrative, and other descriptive materials these features are all part of the larger account of London's and England's laws and customs found in the *Leges Anglorum*. These components appear to have been carefully arranged, and work by Keene has highlighted how the repetition of specific genres and themes in the organization of the compilation's components creates a thematic structure to reflect the way in which London's interests were pursued by its elite and understood within a broader historical and geographical landscape representing the kingdom.[32]

Part of this rhetorical frame is constructed from several descriptions of the kingdom. Early on the compilation contains a quantitative description in the form of the Tribal and Burghal Hidages (Manchester, MS Latin 155, fols. 3^{r}–4^{r}), for which there is a local parallel in the Hidage of Middlesex (London, MS Add. 14525, fol. 126^{r-v}) which appears in the municipal second half of the compilation. During this period, London and Middlesex together formed a single administrative unit under the jurisdiction of a pair sheriffs who would answer for both together at the royal Exchequer.[33] A descriptive preface precedes the Tribal and Burghal Hidages, and at points between these two quantitative accounts appear other narrative descriptions.

A narrative description of Britain (Manchester, MS Latin 155, fol. 70^{r-v}) lifted verbatim from the prologue to Geoffrey of Monmouth's *Historia Regum Britanniae*[34] has been inserted in the middle of the *Leges Edwardi Confessoris*.[35] This description of the island of Britain opens with an account of its natural resources and geography before moving on to enumerated descriptions of the three rivers, twenty-eight cities, and five peoples found there. It is followed by a narrative account of the founding and early history of England that appears to have been heavily influenced by Geoffrey of Monmouth and includes an especially heroic depiction of King Arthur.[36] The founding of London also features with the city as a new Troy, founded by Brutus and given a leading role in the kingdom.

A second French-language description of Britain (London, MS Add. 14252, fols. 101^{r}–104^{v}) is derived from Book 1 of Henry of Huntingdon's *Historia Anglo-*

---

32 Keene, "Text, Visualisation and Politics," 84.

33 John H. Round, *The Commune of London and Other Studies* (Westminster: Archibald Constable, 1899), 257; "Political History," ed. William Page, *A History of the County of Middlesex: Volume 2* (London: Victoria County History, 1911), 15–60, https://www.british-history.ac.uk/vch/middx/vol2/pp15-60.

34 Geoffrey of Monmouth, *Historia Regum Britanniae* 5.24–46, ed. Michael D. Reeve and trans. Neil Wright (Woodbridge, UK: Boydell & Brewer, 2007), 6–7.

35 *Leges Edwardi* 32.D, ed. Liebermann; Manchester, MS Latin 155, fol. 70^{r-v}.

36 *Leges Edwardi* 32.E, ed. Liebermann; Manchester, MS Latin 155, fols. 70^{v}–71^{v}.

rum. In comparison to the description from Geoffrey of Monmouth, this is a longer and more detailed description of the kingdom's natural resources and geography, of its government, and of its inhabitants. The translator of this French-language description may have been working from a Latin text of what Diana Greenway has identified as Redactions A and B of the fifth version of the *Historia Anglorum.*[37] In those witnesses the particular portion of the *Historia Anglorum* adapted for the French-language description appears as a discrete unit corresponding to a single *capitulum,* "Descriptio Britannie insule et de situ et habitu eius" [Description of the island of "Britannia" with regard to both its site and character], the first of a list of *capitula* unique to these redactions and non-authorial.[38] The manuscripts in this group are also notable for their inclusion of the *Tripartita* compilation as an appendix,[39] which as previously mentioned also appears in the *Leges Anglorum.*

The French-language description of Britain is not a direct translation from the *Historia Anglorum,* and there are several additions: a combination of original and potentially derivative material has been identified by Mary Bateson and Claudio Lagomarsini.[40] While it is unclear whether the overall translation could have been the work of the *Leges Anglorum* compiler—neither Bateson nor Lagomarsini believe it to be[41]—there is evidence of the compiler's hand in adapting the work for this compilation. There are interpolations not found in the original passage from the *Historia Anglorum,* such as attributing the need for an assembly to be involved in the rendering of royal justice according to "la uielz lei de iceste Bretaine" [the old law of the aforementioned Britain] (§ 2.5[42]), which mirrors the role of assemblies discussed elsewhere in the *Leges Anglorum.* The repeated use of variations of the phrase "Bretaine, ki ore est apelé Engletere" [Britain, which is now called England][43] echoes variations of the phrase "Anglia quae olim uocabatur Britannia" [England which was formerly

37 Henry of Huntingdon, *Historia Anglorum: The History of the English People,* ed. and trans. Diana Greenway, Oxford Medieval Texts (Oxford: Clarendon Press, 1996), cliii–clvi.

38 Henry of Huntingdon, *Historia Anglorum,* cliv.

39 Henry of Huntingdon, *Historia Anglorum,* cliv.

40 Bateson, "London Municipal Collection," 503–05; Claudio Lagomarsini, "The Prose 'Description of England': A Hitherto Unedited Anglo-Norman Text from BL, Additional MS 14252," *Medium Ævum* 80 (2011): 327.

41 Bateson, "London Municipal Collection," 503; Lagomarsini, "Prose Description of England," 327.

42 Citation of the French-language description of Britain follows editorial subdivisions from the edition of London, MS Add. 14252, fol. 101r–104v in Lagomarsini, "Prose Description of England," 328–31.

43 §§ 1.1, 2.6, 4.2, 12.1, 13.1, and 14.1.

called Britain] found in the compilation's versions of the *Leges Edwardi Confessoris*[44] and the *Articuli Willelmi*,[45] which will be discussed later in more detail.

The *Leges Anglorum* is not unique in making use of only this opening portion of Henry of Huntingdon's text. The twelfth-century Cambridge, Gonville and Caius College, MS 103/55 contains the full text of the *Historia Anglorum*'s opening description of the kingdom (§1.1–8) on two single folios (fols. i^r–ii^r) inserted, in a smaller and earlier hand, before a mostly complete text of the *Historia Regum Britanniae*, a text whose prologue, as mentioned above is also a description of the kingdom.[46] Both texts also appear in a more integrated fashion, that is as part of a single codex with homogenous layout, script, and rubrication and with component texts concluding and beginning on the same folio, as excerpts in Durham, Ushaw College, MS 6[47] (s. xii^2) and as full texts in Rouen, Bibliothèque Municipale, MS 1177 (U.74)[48] (s. $xii^{ex}/xiii^1$). Seen alongside the *Leges Anglorum*, this hints at a wider association between these two texts and indicates that the *Leges Anglorum* compiler's choice was not an isolated incident.

Lagomarsini notes that two of the unique additions to the *Historia Anglorum* source material in this French-language description show parallels to the *Historia Regum Britanniae*.[49] The first is an additional note on the archbishopric of Canterbury "qui jadis fu a Londres en tens de Bretuns" [which formerly was at London in the time of the Britons] (§5.1), according with Geoffrey of Monmouth's inclusion of London alongside York and Caerleon as metropolitan sees during the reign of King Arthur.[50] The second is the addition of the Humber alongside the Thames and Severn as the "tres fluuies ... plus clers e plus precious de altres" [three rivers ... clearer and more precious than others] (§5.41). This

44 *Leges Edwardi* 11.1.A4, ed. Liebermann (Manchester, MS Latin 155, fol. 57^r); 33 Rubric (fol. 71^v); 35.1.A2 (fol. 73^r).

45 *Articuli Willelmi* Incipit and 2; Manchester, MS Latin 155, fol. 52^r. Citation of the *Articuli Willelmi* follows subdivisions from the edition and translation in "Willelmi Articuli Retracti," in *The Laws of the Kings of England from Edmund to Henry I*, ed. and trans. Agnes J. Robertson (Cambridge: Cambridge University Press, 1925), 244–51.

46 Montague R. James, *A Descriptive Catalogue of the Manuscripts in the Library of Gonville and Caius College*, 2 vols. (Cambridge: Cambridge University Press, 1907–1908), 1:103; Julia C. Crick, *The historia regum Britannie of Geoffrey of Monmouth: III. A summary catalogue of the manuscripts* (Cambridge: D.S. Brewer, 1989), 44.

47 Henry of Huntingdon, *Historia Anglorum*, ed. Greenway, cxlii; Crick, *Summary Catalogue*, no. 210.

48 Henry of Huntingdon, *Historia Anglorum*, ed. Greenway, cxxxviii; Crick, *Summary Catalogue*, no. 200.

49 Lagomarsini, "Prose Description of England," 327.

50 Geoffrey of Monmouth, *Historia Regum Britanniae* 156.331–33, ed. Reeve, 210–11.

again accords with Geoffrey of Monmouth[51] but contrasts with the *Historia Anglorum* source material[52] which presents the Thames and Severn as the two rivers in Britain more celebrated than the rest. Elsewhere in the *Leges Anglorum* both Geoffrey of Monmouth and the *Historia Anglorum* appear to have been possible points of reference. For example, material from the *Historia Anglorum* may have been incorporated into the *Leges Edwardi*'s account of Arthur's conquests.[53] The apparent pairing of the two texts in other manuscripts, and their use in the two descriptions of Britain in this compilation, appears structurally to parallel the wide-reaching connecting of the *Historia Anglorum* and *Historia Regum Britanniae*.

The visual appearance of the *Leges Henrici Primi* text in the *Leges Anglorum* points to a further description of the kingdom. Chapter 6 of the *Leges Henrici* opens with a red *capitulum* and a large gold initial "R" on a blue background with red decorative elements.[54] This is noticeably different from the simpler red or blue initials and *capitulum* indicated by smaller lettering and small pen flourishes in the same color as the body of the text that are used elsewhere within both the *Leges Henrici* and other texts of the compilation to mark the start of a new chapter or subsection. This elaborate initial appears at the point in the *Leges Henrici* where the focus of the text shifts from the Church to secular concerns. However, rather than relating to the remainder of the treatise as a whole, the rubric used, "De tripertitione regni Britannie et auersitate [*sic*] legum comitatuum uel prouinciarum" [On the tripartite division of the kingdom of England the diversity (*diversitate*[55]) of laws, counties, and regions], is specific to this particular chapter of the *Leges Henrici* as a description of the subdivisions of the *regnum Anglorum* and of its laws. In the other manuscript witnesses, the fourteenth-century *Leges Anglorum* manuscripts and the other textual tradition represented by the Red Book of the Exchequer and its copy London, British Library, MS Hargrave 313,[56] there is no visual distinction like that found in the *Leges Anglorum*. There the opening initial is identical in style to those used for other chapters of the *Leges Henrici*. In comparison to those copies of the *Leges Henrici*, the distinctive layout for this chapter with its

51 Geoffrey of Monmouth, *Historia Regum Britanniae* 5.35, ed. Reeve, 6–7.

52 Henry of Huntingdon, *Historia Anglorum* 1.6, ed. Greenway, 18–19.

53 Henry of Huntingdon, *Historia Anglorum* 2.18, ed. Greenway, 98–101.

54 Manchester, MS Latin 155, fol. 82ᵛ. Citation of the *Leges Henrici* follows subdivisions from the edition in Leslie J. Downer, ed. *Leges Henrici Primi* (Oxford: Clarendon Press, 1972).

55 This is the word as it appears in the versions of the *Leges Henrici Primi* not in the *Leges Anglorum* tradition; see: Downer, *Leges Henrici Primi*, 96.

56 Downer, *Leges Henrici Primi*, 46–50.

description of the kingdom may have been a one-off effort to highlight this passage. The other two narrative descriptions discussed, however, are not set apart from their surrounding texts more than with the standard expected markers.

These qualitative and quantitative descriptions spread through the *Leges Anglorum*'s chronologically organized account of the laws and customs of London and the *regnum Anglorum* function as part of the organizational framework previously identified by Keene, and their breadth contributes to the compilation's overarching narrative observing the kingdom's long durability. These descriptive accounts covering multiple facets of the *regnum Anglorum* over a long duration can be seen as historic points for contrast with the contracting Angevin realm under King John.

The *Leges Anglorum* compilation also establishes the continuity and long durability of the kingdom through the repeated use of both contemporary and historic names for the kingdom, establishing their equivalence and developing a sense of continuity from the historic to contemporary forms. The compilation's particular use and juxtaposition of the terms "regnum Anglorum" and "regnum Britanniae" is then paralleled elsewhere in the *Leges Anglorum* to provide clarification and historical context. Variations of the phrase "regnum Britanniae modo enim uocatur regnum Anglorum" [the kingdom of Britain, now called the kingdom of the English] appear multiple times throughout the *Leges Anglorum* compilation, in multiple component texts and in a range of forms, contributing a sense of stylistic cohesiveness across the compilation and reiterating that this compilation is a historically rooted account of the laws and customs of London and wider *regnum Anglorum*.

The use of the designations "Angli" and "Britones" does appear in the three earlier versions of the *Leges Edwardi Confessoris*, textual precursors to the version of the text found in the *Leges Anglorum*.[57] However, one of the ways the *Leges Anglorum* compiler's hand is most visible in the *Leges Edwardi* is in the change in how the terms "Angli" and "Britones" and the related forms "Anglia" and "Britannia" are employed and then paralleled elsewhere in the *Leges Anglorum* compilation. As laid out in its prologue, the *Leges Edwardi* are presented as the practices recounted to William I by English nobles as their own rules and customs, those of his predecessor Edward the Confessor, which he then agreed to uphold.[58] As is fitting for this narrative context, wherever the English, the *Angli*, are mentioned in this treatise it is in one of two scenarios: to clar-

57 On the various versions, see: O'Brien, *God's Peace and King's Peace*, 45, 56.

58 *Leges Edwardi* (*Version 2*) Pol.–Prol.1, ed. and trans. Bruce O'Brien, in Bruce O'Brien, *God's Peace and King's Peace: The Laws of Edward the Confessor* (Philadelphia, PA: University of Pennsylvania Press, 1999), 158–59.

ify the English word for particular terms or in reference to a *lex Anglie*, as one would expect from the account of English nobles on their own rules and customs. In this sense, the *Angli* represent a subsection of William's subjects: those who were here before his arrival and with a common name of "Angli" to denote them. There is a single reference to the Britons, specifically to the laws of the *natio Britonum* which are referred to alongside those of the *Anglorum, Pictorum*, and *Scottorum*,[59] the latter an interpolation particular to the *Leges Anglorum*.[60]

However, following usage in Geoffrey of Monmouth, the *Leges Anglorum*'s Version 4 of the *Leges Edwardi* uses *Britannia* as an all-encompassing term referring to both pre- and post-Germanic invasion Britain. The *regnum Britanniae* refers equally to the kingdom of the second-century Lucius, recipient of the well-known letter by Pope Eleutherius on good, Christian kingship,[61] and to the kingdom of Æthelred II (r. 978–1013, 1014–16) and his successors.[62] There are multiple points of reference for the *Angli*. They are the constituent people of the *regnum Anglorum*, as the whole of the present-day kingdom. As in prior versions of the *Leges Edwardi*, they were also a subsection of William I's subjects, those present before his arrival in 1066. Reaching even further back in time, the *Angli* are also the *Angli Germannie* [the *Angli* of *Germania*], from the Germanic invasion of Britain. Through a combination of intermarriage between constituent *gentes/populi* and just laws, an interpolated chapter "on those who lawfully can and ought to cohabit and remain in the *regnum Britanniae*" provides an explanation for the relationship between the *regnum Anglorum* and the *regnum Britanniae*.[63] This passage discusses how, from precedent set during Ine's reign, privileges were granted to the Britons of Amorica (the Bretons), the Jutes, and the continental Saxons in the kingdom on account of ancient kinship ties. Emphasizing the role of integration and intermarriage of the *Angli, Britones, Picti*, and *Scotti* to create one *gens* of the *regnum Anglorum*, the account concludes:

> [...] Et tali modo effecti fuerunt deinde geiis [*sic*] una et populus unus per uniuersum regnum Britanie miseratione diuina. Deinde uniuersi uocauerunt regnum Anglorum, quod ante uocatum fuit regnum Britannie.[64]

59 *Leges Edwardi* (*Version* 2) 34, ed. O'Brien, 191–92.

60 Manchester, MS Latin 155, fol. 71v.

61 *Leges Edwardi* 11.1.A–B, esp. 11.1.A5, ed. Liebermann; Manchester, MS Latin 155, fol. 57v.

62 *Leges Edwardi* 13.1.A Rubric, ed. Liebermann; Manchester, MS Latin 155, fol. 59v.

63 *Leges Edwardi* 32.C.5–6a, ed. Liebermann; Manchester, MS Latin 155, fol. 69v.

64 *Leges Edwardi* 32.C.6a, ed. Liebermann; Manchester, MS Latin 155, fol. 69v.

> [[…] And in such a way one *gens* ["geis"] and one people were brought about through the whole kingdom of Britain by divine compassion. Henceforth all called the kingdom of the English, what previously was called the kingdom of Britain].

The use of variations on the phrase "regnum Britanniae modo enim uocatur regnum Anglorum" [the kingdom of Britain, now called the kingdom of the English] here and in Chapter 11[65] indicates both a distinct chronology and an equivalence between the two names. Later in the *Leges Edwardi*, an account of Edgar Ætheling's sister Margaret's marriage is used as an opportunity to again discuss the Picts, Scots, and Britons,[66] this time their etymological origins. The *Leges Anglorum*-version of the *Leges Edwardi* changes Margaret's title from "regina Scotie" to "domina Albanie" suggesting a subordination of the King of Scotland to fit him within the *regnum Anglorum*.[67]

The use of toponymical legends, particularly the eponymously named peoples and places in this context, can also be seen as a further parallel to Geoffrey of Monmouth, who makes extensive use of them in his own work. There is both Brutus who gave his name to *Britannia* and to the Britons[68] and his sons Locrinus for Loegria, Kamber for Kambria, and Albanactus for Albania.[69] Corineus gave his name to Corineia (Cornwall) and the Corineians,[70] and the Humber River is said to derive its name from Humber, king of the Huns.[71] The *Leges Anglorum*'s etymologies for the *Picti* and *Scotti*, however, are additional and do not feature in Geoffrey's work. The etymological discussion here mirrors the compiler's attentiveness elsewhere to the individual peoples past and present within the *regnum Anglorum*. It also functions as part of the compilation's account of the *regnum Anglorum* as historically comprising many peoples and territories and inviting comparison through the lens of imperial models, where the politically mature and powerful ruler was a ruler of many peoples.[72]

The phrase, "regnum Britanniae modo enim uocatur regnum Anglorum" [the kingdom of Britain, now called the kingdom of the English], should per-

65 *Leges Edwardi* 11.1.A4, ed. Liebermann; Manchester, MS Latin 155, fol. 57^{r}.
66 *Leges Edwardi* 35.1.A2, ed. Liebermann; Manchester, MS Latin 155, fol. 73^{r-v}.
67 *Leges Edwardi* 35.1, ed. Liebermann; Manchester, MS Latin 155, fol. 73^{r}; Liebermann, *Über die Leges Anglorum*, 46; Ullmann, "Geoffrey of Monmouth," 265.
68 Geoffrey of Monmouth, *Historia Regum Britanniae* 21.459–60, ed. Reeve, 28–29.
69 Geoffrey of Monmouth, *Historia Regum Britanniae* 23.5–11, ed. Reeve, 30–31.
70 Geoffrey of Monmouth, *Historia Regum Britanniae* 21.462–65, ed. Reeve, 28–29.
71 Geoffrey of Monmouth, *Historia Regum Britanniae* 24.17–19, ed. Reeve, 30–33.
72 R.R. Davies, "The Peoples of Britain and Ireland 1100–1400: I. Identities," *Transactions of the Royal Historical Society*, 6th series 4 (1994): 13–14.

haps be seen as a stylistic fingerprint of the *Leges Anglorum* compiler and can be found at other points in the compilation. In the previously discussed Chapter 6 of the *Leges Henrici Primi*, an interlinear addition inserts "in regno Britannie" to the first line of the chapter, seemingly to supplement the "regnum Anglorum" already copied.[73] The analogous phrase "Anglia quae olim uocabatur Britannia" [England which was formerly called Britain] is used twice in the *Articuli Willelmi*, an additional clarification of historical context that has been added at both points.[74] The use of the *regnum Britanniae-regnum Anglorum* pairing conveniently highlights continuity in the kingdom's customary practices of justice and administration. The customary practices of the *Angli* are those from days gone by for which the compiler provides the specific Old English terms, such as when he notes that the English term for purchases without guarantors is *fastermannes*.[75] They are also the origins for the customs of the contemporary *Angli* who form the present-day *regnum Anglorum*. This concept of continuity underlies the organization and premise of the legal texts which comprise the bulk of the wider *Leges Anglorum* compilation.

Beyond the legal texts, comparable phrasing also appears in the opening of the geographic preface to the Tribal and Burghal Hidages: "De numero provinciarum et patriarum et comitatuum et insularum que de iure spectant et sine dubio pertinent corone et dignitati regni Britannie scilicet quod modo uocatur regnum Anglorum" [On the number of provinces and countries and shires and islands which by right are situated within and without doubt pertain to the crown and dignity of the kingdom of Britain which is now called the kingdom of the English].[76] And despite the almost exclusive use of *Anglorum* and *Anglie* in the municipal second half of the compilation, in the French-language adaptation of Henry of Huntingdon's description of Britain variations on the phrase "De Bretaine, ki ore est apelé Engletere" [On Britain, which is now called England] appear, including where the *Historia Anglorum* source material uses only "Britannia," suggesting the specific modification of the source material for consistency. The stylistic intervention, reflecting his interest in noting both contemporary and historical terminology, is yet another sign of the comprehensiveness of his editorial work to create a cohesive compilation.

The *Leges Anglorum*'s rubric opening the genealogy of the dukes of Normandy uses the stylistically similar, "Item de ducibus Normannorum in Neustria que modo uocatur Normannia" [Likewise on the dukes of Normandy in

73 Manchester, MS Latin 155, fol. 82v.
74 *Articuli Willelmi* Incipit and 2, ed. Robertson; Manchester, MS Latin 155, fol. 52r.
75 *Leges Edwardi* 38, ed. Liebermann; Manchester, MS Latin 155, fol. 60v.
76 Manchester, MS Latin 155, fol. 3r.

Neustria now called Normandy].[77] By implying continuity between Carolingian Neustria and contemporary *Normannia*, the *Leges Anglorum* compiler is again following terminology from Geoffrey of Monmouth's *Historia Regum Britanniae*, which includes the equivalent "Neustria nunc vocata Normannia" [Neustria now called Normandy]. In the *Historia Regum Britanniae*, Geoffrey uses the contemporary name *Normannia* alongside *Neustria* and *Est(r)usia*.[78] The compiler's etymological flourishes again suggest equivalence between the past and present, underlying the compilation's themes of a traceable legal heritage and continuity. This emphasis on continuity appears to gloss over the upheaval inherent in the Norman historiography between *Neustria* and *Normannia*.[79] However beyond using this place name, there are no other references to the pre-Norman history of Normandy; being a genealogy of the dukes of Normandy, the genealogy opens with Rollo and his baptism. This allusion to the Frankish past however parallels the references to Pepin the Short and his son Charles in the *Leges Edwardi*'s discussion of good kingship.[80]

Both the repeated and strategic appearance of descriptive accounts of the *regnum Anglorum* and the construction of a longue durée account of the peoples of the kingdom place the specific aspects of the kingdom which are an essential part of the *Leges Anglorum*'s contemporarily relevant discussion of the model kingdom at the center of the compilation's structure and organization. Thus, both actively and passively this compilation engages with and highlights the importance of the state of the kingdom as a lens through which to critique the king. The Norman and Angevin dynasties are established as direct heirs to both their historical and legendary predecessors though the compilation's highlighting of continuity and precedent, and thus those predecessors become models to which the contemporary king can be held up against. With regards to the substantial contraction of the Angevin realm under John's watch, the most relevant aspect of the *Leges Anglorum*'s concept of good kingship here is the principle that in maintaining the stability of his kingdom the king ought

77 Manchester, MS Latin 155, fol. 74r.

78 See, for example: Geoffrey of Monmouth, *Historia Regum Britanniae* 155.302, ed. Reeve, 208–09; Hans E. Keller, "Two Toponymical Problems in Geoffrey of Monmouth and Wace: Estrusia and Siesia," *Speculum* 49 (1974): 687–89; John S.P. Tatlock, *The Legendary History of Britain: Geoffrey of Monmouth's Historia Regum Britanniae and its Early Vernacular Versions* (Berkeley, CA: University of California Press, 1950), 90–91.

79 Felice Lifshitz, "The Norman Conquest of Pious Neustria," in *The Norman Conquest of Pious Neustria: Historiographic Discourse and Saintly Relics 684–1090* (Toronto: Pontifical Institute of Mediaeval Studies, 1995), 206–19.

80 *Leges Edwardi* 11.1.A, ed. Liebermann; Manchester, MS Latin 155, fol. 57r.

to be careful not to alienate any rights or land which belong to the crown and consequently also ought to restore those which have been lost.[81]

The model kingdom is expansive, internally peaceful, and stable if not actively growing. This appears twice as interpolations to the *Leges Edwardi*, specifically within the context of the extent of the kingdom. It features as part of the expanded account of the responsibilities of a good, Christian king which precede the compilation's interpolated letter of Pope Eleutherius to Lucius, King of the Britons:[82]

> Debet uero rex de iure omnes terras et honores et omnes dignitates et iura et libertates corone regni huius in integrum cum omni integritate et sine diminucione obseruare et defendere, dispersa et delapidata et ammissa regni iura in pristinum statum et debitum uiribus omnibus reuocare.[83]
>
> [Truly, the king ought to observe and defend, according to law, all lands and honors and all dignities and rights and freedoms of the crown of this kingdom in its entirety with all integrity and without abatement, to restore the kingdom's scattered and dispersed and lost laws to a pristine state and what is owed to all men].

A few folios later, a further interpolation recounts the positive, though not wholly successful, effort by Edward the Confessor (*Bonus rex Eadwardus*) to reverse damages wrought on the kingdom by his predecessors, Cnut and his sons who "multa iura et dignitates et terras et insulas a corona regni huius alienauerunt et delapidauerunt" [alienated and eroded many rights and dignities and lands and islands from the crown of his kingdom].[84]

The account of the atrocities committed by these Scandinavian kings both contrasts with and parallels the extended prologue to I–II Cnut describing Cnut's division of England into administrative units after his invasion for the peaceful ruling of the kingdom.[85] This small account appears to reflect a concern in the *Leges Anglorum* for peaceful relations with foreigners in England, which permeates the compilation more generally. The Danelaw is depicted as having its origins in the inclusion of the Norwegians in Arthur's vast empire, who are eventually integrated in the same way and using the same language as

---

81 Ullmann, "Geoffrey of Monmouth," 262–63.

82 Ullmann, "Geoffrey of Monmouth," 260–63.

83 *Leges Edwardi* 11.1.A2; Manchester, MS Latin 155, fol. 57r.

84 *Leges Edwardi* 13.1.A–A2, ed. Liebermann; Manchester, MS Latin 155, fol. 60r.

85 Manchester, MS Latin 155, fol. 34r–v.

the description of how the intermarriage of the *Angli*, *Britones*, *Picti*, and *Scoti* eventually formed a single *gens Anglorum*.[86] The *Leges Anglorum* goes even further and attributes to Edward the Confessor and his counsel the confirmation of the possessions of the Norwegians' descendants, which fits well with the depiction of a peaceful and harmonious kingdom but is an event which did not occur.[87] Likewise, the *Leges Anglorum*'s text of the *Articuli Willelmi* has been interpolated so that the peace and security which William I's *decreta* are intended to maintain between the English and Normans have been recast to encompass additionally:

> Francigenos et Britones Wallie et Cornubie et Pictos et Scottos Albanie, similiter ... Francos et insulicolas omnium insularum et prouinciarum et patriarum que pertinent ad coronam.[88]
>
> [those of French birth and the Britons of Wales and Cornwall, and the Picts and Scots of Albania, and likewise ... the French and the inhabitants of all the islands, provinces, and countries which appertain to the Crown].

The former vastness of the kingdom, ruled by model kings such as Arthur and Edward the Confessor, to whom William I and his descendants are direct heirs, directly contrasts with the contemporary reality of the shrinking Angevin realm during John's reign.

The de-emphasizing of conquest was obviously an important element for legitimizing the Norman and Angevin dynasties in England. William as Edward's heir is a common trope both here and elsewhere. The desire for continuity over conquest likewise appears in the work of Richard of Devizes, who emphasized a link between Cerdic and Arthur in the founding of the house of Wessex.[89] On the other hand, it also strengthens the tone of rebuke toward John's reign where the shrinking Angevin realm is viewed with concern. The narrative of the kingdom of England as a unified entity needed to be recalibrated to an understanding of an English empire within the British Isles as

---

86 *Leges Edwardi* 32.C.7, E.3–6, ed. Liebermann; Manchester, MS Latin 155, fol. 71^{r-v}.

87 *Leges Edwardi* 32.E.5–6, ed. Liebermann; Manchester, MS Latin 155, fol. 71^{r-v}; Liebermann, *Über die Leges Anglorum*, 48–49.

88 *Articuli Willelmi* 1; Manchester, MS Latin 155, fol. 52^{r}; Translation: *Willelmi Articuli Retracti* 1, ed. Robertson, 244–45.

89 John Gillingham, "Richard of Devizes and 'a rising tide of nonsense': How Cerdic Met King Arthur," in *The Long Twelfth-Century View of the Anglo-Saxon Past*, ed. Martin Brett and David A. Woodman (Farnham: Ashgate, 2015).

well as a need to reflect a reality where Scotland, Wales, and Ireland were sites of conflict and clearly distinct peoples.

This sort of diversity arising from a variety of peoples co-existing within the *regnum Anglorum* would likely have been easily recognizable to Londoners familiar with merchants from many different lands who participated in vast trade networks across the kingdom but centered on London and who benefited from special rights granted to them. The *Leges Anglorum* itself discusses the legal distinctions between the foreigners regularly operating in the city and the franchised Londoners, which were necessary for the arbitration of disputes, as well as specific regulations relating to the conduct of foreigners from places including Lower Lorraine, the Holy Roman Empire, Norway, and Denmark.[90] The *Leges Anglorum*'s discussions of the amalgamation of peoples co-existing within the *regnum Anglorum*, and the multiplicity of jurisdictions within the frame of reference of Londoners could be seen as reminiscent of the special interest found in the "negotiation of settlements," which both Mary P. Richards and Thom Gobbitt note in Cambridge, Corpus Christi College, MS 383,[91] a legal manuscript with links to St Paul's.[92] The two legal compilations in different ways appear to reflect both London's role as an important center of trade and administration within the kingdom, with interactions between parties passing through and traveling to the city, and the complex administrative structures within and for the city itself which were a product of both their development over an extended period of time and the complexity necessarily found in any large urban settlement.

The compilation's attentiveness to the constituent peoples within the kingdom provided a framework for the *Leges Anglorum* to discuss the *regnum Anglorum* in comparison to imperial models: the idea that the politically mature and powerful ruler was a ruler of many peoples. The English kingdom is being highlighted as one where a number of different peoples cohabit the island, in the same way that a number of different peoples had coexisted within the Roman Empire. While the specific term "imperium" does not appear in the *Articuli Willelmi* or in the *Leges Edwardi* in reference to the *regnum Anglorum*,

---

90 London, MS Add. 14252, fols. 99v–100v.

91 Thom Gobbitt, "The Other Book: Cambridge, Corpus Christi College, MS 383 in Relation to the Textus Roffensis," in *Textus Roffesnsis: Law, Language, and Libraries in Early Medieval England*, ed. Bruce O'Brien and Barbara Bombi (Turnhout: Brepols, 2015), 72; Mary P. Richards, "The Manuscript Contexts of the Old English Law: Tradition and Innovation," in *Studies in Earlier Old English Prose*, ed. Paul E. Szarmach (New York: University of New York Press, 1986), 181–82.

92 Kathryn Powell, "The 'Scipmen' Scribe and Cambridge, Corpus Christi College 383," *The Heroic Age* 14 (2010), http://www.heroicage.org/issues/14/powell.php.

if we look again at the geographic preface to the Tribal and Burghal Hidages, the sentiment is definitively expressed: "Uerum de iure potius appellari potest et debet excellencia illustrissime predicte corone imperium quam regnum" [The excellent and illustrious aforementioned crown by right can and ought to be called "imperium" rather than "regnum"].[93]

The vastness of the imperial model is found descriptively in the *Leges Anglorum*'s account of the vastness of King Arthur's conquests stretching from Greenland to Russia. Arthur's realm in the *Leges Anglorum* extends beyond the already vast empire attributed to him by Geoffrey of Monmouth,[94] encompassing:

> Scanciam totam, que modo Norweia uocatur, et omnes insulas ultra Scanciam, scilicet Islandiam et Grenelandiam, que sunt de appendiciis Norweie, et Suetheidam et Yberniam et Gutlandiam et Daciam et Semelandiam et Winelandiam et Curlandiam et Roe et Fenielandiam et Wirlandiam et Estlandiam et Cherrelam et Lappam et omnes alias terras et insulas orientales occeani usque Russiam.[95]
>
> [All Scandinavia, which is now called Norway, and all the islands beyond Scandinavia, namely Iceland and Greenland, which are appendages of Norway, and Sweden and Ireland and Gotland and Denmark and Samland and Vinland and Courland and Ruhnu and Finland and Wirland and Estland and Karelien and Lapland and all other lands and islands of the eastern ocean up to Russia].

This particular passage is the first time that some of these place names appear in an English source.[96] Like several other points in the *Leges Anglorum* compiler's interpolations, "modo" is used adverbially to provide detail and clarify an ancient name; here it is in the phrase "Scanciam totam, que modo Norweia uocatur" [All of Scandinavia, which is now called Norway]. The *Scancia-Norweia* place name information does not come from Geoffrey of Monmouth, who refers throughout his work to *Norguegia* but not *Scancia*.[97] The *Leges*

93 Manchester, MS Latin 155, fol. 3r; Liebermann, *Über die Leges Anglorum*, 6.

94 Geoffrey of Monmouth, *Historia Regum Britanniae* 153.212–351, ed. Reeve, 204–11.

95 *Leges Edwardi*, 32.E, ed. Liebermann; Manchester, MS Latin 155, fol. 70v.

96 Liebermann, *Über die Leges Anglorum*, 47.

97 Geoffrey of Monmouth, *Historia Regum Britanniae* 35.21, ed. Reeve, 48–49; 41.146, 4–55; 80.182, 98–99; 154.236, 204–5; 154.249, 206–7; 155.250, 206–7; 156.346, 210–11; 162.525, 220–21; 178.79, 252–53; 183.120, 254–55.

Anglorum's combined use of both *Scancia* and *Norguegia* may ultimately derive from classical sources; both in Antiquity and later, the Nordic lands were thought of as islands in the ocean.[98] This is the sense of the geography which is used to describe Arthur's kingdom with its multiple references to "omnes insulas" [all the islands] or "multas alias insulas" [the many other islands] beyond *Scancia*. In his *Natural History*, Pliny the Elder used the term *Scandia* in the plural alongside the form *Scadinavia* in his account of the geography of Britain, Ireland, and Thule.[99] This is similar to the earlier account in Pomponius Mela's *De situ orbis*.[100] *Scandia* and *Scancia*, the spellings found in Version 4 of the *Leges Edwardi*, was a common corruption from *Scadnia* and *Scadinavia* which, according to Josef Svennung, appeared in better copies of Pliny's *Natural History*.[101]

This far-reaching kingdom of Britain is attributed to Arthur's prowess as a king and soldier. In the *Historia Regum Britanniae*, Geoffrey envisions an empire, more generally, as "the extension of a king's rule beyond the realm he began with, perhaps to provide apanages for his younger sons as well as revenue and feudal prestige for himself."[102] The *regnum Anglorum* is being highlighted as one where a number of different people cohabit the island as in the way they all coexisted within the Roman Empire. The attention the compiler gives to ideas such as the peaceful coexistence of multiple *gentes* or a king who is able to expand his rule beyond the realm he began with feed into the *Leges Anglorum*'s ideology of good kingship. The compiler's inclusion, or perhaps fabrication, of Pope Eleutherius' letter—the thirteenth-century manuscript of the *Leges Anglorum* is the earliest known appearance of this letter—could also be seen as attributing papal backing for the boundaries of a *regnum Britanniae* extending from the Western Sea all the way to Norway and Denmark.[103] This however is within the *Leges Anglorum*'s expanded account on the law and

98 Josef Svennung, *Scadinavia und Scandia: Lateinisch-nordische Namenstudien*, Acta Societatis Litterarum Humaniorum Regiae Upsaliensis 44:1 (Uppsala: Almqvist & Wiksells, 1963), 12–14.

99 Pliny, *Natural History*, 4.102–4, trans. Harris Rackham, Loeb Classical Library 352 (Cambridge, MA: Harvard University Press, 1942), 2:196–99; Svennung, *Scadinavia und Scandia*, 11, 23.

100 Pomponius Mela, *De situ orbis* 3.54, in *Chorographie*, ed. and trans. Alain Silberman, Collection des universités de France Série latine 283 (Paris: Belles Lettres, 1988), p. 80; Svennung, *Scadinavia und Scandia*, 12.

101 Svennung, *Scadinavia und Scandia*, 11.

102 Tatlock, *Legendary History of Britain*, 305.

103 *Leges Edwardi* 11.1.A3, ed. Liebermann; Manchester, MS Latin 155, fol. 57^{r}.

appendages to the crown of the kingdom of Britain and what the king's office is, which precedes Pope Eleutherius' letter, and the pope is not explicitly granting sovereignty.[104]

While Geoffrey's Arthur is a good, Christian king, the *Leges Edwardi* interpolations go one step further by giving Arthur's annexation of Norway the support of the pope and Roman *curia*. Felix Liebermann suggested that Adrian IV's approval of the Anglo-Norman annexation of Ireland in 1155 may have served as a parallel or model for this account. He noted a similar turn of phrase where Henry II's annexation of Ireland is discussed in the account of Henry II prefacing his royal charters, *Glanvill*, and the Bread Assize.[105]

> Impetrauit enim temporibus illis Arturus Rex a domino papa et a curia Romana quod confirmata fuit Norwegia in perpetuum corone Britannie in augmentum regni huius.[106]
>
> [In those times King Arthur obtained from the lord pope and from the Roman Curia that Norway was confirmed in perpetuity to the British Crown to augment this kingdom.]
>
> Subiugauit eciam iste predictus Rex dignitati corone sue et in augmentum scilicet corone regni sui predicti in perpetuum Yberniam totam cum omnibus appendiciis suis gracia Dei et auctoritate domini pape.[107]
>
> [That aforementioned king [Henry II] also subjugated, to the dignity of his crown and for the augmentation certainly of the crown of his aforementioned kingdom in perpetuity, the whole of Ireland with all its appendages by the grace of God and authority of the lord pope.]

Whether or not this is in fact the case, both episodes contribute toward the *Leges Anglorum*'s depiction of the augmenting of one's kingdom as not only prestigious but also an aspect of good, Christian kingship.

By highlighting the continuity of the kingdom from that time through to the thirteenth century, the compiler suggests continuity with the glory of that vast empire. The practice of an annual oath of fealty via the folkmoots is explained

---

104 *Leges Edwardi* 11.1.A, ed. Liebermann; Manchester, MS Latin 155, fol. 57r; Liebermann, *Über die Leges Anglorum*, 46.

105 Liebermann, *Über die Leges Anglorum*, 48, 77.

106 *Leges Edwardi* 32.E.3, ed. Liebermann; Manchester, MS Latin 155, fol. 71r.

107 Manchester, MS Latin 155, fol. 129r.

as having ancient precedents attributable to King Arthur.[108] The *Leges Anglorum*'s account appears to conflate earlier English practices of oaths of fealty sworn by "omnes populi et gentes uniuerse" [all peoples and groups generally][109] such as those tied with the 1181 and 1205 Assizes of Arms with communal oaths found in some continental cities.[110] This makes Arthur one early, excellent king within a long line of good kings. Stating that King Edgar "excitauit et in lucem erexit. Et illam per totum regnum firmiter obseruare fecit et precepit" [awakened it and brought it into light. And he had it firmly observed and instructed through the whole kingdom][111] establishes that the practice of this oath can then be followed down through a line of legal precedent through the laws of the English kings which the *Leges Anglorum* narrates. The compiler's account contrasts with other historical narratives of the time, including Geoffrey of Monmouth, where the Britons have lost their name and their kingdom upon Cadwalader's death.

In the context of contemporary events, discussion of these particular tenets of good kingship figure as a political critique of the contemporary circumstances of the *regnum Anglorum*, which have been thoroughly integrated within the apparatus of the wider *Leges Anglorum* compilation. This is a compilation where London's customary liberties and its royal charters granting and confirming these and other liberties feature prominently. Texts of Henry I's and Henry II's London charters have been integrated into the chronologically presented account of the laws and customs of the *regnum Anglorum* that began with Ine's law-code. This is complemented by a list of charters found in the city's treasury and considered alongside each other provide an account of the city's royal grants of customs and liberties up to and including John's reign. By using charters of liberties as a defining facet of a city's rights and freedoms, the status of the grantor of those charters is intertwined and made essential to the legitimization of the town's special status being asserted in the documents. In the *Leges Anglorum*, this is emphasized in two ways: one, by the placement of London's royal charters alongside royal law-codes and treatises documenting the customary practices of the kingdom that were protected by royal promises and two, by highlighting where these overlapped with customary municipal practices. It also creates a link between any anxieties about the king or the state of the wider *regnum Anglorum* and the current and future state of the city of London.

108 *Leges Edwardi* 32.A.7–8, ed. Liebermann; Manchester, MS Latin 155, fol. 67r.

109 *Leges Edward* 32.A.5, ed. Liebermann; Manchester, MS Latin 155, fol. 66v.

110 Liebermann, *Gesetze der Angelsachsen*, 1:655, n. h.

111 *Leges Edwardi* 32.A.8, ed. Liebermann; Manchester, MS Latin 155, fol. 67r.

CHAPTER 9

The Inviolable Right: Property and Power in Medieval Scandinavian Laws and Society

Francesco Sangriso

The evolution of land tenure in medieval Nordic society is represented in a range of legal and literary sources, including *Gulatingslova*, Snorri Sturluson's *Heimskringla*, as well as in eddic and skaldic poetry. Analysis of this corpus shows how central the concept of inherited land property is, expressed by the substantive *óðal*, which is a very important element in the foundation of both the elites' power and monarchy's claims to domain.[1] The same linguistic element highlights two different and contrasting ideas of power, whose conflict characterizes Norwegian history during the Middle Ages, from attempts to establish a royal power through until the complete creation of an absolute and centralized monarchy under the reign of Hákon IV, as demonstrated in the *Haralds Saga ins Hárfagra*, in which Snorri Sturluson describes a significant act outlining the rise to power of the Norwegian sovereign:

1 The struggle between royal power and the landed elite characterizes the formation of a centralized monarchy in Norway, from a system based on personal ties between kings and magnates, to a government where the sovereign has its own bureaucratic structure and is not only the supreme leader, but, above all, the holder of the royal office. As Sverre Bagge notes, "Impressive military successes, diplomatic ability and a charismatic personality," along side hereditary succession, are the sources of legitimation for king's right to the throne, and the ownership of real estate becomes an important economic basis for the royal power, Sverre Bagge, *Society and Politics in Snorri Sturluson's Heimskringla* (Berkeley: University of California Press, 1991), 92. With regard to kingship, state formation and the development of Christian kingship ideology in Norway, see Sverre Bagge, *From Gang Leader to the Lord's Anointed: Kingship in Sverris saga and Hákonar saga Hákonarsonar* (Odense: Odense University Press, 1996). Hans Jacob Orning, *Uforutsigbarhet og nærvær: En analyse av norske kongers maktutøvelse i høymiddelalderen* (Oslo: Unipub, 2004). Jón Viðar Sigurðsson, *Det norrøne samfunnet: Vikingen, kongen, erkebiskopen og bonden* (Oslo: Pax, 2008). Sverre Bagge, *From Viking Stronghold to Christian Kingdom: State Formation in Norway, c. 900–1350* (Copenhagen: Museum Tusculanum Press, 2010). Hans Jacob Orning, "Conflict and Social (Dis)order in Norway, c. 1030–1160," in *Disputing Strategies in Medieval Scandinavia*, ed. by Kim Esmark and others (Leiden: Brill, 2013). The sources quoted here, about the conflict between royal power and landed elite, date to a period ranging from the 12th to the 14th centuries.

 | DOI:10.1163/9789004448650_011

> Haraldr konungr setti þann rétt allt þar, er hann vann ríki undir sik, at hann eignaðisk óðǫl ǫll, ok lét alla bóendr gjalda sér landskyldir, bæði ríka ok óríka.[2]
>
> [King Haraldr made this law everywhere he established his dominion over, that he took possession of all *óðǫl* [inherited property] and made all farmers pay him land dues, both rich and poor].[3]

According to *Óláfs Saga Helga*, this also happens when Haraldr subdues the Orkney Islands.[4] A very different case is described in the 31st chapter of the *Haralds Saga ins Hárfagra*. Here the *jarl* Einarr owns all the ancestral property in the Orkney Islands as recovery after he, instead of the farmers, had paid a fine to King Haraldr *inn hárfagri*.[5]

In the introduction to the saga dedicated to the "holy king," Snorri Sturluson emphasizes King Harald's tyrannical nature:

> Þá er Haraldr konungr herjaði land ok átti orrostur, þá eignaðisk hann svá vendiliga allt land ok ǫll óðǫl—bæði byggðir ok sætr ok úteyjar eignaðisk hann, svá markir allar ok alla auðn landsins. Váru allir búendr hans leigumenn ok landbúar.[6]
>
> [When King Haraldr raided land and fought battles, then he gained complete control both of all the land and all *óðǫl* [ancestral property]—both settlements and pasture-land and outlying islands he gained control of, also all forests and wastelands. All farmers were his tenants and landholders].[7]

Similarly, in *Eglis Saga Skalla-Grímssonar*:

---

2 Snorri Sturluson, *Heimskringla I*, ed. Bjarni Aðalbjanarson (Reykjavík: Hið íslenzka fornritafélag, 2002), 98.

3 Snorri Sturluson, *Heimskringla I. The Beginnings to Óláfr Tryggvason*, trans. Alison Finlay and Anthony Faulkes (Exeter: Viking Society for Northern Research, 2011), 56.

4 Snorri Sturluson, *Heimskringla II*, ed. Bjarni Aðalbjanarson (Reykjavík: Hið íslenzka fornritafélag, 2002), 158, 167.

5 Snorri Sturluson, *Heimskringla I*, ed. Bjarni Aðalbjanarson, 134. The same story is reported in the *Orkneyinga Saga*: Finnbogi Guðmundsson, ed. *Orkneyinga Saga* (Reykjavík: Hið íslenzka fornritafélag, 1965), 16.

6 Snorri Sturluson, *Heimskringla II*, ed. Bjarni Aðalbjanarson, 424.

7 Snorri Sturluson, *Heimskringla II Óláfr Haraldsson*, trans. Alison Finlay and Anthony Faulkes (Exeter: Viking Society for Northern Research, 2014), 282.

> Haraldr konungr eignaðisk í hverju fylki óðul ǫll ok allt land, byggt ok óbyggt, ok jafnvel sjóinn ok vǫtnin, ok skyldu allir búendr vera hans leiglendingar.[8]
>
> [Harold claimed as his own through every district all *óðul* [patrimonies], and all land tilled or untilled, likewise all seas and freshwater lakes. All landowners were to be his tenants].[9]

The landed elite was deprived of the full ownership of freehold property which became a precarious detention, subject to precise (and, according to Snorri Sturluson, burdensome) charges. This deprivation then became one of the determining causes of emigration to Iceland which, according to the *Íslendingabók*, was so considerable that the king himself made provisions to avoid the depopulation of Norway:

> En þá varð fǫr manna mikil mjǫk út hingat ýr Norvegi, til þess unz konungrinn Haraldr bannaði, af því at hónum þótti landauðn nema. Þá sættusk þeir á þat, at hverr maðr skyldi gjalda konungi fimm aura, sá er eigi væri frá því skiliðr ok þaðan fœri hingat.[10]
>
> [And then a great many people began to move out here from Norway, until King Haraldr forbade it, because he thought it would lead to depopulation of the land. They then came to the agreement that everyone who was not exempt and travelled here from there should pay the king five ounces of silver].[11]

The same interpretation is given in the *Landnámabók*:

> Geirmundr heljarskinn var herkonungr; hann herjaði í vestrvíking, en átti ríki á Rogalandi. En er hann kom aptr, þá er hann hafði lengi í bruttu verit, þá hafði Haraldr konungr barizk í Hafrsfirði við Eirík Hǫrðakonung ok Súlka konung af Rogalandi ok Kjǫtva enn auðga ok fengit sigr. Hann hafði

8 Sigurður Nordal, ed., *Egils Saga Skalla-Grímssonar* (Reykjavík: Hið íslenzka fornritafélag, 1933), 11–12.

9 W.C. Green, trans., *The story of Egil Skallagrimsson* (London: E. Stock, 1893), accessed September 11, 2020, https://sagadb.org/egils_saga.en.

10 Jakob Benediktsson, ed., *Íslendingabók. Landnámabók* (Reykjavík: Hið íslenzka fornritafélag, 1986), 5–6.

11 Sian Grønlie, trans., *Íslendingabók. Kristni Saga. The Book of Icelanders. The Story of the Conversion* (Exeter: Viking Society for Northern Research, 2006), 4.

> þá lagt undir sik allt Rogaland ok tekit þar marga menn af óðulum sínum. Sá þá Geirmundr øngvan annan sinn kost en ráðask brutt, því at hann fékk þar øngvar sœmdir. Hann tók þá þat ráð at leita Íslands.[12]

> [Geirmund Hell-Skin became a warrior-king. He went on Viking expeditions to the British Isles, but ruled a kingdom in Rogaland. When he came back after a long absence, King Haraldr had fought the Battle of Hafursfjord against King Eirik of Hordaland, King Sulki of Rogaland and Kjotvi the Wealthy, and had defeated them. He'd conquered the whole of Rogaland and driven a good many farmers from their *óðulum* [estates]. Geirmund realized he had no choice but to emigrate, because he had no standing there any more, so he decided to sail to Iceland].[13]

and recurs in several *Íslendingasǫgur*:

> Margir gildir menn, at þeir flýðu óðul sín fyrir ófríki Haralds konungs.[14]

> [Many prestigious men who, as consequence of King Haraldr's tyranny, fled their *óðul* [properties received by inheritance], that they held in free possession].[15]

> Þá váru fyrir vestan haf margir ágætir menn, þeir sem flýit hǫfðu óðul sin ór Nóregi fyrir Haraldi konungi, því at hann gerði alla útlæga, þá sem í móti honum hǫfðu barizk, ok tók undir sik eignir þeira.[16]

> [At that time were many great men west over the Sea, such as had fled from their *óðul* [lands] in Norway before King Harald, because he had made all those outlaws, who had met him in battle, and taken to him their possessions].[17]

12 Jakob Benediktsson, ed., *Íslendingabók. Landnámabók*, 152.

13 Hermann Pálsson and Paul Edwards, trans., *The Book of Settlements. Landnámabók* (Winnipeg: University of Manitoba Press, 2006), 57.

14 Þórhallur Vilmundarson and Bjarni Vilhjálmsson, eds., *Flóamanna Saga* (Reykjavík: Hið íslenzka fornritafélag, 1991), 238.

15 My translation.

16 Guðni Jónsson, ed., *Grettis Saga* (Reykjavík: Hið íslenzka fornritafélag, 1936), 6.

17 William Morris and Eiríkr Magnússon, trans., *The story of Grettir the Strong* (New York: Longmans, Green and Co., 1900), accessed September 11, 2020, https://sagadb.org/grettis_saga.en.

> Margir mikils háttar menn flýðu úr Noregi ok þoldu eigi álögur konungs, þeir sem váru af stórum ættum, ok vildu heldr fyrirláta óðul sín ok frændr ok vini en liggja undir þrælkan og ánauðaroki konungs.[18]
>
> [But many men of account fled from Norway, and would not bear the burden of the king, even men of great kin; for rather would they forego the *óðul* [free lands their fathers owned], their kin and their friends, than lie under the thraldom of the king and the hard days he laid upon them].[19]
>
> Þetta var í þann tíma er Haraldr konungr inn hárfagri gekk til ríkis í Noregi. Fyrir þeim ófriði flýðu margir gǫfgir menn óðul sín af Noregi.[20]
>
> [That was in the days when King Harald Hairfair came to the rule of Norway. Because of that unpeace many noble men fled from their *óðul* [lands] out of Norway].[21]

Haraldr *inn hárfagri* embodies, therefore, a concept of sovereignty whose hallmark is precisely the fulfilment of a plan aimed at depriving the landed elite of the foundation of their power. It would be incorrect, however, to assume a sort of generalized expropriation. Haraldr acted as an early medieval Scandinavian leader, demanding supplies from landowners in case of need, and he received rents from the properties of defeated opponents, but it was certainly not an institutionalized form of taxation, which was unknown at that time in Norway.[22]

---

18 Jóhannes Halldórsson, ed., *Víglundar Saga* (Reykjavík: Hið íslenzka fornritafélag, 1959), 63.

19 William Morris and Eiríkr Magnússon, transl., "The Story of Viglund the Fair," in *Three Northern Love Stories and Other Tales* (New York: Longmans, Green and Co., 1901), accessed September 11, 2020, https://sagadb.org/viglundar_saga.en.

20 Einar Ól. Sveinsson and Matthías Þórðarson, eds., *Eyrbyggja Saga* (Reykjavík: Hið íslenzka fornritafélag, 1935), 3.

21 William Morris and Eiríkr Magnússon, trans., *The Saga of the Ere-Dwellers*, (London: B. Quaritch, 1892), accessed September 11 2020, https://sagadb.org/eyrbyggja_saga.en.

22 Ole Georg Moseng, Erik Opsahl, Gunnar I. Pettersen, and Erling Sandmo, *Norsk Historie 1750–1537* (Oslo: Tano Aschehoug, 2006), 60. See also Narve Bjørgo, "Samkongedøme og einekongedøme", *Historisk Tidsskrift* 49 (1970): 1–33. Helge Salvesen, "The Strength of Tradition: A Historiographical Analysis of Research into Norwegian Agrarian History during the Later Middle Ages," *Scandinavian Journal of History* 7 (1982): 75–133. Claus Krag, "Norge som odel i Harald Hårfagres ætt: Et møte med en gjenganger," *Historisk Tidsskrift* 68 (1989): 288–302; Claus Krag, "Myten om Hårfagreættens 'odel'," *HistoriskTidsskrift* 81(2002): 381–94.

In fact, *Egils saga Skalla-Grímssonar* clearly depicts the existence, during Haraldr *inn hárfagri*'s reign, of an independent agrarian class, not deprived of free possession of its real assets (*bœndr-hǫlðr*), and quite separate from those who had received land from the king (*lendir menn*):

> Haraldr konungr fór þat sumar á Hálogaland, ok váru gǫrvar veizlur í móti honum, bæði þar er hans bú váru, ok svá gerðu lendir menn ok ríkir bœndr.[23]
>
> [King Harold went that summer to Halogaland, and banquets were made ready against his coming, both where his estates were, and also by barons and powerful landowners].[24]
>
> Bjǫrn hlaut annan bústað, góðan ok virðiligan; gerðisk hann ekki handgenginn konungi; því var hann kallaðr Bjǫrn hǫlðr; var hann maðr vellauðigr ok stórmenni mikit.[25]
>
> [Bjorn got for his portion another good and valuable homestead. He did not become a liege-man of the king, wherefore he was called Bjorn Yeoman. He was right wealthy, and a great man].[26]

There are also references to figures of "administrators" of landed property on behalf of the king who, in this respect, in no way differs from any other landowner:

> Þórir þruma [...] var ármaðr Haralds konungs; hann réð fyrir búi hans í Þrumu; þat var mikit bú; sat konungr þar lǫngum, þá er hann var í Víkinni.[27]
>
> [Thorir Thruma [...] he was a steward of king Harold's, manager of his farm at Thruma, a large farm in which the king used to make a long stay when he was in Vik.].[28]

---

23 Sigurður Nordal, *Egils Saga Skalla-Grímssonar*, 28.

24 W.C. Green, trans., *The Story of Egil Skallagrimsson*, accessed September 11, 2020, https://sagadb.org/egils_saga.en.

25 Sigurður Nordal, *Egils Saga Skalla-Grímssonar*, 104.

26 Green, *The Story of Egil Skallagrimsson.*

27 Sigurður Nordal, *Egils Saga Skalla-Grímssonar*, 47.

28 Green, *The Story of Egil Skallagrimsson.*

> Hafði Þórðr Aurland, bæ þann, er faðir þeira hafði búit á; hafði hann gǫrzk konungi handgenginn ok gǫrzk lendr maðr.[29]
>
> [Thord had Aurland, the estate on which his father had dwelt. He had become a liege-man of the king, and was made a baron.][30]

To fully realize the relevance of the passage contained in Snorri Sturluson's saga and of the references that we find in other sources, it is necessary to examine the meaning of the term *óðal*. The substantive is related to the Indo-European root **atos/atta*,[31] from which germ.**aþala* (protonord. **oþila*);[32] and in Germanic languages: ohg. *odhil-uodil*,[33] OE. *eðel*.[34]

Óðal identifies not only a tangible property, but also a precise relations system among all those who, for various reasons, have a link with these goods.

In this regard, the *Gulatingslova* is ideal for investigating *óðal* as this text provides the most complete and well-structured regulation of this matter. The main witness of the law, on which the critical edition of *Gulatingslova* consulted for this study is based, is Copenhagen, Kongelige Bibliotek, MS DonVar 137 4th (*Codex Rantzovianus*)[35] probably drawn up in Bergen, which, according to the almost unanimous orientation of scholars, dates to around 1250 as confirmed by the palaeographic and linguistic evidence.[36] With reference to the composition, the terminus ante quem can be set in 1267, when Magnus *lagabœtir* [law-mender] ordered the review of *Gulatingslova*, a prerequisite for the enactment in 1274 of a discipline for the whole kingdom of Norway (*landslov*). Therefore, "det er all grunn til å tru at det ikkje var noko behov for å skrive

29 Sigurður Nordal, *Egils Saga Skalla-Grímssonar*, 103.

30 Green, *The Story of Egil Skallagrimsson*.

31 Julius Pokorny, *Indogermanisches Etymologisches Wörterbuch* (Bern: Francke, 1959), 71.

32 Terje Spurkland, *Norwegian Runes and Runic Inscriptions* (Woodbridge, UK: Boydell & Brewer, 2005), 11 and 41.

33 [Besitztum, Heimat], Rudolf Schützeichel, *Althochdeutsches Wörterbuch*, 7. Aufl (Berlin: De Gruyter, 2012), 244, 363.

34 [One's own residence or property, inheritance, country, realm, land, dwelling, home], Joseph Bosworth and Thomas Northcote Toller, *An Anglo-Saxon Dictionary* (Oxford: Clarendon Press, 1898), 260. Abbreviations used throughout: fem., feminine; germ., Germanic; masc., masculine.; OE., Old English; ohg., Old High German; protonord., Proto-Nordic; subst., substantive.

35 Knut Helle, *Gulatinget og Gulatingslova* (Leikanger: Skald, 2001), 1. See also Stefan Drechsler's contribution to this volume, "*Production and Content of the Fourteenth-Century Norwegian Law Manuscript Lundarbók*," Chapter 1.

36 See Bjørn Eithun, Magnus Rindal, and Tor Ulset, eds., *Gulatingslova* (Oslo: Riksarkivet, 1994), 7–26, also for the indication of the other witnesses.

av den eldre Gulatingslova etter 1267. Vi har elles heller ingen handskrifter eller fragment av landskaplovene yngre enn ca. 1275, bortsett frå kristenrettane."[37] [There is reason to believe that there was no need to put in writing the ancient law of Gulaþing after 1267. Moreover, we have no manuscript or fragment of territorial laws date back to 1275 ca, apart from the provisions after the introduction of Christianity].[38]

The Gulaþing included the following districts: Firðafylki Sygnafylki and Hǫrðafylki, corresponding to the counties of Sogn and Fjordane and Hordaland.[39]

According to the *Historia Norwegie* (written between 1160 and 1170), instead, the jurisdiction's area included Agder (corresponding to the counties of Vest-Adger and Aust-Adger), Rogaland, Hordaland, Sogn and Fjordane and Sunnmøre (district in the Møre and Romsdal's county), and this text adds Valdres and Hallingdal (nowadays in the counties of Oppland and Buskerud).[40]

The text of *Gulatingslova*, providing for the representatives of each district belonging to the Gulaþing, mentions *horða fylkí* (Hordaland), *rygía fylki* (district in Rogaland's county), *firða fylki* (district in Sogn and Fjordane's county), *sygna fylki* (district in Sogn and Fjordane's county), *egða fylki* (nowadays the counties of Vest-Adger and Aust-Adger), and *sunnmøre* (the southern part of More and Romsdal's county).[41]

The characteristic features of *óðal* that can be drawn from the *Gulatingslova* are the following:

1) *Óðal* is a real landed estate.

> Um oðals iarðer. Nu scal þær iarðer telía. er oðrlom scolo fylgia. Su er eín er ave hever ava leift. Su er onnur er gollden er i mannzgiolld. Su er hin þriðia er i branderfð er tekin. su er hin fiorða er heiðlaunað er. su er hin .v. er dreckulaun er. ef hann þiggr af kononge. setta barnfostr laun hverr sem gefr. siaunda ef maðr skiptir oðalí iorðu sínni í aðra iorð. þær scolo oðrlom fylgia oc allar þær er i oðalí skípti hava komet. með brøðrom oc með frendom þeim. allar aðrar aurum.[42]

37 Eithun, Rindal, and Ulset, *Gulatingslova*, 19.
38 My translation.
39 Sigurður Nordal, *Egils Saga Skalla-Grímssonar*, 154.
40 Inger Ekrem and Lars Boje Mortensen, eds., *Historia Norwegie* (Copenhagen: Museum Tusculanum Press, 2003), 55, 59, 117.
41 Eithun, Rindal, and Ulset, *Gulatingslova*, 33.
42 Eithun, Rindal, and Ulset, *Gulatingslova*, 151–52.

> [Concerning odal land. The various kinds of land that are to be regarded as odal land shall now be enumerated. The first is land that has passed from man to man for [...] successive generations. The second is [land that has been] acquired in payment of wergeld. The third is [land received as] foster inheritance. The fourth is [land received as] a gift [or mark] of honor. The fifth is [land] received from the king as a gift for hospitality. The sixth is land received from some one, whoever it be, as foster payment. The seventh is land received in exchange for odal land. All these kinds of land and all odal land that has been parceled out among brothers and kinsmen shall be regarded as odal land. All other [land] is money [land]].[43]

The third category describes the institution of *branderfð* (the term is made by subst. masc. *brandr* [fire] and subst. fem. *erfð* [inheritance] regulated by the law in the par. 108: "ef maðr tecr mann a hond sér at líufu oc at leiðu. oc føðer hann til brannz oc til báls. kveðr at forno male,"[44] [When a man takes another into his keeping for good or for ill and maintains him to fire and pyre [unto death], as the old saying goes].[45] The property's intended use does not seem relevant, although it may be noted that in *Gulatingslova* there are two different regulations about the division—concerning respectively the land used for *sætr* [grazing] and, in general, the assets indicated as *óðal*, in this latter case with no further indication about the intended use—should demonstrate that in the freehold assets only the land used for cultivation must be included.[46]

2) The owner of this estate exercises a full right, free from whatever burden or obligation and without legal considerations. It is an absolute ownership, free from rent or services due to an overlord.

3) The ownership is made legitimate by inheritance over the generations. *Óðul* are assets that "frændr ok forellrar hafa átt."[47] [kinsmen and forefathers have held].[48] The real estate is owned "at eígn oc at oðrle"[49] [in odal and owner-

43 Laurence Larson, trans., *The Earliest Norwegian Laws* (New York: Columbia University Press, 1935), 178.

44 Eithun, Rindal, and Ulset, *Gulatingslova*, 95.

45 Larson, trans., *The Earliest Norwegian Laws*, 111.

46 Absalon Taranger, "The Meaning of the Words Óðal and Skeyting in the Old Laws of Norway," in *Essays in Legal History read before the International Congress of Historical Studies held in London in 1913*, ed. Paul Vinogradoff (London: Oxford University Press, 1913), 161.

47 Bjarni Aðalbjanarson, *Heimskringla II*, 168.

48 Snorri Sturluson, *Heimskringla. II*, trans. Finlay and Faulkes, 109.

49 Eithun, Rindal, and Ulset, *Gulatingslova*, 146.

ship],[50] and this double statement summarizes both the material relationship and the proof of origin. The distinction between this kind of possession and that resulting from a simple purchase is very important: "scal sía iorð fylgía aurum en eigi oðrlom,"[51] [The land [...] goes by purchase right but not by odal right].[52]

In the *Gulatingslova*, the *óðal*'s regulation is very accurate: to become *óðal*, the real property must be owned by the family for six generations. In the more recent *Frostatingslova*, four generations are enough.[53] When the law regulates quarrels about *óðal*'s retract, it is provided that the owner must demonstrate "langfeðra sínna .v. er átt hava. en sa hínn sette er bæðe atte at eign oc at oðrle."[54] [Ancestors, the five who have owned the land and the sixth who had it both in ownership and in odal].[55] Then the terms were reduced: in the first national law of Norway (1274), the period (both to gain allodium and retract) is reduced to 60 years; in 1604 to 30 years; and in 1687 to 20 years to gain and 10 years to retract. In 1811, an attempt was made to remove the allodium, but the Constitution of 1814 stated that allodium is everlasting.[56] The current Norwegian law (L.28/06/74 n°58) provides for a period of twenty years:

> Odelshevdstid: Odelsrett får odlaren når han har vore eigar med full eigedomsrett i 20 år. Hevdstida blir rekna frå den dagen hevdaren blir eigar med full eigedomsrett. Når ikkje anna er opplyst, reknar ein at han blei eigar då heimelen hans blei tinglyst
>
> [Period required for the acquisition of the freehold qualification: freehold rights the freeholder acquires when he has been the owner with full ownership rights for a period of twenty years. The period of time required is computed from the date on which the holder has gained the full owner-

50 Larson, trans., *The Earliest Norwegian Laws*, 170.
51 Eithun, Rindal, and Ulset, *Gulatingslova*, 157.
52 Larson, trans., *The Earliest Norwegian Laws*, 184.
53 Knut Helle, *Norge Blir en Stat 1130–1319, Handbok i Norges historie* (Bergen: Universitetsforlaget, 1974), 154. Torun Zachrisson, "The Odal and its Manifestation in the Landscape," in *Current Swedish Archaeology* 2, ed. Mats Burström and Anders Carlsson (Stockholm: The Swedish Archaeological Society, 1994), 221.
54 Eithun, Rindal, and Ulset, *Gulatingslova*, 147.
55 Larson, trans., *The Earliest Norwegian Laws*, 171.
56 Arnfin Kjelland, "One Tenant, Several Landlords: The Land Tenure System of Norway until ca. 1800," in *Conference Proceedings: Land, Labour and Tenure: The Institutional Arrangements of Conflict and Cooperation in Comparative Perspective*, University of Leicester, England, August 21–24 (Leicester: University of Leicester: 1996), 2.

ship. If it is not otherwise provided, he is considered as owner when his ownership title has been recorded].[57]

4) The *óðal*, in principle, cannot be transferred to third parties who do not belong to the family:

> Hvessu maðr scal oðals iorð sína selía.
>
> Nu vill maðr selía oðals iorð. þa scal hann a þíng fara um haust. oc bíoða oðalsnautum sínum at kaupa. þa scolo þeir koma til þorsdag i pasca vicu. oc reiða hanom aura slíca sem aðrer menn vílía keypt hava uskylldír. þa scal sunr hans kaupi nestr. Nu vill maðr uskylldr kaupa. oc tyrtryggír sa er nestr er kaupi. at hinn vill sva dýrt keypt hava. þa scolo þeir baðer sverîa kaupi oc sale. at sva vil ec sellt hava oc sva vil ec keypt hava. Nu ef hínn vill eigi sva kaupa. þa scal hann selía til heímíls hveím sem hann vill.[58]
>
> [How a man may sell his odal land. If a man wishes to sell odal land, let him go before the thing in the autumn and offer it for sale to those who share the odal with him. They shall then come on Thursday in Easter week and pay him as much money for the land as other men outside the kindred offer to pay. [In such a case] the man's son has the first [right to] buy. If a man outside the kindred wants to buy [the land] and the one who has the first right to buy doubts that the man is willing to pay as much [as is stated], they shall both [the seller and the purchaser] swear to terms of sale and purchase, stating that "at such a price I wish to buy" and "at such a price I wish to sell". Now if he [the other odal man] does not want to buy at that price, the owner may sell, giving full warranty, to whomever he likes].[59]

5) Each family member is the holder of a right to retract to the prejudice of the subsequent buyer.[60] On this point, the *Gulatingslova* has a detailed regulation that provides a declaratory judgment to ensure continuity of ownership, a requirement for carrying out the reacquisition of the real estate that no longer belongs to the family, The law establishes a priority for the seller's son in the case of sale,[61] but in the *Gulatingslova* there is no prescription that ensures that

57 My translation.
58 Eithun, Rindal, and Ulset, *Gulatingslova*, 153–54.
59 Larson, trans., *The Earliest Norwegian Laws*, 180.
60 Eithun, Rindal, and Ulset, *Gulatingslova*, 154–55.
61 Eithun, Rindal, and Ulset, *Gulatingslova*, 158.

the firstborn has the full and sole right to inherit the *óðal* in case of death of the owner,[62] and, indeed, a provision expressly provides for the possibility of division among the brothers.[63]

Only later do we find the full affirmation of the exclusive right of the firstborn in case of inheritance: "Denne retten kom første gang med i landslova fra 1274. Der ble det bestemt at eldste sønn skulle ha hovedgården udelt og aleine."[64] [This right appears for the first time in the law, valid for the whole Norway, of 1274. It was provided that the eldest son should have, as only owner, the main inherited land property, without any division].[65]

6) The *óðal* is the economic foundation of the community. It is assumed that until at least the middle of the thirteenth century, what in modern terms is usually defined as the gross domestic product, in Norway consisted of 80 percent from agriculture, 13 percent from fishing, and with other sources making up the remaining seven percent.[66]

The *óðal* is, therefore, a typical institution of an agricultural society, where the blood relationship becomes the means by which the free movement of the most important productive resource is severely restricted in order to ensure the integrity and cohesion of the family as institution and, above all, an essential and exclusive economic element.

This is a very important element, also present in the other Scandinavian communities, as Jón Viðar Sigurðsson and Helle Vogt argue:

> In Denmark, it is first in the later provincial laws, i.e. Erik's law and the law of Jutland that we find preemption to inherited land. The Danish word for the institution was *laghbjuthe* (legally offer) which means that who-

---

62 "Etter Gulatings- og Frostatingslovene hadde alle borna krav på kvar sin del av det etterlatne jordegodset," Brynjulv Gjerdhåker, *Til Odel og Eige—Odels- og Åsetesrettane Gjennom eit Millenium med Vekt på dei Siste 250 Åra* (Oslo: Norsk institutt for landbruksøkonomisk forskning, 2001), 15, [According to the *Gulatingslova* and the *Frostatingslova*, all sons were entitled to claim, each for their own part, the landed property bequeathed.] Par. 103 of *Gulatingslova* provides that there is direct inheritance from father to son without any mention of the primogeniture's right, and in par. 129 there are provisions for cases in which the father, at the time of division, favours one of the sons over others and a compensation is determined. Eithun, Rindal, and Ulset, *Gulatingslova*, 93, 101.

63 Eithun, Rindal, and Ulset, *Gulatingslova*, 156.

64 Carolina M. Moland, "Født til å Eie: En Kulturvitenskaplig Analyse av Odelsjenter fra Aust-Agder og Telemark" (Master thesis, Institutt for kulturstudier og kunsthistorie, seksjon for kulturvitenskap Universitetet i Bergen, 2005), 31; See also Brynjulv Gjerdhåker, *Til Odel og Eige*.

65 My translation.

66 Ole Georg Moseng et al., *Norsk Historie 1750–1537*, 225.

> ever wanted to sell their land had to announce their intention and offer it to their kin at the market price at a public assembly. If the seller did not publicly offer the land, his or her kin could demand that the sale be revoked, and the seller was liable to pay a fine to the king and the plaintiff. As in Denmark, preemption was probably introduced in Sweden in the thirteenth century, where it was called *bördsrätt*. *Börd* can mean either birth, kin or rank and *rätt* means right, so *bördsrätt* was a right that arose because of birth. There are variations in the definitions of *bördsrätt* in some of the laws, but the general rule was that the *börds*-land, inherited land, should be offered three times to relatives and if it was not, the sale could be reversed and the seller fined.[67]

The customary practices observed in transferring land are not an exclusive hallmark of Scandinavian society, as Paul Vinogradoff observes:

> Land is not originally regarded as a conveyable or transferable commodity: even after it has been appropriated by separate households some time elapses before the occupiers of the different plots and holdings acquire the right to dispose of them in the market, to give, sell, exchange, mortgage, and bequeath them. The property remains vested in the social group from which individual tenants draw the title and guarantee of their occupation [...] The claim of kinsmen to keep strangers out as to land coming from the kindred and which ought to go back to the kindred is asserted in the primitive legal customs of various tribes, and, to speak only of European nations, we find individual ownership making way against it with some difficulty in the laws of the Greeks and of the Romans, of Celts, Teutons, and Slavs [...] In Denmark as in Sweden, in Norway as in Iceland, the regular act by which the ownership of land was transferred, in consequence of a grant, sale, or exchange, was the *skötning* (*skeyting*), the placing of a sod into the lap of the person acquiring the property, an act reminding us forcibly of the *in laisumn jactare*, the throwing of a stick into the lap of the grantee, in Frankish law. Tradition by passing the sod occurs in English charters of the period preceding the Danish invasions, and we have to consider it, not as an importation from Scandinavian parts,

67 Jón Viðar Sigurðsson and Helle Vogt, "Inheritance and Transfer of Landed Property: The Material Fundament of the Elites," in *Nordic Elites in Transformation, c. 1050–1250, Volume I: Material Resources*, ed. Bjørn Poulsen, Helle Vogt, and Jón Viðar Sigurðsson (New York: Routledge, 2019), 118; For Iceland see Hannah Burrows, "Expertise and Experience: Nuancing Terms for Legal Practitioners in the Íslendingasögur," Chapter 12 in this volume.

> but as a ceremony common to both nations, and probably going back to early Teutonic roots [...] The different customary practices observed in transferring land proceeded from very ancient roots. They are characterized in various degrees by three main traits: symbolic tradition on the part of the principal; proclamation of the validity of the transfer by sureties; and occasional confirmation of the proceedings by the popular court, the *gemót* or *thing*. And the foregoing observations, if accepted, can hardly fail to impress on the mind a sense of the close affinity between Old English and Scandinavian law.[68]

In Norwegian history, *óðal* has had an importance and a very specific meaning that is hardly found in other European countries.

> Odelsloven har hatt stor betydning geografisk, økonomisk, sosialt og historisk. Den norske kulturen og historien er preget av loven. På riksforsamlinga på Eidsvoll i 1814 ble det vedtatt at Stortinget skulle oppdeles i to kammer. Initiativet og framleggingsretten skulle ligge i det største kammeret som fikk navnet Odelstinget. Navnet gir assosiasjoner til odelsrett og viser hvor stor prestisje denne loven hadde i forsamlinga.[69]

> [Óðal's regulation has had a geographical, economic, social and historical extremely prominent significance. Norwegian culture and history are deeply characterized by this regulation. During the Eidsvoll national assembly in 1814, it was decided that the Parliament should have been divided into two chambers. The main chamber had power to initiate legislation and this chamber was called Odelsthing. The name refers immediately to *odelsrett* [right on freehold] and shows how great was the prestige that this regulation had in the constitutional assembly].[70]

The Constitution of Norway contains a provision about allodial rights protection: "Odels- og åsetesretten må ikke oppheves. De nærmere betingelser for hvordan den skal bestå til støtte for staten og til gagn for landallmuen, fastsettes av det første eller annet følgende storting"[71] [Allodial right and the right of primogeniture shall not be abolished. The specific conditions under which

---

68 Paul Vinogradoff, "Transfer of Land in Old English Law," *Harvard Law Review* 20 (1907): 532, 539, 548.

69 Moland, "Født til å Eie," 30.

70 My translation.

71 Norway Constitution, § 117.

these rights shall continue for the greatest benefit of the state and to the best advantage of the rural population shall be determined by the first or second subsequent Storting].[72]

The continued vitality of these values is demonstrated by substantial traces still present in today's Norwegian legislation:

> Odelsloven har vært det juridiske redskapet som samfunnet har gitt landbruket for å ivareta tradisjonene [...]. Selv om odelsloven kun gjelder eiendom på landet har odelsloven gjennomsyret også andre deler av samfunnet. Det viser seg at odelstanken for eksempel har godt rotfeste i norske familiebedrifter der svært mange av de mannlige direktører er eldste sønn til sine foreldre [...] For mange nordmenn oppleves odelsloven som noe unikt norsk og som en del av vår kulturarv.[73]
>
> [The law about allodial property was the legal means that the society provided to the agricultural world to preserve the traditions [...] Although the law applies only to estates, it has also influenced other parts of society. It is demonstrated, for example, that the way of thinking inspired by the *óðal*'s institution has deep roots in Norwegian family businesses, where many male leaders are the firstborn sons of parents already owners of the company [...] For many Norwegians the law about allodial property is conceived as something that belongs exclusively to Norway and as a part of our cultural heritage].[74]

The regulation of freehold has important consequences not only with reference to the ownership of real estate, but also for social relations within the community: "the odal not only stood for the inherited land but it also legitimized the free man's rights in society."[75]

The possession of a freehold not only guarantees the holder a particular legal regulation, but identifies a real class, different from that of the simple landowners.

This distinction is already made clear in mythological and literary works:

---

72 My translation.

73 Moland, "Født til å Eie," 31, 39.

74 My translation.

75 Torun Zachrisson, "The Odal and its Manifestation in the Landscape," 222.

> Kom þar ór runni Rígr gangandi,
> Rígr gangandi, rúnar kendi;
> sitt gaf heiti, son kvez eiga;
> þann bað hann eignaz óðalvǫllo,
> óðalvǫllo, alldnar bygðir.[76]
>
> [Then out of the thicket came Rig walking, Rig came walking, taught him runes; gave him his own name, said he had a son; he told him to take possession of *óðalvǫllo* [ancestral plains], long-established settlements].[77]

Jarl, Rígr's son, is in the *Rigsþula* the symbol of the noble class, whose essence consists of bloodline, represented by the same name of the father, superior knowledge (the runes) and full possession of land property (*óðal*) that will be inherited by future generations.

In poetic language, a precise semantic value of the term *óðal* is already stated, which will be found in historiographical and legal texts. It is a line of continuity that indissolubly links mythical representation, historical narrative and legal provisions, as highlighted in Snorri Sturluson's *Skáldskaparmál*:

> Þar næst eru þeir menn er hǫlðar heita. Þat eru búendr þeir er gildir eru *at ættum ok réttum fullum.[78]
>
> [Next to them are the men called hǫlðar. These are yeomen who have full status as regards their lineage and all their legal rights].[79]

Here, the difference between the landowner and the holder of rights, guaranteed not only by law but also and above all by lineage, is depicted, namely the same distinction that we find in the *Heimskringla* between men who have a common property (*eignir*) and men who have allodial property (*óðǫl eigu*).[80] This difference is fully reflected in the *Gulatingslova*, as confirmed by the law's text in the provision concerning the value limits of purchases effected by women:

---

76 Hans Kuhn, ed., *Edda, Die Lieder des Codex Regius Nebst Veerwandten Denkmälern, I Text*, 7. Aufl. (Heidelberg: Winter, 1983), 285.

77 Carolyne Larrington, trans., *The Poetic Edda* (Oxford: Oxford University Press, 2014), 243.

78 Snorri Sturluson, *Skáldskaparmál 1. Introduction, Text and Notes*, ed. Anthony Faulkes (Exeter: Viking Society for Northern Research, 1998), 80.

79 Snorri Sturluson, *Edda*, trans. Anthony Faulkes (London: Everyman, 1995), 129.

80 Snorri Sturluson, *Heimskringla II*, ed. Bjarni Aðalbjanarson, 87.

> Enn haulld manz kona tveggía aura kaupí. En boanda kona eyris kaupí En lendz mannz kona halfrar mercr kaupí.[81]

> [The wife of a freeman may bargain to [the amount of] one ora; the wife of a hauld to [the amount of] two oras; a baron's wife to [the amount of] half a mark].[82]

Similarly, the gradation of the penalty in case of land's occupancy:

> Boande halvan annan eyrí. Haulldmaðr .ííj. aura.[83]

> [A freeman, to one and one-half oras; a hauld, to three oras].[84]

The *Gulatingslova*, however, does not give an explicit definition of an allodial title holder, which, instead, is found in the *Landslov* of Magnús *lagabœtir*:

> En sa er haullðr er hann hefir oðaul at erfðum tekit bæðe eptir faður oc moðor þau er hans forellrar hafa att aðr firir þeim.[85]

> [Allodial title holder is who has received the estate by inheritance from his father and mother, who, in their turn, had got it from the ascendants, before them].[86]

This particular treatment, which puts the holder of a freehold property in a privileged position, is all the more remarkable considering the aforementioned central role of land asset ownership in the Norwegian society of that time. Therewith, a bond with the land is declared that goes far beyond the material fact. On the contrary, this bond expresses where an individual come from. *Óðal* also means birthplace, identified with reference to the land owned by inheritance, which was then the land of the forefathers.

81 Eithun, Rindal, and Ulset, *Gulatingslova*, 67.

82 Larson, trans., *The Earliest Norwegian Laws*, 76.

83 Eithun, Rindal, and Ulset, *Gulatingslova*, 88.

84 Larson, trans., *The Earliest Norwegian Laws*, 101.

85 Rudolph Keyser and Peter A. Munch, eds., *Norges Gamle Love indtil 1387. Andet Bind* (Christiania: Gröndahl, 1848), 146.

86 My translation.

In this respect, there is full concordance between myth, poetry and historiography. In the *Gylfaginning*, we find the following description of Muspell:

> Fyrst var þó sá heimr í suðrhálfu er Muspell heitir. Hann er ljóss ok heitr. Sú átt er logandi ok brennandi, er hann ok ófoerr þeim er þar eru útlendir ok eigi eigu þar óðul.[87]
>
> [But first there was the world in the southern region called Muspell. It is bright and hot. That area is flaming and burning and it is impassable for those that are foreigners there and and are not *óðul* [native] to it].[88]

In poetry we can quote Þórarinn *svarti* Þórólfsson *máhlíðingr* who, in a *lausavísa*, ("freestanding stanza, loose stanza, a separate stanza or part-stanza which does not belong to a long poem, and which is normally preserved as an integral part of a prose narrative")[89] designates himself as "baugs óðaldraugr" [the tree of the land of the boss],[90] where *óðal* means "native land" or "dwelling," as in the compound *óðalstopt* in the following of Sigvatr Þórðarson's *lausavísa*:

> Geng ek of þvert frá þengils
> (þróask ekki mér) rekka,
> emk sem bast (í brjósti)
> bleikr, verðungar leiki.
> Minnumk ek, hvar manna
> minn dróttinn lék sinna
> opt á óðalstoptum
> orðsæll ok vér forðum.
>
> [I walk away from the game of the bodyguard {of the prince of warriors} [RULER = Sveinn/Magnús]; sobbing sorrows grow in my breast; I am pale as bast. I recall where my praise-blessed lord [Óláfr] and we [I] played often in the past at the *óðalstoptum* [ancestral homesteads] of his people].[91]

---

87 Snorri Sturluson, *Edda. Prologue and Gylfaginning*, ed. Anthony Faulkes (Exeter: Viking Society for Northern Research, 2005), 9.

88 Snorri Sturluson, *Edda*, trans. Faulkes, 9.

89 Diana Whaley, ed., *Poetry from King's Sagas 1* (Turnhout: Brepols, 2012), cxl.

90 Heather O'Donoghue, *Skaldic Verse and the Poetics of Saga Narrative* (Oxford: Oxford University Press, 2005), 98.

91 Text and translation from Whaley, *Poetry from King's Sagas 1*, 727.

The same meaning can also be found in the *Hugsvinnsmál*: "Ver þú óðaljǫrð þína oddi ok eggju,"[92] [Defend your *óðaljǫrð* [native land] with point and edge].

Óðal, as native land where properties are owned, is present in other poetic sources: "Varð Hákon hilmi at sverja eiða þess, es Óláfr bað:at folk-Baldr flýja skyldi óðǫl sín til aldrslita," [Hákon had to swear to the lord oaths concerning that which Óláfr stipulated: that the battle-Baldr ⟨god⟩ [WARRIOR] should flee from his ancestral properties to the end of his life];[93] "En eptir þat óðals á vit fara fráliga fyrðar brezkir," [Then went the British men quickly to their native land].[94]

In Snorri Sturluson's *Heimskringla*, we find further examples. Óláfr Tryggvason meets Gyda and he asks "hvert nafn þessarar konu var, ætt eða øðli," [What the name of this woman was, her descent and origin].[95] When Haraldr Sigurðarson comes into Mikligarðr (Costantinople), "fýsti hann at fara í Norðrlǫnd til óðala sinna," [He longed to return to the North, to his native land].[96] *Óðal*'s ownership expresses, then, both a clear title and real right to an estate and the belonging to a community from the time of birth, and these are the constituents of the landed elite who, from the hereditariness of landed property, take their hallmark as class distinguished by rank or title.

In Snorri Sturluson's text, this element is clearly highlighted in the narratives concerning the conflict between royal power and elites. In these cases, the elites' defeat is always emphasized by reference to deprivation and the forced abandonment of landed property owned by inheritance (*flýja óðal*):

> Mǫrg undr ǫnnur gerði Eysteinn konungr við Þrœndi. Af þeim hernaði ok ófriði flýðu margir hǫfðingjar, ok mart fólk flýði óðǫl sín.[97]
>
> [There were many other surprising things that King Eysteinn did to the Þroendir. Because of this raiding and warfare many of the ruling class fled, and many people fled from their *óðǫl* [ancestral property]].[98]

---

92 Finnur Jónsson, ed., *Den Norsk-Islandske Skjaldedigtning B, Bind 2* (Copenhagen: Gyldendal and Nordisk Forlag, 1915; repr., Copenhagen: Rosenkilde & Bagger, 1973), 187.

93 *Nóregs konunga-tal*; text and traslation from Kari Ellen Gade, ed., *Poetry from King's Sagas II* (Turnhout: Brepols, 2009), 778.

94 Gunnlaugr Leifsson, "*Merlínússpá II*," 62, in *Den Norsk-Islandske Skjaldedigtning B, Bind* 2, ed. Finnur Jónsson, 36.

95 Snorri Sturluson, *Heimskringla I*, ed. Bjarni Aðalbjanarson, 268; Snorri Sturluson, *Heimskringla I*, trans. Finlay and Faulkes, 166.

96 Snorri Sturluson, *Heimskringla III*, ed. Bjarni Aðalbjanarson (Reykjavík: Hið íslenzka fornritafélag, 2002), 85.

97 Snorri Sturluson, *Heimskringla I*, ed. Bjarni Aðalbjanarson, 164–65.

98 Snorri Sturluson, *Heimskringla I.*, trans. Finlay and Faulkes, 97.

Þar var þá með honum Hákon jarl ok Haraldr grenski, son Guðrøðar konungs, ok mart annarra ríkismanna, þeirra er flýit hǫfðu óðǫl sín fyrir Gunnhildarsonum ór Nóregi.[99]

[There with him then were Jarl Hákon and King Guðrøðr's son Haraldr grenski and many others of the ruling class who had fled their *óðǫl* [patrimonies] in Norway because of Gunnhildr's sons].[100]

Erlingr Skjálgsson ok enn margir aðrir lendir menn, þeir er eigi vildu flýja óðǫl sín, fóru norðr til heimila sinna.[101]

[Erlingr Skjálgsson and many other landed men too, who did not want to abandon their *óðǫl* [inherited lands], went north to their homes].[102]

Þeir konungarnir ganga fyrst einir saman á tal. Tók sá fyrst til orða, er kominn var af Raumaríki, ok segir frá ferð Óláfs digra ok þeim ófriði, er hann gerði bæði í manna aftǫkum ok manna meizlum, suma rak hann ór landi ok tók upp fé fyrir ǫllum þeim, er nǫkkut mæltu móti honum, en fór með her manns um landit, en ekki með því fjǫlmenni, er lǫg váru til. Hann segir ok, at fyrir þeim ófriði kvezk hann hafa þangat flýit, kvað ok marga aðra ríkismenn hafa flýit óðǫl sín af Raumaríki.[103]

[These kings at first started making speeches one at a time. The one who was come from Raumaríki began talking first, and speaks about Óláfr digri's travels and the disturbance he was causing in both killing people and maiming people, driving some out of the country and seizing property from all those who opposed him at all, and travelling around the country with a host of men, and not with the numbers that the law provided for. He also says that he declares it is because of this disturbance he has fled to this place, also declaring that many other men of rank have fled their *óðǫl* [ancestral lands] in Raumaríki].[104]

99 Snorri Sturluson, *Heimskringla I*, ed. Bjarni Aðalbjanarson, 240.
100 Snorri Sturluson, *Heimskringla I*, trans. Finlay and Faulkes, 147.
101 Snorri Sturluson, *Heimskringla II*, ed. Bjarni Aðalbjanarson, 67.
102 Snorri Sturluson, *Heimskringla II*, trans. Finlay and Faulkes, 41.
103 Snorri Sturluson, *Heimskringla II*, ed. Bjarni Aðalbjanarson, 102.
104 Snorri Sturluson, *Heimskringla. II*, trans. Finlay and Faulkes, 65.

> Fleiri váru þeir ríkismenn er flýðu ór Orkneyjum óðǫl sín fyrir ríki Einars jarls. Flýðu flestir yfir á Katanes til Þorfinns jarls en sumir flýðu ór Orkneyjum til Nóregs en sumir til ýmissa landa.[105]
>
> [There were other men of the ruling class who fled their *óðǫl* [patrimonies] in Orkney because of Jarl Einarr's tyranny. Most fled across to Katanes to Jarl Þorfinnr, but some fled from Orkney to Norway, and some to various countries].[106]

In contrast, when the king aims to carry out an agreement with the freeholders, he recognizes their rights to ancestral property, like Hákon *inn góði* as soon as he comes into Norway: "bauð hann þeim at gera alla bœndr óðalborna ok gefa þeim óðǫl sín er á bjoggu [...] en þessi Hákon vildi hverjum manni gott ok bauð aptr at gefa bóndum óðǫl sín, þau er Haraldr konungr hafði af þeim tekit," [He offered to make all farmers entitled to their *óðǫl* [patrimony] and to give them their inherited land that they were dwelling in [...] This Hákon wished everyone well and offered to return the farmers their patrimonies which King Haraldr had taken from them.][107]

The leader of the freeholders reminds the king that this is the condition in order that he is recognized as sovereign: "at þá er þú hafðir it fyrsta þing haft hér í Þrándheimi, ok hǫfðum þik til konungs tekinn, ok þegit af þér óðǫl vár." [King Hákon, when you held the first assembly here in Þrándheimr and we had accepted you as king and received from you our *óðǫl* [ancestral rights]].[108]

In the quotations from the *Hákonar saga góða* we see for the first time in the *Heimskringla* the adjective *óðalborinn*, [Freeholder by birth; Born to possession of ancestral property], which depicts the condition of the man who, by right of birth, can be said to be noble and is, thereby, empowered with royal dignity.

The foundation of such dignity lies not in the subjective condition of a royal title transmitted by the ascendants, but in the objective ownership of an ancestral property, in this case also based on inheritance. This is a concept that arises in sharp contrast with the dynastic principle grounded on noble blood, on which the rising Norwegian kingship founds its legitimacy.

---

105 Snorri Sturluson, *Heimskringla II*, ed. Bjarni Aðalbjanarson, 162–63.

106 Snorri Sturluson, *Heimskringla. II*, trans. Finlay and Faulkes, 105.

107 Snorri Sturluson, *Heimskringla I*, ed. Bjarni Aðalbjanarson, 150–51; Snorri Sturluson, *Heimskringla. I*, trans. Finlay and Faulkes, 88.

108 Snorri Sturluson, *Heimskringla I*, ed. Bjarni Aðalbjanarson, 170; Snorri Sturluson, *Heimskringla. I*, trans. Finlay and Faulkes, 100.

In the *Heimskringla*, this dualism is pointed out very clearly in the conflict between King Óláfr *inn helgi* and the Upplǫnd's rulers, who believe themselves fully entitled to gain the royal power because they are *óðalbornir*: "Nú hefir hann í engan stað meira kost en einn hver várr, en því minna, at vér hǫfum nǫkkur lǫnd ok ríki til forráða, en hann hefir alls engi. Erum vér ok eigi síðr óðalbornir til konungdóms." [Now in no respect does he [King Óláfr] have a better chance than any one of us, but rather the less in that we have some lands and power to employ, but he has none at all. We are also no less entitled to kingship by birth].[109]

Their situation would be not much different from that of King Óláfr Tryggvason who "óðalborinn var til konungdóms ok fyrir allra hluta til hǫfðingja fallinn." [Was entitled to the kingdom by birth and in all respects well fitted to be king].[110]

In the aforementioned quotation, the adjective *óðalbornir* was used to found the landed elite's claim to the domain but, later, the same constituent, expressing the landowners' will to act as the powerful élite, is used by those who have a claim to the throne on the basis of their belonging to a royal bloodline, as Óláfr *inn helgi* asserts:

> En yfir þeim eignum sitja útlendir menn, er átti minn faðir ok hans faðir ok hverr eptir annan várra frænda, ok em ek óðalborinn til. Ok láta þeir sér eigi þat einhlítt, heldr hafa þeir undir sik tekit eigur allra várra frænda, er at langfeðgatali erum komnir frá Haraldi inum hárfagra. Miðla þeir sumum lítit af, en sumum með ǫllu ekki. Nú skal því upp lúka fyrir yðr, er mér hefir mjǫk lengi í skapi verit, at ek ætla at heimta fǫðurarf minn, ok mun ek hvártki koma á fund Danakonungs né Svíakonungs at biðja þá né einna muna um, þótt þeir hafi nú um hríð kallat sína eign þat, er var arfr Haralds hárfagra [...] Nú vænti ek um þik, Sigurðr mágr, eða aðra þá menn í landinu, er óðalbornir eru hér til konungdóms at lǫgum þeim, er setti Haraldr hárfagri, þá mun yðr eigi svá mikilla muna á vant, at þér munið upp hefjask at reka af hǫndum frændaskǫmm þessa, at eigi munuð þér alla yðr við leggja at efla þann, er forgangsmaðr vill vera at hefja upp ætt vára.[111]

109 Snorri Sturluson, *Heimskringla II*, ed. Bjarni Aðalbjanarson, 48; Snorri Sturluson, *Heimskringla. II*, trans. Finlay and Faulkes, 29.

110 Snorri Sturluson, *Heimskringla II*, ed. Bjarni Aðalbjanarson, 47; Snorri Sturluson, *Heimskringla. II*, trans. Finlay and Faulkes, 29.

111 Snorri Sturluson, *Heimskringla II*, ed. Bjarni Aðalbjanarson, 43–44.

> [But foreigners have taken over the possessions that my father and his father and one after another of our family had, and that I have an inherited right to. And they do not consider that to be enough, but they have taken control of the possessions of all us kinsmen who are derived in the direct male line from Haraldr *inn hárfagri*. They share a little of it out with some, but with some nothing at all. Now I shall make known to you what has been for a very long time in my mind, that I intend to claim my patrimony, and I go to see neither the king of the Danes nor the king of the Svíar to beg of them any favours, though they have now for a while declared what was the heritage from Haraldr *hárfagri* their own possession [...] Now I expect as regards you, my stepfather Sigurðr, and other men in the land who have an inherited right to kingdoms here according to laws established by Haraldr *hárfagri*, it will not take so very much to make you rise up to get rid of this disgrace to your family that you will not put everything you have got into supporting the one who is willing to be your leader in restoring our family line].[112]

The same idea is expressed in the *Magnúss Saga Góða*, when King Edward the Confessor rejects the claim to the throne of England advanced by Magnús *inn góði*, stating that his father Æthelred "var óðalborinn til ríkis þessa bæði at fornu ok nýju",[113] [was entitled by birth to this kingdom both from earlier times and from more recently].[114]

In this way, the dynastic factor is joined with the territorial element to create the foundations for a full concept of sovereignty, as highlighted in Óláfr *inn helgi*'s words to the Swedish king's envoys:

> Farið nú aptr austr til konungs yðars ok segið honum svá, at snimma í vár mun ek búask at fara austr til landamæris, þar er at fornu hefir skilt ríki Noregskonungs ok Svíakonungs. Má hann þá þar koma, ef hann vill at vit semim sætt okkra, ok hafi þat ríki hvarr okkar, sem óðalborinn er til.[115]

112 Snorri Sturluson, *Heimskringla. II*, trans. Finlay and Faulkes, 26–27.

113 Snorri Sturluson, *Heimskringla III*, ed. Bjarni Aðalbjanarson, 66.

114 Snorri Sturluson, *Heimskringla III Magnús Óláfsson to Magnús Erlingsson*, trans. Alison Finlay and Anthony Faulkes (Exeter: Viking Society for Northern Research, 2015), 39. Magnús claimed to be entitled to the throne of England according to the treaty mentioned in the saga (Snorri Sturluson, *Heimskringla III*, ed. Bjarni Aðalbjanarson, 12–13), which he concluded with Hǫrða-Knútr, son of the Danish King Knútr *inn ríki*.

115 Snorri Sturluson, *Heimskringla II*, ed. Bjarni Aðalbjanarson, 76.

> [Return now to your king and tell him this, that early in the spring I shall set out eastwards to the boundary which in former times separated the realms of the king of Norway and the king of the Svíar. He can then come there if he wants us to reach a settlement with each of us having the realm that we have an inherited right to [*óðalborinn*]].[116]

The boundary between the kingdoms of Sweden and Norway was established not only by ancient borders, but also by taking into account the territories on which each of the two rulers wielded his supremacy as *óðalborinn*. The king's supremacy becomes an absolute right to dispose of land granted in concession to the men in his service who are deprived of the right to transfer such property by inheritance. They are no longer *óðalborinn*, as the "holy king" states:

> En ek man þik láta vera gǫfgastan mann í landinu, þó at ek vilja veizlurnar miðla at sjálfræði mínu, en eigi láta sem ér lendir menn séð óðalbornir til ættleifðar minnar en ek skylda margfǫldum verðum yðra þjónustu kaupa.[117]

> [But I shall have you made the noblest man in the land, even if I decide to assign the revenues according to my own preferences without accepting that you landed men have an inherited right to my patrimonies [*óðal-bornir*], and even if I have to purchase your service at many times its value].[118]

The mutation of the meaning of *óðalborinn* found in Snorri Sturluson's work highlights how the monarchy put as the foundation of its power an institution which, in turn, is the legal, economic and, especially, cultural basis of the social class whose dominance the monarchy attempted to remove—that is, the landed elite. Legitimacy based on descent was, therefore, not an adequate basis to guarantee the monarchy a stable power, as demonstrated in Norwegian history by the vicissitudes concerning the law on succession to the throne, first introduced in 1163 during the civil war era.[119]

---

116 Snorri Sturluson, *Heimskringla. II*, trans. Finlay and Faulkes, 47.

117 Snorri Sturluson, *Heimskringla II*, ed. Bjarni Aðalbjanarson, 78.

118 Snorri Sturluson, *Heimskringla. II*, trans. Finlay and Faulkes, 48.

119 Eithun, Rindal, and Ulset, *Gulatingslova*, 32; Torfin Tobiassen, "Tronfølgelov og Privilegiebrev," *Historisk Tidskrift* 43 (1964): 181–273; Andreas Holmsen, "Erkebiskop Eystein og Tronfølgeloven Av 1163," *Historisk Tidskrift* 44 (1965): 225–66.

Other linguistic elements confirm this appropriation process by the royal power of landed elite's institutions, such as the noun *ǫðlingr* which, in the legal field, defines the possessor of freehold property.

The *-ingr* suffix indicates a relationship of belonging and with it are identified, in particular, those that are part of a specific lineage. Even in *ǫðlingr*, this semantic profile is relevant, aimed at stating the membership of the subject to a particular social group, namely those who are holders of an *óðal*.

The special condition of superiority that comes from such ownership has a precise mythical foundation: in the poetic *Edda*, *ǫðlingr* indicates someone endowed with supernatural qualities which can result from a particular relationship with a deity or from belonging to a noble family, for example, Sigurðr (*Grípispá*), the hero Helgi (*Helgaqviða Hjǫrvarðzsonar*; *Helgaqviða Hundingsbana in fyrri*), Gjuki's sons (*Guðrúnarqviða in fyrsta*, *Oddrúnagrátr*, *Atlaqviða in grœnlenzca*, *Guðrúnarhvǫt*, *Sigurðarqviða in scamma*).[120]

Ǫðlingr, however, appears as *heiti* for "king" in the *þulur*[121] and in the skaldic poetry is equally used with reference to kings across a very wide period, from the beginnings of the Norwegian kingship until the thirteenth century.[122]

In Christian poetry, *ǫðlingr* becomes a constitutive element of *kenningar* that define the Christian God; the substantive no longer expresses belonging to noble descent but is borrowed from the pre-Christian language to depict God's absolute sovereignty: "himins rǫðla ǫðlingr" [the lord of the discs of the sky];[123] "ǫðlinga dǫðlings hirð" [the cohort of the king of kings];[124] "rǫðla

120 Kuhn, *Edda, Die Lieder des Codex Regius*, 130, 134, 135, 144, 146, 167, 204, 205, 208, 235, 247, 266.

121 Finnur Jónsson, ed., *Den Norsk-Islandske Skjaldedigtning B, Bind 1*. (Copenhagen: Gyldendal and Nordisk Forlag, 1912; repr., Copenhagen: Rosenkilde & Bagger, 1973), 671.

122 Haraldr *inn hárfagri*: Þjóðólfr ór Hvini, "Poem about Haraldr hárfagri," in *Den Norsk-Islandske Skjaldedigtning B, Bind 1*, ed. Finnur Jónsson, 18; Whaley, *Poetry from King's Sagas 1*, 61; Haraldr *gráfeldr*: Glúmr Geirason, "*Gráfeldardrápa*," in *Den Norsk-Islandske Skjaldedigtning B, Bind 1*, ed. Finnur Jónsson, 66–67, Whaley, *Poetry from King's Sagas 1*, 255; Óláfr Tryggvason: Anonymous, "*Óláfs drápa Tryggvasonar*," in *Den Norsk-Islandske Skjaldedigtning B, Bind 1*, ed. Finnur Jónsson, 569; Whaley, *Poetry from King's Sagas 1*, 1040; Magnús *inn góði*: Sigvatr Þórðarson, "*Lausavísa*," in *Den Norsk-Islandske Skjaldedigtning B, Bind 1*, ed. Finnur Jónsson, 253; Whaley, *Poetry from King's Sagas 1*, 730; Sigurðr *Jórsalafari*: Einarr Skúlason, "*Sigurðardrápa*," in *Den Norsk-Islandske Skjaldedigtning B, Bind 1*, ed. Finnur Jónsson, 424; Gade, *Poetry from King's Sagas II*, 540; Hákon Hákonarson: Snorri Sturluson, "*Hattatál*," in *Edda. Háttatal*, ed. Anthony Faulkes (Exeter: Viking Society for Northern Research, 2007), 15.

123 Þorleifr *jarlskáld* Rauðfeldarson, *Drápa* about Sveinn *tjúguskegg*; Finnur Jónsson, *Den Norsk-Islandske Skjaldedigtning B, Bind 1*, 133; Whaley, *Poetry from King's Sagas 1*, 374.

124 Einarr Skúlason, "*Geisli*," in *Den Norsk-Islandske Skjaldedigtning B, Bind 1*, ed. Finnur Jónsson, 428.

ǫðlingr" [prince of the suns];[125] "mána tjalds ǫðlingr" [ruler of the tapestry of the moon];[126] "lopthjalms ǫðlingr" [prince of [the helmet of the air] → the sky];[127] "rǫðla salar ǫðlingr" [prince of [the hall of the suns] → the sky];[128] "sunnuǫðlingr" [king of the sun];[129] "aldar allviss ǫðling" [all-knowing prince of mankind];[130] "árs ǫðlingr" [prince of the prosperous season][131]

The same noun *óðal* becomes the linguistic mark of the new royal power with respect to the former title by inheritance, to the element of absolute lordship over the landed property and to the king's fatherland, that is, meanings that, as we have seen in the examination of the provisions contained in *Gulatingslova*, depicted the social status of a single landowner and that now become necessary conditions to found a monocratic sovereignty, as we read in the revelation of Óláfr *inn helgi*'s future:

> En þá er Óláfr konungr lá í Karlsám ok beið þar byrjar ok ætlaði at sigla út til Nǫrvasunda ok þaðan út í Jórsalaheim þá dreymdi hann merkiligan draum, at til hans kom merkiligr maðr ok þekkiligr ok þó ógurligr ok mælti við hann, bað hann hætta ætlan þeiri at fara út í lǫnd: "far aptr til óðala þinna því at þú munt vera konungr yfir Nóregi at eilífu." Hann skilði þann draum til þess, at hann myndi konungr vera yfir landi ok hans ættmenn langa ævi.[132]

> [And while King Óláfr was lying in Karlsár and waiting for a fair wind and planning to sail out to Nǫrvasund and from there out to Jerusalem, then he dreamed a remarkable dream, that there came to him a remarkable and handsome and yet terrifying man and spoke to him, telling him to abandon that plan, of going to distant lands. "Go back to your *óðala*

125 Gamli *kanóki*, "*Harmsól*," in *Den Norsk-Islandske Skjaldedigtning B, Bind 1*, ed. Finnur Jónsson, 552; Anonymous, "*Maríugrátr*," in *Den Norsk-Islandske Skjaldedigtning B, Bind 2*, ed. Finnur Jónsson, 506.

126 Gamli *kanóki*, "*Harmsól*," 556.

127 Anonymous, "*Leiðarvísan*," in *Den Norsk-Islandske Skjaldedigtning B, Bind 1*, ed. Finnur Jónsson, 629.

128 Anonymous, "*Leiðarvísan*," 630.

129 Kolbeinn Tumason, "*Jónsvísur*," in *Den Norsk-Islandske Skjaldedigtning B, Bind 2*, ed. Finnur Jónsson, 46.

130 Ingjaldr Geimundarson, "*Brandsflokkr*," in *Den Norsk-Islandske Skjaldedigtning B, Bind 2*, ed. Finnur Jónsson, 101.

131 Anonymous, "*Líknabraut*," in *Den Norsk-Islandske Skjaldedigtning B, Bind 2*, ed. Finnur Jónsson, 172.

132 Snorri Sturluson, *Heimskringla II*, ed. Bjarni Aðalbjanarson, 25.

[ancestral lands], for you will be king over Norway for ever." He understood this dream to mean that he and his kinsmen would be king over the land for a long time].[133]

It is particularly significant that this meaning of the noun *óðal* finds textual references in poetry, already in the eddic corpus: the compound *óðaltorfa* [Inherited turf; ancestral realm][134] in the Short Lay of Sigurðr (*Sigurðarkviða in skamma*) defines Jonakr's kingdom and in the *Rigsþula* it is said that Danr and Danpr, mythological kings quoted in different sources,[135] have *œðra óðal* [The best inherited domain].[136]

This view gets its definitive consecration in the skaldic poetry, where the kings are celebrated as *óðal*-holders. According to the *Nóregs konunga-tal*, Magnús *inn góði*, after returning to Norway from Russia in 1035, receives all the lands belonging to him by inheritance and gains great power:

Kom ágætr
austan ór Gǫrðum
einkason
Óláfs konungs.
Fekk Magnús
ok mikit ríki
óðalsjǫrð
alla sína.

[The magnificent only son of King Óláfr [= Magnús] came west from Russia. Magnús received all his *óðalsjǫrð* [ancestral land] and great power].[137]

In Valgarðr á Velli's poem about Haraldr *harðráði*, we find the same view when the skald describes Harald's campaign to claim the Norwegian throne:

133 Snorri Sturluson, *Heimskringla. II*, trans. Finlay and Faulkes, 15.

134 Kuhn, *Edda, Die Lieder des Codex Regius*, 21; Beatrice La Farge and John Tucker, *Glossary to the Poetic Edda* (Heidelberg: Winter, 1992), 199.

135 Snorri Sturluson, *Heimskringla I*, ed. Bjarni Aðalbjanarson, 34–35; Bjarni Guðnason, ed., *Skjǫldunga Saga* (Reykjavík: Hið íslenzka fornritafélag, 1982), 9–10; Martin Clarentius Gertz, ed., *Scriptores Minores Historiœ Danicœ*, Vol. 1 (Copenhagen: Selskabet for Udgivelse af Kilder til dansk Historie, 1917), 43–53.

136 Kuhn, *Edda, Die Lieder des Codex Regius*, 287.

137 Text and translation from Gade, *Poetry from King's Sagas II*, 782.

Eik slǫng und þér, yngvi
ógnblíðr, í haf síðan
—rétt vas yðr of ætlat
óðal—frá Svíþjóðu.

[Then the oak-ship sped beneath you into the ocean away from Sweden, battle-rejoicing lord; lawful *óðal* [inheritance] awaited you].[138]

In this case, the poet not only considers the kingdom as *óðal* but also gives a precise evaluation of Harald's claim to legitimacy (*rétt*).[139]

Haraldr had knowledge that, in his absence, the power had fallen into the hands of Magnús Óláfsson, his nephew, and joined forces with Magnus's rival in Denmark (Magnus had also become king of Denmark), the pretender Sweyn II of Denmark. The conflict between Haraldr and Magnús ends with an agreement, and they rule jointly until Magnús's death, as Haraldr becomes the sole ruler of Norway.

Whereas the territorial range on which the king exercises domination is considered private property, this can be inherited as an *óðal* owned by a landed freeholder, as we read in Þjóðolfr Arnórsson's *Sexstefja* ("Six Refrains") concerning Haraldr *harðráði*:

Hár skyli hirðar stjóri
hugreifr sonum leifa
arf ok óðaltorfu
—ósk mín es þat—sína.

[The tall, mind-cheerful commander of the retinue [RULER] shall leave his sons his legacy and *óðaltorfu* [hereditary turf]; that is my wish].[140]

In the Arnórr *jarlaskáld*, Þórðarson's *Hrynhenda Magnússdrápa*, concerning Magnús *inn góði*, the whole of Norway becomes king's *óðal*:

Eignask namt þú óðal þegna
allan Nóreg, gotna spjalli;

138 Text and translation from Gade, *Poetry from King's Sagas II*, 305.

139 Haraldr was Óláfr *inn helgi*'s half-brother and Magnús was an illegitimate son of the same Óláfr.

140 Text and translation from Gade, *Poetry from King's Sagas II*, 147.

manngi ryðr þér mildingr annarr,
Mœra gramr, til landa œri.

[Companion of warriors, you conquered all Norway, the *óðal* [inheritance] of free men; lord of the Mœrir [people of Møre], no other generous king as young as you acquires lands].[141]

In this case, however, the presence of the verb *eigna* highlights that it is not an automatic acquisition of a right but, instead, an action of concrete and tangible seizure of assets that did not belong *ab origine* to the sovereign but to free men (*þegna*), even though "Magnús takes Norway under his rule without bloodshed, welcomed by a people weary of Danish overlordship."[142]

In this context, Sigvatr Þórðarson's *Bersǫglisvísur* ("plain-speaking *Vísur*") is an important exception: "The poem was occasioned by Magnús's heavy-handed treatment of the Norwegian farmers who had participated in the overthrow of his father Óláfr Haraldsson."[143] In this poem *óðal* retains its original meaning as private property owned in free possession, and the rivalry between royal power and landed elites keeps coming up: the poet exhorts the king to moderation ("skal of stytta hǫnd í hófi," [The hand must be held back by moderation])[144] inviting him to pay attention to the farmers ("hlýðið til, hvat búmenn vilja," [You must heed what the farmers want]),[145] and raises his voice against the king's reprisals ("Hverr eggjar þik, hjaldrgegni, hǫggva bú þegna? Es ofrausn jǫfri at vinna þat innanlands," [Who urges you, battle-promoter [WARRIOR], to slay the livestock of your subjects? It is insolence for a prince to do that in his own land]).[146]

The most significant element of the poem is the charge of robbery, addressed to the king, who has (unlawfully) embezzled the farmers' *óðul*:

Eitt es mál, þats mæla:
"minn dróttinn leggr sína
eign á óðǫl þegna";
ǫfgask búendr gǫfgir.

141 Text and translation from Theodor M. Andersson and Kari Ellen Gade, eds., *Morkinskinna* (Ithaca, NY: Cornell University Press, 2000), 101.
142 Gade, *Poetry from King's Sagas II*, 193.
143 Gade, *Poetry from King's Sagas II*, 11.
144 Gade, *Poetry from King's Sagas II*, 21.
145 Gade, *Poetry from King's Sagas II*, 21.
146 Gade, *Poetry from King's Sagas II*, 22.

Rán mun seggr, hinns sína
selr út, í því telja,
flaums at fellidómi
fǫðurleifð konungs greifum.

[They all say the same thing: "my lord appropriates his subjects' *óðal* [ancestral properties]"; proud farmers revolt. That man, who parcels out his patrimony to the king's counts according to precipitate rulings, will call that robbery].[147]

The kingdom is not the king's property but is founded on the appropriation of another's property, just as had happened at the time of Haraldr *hárfagri*.[148] The dualism between territorial sovereignty and royal power persists: King Magnús gets the nickname *inn góði* ("the Good") only after he has recognized the prerogatives of landowners, like his ancient predecessor Hákon, also called *inn góði* and for precisely the same reason.

The conflict between royal power and landed elites, summarized in the semantic versatility of the term *óðal*, would be a constant element in the history of Norwegian kingship during the Middle Ages:

- Royal monocratic power appropriates an institution (*óðal*) belonging to the communities based on family ties;
- *Óðal* becomes a constitutive element of the concept of sovereignty: *óðalborinn*, is the man who by right of birth has royal dignity;
- In the poetic works in which each sovereign is celebrated, *óðal* is the ancerstral land where the king has full and unconditional power.

This evolutionary process finds its fulfillment when royal power became absolute lordship, as highlighted in the *Konungs Skuggsjá* (*Speculum Regale*), drafted between 1240 and 1260 during the reign of Hákon IV: "koningrenn á allt rikit oc sv allt folkit,"[149] [The king owns the entire kingdom as well as all the people in it].[150]

147 Gade, *Poetry from King's Sagas II*, 25.

148 See supra, n. 2.

149 Ludvig Holm-Holsen, ed., *Konungs Skuggsjá* (Oslo: Norsk historisk kjeldeskrift-institutt, 1983), 42.

150 Laurence Larson, trans., *The King's Mirror* (New York: Harvard University Press, 1917), 174.

PART 3

Legal Practice

CHAPTER 10

Juridical Dualism in Medieval Southern Italy: Studies on the *Codex Diplomaticus Cavensis*

Sonia Colafrancesco

The interplay between Lombard and Roman law, although already a well-known matter among scholars and partially documented, still lacks a deeper examination. This dualism led to peculiar juridical situations,[1] in which the distinction between the two laws was quite difficult to clarify. A detailed study of the legal documents presenting this peculiarity, demonstrates that Lombard and Roman law were used together in some particular situations for various reasons, which mainly involved Lombard family law, Roman rural traditions and the Roman Catholic Church. One of the major documentary collections that contains the proofs of interference between Lombard and Roman law, is the *Codex Diplomaticus Cavensis* (CDC) kept in the archives of the Badia of Cava dei Tirreni, near Salerno. The Benedictine Badia of Santissima Trinità of Cava dei Tirreni was one of the most ancient and famous Benedictine abbeys in medieval Southern Italy. It was founded during the Lombard period in 1011 and consecrated to the Blessed Trinity. Soon, the abbey became an important local center and it obtained a gift from Prince Guaimario III and his son Guaimario, the future Guaimario IV, which consisted in a perpetual propriety of the whole lands and territories surrounding the abbey. In addition, the gift included some privileges such us the use of the mill and, above all, legal immunity.[2] The collection includes *chartae* from 792 to 1080, meaning that the acts date back to the Lombard Principality of Salerno.[3]

Today, the so-called "questione longobarda," that is to say the historical, philological and social debate about the importance of the Lombards in the history of Italy and the nature of their actual relationships with the Roman

1 See Brigitte Pohl-Resl, "Legal Practice and Ethnic Identity in Lombard Italy," in *Strategies of Distinction: The Construction of Ethnic Communities 300–800*, ed. Walter Pohl and Helmut Reimitz (Leiden: Brill, 1998), 205–06.

2 See Barbara Kreutz, *Before the Normans: Southern Italy in the Ninth and Tenth Centuries* (Philadelphia, PA: University of Pennsylvania Press, 1991), 95.

3 See Kreutz, *Before the Normans*, 96–115.

 DOI:10.1163/9789004448650_012

population,[4] is even now open and not without its contradictions.[5] Niccolò Machiavelli was perhaps the first one to express an innovative idea about the commixtion between Lombards and Romans. In a passage of his work the *Istorie Fiorentine* [*Florentine Histories*], he claims "Erano stati i Longobardi dugentotrentadue anni in Italia, e di già non ritenevano di forestieri altro che il nome,"[6] [The Lombards had been living in Italy for two hundred and thirty-two years, and by now they were no stranger but for their name].[7] This forms part of the *capitulum* in which Machiavelli describes the Frankish conquest of the Lombard kingdom and how the Pope had strongly influenced Charlemagne's campaign. According to him, after more than two centuries of cohabitation, the Lombards were so well mixed with the Roman population that

4 In particular on Lombard ethnicity and the relations with the Romans see Claudio Azzara, "Forme di acculturazione e di integrazione delle stirpi in Occidente: la testimonianza delle leggi dei Longobardi," in *Archeologia e storia delle migrazioni. Europa, Italia, Mediterraneo fra tarda età romana e alto Medioevo*, Atti del Convegno internazionale di studi, Cimitile-Santa Maria Capua Vetere, 17–18 giugno 2010, ed. Carlo Ebanista and Marcello Rotili (Cimitile: Tavolario, 2011); Nicola Bergamo, "Il problema dell'identità etnica tra Romani e Longobardi nell'Historia Langobardorum di Paolo Diacono," *Porphyra* Anno III, numero VIII (Novembre, 2006): 26–44; Stefano Gasparri, *Prima delle nazioni. Popoli, etnie e regni fra Antichità e Medioevo* (Rome: La Nuova Italia Scientifica, 1997), 141–58; Stefano Gasparri, "I Longobardi, I Romani e l'identità nazionale italiana," *Annales de Historia Antigua, Medieval y Moderna* 39 (2006): 27–39; Stefano Gasparri, "Migrazione, etnogenesi, integrazione nel mondo romano: il caso dei Longobardi," in *Archeologia e storia delle migrazioni. Europa, Italia, Mediterraneo fra tarda età romana e alto Medioevo*, Atti del Convegno internazionale di studi, Cimitile-Santa Maria Capua Vetere, 17–18 giugno 2010, ed. Carlo Ebanista and Marcello Rotili (Cimitile: Tavolario, 2011); Elda Morlicchio, "Dinamiche sociolinguistiche nell'Italia delle 'invasioni barbariche'," in *Archeologia e storia delle migrazioni. Europa, Italia, Mediterraneo fra tarda età romana e alto Medioevo* Atti del Convegno internazionale di studi, Cimitile-Santa Maria Capua Vetere, 17–18 giugno 2010, ed. Carlo Ebanista and Marcello Rotili (Cimitile: Tavolario, 2011); Walter Pohl, "Memory, Identity and Power in Lombard Italy," in *The Use of the Past in the Early Middle Ages*, ed. Yitzah Hen and Matthew Innes (Cambridge: Cambridge University Press, 2000); Walter Pohl, "La discussa identità etnica dei Longobardi," in *I Longobardi e le Alpi*, Atti della Giornata di Studio "Clusae Longobardorum, i Longobardi e le Alpi," Chiusa di San Michele, 6 marzo 2004, ed. CRISM (Susa: Segusium, 2005). In particular, on the situation in Southern Italy see Filippo Burgarella, "Bizantini e Longobardi nell'Italia meridionale," in *I Longobardi dei Ducati di Spoleto e Benevento*, Atti del XVI Congresso internazionale di Studi sull'alto Medioevo, Spoleto, 20–23 ottobre 2002, Benevento, 24–27 ottobre 2002, ed. CISAM (Spoleto: CISAM, 2003); Walter Pohl, "Identità etniche nei ducati di Spoleto e Benevento," in *I Longobardi dei Ducati di Spoleto e Benevento*, Atti del XVI Congresso internazionale di Studi sull'alto Medioevo, Spoleto, 20–23 ottobre 2002, Benevento, 24–27 ottobre 2002, ed. CISAM (Spoleto: CISAM, 2003).

5 See Gasparri, *Prima delle nazioni*, 132–37.

6 Niccolò Machiavelli, *Istorie Fiorentine*, I, 11, (Florence: Le Monnier, 1851), 31.

7 My translation.

the only thing they still maintained of their ancient traditions and customs was their own name.

After this early appearance in Machiavelli, the issue flourished in Italy particularly during the age of Enlightenment and in the Romantic period, but following two opposing ideas. Historians and scholars of the age of Enlightenment assumed that the Lombard period had not been a completely negative experience for Italy, and that the relation between Lombards and Romans, started as a conflict between conquerors and conquered, evolved into an equal social situation across the centuries. Examples of this theory can be found in some passages in the works of Ludovico Antonio Muratori *Antiquitates italicae medii aevi* [Medieval Italian Ancient Events] (1738–1743), Pietro Giannone *Dell'istoria civile del regno di Napoli* [History of the Kingdom of Naples] (1723) and Angelo Fumagalli *Antichità longobardico-milanesi* [Lombard Ancient Events in Milan][8] (1793). On the other hand, Romanticism with its strong nationalistic ideal led to the construction of a parallel between the Lombard domination in Italy and the Austrian one; this association found fertile ground in the ideas of Italian authors and scholars, such as Alessandro Manzoni and Carlo Troya. Manzoni, who wrote the tragedy *Adelchi* based on the life of the Lombard prince, the only male son of the last king of the Lombards, Desiderio, attached an appendix *Discorso sur alcuni punti della storia longobardica in Italia* [On some events during the Lombard Period in Italy][9] to the first edition of the tragedy in 1822, that was also included in the 1845 edition under a slightly different title. The main idea he presented was that the Lombard role was completely negative, and that they had had no contact with the Roman population. According to Manzoni, Romans remained subjugated by the terrible *gens longobarda* for centuries, and their safety came only after the Frankish conquest. On the same wavelength are the theories expressed by Carlo Troya, a medieval historian, in some of his works such as *Della condizione de' romani vinti da' longobardi e della vera lezione d'alcune parole di Paolo Diacono* [The conditions of the Romans defeated by the Lombards and the true manuscript tradition of some words of Paul the Deacon][10] (1841). Both Manzoni and Troya were strongly influenced by the Catholic Church and they were very close to the Neo-Guelf movement.[11]

8 My translation.

9 My translation.

10 My translation.

11 See Enrico Artifoni, "Le questioni longobarde. Osservazioni su alcuni testi del primo Ottocento storiografico italiano," *Mélanges de l'École française de Rome. Moyen-Âge*, v. 119 no. 2 (2007): 297–304.

By the end of the 20th century, one of the most important Italian historians of the Lombards, Gian Piero Bognetti, had started a new approach to the matter, an approach based on every aspect of the Lombard period from politics to law and the social situation.[12] Thanks to this innovative method, modern historiography is able to find new links among the different areas of interest and consequently to highlight the various connections that could have been overlooked in the past, due to the lack of sources available for each single field. Such an approach is fundamental in order to create a more complete survey of the Lombard kingdom in Italy.

Following the above-mentioned new approach, the better way to investigate the "questione longobarda" is by using the available sources, which are mainly represented, in the specific case of the interrelationship of Lombard and Roman law, by documentary collections of legal acts. That is because it was in private acts, like purchase agreements, gifts or testaments, where Lombards and Romans often came in contact. In some of these documents, it is possible to find a relevant number of juridical interferences between Lombard and Roman law, the study of which could provide new clarifying elements for the above-mentioned debate. The focus of such a study is to analyse the where and the when of these commixtures and then to examine the reasons. However, to understand the particular characteristics of the Lombard kingdom in Italy and the social and juridical situation of the period, some crucial points first need to be explained.

Although Italy is considered as the cradle of Mediterranean culture, the peninsula was also a land where some Germanic peoples established their kingdoms. Ostrogoths first and then Lombards who were defeated by Franks in 774, ruled the Italian land, while in the second half of the eleventh century the South of Italy became a Norman kingdom. The Lombard kingdom was certainly an important part of the history of Italy, not only for political matters, but also for the juridical and social involvements. It would be impossible to analyse and

12 See: Gian Piero Bognetti, *L'Età longobarda I–IV* (Milan: Giuffrè, 1966–1968); Enrico Artifoni, "La costituzione e l'ordinamento dei primi stati barbarici nell'Europa occidentale dopo le invasioni barbariche nella Romania," in *Atti del convegno internazionale sul tema Dalla tribù allo stato*, Roma, 13–16 aprile 1961 (Rome: Edizione Accademia nazionale dei Lincei, 1962); Enrico Artifoni, "Storia, archeologia e diritto nel problema dei Longobardi," in *Atti del 1. Congresso internazionale di studi longobardi*, Spoleto 27–30 settembre 1951, ed. CISAM (Spoleto: Accademia spoletina, 1952); Enrico Artifoni, "L' editto di Rotari come espediente politico di una monarchia barbarica," in *Studi in onore di G.M. De Francesco*, vol. 2, ed. Aurelio Candian and Remo Franceschelli (Milan: Giuffrè, 1957); Giulio Vismara, "Gian Piero Bognetti storico dei Longobardi," in *L'età longobarda Vol. 1*, ed. Gian Piero Bognetti (Milan: Giuffrè, 1967).

discuss the entire sequence of the events of the Lombard kingdom here, but it is important to highlight that if the reign ceased to exist after the Frankish conquest, Lombardic customs, law and society did not.

Lombards came to Italy in 568 and quickly conquered the whole territory from North, with the duchies of Turin, Friuli and the city of Pavia, to South with the Duchy of Spoleto and the Duchy of Benevento. The northern duchies of the Lombard kingdom were known as *Langobardia Maior*, while the Duchy of Spoleto and the Duchy of Benevento formed *Langobardia Minor*. *Langobardia Maior* and *Langobardia Minor* were separated by the Byzantine Exarchate of Ravenna in Emilia Romagna and the Duchy of Rome in Lazio. The situation in the South was slightly different from the rest of the country. In fact, although the king in Pavia retained central power, the South and the Duchy of Benevento in particular remained strongly independent.

When Charlemagne conquered the so-called *Langobardia Maior* in 774, Duke Arichis II was ruling Benevento. Instead of bowing to Charlemagne, he assumed the title of Prince in the same year, meaning that Benevento became a Principality, a sovereign state.[13] This act marked the independence of Arichis II from the Frankish conquest but also the persistence, until 1053, of a state ruled by Lombards in southern Italy. In the following centuries, the Principality went through a series of divisions, which led to the formation of two others sovereign states: the Principality of Salerno and the Principality of Capua.[14]

As has already been pointed out, one of the most debated matters regarding the Lombards in Italy was their relationship with the Romans. The Roman population represented the vast majority of the inhabitants, and they belonged to different social classes, from landowners to slaves. The existence of Roman servants and slaves is proved by Rothari, No. 194, where a composition of twelve *solidi* is established for the crime of fornication with a *romana ancilla* "Roman handmaid."[15] Their relationships with the conquerors, Ostrogoths and Lombards, were quite different; in the 490s, the Ostrogoths, ruled by King Theoderic, came to Italy as *foederati*[16] of Byzantium and they started a cooperative cohabi-

13 See Kreutz, *Before the Normans*, 5–9.

14 Kreutz, *Before the Normans*, 32–33.

15 On the ethnic diversity of the inhabitants of Italy in that period and the situation of the Roman landowner during the Lombard kingdom, see Gasparri, *Prima delle nazioni*, 149–151; Chris Wickham, *Early Medieval Italy* (London: Macmillan Press, 1981), 64–79.

16 On treaties between Roman Empire and Germanic people and their consequences, see Guy Halsall, *Barbarian Migrations and the Roman West, 376–568* (New York: Cambridge University Press, 2007), 152–53 and 180–85.

tation with the Romans. They divided social and political powers equally[17] and, at the same time, kept a strong separation between the two ethnic groups.[18] Conversely, the Lombards were truly invaders and they did not cooperate with the Romans, at least in the beginning. Paul the Deacon in his *Historia Langobardorum*[19] described in few passages what happened to the richest Roman landowners. As reported by the Lombard historian: "Hic multos Romanorum viros potentes, alios galdiis extinxit, alios ab Italia exturbavit"[20] [Among the most powerful Roman men, some he killed by sword, some he exiled from Italy][21] and "His diebus multi nobilium Romanorum ob cupitidatem interfecti sunt. Reliqui vero per hospites divisi, ut tertiam partem suarum frugum Longobardis persolverent, tributarii efficiuntur."[22] [In those days, a lot of the most noble Roman men were killed for cupidity. The remaining men were forced to pay a tribute to the strangers, so that they paid the third part of their earnings to the Lombards].[23] According to the source, the wealthy Roman landowners were killed or deported while others were forced to accept the *hospitalitas*, the payment of a tribute same to the third part of their earnings, as usually happened with other Germanic people.[24] In this context, it is clear that coexistence between Lombards and Romans was quite difficult and not free from other implications.

In addition, Lombards and Romans were ruled by two different laws. The Lombards, as all others Germanic people, professed their own *natio* law while the Romans still lived following the Roman territorial law. The Lombard law was the written compilation of their customs, called in Lombard language *cawarfidae*,[25] which King Rothari promulgated for the first time in 643. As with the other *Leges Barbarorum*, the *Edictus Rothari* was written in Latin, following

17 On the political situation during the Ostrogothic Kingdom in Italy see Mario Ascheri, *Istituzioni medievali. Una introduzione* (Bologna: Il Mulino, 1994), 71–76; and Claudio Azzara, *Le invasioni barbariche* (Bologna: Il Mulino, 2003), 76–81.

18 On the Ostrogothic invasion of Italy see Wickham, *Early Medieval Italy*, 20–27.

19 Paul the Deacon (720–99) wrote the *Historia Langobardorum* after his return to Italy from the court of Charlemagne in about 787, more than two centuries after the Lombard conquest.

20 No. 31: Paulus Diaconus, *Historia Langobardorum*, eds. Ludwig Bethmann and Georg Waitz, MGH SS rer. Lang. (Hannover: Hahn, 1878), II, 90.

21 My translation.

22 No. 32: Paulus Diaconus, *Historia Langobardorum*, ed. Bethmann and Waitz, II, 90.

23 My translation.

24 On the *hospitalitas* see Halsall, *Barbarian Migrations*, 422–47; Stefano Gasparri, *Italia longobarda. Il regno, i Franchi, il papato* (Bari: Laterza, 2016), 9–17.

25 Cf. Nicoletta Francovich Onesti, *Vestigia Longobarde in Italia (568–774): lessico e antroponimia* (Rome: Artemide, 1999), 72–73.

the patterns of the Roman law, but mainly with Germanic contents.[26] On the other side, the Roman law consisted of a wide range of laws, from the golden age of the Roman Empire to the most recent law compilations such as the *Corpus Iuris Civilis*, issued by order of Justinian I, or others *codici* of later Byzantine rulers.[27] The Roman law was well established in Italy not only in its official form, but also as rural traditions and customs that had been followed for centuries, especially for land property.[28] They also professed different religions, as, at the outset at least, the Lombards followed Arianism while the Romans' religion was Catholicism.

Such a dualism can be considered quite natural at the beginning of the Lombard domination, when Lombards and Romans shared only the indispensable aspects of social and political life.[29] However, it became more evident that this situation could not be preserved, as far as Lombards and Romans started to create social and cultural links.[30] Their mutual approach was a long process that involved, in the first place, social relationships, like the definitive conversion to Catholicism of the Lombards that led to marriages between them and the Romans.[31] Becoming Catholics also meant introducing new legal aspects into Lombard law, for example the insertion of many new laws, regarding the various religious institutions and the members of the clergy or the ones to regulate the above-mentioned mixed marriages.[32] The fundamental lawmaker for reli-

26 See Claudio Azzara, "... quod cawerfeda antiqua usque nunc sic fuisset. Consuetudine e codificazione nell'Italia longobarda," in *Alto medioevo mediterraneo*, ed. Stefano Gasparri (Florence: Firenze University Press, 2005); Claudio Azzara, "Introduzione al testo," in *Le leggi dei Longobardi. Storia, memoria e diritto di un popolo germanico* ed. Claudio Azzara and Stefano Gasparri (Rome: Viella, 2005), XLIV–XLVII, L–LII; Stefano Gasparri, *La cultura tradizionale dei Longobardi. Struttura tribale e resistenze pagane* (Spoleto: Centro Italiano di Studi sull'Alto Medioevo, 1983), 37–40 and 93–95; Stefano Gasparri, "La memoria storica dei Longobardi," in *Le leggi dei Longobardi. Storia, memoria e diritto di un popolo germanico*, ed. Claudio Azzara and Stefano Gasparri (Rome: Viella, 2005), XXVII–XXX; Gasparri, *Italia Longobarda*, 24–35; Patrick Wormald, "The *Leges Barbarorum*: Law and Ethnicity in the Post-Roman West," in *Regna and Gentes: The Relationship between Late Antique and Early Medieval Peoples and Kingdoms in the Transformation of the Roman World*, ed. Hans-Werner Goetz et al. (Leiden: Brill, 2003).

27 For example, the *Ecloga* issued by Leo III the Isaurian and the *Basilika* and the *Eisagoge* of Basil I the Macedonian.

28 See Francesco Schupfer, *Manuale di storia del diritto italiano*, vol. I, *Leggi e Scienza* (Città di Castello: S. Lapi, 1904), 21.

29 Gasparri, *Prima delle nazioni*, 128–32.

30 Gasparri, *Prima delle nazioni*, 146–54.

31 Gasparri, *Prima delle nazioni*, 148.

32 See Azzara, "Forme di acculturazione e di integrazione," 43–53; Gasparri, *Cultura tradizionale dei Longobardi*, 113–20; Wickham, *Early Medieval Italy*, 43–44.

gious matters was King Liutprand who ruled the Lombard Kingdom from 712 to 744.[33] Two of the first references to religious institutions can be found in the law No. 19 (in 721), which dealt with the property management of a minor and in No. 30 (in 723) where the subjects were women who lived as nuns despite that they were still not ordained by the Church.

Furthermore, purchase agreements between Lombards and Romans were increasing, due to the new socio-economic situation that pushed them towards a different point of view on social interaction. Actually, in some of the articles, the *Edictus Rothari* and its successive additions were inspired by Roman law of property and purchase. The main reason being that traditional Lombard customs were lacking in these particular legal fields, mainly because they had not needed very specific and detailed customs for buying and selling lands and rural administration in the previous time. However, after the settlement in Italy, the necessity for clear regulation of these fields became urgent and the simplest solution was to take it from Roman law and customs.[34] This choice was not so much a matter of convenience, but rather a clever way to make good use of the broad-based Roman customs on landowning and property management. In fact, as Lombards progressively appropriated Roman holdings, they did not modify the structure or the administration of the lands, leaving those under the system provided by Roman law.[35]

Nevertheless, Lombard law was the expression of ancestral traditions of the *gens Langobardorum* and the new legal system needed to be in line with these customs. It would be impossible to exclude the Lombard juridical procedures, because they represented a sign of cohesion of the Lombard people in contrast with the Romans and such a loss of identity would not be accepted.

The Lombards were used to validating purchase agreements and gifts by using old legal customs, the *launegild* and the *wadia* above all. In Lombard language *wadia* (from Gmc. **wadja-, wađja* "agreement, pledge" cf. Got. *wadi*, OHG. *wetti*, OS. *weddi*, OE. *wedd*, ON. *veđ*; from IE. **u̯ādʰ-*, **u̯ədʰ-*, cf. Lat. *vas, vadis* "guarantee, guarantor") means "pledge, collateral", while the *launegild*, according to its etymology, was "a price for the gift", a counter-gift (a compound word: *laun-*, Gmc. **launa-*, **launam* "reward, price", cf. ON. *laun*, OE. *léan*, OFris. *lân*, OS. *lôn*, OHG. *lōn*, from IE. **lõu*; *-geld*, Gmc. **geldan* "payment, fee, money",

33 Thom Gobbitt discusses the treatment of the prologues to Liutprand's various legislative phases in the law-books of the eighth to early-eleventh centuries in this volume, "Liutprand's Prologues in the *Edictus Langobardorum*," Chapter 3.

34 See Wickham, *Early Medieval Italy*, 39–40.

35 See again Schupfer, *Storia del diritto italiano*, 20ff.

cf. OE. *geld*, Got. *gild*, ON. *gjald*, OHG. *gelt*, from IE. **gheldh-* "to pay"). These juridical concepts can be considered two of the most peculiar aspects of the Lombard law. The use of the *wadia* was also common among the Franks and the other Germanic people.[36]

To understand the importance of *launegild* and *wadia* in Lombard law, it is necessary to explain briefly the legal procedures, which were connected to donation and purchase agreements. According to the ancient Lombard customs, a donation agreement cannot be considered valid without a series of specific procedures, some of which were linked to archaic uses that strongly marked the Lombard traditions. One of them was the *launegild*, a counter-gift that the donee gave to the donor to avoid a situation of inferiority that the donation could generate. The idea that a gift could place someone in a subordinate position was a very Germanic point of view, which is also possible to find in Scandinavian culture, for example it is mentioned in the *Landnámabók*, the Icelandic Book of Settlements.[37] The aim of the *launegild* was to put the donee in the same position of the donor, even if this was merely a symbolic counter-gift. Actually, the *launegild* value was never the same as the donation, but rather was just a nominal gift such as a piece of cloth, a garment or other common objects. In the story of Steinuđr and Ingólfr included in the *Landnámabók*, the counter-gift is a multi-colored cloak with a hood (*heklu flekkóta*)[38] and in some acts of the CDC the *launegild* is a piece of cloth (*pannum*)[39] or a kind of tunic (*camiso*).[40] These objects became, in some cases, a sum of money but without losing the symbolic aspect. However, this change is very irregular and not fixed as it can be observed in some of the CDC documents. For example in CDC, I, No. 17 (837 AD) a garment (*westa*) is the counter-gift;[41] in CDC, III, No. 474 (994 AD) the *launegild* is composed of a small cloak (*pallidellum*) and fifteen coins (*et tari boni numerum quindecim*);[42] in CDC, V, No. 819 (1029 AD) a sum of

36 Cf. Rudolf Huebner, *A History of Germanic Private Law* (Boston: Little, Brown, and Company, 1918), 497–98.

37 See Marco Scovazzi, *Il diritto islandese nella Landnámabók* (Milan: Giuffrè, 1961), 46.

38 Scovazzi, *Diritto islandese*, 46.

39 No. 828 (1030 AD): Michele Morcaldi, Mauro Schiani, and Silvano De Stefano, eds., *Codex Diplomaticus Cavensis* (*CDC*) V (Naples, 1878), 196–97. The CDC documents refer to the Morcaldi et alii edition. All references here are taken from this edition.

40 No. 273 (973 AD): Michele Morcaldi, Mauro Schiani, and Silvano De Stefano, eds., *CDC* II (Naples, 1875), 78–79.

41 No. 17 (837 AD): Michele Morcaldi, Mauro Schiani, and Silvano De Stefano, eds., *CDC* I (Naples, 1873), 18–19.

42 No. 474 (994 AD): Michele Morcaldi, Mauro Schiani, and Silvano De Stefano, eds., *CDC* III (Naples, 1876), 22–24.

money (*biginti quatuor auri tari boni*) is used for the *launegild*;[43] in CDC, VII, No. 1079 (1047 AD) the *launegild* is a kind of long tunic (*cammisa larga*);[44] in CDC, VII, No. 1158 (1051 AD) there is again a sum of money (*sexaginta et septem tari ex auro boni*).[45]

In the *Edictus Rothari*, the *launegild* appears several times connected with gift agreements,[46] and its use was deeply assimilated in the procedures. In 726 King Liutprand issued a law to establish the correct use of the *launegild*: no contract would be considered valid unless it was validated by *launegild*, except for donations made in favour of the Church and religious institutions.[47] Such a law highlights how the *launegild* represented an undeniable Lombard custom, an ancestral tradition that characterized the Lombard *gens*, even after a quite long period, during which the Lombard kingdom became increasingly stable and inspired by Roman institutions.

As the *launegild* enforced and validated a donation, the *wadia* made a purchase agreement effective. More precisely, the *wadia* or *guadia*, as integrated loanword in high-medieval Latin, was a pledge that the seller gave to the buyer in order to ensure the validity of the purchase. It represented the vendor's will to sell what the vendee was going to pay for. The act of giving and the *wadia* was known in Lombard law as *datio wadiae/guadiae*.[48]

The Lombard law dedicated many *capitula* to this particular custom,[49] and some of them indicate developments of the socio-economic situation. In fact, the laws regarding buying and selling evolved in both procedure and use based on the needs of the new society.

In ancient times, the *wadia* was an object, a wooden stick that the pledger gave to the pledgee with the intervention of a guarantor.[50] In some particular

---

43 No. 819 (1029 AD): Morcaldi, Schiani, and De Stefano, *CDC* V, 182–83.

44 No. 1079 (1047 AD): Michele Morcaldi, Mauro Schiani, and Silvano De Stefano, eds., *CDC* VII (Naples, 1888), 35–37.

45 No. 1158 (1051 AD): Morcaldi, Schiani, and De Stefano, *CDC* VII, 165–67.

46 Rothari, Nos. 175, 184; Liutprand, Nos. 43, 54, 65, 73; Aistulf, No. 12, numbered as in Friedrich Bluhme, ed. *Edictus Langobardorum*, MGH LL 4 (Hannover: Hahn, 1868), 41, 43–44, 126, 128–89, 134, 137, 199–200.

47 Liutprand, No. 73: Bluhme, "*Edictus Langobardorum*," 137; see also Claudio Azzara and Stefano Gasparri, eds., *Le leggi dei Longobardi. Storia, memoria e diritto di un popolo germanico* (Rome: Viella, 2005), 239–40, n. 56.

48 For more information, see Huebner, *History of Germanic Private Law*, 497–503, and John H. Wigmore, "The Pledge-Idea: A Study in Comparative Legal Ideas," *Harward Law Review* 10, No. 6 (Jan. 25, 1897): 321–50.

49 Rothari Nos. 360–62, 366; Liutprand Nos. 8, 15, 36–40, 61, 96, 128; Ratchis, Nos. 5, 8: Bluhme, *Edictus Langobardorum*, 82–85, 110, 113–14, 125–26, 131–32, 147, 161, 187–90.

50 See Huebner, *History of Germanic Private Law*, 497–98.

situations, the pledge could consist of animals or even people and the *Edictum* issued a series of precise rules for these cases.[51] As it has been already said about the *launegild*, the *wadia* also saw its original nature modified with the use of money instead of wooden sticks.

In order to make the Roman legal procedures on purchase and gifts effective for the Lombard law, the above-mentioned Lombard customs were integrated in the legal acts. The result was a juridical system where the two laws operated together without losing their peculiarities. Lombards and Romans were probably not completely aware of this interpenetration, but they accepted it. Romans used Roman law, but if the other party was a Lombard, then they had to consider the Lombard customs too, and vice-versa. In this sense, there was no written code or law, everything was generated by the socio-economical dynamics, which arose from Lombards and Romans living together.

Nevertheless, at the beginning it was easy to recognize which contracts were drafted using Lombard law and which were with Roman law due to the *professio iuris*, a declaration that the parties made at the beginning of the legal procedures. In this declaration, they stated if they were going to act according to Lombard or Roman law. After centuries, this declaration became in some cases a mere formality, mainly because people had lost the archaic sense of such a legal division and the central point was no longer the distinction between *gens Langobardorum* and the Roman population, but it became the better way to operate for both social and personal wealth. This does not mean that no one cared about ethnicity or correct legal procedures, on the contrary, it represents a social evolution of law which became the perfect instrument to let people take the best advantages in particular situations. In fact, this "legal-mix" was not as arbitrary as it could appear at first sight to be, nor can it be considered a series of notarial mistakes. This theory can be demonstrated with the study of some *chartae* contained in the previously-mentioned CDC.

The diplomatic edition of the CDC was edited by Michele Morcaldi, curator and former abbot of the Badia of Cava dei Tirreni, in collaboration with Mauro Schiani, Silvano De Stefano and Bernardo Geatani d'Aragona.[52] Michele Morcaldi was chosen as curator for the structure after 1866 when, due to a law issued by the then newly-founded Kingdom of Italy, all religious institutions were closed and dismantled, except for some institutions, which were considered culturally and historically relevant. The Badia of Cava became one of

51 Rothari, No. 252: Bluhme, *Edictus Langobardorum*, 61–62.

52 On the history of the edition, see Francesco Senatore, "La storiografia cavense dall'Ottocento ad oggi. Storia del Codex Diplomaticus Cavensis," *Rassegna Storica Salernitana* IX/2, n. 18 (1992): 131–60.

these "Monumenti Nazionali" [National Monuments]. Their edition, published between 1873 and 1893, consists of eight volumes,[53] each one supplied with a *membranarum* (the chronological index of the acts with a brief summary of the content of each document), an *Index alphabeticus* (the index of people that appear in each act and it is divided in sections), a *Civites et Loci* section (the index of cities and places cited in each act) and an appendix which is different in every book. Nearly a century after the publication of the eighth volume, Giovanni Vitolo and don Simeone Leone edited volumes nine and ten in 1984 and 1990.[54] In 2015, volumes eleven and twelve were published by Giovanni Leone with Carmine Carlone and Leone Morinelli.[55]

The CDC presents different types of legal documents; mainly purchase agreements, testaments, gifts, judgments and some public acts of the local authority or the Prince as the *diploma* 764, contained in CDC V,[56] by which Prince Guaimario III made the above-mentioned gift to the Badia in 1025. The legal format can differ from one act to another but, except for the palace's *diplomata*, it is possible to divide them into *chartulae* and *memoratoria*.

Their structure, despite their specificities,[57] is the typical one of medieval legal acts, comprising the protocol, the text and the eschatocol; the text can be further divided into *narratio* and *dispositio*.[58]

Latin was the language of the laws and legal documents, therefore the acts are all written in Latin with the exception of some words in the Lombard language, even if the Germanic terms were often assimilated as loan words. However, the Latin used in the documents is high-medieval Latin, which implies a less grammatical and syntactic coherence and with some variations in the script.[59]

---

53 Comprising: Morcaldi, Schiani and De Stefano, *CDC*, vol. 1 (792–960), vol. 2 (983–993), vol. 3 (993–1000), vol. 4 (1001–1018), vol. 5 (1018–1034), vol. 6 (1034–1045), vol. 7 (1046–1056), vol. 8 (1057–1065) (Naples, 1873–1893).

54 Comprising: Giovanni Vitolo and Simeone Leone, eds. *CDC*, vol. 9 (1065–1072), vol. 10 (1073–1080) (Naples, 1984, 1990).

55 Comprising: Carmine Carlone, Leone Morinelli and Giovanni Vitolo, eds, *CDC*, vol. 11 (1081–1085), vol. 12 (1086–1090) (Salerno, 2015).

56 No. 764 (1025 AD): Morcaldi, Schiani and De Stefano, *CDC* V, 93–95.

57 See Paola Massa, "Documenti, formule e persone nelle carte di Avellino (X–XII secolo)," *Scrineum Rivista* 9 (2012): 45–48.

58 For a complete explanation, see Filippo Valenti, "Il documento medioevale. Nozioni di diplomatica generale e di cronologia," in *Scritti e lezioni di archivistica, diplomatica e storia istituzionale*, ed. Daniela Grana, Pubblicazioni degli Archivi di Stato, Saggi 57 (Città di Castello: Ediprint, 2000).

59 See d'Arco Silvio Avalle, *Bassa latinità: il latino tra l'età tardo-antica e l'alto medioevo con particolare riguardo all'origine delle lingue romanze* (Turin: Giappichelli, 1968).

The use of Latin led the notaries to apply the already known practices of Roman law.[60] Along with the use of Latin, these acts present a typical use of *formulae*, which were inherited from Roman legal practice and the procedures developed over the course of time.[61] Actually, the *formulae* can be applied both to Lombard law and Roman practice, even if originally they were mainly Roman and were adapted by the Lombards to their legal documents.[62] This absence of a definite and clear Lombard legal format counterposed to the Roman one, is another factor which could possibly have helped the interferences and the use of both laws in several documents.

The vast majority of these *formulae* refers to the *launegild* and the *wadia*, but a lot were also used for the so-called *defensio*.[63] It was a custom that contemplated the possibility, for the buyer or the donee, to call to his own defense the seller or the donor in the case of litigation. In fact, for legal reasons, the buyer or donor could keep the documents of a particular plot of land or property after a sale or a gift, with the commitment to present those documents during the eventual trial as proofs in order to settle the case.

The acts selected for this study relate to the period between the 10th and the 11th centuries, a period that can be historically relevant for this type of investigation, in which both Lombard and Roman legal procedures are present.[64] Some documents among the eleven which have been found and studied are

---

60 See Antonella Ghignoli and François Bougard, "Elementi romani nei documenti longobardi?" in *L'héritage byzantin en Italie* (VIIIe–XIIe *siècle*). *I. La fabrique documentaire*, ed. Jean-Marie Martin, Annick Peters-Custot and Vivien Prigent (Rome: École française de Rome, 2011).

61 See Wormald, "*Leges Barbarorum*," 42–44.

62 Cf. Giovanna Nicolaj, "Il documento privato italiano nell'Alto Medioevo," In *Libri e documenti d'Italia: dai Longobardi alla rinascita delle città*, Atti del Convegno dell'Associazione Italiana dei Paleografi e Diplomatisti, Cividale del Friuli (UD), 5–7 ottobre 1994, ed. Cesare Scalon (Udine: Arti grafiche friulane, 1996); Massa, "Documenti, formule e persone," 48–74.

63 Cf. Massa, "Documenti, formule e persone," 51–55.

64 The complete study is contained in my PhD dissertation: Sonia Colafrancesco, "Interferenze e commistioni tra diritto longobardo e diritto romano-bizantino nei documenti del *Codex diplomaticus Cavenis*" [Interferences and Interpenetrations between Lombard Law and Roman-Byzantine Law in the Documents of the *Codex diplomaticus Cavensis*] (PhD Thesis, Università degli Studi "G. d'Annunzio" Chieti-Pescara, 2016), Dottorato di Ricerca in Linguistica, Anglistica, Italianistica e Filologia, XXVIII ciclo, Dipartimento di Lingue, Letterature e Culture Moderne, Università degli Studi "G. d'Annunzio" Chieti-Pescara, tutor Prof.ssa Elisabetta Fazzini, coordinatore del Dottorato Prof. Nicola D'Antuono, April 12, 2016. The dissertation can be consulted at the National Central Library of Rome and at the National Central Library of Florence. The study includes the original text, the translation and the linguistic analysis of all the eleven acts examined.

very helpful for understanding the reasons and conditions of the juridical interference; these comprise act 516 of 998,[65] act 657 of 1012,[66] and act 828 of 1030.[67]

Act 516 is a purchase agreement, a *cartula,* in which one Teodenanda sells her inheritance to Giovanni, Maurone's son. At the beginning of the act, she declares herself to be the lawful owner of her deceased parents' property and that the law allows her to sell it. In addition, even if she speaks in the first person, the woman states that she is accompanied by her husband Urso, "*una mecum adesse ipse ursu viro meo*"[68] [with me comes Urso, my husband],[69] who is involved in the whole purchase. Such an involvement can lead one to think about the Lombard laws regarding the women's proprieties and their limited rights on them. In fact, as Liutprand issued in No. 22 (721) and No. 29 (722/23),[70] a Lombard woman is allowed to sell her properties only with the consent of her husband or her *mundualdo* and with the legal declaration that no compulsion subsisted. In Lombard Law the *mundualdo* was the woman's legal guardian. According to the Lombard Law (Rothari, No. 204),[71] a woman was not allowed to live *selpmundia* that is to say free from the *mundio,* male control and protection. Teodenanda also declares that the sale will be done according to the Roman law.

The propriety is a land in Fonti, a place near the boundary of Salerno, and also including the rights and jurisdictions of the San Felice church built there.

Giovanni, the buyer, is not only going to purchase the land, but also the church with all its jurisdictions, which also includes payment of an annual tribute for the above-mentioned church. The price is agreed at forty golden *tarì,* a type of coin,[72] by common accord, a sum that also includes the guarantee of Teodenanda, Urso and their heirs to respect the agreement. In the act, the term *guadia* is not cited, but the *formula* used to state the guarantee is almost identical to the others found in similar acts, in which the *guadia* is clearly mentioned:[73] "obligamus nos et nostris heredibus amodo et semper antistandum et

---

65 No. 516 (998 AD): Morcaldi, Schiani, and De Stefano, *CDC* III, 81–82.

66 No. 657 (1012 AD): Morcaldi, Schiani, and De Stefano, *CDC* IV, 206.

67 No. 828 (1030 AD): Morcaldi, Schiani, and De Stefano, *CDC* V, 196–97.

68 No. 516: Morcaldi, Schiani, and De Stefano, *CDC* III, 81, l. 4.

69 All the translations of the acts or of portions of them in this paper are my translations.

70 Liutprand, Nos. 22, 29: Bluhme, "*Edictus Langobardorum,*" 117–18, 121.

71 Rothari, No. 204: Bluhme, "*Edictus Langobardorum,*" 50.

72 See Kreutz, *Before the Normans*, 109–10.

73 Nos. 474 (994 AD), 494 (996 AD): Morcaldi, Schiani, and De Stefano, *CDC* III, 22–24, 50–54; Nos. 944 (1039 AD), 951 (1039 AD): Morcaldi, Schiani, and De Stefano, *CDC* VI, 106–07, 117–19.

defensandum tibi tuique heredibus inclita supradicta nostra vindictionem da omnes homines ominque partibus"[74] [we commit ourselves and our heirs from now and forever to stand in front of you and to defend you and your heirs for the whole our above-mentioned sale from anyone and any part].

The sanctions in case of breach are also illustrated in the same way used in the other acts, but with the omission of the word *guadia* in the *formula*. The *defensio* is present and the documents needed for an eventual trial are mentioned as well as the possibility for Teodenanda and Urso to be called as defenders. Before the *defensio* a specific declaration can be found in the act: "de colludio autem legibus vobis iuremus per dei misteria"[75] [and for the collusion according to the law, we swear to you by the divine Mysteries]; this refers to Liutprand, No. 43 (723),[76] which established that the one who cannot provide a guarantee for a gift and is accused of collusion has the opportunity to defend himself by an oath on the Gospel. This oath would free him from all the charges and suspicions. The same *formula* can be found in many other documents of the Cava's collection,[77] and in some of them the link with Lombard law is evident.[78]

According to what is said, the act clearly contains elements of Lombard law even if the *professio iuris* is in favour of the Roman law. In addition, the use of the Roman law is directly authorized by the Prince "per largietate et absolutionem supradicti domni principes."[79] [by concession and absolution of our above mentioned lord the Prince], so it is impossible to consider the declaration to be an error. The main reason could be that Teodenanda is a Roman woman and that, consequently, she uses her native law; however, this theory is refuted by the evidence of her family as contained in previous documents of the Cava collections. In these acts,[80] which mainly concerned the San Felice church and the surrounding lands, her grandfather, father and uncles operate within a strict observance of the Lombard law. For example, they use a garment as *launegild* for a gift,[81] and one of Teodenanda's

74 No. 516: Morcaldi, Schiani, and De Stefano, *CDC* III, 82, ll. 2–4.

75 No. 516: Morcaldi, Schiani, and De Stefano, *CDC* III, 82, l. 10.

76 Liutprand, No. 43: Bluhme, *"Edictus Langobardorum,"* 126.

77 See for example: Nos. 124 (908 AD), 137 (919 AD), 162 (936 AD), 191 (956 AD): Morcaldi, Schiani, and De Stefano, *CDC* I, 158–59, 176–77, 207–08, 246–47.

78 See No. 153 (933 AD): Morcaldi, Schiani, and De Stefano, *CDC* I, 196–97.

79 No. 516: Morcaldi, Schiani, and De Stefano, *CDC* III, 81, ll. 10–11.

80 Nos. 242 (966 AD), 273 (973 AD), 274 (973 AD): Morcaldi, Schiani, and De Stefano, *CDC* II, 37–39, and 78–80; CDC III, No. 486 (995 AD): Morcaldi, Schiani, and De Stefano, *CDC* III, 39–40.

81 No. 237 (966 AD): Morcaldi, Schiani, and De Stefano, *CDC* II, 31–33.

uncles, after her father's death, represents her and her sisters in a case against the other uncle.[82]

It is also possible to assume that Urso, the husband, is Roman, but such a hypothesis does not explain the presence of Lombard elements in the act. In fact, according to the Lombard law, if Urso were Roman and Teodenanda Lombard, she would have become Roman after the wedding,[83] so there are no objective reasons here for the use of Lombard customs.

A further theory focuses not on the people, but on the plot of land and the church: the San Felice church, as with all other religious structures and institutions and the clergy, was ruled by Roman law, because they were all considered subjects to the Pope in Rome, not to the Lombard king. In addition, the plot of land had been gifted and rented out for years by Teodenanda's family,[84] and the possibility that they were only continuing an already extant routine must not be excluded. In other words, Teodenanda's family had arguably purchased or obtained the plot of land and the church, but they left the situation unaltered, without modifying the administrative system nor withdrawing concessions, which were probably based on Roman law.[85]

The presence of the San Felice church, a religious structure subject to Rome on the plot of land, and the persisting concessions are the two factors that can justify the necessity of use of the Roman law in the act. On the other hand, the Lombard legal procedures were similarly necessary in order to validate the purchase agreement for Teodenanda and her husband.

Act 657 contains a gift made by Anna, a widow, under the supervision of her son, Landulo who is her *mundualdo*, as established in the Lombard law.[86] The declaration of compliance to the Lombard law is explicit and reports the expression "sicut mihi congruum est"[87] [as it is appropriate for me]. The donee is the San Massimo church in Salerno, which is represented by Maione, the abbot. The gift consists of a piece of land in Montoro,[88] the native town of Anna's deceased husband Giovanni *Clericus*. This land is part of her *quarta*, the amount of wealth that the husband gives to the wife after the wedding

82 No. 486 (995 AD): Morcaldi, Schiani, and De Stefano, *CDC* III, 39–40.

83 Liutprand, No. 127: Bluhme, "*Edictus Langobardorum*," 160.

84 See the above cited documents.

85 For an overview on the estate administrative system and rural concessions in post-Roman and high-medieval southern Italy see Augusto Lizier, *L'economia rurale dell'età prenormanna nell'Italia meridionale (studi su documenti editi dei secoli IX–XI)* (Palermo: Alberto Reber Libreria della R. Casa, 1907).

86 See Liutprand, Nos. 22, 29: Bluhme, *Edictus Langobardorum*, 117–18, 121.

87 No. 657 (1012 AD): Morcaldi, Schiani, and De Stefano, *CDC* IV, 206, l. 3.

88 A village near Salerno.

night, which consists of a fourth part of his whole property. The *quarta maritalis* was the substitute for the custom, known in Lombard law as *morgingab*, literally "morning gift," which was a common practice among Germanic people.[89] The social evolution and the new richness led Lombard fathers to demand ever more expensive gifts from their future sons-in-law and their families, but sometimes it was the husband to be himself who wanted to demonstrate his wealthy condition by donating a valuable *morgingab*. To limit this situation, Liutprand issued a number of laws (No. 7, in 717, No. 89, in 727, and No. 103, in 728) that contain precise dispositions about the amount of these "gifts," which cannot exceed a fourth part of the husband's properties.[90] The name *quarta maritalis* or *quarta uxoria* is taken from the Roman law, a *novella* by Justinian,[91] according to which Liutprand probably shaped his own law. The *morgingab* along with the *meta* or *metfio* and the *faderfio*[92] were the legitimate proprieties of a married Lombard woman, while a nubile one owned only the *faderfio*. A woman was able to sell and donate her property, but only according to the terms of these laws.

As the Lombard law required, Anna received two *tarì* as a counter-gift for the donation, the *launegild*: "Unde recepi a te iamdicto abbate launegilt tari duo,"[93] [And so I received from you, the previously-mentioned abbot two tarì as *launegild*], and she gives the *guadia* to Maione as a guarantee: "Unde guadia tibi dedi,"[94] [And so I gave to you the *guadia*]. After that, the act does not report the entire *formula* of the sanctions in case of breach, which is replaced by "*etc.*" while the penalty amount is of twenty golden *solidi costantini*, a byzantine golden coin, probably the most valuable in the high-medieval southern Italy.

However, after the *datio guadiae*, there is a reference to the Roman law: "et iuxta lex nostre romanorum me ipsam quindiniiavi"[95] [and our fair Roman law

---

89 See Elisabetta Fazzini, "Condizione sociale e giuridica della donna nelle *Leges Barbarorum*," *Igitur* Anno V, no. 1 (1993): 40–41.

90 Liutprand, Nos. 7, 89, and 103: Bluhme, "*Edictus Langobardorum*," 110, 144, and 149–50.

91 No. 117, 5: Rudolf Schöll and Wilhelm Kroll, eds., *Novellae Constitutiones* (Berlin: Weidmann, 1895) 554–55.

92 On the Germanic traditional wedding gifts and their legal implications, see Antonietta Amati Canta, "Terminologia matrimoniale longobarda nel Codice Diplomatico Barese-Pugliese," in *Presenze longobarde in Italia, il caso della* Puglia, ed. Lucia Sinisi (Ravenna: Longo Editore, 2007); Fazzini, "Condizione sociale e giuridica della donna," 25–72; Luigi Tria, "La disciplina giuridica del matrimonio secondo le consuetudini di terra di Bari." *Iapigia* anno VII, fasc. IV (1937): 404–15.

93 No. 657 (1012 AD): Morcaldi, Schiani, and De Stefano, CDC IV, 206, ll. 17–18.

94 No. 657 (1012 AD): Morcaldi, Schiani, and De Stefano, CDC IV, 206, l. 18.

95 No. 657 (1012 AD): Morcaldi, Schiani, and De Stefano, CDC IV, 206, ll. 18–19.

guarantees for me]. The reference to the Roman law is unexpected and quietly inexplicable, mainly because the act is evidently based on Lombard law. Also in this case, the first option to consider is that Anna is a Roman woman. It has been impossible to investigate the history of her family, because there are no references made to her ancestors, so her origins are not certain. Nevertheless, even if she were Roman, she would have not been able to use the Roman law because she became Lombard after her wedding. The evidence in the act demonstrates that she strictly respects the Lombard customs and legal procedures, which makes no difference as to whether she was Lombard by birth or marriage.

The other possibility is that the use of Roman law is necessary because the donee is a clergy member representing the Church. According to this, the act is well balanced between the necessities of both parts to validate the act. Indeed, there is a clear respect for the Lombard laws, which Anna could not avoid due to her state as the widow of a Lombard man, whatever her origins were. Indeed, the Roman law is also involved in order not to violate the legal customs of the Catholic Church.

Act 828 is a gift in which the brothers Marino and Giovanni donate a plot of land to their sister Teotenanda. The family relationships between the two donors and the donee are quite complicated and involve other people, such as their cousin Mele and Teotenanda's husband Giovanni *Atrianense*. The plot of land is in Vietri, a small town near Salerno, and is the inheritance of Marino, Giovanni and their cousin Mele. Marino and Giovanni are biological brothers and Mele is their first cousin, but the expression used in the act "*consobrino fratrem*" arouses suspicion, and only the word *soror* "sister" designates Teotenanda. In addition, while for Marino and Giovanni there is the usual references to their father and their grandfather, this is absent for Teotenanda and for Mele.

That the two brothers and the cousin have a common inheritance is quite unusual for the period. In fact, an undivided inheritance between the three heirs means that their grandfather was probably still alive at the time of the donation; otherwise, his two hypothetical sons, Giovanni and Marino's father and Mele's father, would have already divided the properties in two parts. However, the Lombard law stated that only the owner is allowed to sell, gift or alienate his or her proprieties and substances.[96] Therefore, Marino and Giovanni would not have been able to give the plot of land to Teotenanda if their grandfather were alive and still its legal owner.

96 See in particular: Rothari, Nos. 169 and 170 on inheritance: Bluhme, "*Edictus Langobardorum*," 39.

In addition, they toss-up to divide the plot of land in half: "… inclita ipsa medietate de predicto campu, quantum quantoque nobis nominati germani exinde in sorte ebenerit da ipsum mele …"[97] [… the entire half of the above-mentioned land, as much as we siblings obtained by lot from Mele …]. In the document the term *sortio* (*-onis*) is used to label the portion of land inherited by Marino and Giovanni, as the word means "hæreditatis portio, quæ forte alicui obvenit" [portion of inheritance which someone obtains by tossing-up].[98] The only reasonable explanation comes from the *datio guadia* moment, when Marino and Giovanni state that they will defend their sister's rights "a pars de ipsa genetrice nostra,"[99] [from our own mother]. The necessity of such a declaration is easily understandable if we hypothesize that Marino and Giovanni's mother is not Teotenanda's mother, and that she, on the contrary, could have legitimate rights to the donated land. Most probably, Teotenanda is the daughter of Marino and Giovanni's father with another woman, which would also explain the lack of references regarding her bloodline. The plot of land that her brothers wanted to donate to her is part of their mother's inheritance, for which Teotenanda should have had no rights. This also clarifies the position of Mele and why he is called *consobrinus*; in fact, in Latin the word *consobrinus* originally means "cousin on the mother's side, related to mother's sister," so it is possible that the relative between them comes from their mother's side. This implies that inheritance could be on maternal line and not paternal, but it still unclear how Marino and Giovanni were able to donate the plot of land if their mother was the rightful owner. It is conceivable that Marino and Giovanni's mother donated the plot of land to her sons and they were consequently able to give it to Teotenanda.

The gift could be considered an "unstinting act" carried out by the brothers in favor of their sister, but the gift is not only for Teotenanda, but also for her heirs and her husband Giovanni. Through the *confinatio*, the description and measurement within the document of the borders of the plot of land, the act reveals that the piece of land adjoins the propriety of Urso *Atrianense*, Teotenanda's husband's brother. The donation therefore also favors Giovanni, who obtains a plot of land near to the brother's one.

Nevertheless, this explanation, which tries to clarify the intricate relationship among the involved parties, does not prove useful for understanding the nature of the interferences in the act. In fact, the document presents a series

97 No. 828 (1030 AD): Morcaldi, Schiani, and De Stefano, *CDC* V, 196, ll. 14–15.

98 See Du Cange et al. ed., "Sortio," in *Glossarium mediæ et infimæ latinitatis*, accessed February 06, 2020, http://ducange.enc.sorbonne.fr/SORTIO.

99 No. 828 (1030 AD): Morcaldi, Schiani, and De Stefano, *CDC* V, 197, l. 11.

of alternate references to Lombard and Roman law, which can be considered as being quite arbitrary. The *professio iuris* is absent, but Marino and Giovanni declare that they are donating the piece of land to their sister "secumdum lex et consuetudo nostre romanorum,"[100] [according to the Roman law and custom], so it appears that they are Roman. However, soon after they receive from Teotenanda and her husband the *launegild*, symbolized by a piece of cloth, but the well-known Lombard custom is described as "iusta lege et consuetudo nostre romanorum,"[101] [our fair Roman law and custom]. The act continues with the *datio guadia* as prescribed by Lombard law but without a clear reference to it in the text. After the *formulae* for the sanctions in the case of breach, the act again cites the *launegild* to better specify the terms of the agreement, and this time they refer to the custom as belonging to Lombard law: "sicud in lex lagnubardorum de donum and launegilt continent,"[102] [as the Lombard law of gift and *launegild* prescribes]. The form "lagnubardorum" is the same reported by Morcaldi in the reference edition.[103]

In this specific situation, theories about the origin of the families or about the involvement of the clergy have not proven to be very useful. No information is given about their bloodline, an omission that makes explaining some crucial points of the act difficult. Moreover, the conclusions do not reveal whether the family were Roman or Lombard. In addition, there are no references at all regarding a church or a monastery or a clergy member, a fact that, as has already been verified, frequently led to the use of the Roman law instead the Lombard one.

According to the legal procedures described, the act is written following the Lombard law and the presence of Roman references is due only to a lack of competence on the scribe's part. The hypothesis, according to which the mistakes are the scribe's faults and not attributable to the notary, finds its foundation in the succession of the incorrect and correct references. In fact, if the notary were totally unaware of the Lombard law and custom, he should have continued to define the *launegild* as a Roman custom throughout the entire act, as he had done in the first two references, and without referring to it correctly in the third. But, if the notary had a scribe at his service, one of the scribe's assignments would have been to take dictation of the acts, a task that only required knowledge of language and not of law. Therefore, if the scribe took dictation of the act, but missed some words, he may have substituted them with terms that,

100 No. 828 (1030 AD): Morcaldi, Schiani, and De Stefano, *CDC* V, 196, ll. 15–16.
101 No. 828 (1030 AD): Morcaldi, Schiani, and De Stefano, *CDC* V, 197, l. 5.
102 No. 828 (1030 AD): Morcaldi, Schiani, and De Stefano, *CDC* V, 197, ll. 12–13.
103 See Morcaldi, Schiani, and De Stefano, *CDC* V, 197, ll. 12–13.

according to him, could have been the right ones. Indeed, for a scribe as for a notary, he should have heard the legal *formulae* many times and so he should have known that a *consuetudo* and a *lex* could be Lombard or Roman.[104] The proof comes from the third reference, where the scribe finally understands the correct word but wrote it incorrectly. This mistake, along with the missed correction of the first two errors, demonstrates that he had no idea of what the legal procedures were that were present in the act.

Along with the other eight acts, these three acts demonstrate that the interpenetration between Lombard and Roman law was not arbitrary nor that it happened without special conditions. The examples clearly show situations in which the two laws had necessarily come into contact: mixed marriages, presence in the act of a member of the clergy, involvement of a religious institution or structure, pre-existing administrative custom of a land.

Each document presents a particular situation that justifies the use of the Lombard law with the Roman one, even if this commixture could appear strange at first sight. However, as this study highlights, each act contains all the elements required to understand the reasons for the legal contact to have occurred, except for a few still obscure points. The hypothesis that those references were nothing more than mistakes is admissible only for those cases where the legal procedures is definitely and clearly Lombard or Roman and there are no objective causes for a juridical commixture. This is the case for the previously-explained act 828, where the entire document is based on Lombard law and for which no other explanation for the references to the Roman law can be found, but for the scribe's error.

The legal interplay is a clear sign of the creation of a new society, where Lombards and Romans evolved from a *status* of forced coexistence to one of reciprocal cooperation. Accordingly, all the speculations made during in the 19th century by many authors and scholars, such as Alessandro Manzoni, cease to make sense.[105] They claimed that the Lombards literally destroyed the Roman population, who remained completely in a servile *status* until the Frankish conquest. But as has been shown, Romans were quite able to survive.

The Lombard role in the development of high medieval Italy should not be underestimated. The Ostrogothic Kingdom, which was in a certain way a continuation of the Western Roman Empire under Byzantine approval, permit-

104 Further discussion of the role of notaries in Lombard legal culture can be found in Daniela Fruscione, "Two Lombard Charters and their Writers," Chapter 13 in this volume.

105 Cf. Giovanni Tabacco, "Manzoni e la questione longobarda," in *Manzoni e l'idea di letteratura*, Atti del convegno di Torino 5–7 dicembre 1987, ed. Liceo linguistico Cadorna (Turin: Tirrenia Stampatori, 1987).

ted the conservation of the major part of the Roman institutions, not only the political ones, but also administrative. After the Gothic War, the Italian peninsula was almost destroyed, the productive system was seriously damaged and the country was deprived of its institutions. In such a difficult situation, without direct and strong help from Byzantium, the reprise could not be taken for granted.

The Lombard invasion, despite its initial violent nature, represented a small "renaissance" for Italy. In fact, as it has been said before, the Lombards, in order to administrate their new territories, started to use Roman law and customs. Moreover, over the years, they conquered and reigned, shaping a new administrative and political system that could guarantee stability, sometimes under the influence of Roman institutions.[106] Despite the absence of a strong royal family and the interferences of the dukes, the Lombard kings created a stable and well-articulated hierarchy that provided royal control on both the public and private sphere. In fact, the king entrusted some portions of the *curtis regia*, the royal demesne,[107] to an official, the *gastaldus* who had civil and judicial powers[108] in his *gastaldia*. For this reason, the *gastald* was loyal to the king contrary to the vast majority of the dukes, and he guaranteed a clear administration of the land and a regular juridical activity.[109]

In order to maintain control across the reign, the Lombard sovereigns adopted a written law, which reflected both the ancient traditions and peculiarities of the Lombard *natio* and the new necessities of the state. The Lombard law, along with the Roman one, created a strong juridical substrate, in which the following dominations put their roots.[110] The South remained a particular case, mainly for its almost total independence from the Frankish kingdom. The echoes of the Lombard traditions and culture can be found there, sometimes tempered and mixed with others, until the beginning of the Modern Era and maybe even beyond.

106 Cf. Katherine Fischer-Drew, "Public vs. Private Enforcement of the Law in the Early Middle Ages: Fifth to Twelfth Centuries," *Chicago-Kent Law Review* 70 (1995): 1584–85.

107 See Gasparri, *Italia longobarda*, 24–27.

108 See Jörg Jarnut, "*Gens*, *Rex* and *Regnum* of the Lombards," in *Regna and Gentes, The Relationship between Late Antique and Early Medieval Peoples and Kingdoms in the Transformation of the Roman World*, ed. Hans-Werner Goetz et al. (Leiden: Brill, 2003), 417–19.

109 See Ascheri, *Istituzioni medievali*, 89–105.

110 For the history of the political, judicial and administrative system in medieval Italy during the Frankish domination, see Ascheri, *Istituzioni medievali*, 131–80.

CHAPTER 11

Mortuary Proxies: Archaeological Contextualization of Medieval Legal Practices

Petar Parvanov

It is perhaps unexpected at first to draw a parallel between the dead recovered from archaeological work and the complicated, often abstract history of law.[1] By all means, this is not a self-evident path for the student of either of these fields due to the very different character of the evidence available and the ontological gap between the facts of things and facts from the word.[2] Yet, when social scientists of the last century delved into the dark side of human society, they revealed the agents of immoral and even criminal behaviour as silenced witnesses for many wider processes occurring within the very same communities that had rejected them.[3] The increased theoretical awareness was backed by refined observations in the field, and started a somewhat forensic turn in bioarchaeological enquiries. On the textual aspects of legal culture, the attempts to transform social control into overreaching written norm by promoting documents like the widely accepted Zakon Sudnyim Lyudem (*Законъ соудный людьмъ*) opens further the dialogue between legal accounts and archaeothanatological assessments. Here, the rare yet complimentary material evidence from the graves of possible law-breakers and written prescriptions for death penalties and physical punishment allows a multifaceted understanding of the less known internal political conditions in which medieval laws developed. A new direction in the emerging pan-European debate concerned with deviant

1 The majority of the quantitative analysis used here was done for: Petar Parvanov, "Medieval Deviant Burials from Bulgaria (7th–14th c.)" (Master's thesis, Central European University, 2016). For the traditional continental approach see, Karl von Amira and Claudius von Schwerin, *Rechtsarchäologie* (Berlin: Ahnenerbe-Stiftung Verlag, 1943); Hermann Baltl, *Rechtsarchäologie des Landes Steiermark* (Graz: Verlag Hermann Böhlaus Nachf., 1957); Witold Maisel, *Rechtsarchäologie Europas* (Vienna: Böhlau Verlag, 1992); Wolfgang Schmale, *Archäologie der Grund- and Menschenrechte in der Frühen Neuzeit. Ein Deutsch-FranzösischesParadigma* (Munich: R. Oldenbourg Verlag, 1997).

2 John Moreland, *Archaeology and Text* (London: Duckworth, 2001), 77–97.

3 Charles R. Tittle, *Control Balance: Toward a General Theory of Deviance* (Boulder, CO: Westview Press, 1995). Ronald Akers, *Social Learning and Social Structure: A General Theory of Crime and Deviance* (London: Transaction Publishers, 2009), 21–46.

 | DOI:10.1163/9789004448650_013

burials is charted by exploring these marginalized finds from *longue durée* south-eastern European perspective. The broad variations among them reflect deeply rooted strategies for establishing and maintaining authority in increasingly complex social context. Arguably, their functionality takes on hybrid secular and spiritual elements in the funerary display. To properly understand this continental phenomenon the growing number of such discoveries in the region can be used to improve the models developed from research on Western and Central European cases.

That explanatory aspect of social deviancy proves most potent as a category to be applied to the archaeological data. The Anglophone term "deviant burial" has faced fierce criticism from continental archaeologists that emphasize its loaded meaning today.[4] Its defenders tend to stress that "deviant" was used by anthropologists in purely statistical terms and is a consequence of a more scientific way of thinking. In this respect, it should be no different than other descriptive words for the specific kind of burial evidence of interest here, for instance atypical or irregular. This is how most of the grave finds from south-eastern Europe would appear in scientific reports.

Essentially, the recognition of burials as deviant is an exercise in structural oppositions between normative and non-normative behaviour observable in the archaeological context. Those who point out that there is significantly more variety in funerary behaviour and a rare grave type should not be simply declared deviant, would be correct.[5] However, the multiple factors at play during the funerary performance make the event a perfect occasion to negotiate any form of status and multiple forms of symbolic interactions, including social denial. Arguably, the labelling theory and its idea of social deviants are best suited to the mortuary context. Following the basic fact that dead people do not bury themselves, the self-image of the labelled person has even less power to resist that labelling. In the case of non-normative burials (for instance, but not limited to, deviant graves), the label applied through the funerary custom is too overwhelming. In practice, its factual correctness has little to do with its impact. In the context created by its application and reactions from others the label becomes real for living and dead alike. Arguably, the uncovered archaeological evidence could be seen to be the final, static outcome from a process deeply rooted in the communal principles and rules. Eventually, this is the basis

4 Edeltraud Aspöck, "What Actually is a Deviant Burial? Comparing German-Language and Anglophone Research on 'Deviant Burials'," in *Deviant Burial in the Archaeological Record*, ed. Eileen Murphy (Oxford: Oxbow Press, 1998).

5 Bruno Boulestin, *Norme funéraire: illusions et vérités, Qu'est-cequ'une sépulture? Humanités et systems funéraires de la Préhistoire à nosjours* (Antibes: Éditions APDCA, 2016), 373–75.

to reconcile archaeology with laws as the written commitment and protection of the same set of norms.

In this sense, the direct treatment of the body, which may evoke negative associations upon contact with it (both in the past or the present), becomes an even more important element in the rites of passage. Much information on the many possible forms of maltreatment is lost after advanced decomposition, but four types of maltreatment which are detectable on skeletal remains appear consistently across medieval Europe, and have attracted significant academic debate and public attention to themselves. They are the following: prone (face-down) positioned inhumations, decapitations, fixations of the corpse inside the grave through weighting down, and mutilations of the postcranial skeleton. This statistically rare and internally diverse group of grave finds is best suited to the contested term deviant burials. As such, they should be primarily considered a past social strategy for maintaining control over the dead. The next step towards a more refined understanding of their social context is to assess empirically the extent to which social norms and law-codes affected mortuary behaviour and vice versa.

So far, the emphasis has been on how deviant burial rites can be understood only in the contexts of their divergence from a recognized standard. This very practical observational technique can be applied to the interpretations of the findings as well. The claim for reconsidering the deviant burials in legal terms as the physical manifestation of judicial activities has a growing support in scholarship and is often a quite plausible alternative to the ethnographically-derived reliance on popular superstitions.[6] Notably, legal discourse is not limited to the provisions of strictly formulated content and variety of narratives and performances could epitomize traditional rules.[7] After all, the law enforcement practice does not exclude rituals for the burials of criminals and wrong-doers. The ritualized behaviour exercised by the authorities reflects their power, sometimes in purely physical means. Therefore, the symbolism will be more transparent and often focus on maltreatment and exclusion. By doing so, the performative strategy applied reverses the emphasis and its visual elements are mobilized to present the deceased as being bad and unacceptable. By sending a message from the grave, a reverse psychology trick establishes a recognizable image to be feared and denied.

6 For a recent and detailed rebuttal of this from Central Europe see, Leszek Gardeła, *Bad Death in the Early Middle Ages. Atypical Burials from Poland in a Comparative Perspective* (Rzeszów: Instytut Archeologii UR, 2017).

7 See Fangzhe Qiu, "Law, Law-books and Tradition in Early Medieval Ireland," Chapter 5 in this volume.

In fact, to consider deviant burials as the remains of law-breakers does not entirely contradict the narrative of superstitious reasoning behind them. The much later ethnological records on which these explanations are based single out individuals as having disobeyed certain social norms. The mode of deviant burial seems to be subject to the social context and the level of authority from which the norm was issued. The laws coming from the top of the state hierarchy are enforced with greater severity and often include serious maltreatment.

The archaeological evidence confirms such a hypothesis. The ninth-century mass grave from Devnya–3 has been discussed elsewhere in great detail, as the archaeological record of executions sanctioned by the monarch himself and displaying multiple forms of maltreatment towards convicted felons and traitors.[8] A remarkable uniformity in the attitude recorded in the *Responsa Nicolai pape ad consulta Bulgarorum* and the violence exhibited on the massacred bodies should raise awareness of the unclear legal status regulating war prisoners and rebels against central authorities in the medieval period.[9] Comparison with another, nearly-contemporary mass grave, the one from Kyulevcha located some 50 km westwards from Devnya, further stressed the differences resulting from state-sanctioned execution in contrast to post-battle practices.[10] The correspondence of isolated deviant burial rites (prone position, decapitation, mutilations and fixations of bodies) from the mass grave in Devnya–3 and in medieval individual graves from the territory of Bulgaria validates a legal explanation of the funerary record.

Naturally, some cases fit such a narrative better, and are better suited for such an interpretation. On the level of single-site analysis the correlation between deviant practices in the mass grave and individual graves in the biritual cemetery are very high in terms of both numbers and repeated elements. One is left to wonder if some post-depositional interventions in graves from Devnya are not also a further elaboration of power demonstration through symbolic punishment over this rebellious community. A similar indication for social

8 Petar Parvanov, "The Mass Grave from Devnya and the Judicial Culture in Early Medieval Bulgaria," in *(Re)lecture archéologique de la justice en Europe médiévale et modern*, ed. Matthieu Vivas (Bordeaux: Ausonius, 2019).

9 The *Responsa* and the mass grave from Devnya are connected for the first time in: Katja Melamed [Катя Меламед], "Към тълкуването на масовия гроб от некропола Девня 3 [Towards an Interpretation of the Mass Grave from Devnya 3]," *Проблеми на прабългарската история и култура* 4 (2007): 147–52.

10 On the mass grave from Kyulevcha see, Kamen Stanev [Камен Станев], "Масов гроб 80 от Кюлевча-опит за историческа интерпретация [Mass Grave No. 80 from Kyulevcha—An Attempt for Historical Interpretation]," *История* 5–6 (2008): 58–59.

seclusion by association was seen in the spatial organization of a burial ground from Na Tynici in Czechia.[11]

Going beyond the reaffirmed necessity for more refined contextualization, the Devnya case opened the dialogue between written accounts and archaeo-thanatological analysis for possible identification of skeletal trauma resulting from law enforcement. An obvious obstacle is the unsatisfactory state of integrated anthropological analysis done on medieval collections from the Balkans. Nevertheless, the medieval legal codes provide enough references to corporeal punishment to justify more intentional effort having been made in that direction.

To compile a short, but not exhaustive list for medieval penal law for the eastern Balkan Peninsula after the seventh century one must begin with the laws issued by khan Krum (803–814). The partial account is described more than a century later in Byzantine sources and although it should not be taken at face value, still proves useful. So, according to Suidas Lexicon, the penalty for slander is death, while thievery was punishable by bodily mutilations. The information from later documents is much more detailed. The most authoritative law-code, utilized in Bulgaria and other Slavic states as well, *Court Law for the People* (*Законъ соудный людьмъ*, henceforth ZSL) dating to the ninth century should definitely be cited in this respect.[12] The ZSL survives in multiple manuscript witnesses, which have been classified into three variants dating from the twelfth to the fifteenth centuries. The so-called short version, best known from thirteenth-century manuscript known as the *Novgorodskij spisok*, is usually considered to represent the earliest text of the law-code as it reached Russia.[13] It was introduced among Slavs soon after the conversion to Christianity and imposes its moral system into the legal sphere of life. Many Byzantine norms (for example, the *Ecloga*) were translated and adapted around that time as well, and their influence on original legal thinking and in the judiciary practice must be acknowledged.[14]

---

11 Ivo Štefan, Petra Stránská, and Hana Vondrová, "The Archaeology of Early Medieval Violence: The Mass Grave at Budeč, Czech Republic," *Antiquity* 90 (2016): 759–76.

12 Stefan Bobchev [Стефан Бобчевъ], *Старобългарски правни паметници* [*Old Bulgarian Legal Documents*] (Sofia: Pechatnicana P.M. Buzhaitov, 1903); more recently see, Kiril Maksimovich [Максимович К. А.], *Законъ соудьныи людьмъ. Источниковедческие и лингвистическиеаспектыисследованияславянскогоюридическогопамятника* [*The Law for Judgment of People. Textual and Linguistic Aspects of a Slavic Judicial Source*] (Moscow: Drevnehranilishte, 2004).

13 Horace W. Dewey and Ann M. Kleimola, eds., Zakon Sudnyi Ljudem (Court Law for the People) (Ann Arbor: Department of Slavic Languages and Literature, 1977).

14 Dimitar Angelov [Ангелов Д], *Образуване на българската народност* [*Formation of the Bulgarian Ethnicity*] (Sofia: Science and Art, 1971), 269.

Many clauses of the ZSL prescribe executions and mutilations, sometimes in very specific ways. In the Conversion period (mid-ninth century) Pope Nicholas I comments on the prescribed death sentence for several crimes against the political or religious authorities, such as high treason, pagan worship, desertion before or during battle, illegal border crossing and even poor maintenance of weaponry.[15] Some of them are confirmed by the Byzantine *Ecloga*, such as the high treason and the heresy.[16] Murder is traditionally punishable by death, unless a financial payment was accepted by the relatives of the victim.[17] The penalty for setting fires or for destruction endangering others and their property is interesting. The convicted has to be slashed with a sword and the law specifically states that this is valid in both rural and urban settlements.[18] Again in the ZSL, the penalty for a slave caught for thievery during night-time is death by hanging.[19] One very telling example and a refreshing reminder for the legal power over multiple subjects already in the Middle Ages is the chapter from ZSL regulating dogs.[20] According to it, a dog can be killed if enters the house from a hole in the wall, but not if it does so through an open door. The list could go on, but what must be stressed here is the variety of possible executions depending on social factors such as the circumstances of the crime or the social status of the wrong-doer.

The clearest example in this respect seems to be grave 81 from Kyulevcha. The grave is close to the mass grave in the peripheral cluster of the biritual necropolis from the eighth to ninth centuries. The male individual buried there was most likely tied before his execution, probably nearby the grave. He was decapitated as part of the disintegration of his body into three parts with a sword, as the cut-marks indicate. Then, his remains were disposed inside a round pit. The torso was prone positioned on top of his head, while the contracted legs and pelvis were in the eastern side of the pit.

Notably, the available law-codes are occasionally very specific in determining the style of execution, while the burial contexts are rarely considered to present distinguishable and related conformity to conventional practice. The

15 Nicholas I, *Responsa Nicolai I papae ad consulta Bulgarorum*, in *Nicolai I. papae epistolae*, ed. Ernst Perels, MGH Epp. 6, 568–600 (Berlin: Weidmann, 1925), Nos. 17, 22, 23, 25, 40.

16 A.G. Monpherratos, ed., *Ecloga Leonis et Constantini* (Athens: Typis fratrum Perri, 1889), 3, 42, 45, 46, 50, 52.

17 Galabina Petrova [ГълабинаПетрова], "Въпроси на наказателното право в Средновековна България. [Issues of Penal Law in Medieval Bulgaria]," *Правна мисъл* 2 (2002): 9–11.

18 *Законъ соудный людьмъ*, XV, in Bobchev, *Old Bulgarian Legal Documents*, 89.

19 Bobchev, *Old Bulgarian Legal Documents*, 46.

20 *Законъ соудный людьмъ*, Onch, in Bobchev, *Old Bulgarian Legal Documents*, 111.

combination of several distinctive elements of deviant burial leaves a strong impression of the severity of the maltreatment and, presumably, the crime which he had committed. It can also serve as an illustration of the types of burial practices most easily associated with the graves of law-breakers. The prone position, decapitation and disintegration can be recognized as a marker of deviant social behaviour and a formidable mode of dying, probably execution. The disintegration has a peculiar meaning in this sense. It is not merely the enforcement act of a capital punishment, but also involves the violent performance of destroying the physical identity of the convicted and by extension, his social personality.

Another potential execution from Varbyane demonstrates that the killing was not always easily done. Despite the lack of proper pathological investigation at the present time, it is possible to argue from the published graphic records that the execution comprised a cutting blow from the top downwards, at an angle of around 45 degrees.[21] The cut, or possibly series of cuts, not only decapitated the individual, but cut part of the chest as well. Within the grave, the skull was placed in a niche, without the mandible, while the clavicle, ribs and vertebrae were misplaced from the anatomical positioning of the skull. However, without closer anthropological examination of the skeleton itself this remains only a guess.

An alternative form of punishment already evident in the Krum legislation is mutilations. It is easy to assume the historically common development of mutilations in use by legal systems across medieval Europe. Mutilation was favored as a compromise penalty of lesser gravity than execution. The deliberate impairment had immediate physical and social implications for the person, and perhaps echoed the medieval mentality for visual recognition and social distinction. In a Christian environment, such an approach would be justified by politically-invested members of the clergy with their ambition to save as many souls as possible by influencing secular law.[22] It is believed that the application of blood-shedding law, especially by secular authorities, was on the rise later in the medieval period.[23] In the legal documents articulated within the

---

21 Hristina Stoyanova [Христина Стоянова], "Обредът "обезвреждане на мъртвите" в езическите некрополи (по данни от района на Плиска и Варна) [The Ritual Against Transfiguration of the Dead in the Pagan Necropoleis (Based on Data from the Area of Pliska and Varna)]," in *Изследвания по българска средновековна археология. Сборник в чест на проф. Рашо Рашев* [Studies in Bulgarian Medieval Archaeology presented to Prof. Rasho Rashev], ed. Pavel Georgiev (Sofia: Faber 2007).

22 See Ben Reinhard, "Wulfstan and the Reordered Polity of Cotton Nero A.i," in this volume, chapter 2.

23 Irina Metzler, *A Social History of Disability in the Middle Ages. Cultural Considerations of*

Byzantine-Balkan context, it is common to recommend the removal of one or more limbs for thievery, trade fraud, crimes against property, and morally unacceptable behaviour.[24]

It is important to remember that the mutilation sometimes targeted soft tissue parts of the body like the eyes, nose, testicles, or ears that can hardly leave traces in the archaeological context, but the methods of impairment could often lead to the death of the person.[25] The ZSL often assigns simultaneous penalties for the same crime under the temporal and church laws. So, for instance, the marriage between god-parents and god-children or an affair with a married woman is sanctioned with cutting off the nose of the man in the temporal law and with penance for fifteen years in the church norms.[26] One valid question is how strictly the local communities handled these situations, and would the offender have received some form of deviant burial in the case where they had passed away before their penitence was completed. A more thorough investigation into the punishments in medieval legal systems can reveal more patterns to be matched by the burial record.

The archaeological data collected from the eastern Balkans at present does not follow the overall European picture. Mutilations as a phenomenon is relatively stable from the seventh to the fourteenth centuries, with peaks in the eighth to tenth centuries and in the twelfth to thirteenth centuries. The first period in which physical impairment intensifies can be matched with the emergence of the codified legal system in the First Bulgarian Khanate/Tsardom. Then again, the interpretation of mutilation burials does not have a single satisfying conclusion. This should not come as a surprise, because the deviant rites including mutilation of the body are the most common and with the most internal diversity. Probably all internal variability requires a different contextualization. To see them as part of law enforcement practices and symbolic behaviour is one plausible solution. Ultimately, the deviant burial rites are linked to the social life of the deceased. The amputation, if survived, was not simply an irreversible sign of criminal activity. It also had a deep impact on the physical identity of the person. It evokes psychological trauma and societal association with limb loss that created the image of an incomplete individual. Additionally, the impairment could impose a dependent lifestyle, which could also contribute to the stigma of a social outcast.[27]

Physical Impairment (London: Routledge, 2013), 13–15, 21.

24 Petrova, "Issues of Penal Law in Medieval Bulgaria," 16–17.

25 Bobchev, *Old Bulgarian Legal Documents*, 20.

26 Bobchev, *Old Bulgarian Legal Documents*, 86.

27 For more on the social consequences of this, see Metzler, *Social History of Disability*.

At this point is useful to go back to well-established tradition of using funerary evidence to comment on social complexity and raise the issue of how this debate can contribute to the historical knowledge tracing the development of judicial systems in medieval polities. Originally, the argument was grounded in the seminal work by Arthur Saxe on the social dimension of mortuary practices.[28] Among his eight cross-cultural hypotheses based on anthropological observations over the West African Ashanti, the Kapauku from New Guinea and the Bontoc Igorot of the Phillipines, Hypothesis No. 7 has explicit significance for the matter of deviant customs. According to Saxe, the simpler a society is, the less variation exists in deviant funerary practices. The logic is clear—a more complex society will develop a more elaborate normative system that will result in differential conduct towards the offenders according to the contextualized seriousness of their act.

The variability of parallel deviant rites in practice, is not the only marker for complexity. The combination of several deviant rites within the same context should also be regarded as a sign for a more complex social network at work. The accumulation of non-normative traits characterizes the deviant burials, and their combination is probably an expression of the sacred and power ideologies embedded in the respective norms, and thereby stresses the gravity of the misconduct. For instance, the synchronicity between physical damage or body fragmentation and symbolic restriction in some graves can be understood in terms of simultaneous preventive acts against the corrupted body and soul. For instance, burials 65 and 89 from Sakardza show the fixation of the individual with stones, even though the feet are also separated from the body.[29] Interestingly, in one of the graves the amputated right foot has been also covered with a stone. Some prone burials are another example of this, notably the individual from Tarnovo exhibiting the combination of decapitation with prone disposal of the skull and fixation by stones targeting the feet.[30]

Building on the legal aspects of their interpretations, Andrew Reynolds also saw deviant burials as another possible indicator of social complexity

---

28 Arthur Saxe, "Social Dimensions of Mortuary Practices," (PhD thesis, University of Michigan; Ann Arbor, University Microfilms Inc., 1970).

29 Kircho Apostolov [Кирчо Апостолов], "Средновековен некропол на хълма Сакарджа край Омуртаг [Medieval Necropolis on the Sakardza Hill Near Omurtag]," in *Eurika. In honorem Ludmilae Donchevae-Petkovae*, ed. Valeri Grigorov, Metodi Daskalov, and Evgenia Komatarova (Sofia: Bulgarian Academy of Sciences, 2009).

30 Boni Petrunova [Бони Петрунова], "Некрополите от XIII-XVII в. Като източник за практикуването на обредите против превъплъщаване [Cemeteries from 13th–17th Century as a Source on Practicing Rituals Against Transfiguration after Death]," in *Конфесия и фолклор*, ed. Rossen Malchev and Konstantin Rangochev (Sofia: ROD, 1998), 70.

in medieval times. His work on the deviant burial customs in early medieval England generated a three-stage model linking judicial culture and political development.[31] As Reynolds urges, the model must be tested in a cross-cultural background. The state of current research is not conclusive for several reasons, but regarding the region in focus it should be highlighted that the territorial extent of the medieval Bulgarian states has not been completely covered; neither the chronological changes nor neighboring polities are fully represented. The data already collected, and some preliminary analysis, leave the suspicion that many potential sites with medieval deviant burials remained undetected or unstudied. That being said, the data allows for some speculations on the topic that only prove the need for more systematic surveys to shed light on the mortuary and administrative landscapes of the medieval Balkans.

The first stages in Reynolds' model are kin-based groups occupying rather small territories. Among these groups the deviant burials are the principal manifestation of casting out people who failed to observe the social order. The archaeologically-visible executions appear to be exceptionally rare, with the individual's families themselves being the agents producing the deviant burials. There is a lack of formalized legislation by the leader, and the tradition of religious beliefs and superstitions dominates the treatment of the wrongdoer.[32]

In the Bulgarian context this closely depicts the period from the late-seventh to the early-ninth centuries. It would seem that the Danubian Bulgar Khanate at the time can be best understood as a chiefdom organized around tribal affiliations, a confederation including a mixture of Bulgar groups and Sclavenes.[33] The khan and the kavhan most likely exercised a form of diarchy regulated by the major aristocratic clans. The best evidence of their importance is recorded in the genealogical *Nominalia* (List) of the Bulgarian Rulers.[34] In this historical account the individual rulers are listed according to their house and time in power. Thus, after the members of the charismatic clan Dulo, the supreme

---

31 Andrew Reynolds, "Judicial Culture and Social Complexity: A General Model from Anglo-Saxon England," *World Archaeology* 45:5 (2013): 708–10. For further consideration on Early English Law in general, see Ben Reinhard in this volume, "Wulfstan and the Reordered Polity of Cotton Nero A.i," Chapter 2.

32 Reynolds, "Judicial Culture," 708.

33 Georgi Nikolov [Георги Николов], *Централизъм и регионализъм в ранносредновековнаБългария* [Centralization and Particularism in Early Medieval Bulgaria] (Sofia: Marin Drinov, 2005), 63–85; for the archaeological manifestation of this in the site system of Pliska see, Andrey Aladzov [Андрей Аладжов (съст.)] *Археологическа карта на Плиска* [Archaeological Map of Pliska] (Sofia: Bulgarian Academy of Sciences, 2013), 185–89.

34 Antoaneta Granberg, "Transferred in Translation: Making a State in Early Medieval Bulgarian Genealogies," *Slavica Helsengiensia* 35 (2008): 50–53.

power shifted between the competing houses of Ermi, Vokil, and Ugain. The Sclavenes, an umbrella term used for the dependent Southern Slavic tribes like the Severes, were also loosely governed by the khan and strategically settled in the frontier zones. Their main responsibility was the defense of southern and western borders and perhaps included the payment of a certain tribute. Generally, the local communities exercised autonomy in dealing with their internal issues and norms were regulated by the local elites. The graves from the period are usually considered to reflect the ethnic diversity during the period. The basic pattern is viewed as a contrast between Slavic urn-fields surrounding a cluster of Bulgar biritual cemeteries in Dobrogea and on both sides of the river Danube. It is believed that this site distribution reflected little co-existence of the two ethnic components within the same burial group.[35] Leaving aside the urge for specific and often speculative ethnic attribution,[36] this can be understood in terms of weaker links between sets of tribal communities.

Non-normative burial rites appear in communal biritual cemeteries from almost the very beginning of the period on sites like Novi Pazar or Balchik. Their frequency and variability slowly increased. Most characteristic features are the tying and fixation of the dead bodies that evolved into more drastic post-mortem mutilations of the dead body. Arguably, the earliest prone burial in Topola also occurred around that time. The geographical distribution remained limited to within what is now north-eastern Bulgaria, which constituted the core territories of the khanate. It is impossible to determine the extent of their presence in the territories where cremation was dominant. However, an ambiguous note for the placement of unburned bones from human feet on top of several cremated remains in the biritual necropolis in Bdintsi could mean that certain bodies were subject to special treatment before the cremation.[37]

The second phase of political development in Reynolds' model is the emergence of supra-local power exploiting the core—periphery dynamics within the large-scale territories under control.[38] This stage is characterized by increased geographical reach of political control and resources for power dis-

35 Uwe Fiedler, *Studien zu Gräberfeldern des 6. Bis 9. Jahrhunderts an der unteren Donau* (Bonn: Dr. Rudolph Habelt GmbH, 1992), 158.

36 Evgeniya Komatarova-Balinova, "The 'Protobulgars' at Balchik and the Nomads in the Field of the 'Protobulgar' Archaeology," *Приноси към българската археология* 8 (2018): 53–4.

37 Zhivka Vazharova [Живка Въжарова], *Славяни и прабългари: по данни на некрополите от VI–XI в. На територията на България* [*Slavs and Protobulgarians Based on Data from the Necropolis from Seventh to Eleventh Century on the Territory of Bulgaria*] (Sofia: БАН, 1976), 143.

38 Reynolds, "Judicial Culture," 709–70.

play. The incorporation of new territories within a larger polity required the performance of the social order as dictated by the remote center. Usually this happens through the codification of the legal system and increased judicial activity at the limits of the state.[39] The formation of distinctive execution sites and burial grounds supplementing a dispersed institutional network are alternative modes for this ideological colonization of the landscape. At the same time, continuation of the earlier rites for burying outsiders in the core regions is to be expected.

The historical processes in the ninth century urged the Bulgarian khanate into the status of supra-local power.[40] The rule of khan Krum at the beginning of the century accelerated the centralization and expansion of state power. His politics were followed by his successors and eventually lead to the conversion to Christianity in Bulgaria. The establishment of far-reaching Bulgar authority carried many elements of legal and administrative culture, increasingly based on an ideology of divine-sanctioned power and codified norms. The aforementioned written laws of Krum are not the only signs of bureaucratic state control exercised through the power of the written word. The stone inscriptions dispersed across the state regulate various aspects of political life, like border control and the allocation of military equipment. For instance, the well-known inscription from Hambarli (in 813) reveals the territorial re-organization of the newly conquered lands south of the Balkan Mountains.[41]

It is interesting to compare this transition to the situation in the Avar khaganate, which by the beginning of the ninth century was overtaken by Carolingians and Bulgars. The Bulgar khanate and the Avar khaganate shared many cultural traits, particularly due to the common political tradition of what is sometimes called the *Pax Nomadica*. Deviant burials appear in Avar cemeteries in what seems to be a very similar manner to the examples from the Lower Danube.[42] Another point that may deserve more credit than traditionally acknowledged by historians is the information that Krum initiated his legislation only after consulting with the vanquished Avars regarding the reasons behind the collapse of the khaganate. The authenticity of this meeting

39 Max Gluckman, *Politics, Law and Ritual in Tribal Society* (Oxford: Blackwell, 1965), 169; Reynolds, "Judicial Culture," 709.

40 Angel Nikolov [Ангел Николов], *Политическ амисъл в ранносредновековна България* [*Political Thought in Early Medieval Bulgaria*] (Sofia: Paradigma, 2006), 32–38.

41 Veselin Beševliev, *Die protobulgarischen Inschriften* (Berlin, Akademie-Verlag, 1963), no. 2.

42 Marija Djurić, Ksenija Djukić, Tamara Pavlović, and Marko Drašković, "'Deviant' Burial in Medieval Avarian Necropolis of Pionirska Ulica (Serbia)," (Research Paper Presented at the 23rd Annual Meeting of the European Association of Archaeologists, Maastricht, the Netherlands, September 01, 2017).

can be challenged for the romanticizing picture of law-making presented by Byzantine authors. Yet again, the undertaking of a historical evaluation on an important threshold in the social processes must be emphasized.

In comparison, the codification initiative resembles the expansion of law books in Carolingian Francia at the same time. The increase in preserved manuscripts demonstrates the introduction of regional written laws containing evidence for inherited influence from the respective customary norms around the Germanic provinces.[43] The codification allowed juxtaposed territorial individuality to coexist in the compendiums of perceived common legal practice. When considered from this angle, the Byzantine story for the introduction of Bulgar legislation highlights the alternatives to Roman law in the face of Germanic and steppe traditions on the expense of the vanquished Avar khaganate. It seems that the secondary literature to date has accepted that the beginnings of territorial governance transformed kin-based tribes into administrative units at that time.[44] Another piece of evidence for the transformed nature of social organization, this time archaeological, is the monumental architectural enterprise in Pliska shaping the city as a fully-formed center of secular and ecclesiastical power.[45] The situation was to some extent similar after the conversion to Christianity and with the further territorial expansion in the second half of the ninth century and the beginning of the tenth century. It seems only natural that the mixture of parallel legal practices evolved into a better functioning legislative body, very much like with other historical situations of coexisting juridical traditions, for instance Lombard Italy.[46]

The deviant burial rites largely confirm this historical reconstruction. The continuation of customs in the core territories between the Danube and the Balkan Mountains is evident. Many deviant burials occur at the limits of communal burial grounds, probably being undertaken by the families of the deceased. However, the frequency of such burials increased into the late ninth-tenth centuries, probably reflecting the development of a more elaborate normative system. Moreover, the positioning of deviant graves in a peripheral posi-

43 Lisi Oliver, *The Body Legal in the Barbarian Law* (Toronto: University of Toronto Press, 2011) 18, 20–22.

44 Daniel Ziemann, *Vom Wandervolk zur Großmacht. Die Entstehung Bulgariens im frühen Mittelalter (7. bis 9. Jh.)* (Cologne: Böhlau, 2007).

45 Rasho Rashev, *Българската езическа култура VII–IX век* [Bulgar Pagan Culture 7th–9th Century] (Sofia: Класика и стил, 2008), 82–98; compare to Vasil Gjuzelev, "Hauptstädte, Residenzen und Hofkultur im mittelalterlichen Bulgarien, 7.–14. Jh. (Vom Nomaden campus bis zum Zarenhof)," *Études balkaniques* 27, no. 2, (1991): 82–105.

46 Sonia Colafrancesco, "Juridicial Dualism in Medieval Southern Italy. Studies on the *Codex Diplomaticus Cavensis*," Chapter 10 in this volume.

tion was regularly implemented, producing a spatial exclusion of the deceased from the more ordinary burials. Isolation was a powerful statement about the deviant character of certain burials and the negative social evaluation surrounding them. The tendency for deviant burials to appear in liminal space is a conspicuous manifestation of this practice. Such strategy for differential treatment is especially noticeable in complexes from this time period, even more so in its pagan phase. Some execution sections and burial grounds clearly developed in key sites like Devnya and Kyulecha to the sides of principal burial grounds. The necessity for a distinguishable arrangement of space to support deviant rites decreases on sites of lesser size and regional importance.

However, the existence and number of isolated burial grounds is likely misrepresented in the archaeological record so far. No doubt, the difficulty of detecting isolated cemeteries and the seeming randomness of such sites contributed to the current state of our knowledge. More often in this period a different orientation of the grave was also followed to increase the message of separation. The elimination of internal resistance from the centralized power can explain the ambiguous geographic characterization of some execution sites. They are found in what is considered to be the core territory of the state, but in its peripheral areas.

In the power center of Pliska during its pagan period the deviant burials were discovered in the common burial grounds spread in the periphery of the city. After the Christianization some deviant burials appear within the city limits in urban cemeteries (the Great Basilica) or isolated (the Southern wall of the Inner City). However, these are later than the burials in question here, and belong instead to the tenth and eleventh centuries.

Another manifestation of this second phase of Reynold's model is evident in the deviant burials from Bulgaria. So far, execution sites and cemeteries from the peripheral lands conquered by the Bulgarian state are a blank spot. However, the core territories of Bulgaria were incorporated into the Byzantine Empire at the time of Basil II Bulgar-Slayer. The next step would be their administrative re-organization into provincial territories subordinate to Constantinople. The consistent decrease in the number of burials with deviant characteristics in the eleventh century can be regarded as the outcome of this process. The pattern is further stressed by the chronological gap registered for the prone burials and the change of their dominant form from complete prone inhumation to a type in which the body was in supine position and with the head being placed, unnaturally, face-down. Of course, a certain national bias can explain the reluctance to ascribe sites to the period of Byzantine domination, but its impact should not be overestimated. Additionally, the recent reinterpretation of the decapitation burial from Madara indicates the re-appraisal of landscapes for judicial purposes, which is a distinctive feature of the model.[47]

The third stage is the one of large-scale power and well-organized state governing.[48] At this point, the social distance between the ruling elite and the majority of people is extended even further and facilitates new forms of expressing power. The demonstrations of judicial activities and the continuous issuing of new laws lead to the proliferation of execution sites and cemeteries within what was the heartland. In the Early English context, the correlation between estate boundaries and execution sites was complete at this point.[49] It would seem therefore that the concern with public attention is on the performance of justice, focusing either on the decision-making or the law enforcement.

Little is known on the internal affairs of the Bulgarian state as a large-scale power in the tenth century, even less regarding the legal culture. Some hints for tightly organized administrative activity like the findings of royal, aristocratic and ecclesiastical seals only makes the lack of preserved written records on the judicial proceedings or local governance even more frustrating. It is accepted that the Byzantine political culture strongly influenced the Bulgarian court, especially after the marriage between Petar I and Maria-Irina in 927.[50] The existing organization must have been maintained until the internal political changes and the shift of the Bulgarian center of power to the west under Samuel. The distribution of lead seals around important political centers can be one sign of active administrative control.

As far as deviant burial rites are concerned, there seems to be a continuation of the practices described above. It is possible that public executions were not the preferred mode of power display, or more likely that such sites have not yet been identified. Nonetheless, a suspected execution site that perfectly fits the expected arrangement is worth mentioning. The prominent location is the so-called *Lobna skala* [The Cliff of Death] in Tarnovo, the capital city during another period of tightly-organized state administration, with an ideological

47 Petar Parvanov, "A Tale of Two Graves: Rethinking the Medieval Reuse of Prehistoric Burial Mounds in Madara," *Annual of Medieval Studies at CEU*, 23 (2017): 11–19; Reynolds, "Judicial Culture," 710.

48 Reynolds, "Judicial Culture," 710.

49 Andrew Reynolds, *Anglo-Saxon Deviant Burial Customs* (Oxford: Oxford University Press, 2009), 180–234.

50 Paul Stephenson, *The Byzantine Balkan Frontier. A Political Study of the Northern Balkans, 900–1204* (Cambridge: Cambridge University Press, 2004), 24.

claim for far-reaching dominion. Allegedly, from this spot the convicted people were thrown down into the river Yantra, most famously the captured Latin emperor of Constantinople, Baldwin I (1172–c. 1205).[51]

At this point of the research, it is apparent that the First Bulgarian Tsardom fits the model to some extent. The evolutionary change from complexity to a large-scale power unifying, more or less, the British Isles is possible due to the geographical and historical specifics of Britain. In the Balkans the competition for dominance in the region and the tendencies for decentralization are much stronger. Another major difference is in the form of Christianity and ecclesiastical organization, particularly when it comes to ideologies of power.

However, the three elements of the model should not necessarily be taken to represent an exclusively linear development. Different social strata and smaller groups generated additional, co-existing norms with different levels of relevance to the rest of the society. Indeed, the main point for resilient and dispersed performance and localization of justice in symbiosis with dominant power structures proves valid. The two-way interactions of authority bottom-up and vice versa, are characteristic for the most successful examples of political systems that do not completely reject the judicial tradition encountered in the subjugated territories. Deviant mortuary treatment is dependent on the ideological charge and social stress impact on the disobedience. The origin of the norms and the immediate context determined the prominence of legal or cult features in the funerary rites.

The deviant burials from the twelfth to fourteenth centuries, or roughly the period of the Second Bulgarian Tsardom, can serve as useful example. Probably, religious symbolism and popular religion revived the various rites. Henceforth, it is likely that many of them continued to exist and re-emerged among small kin-based social groups in rural environments in the twelfth century. The intentional focus on excavating architecturally significant complexes from the High and Late Middle Ages diverted attention from attempts to identify other types of sites, with execution sites and cemeteries having been disregarded in particular. The rural site of Kovachevo provides the link between earlier and later forms of treatment of outcasts. The cemetery is directly adjacent to the settlement and does not have a church operating the activity there.[52] The diversifica-

51 Kazimir Popkonstantinov and Rossina Kostova, "Minorities and Foreigners in Bulgarian Medieval Towns in the Twelfth to Fourteenth Centuries: Literary and Archaeological Fragments," in *Segregation—Integration—Assimilation: Religious and Ethnic Groups in the Medieval Towns of Central and Eastern Europe*, ed. Derek Keene, Balázs Nagy, and Katalin Szende (Farnham: Ashgate, 2009), 136.

52 Peyo Gatev [Пейо Гатев], *Средновековно селище и некропол от 12 век при с. Ковачево,*

tion of the fixation rites also occurs in the period, which provides an interesting insight into the coexistence of regulatory customs in medieval communities experiencing intensified cultural contacts.

Usually the fixation of the deceased inside the grave is symbolically arranged through weighting down with a stone placed on top of the cadaver. The choice of body part to be covered and the size or number of stones varies, but often carries an associated meaning targeting legs, chest or head. After the late twelfth century, the above-mentioned diversification extends not only to the position or quantitative characteristics of the fixation tool, but in its materials as well. Thus, the stone was replaced or substituted by tiles on several occasions. At approximately the same time, the preference shifted completely to ferrous tools in some graves (e.g. Madrets near Stara Zagora and Anevsko kale).[53] The appearance of tiles, plough-heads and sickles in such a role seems to be a rare practice, with a discrete territorial and chronological extent, recorded in present-day southern Bulgaria along the route of the *Via Diagonalis* and coastal Thrace from the twelfth to early-thirteenth centuries.

This zone is one of contested allegiance in the period, being largely a frontier province between Bulgaria, Byzantium and its successor states. Naturally, in the area very dynamic cultural and ethnic contacts and mixtures occurred, with Western and Orthodox Christians, Latin, Greek, Slavonic and Jewish communities engaging in trade and warfare, exchanging ideas and goods. Describing such social mosaics makes a lot of sense when the closest archaeological parallels for the development of the death rite are sought.

For instance, the deposition of sickles in graves is well known from Central Europe, where it has received significant scholarly attention, focused in particular on Slovakia and Poland.[54] Seemingly, sickles appear among the grave goods in the Middle Danube region from the seventh century until the eighteenth century. Interestingly, both Slovakian and Polish sites have a gap of nearly three centuries between the thirteenth and sixteenth century in the recording of such finds. The graves with sickles from Hungary began in the Middle Avar period and appear consistently until the fourteenth century. The introduction of the practice is attributed to part of the Bulgar tribes migrating deep into

---

Пазарджишки окръг [Medieval Village and Cemetery from 12th Century near Kovachevo, District Pazardzhik] (Sofia: National Archaeological Museum, 1985).

53 Ivan Dzambov [Иван Джамбов], "Средновековният некропол край Сопот [Medieval Cemetery near Sopot]," *Известия на музеите в Южна България* 14 (1988): 144–58.

54 Andrzej Janowski and Tomasz Kurasiński, "Rolnik, wojownik czy 'odmieniec?' Próba interpretacji obecności sierpów w grobach wczesnośredniowiecznych na terenie ziem polskich [Farmer, Soldier or Foreigner? An Attempt for the Interpretation of Sickles in Late Medieval Graves from the Polish lands]," *Acta Archaeologica Lodziensia* 56 (2010): 79–96.

the Avar khaganate in the seventh century.[55] The Bulgarian examples correspond to the latest medieval phase of the phenomenon and a direct link on ethnic basis is unlikely. Perhaps naturally, slightly earlier depositions of sickles directly over the body are occasionally discovered elsewhere around the Balkans, as for instance in Matičane (Kosovo).[56] In contrast to social and ethnohistorical aspects, Polish research is emphasizing the apotropaic function of these objects, especially for the later findings.[57] Naturally, such a practice would hardly be directly traceable in the codified written sources, but its existence testifies to a layer of meaning likely connected through memory-work. In this respect the positioning of semantically-charged objects, just like the reopening of graves opens the door to sometimes speculative, yet plausible reconstructions.

On the basis of the Central European analogies it is reasonable to argue that the fixation with ferrous tools appeared in what is today southern Bulgaria under the influence of the Catholic world. Links with the region can also be seen in the fourteenth-century fixation with a tile inside the mouth from Plovdiv.[58] The best analogy to this highly unusual practice is known from Lazzaretto Nuovo in Italy, dated to the fifteenth century.[59] The same measurement, associated with the particularly evil undead (or *Nachzehrer* in German) is frequently recorded in the Baltic region.[60] Ironically, this wide range of similar burials resembles the often-misleading argument that deviant burials signify foreign intruders to local communities or else are, almost instantly, locked within the narrative of vampire beliefs.

Vampirism, as we know and imagine it, is most probably attached to the deviant burial customs in that period. This is not to say that beliefs in evil powers and the dangerous dead were not feared in earlier times. The very existence

---

55 Péter Somogyi, "A Kárpát-meden ceisarlóstemetke zésiszo káseredete [Into the Origin of Burials with Sickles in the Carpathian Basin]," *Archaeológiai Értesítő* 109 (1982): 189–202.

56 Vojislav Jovanović and Ljiljana Vuksanović, "Matičane Nécropole sud-slave de XE et XIE siècle," *Inventaria Archaeologica* 25 (1981): Tombe No. 54.

57 Marek Polcyn and Elzbieta Gajda, "Buried with Sickles: Early Modern Interments from Drawsko, Poland," *Antiquity* 89/348 (2015): 1384–86; Janowski and Kurasiński, "Farmer, Soldier or Foreigner?", 79–96.

58 Elena Bozhilova and Kamen Stanev [Елена Божилова и Камен Станев], "Спасителни археологически разкопки на ул. Рилски метох 3, Пловдив [Rescue Excavations in Rilskimetoh str. 3, Plovdiv]," *Археологически Открития и Разкопки за 2014* (2015): 744–747.

59 David Barrowclough, *Time to Slay Vampire Burials? The Archaeological and Historical Evidence for Vampires in Europe* (Cambridge: Red Dagger Press, 2014), 8.

60 Donat Wehner und Katja Grüneberg-Wehner, "Mit Stein im Mund. Ein Fall von Nachzehrerabwehr in der St. Catharinenkirche am Jellenbek, Kr. Rendsburg-Eckernförde?" *Arkæologii Slesvig / Archäologie in Schleswig* 15 (2014), 62.

of deviant burial rites is one indication for an existing notion of the powerful dead, capable of influencing the world of the living.[61] The belief in bodily resurrection promoted by Christianity (among other mystic religions and cults) must have made those anxieties even more relevant. Rather the social outcasts and criminals treated in particular ways gradually turned into the demographic group recognized as potential vampires. Thus, the rites applied to them were also acknowledged as the appropriate means to deal with supernatural danger. This rationale behind neutralizing a treat to society, either alive or revenant, created common ways in corporal maltreatment, especially when specifically targeting the head. At the level of social judgment, the custom demonstrates a somewhat superstitious form of evaluation, where immediate legal repercussions are replaced by eternal condemnation in afterlife. The argument for the emergence of vampire beliefs from essentially legal practices is still speculative at this point, but reflects better the nature of the available evidence.

The visual dialogue in mortuary display of wrong-doers between Central European and southern Bulgarian forms of fixation is enriched, when seen from the point of view of the arrangements between local communities and central power. The royal charters and international treaties with Italian and Adriatic city-states regulate comprehensive conditions for temporary or permanent residence by foreigners beyond the rights of free trade. They do not prescribe explicitly how the deceased must be treated. Significant judicial freedom is given to consuls from these partnering polities. Extended rights in the continuation of the traditional laws were also granted to minority groups like Jews, Franks (basically Catholics) or Armenians in the urban centers.[62] The Treaty with Genoa, among others, describes in great detail the decision-making process with international parties administered by the Genoese representative, according to the customs of his own people.[63] Nonetheless, the suspicious coincidences likely stream from certain cultural expectations, that might be so unquestionably fitting the gap between the law-code and the criminal body. In this respect, the adoption of varied forms of deviant burials with Central European links may be an additional adaptation of commonly accepted funerary obligation appreciating multiple moral codes. Due to political and economic

61 Mike Parker-Pearson, "The Powerful Dead: Archaeological Relationships Between the Living and the Dead," *Cambridge Archaeological Journal* 3, no. 02 (1993): 203–29.

62 Snezhana Goryanova [Снежана Горянова], "Чужденци в българските средновековни градове през XIII–XIV в.—социален и правен статут [Foreigners in Bulgarian Medieval Towns in 13th–14th c.—Social and Legal Status]," in *Stephanos Archaeologicos in honorem Professoris Stephcae Angelova*, ed. Lyudmil Getov (Sofia: University of Sofia, 2010), 733.

63 Goryanova, "Foreigners in Bulgarian Medieval Towns," 740–41.

benefits, the state allows for the continuous operation of already existing or newly introduced social norms and units, hence employing a plurality of legal systems within a single administrative society.

Some fortified urban centers that at times achieved relative autonomy from Tarnovo and Constantinople tend to demonstrate a larger concentration of deviant burials. The thirteenth-century sites of Assenova Krepost and Voden on the northern slopes of the Rhodope Mountain offered the discoveries of several isolated burials with mutilations of the postcranial skeleton. In the Rhodopes, again during road construction work, the isolated burial ground at Skalishte dating to the twelfth century was discovered, with a large concentration of deviant rites. The site seems to have been used by several settlements to contain the remains of obscure individuals, evidently employing modes of spatial separation. The chance character of its find also hints that other such similar sites still remained unknown.

To continue with this line of thought, one can refer to the decapitations and prone burials dating to twelfth-fourteenth centuries from Kaliakra or Anevsko kale, associated with the medieval city of Kopsis. Both are important aristocratic centers and their rulers probably exercised significant executive powers and feudal rights. The former turned into the center of the Principality of Dobrogea in the fourteenth century, while the latter was the domain of the house Smilets, related to the royal dynasties of Bulgaria, Raska and Byzantium. The presence of graves marked by deviant rites within the communal burial grounds represents the capability of local elites to sustain circumscribed authority in the observance of the social norms. It could be the case that this responsibility was delegated to church representatives, as in Anevsko kale where the graves come from one of the monastic cemeteries with burials of the local population.[64] The clergy as the most-literate of medieval social strata had the easiest access and strongest claim over written laws. Moreover, the church as a norm-inducing organization and dominant agent in funerary activities adopted the strategy for differential treatment of sinful individuals within the realm of consecrated burial grounds. Its acceptance shows the limits and practicalities of maintaining canon-defined normativity. The deviant burial from the churchyard in one of the quarters of Tsarevets in Tarnovo is a rare illustration of this in the capital.[65]

Embracing a diachronic, long-term perspective on law from the distance of its materialized manifestations demonstrates clearly that directly applying the

64 Dzambov, "Medieval Cemetery near Sopot."

65 Atanas Pisarev [Атанас Писарев], "Църква 18 на хълма Царевец в Търново [Church 18 on the Tsarevets hill]," *Годишник на музеите в Северна България* 6 (1981): 18–37.

legislative text to the reality of daily life is neither unproblematic nor straightforward. The law enforcement simultaneously requires and creates a chain stretching to all social levels. Very physical products of this implementation system are the deviant burials. Their continuity and consistency underlie the functionality encoded in the custom, but the patterns and specifics are not immune to changes or particularities. Furthermore, such transformations seem to respond to distinctive historical or intellectual moments redefining the rules of law and authority.

The outstanding character of deviant burials in the funerary practices enables thick descriptions of past processes detected in the *longue durée*. Each body is a reminder of how law happens on the local level, a testament to the invisible roles of different social actors interpreted and implemented by the community for the community. More often than not, this interpretation was rooted in the reception of authoritative texts imposed by political or spiritual powers implementing morality with symbolic acts.

The situation in the eastern Balkan Peninsula, as known from current archaeological data, gives an interactive background for the medieval development of Romano-Byzantine and Bulgarian legal thought. The already emerging patterning opens the discussion to the inherent connection between deviant burial customs and justified maintenance of social control. Furthermore, the judicial tradition in medieval Bulgarian lands, much like everywhere in Europe, seems to be more complex and much more present in the daily life of people from all social strata, when contextualized by death.

CHAPTER 12

Expertise and Experience: Nuancing Terms for Legal Practitioners in the *Íslendingasögur*

Hannah Burrows

The *Íslendingasögur* [Sagas of Icelanders] are famous for their character portraits: the sparing but crucial vignettes that, often when a new figure is introduced, allow audiences to appraise the character, to understand how he or she fits into the social world being described, to assess his or her motivations and even to predict his or her actions. Since the sagas are just as well known for the legal disputes that figure prominently in their plot lines, so legal practitioners are key figures among the cast of characters of many *Íslendingasögur*. Alan Berger has gone so far as to claim that, in the manner of "outlaw sagas" and "poet sagas," subgenres recognized by modern scholarship, certain of the *Íslendingasögur* could fittingly be described as "lawyer sagas."[1]

The Modern English word "lawyer," albeit a convenient term, does not, however, adequately reflect the medieval Icelandic situation (or indeed, the situation elsewhere in Europe in the Middle Ages). Jean-Louis Halpérin, for example, notes the difficulty of identifying "persons we can qualify as lawyers" in cross-temporal and cross-cultural perspectives, suggesting that criteria for a fully professional class such as "the imposition of a detailed curriculum, of examinations, of an enrollment in a guild or association, and including the need to exercise the profession to be recognized as a true lawyer" really only pertain to the West since as late as the nineteenth century.[2] Nonetheless, William Ian Miller observes that in the characters Þórhallr and Njáll in *Njáls saga*, "we might be catching a glimpse of a separation of legal expertise into pleaders on one hand and jurists on the other."[3] Arguably, this separation can be seen in the *Íslendingasögur* much more widely than just in *Njáls saga*, at least

1 Alan Berger, "Lawyers in the Icelandic Family Sagas: Heroes, Villains and Authors," *Saga-Book* 20 (1978–79): 70.

2 Jean-Louis Halpérin, "For a Renewed History of Lawyers," *American Journal of Legal History* 56/1 (2016): 55–56. See also James A. Brundage, *The Medieval Origins of the Legal Profession: Canonists, Civilians, and Courts* (Chicago: University of Chicago Press, 2014), e.g. 56, 61, 70, 88, 99.

3 William Ian Miller, *Why is Your Axe Bloody?: A Reading of Njáls Saga* (Oxford: Oxford University Press, 2014), 272.

 DOI:10.1163/9789004448650_014

when it comes to how characters are perceived (the nature of the legal system means that in practice people often had to take on both roles regardless of their aptitude). An examination of the terms used for legal actors in the *Íslendingasögur* and law texts makes clear that authors and audiences were keenly discerning when it came to their litigants. As will be shown, the vocabulary of the sagas distinguishes between figures either attributed with or remembered in tradition for a particular knowledge of the law (legal experts, or "jurists") and those known for their enthusiasm for and/or success in taking on lawsuits ("pleaders"). While these talents naturally often overlap, nuanced terminology guides understanding of a character's reputation and their role in the legal action of the saga.

Before taking a closer look at the terminology for legal personnel used in the *Íslendingasögur*, it is worth describing early Iceland's unique legal system. Prior to 1262–64, when Iceland became part of the Norwegian realm, the island had developed a bespoke system of administration without a head of state or official infrastructure of governance. The first wave of settlement, largely from Norway and the Scandinavian settlement areas in the British Isles, had begun around 870 and lasted until around 930, according to the twelfth-century historian Ari Þorgilsson and backed up by archaeological evidence. At this point, Ari says, laws were established, based on those of the Gulaþing district of Norway with advice from Þorleifr *enn spaki* [the wise] "hvar við skyldi auka eða af nema eða annan veg setja" [where they should be augmented or taken out or arranged another way].[4] At this time the laws were orally transmitted; they first began to be officially written down in 1117 and survive in two main manuscripts from the thirteenth century as well as in several fragments.[5] The laws of this period are now known collectively as *Grágás*, although they are referred to contemporaneously as *vár lǫg* [our laws].

The person responsible for communicating the law was the *lǫgsǫgumaðr* [lawspeaker]. The Konungsbók manuscript of *Grágás* (Copenhagen, Kongelige Bibliotek, MS GKS 1157 fol) details his duties, responsibilities and rights, in a section called the "Lögsögumannsþáttr" [Lawspeaker's section]. It begins with the fundamental statement: "Sva er eɴ mælt at sa m*að*r s*c*al v*er*a nockoʀ auallt

4 Jakob Benediktsson, ed., *Íslendingabok. Landnámabók*, Íslenzk fornrit 1, 2 vols. (Reykjavík: Hið Íslenzka Fornritafélag, 1986), 1:3. Because of my focus on saga terminology, translations are my own unless otherwise stated (exceptions are generally in the case of the laws, to ensure consistency there).

5 On the legal manuscripts see Vilhjálmur Finsen, ed., *Grágás. Stykker, som findes i det Arnamagnæanske Haandskrift Nr. 351 fol Skálholtsbók og en Række andre Haandskrifter* (Copenhagen: Gyldendal, 1883), xxxvi–lvi.

a l*an*ðe óro er scyldr se ti*l* þess at segia log m*onno*m. *oc* heit*ir* sa lögsogo m*a*ð*r*" [it is also prescribed that there shall always be some man in our country who is required to tell men the law, and he is called the lawspeaker].[6] There are detailed regulations for the lawspeaker's democratic election to the office, which he was to keep for three years, after which he could choose to give it up or to remain in post. His primary duty was "at segia up lög þátto alla a þri*m*r su*m*ro*m* hu*er*io*m*. eɴ þ*in*gscop hu*er*t sumar" [to recite all the sections of the law over three summers and the assembly procedure every summer].[7] This recitation took place at the *Alþing* or General Assembly, held at Þingvellir in southwest Iceland over two weeks of every summer. His fee was "ii. hu*n*droð alna vaðmala af lögretto fiám" [240 ells of homespun from the Law Council's funds], and "hálfar þǽr e*r* a alþ*in*gi ero døm*þ*ar h*er*" [half of all the fines imposed by judgement at the General Assembly].[8] "Lögréttuþáttr" also states that "þess e*r* lögsögo m*a*ð*r* scylldr at segia ollo*m* þei*m* e*r* h*ann* spyria h*er* lögmál bæþi h*er* *oc* hei*ma*, eɴ erat h*ann* fra*m*aʀ scyldr sacraþa við m*enn*" [the Lawspeaker is required to tell everyone who asks him what the article of the law is, both here and at his home, but he is not required to give anyone further advice on lawsuits].[9] The lawspeaker was the official, elected and paid expert in law, then, but his advisory role was limited to stating what the law was, not what one should do about it.

As well as being the venue for the lawspeaker's recitation, the *Alþing* was where court cases were heard and judged. According to Ari's *Íslendingabók*, and *Grágás* (again, in the Konungsbók manuscript), the country was divided into quarters for administrative purposes in the 960s, and each quarter also had three regional *þing* [assemblies; sg. *þing*] (Ari says there were four in the Northern Quarter). These were each convened by three *goðar* (chieftains; sg. *goði*), making a total of 36 (or 39) *goðorð* [chieftaincies; sg. *goðorð*] in the country.[10] There were also what Gunnar Karlsson terms "*ad hoc*" courts, held "at or near the place of action or the place in dispute",[11] and further meetings

---

6 Vilhjálmur Finsen, ed., *Grágás: Islændernes Lovbog i Fristatens Tid, udgivet efter det Kongelige Bibliotheks Haandskrift*, 2 parts (1a, 1b) (Copenhagen: Berling, 1852), 1a:208; Andrew Dennis, Peter Foote, and Richard Perkins, trans., *Laws of Early Iceland: Grágás*, 2 vols, University of Manitoba Icelandic Studies 3 and 5 (Winnipeg: University of Manitoba Press, 1980–2000), 1:187.

7 Finsen, *Grágás: Islændernes Lovbog*, 1a:209; Dennis, Foote and Perkins, *Laws*, 1:187.

8 Finsen, *Grágás: Islændernes Lovbog*, 1a:209; Dennis, Foote and Perkins, *Laws*, 1:188.

9 Finsen, *Grágás: Islændernes Lovbog*, 1a:216; Dennis, Foote and Perkins, *Laws*, 1:193.

10 See Jakob Benediktsson, *Íslendingabok*, 12; Finsen, *Grágás: Islændernes Lovbog*, 1a:38.

11 Gunnar Karlsson, "Social Institutions," in *A Companion to Old Norse-Icelandic Literature and Culture*, ed. Rory McTurk (Oxford: Blackwell, 2005), 507.

in the autumn, called *leið*, which had no judicial function but were a venue for the communication of outcomes from the *Alþing*.[12] At some point before 1030 the regional *þing* seem to have been superseded by separate sessions for each quarter (*fjórðungsdómar* [quarter courts]) held at the *Alþing* rather than locally.[13] A fifth court (*fimmtardómr*) was also established at the *Alþing* in the early eleventh century, which heard appeals, cases that crossed quarter boundaries and procedural disputes.[14] The establishment of the fifth court also led to the establishment of new chieftaincies, so there were 48 in total.[15] In the regional courts, each *goði* appointed 12 judges to the court; at the *Alþing* each nominated one, so that courts in both locations had a total of 36 judges.[16] For the fifth court, all *goðar*, including those holding the newly-established *goðorð*, nominated a judge and 12 were dismissed by the litigants, so that it also had 36 judges.[17]

It should be pointed out that this represents an ideal hypothetical model; the situation continued to develop during the twelfth and thirteenth centuries, until administrative power had become concentrated into the hands of seven families and after 1220 became increasingly entwined with the Norwegian king.[18] The *Íslendingasögur* certainly present a less clear-cut picture of this model, in particular suggesting a higher and fluctuating number of *goðar*, and indeed of local assemblies.[19] What matters here, though, is that both types of sources suggest that anyone of any standing—namely chieftains and *bændr* [householders, sg. *bóndi*][20]—could expect reasonably frequent interaction with the legal system. All *bændr* had to be attached to a *goði* (they were known as his *þingmenn* [assembly men]) and one in nine of those of qualifying wealth had to accompany him to the *Alþing*. Those who remained at home, and were judged to be of sufficient means, had to pay a *þingfararkaupar* [assembly tax] to cover the expenses of the attendees. At the *Alþing* the *þingmenn* were eligible to be selected to serve as a judge (*dómandi*, pl. *dómendr*), with

12 William Ian Miller, *Bloodtaking and Peacemaking: Feud, Law, and Society in Saga Iceland* (Chicago: The University of Chicago Press, 1990), 19.

13 Gunnar Karlsson, "Social Institutions," 510–13.

14 See Finsen, *Grágás: Islændernes Lovbog*, 1a:38–143; Gunnar Karlsson, "Social Institutions," 511.

15 On these see Barði Guðmundsson, "Goðorð forn og ný," *Skírnir* 111 (1937): 56–63; Gunnar Karlsson, "Social Institutions," 513–14.

16 Miller, *Feud, Law, and Society in Saga Iceland*, 17.

17 Gunnar Karlsson, "Social Institutions," 511.

18 Jón Viðar Sigurðsson, *Viking Friendship* (Ithaca, NY: Cornell University Press, 2017), 8.

19 Jón Viðar Sigurðsson, *Viking Friendship*, 8, 17, 30.

20 On the household see Miller, *Feud, Law, and Society in Saga Iceland*, ch. 4 (111–37).

the main selection criterion being that they were impartial to the cases being heard, rather than that they necessarily had any particular expertise in the law (a situation far from unique to Iceland).[21] As Richard Posner puts it, "in effect there were jurors but no judges."[22]

It is perhaps something of a utopian simplification to claim that "law was a living part of the social system that every adult Icelander was expected to know:"[23] the divergences between sagas and law texts, between different sagas, and between different legal manuscripts, attest to, at best, a lack of consensus as to what the law was—albeit a lack perhaps observable only with scholarly hindsight and overview. Individual sources suggest a confidence that there was, in fact, a fixed *lögmál* [article of the law], at the same time as collectively contradicting one another. The fact that it is difficult to date any of *Grágás*'s legal provisions precisely, and that the *Íslendingasögur* were written down more than two centuries (during the thirteenth and fourteenth centuries) after the period they describe (the tenth and early eleventh centuries), is often cited to explain some of this apparent confusion. For some saga episodes, thirteenth-century authors and audiences may have been grappling to understand the legacies of laws no longer in force; for others, the time gap may have given them license to improvise the details.[24] Chris Wickham's observations on gossip provide a useful comparator and additional perspective here, however. He notes that even today, in our highly literate society, in many cases "people go by habitus, by a set of regular improvisations of practice."[25] The "truth" becomes "a truth of meaningfulness, not of 100 per cent re-creation."[26] Communal "memory" of the law, then—the version of the law that all involved were willing to accept as "truth"—would *be* the truth in any given situation. Elsewhere I have described the internal coherence of law within any given saga, whether or not it matches up to law attested in other sources, as a rationalized "saga law," though

21 See for example Brundage, *Medieval Origins*, 53–54.

22 Richard A. Posner, "Medieval Iceland and Modern Scholarship (reviewing William Ian Miller, Bloodtaking and Peacemaking: Feud, Law and Society in Saga Iceland (1990))," *Michigan Law Review* 90 (1992): 1496.

23 David E. Gay, "Review of 'Bloodtaking and Peacemaking: Feud, Law, and Society in Saga Iceland' (Miller)," *Folklore Forum* 23:1/2 (1990): 130, see also Brundage, *Medieval Origins*, 101.

24 Numerous books, articles, and footnotes have been devoted to these problems; for some references and discussion see Hannah Burrows, "Cold Cases: Law and Legal Detail in the *Íslendingasögur*," *Parergon* 26/1 (2009): 35–56.

25 Chris Wickham, "Gossip and Resistance Among the Medieval Peasantry," *Past and Present* 160/1 (1998): 17.

26 Wickham, "Gossip."

it is likely that a meaningful, coherent agreement as to what the law was in a given place, time, and situation, was not simply a literary convenience but a reality.[27]

Offences were against the individual, not against society: if someone with a grievance wanted "justice" or to claim their rights, a third party would pursue it only if the principal (*aðili*), the person responsible for the claim, instigated matters and formally transferred responsibility for the case.[28] In practice, this was likely to be to their *goði* as part of the mutual obligations and support owed between *goðar* and *þingmenn*, although again the *Íslendingasögur* present a more diverse—perhaps more idealized—picture than historians tend to assert was probably actually the case.[29]

Halpérin suggests "we can refer to those people as 'lawyers' who are considered experts in law and, for this reason, are writing about law or acting within the legal system."[30] In early Iceland, though, one could well act within the legal system without being considered expert—especially if one was in a saga. Although court scenes showing litigants in action are in fact quite rare in the *Íslendingasögur*,[31] a panoply of characters are to be found taking up legal cases: as well as numerous instances of *goðar* and prominent *bændr*, there are other free members of the household, fourteen-year-old boys (e.g. *Grettis saga Ásmundarsonar* ch. 16), and women (e.g *Eyrbyggja saga* ch. 38—although in this instance the narrator is quick to point out that the law was soon altered so that "aldri síðan skyldi kona vera vígsakaraðili né yngri karlmaðr en sextán vetra" [never again should a woman be principal in a killing case, nor a boy younger than sixteen years old]).[32] (Actually, in *Grágás* there are certain instances in which women are recognized as a principal, although they could not act in court and would be expected to transfer cases to a male kinsman. They also had legal rights of inheritance and property ownership [including of *goðorð*, although they could not act in the role]; were included in the responsibility for maintenance of dependents and tithe-payments; and

27 Burrows, "Cold Cases," 36.

28 On principals see Dennis, Foote and Perkins, *Laws*, 2:392–93; William Ian Miller, *Hrafnkel or the Ambiguities: Hard Cases, Hard Choices* (Oxford: Oxford University Press, 2017), 62.

29 See e.g. Jón Viðar Sigurðsson, *Viking Friendship*, 15; Gunnar Karlsson, "*Goðar* and *Höfðingjar* in Medieval Iceland," *Saga-Book* 19 (1977): 362–63.

30 Halpérin, "For a Renewed History," 56.

31 Hannah Burrows, "Some Þing to Talk About: Assemblies in the *Íslendingasögur*," *Northern Studies* 47 (2015): 60–62.

32 Einar Ól. Sveinsson and Matthías Þorðarson, ed., *Eyrbyggja saga*, Íslenzk fornrit 4 (Reykjavík: Hið Íslenzka Fornritafélag, 1935), 104.

could undergo ordeal and be prosecuted and outlawed[33]). Those prosecuted in the sagas include revenants (*Eyrbyggja saga* ch. 55) and twelve-year-olds (*Kjalnesingar saga* ch. 3).[34]

It remains a standout and noteworthy skill, however, for someone to be credited with particular legal ability. The term *lǫgmaðr* (pl. *lǫgmenn*), literally lawsman, denotes, in particular, legal expertise, in the sense of thorough knowledge and understanding of the law. Legal knowledge seems to have been passed on through individual teaching rather than through formal education (e.g. *Bárðar saga* chs. 10, 11; *Laxdœla saga* ch. 57; *Njáls saga* ch. 109); there is no evidence for the "academic lawyers" of, for instance, early Ireland.[35] The term *lǫgmaðr* was also enshrined in Icelandic law. In 1271, with the introduction of the law-code *Járnsíða* from Norway, the role of *lögsögumaðr* was supplanted by the royally-appointed office of *Lögmaðr*. *Lögmaðr* was already an official title in Norway, and since the reign of Sverrir Sigurðarson (r. 1184–1202) holders had been appointed by the Crown.[36] However, the term also had a more general sense, used of anyone expert in the law.[37] In Iceland, too, the term already existed and was used to refer to legal experts. Although it was not an official role in the same way as in Norway, *Grágás* uses *lǫgmaðr* to describe people the lawspeaker was allowed to consult before his annual recitation of the law if he felt his own knowledge was unsatisfactory.[38] It also uses it for those whose dictation could supplement the written law texts, as long as they did not contradict what had been codified during the first writing down of the laws.[39] As noted above, the sources give the impression of belief in a sort of "immanent law"—a fixed law that exists to be recalled to memory. An example occurs in *Njáls saga* (ch. 142), where the lawspeaker Skapti Þóroddsson is consulted on a point of law during a court case and replies, "ætlaða ek, at ek einn munda nú kunna þessa lagaréttning, nú er Njáll er dauða, því at hann einn vissa ek

33 See further Dennis, Foote and Perkins, *Laws*, 2:402–03, and references to *Grágás* therein; Miller, *Feud, Law, and Society in Saga Iceland*, 24, 27.

34 I am grateful to Pam Corray for discussion and references relating to children and the law.

35 On the situation in Ireland see Liam Breatnach, "Lawyers in Early Ireland," in *Brehons, Serjeants and Attorneys: Studies in the History of the Irish Legal Profession*, ed. Daire Hogan and William N. Osborough (Dublin: Irish Academic Press in association with The Irish Legal History Society, 1990), 2.

36 Torfinn Tobiassen, "Lagman: Norge," *Kulturhistorisk Leksikon for nordisk middelalder*, edited by Johannes Brønsted et al., 22 vols. (Copenhagen, Gyldendal, 1965): 10: 153–62.

37 Tobiassen, "Lagman."

38 Finsen, *Grágás: Islændernes Lovbog*, 1a: 209.

39 Finsen, *Grágás: Islændernes Lovbog*, 1a:213.

kunna" [I thought that I alone could know this article of law, now that Njáll is dead, because he was the only one I was aware of who knew it].[40] The literary function of highlighting the skill and expertise of the various litigants aside, all involved are perfectly happy to accept Skapti as the repository of an extant law, rather than someone making a personal if expert decision about a situation. However, it is likely that in practice the lawspeaker and *lǫgmenn* "used their knowledge instrumentally, [...] creating a generative reconstruction of history, not a mechanical memorization," as Stefan Brink has written following Jack Goody.[41] The *lǫgmenn* then were probably both people with a good memory, and people whose judgement was trusted.

Interestingly, though, the term *lǫgmaðr* is not used in *Grágás* of the men who sat on the *lǫgrétta* [Law Council], whose job it was to decide and create the law. The *lǫgrétta,* at least in theory, consisted of the holders of the forty-eight *goðorð*, the bishops, and the lawspeaker, all of whom sat on the *miðpallr* [middle bench]; each *goði* also brought along two advisors, who could give counsel but who did not have a vote. "Lögréttuþáttr" refers to these members as "lǫgrétto menn," or even just "menn," or, when referring to matters only applicable to the middle bench, "goðar." Its role in creating and confirming legislation notwithstanding, membership of the *lǫgrétta* was automatic, based on ownership of a *goðorð* rather than (with the exception of the lawspeaker) on any special legal merit.

A similar attempt to denote especial knowledge of the law can be detected in the *Íslendingasögur*. Here the situation is slightly complicated by the fact that some scribes post-1271 seem to have to attempted to avoid confusion with the new official role of *Lǫgmaðr*, and the term *lagamaðr* (lit. man of law), can be found as an alternative to *lǫgmaðr* in the sense of legal expert.[42] In the standard editions, *Eyrbyggja saga*, *Finnboga saga ramma*, *Fljótsdæla saga* and *Laxdæla saga* all use *lagamaðr* and never *lǫgmaðr*. The same is true for the *Sturlunga saga* collection, compiled in the early fourteenth century. Only *Njáls saga* uses both terms, but since it uses *lagamaðr* only once to refer to Mǫrðr *gígja* [fiddle], a character also referred to in the saga as *lǫgmaðr*, it does not appear to be for any reason more significant than variation.

40 Einar Ól. Sveinsson, ed., *Brennu-Njáls saga*, Íslenzk fornrit 12 (Reykjavík: Hið Íslenzka Fornritafélag, 1954), 389–90. For discussion of Skapti's statement see also Miller, *Reading of Njáls Saga*, 261–63.

41 Stefan Brink, "Minnunga mæn: The Usage of Old Knowledgeable Men in Legal Cases," in *Minni and Muninn: Memory in Medieval Nordic Culture*, ed. Pernille Hermann, Stephen A. Mitchell, and Agnes S. Arnórsdóttir (Turnhout: Brepols, 2014), 206.

42 Einar Ól. Sveinsson, *Brennu-Njáls saga*, 5 n. 3.

A survey of the saga corpus at malfong.is reveals that little more than a handful of *Íslendingasaga* characters are awarded one of the epithets *lǫgmaðr* or *lagamaðr*.[43] This tally excludes instances where the office of lawspeaker (*lǫgsǫgumaðr*) is referred to anachronistically as *lǫgmaðr*, and anomalous uses in the late *Svarfdæla saga* and *Hávarðar saga Ísfirðings*, where it appears to refer to some sort of local official. Miller's claim that "numerous people counted as *lǫgmenn* or *lagamenn*" is not restricted to *Íslendingasaga* usage, though is still perhaps generous.[44] In fact, amongst the *Íslendingasögur*, there are only five characters so titled outside *Njáls saga*: Halli Sigurðarson in *Valla-Ljóts saga*; Arnkell *goði* Þórólfsson in *Eyrbyggja saga*; Helgi Droplaugarson in *Fljótsdæla saga* (given the credit by an acquaintance rather than by the narrator), Bersi of Hvammr in *Finnboga saga ramma*; and Þórðr Ingunnarson in *Laxdæla saga*, who is given the credit not by the narrator but by Guðrún Ósvifsdóttir, in her enigmatic response to the question which of her four husbands she loved most: "Þórðr Ingunnarson var maðr þeira vitrastr ok lagamaðr mestr" [Þórðr Ingunnarson was the wisest man among them, and the greatest *lagamaðr*] (ch. 78). (The narrator describes Þórðr as a *sakamaðr* in his introductory portrait (ch. 32); this term will be discussed further below).

Unsurprisingly, *Njáls saga*—dubbed "Die wahre Juristensaga" [the veritable lawyer's saga] by Andreas Heusler[45]—provides a further eight *lǫgmenn*: Mǫrðr *gígja* Sighvatsson, Eyjólfr Bǫlverksson, Njáll himself, Njáll's foster-son Þórhallr Ásgrímsson, the lawspeakers Þórarinn *Ragabróðir* Óleifsson and Skapti Þóroddson, Skapti's father Þóroddr, and Þorkell Geitisson, who is nominated as a *lǫgmaðr* by another character, Flosi Þórðarson, when the latter is asked to think of great *lǫgmenn* (ch. 138). Not content with more than doubling the *Íslendingasögur*'s quota of *lǫgmenn*, *Njáls saga* also insists on emphasising the superlative supremacy of its lawyers. Two characters, Þórhallr Ásgrímsson and Eyjólfr Bǫlverksson, are both referred to as "inn þriði mestr lǫgmaðr á Íslandi" [one of the three greatest legal experts in Iceland][46] (which is actually a slight demotion for Þórhallr, who early in the saga is called "mestr lǫgmaðr á Íslandi" [greatest legal expert in Iceland]).[47] Mǫrðr *gígja* is said to have been "svá mikill lǫgmaðr, at engir þóttu lǫgligir dómar dœmðir, nema hann væri við" [such a great legal expert that no-one thought judgements lawfully judged, unless he

43 Stofnun Árna Magnússonar í íslenskum fræðum, "*Fornritin*," in *Málföng fyrir íslensku*, accessed November 30, 2017, http://www.malfong.is/?pg=fornritin.

44 Miller, *Feud, Law, and Society in Saga Iceland*, 226–27.

45 Andreas Heusler, *Das Strafrecht der Isländersagas* (Leipzig: Duncker & Humblot, 1911), 13.

46 Einar Ól. Sveinsson, *Brennu-Njáls saga*, 279, 359, 363.

47 Einar Ól. Sveinsson, *Brennu-Njáls saga*, 74.

was involved],[48] while Njáll himself is described: "Hann var lǫgmaðr svá mikill, at engi fannsk hans jafningi" [He was such a great legal expert, that his equal could not be found].[49] That said, during the court case after the burning of Njáll, Eyjólfr sends Þorkell to consult the lawspeaker on a point of law: that even these *lǫgmenn* are unsure of the minutiae heightens the tension of the case being built and emphasized the greatness of the legal minds being tested.

Crucially, though, the abilities of these figures are in most cases displayed in a capacity beyond merely acting in court. (Many of them are successful in this regard too, although Miller points out that Mǫrðr's pleading of his own case is "to his manifest detriment"[50]). Njáll, for example, is shown as a teacher to Þórhallr, and directs the serving lawspeaker Skapti on a major constitutional reform, the institution of the fifth court. Njáll's prominence in this innovation is clearly an act of authorial license, but it is still a nice reflex of the *Grágás* definition, which has *lǫgmenn* advising the lawspeaker. Mǫrðr *gígja* is shown speaking "lǫgskil at vanða sínum" [of legal matters, as was his custom] in the *lǫgrétta* (*Njáls saga* ch. 2);[51] Halli Sigurðarson acts as counsellor to the *goði* Guðmundr *inn ríki* Eyjólfsson (*Valla-Ljóts saga* ch. 2). Generalized references in the *Íslendingasögur*, too, confirm this precise sense of sagacity and expertise away from the courtroom: consider *Laxdœla saga*'s explanation that a certain matter "var rannsakað af lǫgmǫnnum" [was examined by *lǫgmenn*] (ch. 25),[52] for example, or Jǫkull's ironic comment in *Vatnsdœla saga* upon hearing that his kinsman Ingólfr has been summoned to a local assembly: "þótt vér sém eigi lǫgmenn, þá munu vér eyða málit með øxarhǫmrum" [although we may not be *lǫgmenn*, we will invalidate their case with the backs of our axes] (ch. 37).[53] *Lǫgmenn*, then, are notable for their legal knowledge whether or not it is manifested by them personally winning cases in the court.

Being recognized as a *lǫgmaðr* is not necessarily correlated with any particular social rank: of the thirteen named above, only two (Arnkell *goði* and Mǫrðr *gígja*) are *goðar* and two (Skapti and Þóroddr) are *hǫfðingjar*. (On the distinction between these two ranks, Miller has an excellent note: "the sagas [...] do not always maintain the *höfðingi/goði* distinction with any great precision. A *höfðingi* might be a *goði* or hold part of a *goðorð*, but he might simply

48 Einar Ól. Sveinsson, *Brennu-Njáls saga*, 5.

49 Einar Ól. Sveinsson, *Brennu-Njáls saga*, 57.

50 Miller, *Reading of Njáls Saga*, 272 n. 24.

51 Einar Ól. Sveinsson, *Brennu-Njáls saga*, 8.

52 Einar Ól. Sveinsson, *Laxdœla saga*, Íslenzk fornrit 5 (Reykjavík: Hið Íslenzka Fornritafélag, 1934), 71.

53 Einar Ól. Sveinsson, ed., *Vatnsdœla saga*, Íslenzk fornrit 8 (Reykjavík: Hið Íslenzka Fornritafélag, 1939), 99.

be a big man, a leader, the head of a large kin-group [...] a *goði* might only be referred to as a *höfðingi* if he has real power"[54]). Most of the other *lǫgmenn* are of notable standing, however: Halli Sigurðarson is "ættstórr" [from an important family],[55] and Eyjólfr Bǫlverksson is "hǫfðingjaefni" [of chieftainly material],[56] while Bersi of Hvammr has become "gildr maðr" [a man of worth], having worked himself up from being the Droplaugarsons' "hleypipiltr" [errand boy].[57] Neither is it (*pace* Guðrún) a guarantee of likeability. Halli is "hávaðamaðr inn mesti" [the most domineering man]; even the lawspeaker Skapti is the subject of downright scorn in *Njáls saga* (chapters 119, 145), as well as coming off as intellectually subordinate to Njáll in the creation of the fifth court.[58]

Even for characters who do not quite achieve recognition as *lǫgmenn*, there are other words that denote their possession of noteworthily advanced legal knowledge. The adjectives *lǫgkœnn* [skilled in the law] and *lǫgvitr* [law-wise or learned in law] seem to imply an intellectual expertise in the law away from its practical application in court: two characters in *Bárðar saga*, for example, are awarded such a description after undergoing particular training (chapters 10, 11). In both cases their being learned in law seems to be what is significant in itself: neither character is shown to act in any legal cases or give legal advice. Again, it is not necessarily an unqualifiedly positive attribute, however: Jón Viðar Sigurðsson highlights the case of Þorgils Hǫlluson in *Laxdœla saga*, described as *lǫgkœnn* but who "was better known for his impulsiveness than for his sharp wit."[59] The small number of instances of these terms in the corpus—the saga corpus at malfong.is (which uses Modern Icelandic orthography) cites 7 instances of *lögkœnn* in the *Íslendingasögur* and 5 of *lögvitur*—means it is difficult to determine any nuanced semantics with confidence, though it is just possible that Þorgils shows up a difference between being *lǫgkœnn* and being a *lǫgmaðr*: the ability to apply knowledge sensibly.

Having considered the proto-"jurists", then, what of the "pleaders"? Miller's reading of *Njáls saga*, of that "glimpse of a separation of legal expertise into pleaders on one hand and jurists on the other," nuances his earlier position that "no evidence suggests that special status was accorded the different aspects of

54 Miller, *Reading of Njáls Saga*, 6 n. 17. See also Gunnar Karlsson, "*Goðar* and *Höfðingjar*".
55 Jónas Kristjánsson, ed., *Eyfirðinga sögur*, Íslenzk fornrit 9 (Reykjavík: Hið Íslenzka Fornritafélag, 1956), 237.
56 Einar Ól. Sveinsson, *Brennu-Njáls saga*, 363.
57 Jóhannes Halldórsson, ed., *Kjalnesinga saga*, Íslenzk fornrit 14 (Reykjavík: Hið Íslenzka Fornritafélag, 1959), 317.
58 Jónas Kristjánsson, *Eyfirðinga sögur*, 233, 237.
59 Jón Viðar Sigurðsson, *Chieftains and Power in the Icelandic Commonwealth* (Odense: Odense University Press, 1999), 90.

legal wisdom and skill".[60] Arguably, legal *skill* in medieval Iceland did not necessarily require a deep knowledge and understanding of the law, but entailed an ability to succeed in legal cases—which could involve more than being technically correct in the minutiae of the law. A talent for public speaking and the ability to present a case clearly and confidently was no doubt highly prized. The word *mál*, after all, means both lawsuits or legal cases and the faculty of speech, related in that *mál* probably earlier referred to a public speech, especially one made at an assembly.[61] There is a nice illustration in the *samtíðarsögur* that *goðar* were measured on their ability to speak well: Oddr Þorgilsson, in *Sturlu saga*, is described as "vitr maðr ok manna snjallastr í máli" [a wise man and of all men most eloquent in speech], in contrast to his successor to the *goðorð*, Einarr: "engi var hann lagamaðr ok blestr í máli" [he was not a *lagamaðr*, and lisped in his speech] (ch. 6).[62] Mǫrðr *gígja* is praised as "allra manna snjallmæltastr" [most eloquent of all men] as he prepares to prosecute Flosi (*Njáls saga* ch. 141).[63] In *Heiðarvíga saga*, Snorri *goði* tricks Þorgísl Arason into pledging peace to his enemies through flattery, saying he has heard persistent rumors "at engi maðr mæli jafnvel fyrir griðum sem þú ok ǫnnur lǫgskil" [that no man can recite the peace-speech or other legal pleadings as well as you] (ch. 33).[64] While this is suggestive of Þorgísl's eloquence, it is also reminiscent of *Grágás*' injunction that the lawspeaker "shall recite all the sections so extensively that no one knows them much more extensively."[65] Although *Njáls saga* (chapters 142–44) suggests that even in the midst of court cases legal advice could be sought from external consultants, admirable pleading likely did include the ability to recite the letter of the law. In fact, in expressing his vision for the fifth court, Njáll declares, "Hér skal ok svá, ef aðrir sœkja rétt, en aðrir rangt, þá skal eptir þeim dœma, er rétt fara með sókn" [Here it shall be like this: if one side pleads correctly, and the other wrongly, the judgement shall go in favour of those who proceed correctly with the case] (*Njáls saga* ch. 97).[66] In *Droplaugarsona saga* everyone present laughs when Helgi Droplaugarson makes a mistake in his pleading (ch. 8)—this may refer to a slip of the tongue, but is more likely

---

60 Miller, *Reading of Njáls Saga*, 272; Miller, *Feud, Law, and Society in Saga Iceland*, 358 n. 13.

61 Tom Markey, "Studies in Runic Origins 1: Germanic **mapl-* /**mahl-* and Etruscan meθum," *American Journal of Germanic Linguistics & Literatures* 10/2 (1998): 154.

62 Jón Jóhannesson, Magnús Finnbogason and Kristján Eldjárn, eds, *Sturlunga saga*, 2 vols. (Reykjavík: Sturlunguútgáfan, 1946), 1:68.

63 Jakob Benediktsson, *Íslendingabok*, 374.

64 Sigurður Nordal and Guðni Jónsson, eds., *Borgfirðinga sögur*, Íslenzk fornrit 3 (Reykjavík: Hið Íslenzka Fornritafélag, 1938), 312.

65 Dennis, Foote, and Perkins, *Laws*, 1:188.

66 Einar Ól. Sveinsson, *Brennu-Njáls saga*, 244.

to be a technical error.[67] Elsewhere in *Njáls saga*, though, the crowd of onlookers in the Burning case is not so confident in its own superior knowledge, or at least is easily swayed by the performances in court to the extent of forming moral judgements of the pleaders: at one moment, "lofuðu nú allir mjǫk Eyjólf ok kǫlluðu engan mundu þurfa við hann at reyna lǫgkœni" [now all praised Eyjólfr highly and said there would be no use anyone challenging his skill at law], but at the next, he is accused of "fara með lǫgvillur einar ok rangyndi" [continuing only with wrongful procedures and unfair dealings].[68]

Brundage equates the term *goðar* with "pleaders or advocates," though he appreciates that "being an advocate or legal expert was by no means a full-time occupation."[69] The legal knowledge of *goðar* is usually taken for granted, because of their role in taking on cases for their *þingmenn*.[70] Nonetheless, the sagas do highlight instances when a *goði*'s legal expertise is outstanding, as with Arnkell Þórólfsson of *Eyrbyggja saga* (ch. 12): "Hann var manna mestr ok sterkastr, lagamaðr mikill ok forvitri [...] hann var ok hofgoði ok átti marga þingmenn" [Arnkell was the greatest of men and the strongest, a great legal expert and very wise [...] he was also a *hofgoði* [temple-chieftain] and had many *þingmenn*].[71] Furthermore, in *Valla-Ljóts saga*, the powerful chieftain Guðmundr *inn ríki* engages the services of Halli in his own legal dealings, and, in the same saga the *goði* Ljótr himself openly admits, "Eigi kann ek lǫgin vel" [I do not know the laws well].[72] It may be recalled, too, that *Grágás* prescribes that each of the *goðar* who sat on the "middle bench" in the *lǫgrétta*—i.e. those who had voting rights in legislative matters—were to bring two advisors with them to its sessions. While a degree of legal knowledge was, in practice, doubtless a useful attribute for the successful *goði*—and one likely to accrue over time, from sitting in the *lǫgrétta* and from taking on cases for their *þingmenn*—*goðar* were not single-handedly expected to have all the answers. They could take advice from those more expert than they were themselves.

The *Íslendingasögur* have other terms to recognize success in court, however, and to reward enthusiasm in the pursuit of court cases as a highly desirable trait in a *goði* or leader. The three terms *málafylgjumaðr*, *málafylgismaðr* and *málamaðr*, rendered by Cleasby and Vigfússon as "helper in lawsuits; taker

67 For discussion of mistakes in pleading and whether they would affect the case, see Miller, *Reading of Njáls Saga*, 266–67.

68 Einar Ól. Sveinsson, *Brennu-Njáls saga*, 386, 389.

69 Brundage, *Medieval Origins*, 101.

70 See, for example, Jón Viðar Sigurðsson, *Chieftains and Power*, 90.

71 Einar Ól. Sveinsson and Matthías Þorðarson, *Eyrbyggja saga*, 20.

72 Jónas Kristjánsson, *Eyfirðinga sögur*, 241.

up of suits," are all associated in the *Íslendingasögur* with success (and popularity) as a leader.[73] The terms are nowhere in the *Íslendingasaga* corpus used of lower status figures. In *Laxdæla saga*, for instance, Þorkell Eyjólfsson "gerðisk hǫfðingi mikill; helt hann sér mjǫk til vinsælda ok virðingar. Hann var maðr heraðríkr ok málamaðr mikill" [became a great chieftain; he maintained much popularity and respect. He was a powerful man in the district and a great *málamaðr*] (ch. 70).[74] In *Bandamanna saga* (Möðruvallabók redaction [Reykjavík, Stofnun Árna Magnússonar, MS AM 132 fol.], ch. 3), when Oddr asks Óspakr to take on his *goðorð*, the latter replies (albeit lying through his teeth, since he "vildi [...] feginn" [wanted it dearly]): "Er þar engi maðr jafnvel til fallinn sem faðir þinn; er hann inn mesti málamaðr ok forvitri" [there is no man better suited to this than your father; he is the greatest *málamaðr*, and a very wise man].[75] Meanwhile, in *Droplaugarsona saga* (ch. 2), two brothers divide their inheritance. Notably, it is Ketill, described as "glaðr maðr ok málamaðr mikill" [a cheerful man and great *málamaðr*] who gets the *goðorð*.[76] That this attribute was a different ability than having expert knowledge of the law is evidenced in that Mǫrðr *gígja* is attributed both qualities: he "var ríkr hǫfðingi ok málafylgjumaðr mikill ok [...] mikill lǫgmaðr" [was a powerful chieftain and a great *málafylgjumaðr* and a great *lǫgmaðr*] (*Njáls saga* ch. 1).[77] Þorkell Geitisson, on the other hand, may be a *lǫgmaðr* but when Flosi is looking for help in building a legal defense, Bjarni Brodd-Helgason warns him "Ekki muni vér hann telja; þótt hann sé lǫgvitr, þá er hann þó forsjáll mjǫk" [We shouldn't consider [Þorkell]; he may be wise in the law, but at the same time he's very cautious] (*Njáls saga* ch. 138).[78]

Málamenn, then, signify in the *Íslendingasögur* leaders who will not stint on pursuing a case to court, and who, presumably, have an attendant reputation for success. In all cases this quality is seen as positive, rather than implying undue litigiousness. Compare also the *goði* Ingimundr Þorsteinsson in *Vatnsdæla saga*: "eigi er hér getit þingdeilda hans, at hann ætti stórmálum at skipta við menn, því at hann varð samhuga við flesta ok óágangsamr" [noth-

73 Richard Cleasby and Guðbrand Vigfusson, *An Icelandic-English Dictionary*, 2nd ed. with a supplement by Sir William A. Craigie (Oxford: Clarendon Press, 1957).

74 Einar Ól. Sveinsson, *Laxdæla saga*, 204.

75 Guðni Jónsson, ed., *Grettis saga Ásmundarsonar*, Íslenzk fornrit 7 (Reykjavík: Hið Íslenzka Fornritafélag, 1936), 303. Interestingly, the Konungsbók (Reykjavík, Stofnun Árna Magnússonar, MS GKS 2845 4to) redaction has *skilamaðr* [trustworthy man] in place of *málamaðr*.

76 Jón Jóhannesson, ed., *Austfirðinga sögur*, Íslenzk fornrit 11 (Reykjavík: Hið Íslenzka Fornritafélag, 1950), 141. See also *Vopnfirðinga saga* ch. 19; *Bolla þáttr* ch. 9.

77 Einar Ól. Sveinsson, *Brennu-Njáls saga*, 5.

78 Einar Ól. Sveinsson, *Brennu-Njáls saga*, 364.

ing is told here about his dealings at the assembly, that he might have had great lawsuits to contest against people, because he was agreeable with most and not aggressive]. It is not necessarily that Ingimundr did not participate in great lawsuits—his reputation for doing so, in a general sense, seems to have persisted—but details of his apparently mundane, peaceful and trouble-calming legal affairs are lost, because after all it is conflict that makes a good story.[79]

The other major support a *goði* could provide was strength in numbers. Although Brundage uses the terms "advocate or legal expert" as if they were synonymous, simply having someone powerful on your side could be equally—if not more—important as knowing the letter of the law. While it might be dystopian to suggest that force, or the threat of force, was always a factor in court cases, problems of this nature are in abundant evidence in the *Íslendingasögur*, where there is a common fear—even assumption—that superior physical force would be a decisive factor, and/or that arbitrated decisions would favour the party with the greatest political sway. So, in *Grettis saga* Þóroddr brings a case against his opponent Atli to the Alþing rather than the Húnavatnsþing "fyrir frændum Atla; hugði hann, at hér myndi hans mál síðr fyrir borð borit" [because of Atli's kinsmen; he thought that here [i.e. at the Alþing] his case would be less likely to be thrown overboard] (ch. 51),[80] while in *Droplaugarsona saga* it is explicitly stated that Helgi Droplaugarson is able to insist on self-judgement because his opponents "hafði ekki lið til at ónýta mál fyrir þeim" [did not have the support to quash his case] (ch. 5).[81] What *þingmenn* needed from their *goði*, therefore, was the support and status that he could command: the force of numbers that would ensure their case was heard and not driven out of court, and the political clout to ensure that decisions and compromises were negotiated in a manner that was as satisfactory as possible to both sides.[82]

---

79 On methods of dispute resolution see Andreas Heusler's famous statistics in *Strafrecht*, 40–41. See also Guðmund Sandvik and Jón Viðar Sigurðsson, "Laws," in *A Companion to Old Norse-Icelandic Literature and Culture*, ed. Rory McTurk (Oxford: Blackwell, 2005), 227; William Ian Miller, "Avoiding Legal Judgment: The Submission of Disputes to Arbitration in Medieval Iceland," *The American Journal of Legal History* 28/2 (1984): 95–134; Jón Viðar Sigurðsson, "The Role of Arbitration in the Settlement of Disputes in Iceland c. 1000–1300," in *Law and Disputing in the Middle Ages: Proceedings of the Ninth Carlsberg Academy Conference on Medieval Legal History 2012*, ed. Per Anderson et al. (Copenhagen: DJØF Press, 2013).

80 Guðni Jónsson, *Grettis saga*, 163.

81 Jón Jóhannesson, *Austfirðinga sögur*, 150. See also e.g *Ljósvetninga saga* ch. 4, *Víga-Glúms saga* ch. 24ff.

82 See e.g. Jesse Byock, *Medieval Iceland: Society, Sagas, and Power* (Berkeley, CA: University

The case of Sámr Bjarnason in *Hrafnkels saga*, though already well studied,[83] nicely draws together a number of matters discussed so far. In status Sámr begins the saga as an ordinary *bóndi*, though he is introduced to the narrative as "lǫgkœnn."[84] It is worth noting here two other of Sámr's attributes. First, "átti hann margt fé" [he had great wealth]. The reason behind his wealth is not made explicit in the saga, but Miller thinks he may have earned it because of his legal skills; he is not a fully professional lawyer, but perhaps one who makes money from taking on lawsuits nonetheless.[85] Second, and in the same breath as his legal knowledge is mentioned, he is described as an "uppivǫzlumaðr," usually rendered as an "overbearing" or "quarrelsome" person. It is possible, then, that Sámr embodies a different, perhaps almost opposite character type to the *málamaðr*—he is not the *goði* always willing to help, but the upstart *bóndi* who is clever when it comes to law and keen to show it off when he thinks he has the upper hand. Indeed, his uncle later criticizes him, "Sýnisk mér slíkum mǫnnum illa farit sem þér, er þykkisk lǫgkœnn vera ok ert gjarn á smásakar, en vilt eigi taka við þessu máli, er svá er brýnt" [It seems to me men like you go about things wrongly, who think themselves to be *lǫgkœnn* and are eager for the small cases, but won't take on this lawsuit, which is such a just cause].[86] When Sámr does become a *goði*, though, he is "vinsæll af sínum þingmǫnnum, því at hann var hœgr ok kyrr ok góðr órlausna" [popular with his *þingmenn*, because he was easygoing and calm and a good help].[87] Miller notes these descriptions are difficult to reconcile, speculating that the *uppivǫzlumaðr* label "might be meant to convey some anti-lawyer animus."[88] The apparent change in character might make sense to a saga audience, though, given his change of status. As a *goði*, Sámr no longer needs to pick fights or agitate contests he can win in order to prove himself; his keenness to participate in lawsuits is now interpreted as useful and supportive rather than as acting above his station.

In the preface to the key court scene of the saga, though, Sámr is still a *bóndi*. Despite holding out little hope, he agrees, reluctantly, to take on a case for his uncle, Þorbjǫrn, against the chieftain Hrafnkell, an "ójafnaðarmaðr mikill"

---

of California Press, 1998), 124; Gunnar Karlsson, "*Goðar* and *Höfðingjar*", 363; Miller, *Feud, Law, and Society in Saga Iceland*, 234 ff.

83 See Miller, *Hrafnkel*, his comments on the saga's critical interest at 15, and references therein.

84 Jón Jóhannesson, *Austfirðinga sögur*, 100.

85 Miller, *Hrafnkel*, 56. Cf. Bersi of Hvammr in *Finnboga saga ramma*, mentioned above.

86 Jón Jóhannesson, *Austfirðinga sögur*, 107. See also Miller, *Hrafnkel*, 55–56.

87 Jón Jóhannesson, *Austfirðinga sögur*, 125.

88 Miller, *Hrafnkel*, 56.

[very unjust man],[89] who "hafi alla menn hrakit af málaferlum þeim, er við hann hafa haft" [had destroyed all the lawsuits of those who had brought them against him] (ch. 3).[90] Just when "flestir hǫfðingjar, þeir er váru á Íslandi" [most of the important chieftains in Iceland] have refused to help Sámr, the mysterious Þorkell Þjóstarsson from the Vestfirðir asks him what he needs.[91] "Liðsinnis ok afla hǫfðingja" [the support and strength of chieftains], Sámr replies, "því at vit eigum málum at skipta við Hrafnkel goða [...] en vit megum vel hlíta okkrum flutningu með þínu fulltingi" [because we have a case to contend with Hrafnkell *goði*, and we can well rely on our pleading with your help] (ch. 4).[92] Later, taking the matter to Þorkell's brother Þorgeirr, who controls the Þjóstarssons' *goðorð*, he reiterates, "styrk þurfum vit af hǫfðingjum, en málaflutning á ek undir mér" [we need the strength of chieftains, but I have the pleading of the case under control] (ch. 4).[93] Sámr is aware that his own legal skills are more than equal to those a *goði* could offer him—he is not looking for someone to take his place in prosecuting the case—but he is afraid he will not get the chance to utilize them. However, with the backing of the Þjóstarssons secured, Sámr is able to take his case to court (ch. 4):

> Sámr gekk þá djarfliga at dóminum. Hann hefr þegar upp váttnefnu ok sótti mál sitt at réttum landslǫgum á hendr Hrafnkeli goða, miskviðalaust með skǫruligum flutningi [...] Sámr sótti málit í dóm, þangat til er Hrafnkeli var boðit [til] varnar [...] Rómr varð mikill at máli Sáms. Kvazk engi vilja lǫgvǫrn fram bera fyrir Hrafnkel.[94]
>
> [Sámr then went boldly to the court. He immediately named witnesses and prosecuted his case against Hrafnkell *goði* according to the true law of the land, without making any slip in the proceedings and with magnificent pleading [...] Sámr prosecuted his case in the court until Hrafnkell was invited to make his defence [...] There was great applause at Sámr's speech. No one declared themselves willing to put forward a defence on behalf of Hrafnkell.]

---

89 Jón Jóhannesson, *Austfirðinga sögur*, 99.
90 Jón Jóhannesson, *Austfirðinga sögur*, 110.
91 Jón Jóhannesson, *Austfirðinga sögur*, 109.
92 Jón Jóhannesson, *Austfirðinga sögur*, 112.
93 Jón Jóhannesson, *Austfirðinga sögur*, 115.
94 Jón Jóhannesson, *Austfirðinga sögur*, 116–17.

True to form, when Hrafnkell hears the case is going well for Sámr, "ætlaði hann at hleypa upp dóminum fyrir Sámi ok hrekja hann af málinu" [he intended to charge up to the court in front of Sámr and drive him off the case].[95] However, the Þjóstarssons' following makes it impossible for him to get near; meanwhile, Sámr "sótti málit til fullra laga" [prosecuted his case to the full extent of the law], and Hrafnkell is outlawed.[96]

Miller's recent book on *Hrafnkels saga* is entitled *Hrafnkel or the Ambiguities*, and sure enough there is ambiguity here as to how much this is a success for law and a triumph of good pleading. On the one hand, the juxtaposition of Sámr's *skǫruligr flutning* and the applause at his speech with the lack of willingness on the part of anyone else to put forward a defense for Hrafnkell could suggest that not only did everyone else think their own pleading skills inferior to Sámr's, but that he had shut down any possible legal objections through his knowledge of the law. On the other hand, it could merely reflect the fact that everyone hated Hrafnkell and all were delighted to see him get his comeuppance after continually blocking everyone else's lawsuits. The voice of the law, through Sámr, is finally able to be heard loudly and clearly—but seems like overkill if there is to be no defense anyway. And the celebration of Sámr's legal skills rings distinctly hollow given he is only able to display them because the Þjóstarssons have kept Hrafnkell and his party out of court by force, the very habit Hrafnkell was so disliked for.[97]

The terms *lǫgspakr* and *lǫgfróðr*, both implying wisdom or learnedness in law, are not found in the *Íslendingasaga* corpus, but there remain a handful of words to mention briefly. In Sámr vs. Hrafnkell, Miller (following Sámr himself) nicely draws the distinction between *flutning* and *fullting*, pleading and "muscle," or brains and brawn.[98] It is worth noting that while *flutning* is used to refer to legal pleading, the associated term *flutningsmaðr* is not employed in a legal sense in the *Íslendingasögur*, but used to mean "spokesman" or "advocate" in a more general sense, such as supporting a marriage proposal (e.g. *Laxdœla saga* ch. 70) or intervening with foreign royalty (e.g. *Egils saga* ch. 36). Clearly the sagas prefer to use more specialised terms for the kind of advocate with a particular aptitude for lawsuits. *Laxdœla saga*'s *sakamaðr* is a hapax legomenon in the *Íslendingasaga* corpus, with only 3 distinct instances in total cited by the *Dictionary of Old Norse Prose*. Its meaning is clear enough, deriving from *sǫk* [lawsuit], and it seems to mean broadly the same as *málamaðr*. Interestingly,

95 Jón Jóhannesson, *Austfirðinga sögur*, 117.
96 Jón Jóhannesson, *Austfirðinga sögur*.
97 See also Miller, *Hrafnkel*, 125.
98 Miller, *Hrafnkel*, 113.

however, Þórðr, the character it is applied to, is not a chieftain, unlike the recipients of the latter label. Another hapax is *saksæll*, literally "lucky in lawsuits," which Bjǫrn thinks himself in *Bjarnar saga hítdœlakappa* (ch. 22). Medieval Icelanders preferred, perhaps, to think of legal success as being down to expertise, experience, or a combination of the two: luck had nothing to do with it.

Berger suggests that the *Íslendingasaga* "lawyer" may have been a stock character type created by the saga author to lend credibility to the details of a plot based around a legal dispute: "if episodes are to turn on points of law, then heroes and villains must be made lawyers to accommodate such conflicts."[99] Helgi Droplaugarson, for instance, "seems to have been known to tradition as a ferocious fighter, but the author of *Droplaugarsona saga* made him a lawyer to handle a series of legal conflicts which finally issued in battle."[100] Conversely, outstanding legal capability—whether expertise or experience—was likely something remembered and celebrated in tradition, perhaps as in the cases of the peaceful litigant Ingimundr Þorsteinsson in *Vatnsdœla saga*, and the *málamaðr* Þorkell Eyjólfsson in *Laxdœla saga* ("þingdeilda hans er hér þó ekki getit" [his assembly-dealings are not mentioned here]).[101] Legal plot lines may have necessitated the creation of legally-able characters, but figures known to tradition as outstanding legal practitioners may also have created legal plot lines, with disputes and cases improvised to show these figures in action.

The attribution of legal success in some form may have become a formulaic character attribute, intended to create a generally positive portrait of a well-rounded chieftain or to indicate a likelihood of social advancement in characters thus endowed. There are, of course, additionally, various circumlocutory phrases, such as "Ǫzurr [...] mjǫk hafðr við mál manna" [Ǫzurr [...] had many lawsuits against people] (*Droplaugarsona saga* ch. 3), that are not possible to cover here but which also demonstrate participation in the legal sphere.[102] The fact that Oddr and Eiðr in *Bárðar saga* become, respectively, "lögvitrari maðr en aðrir menn" [a man more knowledgeable in law than other men] and "allra manna lögvistrastr" [most knowledgeable in law of all men] within a chapter of each other might suggest legal prowess was so formulaic as to be worthy of parody.[103] However, even in that strange saga the descrip-

99 Miller, *Hrafnkel*, 78.
100 Miller, *Hrafnkel*, 78–79.
101 Einar Ól. Sveinsson, *Laxdœla saga*, 204.
102 Jón Jóhannesson, *Austfirðinga sögur*, 143.
103 Þórhallur Vilmundarson and Bjarni Vilhjálmsson eds., *Harðar saga*, Íslenzk fornrit 13 (Reykjavík: Hið Íslenzka Fornritafélag, 1991), 135, 139.

tion has significance in "usher[ing] in a new age" of law over pagan powers, as Eleanor Rosamund Barraclough has pointed out.[104] Where a specific term such as *lǫgmaðr* or *málamaðr* is used, it implies something outstanding and particular in terms of characterization, and in the vast majority of cases has some bearing on the plot.

The lexicon attested in the *Íslendingasögur* is capable of drawing a distinction between those with exceptional knowledge and expertise (*lǫgmenn* and *lagamenn*; those described as *lǫgkœnn* or *lǫgvitr*), and those who were good at winning lawsuits (*málamenn*; *málafylgismenn*/*málafylgjumenn*; *sakamenn*). In some characters, these skills naturally overlap; in others, the distinctions between brains, bravado and brawn (physical or political) are more marked.

To push the consequences of this literary representation further, it is likely that this distinction had some basis in "real life," in that certain people had training and/or aptitude for one or other form of legal ability. It is easy to imagine a shy child sent to learn law who grew into a knowledgeable but mild adult, lacking confidence to plead a winning case; someone interested in attending and pondering the lawspeaker's recitations, but without need or social position to act on knowledge gleaned; or someone who could speak publicly exceptionally well but relied on advisors for the technical details. Although most people would have lacked the leisure time to become learned in law if it were not to have a practical payoff, all indications suggest that advice was a valuable commodity (consider the aforementioned Halli Sigurðarson and Bersi of Hvammr). Legal expertise might be useful (and remunerative) even for a *bóndi* who might not act in court but could cement alliances through giving counsel or be appointed as an advisor to their *goði*. Likewise, certain *goðar* were no doubt thought of more approvingly than others if they were skilled and persistent at winning cases for their *þingmenn*, whether or not they were considered particularly learned.

However, by the time the sagas were written down, even having a choice of *goði* was essentially a literary fiction, as, according to *Sturlunga saga*, was the whole possibility of taking a case to court.[105] The large number of *goðorð* became swallowed up into larger *ríki* [domains], controlled by a handful of powerful families, and the *Alþing* was increasingly bypassed since the less pow-

104 Eleanor Rosamund Barraclough, "Following the Trollish *Baton Sinister*: Ludic Design in *Bárðar saga Snæfellsáss*," *Viking and Medieval Scandinavia* 4 (2008): 29.

105 On the political situation see e.g. Jón Viðar Sigurðsson, "Historical Writing and the Political Situation in Iceland 1100–1400," in *Negotiating Pasts in the Nordic Countries: Interdisciplinary Studies in History and Memory*, ed. Anne Eriksen and Jón Viðar Sigurðsson (Lund: Nordic Academic Press, 2009); on its portrayal in *Sturlunga saga* see Stephen N. Tranter, *Sturlunga Saga: The Rôle of the Creative Compiler* (Frankfurt: Peter Lang, 1987).

erful had no way to enforce its judgements. That is not to say, however, that the *Íslendingasögur* could not imagine (or remember) legal practitioners who knew the law intimately and/or delighted in pursuing its intricacies and opportunities.

CHAPTER 13

Two Lombard Charters and Their Writers

Daniela Fruscione

The analysis of two private documents,[1] written in Tuscany in the eighth century are at the core of the following contribution.[2] One, written in 720, is a *charta dotis*[3] recording a grant made by the *vir magnificus* Pertuald, father of the bishop of Lucca, Peredeus, to a church founded by him; and the other, a *cartula donationis*,[4] records the gift made by Audipert, a landowner in Chiusi, to his nephews Bonipert(ulo) and Leopert, in 770. These Tuscan charters come from the two largest ecclesiastical archives in Italy: the archive of the bishop of Lucca in the north of Tuscany, and the monastery of Monte Amiata in the south of Tuscany, respectively. The volumes of the *Codice Diplomatico Longobardo* (henceforth CDL), comprising documents that record legal transactions from the mid-seventh century to the Carolingian conquest of the Lombard kingdom, reveal that around two-thirds of the documents come from Tuscan archives.[5] The rich availability and constancy in the diplomatic archives of Tuscany, both monastic and episcopal, have made it possible for historians to reconstruct the life of some centres in the eighth and ninth centuries.

The two documents analyzed here were chosen from amongst the vast collection of surviving charters from the Lombard period, as evidence of some important features of early medieval charters.[6] Firstly, the documents show

1 On private documents: Harry Bresslau, *Handbuch der Urkundenlehre für Deutschland und Italien* I (Leipzig: Veit, 1912); Guido Astuti, *Lezioni di storia del diritto italiano. Le fonti. Età romano-barbarica* (Padua: Cedam, 1953); Giovanna Nicolaj, "Il documento privato italiano nell' alto medioevo," in *Libri e documenti d'Italia: dai Longobardi alla rinascita della città* Atti del Convegno Nazionale dell' Associazione Italiana Paleografi e Diplomatisti, Cividale, 5–7 ottobre 1994, ed. Cesare Scalon (Udine: Forum, 1996); François Bougard, "Actes privés et transferts patrimoniaux en Italie centro-septentrionale (VIIIe–Xe siècle)," *Mélanges de l'École Française de Rome* 111 (1999): 539–62.

2 The Lombard private charters were published by Luigi Schiapparelli, ed., *Codice Diplomatico Longobardo* (*CDL*), 2 vols (Rome: Istituto Storico Italiano per il Medio Evo, 1929; repr., 1933); Tuscia's private charters coming from Monte Amiata were published also by Wilhelm Kurze, ed., *Codex Diplomaticus Amiatinus* (*CDA*), 2 vols. (Tübingen: Niemeyer, 1974).

3 No. 28, Schiapparelli, *CDL* 1.

4 No. 248, Schiapparelli, *CDL* 2; No. 17, Kurze, *CDA* 1.

5 Schiapparelli, *CDL*: 1, 2.

6 For a vast bibliography, see: Herbert Zielinski, "Die Charta der Langobarden. Forschungs-

 | DOI:10.1163/9789004448650_015

the relevance of private charters concerning both the Church and lay society. The charters indicate that the interests of laypeople were similar to those of ecclesiastical institutions. All were concerned with securing their rights over property and all had an interest in making use of the added source of legitimacy that was provided by written documents. Secondly, they highlight the connection between the laws and the charters.[7] Most importantly, the evidence shows that charters functioned as a means of integrating precepts of the written law by legitimating transactions that met the agreement of the parties but had no foundation in the laws. This important aspect of charters is envisaged by Liutprand in his legislation: he knew that the literal application of the law would not always be sufficient to anticipate potential areas of dispute.[8]

The charters in question are, however, two very different documents. One provides evidence of a legalistic approach, determined by the need to secure a difficult transaction, while the other takes a legitimating role for the founding of the clerical identity of Peredeus' powerful family. The two charters reveal two very different writers' personalities. The writer of the latter, Firmus, is a very distinguished and proficient man of law, whose understanding of his task as *notarius* goes beyond the merely etymological; and the author of the former, the rather anonymous Petrus, is an occasional writer who records an "easy" transaction enacted by his uncle. In order to understand the relation of bishop Peredeus to documentary practice, two more writers will also be mentioned, who were in connection with the vast production of charters performed by the

---

geschichte und aktuelle Perspektiven," in *Die Privaturkunden der Karolingerzeit*, ed. Peter Erhart, Karl Heidecker and Berhard Zeller (Dietikon-Zürich: Graf, 2009).

7 Daniela Fruscione, "Documenti longobardi e questione dell' effettività delle leggi," *Filologia Germanica* 2 (2010): 105–34; Claudio Azzara, "Le nozze di Anstruda. Codice e prassi nell' Italia di diritto longobardo," in *Carte di famiglia*, ed. Cristina La Rocca and Stefano Gasparri (Rome: Viella, 2005).

8 Liutprand, No. 91 (*De Scrivis*), Friedrich Bluhme, ed., *Edictus Langobardorum*, MGH, LL 4 (Hannover: Hahn, 1868; repr., Hahnsche Buchhandlung, 1984), 144–45; See also, Daniela Fruscione, "Im Spannungsfeld zwischen deutscher Rechtsgeschichte und italienischem Frühmittelalter: Gerhard Dilcher und die Leges Langobardorum," in *Recht—Geschichte—Geschichtsschreibung: Rechts- und Verfassungsgeschichte im deutsch-italienischen Diskurs*, ed. Susanne Lepsius and Bernd Kannowski (Berlin: Erich Schmidt Verlag, 2014), 30. See also Brigitte Pohl-Resl, "Ethnische Bezeichnungen und Rechtsbekenntnisse in langobardischen Urkunden," in *Ethnogenese und Überlieferung. Angewandte Methoden der Frühmittelalterforschung*, ed, Karl Brunner and Brigitte Merta (Vienna: Veröffentlichungen des Instituts für Österreichische Geschichtsforschung, 1994), 163, 166; Nick Everett, "How Territorial was Lombard Law?," in *Die Langobarden. Herrschaft und Identität*, ed. Walter Pohl and Peter Ehrhart (Vienna: Verlag der österreichischen Akademie der Wissenschaften, 2005), 345, 351. See also, Thom Gobbitt, "Liutprand's Prologues in the *Edictus Langobardorum*," Chapter 3 in this volume.

Lucchese church: Osprand, who was the first to copy Petrus' charter, and Fratellus, who wrote several charters for Peredeus. Like Firmus they stand out for their proficiency, but unlike him, who calls himself *notarius* and was probably a layman, they are priests.

The evidence of Lombard charters and Lombard legislation does not allow for the identification of the title of *notarius* as indicating an official recognized by the king, and we have no indication that a *notarius* enjoyed *fides publica.*[9] In the Lombard era a *notarius* only belonged to a profession in an informal sense, his job derived from practice and custom.[10] Moreover, there appears to have been no division between writers who used lay titles and those who used ecclesiastical titles. The variety of titles used by the writers of Lombard charters hint at a broad stratum of persons who could draw up charters.[11] Giorgio Costamagna's survey revealed twenty-three different designations.[12] The title of the writer was not essential for the legitimation of the charter, but rather concordance with the law and the following of a correct procedure for procuring witnesses and their subscriptions; in addition to the legal substance a certain form was due, represented both by the use of correct formulae and by external features like the script-type and the language.

The Latin of the *chartae* cannot be understood without considering the modalities of the relationship between the Lombards, literacy, and the Latin language: around a century before Firmus and the other considered writers were operative, another *notarius*, Ansoald, had used the same language to draw up Rothari's laws. In the first Lombard code this Latin with a non-traditional grammar stands out because it contrasts with the genealogical lists and narrative inserts of the same laws, which are written in a grammatical Latin.[13] The Latin of the Lombard charters therefore reflects the tradition of the laws, a deliberately non-literary language, chosen for its communicative functionality and adapted to the linguistic conditions of the Lombards.[14] Moreover, the ques-

9 Jörg Müller and Hans-Georg Hermann, "Urkunden," *Reallexikon der germanischen Altertumskunde* 31 (2006): 545–49.

10 Nicholas Everett, *Literacy in Lombard Italy, c. 568–774* (Cambridge: Cambridge University Press, 2003), 207.

11 Everett, *Literacy*, 207.

12 Giorgio Costamagna, "L' altomedioevo," in *Alle origini del notariato italiano*, ed. Mario Amelotti and Gorgio Costamagna (Rome: Consiglio Nazionale del notariato, 1975), 157.

13 Claudia Villa and Francesco Lo Monaco, "Cultura e scrittura nell' Italia longobarda," in *Die Langobarden. Herrschaft und Identität*, ed. Walter Pohl and Peter Ehrhart (Vienna: Verlag der österreichischen Akademie der Wissenschaften, 2005); Lidia Capo, "Paolo Diacono e il problema della cultura," in *Langobardia*, ed. Paolo Cammarosano and Stefano Gasparri (Udine: Casamassima, 1990).

14 Attilio Bartoli Langeli, *Notai. Scrivere documenti nell' Italia medievale* (Rome: Viella, 2006),

tion of the charters and their writers is only addressed in the Lombard laws in a fragmentary way. Discussion of the value of the documentary sources therefore must deal with a lack of precise configurations and juridical-institutional definitions.

All of the original Lombard charters were written in a cursive script which is easily recognizable and uniform, despite the range of local and scribal variations. The cursive, the most widespread script of Late Ancient Latin, due to the speed it could be executed writing *currenti calamo*, has two precise structural characters: firstly, the irregular shape of the letters, and, secondly, and above all, the ligatures, which, by altering the shape of the conjoined letters may be added to the alphabet as autonomous graphemes. Compared to the vitality of the southern cursives, the central-northern cursive has an inertial quality; the writers do not show any particular creativity, beyond the variability of individual use and execution.[15] The charters considered here show the graphic capacity of the cathedral cleric, Osprand, who writes in a perfect cursive chancery hand,[16] and the calm and regular writing of Firmus, which shows a strong desire for discipline.[17]

Moreover, little is known about the profession of the writers of charters and their training. However, the quality of the script and the skilled use of the *formulae* in the documents produced by Osprand and Fratellus for bishop Peredeo and his family show the important role of the writing school of the cathedral church of Lucca and its relevance in the development of literate tradition. Also, the charters coming from the cultural landscape of Chiusi, where Firmus is from, bear the influence of the local documentary tradition.[18]

In spite of their formulaic structure, far from being "arid",[19] the charters considered here can be regarded as valuable sources for many aspects of the history of the Early Middle Ages, both in its micro and macro dimensions; indeed, the use and meaning of the charters includes far more than their role as carriers of information about a given transaction.

21; Massimo Vallerani, "Scritture e schemi rituali nella giustizia altomedievale," in *Scrivere e Leggere nell' Alto Medioevo*, ed. CISAM (Spoleto: CISAM, 2012), 102.

15 Armando Petrucci and Carlo Romeo, *"Scriptores in Urbibus". Alfabetismo e cultura scritta nell' Italia altomedievale* (Bologna: Il Mulino, 1992).

16 Everett, *Literacy in Lombard Italy*, 266.

17 Daniela Fruscione, "Documenti Longobardi di Chiusi," in *Goti e Longobardi a Chiusi*, ed. Carla Falluomini (Chiusi: Edizioni Luì, 2009), 86.

18 Fruscione, "Documenti Longobardi di Chiusi," 86–87.

19 Chris Wickham, *Framing the Early Middle Ages. Europe and the Mediterranean: 400–800* (Oxford: Oxford University Press, 2005), 384.

The question of the significance of private documents in a time, the eighth century, when they were not a constitutive element of legal transactions is answered differently in each of these charters, whose actors show different attitudes towards the documentation of a transaction. In order to hold the uncertainties connected with the precarious social position of his nephews in check—they were not free—Audipert's charter exhibits Firmus' deep knowledge of the *lex* as a barrier, whereas in Pertuald's charter the memory of the acquisition and transmission of possessions creates a strong and protecting family identity: the document itself played a role in the social and institutional developments, rather than simply bearing witness to them.

Indeed, both these charters deserve the definition of "carta di famiglia," as an important work edited by Cristina La Rocca and Stefano Gasparri, calls these types of private charter.[20] This is one of the main features of the *chartae* of the Early Middle Ages that makes it possible to gain insight into inheritance and marriage strategies, identity items and to draw conclusions about the principles of name giving.

Moreover, the charters can be considered in the broader contexts of the transition from orality to literacy.[21] The eighth-century evidence shows that Lombard elites had adapted to written forms of administration and legal instruments,[22] and the Lombards had already been working within literate circles for at least a century before the *Edictus Rothari* was drafted.[23] Rothari in the seventh century envisages in his legislation an oral procedure (pledge, oaths, sureties) for most transactions. The charters are obvious reflections of this pro-

20 Cristina La Rocca and Stefano Gasparri, ed., *Carte di famiglia* (Rome: Viella, 2005).

21 Rosamond McKitterick, *The Carolingians and the Written Word* (Cambridge: Cambridge University Press, 1989); Janet Nelson, "Literacy in Carolingian Government," in *The Uses of Literacy in Early Medieval Europe* 258–96 (Cambridge: Cambridge University Press, 1990), 258–96, pointed out the centrality of literacy to laypeople and administration long before the twelfth century, in opposition to an old generation of scholars like Michael Richter, *The Formation of the Medieval West: Studies in the Oral Culture of the Barbarians* (New York: Saint Martin's, 1994), who assumed that the written word was a remnant of the Roman and Christian tradition. On the much debated question of orality and literacy in the Early Middle Ages, and otherwise; Alice Rio, *Legal Practice and the Written Word in the Early Middle Ages* (Cambridge: Cambridge University Press, 2009), 9–26; Matthew Innes, "Memory, Orality and Literacy," *Past and Present* 158 (1998): 3–36.

22 Everett, *Literacy in Lombard Italy*; Gerhard Dilcher, "Langobardisches Recht," *Handwörterbuch zur deutschen Rechtsgechichte* 3 (2016): 624–37; Walter Pohl, "Leges Langobardorum," *Reallexicon Germanischen Altertumskunde* 18 (2001): 208–13.

23 Walter Pohl, "Memory, Identity and Power in Lombard Italy," in *The Uses of the Past in the Early Middle Age*, ed. Yitzhak Hen and Matthew Innes (Cambridge: Cambridge University Press, 2000), 13.

cess of *Verschriftlichung* [textualization], and at the same time are evidence of the coexistence of orality and literacy, both in the field of legal institutions and with regard to forms of communication. Orality and literacy were multifariously interdependent in the charters that recorded agreements made publicly and orally: they could be both dictated to the writer and read out to the participants once they had been written down. An example from the field of legal institutions is provided by the charter written by Firmus, which mentions the symbolic dispensation of a *launegild* in order to confirm the actor's transaction.[24]

In a *charta dotis* issued in Lucca in 720 Pertuald, *vir devotus*, married to Sunderarda,[25] grants to the church of San Michele Arcangelo various possessions.[26] From the beginning of the eighth century there was a growth in the number of private foundations in Tuscany, and Pertuald was himself the founder of the church of St. Michele located near the walls of the town:[27]

> Idcirco ego Pertuald vir devotus offero Deo et tibi ecclesie Beati Sancti arcangeli Michaeli, quem a fundamentis fabricis vestibulis in honore Christi Domini constitui prope domus cellula mea ubi cummanire videor, quam et ad eius monasterium, id est: curte cum fundamento ubi ipse ecclesia vel monasterio sitas sunt per loca designate, fini fossato da occasum solis, finis puteo antique et strata publica.
>
> [For this reason, I, Pertuald, vir devotus, offer to God and to the church of Saint Michael the Archangel, which I founded in honor of Christ the Lord next to my own house where I reside, and also to its monastery: a paved courtyard where church and monastery are located, for which des-

---

24 Giovanna Nicolaj, "Fratture e continuità nella documentazione fra tardo antico e alto medioevo. Preliminari di diplomatica e questioni di metodo," in *Morfologie sociali e culturali in Europa fra tarda antichità e alto medioevo, Settimane di studio del Centro italiano di studi sull' alto medioevo* 45, ed. CISAM (Spoleto: CISAM, 1998). For more on *launegild*, and later activities of Lombard notaries, see Sonia Colafrancesco's contribution in this volume, "Juridical Dualism in Medieval Southern Italy: Studies on the *Codex Diplomaticus Cavensis*," Chapter 10.

25 So Hans-Martin Schwarzmaier, *Lucca und das Reich bis zum Ende des 11. Jahrhunderts* (Tübingen: Niemeyer, 1972), 79.

26 Marco Stoffella, "Crisi e trasformazioni delle élites nella Toscana nord-occidentale nel secolo VIII: esempi a confronto," *Reti Medievali Rivista* 8 (2007): 1–49.

27 Roberto Farinelli, "Churches and Social Elites in Early Medieval Tuscany: A Quantitative-Statistical Approach to the Episcopal Archive of Lucca," in *Churches and Social Power in Early Medieval Europe. Integrating Archaeological and Historical Approaches*, ed. Josè C. Sánchez-Pardo and Michael G. Shapland (Turnhout: Brepols, 2015).

ignated area a ditch acts as boundary, and across the ditch to the west the boundary is an old well and the public road].[28]

In the same charter, Pertuald is named not only as a *vir devotus*, but also a *vir magnificus*, an appellation that reflects his proximity to the Royal Court. This fact is confirmed by the reference to a plot of land (*terra ad Arina*) that was granted to him by the king: "qui mihi a regia potestate concessa est," [which was granted to me from the king].[29]

The *charta* throws some light on the extent of the land owned by and the political power of Pertuald and his family: that is, the grant consists of ten small estates (*casae massaricie*). Pertuald adds to this donation of property the *decima* both from the produce of several pieces of land "decimas de vinea et olibas quemquem hauire videor ad Sancto Pancrazio" and from the new born livestock "et de gregis equorum, armentorum, ouium seu porcorum." The land and jurisdiction of the church of San Michele were so extensive and vast that they would have been sufficient to make a family rich. Moreover, one can assume that Pertuald's generous donation to his church represented only a part of his possessions.

The appurtenance clauses of Pertuald's charter not only account for his wealth; they also give a lively description of the properties and of his tenants, and contain place and personal names of significance.[30] The historical significance of the Italian *chartae* is also due to the textual specificity of these sources. Due to their specific content, private documents contain a good number of place and personal names. Originally private documents, those not recorded as copies are especially tied to the place where they originated. Most of the *massari* bear names with an -l ending, like Maurello, Barinchulo, Pettulo, a feature typical of personal names in the lower social classes in Tuscany.[31]

---

28 No. 28, Schiapparelli, CDL 1.

29 Luca Bertini, *Peredeus vescovo di Lucca* (Pisa: Pacini, 1973), 5.

30 Wolfgang Haubrichs, "Amalgamierung und Identität. Langobardische Personennamen in Mythos und Herrschaft," in *Die Langobarden: Herrschaft und Identität*, ed. Walter Pohl and Peter Erhart (Vienna: Verlag der Österreichischen Akademie der Wissenschaften, 2005); Wolfgang Haubrichs, "Langobardic Personal Names: Given Names and Name-Giving among the Langobards," in *The Lombards Before the Frankish Conquest: An Ethnographic Perspective*, ed. Giorgio Ausenda (Woodbridge, UK: Boydell & Brewer, 2009); Wolfgang Haubrichs, "Sprache und Schriftlichkeit im langobardischen Italien. Das Zeugnis von Namen, Wörtern und Entlehnungen. Ein Kommentar zu Nicholas Everett 'Literacy in Lombard Italy'," *Filologia Germanica* 2 (2010): 133–202.

31 Daniela Fruscione, "Wo waren die Langobarden in den italienischen Urkunden? Identität, Verwandtshaft und Namengebung," *Namenkundliche Informationen* 103/104 (2014): 76–84.

The *chartae* also have the odd feature of being a kind of memory, which is not only related to high officials and the church, and in addition to the personal names of the elite who had a need for institutionalized memory, they also list those of the middle classes, of the small owners. Indeed, there are even several names from the lower social classes and with the unfree emerging as the objects of transactions. Furthermore, frequently data about offices and activities is also to be found in the *chartae*.

The charter appointed by Pertuald deserves the definition of "carta di famiglia" in a very broad way: the charter preserves the memory of Pertuald's transactions for his family and the generations to follow.[32] Moreover, several members of Pertuald's family appear as agents in the production of this impressive document. Pertuald's brother-in-law, Petroni, dictates the provisions of the grant to his own son, Pertuald's nephew, Petrus.[33] As a writer, Petrus does not emerge in the charter: neither his writing (the surviving charter is a copy of the original, written later on in the eighth century, made by a well attested and established *notar* from Lucca, Osprand),[34] nor his technical skills as a *notarius* (the text is dictated by his father) reveal his personality. Petrus is simply an occasional "family writer": "Quam dotalii et monusculi me cartulam Petro nepoti meo, dictante genitore suo Petroni" [Petrus my nephew writes this charter dictated by his father Petroni].[35] Orality here takes the form of a dictation and the complementarity of the oral narrative and the writing is clearly expressed in the charter.

Moreover, in addition to the other members of the Lucchese aristocracy, Pertuald's closest relatives are also among the witnesses: the *charta* is subscribed with a *signum manus* by his sons Sundipert and Peredeus. The participation of Pertuald's relatives in the making of his *charta dotis* informs us of the names of his family members and the relationships among them. Variations on and repetitions of names can be found throughout Pertuald's family genealogy and, above all, alliteration is widely used.[36]

32 Giangiacomo Fissore, "Segni di identità e forme di autenticazione nelle carte notarili altomedievali, fra interpretazione del ruolo e rappresentazione della forma documentaria," in *Comunicare e significare nell' alto medioevo* I, ed. CISAM (Spoleto: CISAM, 2005).

33 On the participation of the author's relatives and friends to the making of the charters see Antonella Ghignoli, "Istituzioni ecclesiastiche e documentazione nei secoli VIII–XI. Appunti per una prospettiva," *Archivio storico italiano* 162 (2004): 624.

34 Anne Mailloux, "L' émergence du notariat à Lucques (VIIIe–Xe siècle). Normes et pratiques d' un corps professionnel," in *Le notaire. Entre métier et espace public en Europe VIIIe–XVIIIe siècle* (Aix en Provence: Publication de l' université de Provence, 2008), 21.

35 No. 28, Schiapparelli, *CDL* 1.

36 Nicoletta Francovich Onesti, *Vestigia Longobarde in Italia (568–774). Lessico e antroponimia* (Rome: Artemide, 2013), 231.

The recognition of and respect for this Lombardian tradition of name-giving can be considered a form of identification within a population group. The value of language and names as signs of identity within a *gens* is the focus of many articles written by Wolfgang Haubrichs.[37] Moreover, in the course of the eighth century the pragmatic and flexible use of this tradition of name-giving, which includes Latin names and focuses on certain sounds, stands as a sign of self-confidence and identity within a family and a social group. In fact, the phonetic identity of this genealogy, rich in voiceless plosives /p/, was also supplemented with the use of non-Lombardic names like Petrus.[38] A Latin-ecclesiastical identity emerges in the name of the "family-scribe", Pertuald's nephew Petrus, who also bears the name of his father, Petroni. The clerical vocation of this family already existed in its onomastic chromosomes.

Moreover, this flexible Germanic form of giving names with a phonetic connection among relatives and across generations created a sense of continuity. In the family of Pertuald, continuity was not only a phonetic device: this continuity of name-giving also corresponded with the possessions and the offices held by this leading family of Lucca.

The family represented in the *charta dotis* written in Lucca in 720 belonged to the Lombard landowning aristocracy and established itself in the Church: Pertuald founded a church,[39] he granted it generous donations and, some thirty-five years later, his son Peredeus became a bishop. This is not limited to the life of Peredeus; several generations after him, in the year 867, a certain Teudilascius, himself the son of another Peredeus, was bishop in Luni, itself an area in which the family had owned land for generations. Even throughout Frankish times, member of this family remained in possession of their rights, and in the first generation following the takeover of the Lombards by the Franks they had already gained new honors.[40]

Peredeus was Bishop of Lucca from 755 up to the Frankish conquest in 774.[41] Indeed, Pertuald had already anticipated such an outcome for his descendants

37 The value of language and names as signs of identity within a *gens* is the focus of many articles written by Wolfgang Haubrichs, for instance: "Amalgamierung und Identität" and "Langobardic Personal Names." On the question of the relationship between ethnic identity and the choice of personal names in the Early Middle Ages see Jörg Jarnut, *Prosopographische und sozialgeschichtliche Studien zum Langobardenreich in Italien (568–774)* (Bonn: Röhrscheid, 1972).

38 Fruscione, "Wo waren die Langobarden in den italienischen Urkunden?," 80.

39 Paolo Delogu, "Devozione longobarda," in *Italy and Early Medieval Europe: Papers for Chris Wickham*, ed. Ross Balzaretti, Julia Barrow and Patricia Skinner (Oxford: University Press, 2018), 457–58.

40 Schwarzmaier, *Lucca und das Reich*, 85.

41 Bertini, *Peredeus vescovo*.

in his charter, and he does not exclude the possibility that one of his sons might start an ecclesiastical carrier: "et si quis de filiis meis in ipso sancto loco Deo seruire uolueret, regulariter agere nulla ei sit contradictio ..." [And if one of my sons should like to serve in this holy place, he can do so because there are no conflicts of interests].[42] Pertuald's charter is not bare routine and descriptive; rather it is narrative, and as such is subject to strategic manipulation. Even if there is no direct causal connection between the founding of a church and, later, getting the bishopric, in the particular case of Peredeus we can state that he received the bishopric because his father Pertuald had created the conditions and the narrative for this thirty-five years before. Considering that the five bishops of Lucca between 713 and 818 were all from the local landowning elite, Pertuald's foundation of a church just outside the town walls and the extremely generous donation to the same institution shows that Pertuald was not only imagining an ecclesiastical future for one of his children but may even have had some bigger plans.[43] While not being of ducal rank, unlike his predecessor Bishop Walprand, son of Walpert, who had been a city duke, Peredeus was instead granted a strong clerical identity via his father Pertuald.[44]

In 720 Peredeus subscribes the donation with a *signum manus*. Forty years later he is established as bishop and has himself become literate—as shown by a *notitia* of May 15, 761, in which he appears as a literate subscriber.[45] We do not know if Peredeus could actually write in 720, as the *signum manus* was not itself indicative of literacy.[46] He may even have still been a child at that time and only capable of the signature, which would mean that not all the witnessing signatures were those of adults.[47]

The participation of Pertuald's relatives in the documentation of a transaction which granted wealth to the "family church" represents the cohesion and the established power of the family of the bishop to be. The charter shows also that the local town churches in Lucca were unifying and dynamic centers for the fortunes of the most eminent family groups. The documentary and archival

42 No. 28, Schiapparelli, *CDL* 1.

43 Farinelli, "Churches and Social Elites," 161.

44 On the political reasons for Peredeus' election see Stoffella, "Crisi e trasformazioni," 13–15.

45 No. 154, Schiapparelli, *CDL* 2.

46 See Antonella Ghignoli and François Bougard, "Elementi romani nei documenti longobardi?," in *L'héritage byzantin en Italie* (*VIIIe–XIIe siècle*). *I. La fabrique documentaire. Études réunies par Jean-Marie Martin*, Collection de l'École française de Rome 449, ed. Annick Peters-Custot and Vivien Prigent (Rome: École Française de Rome, 2011), 267, n. 86.

47 Paola Supino Martini, "Le sottoscrizioni testimoniali lucchesi al documento italiano del secolo VIII: le carte di Lucca," *Bollettino dell'Istituto storico italiano per il medioevo e Archivio muratoriano* 98 (1992): 87–108.

practices of churches and monasteries were influenced by those of the laypeople with whom they were intimately connected.

Wickham considers Peredeo's family to be one of the "seven absolutely richest" documented landowners before 774. A similar picture is offered by the family of the previous bishop Walprand (737–54), whose father Walpert was not only a rich landowner but also of ducal rank. And, in general, the five bishops of Lucca between 713 and 818 were all from the local landowning elite.[48]

Peredeus's role in the promotion and consolidation of documentary writing was relevant to his time. As Lucca is by far the best documented city in Italy,[49] Peredeus is, indeed, the most documented bishop. His name appears in more than fifty charters containing various types of records and transactions: sometimes he is simply referred to as the bishop of Lucca,[50] but most often he acts as an agent in different types of *chartae*. In the documents he appears as a shrewd and powerful administrator, both of the properties of the church of Lucca—as Christian gift-giving to the Church increased, episcopal office could mean the control of substantial estates—and of his own many possessions.[51]

Some of the charters are tenancy agreements that can assume a variety of forms and may or may not include a census.[52] Some of these kinds of transaction were written by a writer called Fratellus, who was probably a pupil of Osprand. He was very skilled in drawing up leases for bishop Peredeus: he did not enforce his own orthography and grammar on what he wrote, but was able to accommodate the formulaic pattern to suit different individual cases and requirements.[53] Moreover, some of the agreements give evidence of exercises of power: so, for instance, a group of documents written after 760, when Bishop Peredeus re-founded the church of St. Colombano.

Between 760 and 774—the year of Peredeus' exile to Francia, immediately after the Carolingian conquest of Italy—the church of St. Colombano was

48 Wickham, *Framing the Early Middle Ages*, 214, n. 16.

49 Francesco Magistrale, "Le pergamene dell' Archivio Arcivescovile di Lucca (secoli VIII–IX): l'esperienza delle "chartae latinae antiquiores"," in *Il patrimonio documentario della chiesa di Lucca. Prospettive di ricerca*, Atti del Convegno Internazionale di Studi, Lucca, 14–15 novembre 2008, ed. Sergio Pagano Pierantonio Piatti (Florence: Edizioni del Galluzzo, 2010).

50 So, for instance, No. 115, Schiapparelli, *CDL* 1.

51 Bertini, *Peredeus vescovo*, 18–19.

52 Delogu, "Devozione longobarda," 458–59.

53 For instance, Nos. 139, 166–67, Schiapparelli, *CDL* 2. On this writer, Giovanna Nicolaj, "*Chartae Latinae Antiquiores*" 32, ed. Jan Olaf Tjäder and Armando Petrucci (Graz: Urs-Graf Verlag, 1985), 77; See also Everett, *Literacy in Lombard Italy*, 226.

granted several donations in the form of estates.[54] The granters, who often retained the usufruct of the properties, were individuals living in an area where Peredeus' family had a particular prominence. These donations were gifts made by clients of Peredeus' family who desired to benefit from their good relationship with Peredeus himself.[55] It became a trend, with the developing power of churches, that new forms of agreement were established through which individuals were permitted the use of land but ultimately had to give over the titles to the churches. This is indicative of the uncertainty about the future and the need for assistance and protection.

The abundance of charters Peredeus enacts, both as bishop—he acts as judge[56] and he is recipient of several pledges[57] and as owner,[58] attests to the importance he ascribed to written documentation as a medium for representing his rank. The organic link between the Lombard elite and the bishop was reinforced by the role of the notary within the town of Lucca. Very often the notaries with ecclesiastical functions within the episcopal curia drafted or copied charters which involved a donation to the Church.[59]

An attention to clerical identity can also be seen in the case of Osprand, a writer identified as a *subdiaconus* between 752 and 758, and then called *diaconus* from 758 to 770, who wrote several *chartae dotis* in favour of the Church of Lucca.[60] He also produced several copies of older donations: it is significant that one of them is Pertuald's charter, the first document that bears witness to the ecclesiastical vocation of Bishop Peredeus's powerful family. It is possible that a copy written by him, a "star" clerical writer—was seen as more appropriate than the original written by the unknown Petrus. Osprand was trained to write charters at the cathedral school in Lucca. Not only was his formal writing competence very good, he also had the skill to manipulate formulaic language in favor of his client and the exigencies of the transaction.

While we still have records of a large amount of transactions related to the land and goods that Peredeus owned or controlled, we only have the one charter issued by his father Pertuald. However, it is an assumption that the *charta dotis* in favor of the church of San Michele was the only charter produced by such an impressive possessor of land and power as Peredeus's father: indeed,

54 For instance, Nos. 219, 276, Schiapparelli, *CDL* 2.
55 Wickham, *Framing the Early Middle Ages*, 166.
56 No. 182, Schiapparelli, *CDL* 2.
57 For instance, Nos. 147, 176, Schiapparelli, *CDL* 2.
58 In No. 139, for instance, he is the recipient of a pledge, and in No. 149 he is an exchanger, Schiapparelli, *CDL* 2.
59 Mailloux, "Émergence du notariat," 13–27.
60 Nos. 170, 173, 175, 176, and 179, Schiapparelli, *CDL* 2.

Pertuald's land holding extended far beyond the Lucchese area and into the southern part of Tuscany (Val di Cornia, Cecina, Roselle).[61] This allows a reflection on the potential that material had not survived.[62]

Furthermore, we know that Pertuald divided his patrimony between his two children, Peredeus and Sundipert. So it is remarkable to discover that the latter is only mentioned in two *notitiae*, issued after his death by his own son Sunderad (761)[63] and by his brother, bishop Peredeus (762),[64] confirming previous transactions and identifying Sundipert as a rich landowner. Sunderad also disappears altogether as an agent of transaction, after the above mentioned *notitia*.[65]

Other family members acting in the *charta* of 720 disappear from our records: neither Peredeus's uncle Petroni nor his cousin Petrus are mentioned again. Indeed, there are no traces left even of Petrus, the cousin who was *litteratus* and who wrote the family charter. The charter issued by Peredeus's father, the eminent *vir magnificus* Pertuald, and written originally by Petrus, has arrived to us as a copy; this prevents us from contrasting/comparing his writing with that of other writers called Petrus active in the Lucchesia in the same period. As they were distinct from the ecclesiastical members of Peredeus's family, the lay members must also have possessed their own charters, but scarcely any of them have survived.[66]

This consideration is a reminder that charters issued and kept by an ecclesiastical institution were more likely to survive over the course of time. One reason why documents survived in the hands of ecclesiastical institutions is that those institutions did not undergo the kinds of changes that led to the dispersal of lay patrimonies and the documents associated with them.[67] The capacities of the church, not only for producing but also in keeping charters, has given consistency and continuity to the properties of the church and to

61 Bertini, *Peredeus vescovo*, 5.

62 Zielinski, "Charta der Langobarden," 53.

63 No. 154, Schiapparelli, *CDL* 2.

64 No. 161 (I, II, III), Schiapparelli, *CDL* 2.

65 He also subscribes as a witness in a *charta offersionis* (768) that granted a donation to the church of St. Colombano, No. 221, Schiapparelli, *CDL* 2.

66 Probably only a fifth of the charters drafted in Lucca in the Early Middle Ages have survived: see, Schwarzmaier, *Lucca und das Reich*, cit. by Anne Mailloux, "Modalité de constitution du patrimoine épiscopal de Lucques, VIIIe–Xe siècle," *Mélanges de l'École française de Rome* 111 (1999): 701.

67 Marios Costambeys, "The Laity, the Clergy, the Scribes and their Archives: The Documentary Record of Eighth- and Ninth-Century Italy," in *Documentary Culture and the Laity in the Early Middle Ages*, ed. Warren Brown et al. (Cambridge: Cambridge University Press, 2013), 254.

the members of the ecclesiastical community. Only the Lombard charters that were preserved in a monastery or in bishopric church funds from if not the beginning then soon after their production, have passed the test of preservation. Moreover, in the Carolingian period, they also had to represent some current interest for the new archive holders.[68]

Lay archives did not benefit from the same level of institutional continuity as religious institutions, and had a lower chance of being preserved. However, the several surviving charters issued by laymen also show that lay society believed in the stability provided by written records. See, for instance, the archive belonging to the Lombard official Alahis, *vir magnificus*. He produced around fifty charters, a dozen of which were royal diplomas of Liutprand. We know about his archive because it was preserved by the nun Ghittia, probably a relative, and then later by the bishop of Pisa.[69]

A lay document,[70] in which neither party carries an explicit clerical designation and that only survived because it was of interest to the ecclesiastical institution (the monastery of Monte Amiata) that absorbed it, is the one written by Firmus *notarius* in Brioni, a place near Turin,[71] who in 770 brought a difficult case before the king. The desire for irrevocability is a salient feature of his charter. The *charta donationis* issued by Audipert has a thematic continuity and common protagonists with another charter written in Chiusi in 763,[72] a *charta venditionis* that provides evidence for the sale of a woman, Boniperga,[73] and her son to the brothers Baroncello and Audipert:

---

68 Ghignoli and Bougard, "Elementi romani nei documenti longobardi?," 263. A similar point is argued by Mailloux, "Modalité de constitution du patrimoine épiscopal," 701 n. 4: "Le fonds de Lucques, en effet, n' a pas connu de dégradations ou de destructions accidentelles majeures: les documents détruits ne l' ont donc pas été fortuitement. Il s' agit souvent de pièces devenues inutiles juridiquement. On peut en conclure qu' il existe une distorsion de l' information disponible: les actes conservés sont surtout représentatifs des pratiques patrimoniales de l' évêché et de l' organisation de son domaine."

69 See Wickham, *Framing the Early Middle Ages*, 179; Costambeys, "The Laity, the Clergy, the Scribes and their Archives," 239.

70 Costambeys, "The Laity, the Clergy, the Scribes and their Archives," 238.

71 Tjäder does not agree with Kurze's suggestion. He leans towards a place near Chiusi, *Chartae Latinae Antiquiores* XXIII, 67.

72 No. 174, Schiapparelli, *CDL* 2; No. 11, Schiapparelli, CDA 1. On the private charters written in Chiusi see Fruscione, "Documenti Longobardi di Chiusi."

73 Nicoletta Francovich Onesti, "L' incontro fra le culture latina e germanica nell'Italia longobarda," in *Akkulturation. Probleme einer germanisch-romanischen Kultursynthese in Spätantike und frühem Mittelalter*, ed. Dieter Hägermann, Wolfgang Haubrichs and Jörg Jarnut (Berlin: De Gruyter, 2004).

> Constat me praenominatus Candidus vinditor vindedisse et vindedimus vobis Audepert et Baroncello, germanis aemptoribus, vindedisse et vindedimus vobis muliere una nomine Boniperga, qui Teudirada, una cum infantulo suo parvulo.
>
> [I, Candidus, the seller, agree to sell to you, the buyers Audepert and Baroncello, a woman named Boniperga, also called Teudirada, with her small son].

The Brioni charter confirms that Baroncello had made the slave Boniperga his companion, had had two children with her and died.[74] The uncle of the two children, Audipert, thinking about his own death, wished to transfer his goods "tam in casis quam vineis, pratjs, pascuis, silvis, movilia et inmovilia," [both in houses and vines, fields, pastures, forests, movable and immovable properties] to his beloved nephews. But this was not as simple as it might seem: between the generous love of Audipert and the transfer of goods stood the *lex*.[75]

The first obstacle: Baroncello had not freed Boniperga when he married her.[76] Therefore she was not *wirdibora*, a "free woman"—literally a "bearer of dignity."[77] According to the *Edictus Rothari* a free man could emancipate a slave whom he intended to marry.[78]

> De ancilla matrimonii gratia. Si quis ancillam suam propriam matrimoniare voluerit sibi ad uxorem, sit ei licentiam; tamen debeat eam libera thingare, sic libera, quod est wirdibora, et legetimam facere per gairethinx.

---

74 Marco Stoffella, "Donne e famiglia nella Toscana occidentale (VIII e IX secolo)," *Genesis. Rivista della società italiana delle storiche* IX/1 (2010): 100.

75 On the relation between the charters and the law, see Fruscione, "Documenti longobardi", and Azzara, "Nozze di Anstruda," 223–36. For an edition of the Lombard laws Claudio Azzara and Stefano Gasparri, eds., *Le leggi dei Longobardi. Storia, memoria e diritto di un popolo germanico*, with introduction, translation and comments (Rome: Viella, 2005). On this also Rémi Oulion, *Scribes et notaires face à la norme dans la Toscane du haut Moyen Âge (VII–XI siècle)* (Clermont-Ferrand: Institute Universitaire Varenne, 2013); Dilcher, "Langobardisches Recht," 624–37; Pohl, "Leges Langobardorum," 208–13.

76 Giulia Rainis, "Per la storia della schiavitù femminile nell' Italia longobarda. Prassi contrattuale e quadri legislativi," *Studi Medievali* 48 (2007): 723–24.

77 Francovich Onesti, *Vestigia longobarde*, 133; Florus van der Rhee, *Die germanischen Wörter in den langobardischen Gesetzen* (Rotterdam: Bronder, 1970), 141–43.

78 Rothari, No. 222, Bluhme, *Edictus Langobardorum*, 54, translation adapted from Katherine Fischer-Drew, trans., *The Lombard Laws* (Cinnaminson, NJ: University of Pennsylvania Press, 1996), 95.

> Tunc intellegatur libera et legetima uxor, et filii, qui ex ea nati fuerint, legetimi heredes patri efficiantur.
>
> [If a man wishes to marry his own woman slave, he may do so. Nevertheless he ought to free her, that is, make her *wirdibora*, and he ought to do it legally by *gairethinx*. She shall then be known as a free and legal wife and her children may become the legal heirs of their father]

As Baroncello had not set Boniperga free, his sons, as a consequence, were not free and could not be considered *legitimi* heirs, but *naturalis*.[79]

Firmus wrote the charter in response to this problematic situation. Since Baroncello's children could not be regarded as legitimate heirs, the transfer of property could only take place by means of a *donatio*. But this would still not be considered legal. In the charter under consideration, the gift, the *donatio*, is bound by various clauses. In particular, two important provisions were required in order to make the *donatio* valid and to secure the position of the "*amantissimi*" nephews.

First, it was necessary for Audipert to state that he had no children: "[...] et neque filius aut filia non abuero, in omnibus vos mihi succidatis [...]" [and if I will not have sons or daughters you will inherit everything]. The *donatio* in favour of his nephews, Bonipertulo and Leopert, would not have been effective in the case that he did have children. In fact, in order to preserve the family goods, donations were traditionally forbidden.[80] As, for instance, we read in Rothari, No. 168 about *De exhereditatione filiorum*. Moreover Rothari, No. 154 allowed natural children to become heirs.

But this was still not enough. Firmus knew that in order to make the *donatio* irrevocable, a further formality was needed: the donees had to dispense

---

79 So in Liutprand, No. 106: "Si quis aldiana alienam aut suam ad oxorem tollere voluerit, faciat eam wirdibora, sicut edictus contenit de ancillam. Nam qui sine ipsa ordinatione eam quasi oxorem habuerit, chartae filii, qui ex ea nati fuerent, non sint legetimi, sed naturalis." [If a man wishes to marry his own aldia or that of another man, he should make her wirdibora, just as the edict decrees concerning a woman slave. But if he marries her without this procedure, her children are not legitimate but natural born], Bluhme, *Edictus Langobardorum*, 151, translation adapted from Fischer-Drew, *Lombard Laws*, 190.

80 On this: Pierluigi Falaschi, "La successione volontaria nella legislazione longobarda," in *Annali della Facoltà giuridica dell'Università di Camerino, Studi in memoria di P. Rasi Caldogno* (Milan: Giuffrè, 1969); Giorgio Vismara, *Storia dei patti successori* (Milan: Giuffrè, 1941; repr., 1986); Walter Ogris, "Schenkung," *Handwörterbuch der deutschen Rechtsgeschichte*, 4 (1990): 1382–84; Franz Dorn, "Schenkung," *Reallexicon Germanischen Altertumskunde* 26 (2004): 623–41.

a *launegild* in return for the donation. But here there was another obstacle. Audipert's unfree nephews could indeed receive a gift, but they could not actively enter into the transactions which were legally necessary for the receipt of the gift. On behalf of his nephews, Audipert was given a gold ring from a certain Aduald as *launechild* to perform the necessary duties for his nephews to inherit:

> Et ut plus magis in vos in ista donatjo firmam persistat, suscipi in persuna vestra launechild ad Aduald anulo aureo uno, ut diximus, in vestra persuna, nam non in persuna Aduald
>
> [Moreover, in order to make this grant more firm, I will receive on your behalf, as launechild, one gold ring from Aduald].

Firmus' *charta donationis* is also an example of the correct application of Rothari No. 175:[81]

> De launegild. Si quis rem suam cuicumque donaverit et postea, qui donavit, launegild requisiverit, tunc ille, qui accepit, aut heredes eius, si ausus non fuerit iurare, quod conpositum sit, reddat ei ferquido, id est similem, quales in illa diae fuit, quando donatum est; et si iuraverit, sit exsolutus.
>
> [On reciprocal gifts. If a man gives his property to someone else and afterwards he who made the gift seeks a reciprocal gift in return, and if he or his heirs cannot swear that a gift in return had been provided, then he or his heirs, shall return the gift singlefold (ferquido), that is to the same amount as on the day it was given. But if he does so swear, he shall be absolved].

And Liutprand, No. 73,[82] which provides for the donation of a symbolic *launegild*.

> De donatione quae sine launegild aut sine thingatione facta est, menime stare deveat. Quiate sic specialiter in edictum non fuit institutum, tamen usque modo sic est iudicatum: ideo pro errore tollendum hoc scribere

81 Rothari, No. 175, Bluhme, *Edictus Langobardorum*, 41, translation adapted from Fischer-Drew, *Lombard Laws*, 83.

82 Liutprand No. 73, Bluhme, *Edictus Langobardorum*, 137, translation adapted from Fischer-Drew, *Lombard Laws*, 175.

in edicti paginam iussimus. Et qui fuerit propinquus parens, ipse succidat, et si ille supraestis fuerit, qui ipsam donationem sine launigild dedit, possiteam a se recollegere. Excepto si in ecclesiam aut in loca sanctorum aut in exeneodochio pro anima sua aliquit quiscumque donaverit, stabile deveat permanere, quia in loga sanctorum aut in exeneodochio nec thinx nec launegild inpedire devit, eo quod pro anima factum est.

[Gift which are made without a return gift or without the formal alienation procedure ought not to be considered lawful at all. Although this heretofore has not been specifically established in the law, it is nevertheless judged lawful now: therefore to make this matter clear, we have ordered this provision to be recorded in the edict. The nearest relative shall succeed, unless the person who first gave the gift still lives, in which case he may receive the return gift for himself. Except in the case where anyone has given a gift to a church or to a holy place or to a hospital for the good of his soul, then it ought to remain firm and neither alienation nor the return gift ought to interfere since gifts to holy places or to hospitals are made for the good of one's soul]

Only when this formality was observed was the gift irrevocably valid. The term launechild/launegild is an almost tautological compound, formed by the Germanic nouns *launa- "prize" and * gelda- "payment, gift."[83] While the laws do not mention what the *launegild* would actually be, the opposite is true in the charters, where the *launegild* is no longer an abstract concept and can be any common object (a piece of cloth, a garment). However, as Anton Val de Lièvre 1877 showed in his work on *launegild,* that such an expensive item as a gold ring was not at all exceptional.[84] The sources show that the *launegild* was not a stereotypical item. The choice of the item was a matter for the parties and they were limited by neither law nor custom. The conditions of each specific case, the scope of the business and the wealth of the people involved were certainly of no small influence when determining what the *launegild* would be. Here one can only suppose that such an expensive item was deemed appropriate to confirm the complex transaction. Moreover, the item chosen as a countergift

83 Rhee, *Die germanischen Wörter*, 94–96; Maria Vòllono, "Methodik und Probleme bei der Erfoschung des Langobardischen am Beispiel einiger juristischer Fachbegriffe: mundoald, launegild, sculdhais," in *Die Langobarden. Herrschaft und Identität*, ed. Walter Pohl and Peter Ehrhart (Vienna: Verlag der österreichischen Akademie der Wissenschaften, 2005).

84 Anton Val de Lièvre, *Launegild und Wadia: eine Studie aus dem langobardischen Rechte* (Innsbruck: Wagner, 1877), 15.

demonstrated the traditional character of Audipert's donation: the significance of gold in the form of rings and in the exchange of gifts, and as a symbol of the commitment between donor and beneficiary, is well known from various Germanic sources.[85] In Old English poetry the lord is called *béaggifa* [he who donates rings], while in the Hildebrandslied, one of the oldest poem in a Germanic language and which surely experienced Lombard influence, Hildebrand tries to offer his son—against whom he is forced to fight—the gold rings he carries on his arm.[86]

Firmus proficient application of the law cannot obscure an important fact: according to the written law, Audipert's nephews could not actively enter into a transaction because they were not free. The important point here is the attempt made in the charter written by Firmus to legitimize a transaction that was outside the precept of written law.[87] Only the private agreement between Audipert and Aduald, who gives him the gold ring on behalf of Bonipertulo and Leopert, makes it possible for the nephews to inherit. The writing down of the private agreement serves here to change the state of things and to circumvent the severe regulations that the Lombard laws had imposed on certain interpersonal transactions between persons of different social status.

In order to secure the position of his nephews, Audipert also arranged that, after his death, they would belong to the monastery of St. Salvatore of Monte Amiata, together with their goods.

Finally, the charter shows that Audipert's concern was not only for the welfare of his nephews; he also arranged that, for the salvation of his own soul, every year they would give a gold coin or the equivalent in wax, oil or in another form to the church of St. Salvatore:

> […] ut per singolos annos persolvere dibeatjs pro anima mea in ecclesia sancti Salbaturi in Amiate, quem bone memorie Erfo abbas a fundamenta edificavet, per quem abueritjs, reddatjs in ipsa ecclesia vel ad eius rectores in auro solido uno, aut per auro aut per cira vel per oleo.
>
> [[…]and every year you must, for my soul, donate to the church of St. Salvatore in Amiata, built by abbot Erfo, or to its rectors one golden coin, or its equivalent value either in gold, in wax or in oil].

85 Heiko Steuer, "Ringgeld: Archeologisches," *Reallexicon Germanischen Altertumskunde* 25 (2003): 16–18; Heinrich Beck, "Ringgeld: Philologisches," *Reallexicon Germanischen Altertumskunde* 25 (2003): 18–19.

86 Rosemarie Lühr, *Studien zur Sprache des Hildebrandslied* (Frankfurt: Peter Lang, 1977).

87 Vallerani, "Scritture e schemi," 102.

Here the life story of the minor land-owner Audipert and of his nephews intersects with "history" and enriches it. By noting that St. Salvatore was founded by Erfo, Audipert's *charta* helps to identify the founder of this important monastery and, indirectly, its foundation year. Audipert's charter is linked to a document written in Friuli in 762 where Erfo's monastery is cited.[88]

With his skillful proficiency in the law, Firmus created an obstacle against any later attempts to deprive Audipert's nephews of their uncle's donation. The charter therefore also suggests Audipert's need for security, projected into the generation of his nephews. In the *charta* this need is expressed by a word that appears three times in the document written by Firmus (and over and over again in other Lombard documents): *firmitas*.[89] As an uncle, Audipert is *donaturis et firmaturis*, the donation is granted and made secure both by writing the document (*concidimus et firmamus dono*) and by respecting certain ritual formalities: "Et ut plus magis in vos in ista donatio firmam persistat, suscipi in persuna vestra launechild," [And moreover, in order to make this donation more firm I receive from you a launechild].

In this *charta*, Firmus exhibits a deep knowledge of the *lex*. He uses the law as a barrier against possible assaults by external parties—other relatives who may assert rights or claims to the estates. But this would still not be enough, and he also has to integrate his precise knowledge of the written law with new contractual solutions.

The charter shows that in order to anticipate a potential area of dispute the literal application of the law was insufficient: It was possible to draw up typologies of acts that allowed the circumvention of the law, by adopting contractual solutions which were clearly *contra legem* but which met with the agreement of both parties.

Firmus behaviour as a *notarius* corresponds to Liutprand's precept: in 726, when the production of documents was increasing significantly, Liutprand promptly adapted his legislation to suit the new situation with the chapter "*de Scrivis*" [In the case of scribes] (No. 91):

> De scrivis hoc prospeximus, ut qui cartulas scribent, sive ad legem langobardorum, quoniam apertissima et pene omnibus nota est, sive ad romanorum, non aliter faciat, nisi quomodo in ipsis legibus contenetur; nam contra legem langobardorum aut romanorum non scribant. Quod si non sciunt, interrogent alteros, et si non potuerent ipsas legis pleniter

88 Fruscione, "Documenti longobardi di Chiusi," 96.

89 On *firmitas*, see Maurizio Lupoi, The *Origins of the European Legal Order* (Cambridge: Cambridge University Press, 2000), 438–57.

> scire, non scribant ipsas cartolas. Et qui aliter facere presumpserit, conponat wirgild suum; excepto si aliquid inter conlibertus convenerit: ut si quiscumque de lege sua subdiscendere voluerit et pactionis aut conveentias inter se facerent, et ambe partis consenserent, isto non inpotetur contra legem, quia ambe partis volontariae faciunt: et illi, qui tales cartolas scribent, culpavelis non inveniantur esse.
>
> [In the case of scribes, we decree that those who prepare charters should write them either according to the law of the Lombards—which is well known and open to all—or according to that of the Romans; they shall not do otherwise than is contained in these laws and they shall not write contrary to the law of the Lombards or of the Romans. If they do not know how to do this, let them ask others, and if they should not know such laws fully, they should not write such charters. He who presumes to do otherwise shall pay his wergild as composition, except in that case where everything is agreed upon among fellow freemen. For if anyone wishes to go outside the law and make a pact or agreement among themselves, and both parties consent, this shall not be regarded as contrary to law since both parties have done it voluntarily, and those who write such charters shall not be found liable to blame].

This chapter from Liutprand, which indicates the concern of the legislator for the proper interpretation of the law in the charters, is quite remarkable for several reasons. To begin with, here the two components of the legal culture, the Roman and the Lombard, are placed side by side—the charters could be issued according to either Roman or Lombard law—which induces us to consider, or perhaps to reconsider, these ideological categories when interpreting the Early Middle Ages.

It would appear that knowledge of the law and the ability to interpret it were regarded as the basic prerequisite when writing documents. The strict adherence of Firmus' charter to the provisions of the law must be thus considered in light of Liutprand's chapter *de scrivis*. Moreover, according to Liutprand No. 91 the writers of the *chartae* were liable to be prosecuted, if their charters contradicted the wording of the law. What is noteworthy here is the fact that an offence concerning the writing of charters, inspired by Roman law could be compensated for with the old restitutive method of the *wirgild*, which came from the Lombard tradition.

Moreover, Liutprand envisages the possibility that the transaction is the result of an agreement between the parties. This spontaneous arrangement outside the *lex* confirms that in the Early Middle Ages, even in Southern Europe, legislation did not constitute a closed system and the regulation of legal issues was not limited to the written text.[90] By admitting in his own legislation the binding role of consensus between private individuals, king Liutprand circumvented the *lex*, the written pact between the king and the people. The consensus between two private parties has a strong oral connotation; charters can thus be considered in the broader issue of the transition from orality to literacy.[91] The *charta*e are monuments of a developing process of "Verschriftlichung" [textualisation] that envisages the movement of members of some social groups to literacy, beginning with different forms of communication. An example of this passage is provided by Audipert's charter, which includes the ritual confirmation of the act: indeed, in the *cartula donationis* Firmus mentions the symbolic dispensation of a *launegild* in order to confirm the transaction.[92]

A further reference to ritual in connection with written charters can also be found some eighty years before Liutprand in the *Edictus Rothari*: in the chapter on the *manumissio* of slaves it is mentioned that the freeing of a slave through the *thingatio* should be remembered in a *cartolam libertatis*.[93]

> Haec sunt quattuor genera manumissionum: Tamen necesse est propter futuri temporis memoriam, ut qualiter liberum aut liberam thingaverit, ipsa manumissio in cartolam libertatis commemoretur. Et si cartolam non fecerit, tamen libertas ei permaneat.
>
> [These are the four kinds of manumission. The possibility of future difficulty requires that the manner in which the man or woman has been freed should be recorded in a charter of freedom. If the charter has not been executed, however, the former slave's freedom remains nevertheless in effect].

90 Fruscione, "Im Spannungsfeld zwischen deutscher Rechtsgeschichte und italienischem Frühmittelalter," 30.

91 Hanna Vollrath "Gesetzgebung und Schriftlichkeit. Das Beispiel der angelsächsischen Gesetze," *Historisches Jahrbuch* 99 (1979): 28–54, Vollrath explored and introduced the theme of the limits and inconsistency of medieval law in the broader question of the transition from orality to literacy.

92 Nicolaj, "Fratture e continuità," 963–84. For more on *launegild*, see Colafrancesco "Juridical Dualism," Chapter 3 in this volume.

93 Rothari, No. 224, Bluhme, *Edictus Langobardorum*, 54–55, translation adapted from Fischer-Drew, *Lombard Laws*, 96.

From this law, which relates the writing of a charter and memory, one can deduce that in the seventh century various forms of ritual confirmation of a legal action are still given exclusive and absolute binding value. The charters themselves are merely a form of reminder and further security. Given the absence of the obligation to employ the written record, the significance of the charters in the beginning was not the normative regulation of transactions, but the fulfilment of a personal need. Charters mainly represented a desire for security; the reason for writing them was more sociological and psychological than legal in origin. Such a need not only shapes Firmus' charter, it also reveals some hidden aspects of the recorded agreements in the Lucchese area. Some of Peredeus' documents describe a not uncommon transaction: after donating or selling his property to an ecclesiastical institution, the actor of the charter receives the use of that property in exchange.[94] Though it is reasonable to ask why a free owner decided to become a tenant or a subject, even though this step meant a lowering in their social status, it is probable that a written lease agreement would have given more security than a possession based on custom: protection was worth the sale of one's own land. The Lucchese charters are not an exception to this. In the eighth century, almost all similar charters were the rental contracts enacted by the monastery of St. Salvatore, the most prominent landowner in a vast territory in the south of Tuscany.[95]

Firmus' charter clearly shows that this need for security was not only in regard to earthly life but extended also into the afterlife, which the church was extremely prompt to realize and make the best use of. Following the reception of the Christian message of salvation inherited from the patristic era, the clergy progressively established itself as the mediator in exchanges between men and God:[96] monasteries and churches received donations of land and of other property, and in return recompensed the donors with spiritual counter-gifts.[97] In the eighth century, donations with a view to redemption started expanding within

94 For instance, Nos. 140, 170, 219, 239, 276, Schiapparelli, *CDL* 2.

95 Cristina La Rocca, "La trasformazione del territorio in occidente," in *Morfologie sociali e culturali in Europa fra tarda antichità e alto medioevo*, ed. CISAM (Spoleto: CISAM, 1998), 266: "... la ripresa della documentazione scritta pare ovunque in stretta correlazione con il trasferimento delle proprietà fondiarie da gruppi famigliari a enti monastici: grazie a uno spontaneo orientamento delle aristocrazie nell' Italia dell' VIII secolo."

96 Eliana Magnani, "Almsgiving, *Donatio Pro Anima* and Eucharistic Offering in the Early Middle Ages of Western Europe (4th–9th century)," in *Charity and Giving in Monotheistic Religions* ed. Miriam Frenkel and Yaacov Lev (Berlin: De Gruyter, 2009).

97 Arnold Angenendt, "*Donationes pro anima*: Gift and Countergift in the Early Medieval Liturgy," in *The Long Morning of Medieval Europe: New Directions in Early Medieval Studies*, ed. Jennifer R. Davis and Michael McCormick (Aldershot: Ashgate, 2008).

a new, very precise documentary context. The legal basis for this significant increase is a royal edict of 713 which permitted donations *pro anima*, without other formalities, for "Longobardus" men who were ill or infirm.[98]

> Si quis longobardus, ut habens casus humanae fragilitatis, egrotaverit, quamquam in lectolo reiaceat, potestatem habeat, dum vivit et recte loqui potest, pro anima sua iudicandi vel dispensandi de rebus suis, quid aut qualitercui voluerit; et quod iudicaverit, stabilem debeat permanere.
>
> [If a Lombard, suffering from human infirmity, is ill, even though he is confined to his bed he has the right, while he lives and is able to speak rationally, to make decisions on behalf of his soul or to dispose of his property in whatever manner and to whatever extent is pleasing him. And that which he decides shall remain firmly in effect]

The charter of Firmus, the proficient *notarius* from Chiusi, starts as a transaction in favor of Audipert's nephews, but reveals itself as a bilateral *pro anima* act. In preparation for his own death, Audipert, in the hope for eternal life, stated a condition: his nephews must give a *donatio* every year in favor of the church of St. Salvatore for the salvation of his own soul. In the Early Middle Ages the *pro anima* bequest provided the most expedient provision that could be made to ease the actor's passage into the next world and secure everlasting life with the Lord.[99]

Like windows onto different landscapes, the two documents under consideration here open onto different scenery and actions: the social positions of both the actors and the cultural backgrounds of the writers differ notably. Moreover, the two charters owe their production to the desire to secure two very different types of transaction. Conversely, both charters date from the last fifty years of the Lombard reign in Italy. One is a *donatio* enacted within a family group in Chiusi, made according to the reciprocal traditions of the *lex langobardorum*, whereas the other is a typical *charta dotis* that records the unilateral donation of land and movable goods to a Lucchese church by its founder.

98 Liutprand, No. 6, Bluhme, *Edictus Langobardorum*, 109, Fischer-Drew, *Lombard Laws*, 146; See also Chris Wickham, "Economic and Social Institutions in Northern Tuscany in the Eighth Century," in *Istituzioni ecclesiastiche della Toscana medievale*, ed. Chris Wickham, et al. (Galatina: Congedo, 1980), 23–26.

99 Francine Michaud, "Wills and Testaments," in *Death in Medieval Europe: Death Scripted and Death Choreographed*, ed. Joelle Rollo-Koster (London: Routledge, 2017), 116.

The widespread use of documents and the preservation of legal records as well as the existence of a sophisticated notarial tradition centered in Tuscany does not at all imply the disappearance of forms of orality in Lombard Italy. The nature and the use of charters supports the so called "weak thesis" for legal literacy that does not oppose orality to literacy but rather puts stress on the coexistence and complementarity of written communication and other modes (orality and gestures).[100] Pertuald's charters not only records his generous donation, but it also records the oral performance of Petroni, who dictates the charter to his son Petrus. Moreover, the writing down of a *cartula* also entailed its reading out to the participants.

The charter written by Firmus is also evidence of the coexistence of written legal instruments and oral procedure: in fact, part of his legal script revolves around the symbolic dispensation of a *launegild* in order to confirm the transaction. Indeed, the sources of the seventh and eighth centuries clearly indicate that the writing of a document could not ignore the symbolic confirmation that, alone, represents the binding aspect of the agreement. The production of a *cartula* could prove useful in the case of conflict, but conversely a written agreement could be canceled in the absence of a symbolic confirmation.[101]

The historian of law is confronted here by some important aspects of, and developments in, early medieval donation: Firstly, in the *cartula donationis*, written by Firmus in 770, the gift is followed by a symbolic countergift, a *launechild* in the form of *anulo aureo uno* [one gold ring], which is an example of the relationship between the symbolic and the written validation of a transaction. Moreover, Firmus' document offers a good case for the interaction of charter and written law: it shows how far legal constraints could condition property donations but also reveals the extent to which laws could be subject to adjustment.

In the case of Pertuald, the *charta dotis* records the *donatio* to his own church as a non-reciprocal transaction, as indicated in the *lex*, Liutprand, No. 73, which gives up the need for reciprocity in the case of a Lombard's donation to the Church. Moreover, considered within its historical and social background, Pertuald's *donatio* is not altogether unilateral, at least not in its social consequences. The connection between churches and monasteries and the families that founded and patronized them was a two-way relation. In Lucca in the eighth century, churches were endowed with land by their founders as a strategy to consolidate social status: Pertuald's foundation of a church and the

100 On the strong vs weak theses for legal literacy, see Rio, *Legal Practice and the Written Word*, 11–15; also Innes, "Memory, Orality and Literacy," 3–36.

101 No. 163, Schiapparelli, *CDL* 2.

following donation of land initiated his privileged position within Lucchese society and promoted the election of his son to the seat of a bishop.

Secondly, the charter also reflects on the close relation between the social elite and the episcopacy. To remain close to the churches they founded, it was the strategy of the elite to record and preserve documents, the result here being the Lucca archive. Bishop Peredeus' vast production of documents is indicative of one of the aspects of the protagonism of the Church in the eighth century in Lombard Italy. In keeping with his powerful position, not only transactions that were in favor of the Church were recorded and saved, but also the recorded validations through the work of established ecclesiastical writers, whose technical and intellectual training took place within the episcopal curia.

As an example, the donation by Pertuald to the church of San Michele in Lucca does not now survive in its original form, but instead as a copy written by the popular *diaconus* Osprandus: the charter thus owes its existence not to a spontaneous need for a written draft of a legal action, but within a strategy related to the Church of Lucca's intentions to secure and confirm its already existing rights as established by the original documents.[102] Thus, documentary and archival practice was as central to the formation of both institutional and family identity as was the movement of property.

In the instance of the document written by Firmus, the ready need for security can be clearly seen; it indicates a flexible legalistic approach, which may be determined from the need to write a charter that would stand firmly against any assault to the unfree donees, whose fragility the *notarius* was aware of. Audipert's donation derives its "unassailable firmitas" from the technical skill of the lay *notarius* and not from his established social position inside an ecclesiastical milieu.

Moreover, the charter written by Firmus reveals a level of writers from the laity who took inspiration from ancient models and adapted them to the new Lombard reality. A clue to Firmus professional background and culture is given by the unusual *inscriptio* of his charter, "dilectissimi mihi semperque amantissimis Bonipertulo et Leopert neputibus meis," [my dearest and beloved nephews Bonipertulo and Leopert] that, in spite of the somewhat personal tone, represents a common formula in the documents from Ravenna.[103] As a Byzantine *tabellion*, Firmus (who calls himself *notarius* in all the charters he

102 Paola Supino Martini, "Cultura grafica nella Langobardia maior," in *Visigoti e Longobardi*, ed. Paolo Delogu and Javier Arce (Florence: All' insegna del Giglio, 2001), 372.

103 Fruscione, "Carte longobarde di Chiusi," 96; on Byzantine influences in Chiusi also Mario Marrocchi, "Le istituzioni civili e religiose a Chiusi (secoli V–VIII)," in *Goti e Longobardi a Chiusi*, ed. Carla Falluomini (Chiusi: Edizioni Luì, 2009).

wrote)[104] shows indeed that he values his task: his controlled and considered writing is indicative of a strong tendency towards self-control, his focus on the law as a means to validate and secure a transaction, but also his ability to adapt the law to Audipert's advantage emerges within the elaborate world of Italian charters.

104 Nos. 192, 253, Schiapparelli, *CDL* 2.

PART 4

Text and Edition

CHAPTER 14

Lombard Juridical Tradition: A New Edition of Turin, Biblioteca Nazionale Universitaria, MS F.IV.1 fr. 11 (Turin, BNU), a Fragment of the *Lombarda* with Glosses

Chiara Simbolotti

The choice to re-examine the bifolium Turin, Biblioteca Nazionale Universitaria, MS F.IV.1 fr. 11—first edited in 2012—[1] originated from an interest in exploring the possibilities offered by the digital restoration of damaged parchments.

In order to release a more complete and improved reading of this text—of some interest both for its plausible dating to the late-eleventh or the early-twelfth century and for preserving some Lombard terms in their original form—the fragment has been re-inspected both physically and by means of digital photography using multispectral imaging techniques in ultraviolet (UV), visible, and near-infrared (IR) wavebands of light. The images have been taken *in situ* by Dr. Gianluca Poldi (University of Bergamo) using a specifically modified camera (20Mpx). An UV bulb MPXL technology source (365 nm emission peak, 35 W) was used for UV-fluorescence and for reflected UV, while a halogen lamp was employed for RGB and IR images.

Multispectral imaging, although not performed in optimum conditions, as it was not permitted to take the fragment out of the manuscript reading room and capture images in a dark space with no other light sources than those specified, nevertheless allowed for a rather satisfying digital restoration of the text, particularly in some circumstances. While it has not been possible to re-establish the entire text, especially in the most damaged areas of the parchment, it has been useful to emend some previously imprecise readings, and decisively intervene in more than one dubious case. In addition, for the physical inspection, it was sometimes useful to employ a polarized light dermatoscope.[2]

1 Chiara Simbolotti, "Tradizione giuridica longobarda. Un inedito frammento della Lombarda con glosse (Torino, BNU, F. IV. 1 fr. 11)," *Rivista Internazionale di Diritto Comune* 23 (2012): 223–55.

2 Kindly loaned by Prof. Pietro Quaglino (Dipartimento di Scienze Mediche, University of Turin).

 | DOI:10.1163/9789004448650_016

The bifolium is a membrane fragment, part of a documental series from Bobbio Abbey, nowadays kept in the Turin National Library, thanks to the efforts of the philologist and professor of Classical and Oriental Literatures, Amedeo Peyron, appointed in 1820 by the Italian Interior Ministry with the objective of recovering the lost codices from Bobbio.[3]

Nothing is known about the fragment before its appearance in Turin, except that it may have been compiled at the monastery in Emilia.[4] The codex that it was formerly a part of, however, was probably lost or dismembered in the sixteenth century at the latest, since, from then on, the surviving bifolium was used for an unknown period of time as the flyleaf of a protocol.[5] This seems to be confirmed by two features of the parchment, which will be discussed shortly.

Turin, MS F.IV.1 fr. 11 is now kept in the same miscellaneous box containing the much more famous *Codex Taurinensis* (Turin, MS F.IV.1 fr. 10)—four folios of a palimpsest whose *scriptio inferior* preserves, beneath Saint Gregory the Great's *Homeliae in Ezechielem*, passages of Ulfila's Gothic translation of the Bible. Ottino describes the entire contents of box F.IV.1 as "*varia fragmenta codicum*," a miscellany of seventeen fragments already consecutively numbered from I to XVII. Carlo Cipolla also talks of the heterogeneous contents of F.IV.1, holding parchments from different and non-contemporaneous manuscripts.[6]

As with the other documents in the box, F.IV.1 fr. 11 bears clear signs of damage caused by flames and water to which it was exposed during the great fire that broke out at the original site of the library,[7] in the night between January the 25th and 26th, 1904, causing the destruction of five rooms, includ-

3 Giuseppe Ottino, *I Codici Bobbiesi nella Biblioteca Nazionale di Torino indicati e descritti da Giuseppe Ottino* (Turin, Palermo: Carlo Clausen, 1890), VI. On the activity and decadence of the Bobbio *scriptorium* and library during the Langobardic age see Alessandro Zironi, *Il monastero longobardo di Bobbio. Crocevia di uomini, manoscritti e culture*, Istituzioni e società 3 (Spoleto: Fondazione CISAM, 2004), 47–76. This study describes, moreover, several manuscripts from Bobbio (121–66), but not Turin, MS F.IV.1 fr. 11.

4 See Federico Patetta, "Nuove ipotesi sulla patria della così detta Lombarda," in *Studi sulle fonti giuridiche medievali*, ed. Guido Astuti (Turin: Bottega d'Erasmo, 1967), 939, reprinted from *Festschrift Heinrich Brunner zum siebzigsten Geburtstag dargebracht von Schülern und Verehrern* (Weimar: H. Böhlaus Nachfolger, 1910), 361 n. 2. Without supporting his statement with any evidence, the scholar affirms that the Turin fragment was probably found in Piedmont.

5 Federico Patetta, *Le Ordalie. Studio di Storia del Diritto e Scienza del Diritto Comparato* (Turin: Fratelli Bocca Editori, 1890), 294 n. 2.

6 See Ottino, *Codici Bobbiesi*, 22 and Carlo Cipolla, *Codici Bobbiesi della Biblioteca Nazionale Universitaria di Torino* (Milan: Ulrico Hoepli Editore Libraio della Real Casa, 1907), 75.

7 Known as Regia Biblioteca Universitaria, it was sited within the university palace in Via Po 17. On October 15th, 1973, the library was transferred to its current site in Piazza Carlo Alberto 3.

ing the one housing the manuscripts.[8] Carlo Cipolla, in his inventory of the surviving codices, published immediately after the terrible event,[9] noted that box F.IV.1 was complete but damaged, except for the documents contained in folders 1, 5, 8 and 15, all of which appeared to be in good or passable condition.[10] Within the first two decades of the nineteenth century,[11] the entire box underwent conservation at Carlo Marré's workshop,[12] through which its present condition was established. Although Cipolla did not number our fragment among the less damaged pieces, we can ascertain that the manuscript is in relatively good state, especially as far as the main text is concerned, which is fairly legible; the same cannot be said for some of the interlinear and marginal glosses—particularly, but not only, those on the upper margins of fol. 1r and fol. 2v—where the parchment has been so seriously damaged as to make the text extremely difficult to read and, in some cases, not completely decipherable.

The fragment is now contained in a dark purple canvas board folder (dating to the early nineteenth century), which is in turn within a modern board box clad in ecru canvas. The open bifolium is protected by its own paper folder, marked in red and blue pencil "F.IV.1" (11). In this same folder, there is also a paper flyleaf, originally folded in two and now flattened and fastened to a thick paper sheet, therefore, its *verso* is inaccessible, although an inspection in trans-

8 For a summary regarding the fire and subsequent efforts to recover the damaged collections, see Angelo Giaccaria, *I manoscritti danneggiati nell'incendio del 1904. Mostra di recuperi e restauri: Torino Febbraio–Marzo 1986*, Quaderni della Biblioteca Nazionale Universitaria di Torino 9 (Turin: Turingraf, 1986), 5–10, and Angelo Giaccaria, "Nuove identificazioni di manoscritti greci e latini della Biblioteca Nazionale Universitaria di Torino," *Aevum* 81/2 (2007): 429–33. In addition, Giovanni Gorrini, *L'incendio della Biblioteca Nazionale di Torino* (Turin: Edizioni Renzo Streglio e C.ia, 1905).

9 Carlo Cipolla, Gaetano De Sanctis, and Carlo Frati, "Inventario dei codici superstiti greci e latini antichi della Biblioteca Nazionale di Torino," *Rivista di filologia e d'istruzione classica* 32 (1904): 385–588. The section edited by Cipolla and Frati (436–56) was republished as an appendix to Gorrini's Italian-French work. See Gorrini, *Incendio della Biblioteca*, 273–92.

10 See Cipolla, De Sanctis, and Frati, "Inventario dei codici": 439 or Gorrini, *Incendio della Biblioteca*, 277.

11 By 1912—according to a note from the library record concerning this box—and certainly before 1922, since in Francesco Cosentini and Albano Sorbelli, *Inventari dei manoscritti delle Biblioteche d'Italia*. Vol. 28 *Torino* (Florence: Libreria Editrice Leo S. Olschki, 1922), 91, the reference number for the box F.IV.1 is R 882, where R indicates it has been restored. Nevertheless, in this catalogue the various fragments of the miscellany are identified with a number that differs from the traditional reference. Fr. 11, in particular, is indicated as number 4. On the inaccuracy of this inventory see Angelo Giaccaria, "I fondi medievali della Biblioteca Nazionale Universitaria di Torino," *Pluteus* 2 (1984): 188.

12 Giaccaria, "Fondi medievali," 179.

parency demonstrates that it is empty. The flyleaf bears on its first page the red ink mark of the library and, in a nineteenth-century hand, the heading: "Fragmentum XI. Duo folia membranacea in 4°. Frag. Legum Longobardicarum F.IV.1" [Fragment XI. Two membrane folios in 4°. Fragment of Lombard Laws F.IV.1], beneath this header, the note *Legum longobardicarum fragm*[…], now partially damaged by the fire, was rewritten in pencil. A second, smaller sheet of paper, containing notes from the *Codex Eporedianus* XXXIV, is likewise fixed onto a paper support which, nevertheless, leaves both recto and verso perfectly visible. The flyleaf, the page of notes and the membrane fragment show clear signs of burning.

The bifolium comprises two leaves numbered on both sides on the low outer corners of the pages; this modern foliation is in Arabic numerals, marked with a pencil ("1^r", "1^v", "2^r" and "2^v"). In the lower part of the outer margin of fol. 1^r, in addition to the foliation there is an extra indication in pencil, "F.IV.1 Frammento XI".[13] The parchment measures approximately 250×332 mm; interestingly, Ottino gives dimensions of 26.5×18 cm for MS F.IV.1 fr. 11. Even assuming, as Giaccaria also argues, that there are frequent inaccuracies in Ottino's catalogue,[14] such a difference in the measurements indicated here can hardly be ascribed to an oversight; clearly Ottino measured only the single leaf—that is just half of a bifolium. In this way, without forgetting to double the length, if Ottino's measurements are compared with the current ones, it is possible to have an idea of the extent of the fire damage to the margins. The bifolium is blind-ruled in hardpoint from the flesh side, with thirty-two text lines and with a pair of verges flanking the written area on each page. The distance between the lines is 6 mm, while the width of the verges columns is 5 mm.

In both of the outer margins it is still possible to see the signs of the pricking used to guide the ruling. Considering the set of text lines determined in the layout, however, on fol. 2^r the presence of an extra written (but not ruled) line can be observed, positioned between the twelfth and the thirteenth ruled lines. Since this feature does not appear to be a later addition made by another scribal hand, it could be possible that it originated from the necessity to acquire some more space, perhaps in order to manage a scribal omission, maybe *ex homeoteleuto* due to the three times repeated *incipit* "Siquis seruum alienum".

Other interesting features are: two *notabilia*—one in the outer margin of fol. 2^r, level with ll. 25–26, the other in the inner margin of fol. 2^v, parallel to ll. 5–6—represented by a monogram for the word "NOTA"; in the inner and

13 The paper flyleaf and the page of notes, on the contrary, are numbered in pencil with Roman numerals (I, II).

14 See Ottino, *Codici Bobbiesi*, 24 and Giaccaria, "Fondi medievali," 189.

outer margins of fol. 2^r^ there are two single letters an ọ̄ and a g· corresponding to the first and second lines, respectively; in addition, in the inner margin, approximately midway up the leaf we read "NON LEGITUR" in majuscule letters of different size, overlapping each other and sharing one or more strokes. Finally, in the upper margin of fol. 2^v^ there are some Arabic numerals, probably "1850 4 12". In practice, only the "1," "8" and "0" are clearly readable, while the "5" is barely distinguishable. The same happens with the number "4," and the "12" may in fact be only "2." Presumably these numerals indicate an old reference number, but there is no certainty about it. Moreover, in the upper outer margin of fol. 2^v^ there is a trace of the original foliation of the codex to which the bifolium initially belonged. It is an apparently three-figure number written in ink—perhaps 147.

Two pieces of evidence suggest that the bifolium was used, as said previously, as the flyleaf of a protocol: in addition to an upside-down inscription in the lower margin of fol. 2^v^, "Protocollo 1578 B," there is also a series of tiny, regular prickings—two pairs on each leaf—converging two by two from the outer margins towards the center of the text area. The series is mirrored across the two leaves, so that by—hypothetically—folding the bifolium in half along the spine, it should be possible to superimpose them. It seems very probable that these are the marks left by stitches fixing the strings of a folder, created by reusing a discarded piece of parchment. Small parchment fillings applied during conservation in order to strengthen some fragile or damaged parts of the surface, especially in the upper margin, are clearly visible. This method was particularly used for the repair of two lacerations which had partially compromised the text of the gloss apparatus: the first, of elongated shape—about 20 × 3 mm—extends obliquely from the outer margin of fol. 1, the second—about 7 × 5 mm—is in the upper margin of the same leaf.

The dense and tiny Carolingian minuscule script was realized in a dark-brown ink, whereas a red ink was used for rubrics and some capital initials only.[15] Finally, another scribe added some distinctly visible amendments to the text using a darker ink. The plain aspect, the lack of ornamentation,[16] the presence of marginal and interlinear explanatory glosses and *allegationes*, and

---

15 Traced in red ink: on fol. 1^r^ the capital initials ⟨R⟩ of "Recolimus" (ll. 6 and 32), on fol. 1^v^ the initial ⟨I⟩ of "Item" (l. 24), on fol. 2^r^ the capital letters ⟨R⟩, ⟨S⟩, ⟨N⟩ of "Rex," "Siquis," "Nullus" (ll. 5, 6, 10, 12, 13, 15, 19, 24, 27) and the rubric "R de homicidio seruorum uel aldiorum" (outer margin, l. 4); on fol. 2^v^ the capital initials ⟨R⟩, ⟨S⟩ of "Rex" and "Siquis" (ll. 8, 15, 20, 28) and the rubrics "R de sepulchro uiolato et de eo qui hominem mortuum expoliauerit" and "R ne ad regem uenientibus iniuria fiat" (inner margin, ll. 7, 8, 19, 20).

16 The initials are undecorated, and some clauses are not even rubricated. Instead, these letters are simply larger.

the use of *maniculae*,[17] in order to draw the attention to particular passages of the text, are all features that generally suggest a practical purpose for the manuscript, and that it was mainly used for study and consultation.

Over the course of time, the manuscript was simply ascribed to the twelfth century,[18] without any attempt to date it more precisely. While somewhat broad and vague, this might not be an unrealistic indication, especially considering the relevant graphic changes that came in succession throughout this century.

It is certainly very difficult to date manuscripts in Carolingian minuscule, particularly where the eleventh and twelfth centuries are concerned; for this reason, it is preferable to adopt cautious and flexible criteria,[19] without claiming an exact date for the script. However, it seems to be particularly interesting—following Bernhard Bischoff, Armando Petrucci and Alessandro Pratesi[20]—to underline certain features coexisting in this manuscript, some of which still belong to the eleventh-century Carolingian script, while others are already typical of its evolution between the eleventh century and the first decades of the twelfth. Obviously, paleographical description has to consider both the main text and the glosses, which, are most likely—although not certainly—by a different hand. Moreover, it must be remembered that only some of these glosses are clearly readable.

First of all, the script no longer slants to the left, a typical characteristic of early Carolingian writing, a change already begun between the tenth and the eleventh century; the letters are now less rounded, but their shading is not particularly noticeable and no angular shapes or broken lines—a prelude to the Gothic script—have yet been developed.

Considering some interesting graphical features of the manuscript, both in the main text and the glosses, two strokes are still not used on the double ⟨ii⟩ in order to distinguish them from ⟨u⟩, a characteristic that began to spread in Italy from the end of the eleventh century, and became established in the second half of the twelfth.[21] The cedillated ⟨ę⟩, which developed during the eleventh

17 Two are on fol. 1ʳ, four on fol. 1ᵛ, indicating Liutprand, Nos. 21, 92, 118 and 136; one is on fol. 2ʳ at the end of Rothari, No. 137, and the last is on fol. 2ᵛ, indicating Rothari, No. 16.

18 See Ottino, *Codici Bobbiesi*, 24; Patetta, *Ordalie*, 294; Patetta, "Nuove ipotesi," 938–39 n. 2.

19 Armando Petrucci, "Censimento dei codici dei secoli XI–XII. Istruzioni per la datazione," *Studi Medievali*, s. III, IX (1968): 1115–17.

20 See Bernhard Bischoff, *Paleografia Latina. Antichità e Medioevo* (Padua: Editrice Antenore, 1992), 169–83; Paolo Cherubini and Alessandro Pratesi, *Paleografia Latina. L'avventura grafica del mondo occidentale* (Vatican City: Scuola Vaticana di Paleografia, Diplomatica e Archivistica, 2010), 399–402; Petrucci, "Censimento dei codici," 1115–25.

21 Bischoff, *Paleografia Latina*, 176.

century, normally to indicate the diphthong ⟨æ⟩, is still used here for ⟨*-ae*⟩ at the end of words, but is clearly not yet replaced by a simple ⟨e⟩.

Although such a feature dates to between the end of the eleventh and the beginning of the twelfth century, in this manuscript the ⟨r⟩ *rotunda*, shaped like the numeral 2, is not yet a regular presence within words after the letter ⟨o⟩; on the contrary, the scribal abbreviation for "-rum"—a rounded ⟨r⟩ with a left-slanting cut on its horizontal bar—is still used here not only for the genitive masculine plural suffix "-orum," but, in the glosses, also for the feminine "-arum," a trait which emerged within the first two decades of the twelfth century.[22]

In Turin, MS F.IV.1 fr. 1, there are too few occurrences of the minuscule "round ⟨s⟩" at the end of a line to judge its use. On the contrary, its presence at the end of a word—which could possibly represent a more recent feature[23]—apparently prevails in the main text, while in the glosses minuscule tall ⟨s⟩ seems to be more frequent in the same position.

In order to date the fragment, there is another element which also suggests that it was written relatively early in the twelfth century: the near-complete absence of the ⟨ɔ⟩ *retroversus* for the prefixes "con-" and "cum-," it occurs only twice in *contigerit* and *consilio* in the problematic marginal gloss on fol. 1r.[24] But the constant use of the Tironian note ⟨⁊⟩ for the conjunction "et,"[25] never replaced here with the mark ⟨&⟩, represents instead a later scribal trait. The Tironian note is also used to shorten *et* in word endings—es. *s⁊* for *set/sed, hab⁊* for *habet.*

The tall ligature appears only for the letters ⟨st⟩ and not for ⟨ct⟩. Its rather narrow and elongated shape shows the form that had already developed during the first half of the eleventh century; the horizontal stroke of the ⟨t⟩ tends to approach, and sometimes touches, the vertical stroke of the tall ⟨s⟩.

It therefore seems possible to conclude that, while some typical features of the late Caroline minuscule, which evolved at the end of the eleventh century and during the twelfth, are either not prevalent or are completely absent, some other older traits endure. On the other hand, the survival of conservative elements is not necessarily a suitable parameter to push the dating of a manuscript further back; indeed, it could possibly depend on the scribes' personal style, on their age and training or, perhaps, on the influence of the

22 Cherubini and Pratesi, *Paleografia Latina*, 401.

23 Petrucci, "Censimento dei codici": 1123.

24 See below, gloss (a), p. 364; See also Cherubini and Pratesi, *Paleografia Latina*, 401; Petrucci, "Censimento dei codici," 1123–24.

25 Cherubini and Pratesi, *Paleografia Latina*, 400.

antigraph available to them, which could be particularly true for the main text: the edict that ought to be preserved in its original content and form. For the explanatory glosses, on the other hand, the scribe may have been a little freer in following their own style.

From these paleographical observations, it appears reasonable to conclude that the fragment is ascribable to the period spanning the end of the eleventh and first decades of the twelfth centuries. Considering that the systemization of the *Lombarda* has been placed in the scholarship in the second half, sometimes more specifically at the end, of the eleventh century,[26] such a dating of Turin, MS F.IV.1 fr. 11—a fragment that apparently contains a selection from the *Lombarda Vulgata*, as discussed further—could suggest a relatively fast stabilization of the *Lombarda* itself, if a summa appeared so close to its codification.

Before Federico Patetta, the first scholar to establish what the contents of the bifolium were more exactly, Turin, MS F.IV.1 fr. 11 was identified and described in very general terms by those who, in the course of time, had worked on the rearrangements of the library collections. In *Appendice al Pasini*, f. 109r, the fragment is registered under the heading *Leges* as: *Legum Langobardicarum fragmenta* (*V in theca*), with the actual reference number;[27] Ottino instead indicates the fr. 11 as: "*XI. Lex Lombarda vulgata.* Frammento di codice del secolo XII. Membranaceo, 26,5×18. Carte due, con glosse interlineari e marginali, contiene: Libro I, Titolo IX, cap. 20–24. Titolo X, legge finale. Titolo XI, cap. 1–9."[28]

Patetta first mentioned the fragment in two notes to his study of the ordeal;[29] on that occasion, he defined it respectively: a series of ample extracts from the *Expositio* to the *Liber Papiensis*, and fragments of a law miscellany known as the *Lombarda*. The collections of laws known as *Liber Papiensis* and *Lombarda*, thrived with their many redactions between the eleventh and the twelfth century, aimed to re-organize the juridical matters of the Lombard kings' edicts,

26 See Guido Astuti, "Lombarda," in *Novissimo Digesto Italiano* IX, ed. Antonio Azara and Ernesto Eula (Turin: UTET, 1963), 1068; Patetta, "Nuove ipotesi," 930; Charles M. Radding, *The Origins of Medieval Jurisprudence: Pavia and Bologna, 850–1150* (London: Yale University Press, 1988), 128.

27 The *Appendice al Pasini*—in Turin, Biblioteca Nazionale Universitaria, MS Cons.Mss.8 Pasini 1/3, without giving any indication as to the author or year of compilation (See Ottino, *Codici Bobbiesi*, VII)—continues the catalogue edited by Giuseppe Pasini in 1759 (*Catalogo del Pasini*). For the ascription of the *Appendice* to Bernardino Peyron, Amedeo Peyron's nephew, and its possible dating to around 1860–65, see Giaccaria, "Fondi medievali," 187; Silvia Bellocchio and Vittoria Dolcetti Corazza, "Il *Codex Taurinensis* F.IV.1 fr. 10," in *Le rune. Epigrafia e letteratura*, ed. Vittoria Dolcetti Corazza and Renato Gendre, Bibliotheca Germanica. *Studi e testi* 26 (Alessandria: Edizioni dell'Orso, 2009), 87.

28 See Ottino, *Codici Bobbiesi*, 24.

29 Patetta, *Ordalie*, 294 n. 2; 438 n. 3.

integrating them with the imperial capitularies for Italy (*Capitulare Italicum*), covering a period from king Rothari (636–52) to the Emperor Henry II (1014–24).[30] Later, Patetta confirmed this second identification definitively in his contribution regarding the possible place of origin of the *Lombarda*,[31] where he ascribed the Turin fragment to the manuscript tradition of this collection of laws, which originated between the eleventh and the twelfth century and comprised a systematic reorganization of the Lombard-Frankish juridical *corpus*.

Certainly, such a brief and incomplete text is insufficient to allow a close examination of the structure and content of the codex to which this bifolium once belonged, although some considerations are possible.

Firstly, it is quite evident that the fragment was not the central bifolium of a quire, since the content between fols. 1^{v} and 2^{r} changes, making it clear that other sheets were interposed between the two leaves. Fol. 1^{r-v} bears a part of Liutprand, No. 21 from "et in eo ordine" to the end,[32] then proceeds with Nos. 62, 92, 118 and the beginning of 136—from "Item annuntiatum est nobis" to "et nostris iu"[33]—of the same king. On fol. 2^{r-v} there is, instead, the end of king Henry I, No. 2 from "penitentie subdatur,"[34] and then some of Rothari, Nos. 129–137, 376, 16, 15, 17 and 18.[35]

Despite the hiatus between the two leaves—a lacuna in the text equal to at least another bifolium's worth of material—it is immediately clear that the law chapters are organized by subject, since almost all the chapters concern different forms of homicide, voluntary or involuntary, by accident, in self-defense or murder, perpetrated against freemen or servants, men, women or minors. The

30 See the prefaces to the MGH volumes—Alfred Boretius, ed., *Liber Legis Langobardorum Papiensis dictus*, MGH LL 4 (Hannover: Hahn, 1868), 46–98 and Friedrich Bluhme, ed., *Leges Langobardorum*, MGH LL 4 (Hannover: Hahn, 1868), 98–111; Guido Astuti, "*Liber Papiensis*," in *Novissimo Digesto Italiano* IX, ed. Azara and Eula, 829–30; and Astuti, "*Lombarda*," 1068–70. See also: Guido Astuti, *Lezioni di storia del diritto italiano. Le fonti. Età romano-barbarica* (Padua: CEDAM, 1968), 157–70 and 358–76; Manlio Bellomo, *Società e Istituzioni in Italia dal Medioevo agli inizi dell'Età moderna* (Catania, Rome: Editrice Giannotta e Il Cigno Galileo Galilei, 1991; 1st ed. Catania, 1976), 186–87; Francesco Calasso, *Il Medio Evo del diritto*. I. *Le fonti* (Milan: A. Giuffrè Editore, 1954), 309–15; Ennio Cortese, *Il diritto nella storia medievale*. II. *Il basso Medioevo* (Rome: Il Cigno Galileo Galilei, 1995), 16–22. See also Gobbitt, "Liutprand's Prologues," Chapter 3.

31 Patetta, "Nuove ipotesi," 938–39 n. 2.

32 For the first part of Liutprand, No. 21, see Boretius, *Liber Legis Langobardorum Papiensis dictus*, 417.

33 For the rest of the chapter see Boretius, *Liber Legis Langobardorum Papiensis dictus*, 466.

34 For the first part of the chapter see Boretius, *Liber Legis Langobardorum Papiensis dictus*, 582.

35 The clause numbering follows Bluhme, ed., *Edictus Langobardorum*, MGH LL 4 (Hannover: Hahn, 1868).

text focuses on this offence from fol. 1r up to the beginning of fol. 2v (line 7), suggesting therefore that it might very probably also have been the subject of the now missing interposed folios; a fact partially supported by the presence, at the beginning of fol. 2r, of the final part of the chapter of Henry I's additions. This rule, in fact, also concerns in particular killings that were committed against parents or relatives for motives of inheritance, which certainly reinforces the impression of a thematic unity. On fol. 2v (line 8) the subject then changes and the four last chapters of Rothari deal with different crimes.

As this order by subject confirms Patetta's identification of the text, a detailed comparison between the inner structure of Turin, MS F.IV.1 fr. 11 and the *Lombarda* order of juridical matters by books and headings helps to establish in which of the two *Lombarda* textual traditions—*Cassinese* and *Vulgata*—this bifolium may be placed.

The fragment follows exactly the arrangement of chapters in the *Vulgata* partition of them, although sometimes only selecting some clauses. Conversely, there is a certain divergence from the ordering of materials found in the *Cassinese*. A specific difference consists of the particular tendency towards thematic unity that links the Turin manuscript and the *Vulgata*, since both of them arrange all of the chapters on homicide into contiguous groups, unlike the *Cassinese*.[36]

The scheme detailed in Table 13.1 can be useful for providing a clearer view of common traits and differences in the order of juridical matters.

Considering the structure of the two *Lombarda* redactions and Turin, MS F.IV.1 fr. 11, there is an element common to all of them: Rothari, Nos. 16 and 15 are in reverse order in regard to their regular sequence of transmission in both the *Edictus Rothari* and the *Liber Papiensis*,[37] nevertheless, the rubric introduces the two chapters in their correct order.

A significant chronological gap of some three to four centuries separates our fragment from the Edicts originally issued by the Lombard kings, but the existence of later law collections, such as the one partially preserved here, clearly indicates how ancient juridical matters continued to hold some significance long after the end of the Lombard reign in Italy (in 773–74), and testify, moreover, to the survival of a social group who were still following Lombard law, as can also be inferred from public and private documental production.[38]

36 Friedrich Bluhme, ed., "*Legis Langobardorum libri tres sive syntagmata duo Lombarda vulgo dicta ex libro Papiensi confecta,*" MGH LL 4 (Hannover: Hahn, 1868), 607–40.

37 Bluhme, *Edictus Langobardorum*, 15; Boretius, *Liber Legis Langobardorum Papiensis dictus*, 298.

38 See also the contributions by Sonia Colafrancesco, "Juridical Dualism in Medieval South-

TABLE 13.1 Comparison of clause arrangement between, *Lombarda Cassinensis*, *Lombarda Vulgata* and Turin, MS F.IV.1 fr. 11

	Lombarda Cassinensis	*Lombarda Vulgata*	Turin, MS F. IV. 1 fr. 11
Liutprand	nn. 20–24, lib. I, R 3 *De homicidiis*	nn. 20–24, lib. I, tit. IX *De homicidiis liberorum hominum*	nn. 21, 62, 92, 118, 136, f. 1r–v
Henry I	n. 4, lib. I, R 4 *De parricidiis*	n. 5, lib. I, tit. X *De parricidiis*	n. 2, f. 2r
Rothari	nn. 1–2, lib. I, R 5 *De sepulcro violato et homine mortuo expoliato*	nn. 1–9, lib. I, tit. XI *De homicidiis servorum vel aldiorum*	nn. 129–137, 376, f. 2r–v *De homicidio seruorum uel aldiorum*
Rothari	nn. 1–2, lib. I, R 6 *Ne quis ad regem venientibus iniuria fiat*	nn. 1–2, lib. I, tit. XII *De sepulcro violato et de eo qui hominem mortuum expoliaverit*	nn. 16, 15, f. 2v *De sepulchro uiolato et de eo qui hominem mortuum expoliauerit*
Rothari	nn. 1–9, lib. I, R 18 *De homicidiis servorum aut aldiorum*	nn. 1–2, lib. I, tit. XIII *Ne ad regem venientibus iniuria fiat*	nn. 17, 18, f. 2v *Ne ad regem uenientibus iniuria fiat*

In such later collections, the original edicts necessarily underwent textual changes, introducing modifications generally of little relevance from a juridical point of view, but perhaps substantial for linguistic studies, as highlighted by Guido Astuti.[39] This is the case, for example, of Lombard edictal terms replaced in time with a Latin word. In Turin, MS F.IV.1 fr. 11, for example, two specific *nomina actionis* were lost:[40] *crapworfin* [grave profanation] and *rairaub* [corpse despoliation].[41] Originally used in the headings of Rothari's chapters 15 and 16, these words, were not linguistically assimilated into Latin and, for this reason, are undeclined, but were nevertheless preceded with the Latin preposition "de";

ern Italy: Studies on the *Codex Diplomaticus Cavensis*," Daniela Fruscione, "Two Lombard Charters and their Writers," and Thom Gobbitt "Liutprand's Prologues in the *Edictus Langobardorum*," in this collection, Chapters 10, 13 and 3, respectively, in this volume.

39 Astuti, *Lezioni di storia del diritto italiano*, 158.

40 Bluhme, *Edictus Langobardorum*, 15.

41 Nicoletta Francovich Onesti, *Vestigia longobarde in Italia (568–774). Lessico e antroponimia* (Rome: Artemide Edizioni, 1999), 74, 112–13.

in the fragment they were joined and substituted by only one rubric, combining both concepts: "de sepulchro uiolato et de eo qui hominem mortuum expoliauerit" [concerning violation of graves and concerning he who despoliates the dead].

Considering its content and shortness, Turin, MS F.IV.1 fr. 11 certainly does not offer any new contributions to current knowledge of Lombard vocabulary. As no written testimonies of the Lombard idiom remain, scholars are only able to examine the lexical elements surviving in the law and documental *corpora*, as well as those present in the historical sources, above all Paolo Diacono's *Historia Langobardorum*, loan words in modern languages, for example in different Italian vernaculars and then in the Italian language itself, as well as their traces in onomastics and toponymy.[42]

Turin, MS F.IV.1 fr. 11 preserves the same Lombard words already used in the respective edictal chapters, terms that, by now, scholars have extensively examined and discussed, both from an etymological and linguistic point of view, or,

42 See: Wilhelm Bruckner, *Die Sprache der Langobarden*, Quellen und Forschungen zur Sprach- und Culturgeschichte der germanischen Völker 75 (Strassburg: Karl J. Trubner, 1895; anast. repr. Berlin: De Gruyter, 1969); Carl R. Meyer, *Sprache und Sprachdenkmäler der Langobarden: Quellen, Grammatik, Glossar*, Bibliothek der ältesten deutschen Litteratur-Denkmäler 14 (Paderborn: Druck und Verlag von Ferdinand Schöningh, 1877) and Ernst Gamillscheg, *Romania germanica. Sprach- und Siedlungsgeschichte der Germanen auf dem Boden des alten Romerreichs*, vol. 2 (Berlin: De Gruyter, 1935). More recently: Maria Vittoria Molinari, "Lessico germanico nelle leggi longobarde," *Linguistica e filologia. Quaderni del dipartimento di linguistica e letterature comparate dell'Università di Bergamo* 1 (1995): 5–20; Francovich Onesti, *Vestigia longobarde*, gathers everyday vocabulary and onomastics from the sixth century to the end of the Lombard kingdom in Italy (568–714), and underlies my discussion of the Lombard words in the fragment. Regarding the Lombard lexicon within documental material see: Piergiuseppe Scardigli, "Appunti longobardi," in *Goti e Longobardi. Studi di Filologia Germanica* (Rome: Istituto italiano di Studi germanici, 1987), 191–246; repr. *Filologia e critica. Studi in onore di Vittorio Santoli*, ed. Paolo Chiarini (Rome: Bulzoni Editore, 1976), 91–131; Piergiuseppe Scardigli, "All'origine dei longobardismi in italiano," in *Goti e Longobardi*, 269–93; repr. *Sprachliche Interferenz. Festschrift für Werner Betz zum 65. Geburtstag*, ed. Herbert Kolb and Hartmut Lauffer (Tübingen: Max Niemeyer Verlag, 1977), 335–54; Piergiuseppe Scardigli, "Le parole longobarde per l'ecdotica dell'Editto di Rotari," in *Goti e Longobardi*, 303–29; repr. *Medioevo e Rinascimento. Annuario del Dipartimento di Studi sul Medioevo e il Rinascimento dell'Università di Firenze* 1 (1987): 53–73; Giovanna Princi Braccini, "Germanismi editi e inediti nel *Codice diplomatico longobardo*: anticipi da uno spoglio integrale e commentato di fonti latine in vista di un *Tesoro* longobardo," *Quaderni del Dipartimento di Linguistica dell'Università degli Studi di Firenze* 9 (1998/1999): 191–240; Giovanna Princi Braccini, "Germanismi editi e inediti nel *Cartulario di S. Benedetto di Conversano (901–1265)*," *Quaderni del Dipartimento di Linguistica dell'Università degli Studi di Firenze* 10 (2000): 1–41.

in the case of words indicating juridical figures and institutions, for their historical and social significance. Therefore, a brief mention about them can be sufficient.

The first in order of appearance is *guidrigild* [wergild],[43] namely the monetary compensation due in case of personal injuries or manslaughter, and depending on the victim's social status: an indemnity intended to limit the recourse to the *faida*. In the fragment, *guidrigild* appears only in the glosses (a)[44] and (g) of Liutprand, No. 21,[45] and in a form representative of a later variant—however undeclined—linguistically different from *wergild*, equally recurring in the Lombard laws, particularly in the edicts of Rothari and Liutprand. In fact, if *guidrigild* is a compound of the Germanic adverb **wiþr(o)* "against" and the substantive **gelða* "reward" from which the meaning of "compensation" originates; the original term *wergild* derives from **gelða* preceded by the substantive *wer* "freeman" (Germ. **wera-z, wira-z*), thereby highlighting the concept of a compensation for an offence made against a person.[46]

The word *gasindius* [king's officer, king's follower],[47] in the manuscript occurs in Liutprand, No. 62,[48] and its related glosses (e) and (h), inflected according to the Latin forms of the plural nominative and ablative: *gasindii* and *gasindiis*. On this subject, it is interesting that there is no explanatory Latin gloss to the Lombard word in the law text; on the contrary, both *gasindiis* and *gasindii* are used in the glosses to annotate the Latin terms *minimis* and *maiores*, two words that are by no means so unfamiliar as to require some sort of translation into the Lombard language, making it clear that the gloss had, in this case, the mere function of connecting those generic *maiores* and *minimi* to the particular functionaries just mentioned. Nevertheless, the use of Lombard words by the commentator is a sign of a still living familiarity with some remnants of this idiom.

Certainly, the assimilation of Lombard terms into Latin forms was not an innovation specific to the later law collections, but dates back to the original edictal texts. If, as has been said, *guidrigild* remains undeclined, the same does

43 Francovich Onesti, *Vestigia longobarde*, 131–32.

44 As far as the poor state of the parchment allows us to read this marginal gloss, this word occurs twice. Perhaps the first time following the graphical variant *uuidrigild*, but the reading is really uncertain.

45 Bluhme, ed., *Edictus Langobardorum*, 117; Boretius, ed., *Liber Legis Langobardorum Papiensis dictus*, 417–18.

46 See Francovich Onesti, *Vestigia longobarde*, 131.

47 Onesti, *Vestigia longobarde*, 91.

48 Bluhme, *Edictus Langobardorum*, 132; Boretius, *Liber Legis Langobardorum Papiensis dictus*, 432–33.

not happen with the nominatives *castaldius* [king's administrator] and *sculdasius* [king's collector],[49] (Rothari, No. 15).[50] In particular, the Latinised form *sculdasius*, present in Turin, MS F.IV.1 fr. 11, seems to be absent in the manuscript traditions of both of the *Edictis langobardorum* and the *Liber Papiensis*.[51] Similarly, *aldium* [semi-free man], its feminine *aldiam* [semi-free woman, maid],[52] (Rothari, Nos. 129 and 376),[53] and *camphionem*, [warrior, champion],[54] specifically hired to substitute a contender in a trial by combat (Liutprand, No. 118 text and gloss (i); Henry I, No. 2),[55] follow the accusative Latin declension.

Some final outstanding examples are: the ablative *sala* [master's house], *pars dominica*[56] (Rothari, Nos. 133 and 136),[57] in the expression *de sala*, the genitive ethnonym *Longobardorum*[58]—Liutprand, No. 118,[59] and related gloss (k)—and the particular case of *asto*,[60] a term morphologically difficult to classify, because of its three possible functions,[61] all represented in this fragment. In Liutprand, No. 118 and its glosses, *asto* is in fact respectively: an adjective inflected in the ablative of manner: *asto animo* [with malicious attitude, namely, deliberately with malice]; a substantive in the expression *de asto iurare* [to swear about the willfulness] (f), and also as an adverb *asto* [voluntarily] (j).

What is significant about these few and well-known Lombard words preserved in Turin, MS F.IV.1 fr. 11 is their survival itself. Whether they had been formally assimilated into Latin, testifying their complete acceptance into familiar vocabulary, or if they had maintained their early form, they were evidently

49 Francovich Onesti, *Vestigia longobarde*, 92, 118–19.

50 Bluhme, *Edictus Langobardorum*, 15; Boretius, *Liber Legis Langobardorum Papiensis dictus*, 298.

51 Bluhme, *Edictus Langobardorum*, 15 n. t; Boretius, *Liber Legis Langobardorum Papiensis dictus*, 298.

52 Francovich Onesti, *Vestigia longobarde*, 54, 57.

53 Bluhme, *Edictus Langobardorum*, 30, 80; Boretius, *Liber Legis Langobardorum Papiensis dictus*, 310, 394.

54 Francovich Onesti, *Vestigia longobarde*, 71–72.

55 Bluhme, *Edictus Langobardorum*, 156; Boretius, *Liber Legis Langobardorum Papiensis dictus*, 457–59, 582–83.

56 Francovich Onesti, *Vestigia longobarde*, 113–14.

57 Bluhme, *Edictus Langobardorum*, 31; Boretius, *Liber Legis Langobardorum Papiensis dictus*, 311.

58 Francovich Onesti, *Vestigia longobarde*, 99.

59 Bluhme, *Edictus Langobardorum*, 156; Boretius, *Liber Legis Langobardorum Papiensis dictus*, 457–59.

60 Francovich Onesti, *Vestigia longobarde*, 65–66.

61 Onesti, *Vestigia longobarde*, 66.

still so comprehensible that they were not only pedestrianly copied, transcribing the edictal texts, but were also used appropriately in the complementary glosses too.

The references used for the publication of Turin, MS F.IV.I fr. 1 are those of the *Liber Papiensis*, edited by Alfred Boretius,[62] as well as the *Lombarda Vulgata* edited by Frederick Bluhme,[63] the latter, however, indicates only the heading and *incipit* of each law chapter; the source of the single chapters is, in fact, the *Liber Papiensis*, a collection which shares the same juridical content with the *Vulgata*, but is, however, arranged by subject rather than chronologically. Bluhme's edition of the *Leges Langobardorum*,[64] and, when needed, that of Claudio Azzara and Stefano Gasparri,[65] have been useful for further comparisons between the juridical material of the fragment and the edicts of Rothari and Liutprand.

Stephan Kuttner's editing guidelines have been followed for the transcription of the bifolium,[66] although they have been adapted to suit the needs of the text. While this is not meant to be a strictly diplomatic transcription, it seems useful to indicate the partition of the written lines with a single vertical line | at every line change. Two lines || mark the end of a page and the passage to the following one. However, for the transcription of the marginal or interlinear glosses and rubrics, since they lack their own proper ruling, when they take more than one line, they are transcribed without marking any partition.

The foliation is indicated at the beginning of each leaf. The alphabetical superscripts refer to the glosses put under their corresponding law chapter; these superscripts have been placed in an attempt to reproduce, as far as possible, the original correspondence between the gloss and its textual referent; unfortunately the almost complete absence of reference-marks in the manuscript, sometimes makes it extremely difficult to unambiguously position the glosses—which begin with an angular paragraph mark—even when they are close to the terms or passages they expand upon. On three occasions, however, in order to link a passage from the text with its gloss the scribe used a reference-mark comprising two or three small dots placed over the term or part it explains, and over the gloss *incipit* as well: at fol. 1^{r}, at the end of the

---

62 Boretius, *Liber Legis Langobardorum Papiensis dictus*, 290–585.

63 Bluhme, *Legis Langobardorum libri tres*, 607–40.

64 Bluhme, *Edictus Langobardorum*, 1–225.

65 Claudio Azzara, and Stefano Gasparri, eds., *Le leggi dei Longobardi. Storia, memoria e diritto di un popolo germanico* (Rome: Viella, 2005).

66 Stephan Kuttner, "Notes on the Presentation of Text and Apparatus in Editing Works of the Decretists and Decretalists," *Traditio* 15 (1959): 452–64.

tenth written line, three dots connect *persona* to the outer marginal note *libera*; at the beginning of the fourteenth line two dots link the verb *seruire* with the inner marginal gloss *idest ualde seruire*. At fol. 2^{v}, approximately in the middle of the tenth line, three dots apparently relate *mortui* to *eo* at the beginning of the underlying interlinear gloss. In the present edition, the marginal or interlinear position of each gloss within the leaf and with respect to its referent has been clearly indicated.

The numeral superscripts refer to the critical apparatus. As the transcription is based only on Turin, MS F.IV.1 fr. 11, the original spelling has been preserved without any graphic standardization. In the case of scribal abbreviations for *haec, prae-, quae* that, considering the late dating of the text, could have been expanded *hec, pre-, que*, the classical Latin spelling has been preferred for the sake of clarity.

The use of the capital letters tends likewise to reproduce what appears in the original text, except for some obvious cases like the *nomina sacra*, the anthroponyms and the ethnonyms, generally written in small letters in the manuscript, but here transcribed with a capital initial—in particular: *Dei* (fol. 1^{r-v}), *Euangelia* e *Euangelii* (fol. 1^{r-v}), *Rothar* (fols. 1^{v}, 2^{r-v}),[67] *Gallos* (fol. 1^{v}), *Longobardorum* (fol. 1^{v}), *Octonis* (fol. 1^{v}), *Karoli* and *Liutprandi* (fol. 2^{v}). Also, the headings of the *Lombarda* books and *incipit* to the law chapters quoted in the allegations present in the notes are always introduced by a capital letter and placed between double quotes.

The supply of punctuation is limited to the minimum, in an endeavor to conciliate the textual forms and the actual orthography.

Where the script proves to be hopelessly illegible because of the fire damage, the sign [...] generically represents the loss of a definite, but not precisely quantifiable, number of words or letters. The size of the lacuna is, as far as possible, discussed in the critical apparatus; those glosses which are barely visible—hardly perceptible text fragments or single letters—which were perhaps already erased and therefore are, obviously, unattributed to any textual referent, are also discussed in the apparatus.

Both the position of each law clause within the *Lombarda Vulgata* and its number in its own edictal collection are indicated in square brackets. Where these diverge, the number of the clause per the *Liber Papiensis* is placed in round brackets.

No mention is made here where there are variants from Boretius' edition, when the German editor registers them as acceptable alternatives testified in

67 On only two occasions is the name "*Rothar*" written with a capital initial (fol. 2^{r-v}).

various manuscripts. On the contrary, scribal errors, or at least forms unattested in the tradition, and even a simple reversal of words, are indicated.

Conspectus Siglorum

⟨ ⟩	editor's reading
⟦ ⟧	scribal expunction
[...]	illegible text
|	end of the written line
||	end of the page
EL	*Edictus Langobardorum* (ed. Bluhme)[68]
Lomb.	*Lombarda Vulgata* (ed. Bluhme)[69]
LP	*Liber Papiensis* (ed. Boretius)[70]
Charl.	Charles the Great
Henr.	Henry I of Germany
Liut.	Liutprand
Roth.	Rothari
chap.	chapter
fol.	*folio*
fr.	fragment
lo.int.	lower interlinear space
up.int.	upper interlinear space
in.marg.	inner margin
out.marg.	outer margin
lo.marg.	lower margin
up.marg.	upper margin
n.	note
p.	page

68 Bluhme, *Edictus Langobardorum*, 1–225.

69 Bluhme, *Legis Langobardorum libri tres*, 623–640.

70 Boretius, *Liber Legis Langobardorum Papiensis dictus*, 290–585.

1r [***Lomb*. I, IX, 20, Liut. 21**] et[(a)][1] in eo ⟦uero⟧[2] ordine[(b)] sicut supra adnexum est[(c)]. Et[3] si dominus eius | negauerit[(d)] quod per ipsius consilium factum non fuisset[(e)], pu|rificet se ad legem Dei[(f)][4], et componat ipsum mortuum sicut | antea fuit consuetudo[(g)], et ipsum insuper seruum tradat[(h)] | in manibus parentum defuncti[(i)]. |

a) up./out.marg.[5]: Si seruus duorum vel plurium [...] superueniens liberum hominem occiderit quamquam [...] singuli tamen domini res suas debent amittere quia p[...]. Si uero absque iussu dominorum liberum hominem occiderit, singuli seruum tradentes pro portione serui uuidrigild componant. Si uero seruus p[...] occid[...] iussu unius domini ceteris non iubentibus, ille qui iussit res suas omnes amittat ceteris dominis dantibus guidrigild iubentis.

Siquis habens inimicum seruo suo dixerit "ille taliter est michi inimicus, uide ne eum assalias set si te assalierit et te defendendo eum occidere poteris, non euadat", et si ita contigerit, dicebant antiqui q[...][6] omnes res suas deberet amittere, ideo scilicet, quia ⟨seruus⟩[7] consilio domini [...][8] ⟨per⟩petrauerat[9]. Set exorbitabant quia haec lex non in alio casu omnes suas substantias perdere praecepit, nisi quando seruus super alium ambulando homicidium fec[...] euidens inconueniens sequeretur.

In.marg.: supra titulum c. "Si seruus aut ancilla" [= *Lomb*. I, IX, 7] capitulum;

b) up.int.: idest casu, scilicet cum fuit homicidium super alium ambulando;

c) up./lo.int.: idest per supradictam legem "Siquis liber" set non amittat uel etiam sicut dicit "Siquis liber" [= *Lomb*. I, IX, 19] quod melius est;

d) in.marg.: infra "Qualiter quis se defendere". "Si pro quacumque causa" [= *Lomb*. II, LV, 9];

e) lo.int.: scilicet de consilio;

f) up.int.: idest per sacramentum Euangelii lex uocantur [...][10];

g) up.int.: idest guidrigild[11];

1 *et*] not in *LP*.

2 *uero*] expunged by the scribe.

3 Between the lines, the abbreviation *c̃p̃* is neither easy to place, nor to interpret. In fact, it is quite similar in size to the rest of the main text, but certainly not part of it.

4 *Dei*] Patetta—*Ordalie*, 294 n. 2—reads *ad legem Dei* as "oath on the New Testament".

5 It is a gloss that is extremely difficult to read due to the fire damage, some passages are illegible, in particular the first two lines in the upper margin.

6 An already mentioned hole in the outer margin, partially compromises the gloss text.

7 *seruus*] completed according to Boretius' edition (*LP*, chap. 21, p. 417). Here the text shows an almost unidentifiable sign.

8 Before the lacuna there is an illegible word.

9 *perpetrauerat*] completed following Boretius' reading: *homicidium perpetraverat* (*LP*, chap. 21, p. 417). In the text only *-petrauerat* is legible, the first part of the word is missing due to a parchment lacuna.

10 Hereunder and in the underlying interlinear space up to the next gloss, some almost illegible words, possibly deliberately erased, can be discerned. What can be distinguished is: [...] *filium habuit* [...] *est*.

11 As with the previous gloss, here too, some practically unidentifiable words follow, possibly erased on purpose; *est* [...] *infra "Siquis* [...]" is barely visible.

h) in.marg.: infra "De culpis seruorum" [= *Lomb.* I, XXXVI][12];
i) line and out.marg.: hoc detrahit uel addit legi, "Si seruus talem" infra "de culpis seruorum" [= *Lomb.* I, XXXVI, 5].

[***Lomb.* I, IX, 21, Liut. 62 (*LP* 61)**] Recolimus qualiter iam statuimus, ut qui hominem liberum oc|cidere praesumpserit(a), ut res suas in integrum perdat, et qui se de|fendendo hominem occiderit, componat secundum qualitatem per|sonę(b). Nunc autem statuere praeuidimus, quo modo sit ipsa quantitas[13] | consideranda. Consuetudo enim est, ut pro minima persona(c) quae | ⟦quae⟧[14] exercitalis homo inuenitur,[15] CL solidos componatur, et qui primus est(d), | CCC solidos. De gasindiis uero nostris uolumus, ut quicumque | ex minimis(e) in tali ordine(f) occisus fuerit, pro eo | quod nobis deseruire(g) uidetur, CC solidos fiat compositus. Ma|iores(h) uero secundum quales personę fuerint(i), ut in nostra conside|ratione uel successorum nostrorum debeat permanere, quomodo[16] usque | ad CCC solidos compositio ipsa debeat[17] ascendere. |

a) Up.int.: super alium ambulando et nulla iusta causa praecedente;
b) up.int., inf. and out.marg.: persone qualitas quae hac in lege[18] discernitur, non solum in homicidio a se defendente set etiam a nolente commisso tam in femina quam in masculo perspici debet;
c) out.marg. with reference mark: libera;
d) up.int. and out.marg.: idest maior inter exercitales;
e) up.int.: scilicet gasindiis;
f) up.int., inf. and out.marg.: idest quod obtineat fieri compositio secundum qualitatem persone uel aliter in tali ordine, idest defendendo uel nolendo;
g) in.marg. with reference mark: idest ualde seruire;
h) up.int. and out.marg.: gasindii;
i) up.int.: set uolumus.

[***Lomb.* I, IX, 22, Liut. 92 (*LP* 91)**] Siquis liber homo in terra aliena residens[19] libellario | nomine, homicidium fecerit, et fuga lapsus fuerit, tunc ille | in

12 This gloss is difficult to read.
13 *quantitas*] *LP qualitas.*
14 *quae*] scribal expunction due to its reduplication at the beginning of the following line.
15 *inuenitur*] *LP esse invenitur.*
16 *quomodo*] *-modo* abbreviated and added between the lines with an omission mark by the corrector.
17 *debeat*] *-b-* added between the lines with an omission mark by the corrector.
18 *hac in lege*] *LP in hac lege.*
19 *residens*] corrected from *resideret* by the scribe himself; *-ret* has been expunged and above the second *-e-* has been placed the abbreviation mark indicating the presence of a nasal, the final *-s* is in superscript.

cuius terra ipse homicida laborauit aut[20] inhabita|uit[21], habeat spatium[22], in mense uno ad[23] ipsum hominem perqui|rendum[24]; et si eum inuenerit, habeat licentiam ipsum hominem, | quamuis liber sit, comprehendendi et tradendi in manu[25] | illius cui homicidium fecit; et si hoc non fecerit, dare debet | medietatem de omnibus rebus mobilibus, excepto[26] tecto[27], quas[28] | in ipsa casa habuerit ipse homicida[29]. Quod si nec | hoc facere uoluerit[30], ipse cuius terra est, dare debeat libel|lario nomine ipsam terram ei cui homicidium factum est, ut | reddat ei sicut exinde[31] reddebat[32] qui ipsum homici|dium fecit. Tamen[33] de his tribus capitulis, in illius sit po|testate eligendi cuius terra est, et faciat exinde qualiter uoluerit[34]. |

20 *aut*] placed between the lines by the corrector, substituting an original *et*.

21 *laborauit aut inhabitauit*] LP *habitavit*.

22 *spatium*] corrected from *spatio*; the corrector espunged -*o* and placed above it -*u* with the abbreviation mark for the presence of a nasal.

23 *ad*] added between the lines with an omission mark by the corrector.

24 *perquirendum*] corrected from *perquirendo*; the reviser expunged -*o* and placed -*u* above it with the abbreviation mark for the presence of a nasal. Also the following punctuation mark has been emended.

25 *comprehendendi et tradendi in manu*] LP *comprehendendum et tradendum in manus*.

26 *excepto*] -*ce*- added between the lines with an omission mark by the corrector.

27 *tecto*] LP *tectora* and in its apparatus only the variant *tecta*.

28 *quas*] -*a*- added between the lines by the corrector above *q*-. LP *quae*. Evidently here the relative agrees only with the feminine *rebus*, unless it is a grammatical mistake.

29 *habuerit ipse homicida*] LP *ipse homicida habuit*.

30 *facere uoluerit*] LP *voluerit facere*.

31 *sicut exinde*] LP *ei exinde, sicut ille*.

32 *reddebat*] on -*a*- the scribe cancelled the nasal abbreviation mark.

33 *Tamen*] shortened and added by the corrector between the lines above the expunged *uel inde*.

34 *uoluerit*] taken down.

[*Lomb.* I, IX, 23, Liut. 118 (*LP* 117)] Recolimus enim quod statuimus cum nostris iudicibus ||

ut qui hominem liberum occidere praesumpserit[(a)], omnem substantiam | suam amittat. Modo uero, dum repeterent singuli | homines quos forte aliqua duritia detinebat, quod[(b)] | parens eorum qui in lectulo mortuus[1] fuerat[2] per ue|nenum occisus esset, et dum per pugnam ipsam causam, | sicut antiqua fuerat consuetudo, querere dispone|bant grauis causa nobis esse comparuit, ut sub uno | scuto per pugnam omnem substantiam suam homo amitteret[(c)]. | Ideoque statuere praeuidimus ut, si ammodo talis causa e|merserit, quod ille qui[3] mortem parentis sui per pug|nam probare uoluerit,[4] quod eum per uenenum occidisset, ob|seruatis his quae[5] in anteriore edicto affiximus[(d)6], ut per | Euangelia affirmet[(e)] quod asto animo causam ipsam non di|cat[(f)] vel querat[7], nisi quod[8] ei certa suspitio sit, postea potestatem habeat | querere per pugnam, sicut antiqua fuit consuetudo[(g)], | et si ei ferita uenerit[(h)] cui ipsum crimen[9] mittitur, aut | ad camphionem[(i)] ipsius quem conductum habuerit, | non amittat omnem substantiam suam, set componat[10] secundum qualita|tem personę, sicut antea fuit lex[(j)] componendi; quia incerti | sumus de iudicio Dei[11] et multos audiuimus per pug|nam sine iusta causa[(k)] suam causam perdere[(l)12], set propter consu|etudinem gentis nostrę Longobardorum, legem ipsam[(m)] | uetare non possumus. | 1ᵛ

1 *mortuus*] corrected from *mortuis*, *-u-* is placed above the expunged *-i-*.

2 *qui in lectulo mortuus fuerat*] *LP qui in lectulo suo mortuus fuerat.*

3 *quod ille qui*] *LP ut ille qui*; the manuscript tradition documents also *quod ille quis*. Our text shows an emendation after the *q-* that transforms an original *qui illi* in *quod ille.*

4 *probare uoluerit*] *LP querere voluerit.*

5 *obseruatis his quae*] *LP obseruato eo quod* or *obseruatis eis quae*. The fragment variant is attested in the edictal tradition (*EL*, chap. 118, p. 156 nn. x, y).

6 *affiximus*] the first *-f-* has been added by the scribe with an omission mark between the lines above *a-*.

7 *non dicat uel querat*] *LP non querat.* In the manuscript *uel querat* has been added between the lines above *dicat.*

8 *quod*] added by the scribe between the lines with the omission mark between *nisi* and *ei certa.*

9 *ipsum crimen*] *LP crimen ipsum.*

10 *set componat*] *LP sed componat eum.*

11 *Dei*] added by the corrector between the lines with the omission mark.

12 *sine iusta causa suam causam perdere*] *LP sine iustitia causam suam perdere.* The fragment variant is attested in the edictal tradition (*EL*, chap. 118, p. 156 nn. l, m).

a) Up.marg. and lo.int.[13]: super eum ambulando uel nulla iusta causa praecedente;
b) up.int. and in.marg.: scilicet dicendo;
c) out.marg.: Grauis[14] causa est ut sub uno scuto homines substantiam suam amittere debeant;
d) in.marg.: infra "Qualiter quis se defendere". "Siquis alium" [= *Lomb.* II, LV, 16];
e) up.int.: quotiens enim aliquis pugnam querit de asto iurare debet;
f) out.marg.: [...] hoc quod dicitur pugnam praecipit, uidetur contra legem "Si liber homo" set [...] et certum est aliquem homicidium commisisset super eum ambulando et hic cum incertum est;
g) up.int.: scilicet ut duo tantum cum scutis et fustibus certarent;
h) up.int.: ita ut cadat[15];
i) up./lo.int.: cum talis persona sit cui per camphionem pugnare licet ut puer uel ille qui est in decrepita etate ut in lege ulti "De parricidiis" [*Lomb.* I, X, 5], alioquin obuiaretur huic a lege Octonis "Laicorum uero nullum" infra "De aduocatis uicedominis" [= *Lomb.* II, XLVII, 11] et a lege "Quicumque" infra "Qualiter quis se defendere" [= *Lomb.* II, LV, 30];
j) out.marg. with reference mark: scilicet Rothar quae est "Siquis alii uenenum" [= *Lomb.* I, IX, 6]. Supra idest asto;
k) up./lo.int.: ut in lege "De furtis". "Siquis alium" [= *Lomb.* I, XXV, 59], uel dicit hoc propter Gallos cisalpine terrę, qui iniuste per pugnam Longobardorum causam, idest patriam[16] suam ammisere[17];
l) out.marg.: Multos audiuimus propter pugnam causam suam perdere. [...] x[...] "Si liber homo se defendendo" [= *Lomb.* I, IX, 19] contradicit, qui enim ueneno alium occidit [...] iubendo occidit huic et illi derogatur per legem quicumque ueneficio [= *Lomb.* I, IX, 40];
m) in.marg.: idest consuetudinem uel pugnam.

[***Lomb.* I, IX, 24, Liut. 136 (*LP* 135)**] Item annuntiatum est nobis, quod quidam[18] habebat pu|teum[19] in curte sua et secundum consuetudinem furcam | et tol-

13 This gloss is almost illegible; however, its content can be reasonably reconstructed considering what we can see at the beginning (*super*) and in the end (*-cedente*) and then comparing it with other textual passages, namely the gloss (a) of the chapter *Lomb.* I, IX, 21, LIUT. 62 (*LP* 61).

14 In the outer margin, before the *G-* of *Gravis* some undecipherable signs are visible.

15 *ita ut cadat*] it is effectively a gloss—See also Patetta, *Ordalie*, 438 n. 3—even though it apparently looks more like an interlinear addition to the main text. The size of its letters is in fact considerably larger than that normally used for the marginal and interlinear notations.

16 *patriam*] *-i-* added by the scribe above *-a-*.

17 *ammisere*] perhaps better *amisere* but clearly above *a-* there is an abbreviation mark indicating the presence of a nasal. Moreover, with regards to this entire gloss, Patetta ("Nuove ipotesi", 938–39 n. 2) discussing new theories on the place of origin of *Lex Lombarda*, highlights how this expression "*cisalpinae terrae*", considering the territorial partition at that time, could possibly indicate both Lombardy and Piedmont.

18 *quidam*] *LP quidam homo.*

19 *puteum*] originally *putheum*, then *t* and *h* were expunged and the round stroke of *h* transformed in a *t*.

lenum ad auriendam aquam.[20] Ueniens autem alter[21] homo, | stetit sub ipso tolleno, et cum[22] uenisset quidam ad | auriendam aquam de ipso putheo et incaute | ipsum tollenum dimississet, uenit super eum qui sub | ipso stabat et mortuus est sub ipso[23]. Dum autem re|quisitio de morte eius fieret[24], quis eum deberet compo|nere, et nobis relatum fuisset, ita nobis et nostris iu ||

20 *ad auriendam aquam*] LP *ad auriendum aquam.* The variant of the fragment appears instead in the edictal tradition (EL, chap. 136, p. 166 n. k).

21 *alter*] added between the lines with the omission mark.

22 *et cum*] LP *cum autem.* The variant of the fragment appears instead in the edictal tradition (EL, chap. 136, p. 166 n. n).

23 *sub ipso*] not present in EL and LP, not even as a textual variant of the manuscript testimonies.

24 *de morte eius fieret*] LP *eiusdem mortui facta fuerit.*

2r [*Lomb.* I, X, 5, (*LP* Henr. 2)] penitentie subdatur[1]. Quod si ille cui crimen arguitur[2] | negare uoluerit, per se pugnam faciat, nec lice|at[3] camphionem pro se dare, nisi decrepita etas, | aut iuvenilis, aut infirmitas pugnare prohibuerit. |

[*Lomb.* I, XI, 1, Roth. 129] R. DE HOMICIDIO SERUORUM UEL ALDIORUM[4] Rex Rothar(a). Siquis aldium alienum occi|derit(b), componat solidos LX.

a) In.marg.: infra "Qualiter quis se" capitulum uadie legis[5] [= *Lomb.* II, LV, 5];
b) up.int., inf.: [...] et sic in sequentibus.
Out.marg.: Supra capitula homicidio liberorum nomine [= *Lomb.* I, IX]. Ist[...] non le[...] de homicidio [...] "De homicidio seruorum uel aldiorum" [= *Lomb.* I, XI][6].

[*Lomb.* I, XI, 2, Roth. 130] Siquis seruum ministerialem pro|batum ut supra(a) aut doctum occiderit domi(b), componat solidos | L.

a) Up.int.: idest in prima lege "De plagis seruorum" [= *Lomb.* I, VIII, 3];
b) up.int. and out.marg.: scilicet palam alioquin infirmata lege supra posita "Siquis homicidium absconse perpetrauit" [= *Lomb.* I, IX, 3].

[*Lomb.* I, XI, 2, Roth. 131] De alio uero seruo[7] ministeriali qui secundus eius(a) inuenitur | esse[8], tamen nomen ministeriale[9] habet, siquis occiderit, componat solidos XXV[10]. |

a) Up.int.: idest qui non ita eruditus est.

[*Lomb.* I, XI, 3, Roth. 132] Siquis seruum alienum massarium | occiderit, componat XX solidos[11]. |

1 *subdatur*] *LP subdetur.*
2 *Quod si ille cui crimen arguitur*] *LP Quod si ille qui crimine arguitur.*
3 *liceat*] *LP liceat ei.*
4 Rubric placed in the outer margin corresponding to the fourth line.
5 Above this gloss, in the inner margin, in correspondence to the second line of writing, another note is barely visible: indeed, only the abbreviated words: *idest* [...] *contra legem* [...], are quite legible; another few letters are just perceptible. Considering that this area of the parchment is apparently intact, this gloss may have been intentionally erased.
6 What was said in the previous note applies here too, except that in this case perhaps something more is readable. The interlinear part is almost illegible, the first marginal line a little more visible, whereas a second one is barely perceivable. It is possible, however, to discern some brief juxtaposed glosses.
7 *seruo*] not in *LP*, but attested in the edictal tradition (*EL*, chap. 131, p. 30 n. b).
8 *secundus eius inuenitur esse*] *LP secundus ei invenitur.*
9 *ministeriale*] *LP ministerialis.*
10 *componat solidos XXV*] taken down.
11 *XX solidos*] *LP solidos XX.*

[*Lomb.* I, XI, 4, **Roth.** 133] Siquis[(a)] seruum alienum bobulcum de sala[(b)] | occiderit, componat solidos XX[12]. |

a) Up.int.: uerna [...][13];
b) up.int.: idest de domo donicata uel casa.

[*Lomb.* I, XI, 5, **Roth.** 134] Siquis[(a)] seruum alienum rusticanum qui sub | massario[14] est occiderit, componat solidos XVI[(b)]. |

a) Up.int.: Mirabile cum tantum pro morte componat quantum si ei ante stetisset;
b) in.marg.: capitula.

[*Lomb.* I, XI, 6, **Roth.** 135] Siquis porcarium[(a)] alienum occiderit, magistrum tamen il|lum, qui sub se discipulos habet duos aut III aut | amplius, componat solidos L. De inferioribus autem porcariis, | siquis occiderit, componat solidos XXV. |

a) Up.int.: seruum.

[*Lomb.* I, XI, 7, **Roth.** 136] Siquis pecorarium[15], aut caprarium, seu armentarium occiderit, | magistrum tamen[16], componat solidos XX. Pro discipulis autem, | qui sequentes sunt, siquis occiderit, componat solidos XVI. De | illis uero pastoribus dicimus, qui ad liberos homines seruiunt | et de sala propria exeunt. |

[*Lomb.* I, XI, 8, **Roth.** 137] Siquis infantem paruulum de seruo massario[(a)] casu | faciente nolendo[17] occiderit[(b)], arbitretur a iudice[(c)] et[18] | secundum qualem habuit etatem, aut quale lucrum facere poterat, ita componatur[(d)19]. |

a) Up./lo.int.: similiter de infantibus [...]e[...]orum seruorum pena arbitrata est imponenda;
b) in.marg.: capitula haec uero nolendo cum supra uolendo;

---

12 *componat solidos XX*] taken down.
13 The rest of the brief gloss is illegible due to some discoloration, marginally affecting, without serious consequences, the main text too.
14 *massario*] the first -*s*- added between the lines.
15 *pecorarium*] corrected from *porcarium* placing -*e*- above an expunged -*o*-, converting -*rc*- in -*co*- and adding an abbreviation mark for -*r*- above -*oa*-.
16 *Siquis pecorarium aut caprarium seu armentarium magistrum tamen occiderit*] *LP De pecorario, caprario seu armentario occiso magistro tamen siquis occiderit*. However, *LP* indicates the here attested variant as present in some testimonies, with the difference of the occurrence of *porcarium* instead of *pecorarium* (*LP*, chap. 136, p. 311 n. a).
17 *nolendo*] neither in *LP* nor in the manuscripts of the Edict (*EL*, chap. 137, 31).
18 *et*] not in *LP*.
19 -*cere poterat, ita componatur*] taken down.

c) up./lo.int. and out.marg.: non exprimit çertam compositionem ut supra quoniam uoluit distinguere uolendo uel nolendo delinquentes. Illos grauiori pena et ultra damnum extensa affligendo hos uero in sola damni ratione multando, quidem hodie recte considerantibus contra uidebitur punitis leuius grauius delinquentibus et hoc uilitate monente contra mentem certe legislatorum accidit. Cum enim nolendo peccantes da[...]one afflixerunt multomagis uolendo affligunt, ea propter iustum est electione penę suprascriptę damn[...]est quae malit accipere domino tribui;
d) out.marg.: Nota. Quocumque modo datum damnum componi debere;

[**_Lomb._ I, XI, 9, Roth.** 376 (*LP* 377)] Nullus praesumat al|diam alienam, aut ancillam quasi strigam, quae dicitur ma|sca occidere[(a)], quia christianis[20] mentibus nullatenus est | credendum[21], nec possibile est, ut mulier hominem | uiuum intrinsecus possit commedere. Siquis deinceps | talem illicitam et nefandam rem perpetrare praesump|serit, si aldiam occiderit, componat pro statu eius solidos LX[(b)] ||

a) out.marg.: Ista contradicit legem II "De iniuriis mulierum" [= *Lomb.* I, XVI, 2] uidetur enim precipere fieri p[...]. Set sane intellegentibus tantum de fornicatione ·p· fieri p[...]et.
b) in.marg.: Infra depositi capitulum[22] [= *Lomb.* II, XXVI, 1];

20 *christianis*] the corrector emended *christianis* in *humanis* placing *huma* above *christia-*. The variant *humanis* is present neither in the manuscripts of the *LP*, nor in the testimonies of Rothari's Edict (*EL*, chap. 376, 87). Moreover, the corrector evidently acted before the compilation of the gloss apparatus, since the interlinear annotations had to adjust here to the presence of this correction.

21 *est credendum*] *LP credendum est.*

22 I put this gloss here, even though between this *allegatio* and the chapter of the law in question there is no direct nexus that allows us to place it more precisely. There is, however, a relation between this gloss and what is expressed in the marginal and interlinear note added to the first lines of fol. 2ᵛ. Finally, above this gloss, some traces are barely perceivable of another, now illegible note.

LX[1], et insuper addat pro culpa solidos C[(a)], medieta|tem regi et medietatem cuius aldia fuerit. Si autem ancilla | fuerit, componat pro statu eius sicut supra constitutum est. Siue[2] mi|nisterialis aut rusticana fuerit[(b)], et insuper pro culpa | solidos LX, medietatem regi et medietatem cuius ancilla fuerit[3]; si | uero iudex hoc malum[4] perpetrare iusserit, ipse de suo | proprio penam suprascriptam componat[(c)]. | 2v

a) Up.marg. and interl.: Non obuiat huic lex Liutprandi [= Liut. 131, *LP* 130] ex una causa alicui duas calumnias imponi prohibens quia illa loquitur quando ex uno facto idest maleficio plures nascuntur actiones. Set de hac culpa idest maleficio licet LX pro seruis et insuper C pro culpa componi praecipiat non idem dicere ex hoc maleficio concurrunt actiones set C solidos furis prioris pene exaggeratio uel illa est specialis in deposito;
b) out.marg. with reference mark: et superiores leges de occisione seruorum loquentes pro ancilla ministeriali solidos XXV et ancilla ministeriali et probata L et pro rusticana solidos XX;
c) in.marg.: Nota. Qui iussu iudicis delinquit non teneri.

[*Lomb.* I, XII, 1, **Roth. 16**] R. DE SEPULCHRO UIOLATO ET DE EO QUI HOMINEM MORTUUM EXPOLIAUERIT[5]. Rex Rothar. Siquis[(a)] hominem[(b)] | mortuum in flumine[(c)] aut foris[(d)] inuenerit et eum[6] expo|liauerit[(e)] et celauerit, componat parentibus mortui[(f)] solidos LXXX, | etsi eum inuenerit et exspoliauerit et mox uicinis pa|tefecerit et cognoscetur[7] quia pro mercedis causa fecerit, | nam non furandi animo, reddat spolia quae super eum inuenit, | et amplius ei calumpnia non generetur[(g)]. |

a) Up.int.: liber uel seruus;
b) up.int.: liberum uel seruum;
c) up.int.: infra, dicta ratione;
d) up.int.: scilicet in ripa fluminis;
e) interlinear space after *eum* and in.marg.: scilicet anima lucrandi intercipiendi.
Moreover in.marg.: Supra "De homicidiis liberorum hominum". "Siquis hominem" [= *Lomb.* I, IX, 17].
Out.marg.: h[...] qu[.]m hanc publicam occasionem exponit illa crimina [...] publica[8].

---

1 *lx*] dittography; it is in fact already present at the end of fol. 2r.
2 *siue*] *LP si*. At first also our scribe copied *si*, then he added to it *-ue* between the lines with an omission mark.
3 *fuerit*] corrected from an abbreviated *fuarit* placing *-i-* above *-a-*.
4 *hoc malum*] *LP hoc opus malum*. The textual variant is instead present in the edictal tradition (*EL*, chap. 376, p. 87 text and notes v, w).
5 Rubric placed on the line and the inner margin in correspondence to the seventh and eighth lines.
6 *eum*] not in *LP*.
7 *cognoscetur*] *LP cognoscitur*.
8 This gloss is difficult to decipher since it is particularly discoloured.

Infra "De eo qui peculium in dampno inuenerit". "Siquis porcos" [= *Lomb.* I, XXIII, 7] capitulum. Set non obuiat, quia illa loquitur de rebus alterius heredis esse nullius. Res enim mortui in nullius bonis intelliguntur uel lex illa imponit penam nomine rerum malo ordine ablatarum haec uero nomine corporis expoliati;

f) lo.int. with reference mark: eo scilicet quod spoliauit eo uero quod malo ordine contractauit si petitum fuit sibi nonum reddat;

g) out.marg.: Infra "De his qui in ecclesiis confugium fecerint" capitulum "Siquis in" [= *Lomb.* II, XXXIX, 5]. Set illa de alio damno in emunitate commisso loquitur, quia lex illa quae est inuenta eorum fauore quibus damnum datur in emunitate, in hoc casu loqueretur tam quam fauore quorum [...] introductum ad eorum lesionem conuerteretur.

[***Lomb.*** **I, XII, 1, Roth. 15**] Siquis(a) sepulturam hominis(b) mortui ruperit(c) et corpus ex|poliauerit(d) aut foras(e)[9] iactauerit, DCCCC solidos sit cul|pabilis(f) parentibus defuncti, et si parentes proximi non[10] | fuerint, tunc castaldius regis aut sculdasius[11] requi|rat culpam ipsam et ad curtem regis exigat. |

a) Up.int.: liber vel seruus;

b) up.int.: liberi;

c) up.marg.[12]: liber vel seruus neminis ob id quod inf[...] [...]p[...] defuncti lex iusta g[...] [...] sepultura [...] specialiter fin[...] de sepultura liberi [...] ideo de s[...][...] facit.

[...] sepulturam uiolauit aut tantum corpus expoliauit quod componi debeat haec lex non diffinit. Set si in emunitate utrumque fecerit hanc compositionem faciat et DC solidos in emunitate componat. Si non tantum ruperit et si expoliaverit [...] [...], DC solidos in emunitate componat.

d) in.marg. after *ex-*: infra "De culpis seruorum". "Si seruus talem" [= *Lomb.* I, XXXVI, 5] capitulum;

e) up.int.: scilicet extra sepulturam;

f) up.int.: scilicet liber, de seruo uero itur per legem igitur.

Moreover up.int.: per hoc dici non potest de liberis tantum loqui, generaliter enim incipit et specialiter finit.

[***Lomb.*** **I, XIII, 1, Roth. 17**] R. NE AD REGEM UENIENTIBUS INIURIA FIAT[13]. Rex Rothar(a). Siquis ex baronibus(b) nostris ad | nos uenire uoluerit, securus ueniat, et illesus | ad suos reuertatur, et nullus de aduersariis illius | aliquam[14] iniuriam

9 *foras*] LP *foris*. The variant of the fragment is instead attested in the edictal tradition (*EL*, chap. 15, p. 15 n. g).

10 In the outer margin, in correspondence to this seventeenth line, before *-pabilis* appears the siglum for *idest*, without any other references.

11 *sculdasius*] LP *sculdais*. Also in the Edict this term remains un-Latinized (*EL*, chap. 15, p. 15 text and n. t).

12 This marginal gloss, like the one on fol. 1r, is extremely difficult to read because of the damage to the parchment. In each of the irreparable lacunae more than one word is missing.

13 Rubric placed in the inner margin in correspondence to the nineteenth and twentieth lines.

14 *aliquam*] LP *aliquam ei*.

in itinere aut molestiam facere praesumat; | tantum est, ut ille qui ad regem uenire festinat, ho|neste ueniat(c), et nullam lesionem aut dampnum | cuique[15] in ipso itinere ad regem ueniendo aut rede|undo faciat. Nam si fecerit, sicut subter in hoc edicto | scriptum est(d) componat[16]. |

a) Out.marg.: explicito tractatu illo quo prohibetur iniuria fieri mortuis, ponit illum ne iniuria fiat uiuis et primum ne uenientibus ad regem fiat;
b) up.int.: fidelibus;
c) in.marg.: infra "De iterantibus" [= *Lomb.* III, IV, 3];
d) up.int.: Respexit ad compositiones plagarum et feritarum quas post hanc legem "De plagis et feritis" [= *Lomb.* I, VII] fieri iussit.

[***Lomb.* I, XIII, 1, Roth. 18**] Siquis ex aduersariis manu arma|ta[17] super quemcumque hominem ad regem uenientem(a) iniecerit[18], | pro(b) sua iniuria propter[19] qualemcumque culpam uindican|dam, DCCCC solidos sit culpabilis, medietatem regi et | medietatem cui iniuria illata fuerit. ||

a) Up./lo.int., in./lo.marg.: Capitula. Set hic ibat ad regem pro sua utilitate cum ille de quo sequens lex loquitur, iret pro missatico a rege sibi iniuncto.
Idem est de redeunte secundum quosdam ad ea enim quae sepius contingunt iura aptantur set melius est ut uadat in praesentia regis per capitulum Karoli "De his qui legem obseruare contempserint ut per fideiussores in praesentia regis deducantur" [= *LP* Charl. 91], quemadmodum legis contemptor; qui sit legis contemptor uidere possumus per legem quae est: "Siquis ex baronibus" in hoc quod dicit "illesus reuertatur" [= Roth. 17];
b) out.marg.: eis non fit iniuria set dominus per eos fieri uidetur.

15 *cuique*] *sic* in the text; instead correctly *LP cuicumque.*

16 *scriptum est, componat*] *LP constitutum est, componat.* The variant of the fragment is not even attested in the edictal tradition (*EL*, chap. 17, p. 16 text and n. b); *scriptum est, componat* taken down. The corrector emended *scriptum* partially by scraping and partially, perhaps, by modifying a previous *certum*; *-ip-* has been added between the lines with an omission mark.

17 *manu armata*] *LP manum armatam.*

18 *iniecerit*] the second *-i-* appears to be a corrector's emendation.

19 *propter*] *LP aut.* The textual variant is not even present in the edictal tradition (*EL*, chap. 18, p. 16 n. e). Moreover, on *propter*, abbreviated and preceded by a scrape, the hand of the corrector partially acted.

CHAPTER 15

'A Rather Laborious and Harassing Occupation': The Creation of the *Ancient Laws and Institutes of Wales* (1841)

Sara Elin Roberts

The laws of medieval Wales are a rich and valuable mine of information on all aspects of life and society in Wales in the Middle Ages, and as such are a crucial historical source. It would be expected that editions of such important texts would abound; but the study of the manuscripts of the Welsh laws, and the links (or lack thereof) between the texts, caused the early editors untold problems. The present author is not in a position to judge whether working on editions of the texts of Welsh law causes issues such as drinking problems, sexual misdemeanors, financial issues and debts, or whether such problems arise as a result of the work. One of the early editors died as a result of a brawl outside a tavern; another, using Welsh law as rehabilitation, lost his clerical position due to financial and other problems and was unable to go to England because of his creditors. It is a worry that working on the Welsh lawtexts is linked to such difficulties—perhaps even causes them. But there is no denying that untangling the complex texts of the Welsh lawtexts is a big task, although the work is perhaps best done sober.

With the problems of previous editors in mind, the present chapter looks at the first modern edition of the Welsh lawtexts, Aneurin Owen's *Ancient Laws and Institutes of Wales* (1841). It will consider how Owen approached his work, and how he dealt with the multiplicity of texts and versions of the laws in the manuscripts which he viewed. His textual decisions in his edition have led to the laws being viewed in a particular way even today, but the suggestion being made here is that this is misleading and that the manuscripts should be viewed as complete texts, moving away from the coloring by earlier editors.

"The literature produced by a profession is often the clearest guide to the state of its intellectual development."[1] There are around forty manuscripts dating from the mid-thirteenth to the sixteenth century preserving a text of

1 John H. Baker, *An Introduction to English Legal History*, 4th ed. (London: Butterworths, 2002), 175.

 | DOI:10.1163/9789004448650_017

medieval Welsh law, and this means that law manuscripts make up the biggest genre of surviving literature in Middle Welsh.[2] The manuscripts themselves are varied, with most of them presenting a unique text of the laws, or at least a text with unique features, which shows that the law was a constantly changing field with the texts being edited and added to throughout the period of development in the thirteenth century and beyond. While this reveals an exciting and lively subject area, and huge interest in the laws in the Middle Ages, it also makes for a complex textual history and the study of the Welsh law manuscripts and texts is a subject in itself.

Medieval Wales, unlike England, was made up of various territories or regions, each with their own ruler, although there were periods in its history when large parts of the country were unified under one king or prince.[3] The borderlands between England and Wales, which also spread across the south of Wales and up as far as Carmarthen and west as far as Pembrokeshire, were Norman territories known as The March. This was a collection of lordships, with some rulers having palatine powers.[4] On the whole, therefore, medieval Wales was not a single entity and there was considerable variety in language, fortune, rule, politics and foreign policy in the various kingdoms of medieval Wales and the March. However, there were some unifying factors, and one of these was the law, which distinguished Wales as a separate country with its own legal system which applied to all the inhabitants of Wales, regardless of ruler or region. Known as "Cyfraith Hywel" (the Law of Hywel), this was a home-grown *volksrecht* system, a law of the people, but perhaps more accurately lawyer-made law. The law of Wales was separate to both Common Law and Canon Law. It may have early origins, and is linked to the ruler Hywel ap Cadell (Hywel Dda, "The Good", d. 950) but there is no actual evidence outside of the lawtexts for any lawmaking activities by Hywel Dda. The link, set out in a story which forms

2 There are also several law manuscripts in Latin, but these are not the focus of this present article. More information can be found in Hywel D. Emanuel, *The Latin Texts of the Welsh Laws* (Cardiff: University of Wales Press, 1967); and Paul Russell, *Welsh Law in Medieval Anglesey. British Library, Harleian MS 1796 (Latin C)*, Texts and Studies in Medieval Welsh Law 2 (Cambridge: Seminar Cyfraith Hywel, 2011).

3 Studies of this period and these rulers include the excellent introduction by Kari Maund, *The Welsh Kings: The Medieval Rulers of Wales* (Stroud: Tempus, 2000).

4 For studies on the March, see for example Robert Rees Davies, *Lordship and Society in the March of Wales* (Oxford: Oxford University Press, 1978); William Rees, *South Wales and the March, 1284–1415* (Oxford: Oxford University Press, 1924); Max Liebermann, *The March of Wales 1067–1300* (Cardiff: University of Wales Press, 2008); Max Liebermann, *The Medieval March of Wales: The Creation and Perception of a Frontier, 1066–1283* (Cambridge: Cambridge University Press, 2010); John Goronwy Edwards, "The Normans and the Welsh March," *Proceedings of the British Academy* 42 (1956): 155–77.

the Prologue of the law manuscripts, is likely to have been formed to protect the laws from attacks from Norman churchmen.[5]

The earlier lawtexts are presented as a code of law, a single book with the intention of suggesting that they contain all of the law of Wales. It was a compensation-based system, with every individual expected to be responsible for his own actions and his property, and compensation was to be paid for any action which caused injury or loss to others. Rather than being a disorganized text, the law manuscripts are subdivided into recognizable sections called tractates, and these are thematically organized. Tractates include the Laws of Court, usually the lengthy opening book in a law manuscript, detailing the royal court and the officials of the king, and giving the laws a royal link. The laws of country are made up of several shorter tractates, including *inter alia* the law of women, land law, suretyship (contract), the Three Columns of Law (homicide, theft and fire) and sections of law on animals and agriculture. A collection of triads, sentences listing legal rules or situations in threes, also form a tractate included in most of the law manuscripts.[6]

Dating the laws is a difficult task, since the laws are unlikely to have been written in their entirety at one point in time—rather, there was development of the text, and re-working of some sections. The laws do not show evidence of being written in Old Welsh, although some sections of the law are clearly early, even if not from the time of Hywel ap Cadell. However, there is evidence that at least some parts of the laws were in operation in certain regions in the thirteenth century, and this is likely to be the case in the twelfth century also, if not earlier than that. The earliest manuscripts date to the mid-thirteenth century, although there are no Welsh manuscripts at all before then, so some of the Welsh law manuscripts are among the earliest texts in Middle Welsh. Wales was conquered by Edward I of England in 1282, and the consolidation of the conquest included making provisions for the law in Wales, and this was done in the Statute of Rhuddlan, 1284, the legal document which set out the constitutional situation for the government of the new Principality of North Wales.[7] The Statute of Rhuddlan appeared to abolish Welsh law in favor of English law in criminal cases, but the situation was far from clear cut, and of course the Statute of Rhuddlan only applied to the conquered territories, and did not include large parts of south Wales or the Marcher lordships.[8] Some manuscripts of Welsh law

5 Dafydd Jenkins, *The Law of Hywel Dda: Lawtexts from Medieval Wales* (Llandysul: Gomer, 1986), xiii.
6 Sara Elin Roberts, *The Legal Triads of Medieval Wales* (Cardiff: University of Wales Press, 2007).
7 Llinos Beverley Smith, "The Statute of Wales, 1284," *Welsh History Review* 10 (1980): 134.
8 Smith, "Statute of Wales," 134; Paul Brand, "An English Legal Historian Looks at the Statute

post-date the conquest of 1282, and the later lawmaking can occasionally be seen reflected in the text. These later lawtexts, including the fifteenth-century manuscripts, can be attributed to early antiquarian interest in the laws, but it is certain that some parts of the laws were still in use in some regions after the conquest, and so the lawtexts were still applicable and necessary.

There is considerable repetition of material across the forty or so law manuscripts, and while each manuscript is a unique text of the law, the majority can be assigned to a group or redaction, with manuscripts of that group showing similarities in order and content. There are, however, several non-redaction law manuscripts which are more miscellaneous in nature. It is this aspect that caused such problems to the early editors of the lawtexts, since they had a multiplicity of manuscripts with similarities, and yet huge differences between the texts. The first stage in looking at the law manuscripts has always traditionally been distributing the manuscripts into groups and organizing the large bulk of material.

The Welsh laws had been a subject of study from an early period, but the manuscripts and different versions regularly proved to be a difficulty for the authors and editors. Perhaps the first edition, in manuscript form, was William Maurice's "Deddfgrawn" ("law anthology"), or "Corpus Hoelianum", created 1660–63 and preserved in Aberystwyth, National Library of Wales (NLW), MSS Wynnstay 37 and 38.[9] Maurice was an antiquary and manuscript collector, the owner of several important Welsh manuscripts including one fine law manuscript, and he also spent time studying and copying those manuscripts. His legal compilation is the first attempt to categorize and distribute the contents of the Welsh law manuscripts, and there is diligent editing work giving variant readings from at least ten manuscripts.[10] Aneurin Owen drew upon his work in his own *Ancient Laws*, but William Maurice's "Deddfgrawn" was not used for the first printed edition of the Welsh laws.

William Wotton and Moses Williams published *Leges Wallicae* in 1730, after Wotton's death.[11] Moses Williams (1685–1742) was a cleric and scholar, with considerable expertise in Welsh manuscripts; he had access to several impor-

of Wales," in *Y Cyfraniad Cymreig: Welsh Contributions to Legal Development*, ed. Thomas Glyn Watkin (Bangor: Welsh Legal History Society, 2005), 37, and *passim*.

9 Dafydd Jenkins, "Deddfgrawn William Maurice," *National Library of Wales Journal* 2 (1941): 33.

10 Daniel Huws, "Maurice, William (1619/20–1680)," in *Oxford Dictionary of National Biography* (Oxford University Press, 2004, online ed., January 2008), accessed October 20, 2017, http://www.oxforddnb.com/view/article/18388.

11 William Wotton and Moses Williams, eds., *Cyfreithjeu Hywel Dda Ac Ereill Seu Leges Wallicae Ecclesiasticae & Civiles Hoeli Boni Et Alconium Wallicae Principium* (London, 1730).

tant libraries.[12] The work had been started by William Wotton (1666–1727). Wotton, a child prodigy and incredibly talented linguist, had been destined for a high career in the church, but his drinking and whoring led to serious debts. As a result, he and his wife and daughter fled his living in Milton Keynes and escaped to Carmarthen, where he lived in disguise as Dr. Edwards. Wotton's former sponsor, Bishop Wake, suggested that Wotton could work on the laws, as a way to occupy him and help him move on from his financial difficulties and his drinking problems and back into favor, and eventually perhaps regaining his career in the church. Wake presumably expected a study of one manuscript, but the task did not work out as planned. Wotton had to learn Welsh to work on the laws—which he did in just over a year—and he translated the Welsh texts into Latin in the multi-text edition. However, the attempt to organize the various texts of the Welsh law manuscripts caused Wotton untold distress.[13] He had many difficulties, including his problems in gaining access to the manuscripts—he could not go to England because of his creditors—but his collaborator Moses Williams had no such blots on his character and helped Wotton by bringing him manuscripts, as well as making considerable contributions to the text itself. Dafydd Jenkins suggested that looking at William Maurice's manuscripts would have shown a better classification of the lawtexts to Wotton and Williams, but Moses Williams did not visit Llanforda (where the manuscripts were kept at that time) until 1728, when the *Leges Wallicae* must have already gone to press.[14]

The first modern edition of the Welsh laws, *Ancient Laws and Institutes of Wales*, was published in two volumes in 1841, and the editor appears to have escaped the personal problems faced by some of the previous editors of the Welsh lawtexts.[15] Aneurin Owen (1792–1851) was the only son of the well-known antiquarian and London Welsh literary figure William Owen Pughe.[16] Although Aneurin Owen had attended school for a short while, he was mainly educated by his father.[17] Glenda Carr, in her biography of Owen's father, Pughe, argues

12 Geraint Bowen, "Moses Williams (1685–1742)," in *Dictionary of Welsh Biography* (National Library of Wales), accessed October 20, 2017, http://yba.llgc.org.uk/en/s-WILL-MOS-1685.html.

13 David Stoker, "William Wotton's Exile and Redemption: an Account of the Genesis and Publication of *Leges Wallicae*," *Welsh Book Studies* 7 (2006): 7–106.

14 Jenkins, "Deddfgrawn William Maurice," 36.

15 Aneurin Owen, ed., *Ancient Laws and Institutes of Wales*, 2 vols (London: Record Commission, 1841).

16 For the life of William Owen Pughe, see the excellent biography by Glenda Carr: *William Owen Pughe* (Cardiff: University of Wales Press, 1983). She also discusses Aneurin Owen.

17 J.E. Lloyd, "Owen, Aneurin (1792–1851)," in *Oxford Dictionary of National Biography*, rev.

that Aneurin Owen is unlikely to have been the true author of *Ancient Laws and Institutes of Wales*: apart from allegedly not being able to speak Welsh fluently until his marriage at the age of twenty-seven, there is evidence from Pughe's diaries that he was helping Aneurin learn his craft as a scholar, and was even responsible for copying manuscripts, translating texts and organizing the work for Aneurin: indeed, Carr states "Rhaid gofyn yn ddifrifol faint o ôl llaw William Owen Pughe sydd ar waith ei fab." [It must be asked in all seriousness how much of William Owen Pughe's handprint is on the work of his son.][18] They visited libraries together, and Pughe was in London more often than Aneurin was, since Aneurin farmed at the family farm of Nantglyn in Denbighshire, and it was Pughe who met regularly with Henry Petrie, the overseer of the bigger project in which the work on the Welsh laws was included.[19] Whoever was the true author of the work, Aneurin Owen is the one who is credited with it, and there was no mention of his father (who had died by that time) in his acknowledgements—whether that omission is significant is debatable.[20]

The idea of a study of the Welsh laws originated not with Aneurin Owen but with an earlier scholar, John Humphreys Parry, a London Welshman like Pughe who was involved in the literary work which was being undertaken in the city at the time. Parry became the secretary of the Cymmrodorion society, and established the literary magazine *The Cambro-Briton*.[21] He had a troubled life, with financial difficulties, and died young following a brawl near the Prince of Wales tavern in Pentonville.[22] Before his death, he had started working on the Welsh chronicle *Brut y Tywysogion* and also on Welsh law, with the intention of publishing an edition of both, and his papers were inherited by Pughe, who came to know Henry Petrie as a result.[23] Petrie, a Fellow of the Society of Antiquaries, was the keeper of records in the Tower of London, and he was tasked with producing a "corpus historicum" of all materials on English history, and John Humphreys Parry's plan of publishing an edition of all early Welsh history works, the *Monumenta Historica Britannica*, was incorporated into this wider plan.[24] The work was publicly funded and published by the Record Commis-

Brynley F. Roberts (Oxford University Press, 2004, online ed., January 2008), accessed May 18, 2016, http://www.oxforddnb.com/view/article/20985. Henceforth *ODNB*.

18 Carr, *William Owen Pughe*, 247–48.

19 Carr, *William Owen Pughe*, 248.

20 Carr, *William Owen Pughe*, 250.

21 Carr, *William Owen Pughe*, 203. The Honourable Society of the Cymmrodorion is the only one of the London Welsh learned societies which is still going today.

22 Carr, *William Owen Pughe*, 211.

23 Carr, *William Owen Pughe*, 212.

24 Albert F. Pollard, "Petrie, (Frederick) Henry (*bap.* 1772, *d.* 1842)," in *Oxford Dictionary of*

sion, and Aneurin Owen became involved in this work from the late 1820s when he took over Parry's role, probably organized for him through his father's connections.[25] Owen's Welsh work was divided into two: an edition of the laws, and an edition of the "Chronicle of the Princes," but despite the problems in gaining a usable reading of the texts, the work on the laws was the first to appear, in 1841, as *Ancient Laws and Institutes of Wales*. Although the *Ancient Laws* were highly praised—at the time, Owen was particularly commended in his "improved edition of Wotton's *Leges Cambriae*" for dividing the Welsh material into the three redactions[26]—Owen's work on the chronicles towards the same aim was not published. However, the version of *Brut y Tywysogion* edited by ab Ithel in 1860 was claimed—in print—to be the work of Owen, uncredited, "with a trifling verbal alteration in certain sentences."[27] The reviewer had a high opinion of Owen's work:

> No Welsh archaeologist since the days of Edward Lhwyd has appeared superior to Aneurin Owen. He was employed by the Record Commissioners for the Welsh part of their labours, and he *exhausted* the subject. We look into his *reliquia*, we test his accuracy, we go over his ground: it is all done, it is all correct; we have all that we want, as far as the state of archaeological research extended at the date of Aneurin Owen's decease. His *magnum opus* is undoubtedly the *Laws of Howel Dda*: the two Chronicles, which he edited, are but *opuscula*: still they are of very great value, and they reflect the highest credit on his memory … Nobody has undertaken such a task since; and very few have been qualified for it.[28]

Despite succeeding in his work and producing a masterpiece which was highly praised at the time of publication, and which is still in use today (although with some caveats), Aneurin Owen struggled with his edition of the laws. Tasked with the work of creating an edition of the Welsh law manuscripts, Owen discovered that his original plan of adapting or working from the basis of the earliest printed edition of the laws, *Leges Wallicae*, was not feasible and so it was "reluctantly abandoned."[29] The reason for changing the scheme and starting

---

National Biography, rev. Bernard Nurse (Oxford University Press, 2004, online ed., January 2008), accessed January 16, 2017, http://www.oxforddnb.com/view/article/22052.

25 Carr, *William Owen Pughe*, 212.

26 Review of *Brut y Tywysogion*, *Archaeologia Cambrensis*, 3rd ser., 25 (1861): 94.

27 Review of *Brut y Tywysogion*, 95.

28 Review of *Brut y Tywysogion*, 94.

29 Owen, *Ancient Laws*, Introduction, viii.

afresh was explained in his Introduction and was said to be due to the nature of the material in the manuscripts:

> It was apparent that the sense of the text was admirably rendered, and the notes and glossary worthy of the accomplished coadjutors in these labours: but the plan upon which Dr. Wotton proceeded with the *Leges Wallicae* was the adoption of one form of laws as the foundation of his text, interspersed with which were various readings, which differed widely from the text, and sometimes were contradictory of it. The cause of this anomaly was unexplained, and upon its being investigated it appeared that there were three distinct forms of laws existing, the parts of which had been dislocated by the Editor, and so arranged as to suit the order of the manuscript which he had adopted as his text, from the conviction of its being the most ancient and uniform of the whole... It was therefore evident that justice could not be done to the subject without allotting to each respectively its proper station, by which the discrepancies above alluded to are satisfactorily explained, the contrary usages of each district rightly attributed, and the consistency of each class of Codes preserved. Consequently, a re-modelling of the materials became necessary.[30]

Owen was happy with the new division and the way this presented the material in a more orderly fashion, saying so in one of his letters to Henry Petrie:

> The division of the laws into 3 codes has simplified the coup d'œil, & rendered the investigation to the reader more satisfactory. In Wotton we are surprized at the very great & unaccountable variance in the Mss. but the distribution of each to its respective province, the courts of N & S Wales being differently constituted & the practise dissimilar, explains the anomaly.[31]

The task that faced Aneurin Owen was huge. He had to see all of the extant manuscripts of medieval Welsh law, and work out a scheme for presenting those texts. Since the texts are almost all unique, editorial decisions had to be made about determining a base text, and how to deal with the other manuscripts—it would not have been practical to present each manuscript indi-

30 Owen, *Ancient Laws*, Introduction, viii.

31 London, The National Archives, Kew, PRO 36/44, 5.

vidually since all of the manuscripts are lengthy. Owen worked out that the manuscripts could be put into groups showing similarities in content and order, and he decided on three groups for the Welsh manuscripts which he had seen: this was a concept first discovered by William Maurice in his manuscript edition of the laws, but it was not a strategy employed by Wotton and Williams, which is why Aneurin Owen felt that he could not replicate that work. While it is not stated in the book, Aneurin Owen did use William Maurice's edition and drew upon it, particularly in his first volume. William Maurice's manuscripts were at the Wynnstay library by that time, and there is a slip acknowledging the return of several law manuscripts, including Maurice's edition in Aberystwyth, MSS Wynnstay 37 and 38.[32]

For his magnum opus, Owen set about viewing all of the Welsh law manuscripts available to him, and he viewed twenty-nine Welsh manuscripts, plus three Latin manuscripts, texts of the Statute of Rhuddlan (the post-conquest legal settlement for Edward I's territories in the Principality), and a section taken from *The Myvyrian Archaiology of Wales*, the work of the antiquary and eccentric scholar Iolo Morganwg, containing what are now known to be forgeries.[33] Most of the Welsh law manuscripts were given an identifying siglum by Owen, for easy reference, using letters of the alphabet and—since he had more manuscripts than letters of the alphabet—Old English characters.[34] These sigla are still used today in referring to the law manuscripts although the Old English characters have now been replaced with sigla which can be more easily reproduced. Three of the Latin manuscripts were presented as "a few Latin transcripts" and while Owen was familiar with all five versions of the laws in Latin, he did not give the Latin manuscripts as much attention as he afforded to the Welsh manuscripts.[35] As such, the Latin manuscripts are not the focus of this present study, since Owen only offered transcripts with very little discussion.

Once he had gathered together his manuscripts, Owen categorized them, following a similar method to that employed by William Maurice. In his Introduction, Owen demonstrated that he perceived geographical links to the law manuscripts, and he had a concept of original books created at the instigation of King Hywel ap Cadell.[36] Owen appears to have taken the story describing Hywel as a lawmaker in the Prologues at face value—"To him are we indebted for the collections of laws which pass under the name of the Laws of Hywel

32 Jenkins, "Deddfgrawn William Maurice," 36.

33 Owen, *Ancient Laws*, Introduction, xxv–xxxiv.

34 Owen, *Ancient Laws*, Introduction, xxv–xxxii.

35 Owen, *Ancient Laws*, title pages; *Ancient Laws*, Introduction, xxxiii–xxiv. See also n. 2.

36 Owen, *Ancient Laws*, Introduction, xviii–xxi.

dda"[37]—and so Owen believed that the three books said (in the Prologues) to be deposited in the three Welsh royal courts at Aberffraw, Dinefwr and Mathrafal were genuine, and also uniform texts, but that "shortly after a variance must have occurred" which caused the variety in the manuscripts he viewed.[38] He saw the manuscripts of Welsh law as containing a "Code" of law, with three different forms for different regions of Wales, and this idea was the basis of his edition. The Welsh manuscripts he used were therefore placed into three Codes, and they were named after geographical regions of Wales: the Venedotian Code (of Gwynedd), the Dimetian Code (Dyfed in South Wales) and the Gwentian Code (of Gwent, also in South Wales). These Codes form Owen's first volume, and the division made by Owen still stands to a great extent as the Redactions of Welsh law, although some manuscripts were misplaced by him, and the names of the Codes have been changed.[39]

Owen's Venedotian Code consisted of manuscripts A–H.[40] Owen saw A, "The Black Book of Chirk," as the oldest version of the laws in Welsh but this is no longer considered to be the case.[41] Manuscripts F and H are no longer included in this redaction but are largely manuscripts not containing a redaction-text; manuscript K has been moved to this redaction; and Aberystwyth, MS Peniarth 39, Lew, was discovered after Owen's time and belongs in this group. The manuscripts in Owen's Venedotian Code are well-organized texts and they are very close in order and content. The extant texts were for the most part a new edition made in Gwynedd in the early- to mid-thirteenth century by a jurist called Iorwerth ap Madog.[42] Each manuscript has a tripartite structure, consisting of the Laws of Court, the Laws of Country, and the Justices' Test Book ("Proof Book" according to Owen) which contained everything

37 Owen, *Ancient Laws*, Introduction, x.

38 Owen, *Ancient Laws*, Introduction, xviii.

39 See Arthur W. Wade-Evans, *Welsh Medieval Law, Being a Text of the Laws of Howel the Good* (Oxford: Clarendon Press, 1909; repr., Darmstadt: Scientia Verlag Aalen, 1979), vii–xii.

40 See Appendix.

41 See Paul Russell, "Scribal (In)Competence in Thirteenth-Century North Wales: The Orthography of the Black Book of Chirk (Peniarth MS. 29)," *National Library of Wales Journal* 29 (1995–6): 129–76; Thomas M. Charles-Edwards, *The Welsh Laws* (Cardiff: University of Wales Press, 1989), 23–24; 29–30; and the full study of the manuscript and its history in Daniel Huws, "The Manuscripts: Cotton Caligula A iii," in *Lawyers and Laymen. Studies in the History of Law Presented to Professor Dafydd Jenkins*, ed. Thomas M. Charles-Edwards, Morfydd E. Owen and Dafydd B. Walters (Cardiff: University of Wales Press, 1986). On the redaction see the introduction in Aled Rhys Wiliam, *Llyfr Iorwerth* (Cardiff: University of Wales Press, 1960).

42 Charles-Edwards, *Welsh Laws*, 29–30.

a lawyer needed to know in order to practice law. This group is now called the Iorwerth redaction.

Owen's largest group was his Dimetian Code, consisting of manuscripts I–T.[43] These manuscripts do have a South Wales link, but are not confined to Dyfed. Since Owen's time, five manuscripts have been added to this group—Cambridge, Trinity College, MS 1329, known as Tr, and Bost, now Aberystwyth, MS 24029A which had gone to Boston, Massachusetts, by the time Owen was working, but which was used for the earlier *Leges Wallicae*;[44] both were unknown to Owen. Ep, Aberystwyth, MS Peniarth 258, was not assigned to a redaction by Owen but is a full copy of manuscript Q and belongs in this group;[45] and Tim, Aberystwyth, MS Llanstephan 116, and Llan, Aberystwyth, MS Llanstephan 29 were presumably not known to Owen. This is now known as the Blegywryd redaction.

The Gwentian Code was the smallest of Owen's groups and the most problematic since the manuscripts did not show very much similarity. Owen's Gwentian Code had six manuscripts, U–Z, to which today is added Mk, the Meyrick manuscript which was then—as now—in private ownership and of which Owen was not aware.[46] Y has been reconsidered and is a composite text: The Laws of Court are from the Cyfnerth redaction (Owen's Gwentian Code), but the remainder of the manuscript is largely Blegywryd material (Owen's Dimetian Code).[47] The Gwentian Code has been renamed the Cyfnerth redaction.

Once Owen had viewed the manuscripts and presumably transcribed them in their entirety, his aim was to present the text in a usable form.

> The operose task of collating the various matters contained in these Manuscripts and distributing them in their respective classes having been gone through, the enquirer may now ascertain the reading of every existing Manuscript of each description, with the exception of some fragments of no importance, and may also estimate the form and character of each

---

43 See Appendix.

44 Morfydd E. Owen, "Llawysgrif Gyfreithiol Goll," *Bulletin of the Board of Celtic Studies* 22 (1966–68): 338–43.

45 Sara Elin Roberts, "Creu Trefn o Anhrefn: Gwaith copïydd Testun Cyfreithiol," *Cylchgrawn Llyfrgell Genedlaethol Cymru* [National Library of Wales Journal] 32 (2002): 402.

46 See Appendix.

47 See Daniel Huws, "Descriptions of the Welsh Manuscripts: National Library of Wales, MS 20143A," in *The Welsh King and His Court*, ed. Thomas M. Charles-Edwards, Morfydd E. Owen, and Paul Russell (Cardiff: University of Wales Press, 2000), 420.

> version, and scrutinize the validity of the conclusions that induced the classifications here adopted ...[48]

Owen's working method can still be viewed as a standard and sensible approach today. Although he does not reveal the details of his method in his Introduction, his working process appears to have been to choose a base manuscript: in the case of his Venedotian and Dimetian codes, he selected the manuscript which was in his view the oldest version of the text; for his Gwentian code he used the manuscript "not from any superiority, but as being the simplest; most of the others being anomalous, and containing much matter extracted from the Dimetian form."[49] The text for each of his Codes would be taken from his base manuscript and presented as it appeared in the manuscript, with "no transpositions of matter, nor ... any incongruity of arrangement."[50] In that sense, this is a very useful method since Owen was not combining texts, and his statement that the order of the base manuscripts were followed is in fact accurate throughout his work—it is also true of the texts in his second volume, The Anomalous Laws. Once he had selected the base manuscript for his text, a loosely edited transcript was presented, along with an English translation on the facing page. For the Welsh text, variant readings were given from the other manuscripts of the same code where possible, although Owen would occasionally admit that things did not always work to plan. For example, when it came to the complex Gwentian Code he struggled with some of the manuscripts and by the time he had reached Book II of the Gwentian Code, after the Laws of Court, he took drastic measures, and decided to stop giving variant readings from Z, Aberystwyth, MS Peniarth 259B: "... Z. is carelessly transcribed and has many chasms ... will only be noticed when important variations or new matter occur."[51] Occasionally, a different version of the text would be presented at the bottom of the page, when the version was too different for Owen to incorporate it into his main text or present it using his usual method of giving variant readings.[52] Corrections or additions to his main text were presented in square brackets in the text, with a numbered footnote giving the base manuscript for the variation.

48 Owen, *Ancient Laws*, Introduction, xxxv.

49 Owen, *Ancient Laws*, Introduction, xxxi.

50 Owen, *Ancient Laws*, Introduction, xxxv.

51 Owen, *Ancient Laws*, GC II.i n. 11; see also Sara Elin Roberts, *Llawysgrif Pomffred: An Edition and Study of Peniarth MS 259B* (Leiden: Brill, 2011), 20. Owen did not note anything else from Z after that statement.

52 See, for example, Owen, *Ancient Laws*, VC III.i.10–VC III.ii.13.

The apparatus itself often appears to be intractable, but a variation of Owen's method is still used today for critical texts, although in a simplified form, and omitting the confusing "ticks":

> The notes are commonly referred to by a small numeral: thus, ([1]); and in special cases by a small Italic letter: thus, (*[a]*). Explanatory foot-notes are distinguished by a Roman letter: thus, ([a]). There is also used another mark, called a tick: thus, ('). In the body of the text this mark shows the end of the passage, for which a various reading is to be found; and in the notes a corresponding tick has been placed immediately after the numeral or Italic letter. In cases where two or more Manuscripts vary as to the length of the passage about which they differ, the point in the text at which each terminates is marked by one or more ticks, according to the number of conflicting Manuscripts: thus, (') (") (''') ('''') and so on.[53]

Despite sounding horrifically complex, the process does in fact work well, if a little confusing to a new reader. The benefits are that a good sense can be had of the manuscripts, although the order of the contents of the manuscripts used for variant readings is less clear, mainly because page or folio numbers are not used in the edition. But generally speaking, the Codes in *Ancient Laws* still function as a usable text, with a focus on the base text, and a guide to where else the material is available.

However, fairly early on in his work, Owen discovered that the Welsh law manuscripts did not work effectively and tidily into the scheme which he had in mind. This was so problematic that it caused some delay: "The labour incurred in the collation, and in the care required in the printing and correction of such complicated matter, were the causes of a longer delay in the publication than could have been anticipated, and which the Editor greatly regrets."[54] Owen's worry and the troublesome nature of his work is apparent in that statement: in a letter to Henry Petrie, he describes the work as "a rather laborious and harassing occupation."[55] Owen still had the material which he could not fit into his neat organized structure, and appeared to be extraneous to his Codes. Owen's answer to making the material fit together neatly was to introduce his division of the work, with the Codes in the first volume, versus the "Anomalous Laws" in his second volume. This structure produced a synthetic form to the Welsh laws,

53 Owen, *Ancient Laws*, Introduction, xxiv.
54 Owen, *Ancient Laws*, Introduction, xxxv.
55 London, The National Archives, Kew: PRO 36/44.

something which does not exist, although this is naturally a problem with any edited work. Owen was aware of this issue and raised it in his introduction:

> The ANOMALOUS or WELSH LAWS constitute an important portion of the Work. Under this head are given such anomalous chapters as are respectively found in those Manuscripts which afforded the texts for the regular Codes, and also all additional and later matter, wherever found. Herein are comprehended legal dicta and decisions, pleadings, and elucidatory matter.[56]

Owen used "Anomalous" in a specific sense, it appears, and he had a clear idea of what the anomalous material constituted. Some clues to the division are referred to in the law manuscripts themselves: Charles-Edwards points out that manuscript U marks the division between the main text and the *damweiniau* (a collection of sentences which give special circumstances, often called "eventualities") by saying that it is turning to looking at customs.[57] Aneurin Owen refers to anomalous material which occurred in his manuscripts, but this is not always material found interrupting his neat codes—rather, it was material appended to the main Code in his manuscripts, and material which is now sometimes seen to be the "tail" of the manuscripts. In his description of manuscript U, Owen uses "anomalous" in a very specific sense—the anomalous material was anything which interrupted his basic Gwentian text, and that could be material taken from another Code (the Dimetian, in this case).[58] He also seemed to have very clear ideas of how the manuscripts were formed, and extremely strict views on which material belongs in which class or Code.

As stated, there are some manuscripts which defy categorization into the recognizable groups, and Owen was aware of some of these manuscripts, since he listed them after the manuscripts in the Codes, under the (puzzling) heading "The Welsh or Anomalous Laws."[59] His use of "Welsh" here is not explained, but may refer to a more general or unknown geographical origin, as opposed to the "regional" texts found in his Codes. These manuscripts, four of them in all, were assigned "characters from the Saxon alphabet," since Owen had exhausted letters of the Roman alphabet, which has had the unfortunate effect of contributing to their classification as "other" or even "weird," and has made referring to them problematic on modern computers. This group has been expanded since

56 Owen, *Ancient Laws*, Introduction, xx.
57 Charles-Edwards, *Welsh Laws*, 26.
58 Owen, *Ancient Laws*, Introduction, p. xxxi.
59 Owen, *Ancient Laws*, Introduction, p. xxxii.

other manuscripts have come to light after Owen's time, and some manuscripts have been moved into this group from the main Codes.

Much of the material from these manuscripts can be found in Aneurin Owen's Second Volume, "The Anomalous Laws," along with material from manuscripts which fit into one of his Codes but which have more material than other manuscripts. The Anomalous Laws is thematic and well-organized. Owen's *modus operandi* seems to have been to work through his manuscript by Code, and anything he found which he felt to be an addition to the Code (and this would largely be at the end of the manuscript rather than removing material from the main section providing his Code) would be put in the second volume. However, there was more of an element of selection in his Anomalous Laws, since the material was thinned down to some extent, to avoid repetition with the material found in the Codes. So, if a version of a text from, say, manuscript H appeared similar to something he had already edited in his Code—such as a triad from his Dimetian Code—he would not include the variant version in his Anomalous Laws. This reduced the size of the volume, naturally, but it does make it difficult when examining a Welsh law manuscript to find which of the material is in *Ancient Laws*, and more importantly, which is not.

The Anomalous Laws is organized thematically, and is divided into Books IV–XIV. The first six books are arranged by different genres: Books IV–VI present *damweiniau* (eventualities), collections of sentences stating "if X happens, then Y is to follow."[60] Books VII–IX are collections of *cynghawsedd*, model pleadings.[61] Book XII is also thematic, looking at plaints, the initial statement in a legal process.[62] The remaining books are organized by individual manuscripts: Book X is material taken from Q; XI is from S; and XIV is from H. Book XIII was also manuscript based but the manuscript was a later forgery and is not counted amongst the law manuscripts today.

So, the Anomalous Laws is not disorganized, and neither does it appear to have been an afterthought, and Owen himself was aware of the importance of the material in his second volume. But his very act of dividing the material—for convenience, or due to his concept of the original books of law—led to the

60 Charles-Edwards, *Welsh Laws*, 49.

61 Thomas M. Charles-Edwards, "*Cynghawsedd*: Counting and Pleading in Medieval Welsh Law," *Bulletin of the Board of Celtic Studies* 33 (1986): 188–98; Robin Chapman Stacey, "Learning to Plead in Medieval Welsh Law," *Studia Celtica* 38 (2004): 107–24; and Charles-Edwards, *Welsh Laws*, 53–67.

62 Sara Elin Roberts, "Plaints in Mediaeval Welsh Law," *The Journal of Celtic Studies* 4 (2004): 219–61; and Sara Elin Roberts, "More Plaints in Medieval Welsh Law," *Studia Celtica* 48 (2014): 171–99.

material being viewed differently, and this division has affected the study of the Welsh lawtexts and continues to do so today. Owen created his second volume because of his concept of the basic texts, the original books, of Welsh law, with elements which he felt were old and general to all of the Codes—some of them he even traced back to some early "White House book." As such, the material in his second volume did not fit in with this scheme—it had a more practical aspect, and the material was different and indeed probably later than the material in his first volume. But the division is not realistic, and is problematic. The fact that the material in the second volume occurs in genre-based collections suggests a degree of organization which would be lacking if it was really anomalous, miscellaneous or additional. A further problem is that the material in the manuscript-based books of the Anomalous Laws is taken from some of the same manuscripts used in his first volume, since they also contain a "Code" of law. This points to the fact that the creators or redactors of the lawbooks did not see a definite division in their material: if the manuscript contained a "Code" as well as material in Owen's "Anomalous Laws" then the suggestion is that this is all law, and all part of the same book, rather than being material which needed to be divided in any way.

Owen's division of the material had a significant impact on later studies of the Welsh law manuscripts. Traditionally, editions of the laws presented single manuscripts from particular redactions, and the division of the Code versus the Anomalous material held its ground. The edition of the Blegywryd redaction (Owen's Dimetian Code) in *Llyfr Blegywryd* (1942) was based on O, and its sister text Tr, with lacunae filled from manuscript L.[63] This edition is often seen as presenting the "basis" of the Blegywryd redaction, but the editor J. Enoch Powell (today better known as an English politician) had his own ideas about material which did not belong in the original lawbook.[64] In addition, the editors omitted material which is found near the end of manuscript L, although that material was included in Owen's Dimetian Code rather than in his Anomalous Laws, thus reducing the texts included in the Blegywryd redaction.[65]

The editor of the only edition to date of Owen's Venedotian Code, Aled Rhys Wiliam, focused on manuscript B, but stopped his edition before the collection of model pleadings at the end of the manuscript—this is material which was in Owen's Anomalous Laws, in Book VII—and so divided his manuscript in

63 See *Llyfr Blegywryd*, xxxix.

64 *Llyfr Blegywryd*, xxxix–xlvi. For a discussion on Powell's "Floating Sections" theory see Roberts, *Legal Triads*, 11–15.

65 Owen, *Ancient Laws*, DC III.

the same way that it had been divided in *Ancient Laws*.[66] Likewise, Jenkins' edition of the early manuscript Col also presented the first part of the manuscript, omitting the large collection of *damweiniau* (material in the Anomalous Laws) but later published the *damweiniau* in a separate book.[67]

Aled Rhys Wiliam also published an important study of manuscripts which he termed "Deddfgronau" (legal compilations or anthologies), focusing on manuscripts with little or no material from Owen's Codes.[68] Wiliam's title may have been a useful name for such law manuscripts, but again it assumes that the material is "additional" if not independent of the law manuscripts, which may not be the case in reality. The edition of manuscript J was an important step in the study of the legal manuscripts. A beautiful manuscript, J has what could be called a basic text of the laws from Blegywryd followed by material from another redaction, and the introduction gave this the attention it deserved, although the division of the text as set out in *Llyfr Blegywryd* was maintained, with the remainder of the manuscript called a "tail."[69] This has become the standard way of referring to the lengthier manuscripts—those with a "tail," or those containing "additional material." The issue that is less clear is that of what the material is additional to—and the answer is that it is additional to an early editorial decision and a concept of basic legal material. This division is not reflected in the manuscripts.

Looking at the manuscripts themselves, of the thirty-six Welsh manuscripts, very few of them present the so-called basic text only (i.e. that in *Llyfr Blegywryd* with no material in addition; or the same for *Llyfr Iorwerth*), and many of the manuscripts have their end wanting in any case. Of the eight Iorwerth (formerly Venedotian) redaction manuscripts, all but one have a collection of *damweiniau* in the latter part of the manuscript, with the exception of B which has a collection of *cynghawsedd* instead. The earliest manuscript, C, is incomplete. This suggests that Iorwerth manuscripts were expected to have a collection of *damweiniau*, and that it was part of the text rather than something which was added later or omitted. The Cyfnerth (previously Gwentian) manuscripts do not have a fixed form and therefore it is more difficult—if not impossible—to set out a "basic text" for this redaction, but that may be telling

---

66 Aled Rhys Wiliam, *Llyfr Iorwerth* (Cardiff: University of Wales Press, 1960).

67 D. Jenkins, *Llyfr Colan* (Cardiff: University of Wales Press, 1963); D. Jenkins, *Damweiniau Colan* (Aberystwyth: Cymdeithas Llyfrau Ceredigion, 1973).

68 Aled Rhys. Wiliam, "Y Deddfgronau Cymraeg," *National Library of Wales Journal* 8 (1953): 97.

69 Melville Richards, ed. *Cyfreithiau Hywel Dda yn ôl Llawysgrif Coleg yr Iesu LVII*, rev. ed. (Cardiff: University of Wales Press, 1990), xiii. The term "tail" was applied earlier than this.

in itself; the early texts in the Cyfnerth manuscripts may be the example that shows that there was no such thing as a standard text of the law. Manuscript Z is considerably longer than the other Cyfnerth manuscripts and has a "tail" of material which was circulating in north-east Wales.[70] The largest group, Blegywryd (formerly Dimetian), has sixteen manuscripts, but several of these are not complete and/or have their end wanting; manuscripts which have their end wanting are missing the very place where the "additional" material would be copied in the first place. Some of the manuscripts in this group are very lengthy and Q and S formed the basis of Books in Owen's Anomalous Laws. Looking at the material in this way shows that most law manuscripts have "additional" material of some form or another, and so there is apparently no such thing as a complete law manuscript only containing a version of the Law of Hywel, with no additional material or losses.[71]

Turning to the lengthier texts, on the whole there is nothing to mark out the second part of the manuscript as being "additional" or different in any way to the material which was recognized as forming a Code. In the Iorwerth redaction, the *damweiniau* collection carries on from the previous text with nothing to mark it out as being anything other than a continuation, although one extant manuscript has a sentence stating what has come before, and that *damweiniau* follow:

> Hyt hyn y traeth[ir] affam k'eu llys a chyfreitheu yr gwlat. O hyn allan or damweineu.
>
> [Up to now has been spoken of the laws of court and the laws of country. From now on of the *damweiniau*.][72]

This is a standard thing which occurs throughout the lawbooks and is not indicative of importance, only of a change of subject. The same is true of the lengthier Blegywryd manuscripts; some of them have nothing to mark a change of subject, but there is a dividing sentence in some of the manuscripts. L, Bost and J continue where *Llyfr Blegywryd* ends, and the texts are closely related; they also have the same colophon.[73]

---

70 Roberts, *Llawysgrif Pomffred*, 41–43.

71 Charles-Edwards, *Welsh Laws*, 17: "Some legal manuscripts contain only a version of the law of Hywel."

72 Arthur W. Wade-Evans, "Text of Pen. MS. 37 (fols. 61–76) with Translation," *Y Cymmrodor* 17 (1904): 132. My translation.

73 Owen, *Ancient Laws*, DC III.i.26, taken from L.

> Dywededic yw hyt hynn o gyureith Hywel da, a'e arueroed, a'e gynneuodeu. Dywedadwy yw rac llaw o achwannec kyureith dylyedus y chynnal a gossodedic trwy gyuundeb gwlat ac arglwyd. Nyt amgen no'r dynnyon hynn yma ny dyly eu tystolyaeth seuyll yn vnn lle.
>
> [Up to now has been spoken of the law of Hywel Dda, and its practices, and its customs. Henceforth will be spoken of additional law which ought to be maintained and which is set by the agreement of country and lord. Namely of these men here whose testimony ought not to stand in any place.]

While this could be seen as marking the start of a "tail," it may simply indicate a change of subject, and the use of "stated up to now" is not final and leaves open the possibility of adding more material. Although it is written in red ink, the colophon is not closing the law completely, and leaves an appropriate frame for more material. It also states what this material will be: "additional law which ought to be maintained" and notes its official nature. It does use the word "additional," *achwannec*, but perhaps it should simply be interpreted as "more of the same," and suggests a more flexible view of what the lawbooks should contain.

As the ninety-one sections in *Llyfr Blegywryd* have been taken as forming the "core" Blegywryd text, and in the same way the 160 sections of *Llyfr Iorwerth*, with everything else being "additional," one consideration is whether there is any difference between this material and the texts found in the Anomalous Laws. Often, the so-called "additional material" or the "tails" are seen as a bundling of all sorts of material, but this may not be the case. Several of the "tails" are highly organized: either by genre, or in some cases by exemplar. The lengthy manuscripts Z, Q and S are actually very well organized and carefully planned and edited. Another comment which is often made of the "additional material" is that it is later in date, but again, there are some early sections in some of the lengthier manuscripts, and the Codes themselves have material from different periods interspersed, with parts of the Iorwerth lawbooks seen to be "current" law broadly contemporary to the date of the manuscripts. The *damweiniau* form a lengthy collection, but the same is true of the triads included in *Llyfr Blegywryd*. *Damweiniau* are also attested within *Llyfr Iorwerth*, and an important part of Land Law in Iorwerth is the legal case, very similar to the *cynghawsedd* which is found in the Anomalous Laws. It is rather difficult to justify setting any of this material apart, since it is all on the same topic—law. An important point which may be crucial to the understanding of the material in the law manuscripts is that in medieval Wales it seems that legal material was always confined to the law manuscripts. There are no fragments or short sections of law found separate to the law manuscripts, or copied into books of other material such as poetry; sections of law copied into miscellaneous manuscripts or compilations are also extremely rare. The law material is always found within subject-specific manuscripts. This is an interesting factor, and one consideration is why this is the case. A possible answer is that the law manuscripts are subject-specific, very topic-focused, and therefore the material is self-contained; and this may mean that distinguishing or dividing the legal material within the law manuscripts was not something which was intended by the original compilers. All of this raises questions regarding Aneurin Owen's division of the material, and that the division between his Code or main text and the "additional" material is not at all clear. It may be that the main point to bear in mind when looking at the law manuscripts is that modern constructs and divisions were first applied in the nineteenth century, and were then not superseded by anything later.

Despite the early date of the publication, *Ancient Laws* remains a valuable work for studying the Welsh law manuscripts, and credit is due to Aneurin Owen who made the field accessible and who made great strides in dealing with the large bulk of legal material by categorizing it and giving it some kind of order. The sigla assigned by Owen are still in use, and the three groups of the Welsh manuscripts also still stand albeit with newer names. His text is still valuable even though it can sometimes be difficult to get back to the original reading in some of the manuscripts, but as a starting point, Owen's edition is excellent. His English translations are now dated, but they show that he had a superb understanding of the law manuscripts and of legal terms. However this material is viewed, in his *Ancient Laws and Institutes of Wales* Aneurin Owen went beyond laying the foundations for dealing with the Welsh law manuscripts and material, and without his contribution and back-breaking work, the field of Welsh law would be far less advanced than it is today.

Appendix: The Welsh Law Manuscripts

Below is a list of manuscripts used by Aneurin Owen and included in his edition of *Ancient Laws and Institutes of Wales*. The sigla are the ones assigned by Owen and they continue to be used today, along with their modern shelfmarks.

"The Venedotian Code" (Iorwerth Redaction)

A Aberystwyth, National Library of Wales (NLW), MS Peniarth 29. Mid-thirteenth century.

B	London, British Library (BL), MS Cotton Titus D II. Second half thirteenth century.
C	London, BL, MS Cotton Caligula A III, Mid-thirteenth century.
D	Aberystwyth, NLW, MS Peniarth 32. c. 1404
E	London, BL, MS Additional 14931. Second half thirteenth century.
F	Aberystwyth, NLW, MS Peniarth 34. Second half fifteenth century. *Non-redaction.*
G	Aberystwyth, NLW, MS Peniarth 35. First half fourteenth century.
H	Aberystwyth, NLW, MS Peniarth 164. Second half fourteenth century. *Non-redaction.*

"The Dimetian Code" (Blegywryd Redaction)

I	Aberystwyth, NLW, MS Peniarth 38. Fourteenth/fifteenth century.
J	Oxford, Jesus College, MS LVII. Fourteenth/fifteenth century.
K	Aberystwyth, NLW, MS Peniarth 40. Before 1469. *Iorwerth.*
L	London, BL, MS Cotton Titus D IX. Mid-fourteenth century.
M	Aberystwyth, NLW, Peniarth MS 33. First half fourteenth century.
N	Aberystwyth, NLW, Peniarth MS 36B. First half fourteenth century.
O	Aberystwyth, NLW, Peniarth MS 36A. First half fourteenth century.
P	Aberystwyth, NLW, MS Peniarth 259A. Second half fifteenth century. *Copy of Q.*
Q	Aberystwyth, NLW, MS Wynnstay 36. First half fifteenth century.
R	Aberystwyth, NLW, Peniarth MS 31. First half fourteenth century.
S	London, BL, MS Additional 22356. Mid-fifteenth century.
T	London, BL, MS Harleian 958. Mid-fourteenth century.

"The Gwentian Code" (Cyfnerth Redaction)

U	Aberystwyth, NLW, MS Peniarth 37. First half fourteenth century.
V	London, BL, MS Harleian 4353. First half fourteenth century.
W	London, BL, MS Cotton Cleopatra A XIV. First half fourteenth century.
X	London, BL, MS Cotton Cleopatra B V. Mid-fourteenth century.
Y	Aberystwyth, NLW, MS 20143A. Mid-fourteenth century. *Cyfnerth Laws of Court, remainder is Blegywryd.*
Z	Aberystwyth, NLW, MS Peniarth 259B. Sixteenth century copy of a mid-fourteenth century text.

"The Anomalous or Welsh Manuscripts" (Non-redaction Texts)

Ep	Aberystwyth, NLW, MS Peniarth 258. Second half fifteenth century. *Blegywryd, copy of Q.*
As	Aberystwyth, NLW, MS Peniarth 175. Second half fifteenth century.

Mor Aberystwyth, NLW, MS Peniarth 36C. Second half fifteenth century.

Dd London, BL, MS Additional 31055. *Copy of the lost 'White Book of Hergest' and only contains Plaints as legal material.*

The following manuscripts were not used by Aneurin Owen and are designated by newer sigla. If the manuscripts belong to a redaction it is noted here in italic.

Mk Bodorgan Manuscript, in private ownership. First half fourteenth century. *Cyfnerth.*

Llan Aberystwyth, NLW, MS Llanstephan 29. Fifteenth/sixteenth century. *Blegywryd.*

Tim Aberystwyth, NLW, MS Llanstephan 116. Mid-fifteenth century. *Blegywryd, same hand as S.*

Bost Aberystwyth, NLW, MS 24029A. Second half fourteenth century. *Blegywryd.*

Tr Cambridge, Trinity College MS 1329. First half fourteenth century. *Blegywryd.*

Lew Aberystwyth, NLW, MS Peniarth 39. Mid-fifteenth century. *Iorwerth.*

Col Aberystwyth, NLW, MS Peniarth 30. Mid-thirteenth century. *Linked to Iorwerth.*

An Aberystwyth, NLW, MS Peniarth 166. Sixteenth century. *Non-redaction.*

Bibliography

Primary Sources

Adam of Bremen. *History of the Archbishops of Hamburg-Bremen*. Translated by Francis J. Tschan, with new introduction by Timothy Reuter. New York: Columbia University Press, 1959. Reprint, 2002.

Andersson, Theodore M., and Kari Ellen Gade, eds. *Morkinskinna*. Ithaca, NY: Cornell University Press, 2000.

Astronomer. *Vita Hludowici imperatoris*. Edited by Ernst Tremp, MGH SSRG 64, 280–554. Hannover: Hahnsche Buchhandlung, 1995.

Aurelius Augustine. *Enarrationes in Psalmos*. Edited by Jacques-Paul Migne, PL 36:67–1027. Paris: Imprimerie Catholique 1844–1855.

Aurelius Augustine. *Sermones Ad Populum. Classis II. De Tempore*. Edited by Jacques-Paul Migne, PL38:995–1248. Paris: Imprimerie Catholique 1844–1855.

Azara, Antonio, and Ernesto Eula. "*Liber Papiensis.*" In *Novissimo Digesto Italiano*, IX. Turin: UTET, 1963.

Azzara, Claudio, and Stefano Gasparri, ed. and trans. *La Leggi dei Longobardi. Storia, memoria e diritto di un popolo germanico*. Rome: Viella, 2005.

Barney, Stephen A., W.J. Lewis, J.A. Beach, and Oliver Berghof, eds. *The Etymologies of Isidore of Seville*. Cambridge: Cambridge University Press, 2006.

Binchy, Daniel A., ed. "Bretha Crólige." *Ériu* 12 (1938): 1–77

Binchy, Daniel A., ed. *Críth Gablach*. Dublin: Dublin Institute for Advanced Studies, 1941.

Binchy, Daniel A., ed. "The Saga of Fergus Mac Léti." *Ériu* 16 (1952): 33–48.

Binchy, Daniel A., ed. "Bretha Déin Chécht." *Ériu* 20 (1966): 1–66.

Binchy, Daniel A., ed. "An Archaic Legal Poem." *Celtica* 9 (1971): 152–68.

Binchy, Daniel A., ed. *Corpus Iuris Hibernici*, 6 vols. Dublin: Dublin Institute for Advanced Studies, 1978.

Bjarni Guðnason, ed. *Skjǫldunga Saga*. Reykjavík: Hið Íslenzka Fornritafélag, 1982.

Bluhme, Friedrich, ed. *Leges Langobardorum*. MGH LL 4, 1–225. Hannover: Hahn, 1868.

Bluhme, Friedrich, ed. *Legis Langobardorum libri tres sive syntagmata duo Lombarda vulgo dicta ex libro Papiensi confecta*. MGH LL 4, 607–40. Hannover: Hahn, 1868.

Bluhme, Friedrich, ed. *Edictus Langobardorum*. MGH LL 4, 1–225. Hannover: Hahn, 1868. Reprint, 1984.

Bobchev, Stefan [Стефан Бобчевъ]. *Старобългарски правни паметници* [*Old Bulgarian Legal Documents*]. Sofia: Pechatnicana P.M. Buzhaitov, 1903.

Boretius, Alfred, ed. *Liber Legis Langobardorum Papiensis Dictus*. MGH LL 4, 289–585. Hannover: Hahn, 1868. Reprint, Hannover: Hahnsche Buchhandlung, 1984.

Breatnach, Liam, ed. *Córus Bésgnai: An Old Irish Law Tract on the Church and Society*. Early Irish Law Series 7. Dublin: Dublin Institute for Advanced Studies, 2017.

Buma, Wybren Jan, and Wilhelm Ebel, eds. *Das Rüstringer Recht*. Altfriesische Rechtsquellen 1. Göttingen: Musterschmidt, 1963.

Buma, Wybren Jan, and Wilhelm Ebel, eds. *Das Emsiger Recht*. Altfriesische Rechtsquellen 3. Göttingen: Vandenhoeck & Ruprecht, 1967.

Buma, Wybren Jan, and Wilhelm Ebel, eds. *Das Hunsingoer Recht*. Altfriesische Rechtsquellen 4. Göttingen: Vandenhoeck & Ruprecht, 1969.

Buma, Wybren Jan, and Wilhelm Ebel, eds. *Das Fivelgoer Recht*. Altfriesische Rechtsquellen 5. Göttingen: Vandenhoeck & Ruprecht, 1972.

Buma, Wybren Jan, and Wilhelm Ebel, with Martina Tragter-Schubert, eds. *Westerlauwersches Recht I: Jus municipale Frisonum*. 2 vols. Altfriesische Rechtsquellen 6. Göttingen: Vandenhoeck & Ruprecht, 1977.

Buma, Wybren Jan, and Wilhelm Ebel, with Martina Tragter-Schubert, eds. *Codex Aysma. Die altfriesische Texte herausgegeben und übersetzt*. Assen: van Gorcum, 1993.

Calendar of the Close Rolls Preserved in the Public Record Office: Edward II, 1313–18, edited by Great Britain Public Record Office. London: H. M. S. O., 1893.

Camargo, Martin, ed. *Medieval Rhetorics of Prose Composition. Five English* Artes Dictandi *and their Tradition*. Binghampton: Medieval & Renaissance Texts & Studies, 1995.

"Cambridge, Corpus Christi College, MS 265: Wulfstan's Handbook and other Ecclesiastical Extracts." *Parker Library on the Web*. Accessed July 16, 2018, https://parker.stanford.edu/parker/catalog/nh277tk2537.

Campbell, Alistair, ed. *Thet Freske Riim. Tractatus Alvini*. The Hague: Martinus Nijhoff, 1952.

Carey, John, ed. "A Tract on the Creation." *Éigse* 21 (1986): 1–9.

Carey, John, ed. "An Edition of the Pseudo-Historical Prologue to the Senchas Már." *Ériu* 45 (1994): 1–32.

Carlin, Martha, and David Crouch, eds. *Lost Letters of Medieval Life. English Society, 1200–1250*. Philadelphia, PA: Penn, 2013.

Carlone, Carmine, Leone Morinelli, and Giovanni Vitolo, eds. *Codex Diplomaticus Cacensis*, vols 11–12. Salerno: Badia di Cava, 2015.

"Cava de'Tirreni, Biblioteca della Badia, 4." In *Bibliotheca Legum: A Database on Carolingian Secular Law Texts*, edited by Karl Ubl. Accessed November 06, 2019. http://www.leges.uni-koeln.de/en/mss/codices/cava-dei-tirreni-bdb-4/.

"Cava de'Tirreni, Biblioteca della Badia, 4." In *Capitularia: Edition der fränkischen Herrschererlasse*, edited by Karl Ubl. Accessed November 06, 2019. https://capitularia.uni-koeln.de/en/mss/cava-dei-tirreni-bdb-4/.

Chartularium Studii Bononiensis. Documenti per la Storia Dell'Università di Bologna

Da'alle Origini Fino al Secolo XV. 13 Vols. Bologna: Istituto per la storia dell'Università di Bologna, 1907–40.

Cipolla, Carlo. *Codici Bobbiesi della Biblioteca Nazionale Universitaria di Torino*. Milan: Ulrico Hoepli Editore Libraio della Real Casa, 1907.

Cipolla, Carlo, Gaetano De Sanctis, and Carlo Frati. "Inventario dei codici superstiti greci e latini antichi della Biblioteca Nazionale di Torino." *Rivista di filologia e d'istruzione classica* 32 (1904): 385–588.

Close Rolls of the Reign of Henry III: Preserved in the Public Record Office, edited by Great Britain Public Record Office. 14 vols. London: H. M. S. O., 1902–38.

Cosentini, Francesco, and Albano Sorbelli. *Inventari dei manoscritti delle Biblioteche d'Italia*. Vol. 28. *Torino*. Florence: Libreria Editrice Leo S. Olschki, 1922.

Davis, Henry W.C., Robert J. Whitwell, Charles Johnson, and Henry A. Cronne, eds. *Regesta Regum Anglo-Normannorum 1066–1154*. 4 vols. Oxford: Clarendon Press, 1913–1969.

Delisle, Léopold, and Élie Berger, eds. *Recueil des actes d'Henri II, roi d'Angleterre*. 3 vols. Paris: Imprimerie Nationale, 1916–1927.

Dennis, Andrew, Peter Foote, and Richard Perkins, trans. *Laws of Early Iceland: Grágás*, 2 vols. University of Manitoba Icelandic Studies 3 and 5. Winnipeg: University of Manitoba Press, 1980–2000.

Dewey, Horace W., and Ann M. Kleimola, eds. *Zakon Sudnyi Ljudem* [Court Law for the People]. Ann Arbor: Department of Slavic Languages and Literature, 1977.

Dillon, Myles, ed. "Stories from the Law-tracts." *Ériu* 11 (1932): 42–65.

Dillon, Myles, ed. *Lebor na Cert: The Book of Rights*. Irish Texts Society 46. London: Irish Texts Society, 1962.

Downer, Leslie J., ed. *Leges Henrici Primi*. Oxford: Clarendon Press, 1972.

Ebbo of Rheims. *Apologetici Ebonis forma prior*. Edited by Albert Werminghoff, MGH Conc. 2/2, 794–798 Hannover: Hahn, 1908.

Einar Ól. Sveinsson, ed. *Laxdœla saga*. Íslenzk fornrit 5. Reykjavík: Hið Íslenzka Fornritafélag, 1934.

Einar Ól. Sveinsson, ed. *Brennu-Njáls saga*. Íslenzk fornrit 12. Reykjavík: Hið Íslenzka Fornritafélag, 1954.

Einar Ól. Sveinsson, ed. *Vatnsdœla saga*. Íslenzk fornrit 8. Reykjavík: Hið Íslenzka Fornritafélag, 1939.

Einar Ól. Sveinsson, and Matthías Þorðarson, eds. *Eyrbyggja saga*. Íslenzk fornrit 4. Reykjavík: Hið Íslenzka Fornritafélag, 1935.

Eithun, Bjørn, Magnus Rindal, and Tor Ulset, eds. *Gulatingslova*. Oslo: Riksarkivet, 1994.

Elliott, J.K., ed. *The Apocryphal New Testament. A Collection of Apocryphal Literature in an English Translation*. Oxford: Clarendon Press, 1993.

Emanuel, Hywel D. *The Latin Texts of the Welsh Laws*. Cardiff: University of Wales Press, 1967.

Finnbogi Guðmundsson, ed. *Orkneyinga Saga*. Reykjavík: Hið Íslenzka Fornritafélag, 1965.

Finnur Jónsson, ed. *Den Norsk-Islandske Skjaldedigtning B, Bind 1*. Copenhagen: Gyldendal and Nordisk Forlag, 1912. Reprint, Copenhagen: Rosenkilde & Bagger 1973.

Finnur Jónsson, ed. *Den Norsk-Islandske Skjaldedigtning B, Bind 2*. Copenhagen: Gyldendal and Nordisk Forlag, 1915. Reprint, Copenhagen: Rosenkilde & Bagger, 1973.

Finsen, Vilhjálmur, ed. *Grágás. Stykker, som findes i det Arnamagnæanske Haandskrift Nr. 351 fol Skálholtsbók og en Række andre Haandskrifter*. Copenhagen: Gyldendal, 1883.

Finsen, Vilhjálmur, ed. *Grágás: Islændernes Lovbog i Fristatens Tid, udgivet efter det Kongelige Bibliotheks Haandskrift*, 2 parts (1a, 1b). Copenhagen: Berling, 1852.

Fischer-Drew, Katherine, trans. *The Lombard Laws*. Cinnaminson, NJ: University of Pennsylvania Press, 1996.

Flechner, Roy, ed. *The Hibernensis*, 2 vols. Washington, D.C.: Catholic University of America Press, 2019.

Fry, Timothy, ed. *RB 1980: The Rule of St. Benedict in Latin and English with Notes*. Collegeville: The Liturgical Press, 1981.

Gade, Kari Ellen, ed. *Poetry from King's Sagas II*. Turnhout: Brepols, 2009.

Geoffrey Chaucer. *The Riverside Chaucer*. Edited by Larry Benson. 3rd ed. Oxford: Oxford University Press, 1988. Reprint, 2008.

Geoffrey of Monmouth. *The History of the Kings of Britain: An edition and translation of the De gestis Britonum (Historia Regum Britanniae)*. Edited by Michael D. Reeve. Translated by Neil Wright. Woodbridge, UK: Boydell & Brewer, 2007.

Gerbenzon, Pieter, ed. *Rudolfsboek–materiael*. Estrikken 32. Groningen: Frysk Ynstitút, Rijksuniversiteit Groningen, 1961.

Gertz, Martin Clarentius, ed. *Scriptores Minores Historiæ Danicæ*, vol. 1. Copenhagen: Selskabet for Udgivelse af Kilder til dansk Historie, 1917.

"Gotha, Forschungsbibliothek, Memb. I 84." In *Bibliotheca Legum: A Database on Carolingian Secular Law Texts*, edited by Karl Ubl. Accessed November 06, 2019. http://www.leges.uni-koeln.de/en/mss/codices/gotha-flb-memb-i-84/.

"Gotha, Forschungsbibliothek, Memb. I 84." In *Capitularia: Edition der fränkischen Herrschererlasse*, edited by Karl Ubl. Accessed November 06, 2019. https://capitularia.uni-koeln.de/en/mss/gotha-flb-memb-i-84/.

Green, William Charles, trans. *The Story of Egil Skallagrimsson*. London: E. Stock, 1893. Accessed September 11, 2020, https://sagadb.org/egils_saga.en.

Gregory the Great. *Homiliarum in Evangelia Libri Duo*. Edited by Jacques-Paul Migne, PL 76:1075–1312C. Paris: Imprimerie Catholique, 1844–1855.

Gregory the Great. *Regula Pastoralis*. Edited by Floribert Rommel. Turin: Città Nuova, 2008.

Grønlie, Sian, trans. *Íslendingabók. Kristni Saga. The Book of Icelanders. The Story of the Conversion*. Exeter: Viking Society for Northern Research, 2006.

Guðni Jónsson, ed. *Grettis saga Ásmundarsonar.* Íslenzk fornrit 7. Reykjavík: Hið Íslenzka Fornritafélag, 1936.

Gwynn, Edward John, ed. *The Metrical Dindshenchas.* 5 vols. Dublin: Hodges & Figgis, 1935. Reprint, Dublin: Dublin Institute for Advanced Studies, 1991.

Hadrian II, *Epistola 3*, MGH *Epistola* 6, edited by Ernst Dümmler, Ernst Perels et al., 699–700. Berlin: Weidmannsche, 1925.

Hardy, Thomas D., ed. *Rotuli Litterarum Patentium in Turri Londinensi asservati.* London: Eyre & Spottiswoode, 1835.

Henry of Huntingdon. *Historia Anglorum: The History of the English People.* Edited and translated by Diana Greenway. Oxford Medieval Texts. Oxford: Clarendon Press, 1996.

Hermann Pálsson and Paul Edwards, trans. *The Book of Settlements. Landnámabók.* Winnipeg: University of Manitoba Press, 2006.

Hettema, Montanus. *Jurisprudentia Frisica, of Friesche Regtskennis.* 2 vols. Leeuwarden: H.C. Schetsberg, 1834–35.

Hincmar of Reims. *De Divortio Lotharii regis et Theutbergae reginae.* Edited by Letha Böhringer. MGH Conc. 4, sup. 1. Hannover: Hahnsche Buchhandlung, 1992.

Hincmar of Reims. *Visio Bernoldi*: edited by Maaike van der Lugt, "Tradition and Revision. The textual tradition of Hincmar of Reims' *Visio Bernoldi*. With a New Critical Edition." *Archivum Latinitatis Medii Aevi* 52 (1994): 140–48.

Hoekstra, Jelle. *De Eerste en de Tweede Hunsinger Codex.* Oudfriese Taal- en Rechtsbronnen 6. The Hague: Martinus Nijhoff, 1950.

Holm-Holsen, Ludvig, ed. *Konungs Skuggsjá.* Oslo: Norsk historisk kjeldeskrift-institutt, 1983.

Hormisdas. *Epistola per Universas Provincias.* Edited by Jacques-Paul Migne, PL 63: 527C–529D. Paris: Imprimerie Catholique, 1844–1855.

Huitfeldt-Kaas, Henrik J., Christopher Brinchmann, and Oluv Kolsrud, eds. *Norske Sigiller fra Middelalderen, Første Bind: Verdslige Sigiller indtil aar 1400.* Oslo: Kristiana Lithografiske Aktiebolag og Det Mallingske Boktrykkeri, 1899–1950.

"Ivrea, Biblioteca Capitolare, XXXIV (5)." In *Bibliotheca Legum: A Database on Carolingian Secular Law Texts*, edited by Karl Ubl. Accessed May 04, 2020. http://www.leges.uni-koeln.de/en/mss/codices/ivrea-bc-xxxiv-5/.

"Ivrea, Biblioteca Capitolare, XXXIV." In *Capitularia: Edition der fränkischen Herrschererlasse*, edited by Karl Ubl. Accessed May 04, 2020. https://capitularia.uni-koeln.de/en/mss/ivrea-bc-xxxiv/.

Jakob Benediktsson, ed. *Íslendingabok. Landnámabók.* Íslenzk fornrit 1. 2 vols. Reykjavík: Hið Íslenzka Fornritafélag, 1986.

James, Montague R., ed. *A Descriptive Catalogue of the Manuscripts in the Library of Lambeth Palace. The Mediaeval Manuscripts.* Cambridge: Cambridge University Press, 1932.

Jenkins, Dafydd. *Llyfr Colan*. Cardiff: University of Wales Press, 1963.

Jenkins, Dafydd. *Damweiniau Colan*. Aberystwyth: Cymdeithas Llyfrau Ceredigion, 1973.

Jenkins, Dafydd. *The Law of Hywel Dda: Lawtexts from Medieval Wales*. Llandysul: Gomer, 1986.

Jóhannes Halldórsson, ed. *Kjalnesinga saga*. Íslenzk fornrit 14. Reykjavík: Hið Íslenzka Fornritafélag, 1959.

Jóhannes Halldórsson, ed. *Víglundar Saga*. Reykjavík: Hið Íslenzka Fornritafélag, 1959.

Jón Jóhannesson, ed. *Austfirðinga sögur*. Íslenzk fornrit 11. Reykjavík: Hið Íslenzka Fornritafélag, 1950.

Jón Jóhannesson, Magnús Finnbogason, and Kristján Eldjárn, eds. *Sturlunga saga*. 2 vols. Reykjavík: Sturlunguútgáfan, 1946.

Jónas Kristjánsson, ed. *Eyfirðinga sögur*. Íslenzk fornrit 9. Reykjavík: Hið Íslenzka Fornritafélag, 1956.

Jost, Karl, ed. *Die "Institutes of Polity, Civil and Ecclesiastical": Ein Werk erzbischof Wulfstans von York*. Swiss Studies in English 47. Bern: Francke, 1959.

Kelly, Fergus, ed. *Audacht Morainn*. Dublin: Dublin Institute for Advanced Studies, 1976.

Ker, Neil R., ed. *The Pastoral Care*. Early English Manuscripts in Facsimile 6. Copenhagen: Rosenkilde and Bagger, 1956.

Keyser, Rudolph, and Peter A. Munch, eds. *Norges Gamle Love indtil 1387. Andet Bind*. Christiania: Gröndahl, 1848.

Keyser, Rudolph, and Peter A. Munch, eds. *Norges Gamle Love indtil 1387. Tredie Bind*. Christiania: Gröndahl, 1849.

Kirkus, A. Mary, ed. *Pipe Roll 9 John*. Pipe Roll Society 60. London: J.W. Ruddock 1946.

Kuhn, Hans, ed. *Edda, Die Lieder des Codex Regius Nebst Veerwandten Denkmälern, I Text*. 7. Aufl. Heidelberg: Winter, 1983.

Kurze, Wilhelm, ed. *Codex Diplomaticus Amiatinus*. 2 vols. Tübingen: Niemeyer, 1974.

Kuttner, Stephen, and Reinhard Elze, eds. *A Catalogue of Canon and Roman Law Manuscripts in the Vatican Library*. 2 vols. Vatican City: Biblioteca Apostolica Vaticana, 1986–87.

Larrington, Carolyne, trans. *The Poetic Edda*. Oxford: Oxford University Press, 2014.

Larson, Laurence, trans. *The King's Mirror*. New York: Harvard University Press, 1917.

Larson, Laurence, trans. *The Earliest Norwegian Laws*. New York: Columbia University Press, 1935.

Leo I. *Epistolae*. Edited by Jacques-Paul Migne, PL 54:551–1218B. Paris: Imprimerie Catholique, 1844–1855.

Liebermann, Felix, ed. *Die Gesetze der Angelsachsen*. 3 vols. Halle: Max Niemeyer, 1903–1916.

Mac Cana, Proinsias, ed. *The Learned Tales of Medieval Ireland*. Dublin: Dublin Institute for Advanced Studies, 1980.

Macray, William D., ed. *Chronicon Abbatiae de Evesham ad annum 1418*. London: Longman, Green, Longman, Roberts and Green, 1863.

"Madrid, Biblioteca Nacional, 413." In *Bibliotheca Legum: A Database on Carolingian Secular Law Texts*, edited by Karl Ubl. Accessed November 06, 2019. http://www.leges.uni-koeln.de/en/mss/codices/madrid-bn-413/.

"Madrid, Biblioteca Nacional, MS 413." In *Early Medieval Laws and Law-Books*, edited by Thom Gobbitt. Last modified April 01, 2019. https://thomgobbitt.files.wordpress.com/2018/04/madrid_bn_ms413_april2018.pdf.

Meyer, Kuno, ed. *Cáin Adamnáin: An Old Irish Treatise on the Law of Adamnan*. Oxford: Oxford Clarendon Press, 1905.

Meyer, Kuno, ed. *Tecosca Cormaic: The Instructions of King Cormac Mac Airt*. Todd Lecture Series, vol. 15. Dublin: Hodges & Figgis, 1909.

"Miscellany: Law." In *Alvin: Platform for Digital Collections and Digitized Cultural Heritage*. Universitetsbiblioteket, Lund. Accessed October 15, 2019. https://www.alvin-portal.org/alvin/view.jsf?pid=alvin-record:14709.

Monpherratos, A.G., ed. *Ecloga Leonis et Constantini*. Athens: Typis fratrum Perri, 1889.

Morcaldi, Michele, Mauro Schiani, and Silvano De Stefano, eds. *Codex Diplomaticus Cacensis*. vols 1–8. Naples, 1873–1893.

Morris, Richard, ed. *The Blickling Homilies of the Tenth Century, Early English Texts Society* 58, 63, 73. London: 1874–80.

Morris, William and Eiríkr Magnússon, trans. *The Saga of the Ere-Dwellers*. London: B. Quaritch, 1892. Accessed September 11, 2020, https://sagadb.org/eyrbyggja_saga.en.

Morris, William and Eiríkr Magnússon, trans. *The story of Grettir the Strong*. New York: Longmans, Green and Co., 1900. Accessed September 11, 2020, https://sagadb.org/grettis_saga.en.

Morris, William and Eiríkr Magnússon, trans. "The Story of Viglund the Fair." In *Three Northern Love Stories and Other Tales*. New York: Longmans, Green and Co., 1901. Accessed September 11, 2020, https://sagadb.org/viglundar_saga.en.

Nicholas I. *Responsa Nicolai I papae ad consulta Bulgarorum*. In *Nicolai I. papae epistolae*, edited by Ernst Perels, MGH Epp. 6, 568–600. Berlin: Weidmann, 1925.

Nordal, Sigurður, ed. *Egils Saga Skalla-Grímssonar*. Reykjavík: Hið Íslenzka Fornritafélag, 1933.

Nordal, Sigurður, and Guðni Jónsson, eds. *Borgfirðinga sögur*. Íslenzk fornrit 3. Reykjavík: Hið Íslenzka Fornritafélag, 1938.

O'Brien, Bruce. *God's Peace and King's Peace: The Laws of Edward the Confessor*. Philadelphia, PA: University of Pennsylvania Press, 1999.

O Daly, Máirín. "A Poem on the Airgialla." *Ériu* 16 (1952): 179–88.

O Daly, Máirín, ed. *Cath Maige Mucrama: the Battle of Mag Mucrama*. Irish Texts Society 50. London: Irish Texts Society, 1975.

Ó Néill, Pádraig, and David Dumville, eds. *Cáin Adomnáin and Canones Adomnani.* Cambridge: Department of Anglo-Saxon, Norse, and Celtic, University of Cambridge, 2003.

Orderic Vitalis. *The Ecclesiastical History of Orderic Vitalis.* Edited and Translated by Marjorie Chibnall. 6 vols. Oxford Medieval Texts. Oxford: Clarendon Press, 1969–1980.

Ottino, Giuseppe. *I Codici Bobbiesi nella Biblioteca Nazionale di Torino indicati e descritti da Giuseppe Ottino.* Turin, Palermo: Carlo Clausen, 1890.

Owen, Aneurin, ed. *Ancient Laws and Institutes of Wales.* 2 vols. London: Record Commission, 1841.

"Paris, Bibliothèque Nationale, Lat. 4613." In *Bibliotheca Legum: A Database on Carolingian Secular Law Texts*, edited by Karl Ubl. Accessed November 06, 2019. http://www.leges.uni-koeln.de/en/mss/codices/paris-bn-lat-4613/.

"Paris, Bibliothèque Nationale, Lat. 4613." In *Capitularia: Edition der fränkischen Herrschererlasse*, edited by Karl Ubl. Accessed November 06, 2019. https://capitularia.uni-koeln.de/en/mss/paris-bn-lat-4613/.

"Paris, Bibliothèque Nationale de France, MS Lat. 4613." In *Early Medieval Laws and Law-Books*, edited by Thom Gobbitt. Last modified February 06, 2020. https://thomgobbitt.files.wordpress.com/2020/02/paris-bnf-ms-lat-4613.pdf.

"Paris, Bibliothèque Nationale, Lat. 4614." In *Bibliotheca Legum: A Database on Carolingian Secular Law Texts*, edited by Karl Ubl. Accessed November 06, 2019. http://www.leges.uni-koeln.de/en/mss/codices/paris-bn-lat-4614/.

Patent Rolls of the Reign of Henry III: Preserved in the Public Record Office. Edited by Henry C. Maxwell Lyte. 6 vols. London: H. M. S. O., 1901–13.

Paulus Diaconus. *Historia Langobardorum.* Edited by Ludwig Bethmann and Georg Waitz, MGH SS rer. Lang., 12–187. Hannover: Hahn, 1878.

Pini, Virgilio, ed. "La "Summa de Vitiis et virtutibus" di Guido Faba." *Quadrivium* 1 (1956): 41–152.

Pliny. *Natural History, Volume II: Books 3–7.* Translated by Harris Rackham. Loeb Classical Library 352. Cambridge, MA: Harvard University Press, 1942.

Pomponius Mela. *Chorographie.* Edited and Translated by Alain Silberman. Collection des universités de France Série latine 283. Paris: Belles Lettres, 1988.

Richards, Melville, ed. *Cyfreithiau Hywel Dda yn ôl Llawysgrif Coleg yr Iesu LVII.* Rev. ed. Cardiff: University of Wales Press, 1990.

Rindal, Magnus, and Bjørg Dale Spørck, eds. *Kong Magnus Håkonsson Lagabøtes landslog.* Norrøn tekst med fullstendig variantapparat, del I. Oslo: Arkivverket, 2018.

Roberts, Sara Elin. *The Legal Triads of Medieval Wales.* Cardiff: University of Wales Press, 2007.

Roberts, Sara Elin. *Llawysgrif Pomffred: An Edition and Study of Peniarth ms 259B.* Leiden: Brill, 2011.

Robertson, Agnes J., ed. and trans. *The Laws of the Kings of England from Edmund to Henry I*. Cambridge: Cambridge University Press, 1925.

Russell, Paul. *Welsh Law in Medieval Anglesey. British Library, Harleian ms 1796 (Latin C)*. Texts and Studies in Medieval Welsh Law 2. Cambridge: Seminar Cyfraith Hywel, 2011.

Schiapparelli, Luigi, ed. *Codice Diplomatico Longobardo*. 2 vols. Rome: Istituto Storico Italiano per il Medio Evo, 1929. Reprint, 1933.

Sipma, Pieter, ed. *De Eerste Emsinger Codex*. Oudfriese Taal- en Rechtsbronnen 4. The Hague: Martinus Nijhoff, 1942.

Snorri Sturluson. *Edda*. Translated by Anthony Faulkes. London: Everyman, 1995.

Snorri Sturluson. *Edda. Háttatal*. Edited by Anthony Faulkes. Exeter: Viking Society for Northern Research, 2007.

Snorri Sturluson. *Edda. Prologue and Gylfaginning*. Edited by Anthony Faulkes. Exeter: Viking Society for Northern Research, 2005.

Snorri Sturluson. *Heimskringla I*. Edited by Bjarni Aðalbjanarson. Reykjavík: Hið Íslenzka Fornritafélag, 2002.

Snorri Sturluson. *Heimskringla I. The Beginnings to Óláfr Tryggvason*. Translated by Alison Finlay and Anthony Faulkes. Exeter: Viking Society for Northern Research, 2011.

Snorri Sturluson. *Heimskringla II*. Edited by Bjarni Aðalbjanarson. Reykjavík: Hið Íslenzka Fornritafélag, 2002.

Snorri Sturluson. *Heimskringla II. Óláfr Haraldsson*. Translated by Alison Finlay and Anthony Faulkes. Exeter: Viking Society for Northern Research, 2014.

Snorri Sturluson. *Heimskringla III*. Edited by Bjarni Aðalbjanarson. Reykjavík: Hið Íslenzka Fornritafélag, 2002.

Snorri Sturluson. *Heimskringla III. Magnús Óláfsson to Magnús Erlingsson*. Translated by Alison Finlay and Anthony Faulkes. Exeter: Viking Society for Northern Research, 2015.

Snorri Sturluson. *Skáldskaparmál 1. Introduction, Text and Notes*. Edited by Anthony Faulkes. Exeter: Viking Society for Northern Research, 1998.

Stone, Rachel, and Charles West, trans. *The Divorce of King Lothar and Queen Theutberga: Hincmar of Rheims's* De Divortio. Manchester: Manchester University Press, 2016.

Sweet, Henry, ed. *King Alfred's West-Saxon Version of Gregory's Pastoral Care*. Early English Text Society 45. London: Oxford University Press, 1871.

Thegan. *Gesta Hludowici imperatoris*. Edited by Ernst Tremp, MGH SSRG 64, 168–258. Hannover: Hahnsche Buchhandlung, 1995.

Theoderich of Cambrai. *Libellus Theoderici Cameracensis*. Edited by Wilfried Hartmann, MGH Conc. 3, 290–93. Hannover: Hahnsche Buchhandlung, 1984.

Thomson, Rodney M., ed. *A Descriptive Catalogue of the Medieval Manuscripts of Merton College, Oxford*. Cambridge: Cambridge University Press, 2009.

Thomson, Rodney M., ed. *A Descriptive Catalogue of the Medieval Manuscripts of Corpus Christi College, Oxford*. Cambridge: Cambridge University Press, 2011.

Thomson, Rodney M., and Michael Gullick, eds. *A Descriptive Catalogue of the Medieval Manuscripts in Worcester Cathedral Library*. Woodbridge, UK: D.S. Brewer, 2001.

Thorpe, Benjamin. *Ancient Laws and Institutes of England*. Vol. 2. London: Eyre and Spottiswode, 1840.

"Vatican, Biblioteca Apostolica Vaticana, Vat. Lat. 5359." In *Bibliotheca Legum: A Database on Carolingian Secular Law Texts*, edited by Karl Ubl. Accessed November 06, 2019. http://www.leges.uni-koeln.de/en/mss/codices/vatikan-bav-vat-lat-5359/.

"Vatican, Biblioteca Apostolica Vaticana, Vat. Lat. 5359." In *Capitularia: Edition der fränkischen Herrschererlasse*, edited by Karl Ubl. Accessed November 06, 2019. https://capitularia.uni-koeln.de/en/mss/vatikan-bav-vat-lat-5359/.

"Vercelli, Biblioteca Capitolare Eusebiana, CLXXXVIII." In *Bibliotheca Legum: A Database on Carolingian Secular Law Texts*, edited by Karl Ubl. Accessed November 06, 2019. http://www.leges.uni-koeln.de/en/mss/codices/vercelli-bce-clxxxviii/.

Vitolo, Giovanni, and Simeone Leone, eds. *Codex Diplomaticus Cacensis*, vols 9–10. Naples: Cava dei Tirreni, 1984. Reprint, 1990.

Wade-Evans, Arthur W. "Text of Pen. ms. 37 (fols. 61–76) with Translation." *Y Cymmrodor* 17 (1904): 129–63.

Wade-Evans, Arthur W. *Welsh Medieval Law, Being a Text of the Laws of Howel the Good*. Oxford: Clarendon Press, 1909. Reprint, Darmstadt: Scientia Verlag Aalen, 1979.

Waitz, Georg, ed. *Annales Bertiniani*. MGH SSRG 5. Hannover: Hahn, 1883.

Wasserschleben, Hermann, ed. *Die irische Kanonensammlung*. Giessen: J. Rickersche Buchhandlung, 1874.

Watkins, Calvert, ed. "Varia III." *Ériu* 29 (1978): 155–65.

Weinbaum, Martin. *London unter Eduard I und II*. 2 vols. Beihefte zur Vierteljahrschrift für Sozial- und Wirtschaftsgeschichte 28–29. Stuttgart: W. Kohlhammer, 1933.

Weinreich, C. William, ed. and trans. *Commentaries on Revelation by Victorinus of Petovium, Apringius of Beja, Caesarius of Arles, and Bede the Venerable*. Downers Grove, IL: Intervarsity Press, 2011.

Werminghoff, Albert, ed. *Episcoporum de poenitentia, quam Hludowicus imperator professus est, relatio Compendiensis*. MGH Conc. 2/2, 695. Hannover: Hahn, 1908.

Whaley, Diana, ed. *Poetry from King's Sagas 1*. Turnhout: Brepols, 2012.

Wiarda, Tilemann D. *Asega-Buch. Ein Altfriesisches Gesetz-buch der Rüstringer*. Berlin: Friedrich Nicolai, 1805.

Wild, Benjamin Linley, ed. *The Wardrobe Accounts of Henry III*. Publications of the Pipe Roll Society, n.s. 58. London: Pipe Roll Society, 2012.

Wiliam, Aled Rhys. *Llyfr Iorwerth*. Cardiff: University of Wales Press, 1960.

"Wolfenbüttel, Herzog August Bibliothek, Cod. Guelf. 130 Blank." In *Bibliotheca Legum: A Database on Carolingian Secular Law Texts*, edited by Karl Ubl. Accessed November 06. 2019, http://www.leges.uni-koeln.de/en/mss/codices/wolfenbuettel-hab-blankenb-130/.

"Wolfenbüttel, Herzog August Bibliothek, Cod. Guelf. 130 Blank." In *Capitularia: Edition der fränkischen Herrschererlasse*, edited by Karl Ubl. Accessed November 06, 2019. https://capitularia.uni-koeln.de/en/mss/wolfenbuettel-hab-blankenb-130/.

Wotton, William, and Moses Williams, eds. *Cyfreithjeu Hywel Dda Ac Ereill Seu Leges Wallicae Ecclesiasticae & Civiles Hoeli Boni Et Alconium Wallicae Principium*. London, 1730.

Þórhallur Vilmundarson, and Bjarni Vilhjálmsson, eds. *Harðar saga*. Íslenzk fornrit 13. Reykjavík: Hið Íslenzka Fornritafélag, 1991.

Secondary Literature

Ahlqvist, Anders. *The Early Irish Linguist: An Edition of the Canonical Part of the Auraicept na nÉces*. Helsinki: Societas Scientiarum Fennica, 1982.

Ahlqvist, Anders. "Old Irish *Airaiccecht* 'Primer, etc.'." In *Medieval Irish Law: Texts and Contexts*, edited by Anders Ahlqvist and Pamela O'Neill, 221–36. Sydney: University of Sydney, 2013.

Airlie, Stuart. "Private Bodies and the Body Politic in the Divorce Case of Lothar II." *Past & Present* 161 (1998): 3–38.

Akers, Ronald. *Social Learning and Social Structure: A General Theory of Crime and Deviance*. London: Transaction Publishers, 2009.

Aladzov, Andrey [Андрей Аладжов], ed. *Археологическа карта на Плиска* [Archaeological Map of Pliska]. Sofia: Bulgarian Academy of Sciences, 2013.

Alexander, Jonathan J.G. *Medieval Illuminators and Their Methods of Work*. New Haven, CT: Yale University Press, 1992.

Algra, Nikolaas E. *Zeventien Keuren en Vierentwintig Landrechten*. Doorn: Graal, 1991.

Amati Canta, Antonietta. "Terminologia matrimoniale longobarda nel Codice Diplomatico Barese-Pugliese." In *Presenze longobarde in Italia, il caso della Puglia*, edited by Lucia Sinisi, 141–172. Ravenna: Longo Editore, 2007.

Amira, Karl von, and Claudius von Schwerin. *Rechtsarchäologie*. Berlin: Ahnenerbe-Stiftung Verlag, 1943.

Andersen, Merete Geert. *Katalog over AM Accessoria 7. De latinske fragmenter*. Copenhagen: C.A. Reitzels Forlag, 2008.

Andersen, Per, Mia Münster-Swendsen, and Helle Vogt, eds. *Law Before Gratian: Law in Western Europe c. 500–1100*. Copenhagen: DJØF, 2007.

Angelov, Dimitar [Ангелов Д]. *Образуване на българската народност* [*Formation of the Bulgarian Ethnicity*]. Sofia: Science and Art, 1971.

Angenendt, Arnold. "*Donationes pro anima*: Gift and Countergift in the Early Medieval

Liturgy." In *The Long Morning of Medieval Europe: New Directions in Early Medieval Studies*, edited by Jennifer R. Davis and Michael McCormick, 131–54. Aldershot: Ashgate, 2008.

Apostolov, Kircho [Кирчо Апостолов]. "Средновековен некропол на хълма Сакарджа край Омуртаг [Medieval Necropolis on the Sakardza Hill Near Omurtag]." In *Eurika. In honorem Ludmilae Donchevae-Petkovae*, edited by Valeri Grigorov, Metodi Daskalov, and Evgenia Komatarova, 185–98. Sofia: Bulgarian Academy of Sciences, 2009.

Archan, Christophe. *Les Chemins du Jugement. Procédure et Science du Droit dans l'Irlande Médiévale*. Romanité et Modernité du Droit. Paris: De Boccard, 2007.

Archan, Christophe. "Les Règles de Droit dans la Prose du Dindshenchas de Rennes." *Droit et Cultures* 64.2 (2012): 91–113. Arnamagnæan Commission. *Dictionary of Old Norse Prose* online. http://onp.ku.dk/.

Artifoni, Enrico. "Storia, archeologia e diritto nel problema dei Longobardi." In *Atti del 1. Congresso internazionale di studi longobardi*, Spoleto 27–30 settembre 1951, edited by CISAM, 71–136. Spoleto: Accademia spoletina, 1952.

Artifoni, Enrico. "L'editto di Rotari come espediente politico di una monarchia barbarica." In *Studi in onore di G.M. De Francesco*, vol. 2, edited by Aurelio Candian and Remo Franceschelli, 235–256. Milan: Giuffrè, 1957.

Artifoni, Enrico. "La costituzione e l'ordinamento dei primi stati barbarici nell'Europa occidentale dopo le invasioni barbariche nella Romania." In *Atti del convegno internazionale sul tema Dalla tribù allo stato*, Roma, 13–16 aprile 1961, 67–78. Rome: Edizione Accademia nazionale dei Lincei, 1962.

Artifoni, Enrico. "Le questioni longobarde. Osservazioni su alcuni testi del primo Ottocento storiografico italiano." *Mélanges de l'Ecole française de Rome. Moyen-Age*, v. 119 n. 2 (2007): 297–304.

Ascheri, Mario. *Istituzioni medievali. Una introduzione*. Bologna: Il Mulino, 1994.

Aspöck, Edeltraud. "What Actually is a Deviant Burial? Comparing German-Language and Anglophone Research on 'Deviant Burials'." In *Deviant Burial in the Archaeological Record*, edited by Eileen Murphy, 17–34. Oxford: Oxbow Press, 1998.

Assmann, Jan. *Religion und kulturelles Gedächtnis. Zehn Studien*. Munich: Beck, 2000.

Astuti, Guido. *Lezioni di storia del diritto italiano. Le fonti. Età romano-barbarica*. Padua: CEDAM, 1953. Reprint, 1968.

Astuti, Guido. "*Liber Papiensis*." In *Novissimo Digesto Italiano* IX, edited by Antonio Azara and Ernesto Eula, 829–30. Turin: UTET, 1963.

Astuti, Guido. "Lombarda." In *Novissimo Digesto Italiano* IX, edited by Antonio Azara and Ernesto Eula, 1068–70. Turin: UTET, 1963.

Avalle, d'Arco Silvio. *Bassa latinità: il latino tra l'età tardo-antica e l'alto medioevo con particolare riguardo all'origine delle lingue romanze*. Turin: Giappichelli, 1968.

Azzara, Claudio. *Le invasioni barbariche*. Bologna: Il Mulino, 2003.

Azzara, Claudio. "… quod cawerfeda antiqua usque nunc sic fuisset. Consuetudine e codificazione nell'Italia longobarda," in *Alto medioevo mediterraneo*, edited by Stefano Gasparri, 251–57. Florence: Firenze University Press, 2005.

Azzara, Claudio. "Le nozze di Anstruda. Codice e prassi nell'Italia di diritto longobardo." In *Carte di famiglia*, edited by Cristina La Rocca and Stefano Gasparri, 223–36. Rome: Viella, 2005.

Azzara, Claudio. "Introduzione al testo." In *Le leggi dei Longobardi. Storia, memoria e diritto di un popolo germanico*, edited by Claudio Azzara and Stefano Gasparri. Rome: Viella, 2005.

Azzara, Claudio. "Forme di acculturazione e di integrazione delle stirpi in Occidente: la testimonianza delle leggi dei Longobardi." In *Archeologia e storia delle migrazioni. Europa, Italia, Mediterraneo fra tarda età romana e alto Medioevo*. Atti del Convegno internazionale di studi, Cimitile-Santa Maria Capua Vetere, 17–18 giugno 2010, edited by Carlo Ebanista and Marcello Rotili, 43–53. Cimitile: Tavolario, 2011.

Bagge, Sverre. *Society and Politics in Snorri Sturluson's Heimskringla*. Berkeley: University of California Press, 1991.

Bagge, Sverre. *From Gang Leader to the Lord's Anointed: Kingship in Sverris saga and Hákonar saga Hákonarsonar*. Odense: Odense University Press, 1996.

Bagge, Sverre. *From Viking Stronghold to Christian Kingdom: State Formation in Norway, c. 900–1350*. Copenhagen: Museum Tusculanum Press, 2010.

Baker, John H. *An Introduction to English Legal History*. 4th ed. London: Butterworths, 2002.

Ballard, Adolphus, ed. *British Borough Charters 1042–1216*. Cambridge: Cambridge University Press, 1913.

Baltl, Hermann. *Rechtsarchäologie des Landes Steiermark*. Graz: Verlag Hermann Böhlaus Nachf., 1957.

Barraclough, Eleanor Rosamund. "Following the Trollish *Baton Sinister*: Ludic Design in *Bárðar saga Snæfellsáss*." *Viking and Medieval Scandinavia* 4 (2008): 15–43.

Barratt, Nick. "The Impact of the Loss of Normandy on the English Exchequer: the Pipe Roll Evidence." In *Foundations of Medieval Scholarship: Records edited in honour of David Crook*, edited by Paul Brand and Sean Cunningham, 133–40. York: Borthwick Institute / National Archives, 2008.

Barrowclough, David. *Time to Slay Vampire Burials? The Archaeological and Historical Evidence for Vampires in Europe*. Cambridge: Red Dagger Press, 2014.

Bartlett, Robert. *Trial by Fire and Water: The Medieval Judicial Ordeal*. Oxford: Oxford University Press, 1986.

Bartoli Langeli, Attilio. *Notai. Scrivere documenti nell'Italia medievale*. Rome: Viella, 2006.

Barton, John L. "The Study of Civil Law before 1380." In *A History of the University of*

Oxford. Volume 1—The Early Oxford Schools, edited by Jeremy I. Catto, Trevor Henry Aston, and Ralph Evans, 519–30. Oxford: Oxford University Press, 1984.

Barði Guðmundsson. "Goðorð forn og ný." *Skírnir* 111 (1937): 56–83.

Bates, David. "Rouen from 900 to 1204: From Scandinavian Settlement to Angevin 'Capital'." In *Medieval Art, Architecture and Archaeology at Rouen*, edited by Jenny Stratford. British Archaeological Association Conference Transactions, 1–11. London: British Archaeological Association, 1993.

Bateson, Mary. "A London Municipal Collection of the Reign of John." *English Historical Review* 17 (1902): 480–511, 707–30.

Bauer, Andreas. "Das Recht im Bild. Bildquellen des Mittelalters als Informationsträger für die Rechtsgeschichte." In *Kloster und Bildung im Mittelalter*, edited by Nathalie Kruppa and Jürgen Wilke, 263–300. Göttingen: Vandenhoeck & Ruprecht, 2006.

Bauman, Richard. "Mediational Performance, Traditionalization, and the Authorization of Discourse." In *Verbal Art Across Cultures: The Aesthetics and Proto-aesthetics of Communication*, ed. Hubert Knoblauch and Helga Kotthoff, 91–117. Tübingen: Gunter Narr, 2001.

Bauman, Richard, and Charles Briggs. "Genre, Intertextuality, and Social Power." *Journal of Linguistic Anthropology* 2 (1992): 131–72.

Baumgarten, Rolf. "Etymological Aetiology in Irish Tradition." *Ériu* 41 (1990): 115–22.

Baumgarten, Rolf. "Discourse Markers in Medieval Irish Texts: Cs̄, Cair, Nī and Similar Features." *Ériu* 43 (1992): 1–37.

Baumgarten, Rolf. "Creative Medieval Etymology and Irish Hagiography (Lasair, Columba, Senán)." *Ériu* 54 (2004): 49–78.

Baxter, Stephen, Catherine E. Karkov, Janet L. Nelson, and David Pelteret, eds. *Early Medieval Studies in Memory of Patrick Wormald*. Bodmin: Ashgate, 2009.

Beck, Heinrich. "Ringgeld: Philologisches." *Reallexicon Germanischen Altertumskunde* 25 (2003): 18–19.

Bellocchio, Silvia, and Vittoria Dolcetti Corazza. "Il *Codex Taurinensis* F.IV.1 fr. 10." In *Le rune. Epigrafia e letteratura*, edited by Vittoria Dolcetti Corazza and Renato Gendre, 65–115. Bibliotheca Germanica. *Studi e testi* 26. Alessandria: Edizioni dell'Orso, 2009.

Bellomo, Manlio. *Società e Istituzioni in Italia dal Medioevo agli inizi dell'Età moderna*. Catania, Rome: Editrice Giannotta e Il Cigno Galileo Galilei, 1991; 1st ed. Catania, 1976.

Bellomo, Manlio. *The Common Legal Past of Europe 1000–1800*. Translated by Lydia G. Cochrane. Washington DC: Catholic University of America Press, 1995. Originally published as *L'Europa del diritto commune*. Rome: Il Cigno Galileo Galilei, 1988.

Benham, Jenny, ed. *Early Medieval Law in Context. Historical Research* 86 (2013): 443–64.

Berg, Knut. "The Illuminations in No. 1154 Folio in the Old Royal Collection, Copenhagen." In *King Magnus Håkonsson's Laws of Norway and other legal texts*, edited by

Knut Berg and Magnus Rindal, 26–35. Oslo: Selskapet til Utgivelse av gamle Norse håndskrifter, 1983.

Bergamo, Nicola. "Il problema dell'identità etnica tra Romani e Longobardi nell'Historia Langobardorum di Paolo Diacono." *Porphyra* Anno III, numero VIII (Novembre, 2006): 26–44.

Berger, Alan. "Lawyers in the Icelandic Family Sagas: Heroes, Villains and Authors." *Saga-Book* 20 (1978–79): 70–79.

Bertini, Luca. *Peredeus vescovo di Lucca*. Pisa: Pacini, 1973.

Best, Richard Irvine. "Cuchulainn's Shield." *Ériu* 5 (1911): 72.

Beševliev, Veselin. *Die protobulgarischen Inschriften*. Berlin, Akademie-Verlag, 1963.

Bethurum, Dorothy L. *The Homilies of Wulfstan*. Oxford: Clarendon, 1957.

Bethurum, Dorothy L. "A Letter of Protest from the English Bishops to the Pope." In *Philologica: the Malone Anniversary Studies*, edited by Thomas A. Kirby and Henry Bosley Woolf, 97–104. Baltimore: Johns Hopkins Press, 1949.

Binchy, Daniel A. "The Date and Provenance of *Uraicecht Becc*." *Ériu* 18 (1958): 44–54.

Bischoff, Bernhard. "Turning Points in the History of Latin Exegesis in the Early Irish Church." Translated by Colm O'Grady. In *Biblical Studies: The Medieval Irish Contribution*, edited by Martin McNamara, 74–149. Dublin: Irish Biblical Association, 1976.

Bischoff, Bernhard. *Paleografia Latina. Antichità e Medioevo*. Padua: Editrice Antenore, 1992.

Bjørgo, Narve. "Samkongedome kontra einekongedome. Ein analyse av norsk kjeldemateriale i historiografisk perspektiv." *Historisk Tidsskrift* 49 (1970): 1–33.

Bof, Riccardo, and Conrad Leyser. "Divorce and Remarriage Between Late Antiquity and the Early Middle Ages: Canon Law and Conflict Resolution." In *Making Early Medieval Societies Conflict and Belonging in the Latin West, 300–1200*, edited by Kate Cooper and Conrad Leyser, 155–180. Cambridge: Cambridge University Press, 2016.

Bognetti, Gian Piero. *L'Età longobarda I–IV*. Milan: Giuffrè, 1966–1968.

Booker, Courtney. *Past Convictions: The Penance of Louis the Pious and the Decline of the Carolingians*. Philadelphia, PA: University of Pennsylvania Press, 2009.

Bos-Van der Heide, Henny S.E. *Het Rudolfsboek*. Assen: van Gorcum, 1937.

Bosworth, Joseph, and Thomas Northcote Toller. *An Anglo-Saxon Dictionary*. Oxford: Clarendon Press, 1898.

Bougard, François. *La Justice Dans le Royaume d'Italie: De la Fin du VIIIe Siècle au Debut du XIe Siècle*. Rome: École Française de Rome, Palais Farnèse, 1995.

Bougard, François. "Actes privés et transferts patrimoniaux en Italie centro-septentrionale (VIIIe–Xe siècle)." *Mélanges de l'École Française de Rome* 111 (1999): 539–62.

Boulestin, Bruno. *Norme funéraire: illusions et vérités, Qu'est-ce qu'une sépulture? Humanités et systems funéraires de la Préhistoire à nos jours*. Antibes: Éditions APDCA, 2016.

Bowen, Geraint. "Moses Williams (1685–1742)." In *Dictionary of Welsh Biography*. National Library of Wales. Accessed October 20, 2017. http://yba.llgc.org.uk/en/s-WILL-MOS-1685.html.

Bozhilova, Elena [Елена Божилова], and Kamen Stanev [Камен Станев]. "Спасителни археологически разкопки на ул. Рилски метох 3, Пловдив [Rescue Excavations in Rilskimetoh str. 3, Plovdiv]." *Археологически Открития и Разкопки за 2014* (2015): 744–747.

Braccini, Giovanna Princi. "Germanismi editi e inediti nel *Codice diplomatico longobardo*: anticipi da uno spoglio integrale e commentato di fonti latine in vista di un *Tesoro* longobardo." *Quaderni del Dipartimento di Linguistica dell'Università degli Studi di Firenze* 9 (1998/1999): 191–240.

Braccini, Giovanna Princi. "Germanismi editi e inediti nel *Cartulario di S. Benedetto di Conversano (901–1265)*." *Quaderni del Dipartimento di Linguistica dell'Università degli Studi di Firenze* 10 (2000): 1–41.

Brand, Paul. *The Origins of the English Legal Profession*. Oxford: Blackwell, 1992.

Brand, Paul. "An English Legal Historian Looks at the Statute of Wales." In *Y Cyfraniad Cymreig: Welsh Contributions to Legal Development*, edited by Thomas G. Watkin, 20–56. Bangor: Welsh Legal History Society, 2005.

Breatnach, Liam. "Canon Law and Secular Law in Early Ireland: The Significance of *Bretha Nemed*." *Peritia* 3 (1984): 439–59.

Breatnach, Liam. "The Ecclesiastical Element in the Old-Irish Legal Tract *Cáin Fhuithirbe*." *Peritia* 5 (1986): 36–52.

Breatnach, Liam. "Lawyers in Early Ireland." In *Brehons, Serjeants and Attorneys: Studies in the History of the Irish Legal Profession*, edited by Daire Hogan and William N. Osborough, 1–13. Dublin: Irish Academic Press, 1990.

Breatnach, Liam. "On the Original Extent of the 'Senchas Már'," *Ériu* 47 (1996): 1–43

Breatnach, Liam. *A Companion to the Corpus Iuris Hibernici*. Early Irish Law Series 5. Dublin: Dublin Institute for Advanced Studies, 2005.

Breatnach, Liam. *The Early Irish Law Text Senchas Már and The Question of Its Date*, E.C. Quiggin Memorial Lectures 13. Cambridge: Department of Anglo-Saxon, Norse, and Celtic, University of Cambridge, 2011.

Bremmer Jr, Rolf H. *'Hir is eskriven'. Lezen en schrijven in de Friese landen rond 1300*. Hilversum: Verloren, 2004.

Bremmer Jr, Rolf H. *Introduction to Old Frisian. History, Grammar, Reader, Glossary*. Amsterdam: John Benjamins, 2009.

Bremmer Jr, Rolf H. "From Alien to Familiar: Christ in Language and Law of Medieval Frisia." In *Myths, Martyrs, and Modernity. Studies in the History of Religions in Honour of Jan N. Bremmer*, edited by Jitse Dijkstra, Justin Kroesen, and Yme Kuiper, 531–552. Leiden: Brill, 2010.

Bremmer Jr, Rolf H. "Leiden, Vossianus Lat. Q. 69 (Part 2): Schoolbook or Proto-Encyclopaedic Miscellany?" In *Practice in Learning: The Transfer of Encyclopaedic Knowledge in the Early Middle Ages*, edited by Rolf H. Bremmer Jr and Kees Dekker, 19–53. Leuven: Peeters, 2010.

Bremmer Jr, Rolf H. "The Orality of Medieval Frisian Law." In *Directions for Old Frisian Philology*, edited by Rolf H. Bremmer Jr, Stephen Laker, and Oebele Vries, 1–48. Amsterdamer Beiträge zur älteren Germanistik 73. Amsterdam: Rodopi, 2014.

Bremmer Jr, Rolf H. "Codifying the Law: Frisian Legal Manuscripts around 1300." In *Vernacular Manuscript Culture 1000–1500*, edited by Erik Kwakkel, 143–85. Leiden: Leiden University Press, 2018.

Bremmer Jr, Rolf H. "'The Fleeing Foot is the Confessing Hand': Proverbs in the Old Frisian Laws." In *La tradizione gnomica nelle letterature germaniche medievali*, edited by Marina Cometta, Elena di Venosa, Andrea Meregalli, and Paola Spazzali, 79–100. Collana Di/Segni 13. Milan: Ledizioni, 2018.

Bresslau, Harry. *Handbuch der Urkundenlehre für Deutschland und Italien* I. Leipzig: Veit, 1912.

Briggs, Charles F. *Giles of Rome's* De Regimine Principum. *Reading and Writing Politics at Court and University, c.1275–c.1525*. Cambridge: Cambridge University Press, 1999.

Brink, Stefan. "Minnunga mæn: The Usage of Old Knowledgeable Men in Legal Cases." In *Minni and Muninn: Memory in Medieval Nordic Culture*, edited by Pernille Hermann, Stephen A. Mitchell, and Agnes S. Arnórsdóttir, 197–210. Turnhout: Brepols, 2014.

Brooke, Christopher N.L., and Gillian Keir. *London 800–1216: The Shaping of a City*. Berkeley, CA: University of California Press, 1975.

Bruckner, Wilhelm. *Die Sprache der Langobarden*, Quellen und Forschungen zur Sprach- und Culturgeschichte der germanischen Völker 75. Strassburg: Karl J. Trubner, 1895; anast. repr. Berlin: De Gruyter, 1969.

Brundage, James A. *Medieval Canon Law*. London: Longman, 1995.

Brundage, James A. *The Medieval Origins of the Legal Profession: Canonists, Civilians, and Courts*. Chicago: University of Chicago Press, 2014.

Buc, Philip. *The Dangers of Ritual: Between Early Medieval Texts and Social Scientific Theory*. Princeton: Princeton University Press, 2001.

Burgarella, Filippo. "Bizantini e Longobardi nell'Italia meridionale." In *I Longobardi dei Ducati di Spoleto e Benevento*. Atti del XVI Congresso internazionale di Studi sull'alto Medioevo, Spoleto, 20–23 ottobre 2002, Benevento, 24–27 ottobre 2002, edited by CISAM, 181–204. Spoleto: CISAM, 2003.

Burnyeat, Abigail. "The Early Irish *Grammaticus*?" *Aiste* 1 (2007): 181–217.

Burrows, Hannah. "Cold Cases: Law and Legal Detail in the *Íslendingasögur*." *Parergon* 26/1 (2009): 35–56.

Burrows, Hannah. "Some Þing to Talk About: Assemblies in the *Íslendingasögur*." *Northern Studies* 47 (2015): 47–75.

Burt, Caroline. *Edward I and the Governance of England, 1272–1307*. Cambridge: Cambridge University Press, 2013.

Byock, Jesse. *Medieval Iceland: Society, Sagas, and Power*. Berkeley, CA: University of California Press, 1998.

Byrne, Francis John. "Senchas: The Nature of Gaelic Historical Tradition." *Historical Studies* 9 (1974): 137–59.

Byrne, Francis John. *Irish Kings and High-kings*. Dublin: Four Courts Press, 1987.

Cahn, Walter. *Romanesque Manuscripts: The Twelfth Century, Volume One: Texts and Illustrations*. London: Harvey Miller, 1994.

Calasso, Francesco. *Il Medio Evo del diritto*. I. *Le fonti*. Milan: Giuffrè, 1954.

Calder, George. *Auraicept na n-Éces: The Scholars' Primer*. Edinburgh: J. Grant, 1917.

Camargo, Martin. "The English Manuscripts of Bernard of Meung's *Flores Dictaminum*." *Viator* 12 (1981): 197–220.

Camargo, Martin. "Beyond the *Libri Catoniani*: Models of Latin Prose Style at Oxford University ca. 1400." *Mediaeval Studies* 59 (1994): 165–87.

Camargo, Martin. *Essays on Medieval Rhetoric*. Farnham: Ashgate, Variorum, 2012.

Camargo, Martin. "Vinsauf, Geoffrey of [called Galfridus Anglicus] (fl. 1208–1213), Poet and Teacher of Grammar and Rhetoric." *Oxford Dictionary of National Biography*. Accessed December 11, 2017. http://www.oxforddnb.com/view/10.1093/ref:odnb/9780198614128.001.0001/odnb-9780198614128-e-28326.

Cameron, Euan. *Waldenses: Rejections of Holy Church in Medieval Europe*. Oxford: Blackwell, 2000.

Canning, Joseph P. "Ideas of the State in Thirteenth and Fourteenth-Century Commentators on the Roman Law." *Transactions of the Royal Historical Society*, 5th series 33 (1983): 1–27.

Capo, Lidia. "Paolo Diacono e il problema della cultura." In *Langobardia*, edited by Paolo Cammarosano and Stefano Gasparri, 169–235. Udine: Casamassima, 1990.

Carey, John. "Cosmology in Saltair na Rann." *Celtica* 17 (1985): 33–52.

Carey, John. *The Irish National Origin-Legend: Synthetic Pseudohistory*. Cambridge: Department of Anglo-Saxon, Norse, and Celtic, University of Cambridge, 1994.

Carlin, Martha. "Fetcham [Peckham], Peter of [Pierre d'Abernon] (fl. 1267–1276), Translator and Poet." *Oxford Dictionary of National Biography*. Accessed December 11, 2017. http://www.oxforddnb.com/view/10.1093/ref:odnb/9780198614128.001.0001/odnb-9780198614128-e-52678.

Carr, Glenda. *William Owen Pughe*. Cardiff: University of Wales Press, 1983.

Carruthers, Mary. *The Book of Memory. A Study of Memory in Medieval Culture*. Cambridge: Cambridge University Press, 2008.

Carus-Wilson, Eleonora M. "The Effects of the Acquisition and of the Loss of Gascony on the English Wine Trade." In *Medieval Merchant Ventures: Collected Studies*, 265–78. London: Methuen, 1954.

Catto, Jeremy I. “Andrew Horn: Law and History in Fourteenth-Century England.” In *The Writing of the Middle Ages: Essays Presented to Richard William Southern*, edited by Ralph Henry C. Davis and John Michael Wallace-Hadrill, 367–91. Oxford: Clarendon Press, 1981.

Cavanaugh, Susan H. “Royal Books: King John to Richard II.” *The Library: Transactions of the Bibliographical Society*, 6th series 10:4 (1988): 304–16.

Chapman Stacey, Robin. “Learning to Plead in Medieval Welsh Law.” *Studia Celtica* 38 (2004): 107–24

Chapman Stacey, Robin. “Law and Literature in Ireland and Wales.” In *Medieval Celtic Literature and Society*, edited by Helen Fulton, 65–82. Dublin: Four Courts Press, 2005.

Charles-Edwards, Thomas M. “Honour and Status in Some Irish and Welsh Prose Tales.” *Ériu* 29 (1978): 123–41.

Charles-Edwards, Thomas M. “Review Article: the *Corpus Iuris Hibernici.*” *Studia Hibernica* 20 (1980): 141–62.

Charles-Edwards, Thomas M. “*Cynghawsedd*: Counting and Pleading in Medieval Welsh Law.” *Bulletin of the Board of Celtic Studies* 33 (1986): 188–98.

Charles-Edwards, Thomas M. *The Welsh Laws*. Cardiff: University of Wales Press, 1989.

Charles-Edwards, Thomas M. *The Early Mediaeval Gaelic Lawyer*. ASNC Publications 4. Cambridge: Cambridge University Press, 1999.

Charles-Edwards, Thomas M. “Geis, Prophecy, Omen, and Oath,” *Celtica* 23 (1999): 38–59.

Cherubini, Paolo, and Alessandro Pratesi. *Paleografia Latina. L’avventura grafica del mondo occidentale*. Vatican City: Scuola Vaticana di Paleografia, Diplomatica e Archivistica, 2010.

Christie, Neil. *The Lombards*. Oxford: Blackwell, 1995.

Clarke, Peter D. “The Growth of Canon and Civil Law Studies, 1070–1535.” In *Illuminating the Law: Legal Manuscripts in Cambridge Collections*, edited by Susan L’Engle and Robert Gibbs, 22–38. London: Harvey Miller, 2001.

Clarke, Peter D. “Peter the Chanter, Innocent III and Theological Views on Collective Guilt and Punishment.” *Journal of Ecclesiastical History* 52 (2000): 1–20.

Cleasby, Richard, and Gudbrand Vigfusson. *An Icelandic-English Dictionary*. 2nd ed. with a supplement by Sir William A. Craigie. Oxford: Clarendon Press, 1957.

Clement, Richard W. “A Handlist of Manuscripts Containing Gregory’s *Regula Pastoralis.*” *Manuscripta* 28 (1984): 33–44.

Coates, Alan. *English Medieval Books: The Reading Abbey Collections from Foundation to Dispersal*. Oxford: Oxford University Press, 1999.

Cobban, Alan B. “Edward II, Pope John XXII and the University of Cambridge.” *Bulletin of the John Rylands Library* 47:1 (1964): 49–78.

Colafrancesco, Sonia. “Interferenze e commistioni tra diritto longobardo e diritto romano-bizantino nei documenti del *Codex diplomaticus Cavenis*" [Interferences and Interpenetrations between Lombard Law and Roman-Byzantine Law in the Documents of the *Codex diplomaticus Cavensis*]. PhD Thesis, Università degli Studi "G. d'Annunzio" Chieti-Pescara, 2016.

Constable, Giles. *Letters and Letter-Collections*. Turnhout: Brepols, 1976.

Cortese, Ennio. *Il diritto nella storia medievale*. II. *Il basso Medioevo*. Rome: Il Cigno Galileo Galilei, 1995.

Costamagna, Giorgio. "L'altomedioevo." In *Alle origini del notariato italiano*, edited by Mario Amelotti and Giorgio Costamagna, 147–314. Rome: Consiglio Nazionale del notariato, 1975.

Costambeys, Marios. "The Laity, the Clergy, the Scribes and their Archives: The Documentary Record of Eighth- and Ninth-Century Italy." In *Documentary Culture and the Laity in the Early Middle Ages*, edited by Warren Brown, Marios Costambeys, Matthew Innes, and Adam Kosto, 231–58. Cambridge: Cambridge University Press, 2013.

Crick, Julia C. *The historia regum Britannie of Geoffrey of Monmouth: III. A summary catalogue of the manuscripts*. Cambridge: D.S. Brewer, 1989.

Cross, James E. "Missing Folios in Cotton MS. Nero A.I." *British Library Journal* 16 (1990): 99–100.

Cross, James E., and Andrew Hamer. *Wulfstan's Canon Law Collection*. Cambridge: D.S. Brewer, 1999.

Cubitt, Catherine. "'As the Lawbook Teaches': Reeves, Lawbooks and Urban Life in the Anonymous Old English Legend of the Seven Sleepers." *English Historical Review* 124 (2009): 1021–49.

Davies, Morgan Thomas. "Protocols of Reading in Early Irish Literature: Notes on Some Notes to 'Orgain Denna Ríg' and 'Amra Coluim Cille'." *Cambrian Medieval Celtic Studies* 32 (Winter 1996): 1–24.

Davies, R.R. *Lordship and Society in the March of Wales*. Oxford: Oxford University Press, 1978.

Davies, R.R. "The Peoples of Britain and Ireland 1100–1400: I. Identities." *Transactions of the Royal Historical Society*, 6th series 4 (1994): 1–20.

Dekker, Kees. "The Old Frisian Studies of Jan van Vliet (1622–1666) and Thomas Marshall (1621–1685)." In *Approaches to Old Frisian Studies*, edited by Rolf H. Bremmer Jr, Thomas S.B. Johnston, and Oebele Vries, 113–38. Amsterdamer Beiträge zur älteren Germanistik 49. Amsterdam: Rodopi, 1998.

Delogu, Paulo. "Lombard and Carolingian Italy." In *The New Cambridge Medieval History*, vol. ii, *c. 700–c. 900*, edited by Rosamond McKitterick, 290–319. Cambridge: Cambridge University Press, 1995.

Delogu, Paulo. "Devozione longobarda." In *Italy and Early Medieval Europe: Papers for Chris Wickham*, edited by Ross Balzaretti, Julia Barrow, and Patricia Skinner, 441–59. Oxford: Oxford University Press, 2018.

Denholm-Young, Noel. "The Cursus in England." In *Collected Papers*, 42–73. Cardiff: University of Wales Press, 1969.

Derolez, Albert. *The Palaeography of Gothic Manuscript Books: From the Twelfth to the Early Sixteenth Century*. Cambridge: Cambridge University Press, 2003.

Devisse, Jean. *Hincmar, archevêque de Reims, 845–882*. 3 vols. Genève: Droz, 1975–1976.

Dilcher, Gerhard. "Langobardisches Recht." *Handwörterbuch zur deutschen Rechtsgechichte* 3 (2016): 624–37.

Dilcher, Gerhard, and Eva-Marie Distler, eds. *Leges, Gentes, Regna: zur rolle von germanischen Rechtsgewohnheiten und lateinischer Schrifttradition bei der Ausbildung der frühmittelalterlichen Rechtskultur*. Berlin: Erich Schmidt Verlag, 2006.

Dion, Roger. *Histoire de la vigne et du vin en France des origines au XXe siècle*. Paris: CNRS, 1959.

Djurić, Marija, Ksenija Djukić, Tamara Pavlović, and Marko Drašković. "'Deviant' Burial in Medieval Avarian Necropolis of Pionirska Ulica (Serbia)." Research Paper Presented at the 23rd Annual Meeting of the European Association of Archaeologists. Maastrich, Niederlands, September 2017.

Donald Logan, F. "An Early Thirteenth-Century Papal Judge-Delegate Formulary of English Origin." *Studia Gratiana* 14:4 (1967): 75–87.

Dorn, Franz. "Schenkung." *Reallexicon Germanischen Altertumskunde* 26 (2004): 623–41.

Dorndop, Harry, and Eltjo J.H. Schrage. "The Sources of Medieval Learned Law." In *The Creation of the ius commune: From Casus to Regula*, edited by John W. Cairns and Paul J. du Plessis, 7–56. Edinburgh: Edinburgh University Press, 2010.

Drechsler, Stefan. "The Illuminated Þjófabálkr in Fourteenth-Century Icelandic Jónsbók Manuscripts." *Viking and Medieval Scandinavia* 12 (2016): 1–40.

Drechsler, Stefan. "Illuminated Manuscript Production in Western Iceland in the Thirteenth and Early Fourteenth Centuries." *Gripla* XXVIII (2017): 169–96.

Du Cange, Charles Du Fresne et al., eds. "Sortio," in *Glossarium mediæ et infimæ latinitatis*. Accessed February 06, 2020. http://ducange.enc.sorbonne.fr/SORTIO.

Dzambov, Ivan [Иван Джамбов]. "Средновековният некропол край Сопот [Medieval Cemetery near Sopot]." *Известия на музеите в Южна България* 14 (1988): 144–58.

Ebel, Friedrich, Andreas Fijal, and Gernot Kocher. *Römisches Rechtsleben im Mittelalter. Miniaturen aus den Handschriften des Corpus iuris civilis*. Heidelberg: C.F. Müller, 1988.

Ekrem, Inger, and Lars Boje Mortensen, eds. *Historia Norwegie*. Copenhagen: Museum Tusculanum Press, 2003.

Eliot, Simon, and Jonathan Rose, eds. *A Companion to The History of the Book*. Oxford: Blackwell, 2007.

Eriksen, Stefka Georgieva. "Litterær kultur i Norge i Eufemias tid." In *Eufemias. Oslos Midelalderdronning*, edited by Bjørn Bandlien, 157–72. Oslo: Dreyers Forlag, 2012.

Everett, Nicholas. "Literacy and the Law in Lombard Government." *Early Medieval Europe* 9 (2000): 93–127.

Everett, Nicholas. *Literacy in Lombard Italy, c. 568–774*. Cambridge: Cambridge University Press, 2003.

Everett, Nicholas. "How Territorial was Lombard Law?" In *Die Langobarden. Herrschaft und Identität*, edited by Walter Pohl and Peter Ehrhart, 345–60. Vienna: Verlag der österreichischen Akademie der Wissenschaften, 2005.

Falaschi, Pierluigi. "La successione volontaria nella legislazione longobarda." In *Annali della Facoltà giuridica dell'Università di Camerino, Studi in memoria di P. Rasi Caldogno*, 194–300. Milan: Giuffrè, 1969.

Farinelli, Roberto. "Churches and Social Elites in Early Medieval Tuscany: A Quantitative-Statistical Approach to the Episcopal Archive of Lucca." In *Churches and Social Power in Early Medieval Europe. Integrating Archaeological and Historical Approaches*, edited by Josè C. Sánchez-Pardo and Michael G. Shapland, 157–73. Turnhout: Brepols, 2015.

Farinelli, Roberto. "How Territorial was Lombard Law?" In *Die Langobarden: Herrschaft und Identität*, edited by Walter Pohl and Peter Erhart, 345–60. Vienna: Verlag der Österreichischen Akademie der Wissenschaften, 2005.

Faulkner, Thomas. "Carolingian Kings and the *Leges Barbarorum*." In *Early Medieval Law in Context*, edited by Jenny Benham, *Historical Research* 86 (2013): 443–64.

Faulkner, Thomas. *Law and Authority in the Early Middle Ages*. Cambridge: Cambridge University Press, 2016.

Fazzini, Elisabetta. "Condizione sociale e giuridica della donna nelle *Leges Barbarorum*." *Igitur* Anno V, n. 1 (1993): 25–72.

Fehr, Bernhard. *Die Hirtenbriefe Ælfrics*. Bibliothek der angelsächsischen Prosa IX. Hamburg: Henri Grand, 1914.

Fell, Christine E. "Some Questions of Layout and Legal Manuscripts." In *'Lastworda Betst' Essays in Memory of Christine E. Fell with her Unpublished Writing*, edited by Carole Hough and Kathryn Lowe, 229–41. Donington: Tyas, 2002.

Fiedler, Uwe. *Studien zu Gräberfeldern des 6. Bis 9. Jahrhunderts an der unteren Donau*. Bonn: Dr. Rudolph Habelt GmbH, 1992.

Figueira, Robert C. "Decretalists, Medieval Papal Legislation, and the Roman Law of Offices and Jurisdiction." *Res Publica Litterarum: Studies in the Classical Tradition* 9 (1986): 110–35.

Firey, Abigail. *A Contrite Heart: Prosecution and Redemption in the Carolingian Empire*. Boston: Brill, 2009.

Fischer-Drew, Katherine. "Notes on Lombard Institutions / Lombard Laws and Anglo-Saxon Dooms." *Rice Institute Pamphlet* 43 (1956): i–ix, 1–125.

Fischer-Drew, Katherine. "Public vs. Private Enforcement of the Law in the Early Middle Ages: Fifth to Twelfth Centuries." *Chicago-Kent Law Review* 70 (1995): 1583–92.

Fissore, Giangiacomo. "Segni di identità e forme di autenticazione nelle carte notarili altomedievali, fra interpretazione del ruolo e rappresentazione della forma documentaria." In *Comunicare e significare nell'alto medioevo* I, edited by CISAM, 285–333. Spoleto: CISAM, 2005.

Flower, Robin. "Quidam Scotigena .i. Discipulus Boëthii or Boëthius and the Four Conditions of a Tale." *Ériu* 8 (1916): 150–54.

Foss, Edward. *The Judges of England, From the Time of the Conquest*. 9 vols. London: Longman, Brown, Green and Longmans, 1948–64.

Francovich Onesti, Nicoletta. *Vestigia longobarde in Italia (568–774). Lessico e antroponimia*. Rome: Artemide, 1999. Reprint 2013.

Francovich Onesti, Nicoletta. "L'incontro fra le culture latina e germanica nell'Italia longobarda." In *Akkulturation. Probleme einer germanisch-romanischen Kultursynthese in Spätantike und frühem Mittelalter*, edited by Dieter Hägermann, Wolfgang Haubrichs, and Jörg Jarnut, 204–20. Berlin: De Gruyter, 2004.

Fruscione, Daniela. "Documenti Longobardi di Chiusi." In *Goti e Longobardi a Chiusi*, edited by Carla Falluomini, 85–103. Chiusi: Edizioni Luì, 2009.

Fruscione, Daniela. "Documenti longobardi e questione dell'effettività delle leggi." *Filologia Germanica* 2 (2010): 105–34.

Fruscione, Daniela. "Wo waren die Langobarden in den italienischen Urkunden? Identität, Verwandtshaft und Namengebung." *Namenkundliche Informationen* 103/104 (2014): 76–84.

Fruscione, Daniela. "Im Spannungsfeld zwischen deutscher Rechtsgeschichte und italienischem Frühmittelalter: Gerhard Dilcher und die Leges Langobardorum." In *Recht—Geschichte—Geschichtsschreibung: Rechts- und Verfassungsgeschichte im deutsch-italienischen Diskurs*, edited by Susanne Lepsius and Bernd Kannowski, 17–31. Berlin: Erich Schmidt Verlag, 2014.

Gade, Kari Ellen. "Hanging in Northern Law and Literature." *Maal og Minne* (1986): 159–83.

Gallagher, Edmon L. *Hebrew Scripture in Patristic Biblical Theory: Canon, Language, Text*. Leiden: Brill, 2012.

Gamillscheg, Ernst. *Romania germanica. Sprach- und Siedlungsgeschichte der Germanen auf dem Boden des alten Romerreichs*, vol. 2. Berlin: De Gruyter, 1935.

Ganz, Peter, ed. *The Role of the Book in Medieval Culture: Proceedings of the Oxford International Symposium 26 September–1 October 1982*. Turnhout: Brepols, 1986.

Gardeła, Leszek. *Bad Death in the Early Middle Ages. Atypical Burials from Poland in a Comparative Perspective*. Rzeszów: Instytut Archeologii UR, 2017.

Garrison, Mary. "Divine Elections for Nations—A Difficult Rhetoric for Medieval Scholars?" In *The Making of Christian Myths in the Periphery of Latin Christendom* (*c. 1000–1300*), edited by Lars B. Mortensen, 275–314. Copenhagen: Museum Tusculanum Press, 2006.

Gasparri, Stefano. *La cultura tradizionale dei Longobardi. Struttura tribale e resistenze pagane*. Spoleto: Centro Italiano di Studi sull'Alto Medioevo, 1983.

Gasparri, Stefano. *Prima delle nazioni. Popoli, etnie e regni fra Antichità e Medioevo*. Rome: La Nuova Italia Scientifica, 1997.

Gasparri, Stefano. "Kingship Rituals and Ideology in Lombard Italy." In *Rituals of Power: From Late Antiquity to the Early Middle Ages*, edited by Frans Theuws and Janet L. Nelson, 95–114. Leiden: Brill, 2000.

Gasparri, Stefano. "La memoria storica dei Longobardi." In *Le leggi dei Longobardi. Storia, memoria e diritto di un popolo germanico*. Edited by Claudio Azzara and Stefano Gasparri. Rome: Viella, 2005.

Gasparri, Stefano. "I Longobardi, I Romani e l'identità nazionale italiana." *Annales de Historia Antigua, Medieval y Moderna* 39 (2006): 27–39.

Gasparri, Stefano. "Migrazione, etnogenesi, integrazione nel mondo romano: il caso dei Longobardi." In *Archeologia e storia delle migrazioni. Europa, Italia, Mediterraneo fra tarda età romana e alto Medioevo*. Atti del Convegno internazionale di studi, Cimitile-Santa Maria Capua Vetere, 17–18 giugno 2010, edited by Carlo Ebanista and Marcello Rotili, 31–42. Cimitile: Tavolario, 2011.

Gasparri, Stefano. *Italia longobarda. Il regno, i Franchi, il papato*. Bari: Laterza, 2016.

Gatev, Peyo [Пейо Гатев]. *Средновековно селище и некропол от 12 век при с. Ковачево, Пазарджишки окръг* [Medieval Village and Cemetery from 12th Century near Kovachevo, District Pazardzhik]. Sofia: National Archaeological Museum, 1985.

Gay, David A. "Review of 'Bloodtaking and Peacemaking: Feud, Law, and Society in Saga Iceland' (Miller)." *Folklore Forum* 23:1/2 (1990): 129–30.

Gerbenzon, Pieter. *Excerpta legum. Onderzoekingen betreffende enkele Friese rechtsboeken uit de vijftiende eeuw*. Groningen: J.B. Wolters, 1956.

Gerbenzon, Pieter. *Zeer voorlopige lijst van de belangrijkste middeleeuwse rechtsbronnen uit het Groot-Friese gebied tussen Vlie en Wezer*. 2nd ed. Groningen: Juridisch Instituut, Rijksuniversiteit, 1975.

Gerbenzon, Pieter. "Aantekeningen over de *Jurisprudentia Frisica*, een laat-vijftiende-eeuwse Westerlauwers-Friese bewerking van de *Exerpta legum*." *Tijdschrift voor Rechtsgeschiedenis/Legal History Review* 57 (1989): 21–67, 339–84.

Gerriets, Marilyn. "The King as Judge in Early Ireland." *Celtica* 20 (1988): 29–52.

Gerriets, Marilyn. "Theft, Penitentials and the Compilation of the Early Irish Laws." *Celtica* 22 (1991): 18–32.

Ghignoli, Antonella. "Istituzioni ecclesiastiche e documentazione nei secoli VIII–XI. Appunti per una prospettiva." *Archivio storico italiano* 162 (2004): 619–66.

Ghignoli, Antonella, and François Bougard. "Elementi romani nei documenti longobardi?" In *L'héritage byzantin en Italie* (*VIIIe–XIIe siècle*). *1. La fabrique documentaire*, edited by Jean-Marie Martin, Annick Peters-Custot, and Vivien Prigent, 241–301. Rome: École française de Rome, 2011.

Giaccaria, Angelo. "I fondi medievali della Biblioteca Nazionale Universitaria di Torino." *Pluteus* 2 (1984): 175–94.

Giaccaria, Angelo. *I manoscritti danneggiati nell'incendio del 1904. Mostra di recuperi e restauri: Torino Febbraio-Marzo 1986*. Quaderni della Biblioteca Nazionale Universitaria di Torino 9. Turin: Turingraf, 1986.

Giaccaria, Angelo. "Nuove identificazioni di manoscritti greci e latini della Biblioteca Nazionale Universitaria di Torino." *Aevum* 81/2 (2007): 429–33.

Giliberto, Concetta. "The Fifteen Signs of Doomsday in the Rüstring Manuscript." In *Advances in Old Frisian Philology*, edited by Rolf H. Bremmer Jr, Stephen Laker, and Oebele Vries, 129–52. Amsterdamer Beiträge zur älteren Germanistik 64. Amsterdam: Rodopi, 2007.

Giliberto, Concetta. "Theological and Doctrinal Texts in the Old Frisian *Thet Autentica Riocht*." *Philologia Frisica anno 2014* (2015): 136–53.

Gillingham, John. "Richard of Devizes and 'a rising tide of nonsense': How Cerdic Met King Arthur." In *The Long Twelfth-Century View of the Anglo-Saxon Past*, edited by Martin Brett and David A. Woodman, 141–56. Farnham: Ashgate, 2015.

Gillingham, John. "Stupor mundi: 1204 et un obituaire de Richard Coeur de Lion depuis longtemps tombé dans l'oubli." In *Plantagenêts et Capétiens: confrontations et héritages*, edited by Martin Aurell and Noël-Yves Tonnerre, 397–411. Turnhout: Brepols, 2006.

Gjerdhåker, Brynjulv. *Til Odel og Eige—Odels- og Åsetesrettane Gjennom eit Millenium med Vekt på dei Siste 250 Åra*. Oslo: Norsk institutt for landbruksøkonomisk forskning, 2001.

Gjerløw, Lilli. *Liturgica Islandica*, 1. Copenhagen: C.A. Reitzels Forlag, 1980.

Gjuzelev, Vasil. "Hauptstädte, Residenzen und Hofkultur im mittelalterlichen Bulgarien, 7.–14. Jh. (Vom Nomaden campus bis zum Zarenhof)." *Études balkaniques* 27, no. 2 (1991): 82–105.

Gluckman, Max. *Politics, Law and Ritual in Tribal Society*. Oxford: Blackwell, 1965.

Gobbitt, Thom. "Codicological Features of a Late-Eleventh-Century Manuscript of the Lombard Laws." *Studia Neophilologica* 86 (2014): 48–67.

Gobbitt, Thom. "Materiality, Stratigraphy and Artefact Biography: Codicological Features of a Late-Eleventh-Century Manuscript of the Lombard Laws." *Studia Neophilologica* 86 (2014): 48–67.

Gobbitt, Thom. "Palaeographic Preferences and Manuscript Contexts of a Mid-Eleventh-Century English Legal Collection: London, British Library, Cotton MS Nero A. I (Part A)." *Scriptorium* 69 (2015): 61–77.

Gobbitt, Thom. "The Other Book: Cambridge, Corpus Christi College, MS 383 in Relation to the Textus Roffensis." In *Textus Roffesnsis: Law, Language, and Libraries in Early Medieval England*, edited by Bruce O'Brien and Barbara Bombi, 69–82. Turnhout: Brepols, 2015.

Gobbitt, Thom. "Scribal Communities and Lombard Law-Books: Charlemagne's Herstal Capitulary within the Eleventh-Century *Liber Papiensis*." In *Creating Communities and Others in Early Medieval Europe*, edited by Richard Broome. Leeds: Kismet Press, forthcoming.

Gobbitt, Thom. *The Liber Papiensis in the Long Eleventh Century: Manuscripts, Materiality and Mise-en-Page*. Leeds: Kismet Press, 2021.

Gödel, Vilhelm. *Fornnorsk-isländsk litteratur i Sverige*, 1. Stockholm: Hæggström boktrykkeri, 1897.

Gödel, Vilhelm. *Katalog öfver Kongl. bibliotekets fornisländska och fornnorska handskrifter*. Stockholm: Kongelige Biblioteket, 1897–1900.

Goronwy Edwards, John. "The Normans and the Welsh March." *Proceedings of the British Academy* 42 (1956): 155–77.

Goryanova, Snezhana [Снежана Горянова]. "Чужденци в българските средновековни градове през XIII–XIV в.—социален и правен статут [Foreigners in Bulgarian Medieval Towns in 13th–14th c.—Social and Legal Status]." In *Stephanos Archaeologicos in honorem Professoris Stephcae Angelova*, edited by Lyudmil Getov. Sofia: University of Sofia, 2010.

Gneuss, Helmut, and Michael Lapidge. *Anglo-Saxon Manuscripts: A Bibliographical Handlist of Manuscripts and Manuscript Fragments Written or Owned in England up to 1100*. Toronto Anglo-Saxon Series 15. Toronto: University of Toronto Press, 2015.

Gorrini, Giovanni. *L'incendio della Biblioteca Nazionale di Torino*. Turin: Edizioni Renzo Streglio e C.ia, 1905.

Granberg, Antoaneta. "Transferred in Translation: Making a State in Early Medieval Bulgarian Genealogies." *Slavica Helsengiensia* 35 (2008): 49–58.

Gray, Nick. "Langland's Quotations from Penitential Tradition." *Modern Philology* 84 (1986): 53–60.

Greenfield, Stanley. *A Critical History of Old English Literature*. New York: New York University Press, 1965.

Grévin, Benoit. "Writing Techniques in Thirteenth- and Fourteenth-Century England: The Role of the Sicilian and Papal Letter Collections as Practical Models for the Shaping of Royal Propaganda." In *Fourteenth-Century England VII*, edited by Mark Ormrod, 1–29. Woodbridge, UK: Boydell & Brewer, 2012.

Grigg, Julianna. "Aspects of the *Cáin*: Adomnán's *Lex Innocentium*." *Journal of the Australian Early Medieval Association* 1 (2005): 41–50.

Grisé, C. Annette. "The Textual Community of Syon Abbey." *Florilegium* 19 (2002): 149–62.

Gumbert, Johann Peter. "One Book with Many Texts: The Latin Tradition." In *Codices Miscellanearum*, edited by Ria Jansen-Sieben and Hans van Dijk, 27–36. Brussels: Archives et Bibliothèques de Belgique, 1999.

Gumbert, Johann Peter. "Skins, Sheets and Quires." In *New Directions in Later Medieval Manuscript Studies. Essays from the 1998 Harvard Conference*, edited by Derek Pearsall, 81–90. York: York University Press, 2000.

Gumbert, Johann Peter. "Codicological Units: Towards a Terminology for the Stratigraphy of the Non-Homogenous Codex." *Segno E Testo* 2 (2004): 17–42.

Gunnar Karlsson. "Goðar and Höfðingjar in Medieval Iceland." *Saga-Book* 19 (1977): 358–70.

Gunnar Karlsson. "Social Institutions." In *A Companion to Old Norse-Icelandic Literature and Culture*, ed. Rory McTurk, 503–17. Oxford: Blackwell, 2005.

Guðvarður Már Gunnlaugsson. "Færeyskar málheimildir." *Frændafundur* 3 (2000): 91–105.

Guðvarður Már Gunnlaugsson. "Voru scriptoria i íslenskum klaustrum?" In *Íslensk klausturmenning á miðöldum*, edited by Haraldur Bernharðsson, 173–200. Reykjavík: Háskólaútgáfan, 2014.

Hall, Thomas N. "Wulfstan's Latin Sermons." In *Wulfstan, Archbishop of York: The Proceedings of the Second Alcuin Conference*, edited by Matthew Townend, 93–140. Studies in the Early Middle Ages 10. Turnhout: Brepols, 2004.

Halpérin, Jean-Louis. "For a Renewed History of Lawyers." *American Journal of Legal History* 56/1 (2016): 53–59.

Halsall, Guy. *Barbarian Migrations and the Roman West, 376–568*. New York: Cambridge University Press, 2007.

Hanna, Ralph. *London Literature, 1300–1380*. Cambridge: Cambridge University Press, 2004.

Harris, Joseph, and Karl Reichl, eds. *Prosimetrum: Crosscultural Perspectives on Narrative in Prose and Verse*. Cambridge: D.S. Brewer, 1997.

Harrison, Dick. *The Early State and the Towns: Forms of Integration in Lombard Italy AD 568–774*. Lund: Lund University Press, 1993.

Harrison, Dick. "Political Rhetoric and Political Ideology in Lombard Italy." In *Strategies of Distinction: The Construction of Ethnic Communities, 300–800*, edited by Walter Pohl and Helmut Reimitz, 241–54. Leiden: Brill, 1998.

Hartmann, Wilfried. *Die Synoden der Karolingerzeit im Frankenreich und in Italiën*. Paderborn: F. Schöningh, 1989.

Haubrichs, Wolfgang. "Amalgamierung und Identität. Langobardische Personennamen in Mythos und Herrschaft." In *Die Langobarden: Herrschaft und Identität*, edited by Walter Pohl, 67–102. Vienna: Verlag der Österreichischen Akademie der Wissenschaften, 2005.

Haubrichs, Wolfgang. "Langobardic Personal Names: Given Names and Name-Giving among the Langobards." In *The Lombards Before the Frankish Conquest: An Ethnographic Perspective*, edited by Giorgio Ausenda, 195–250. Woodbridge, UK: Boydell & Brewer, 2009.

Haubrichs, Wolfgang. "Sprache und Schriftlichkeit im langobardischen Italien. Das Zeugnis von Namen, Wörtern und Entlehnungen. Ein Kommentar zu Nicholas Everett 'Literacy in Lombard Italy'." *Filologia Germanica* 2 (2010): 133–202.

Haugen, Odd Einar. "The Development of Latin Script I: In Norway." In *The Nordic Languages: An International Handbook of the History of the North Germanic Languages*, edited by Oskar Bandle, Kurt Braunmüller, Ernst Hakon Jahr, Allan Karker, Hans-Peter Naumann, Ulf Telemann, Lennart Elmevik, and Gun Widmark, 824–32. Berlin: De Gruyter, 2002.

Hearne, Thomas. *Johannis, confratris & monachi Glastoniensis, chronica sive historia de rebus Glastoniensibus*. 2 vols. Oxford, 1726.

Heidecker, Karl. "Gathering and Recycling Authorative Texts: The Importance of Marginalia in Hincmar of Rheims' *De Divortio*." In *Organizing the Written Word: Proceedings of the First Utrecht Symposium on Medieval Literacy, Utrecht 5–7 June 1997*, edited by Marco Mostert. Turnhout: Brepols, forthcoming.

Heidecker, Karl. *The Divorce of Lothar II: Christian Marriage and Political Power in the Carolingian World*. Translated by Tanis M. Guest. Ithaca: Cornell University Press, 2010.

Helle, Knut. *Kong og gode men i norsk riksstyring ca. 1150–1319*. Bergen: Universitetsforlaget, 1972.

Helle, Knut. *Norge blir en stat 1130–1319, Handbok i Norges historie*. Bergen: Universitetsforlaget, 1974.

Helle, Knut. *Gulatinget og Gulatingslova*. Leikanger: Skald, 2001.

Hennings, Lucy. "*Haec detestabilis adjectio*: The Clause *non obstante* and the Governance of England During the Personal Rule of Henry III, 1230–1250." *Proceedings of the Fifteenth International Congress of Medieval Canon Law* (forthcoming).

Herde, Peter. "Literary Activities of the Imperial and Papal Chanceries during the Struggle Between Frederick II and the Papacy." In *Intellectual Life at the Court of Frederick II Hohenstaufen*, edited by William Tromzo, 226–39. Washington, DC: National Gallery of Art, 1994.

Herde, Peter. "Papal Formularies for Letters of Justice (13th–16th Centuries): Their Development and Significance for Medieval Canon Law." In *Diplomatik, Kanonistik, Paläographie: Studien zu den Historischen Grundwissennschaften*, 123–51. Stuttgart: Anton Hiersemann, 2008.

Herzog, Tamar. *A Short History of European Law: The Last Two and a Half Millennia*. Cambridge, MA: Harvard University Press, 2018.

Heusler, Andreas. *Das Strafrecht der Isländersagas*. Leipzig: Duncker & Humblot, 1911.

Hill, Joyce. "Ælfric, Authorial Identity, and the Changing Text." In *The Editing of Old*

English, edited by Donald G. Scragg and Paul E. Szarmach, 177–90. Cambridge: D.S. Brewer, 1994.

Hoekstra, Jelle. *Die gemeinfriesische siebzehn Küren*. Assen: van Gorcum, 1940.

Hoffman Berman, Constance. *The Cistercian Evolution: The Invention of a Religious Order in Twelfth-Century Europe*. Philadelphia, PA: University of Pennsylvania Press, 2000.

Hollis, Stephanie. "Old English 'Cattle-Theft Charms': Manuscript Contexts and Social Uses." *Anglia: Zeitschrift für Englische Philologie* 115 (1997): 139–64.

Holmsen, Andreas. "Erkebiskop Eystein og Tronfølgeloven Av 1163." *Historisk Tidskrift* 44 (1965): 225–66.

Holt, James C. *Magna Carta*. Edited by George Garnett and John Hudson. 3rd ed. Cambridge: Cambridge University Press, 2015.

Horn, Anna Catharina. *Lov og tekst i middelalderen. Produksjon og resepsjon av Magnus lagabøtes landslov*. Gothenburg: Institutionen för svenska språket, 2016.

Hreinn Benediktsson. *The Life of St. Gregory and his Dialogues: Fragments of an Icelandic Manuscript from the 13th Century*. Copenhagen: Munksgaard, 1963.

Hudson, John. *The Oxford History of the Laws of England. Volume II: 871–1216*. Oxford: Oxford University Press, 2012.

Huebner, Rudolf. *A History of Germanic Private Law*. Boston: Little, Brown, and Company, 1918.

Hull, Vernam. "The Later Version of the Expulsion of the Déssi." *Zeitschrift für Celtische Philologie* 27 (1959): 14–65.

Hunt, Richard William. "The Introductions to the 'Artes' in the Twelfth Century." In *Studia Mediaevalia in Honorem Admodum Reverendi Patris Raymundi Josephi Martin Ordinis Praedicatorum s. theologiae magistri LXXUM natalem diem agentis*, 85–112. Bruges: De Tempel, 1948.

Huws, Daniel. "The Manuscripts: Cotton Caligula A iii." In *Lawyers and Laymen. Studies in the History of Law Presented to Professor Dafydd Jenkins*, edited by Thomas M. Charles-Edwards, Morfydd E. Owen and Dafydd B. Walters, 119–135. Cardiff: University of Wales Press, 1986.

Huws, Daniel. "Descriptions of the Welsh Manuscripts: National Library of Wales MS 20143A." In *The Welsh King and His Court*, edited by Thomas M. Charles-Edwards, Morfydd E. Owen, and Paul Russell, 415–24. Cardiff: University of Wales Press, 2000.

Huws, Daniel. "Maurice, William (1619/20–1680)." In *Oxford Dictionary of National Biography*. Oxford University Press, 2004, online ed., January 2008. Accessed October 20, 2017. http://www.oxforddnb.com/view/article/18388.

Innes, Charles. "Charlemagne, Written Law and Justice." In *Law, Custom and Justice in Late Antiquity and the Early Middle Ages*, edited by Alice Rio, 155–204. London: Centre for Hellenic Studies, 2011.

Innes, Matthew. "Memory, Orality and Literacy." *Past and Present* 158 (1998): 3–36.

Irvine, Martin. *The Making of Textual Culture: "Grammatica" and Literary Theory, 350–1100*. Cambridge: Cambridge University Press, 1994.

Jackson, Deirdre, Nigel Morgan, and Stella Panayotova. *A Catalogue of Illuminated Western Books in the Fitzwilliam Museum and the Cambridge Colleges, Part Three: France*. London: Harvey Miller, 2014.

Jakob Benediktsson. *Skarðsbók: Jónsbók and Other Laws and Precepts: MS. No. 350 fol. in The Arna-Magnæan Collection at the University Library of Copenhagen*. Copenhagen: Munksgaard, 1942.

Jakobi-Mirwald, Christine. "Gratian in Schäftlarn." In *AusBILDung des Rechts. Systematisierung und Vermittlung von Wissen in mittelalterlichen Rechtshandschriften*, edited by Kristin Böse and Susanne Wittekind, 83–98. Frankfurt: Peter Lang, 2009.

Jakobsen, Alfred. *Studier i Clarus saga: Til spørsmålet om sagaens norske proveniens*. Bergen: Årbok for Universitetet i Bergen, 1964.

Janowski, Andrej, and Tomasz Kurasiński. "Rolnik, wojownik czy 'odmieniec?' Próba interpretacji obecności sierpów w grobach wczesnośredniowiecznych na terenie ziem polskich [Farmer, Soldier or Foreigner? An Attempt for the Interpretation of Sickles in Late Medieval Graves from the Polish lands]." *Acta Archaeologica Lodziensia* 56 (2010): 79–96.

Jarnut, Jörg. *Prosopographische und sozialgeschichtliche Studien zum Langobardenreich in Italien (568–774)*. Bonn: Röhrscheid, 1972.

Jarnut, Jörg. "*Gens*, *Rex* and *Regnum* of the Lombards." In *Regna and Gentes, The Relationship between Late Antique and Early Medieval Peoples and Kingdoms in the Transformation of the Roman World*, edited by Hans-Werner Goetz, Jörg Jarnut, and Walter Pohl, 409–27. Leiden: Brill, 2003.

Jenkins, Dafydd. "Deddfgrawn William Maurice." *National Library of Wales Journal* 2 (1941): 33–36.

Johansson, Karl Gunnar, and Lena Liepe. "Text and Images in Norwegian and Icelandic Fourteenth-Century Legal Manuscripts." In *The Power of Book: Medial Approaches to Medieval Nordic Legal Manuscripts*, edited by Lena Rohrbach, 129–56. Berlin: Nordeuropa-Institut der Humboldt-Universität, 2014.

Johnston, Thomas S.B. "'*Ene zie borch tho bouwenn*': A New Look at the Pan-Frisian Dike Law of a Low German Ommeland Version." *Us Wurk* 44 (1995): 1–37.

Johnston, Thomas S.B. "Old Frisian Law and the Frisian Freedom Ideology: Text and Manuscript Composition as a Marketing Device." In *Approaches to Old Frisian Philology*, edited by Rolf H. Bremmer Jr, Thomas S.B. Johnston, and Oebele Vries, 179–214. Amsterdamer Beiträge zur älteren Germanistik 49. Amsterdam: Rodopi, 1998.

Jolliffe, John Edward Austin. "The Chamber and the Castle Treasuries under King John." In *Studies in Medieval History Presented to Frederick Maurice Powicke*, edited by Richard William Hunt, William Abel Pantin, and Richard W. Southern, 117–42. Oxford: Clarendon Press, 1948.

Jón Viðar Sigurðsson. *Chieftains and Power in the Icelandic Commonwealth*. Odense: Odense University Press, 1999.

Jón Viðar Sigurðsson. *Det norrøne samfunnet: Vikingen, kongen, erkebiskopen og bonden*. Oslo: Pax, 2008.

Jón Viðar Sigurðsson. "Historical Writing and the Political Situation in Iceland 1100–1400." In *Negotiating Pasts in the Nordic Countries: Interdisciplinary Studies in History and Memory*, edited by Anne Eriksen and Jón Viðar Sigurðsson, 59–78. Lund: Nordic Academic Press, 2009.

Jón Viðar Sigurðsson. "The Role of Arbitration in the Settlement of Disputes in Iceland c. 1000–1300." In *Law and Disputing in the Middle Ages: Proceedings of the Ninth Carlsberg Academy Conference on Medieval Legal History 2012*, edited by Per Anderson, Kirsi Salonen, Helle Møller Sigh, and Helle Vogt, 123–35. Copenhagen: DJØF Press, 2013.

Jón Viðar Sigurðsson. *Viking Friendship*. Ithaca, NY: Cornell University Press, 2017.

Jón Viðar Sigurðsson, and Helle Vogt. "Inheritance and Transfer of Landed Property: The Material Fundament of the Elites." In *Nordic Elites in Transformation, c. 1050–1250, Volume 1: Material Resources*, edited by Bjørn Poulsen, Helle Vogt, and Jón Viðar Sigurðsson, 107–29. New York: Routledge, 2019.

Jong, Mayke de. "What was Public about Public Penance? *Paenitentia publica* and Justice in the Carolingian World." In *La Giustizia Nell'Alto Medioevo (Secoli IX–XI), 11–17 aprile 1996, Settimane di studio del centro italiano di studi sull'alto medioevo* 44, 2:863–904. 2 vols. Spoleto: Presso La Sede del Centro, 1997.

Jong, Mayke de. *The Penitential State: Authority and Atonement in the Age of Louis the Pious, 814–840*. Cambridge: Cambridge University Press, 2009.

Jost, Karl. *Wulfstanstudien*. Swiss Studies in English 23. Bern: Francke, 1950.

Jovanović, Vojislav, and Ljiljana Vuksanović. "Matičane, Nécropole sud-slave de XE et XIE siècle." *Inventaria Archaeologica* 25 (1981): 239–248.

Jurasinski, Stefan, Lisi Oliver, and Andrew Rabin, eds. *English Law before Magna Carta: Felix Liebermann and Die Gesetze der Angelsachsen*. Leiden: Brill, 2010.

Kålund, Kristian. *Katalog over den Arnamagnæanske håndskriftsamling*, I. Copenhagen: Gyldendalske Boghandel, 1889.

Kantorowicz, Ernst. "Petrus de Vinea in England." *Mitteilungen des Instituts für Österreichische Geschichtsforschung* 51 (1937): 43–88.

Kantorowicz, Ernst. "The Prologue to *Fleta* and the School of Petrus de Vinea." *Speculum* 32 (1957): 231–49.

Kantorowicz, Ernst. "An "Autobiography" of Guido Faba." In *Selected Studies*, 194–212. Locust Valley, NY: J.J. Augstin, 1965.

Kantorowicz, Ernst. "Kingship under the Impact of Scientific Jurisprudence." In *Selected Studies*, 151–66. Locust Valley, NY: J.J. Augstin, 1965.

Keene, Derek. "Text, Visualisation and Politics: London, 1150–1250." *Transactions of the Royal Historical Society*, 6th series 18 (2008): 69–99.

Keller, Hans E. "Two Toponymical Problems in Geoffrey of Monmouth and Wace: Estrusia and Siesia." *Speculum* 49 (1974): 687–98.

Kelly, Fergus. "An Old-Irish Text on Court Procedure," *Peritia* 5 (1986): 74–106.

Kelly, Fergus. *A Guide to Early Irish Law*. Dublin: Dublin Institute for Advanced Studies, 1988.

Kelly, Fergus. "Texts and Transmissions: The Law-Texts," in *Irland und Europa im früheren Mittelalteren: Texte und Überlieferung*, edited by Próinséas Ní Chatháin and Michael Richter, 230–42. Dublin: Four Courts Press, 2002.

Ker, Neil R. "Liber Custumarum, and Other Manuscripts Formerly at the Guildhall." *Guildhall Miscellany* 3 (1954): 37–45.

Ker, Neil R. *Medieval Libraries of Great Britain: A List of Surviving Books*. 2nd ed. London: Royal Historical Society, 1964.

Ker, Neil R. "The Handwriting of Archbishop Wulfstan." In *England Before the Conquest: Studies in Primary Sources Presented to Dorothy Whitelock*, edited by Peter Clemoes and Kathleen Hughes, 315–31. Cambridge: Cambridge University Press, 1971.

Ker, Neil R. "Books at St. Paul's Cathedral Before 1313." In *Books, Collectors and Libraries: Studies in the Medieval Heritage*, edited by Andrew G. Watson, 209–42. London: Hambledon, 1985.

Kjelland, Arnfin. "One Tenant, Several Landlords: The Land Tenure System of Norway until ca. 1800." In *Conference Proceedings: Land, Labour and Tenure: The Institutional Arrangements of Conflict and Cooperation in Comparative Perspective*, August 21–24. University of Leicester, England. Leicester: University of Leicester: 1996.

Klemm, Elisabeth. *Die romanischen Handschriften der Bayrischen Staatsbibliothek*, 2. Wiesbaden: Reichert, 1980.

Kocher, Gernot. *Zeichen und Symbole des Rechts. Eine historische Ikonographie*. Berlin: De Gruyter, 1992.

Komatarova-Balinova, Evegeniya. "The 'Protobulgars' at Balchik and the Nomads in the Field of the 'Protobulgar' Archaeology." *Приноси към българската археология* 8 (2018): 47–92.

Krag, Claus. "Norge som odel i Harald Hårfagres ætt: Et møte med en gjenganger." *Historisk Tidsskrift* 68 (1989): 288–302.

Krag, Claus. "Myten om Hårfagreættens 'odel'." *Historisk Tidsskrift* 81 (2002): 381–94.

Kreutz, Barbara. *Before the Normans: Southern Italy in the Ninth and Tenth Centuries*. Philadelphia, PA: University of Pennsylvania Press, 1991.

Krogh, Knud J. *Kirkjubøarstólarnir og Kirkjubøur, Brot úr søgu føroyska biskupssøtisins*. Tórshavn: Emil Thomsen, 1988.

Krolis-Sytsema, Johanneke. "De weirekke tsiende Kêst. Oer in ûnbekende ferzy fan de 17 Kêsten." *It Beaken* 55 (1993): 83–95.

Kottje, Raymond. "Buße oder Strafe? Zur '*iustitia*' in den '*libri paenitentiales*'." In *La giustizia nell'alto Medioevo (Secoli V–VII), 7–13 aprile 1994, Settimane di studio del centro italiano di studi sull'alto medioevo* 42, 1:443–74. 2 vols. Spoleto: Presso La Sede del Centro, 1995.

Kuttner, Stephan. "Notes on the Presentation of Text and Apparatus in Editing Works of the Decretists and Decretalists." *Traditio* 15 (1959): 452–64.

Kuttner, Stephan. *The History of Ideas and Doctrines of Canon Law in the Middle Ages*, 1–16. 2nd ed. Aldershot: Variorum Reprints, 1992. Originally published as "Harmony from Dissonance: An Interpretation of Medieval Canon Law," *Wimmer Lecture X, 1956, St. Vincent College*. Latrobe, PA: Archabbey Press, 1960.

Kwakkel, Erik. "Towards a Terminology for the Analysis of Composite Manuscripts." *Gazette du livre médiéval* 41 (2002): 12–19.

Kwakkel, Erik, ed. *The European Book in the Twelfth Century*. Cambridge: Cambridge University Press, 2018.

Kwakkel, Erik, Rosamond McKitterick, and Rodney Thomson. *Turning Over a New Leaf: Change and Development in the Medieval Manuscript*. Chicago: University of Chicago Press, 2012.

La Farge, Beatrice, and John Tucker. *Glossary to the Poetic Edda*. Heidelberg: Winter, 1992.

La Rocca, Cristina. "La trasformazione del territorio in occidente." In *Morfologie sociali e culturali in Europa fra tarda antichità e alto medioevo*, edited by CISAM, 257–90. Spoleto: CISAM, 1998.

La Rocca, Cristina, and Stefano Gasparri, eds. *Carte di famiglia*. Rome: Viella, 2005.

Lagomarsini, Claudio. "The Prose 'Description of England': A Hitherto Unedited Anglo-Norman Text from BL, Additional MS 14252." *Medium Ævum* 80 (2011): 325–35.

LaVoy, Hayley. "Hirmindrut Sculdarissa: A Ninth-Century Woman's Original Letter and its Implications." *Journal of Medieval Latin* 25 (2015): 29–50.

Law, Vivien. *Wisdom, Authority and Grammar in the Seventh Century*. Cambridge: Cambridge University Press, 1995.

Lawrence, C.H. "Somercotes [Somerton], Laurence of (fl. 1245–1258), Ecclesiastic and Canonist." *Oxford Dictionary of National Biography*. Accessed December 11, 2017. http://www.oxforddnb.com/view/10.1093/ref:odnb/9780198614128.001.0001/odnb-9780198614128-e-25998.

Leeson, Peter T. "'God Damn': The Law of Economics of Monastic Malediction." *Journal of Law, Economics and Organization* 30.1 (2012): 193–216.

L'Engle, Susan. "Layout and Decoration." In *Illuminating the Law: Legal Manuscripts in Cambridge Collections*, edited by Susan L'Engle and Robert Gibbs, 54–74. London: Harvey Miller, 2001.

Liebermann, Felix. "A Contemporary Manuscript of the 'Leges Anglorum Londoniis Collectae'." *English Historical Review* 28 (1913): 732–45.

Liebermann, Felix. *Über die Leges Anglorum saeculo XIII. ineunte Londoniis collectae*. Halle: Max Niemeyer, 1894.

Liebermann, Max. *The March of Wales 1067–1300*. Cardiff: University of Wales Press, 2008.

Liebermann, Max. *The Medieval March of Wales: The Creation and Perception of a Frontier, 1066–1283*. Cambridge: Cambridge University Press, 2010.

Liepe, Lena. *Studies in Icelandic Fourteenth Century Book Painting*. Reykholt: Snorrastofa, 2009.

Lifshitz, Felice. "The Norman Conquest of Pious Neustria." In *The Norman Conquest of Pious Neustria: Historiographic Discourse and Saintly Relics 684–1090*, 180–219. Toronto: Pontifical Institute of Mediaeval Studies, 1995.

Linde, Cornelia. "Twelfth-Century Notions of the Canon of the Bible." In *Reading the Bible in the Middle Ages*, edited by Jinty Nelson and Damien Kempf, 7–18. London: Bloomsbury, 2015.

Lionarons, Joyce Tally. *The Homiletic Writings of Archbishop Wulfstan*. Woodbridge: D.S. Brewer, 2010.

Lizier, Augusto. *L'economia rurale dell'età prenormanna nell'Italia meridionale (Studi su documenti editi dei secoli IX–XI)*. Palermo: Alberto Reber Libreria della R. Casa, 1907.

Lloyd, J.E. "Owen, Aneurin (1792–1851)." In *Oxford Dictionary of National Biography*, rev. Brynley F. Roberts. Oxford University Press, 2004, online ed., January 2008. Accessed May 18, 2016. http://www.oxforddnb.com/view/article/20985.

Loyn, Henry R. *A Wulfstan Manuscript (British Museum Cotton Nero A.i), Early English Manuscripts in Facsimile* 17. Copenhagen: Rosenkilde and Bagger, 1971.

Lühr, Rosemarie. *Studien zur Sprache des Hildebrandslied*. Frankfurt: Peter Lang, 1977.

Lupoi, Maurizio. The *Origins of the European Legal Order*. Cambridge: Cambridge University Press, 2000.

Mac Airt, Seán, and Gearóid Mac Niocaill, eds. *The Annals of Ulster (to A.D. 1131) Part I, Text and Translation*. Dublin: Dublin Institute for Advanced Studies, 1983.

Mac Cana, Proinsias. "The Three Languages and the Three Laws." *Studia Celtica* 5 (1970): 62–78.

Mac Cana, Proinsias. "Notes on the Combination of Prose and Verse in Early Irish Narrative." In *Early Irish Literature: Media and Communication*, edited by Stephen N. Tranter and Hildegard L.C. Tristram, 125–47. Tübingen: Narr, 1989.

Mac Cana, Proinsias. "Narrative Openers and Progress Markers in Irish." In *A Celtic Florilegium: Studies in Memory of Brendan O Hehir*, edited by Kathryn A. Clar, Eve E. Sweetser, and Claire Thomas, 104–20. Lawrence, MA: Celtic Studies Publications, 1996.

MacNamara, Martin. "The (Fifteen) Signs of Doomsday in Irish Tradition." *Warszawskie Studia Teologiczne* 20.2 (2007): 223–54.

Machiavelli, Niccolò. *Istorie Fiorentine*. Florence: Le Monnier, 1851.

Magistrale, Francesco. "Le pergamene dell'Archivio Arcivescovile di Lucca (secoli VIII–

IX): l'esperienza delle "chartae latinae antiquiores"." In *Il patrimonio documentario della chiesa di Lucca. Prospettive di ricerca.* Atti del Convegno Internazionale di Studi, Lucca, 14–15 novembre 2008, edited by Sergio Pagano and Pierantonio Piatti, 73–91. Florence: Edizioni del Galluzzo, 2010.

Magnani, Eliana. "Almsgiving, *Donatio Pro Anima* and Eucharistic Offering in the Early Middle Ages of Western Europe (4th–9th century)." In *Charity and Giving in Monotheistic Religions* edited by Miriam Frenkel and Yaacov Lev, 111–21. Berlin: De Gruyter, 2009.

Mailloux, Anne. "Modalité de constitution du patrimoine épiscopal de Lucques, VIIIe–Xe siècle." *Mélanges de l'École française de Rome* 111 (1999): 701–723.

Mailloux, Anne. "L'émergence du notariat à Lucques (VIIIe–Xe siècle). Normes et pratiques d'un corps professionnel." In *Le notaire. Entre métier et espace public en Europe VIIIe–XVIIIe siècle*, 13–27. Aix en Provence: Publication de l'université de Provence, 2008.

Maisel, Witold. *Rechtsarchäologie Europas*. Vienna: Böhlau Verlag, 1992.

Maksimovich, Kiril [Максимович К. А.]. *Законъ соудьныи людьмъ. Источниковедческие и лингвистическиеаспектыисследованияславянскогоюридическогопамятника* [*The Law for Judgment of People. Textual and Linguistic Aspects of a Slavic Judicial Source*]. Moscow: Drevne hranilishte, 2004.

Már Jónsson. Introduction to *Jónsbók. Lögbók Íslendinga hver samþykkt var á alþingi árið 1578*. Reykjavík: Háskólaútgáfan, 2004.

Markey, Tom. "Studies in Runic Origins 1: Germanic **mapl-* /**mahl-* and Etruscan meθum." *American Journal of Germanic Linguistics & Literatures* 10/2 (1998): 153–200.

Marrocchi, Mario. "Le istituzioni civili e religiose a Chiusi (secoli V–VIII)." In *Goti e Longobardi a Chiusi*, edited by Carla Falluomini, 73–83. Chiusi: Edizioni Luì, 2009.

Massa, Paola. "Documenti, formule e persone nelle carte di Avellino (X–XII secolo)." *Scrineum Rivista* 9 (2012): 5–86.

Maund, Kari. *The Welsh Kings: The Medieval Rulers of Wales*. Stroud: Tempus, 2000.

McCone, Kim. "Zur Frage der Register im frühen Irischen." In *Early Irish Literature: Media and Communication*, edited by Stephen N. Tranter and Hildegard L.C. Tristram, 57–97. Tübingen: Narr, 1989.

McKenna, Lambert, ed. *Iomarbhagh na Bhfileadh: The Contention of the Bards*. London: Irish Texts Society, 1920.

McKitterick, Rosamond. "Some Carolingian Law Books and their Function." In *Authority and Power: Studies on Medieval Law and Government Presented to Walter Ullman on his 70th Birthday*, edited by Peter Linehan and Brian Tierney, 13–27. Cambridge: Cambridge University Press, 1980.

McKitterick, Rosamond. *The Carolingians and the Written Word*. Cambridge: Cambridge University Press, 1989.

McKitterick, Rosamond. "Script and Book Production." In *Carolingian Culture: Emulation and Innovation*, 221–47. Cambridge: Cambridge University Press, 1994.

McKitterick, Rosamond. "The Uses of Literacy in Carolingian and Post-Carolingian Europe: Literate Conventions of Memory." In *Scrivere e leggere nell'alto Medioevo, Settimane di studio della fondazione centro italiano di studi sull'alto medioevo* 59, 179–211. Spoletto: CISAM, 2012.

McLeod, Neil. "Di Ércib Fola." *Ériu* 52 (2002): 123–216.

McLeod, Neil. "A True Companion to the *Corpus Iuris Hibernici* [Review of: Liam Breatnach, *A Companion to the Corpus Iuris Hibernici*, Early Irish Law Series 5 (Dublin, 2005)]." *Peritia* 19 (2005): 136–63.

McLeod, Neil. "*Cáin Adomnáin* and the Lombards." In *Language and Power in the Celtic World*, edited by Anders Ahlqvist and Pamela O'Neill, 241–66. Sydney: University of Sydney, 2011.

Meijering, Hendrik D. *De Willekeuren van de Opstalsboom (1323). Een filologisch-historische monografie*. Groningen: V. R. B.-Offsetdrukkerij, 1974.

Melamed, Katja [Катя Меламед]. "Към тълкуването на масовия гроб от некропола Девня 3 [Towards an Interpretation of the Mass Grave from Devnya 3]." *Проблеми на прабългарската история и култура* 4 (2007): 147–52.

Melnikas, Anthony. *The Corpus of the Miniatures in the Manuscripts of Decretum Gratiani*, I–III. Rome: Libreria Ateneo Salesiano, 1975.

Merkel, Johannes. *Die Geschichte des Langobardenrechts*. Berlin: Verlag von Wilhelm Hertz, 1850.

Metzger, Bruce, and Bart D. Ehrman. *The Text of the New Testament: Its Transmission, Corruption, and Restoration*. Oxford: Oxford University Press, 2005.

Metzler, Irina. *A Social History of Disability in the Middle Ages. Cultural Considerations of Physical Impairment*. London: Routledge, 2013.

Meyer, Carl R. *Sprache und Sprachdenkmäler der Langobarden: Quellen, Grammatik, Glossar*. Bibliothek der ältesten deutschen Litteratur-Denkmäler 14. Paderborn: Druck und Verlag von Ferdinand Schöningh, 1877.

Meyer, Kuno. *The Triads of Ireland*. Todd Lecture Series, vol. 13. Dublin: Hodges & Figgis, 1906.

Meyer, Kuno. "The Expulsion of the Déssi." *Ériu* 3 (1907): 135–42.

Michaud, Francine. "Wills and Testaments." In *Death in Medieval Europe: Death Scripted and Death Choreographed*, edited by Joelle Rollo-Koster, 114–29. London: Routledge, 2017.

Miller, Edward, and John Hatcher. *Medieval England: Towns, Commerce and Crafts, 1086–1348*. London: Longman, 1995.

Miller, William Ian. "Avoiding Legal Judgment: The Submission of Disputes to Arbitration in Medieval Iceland." *The American Journal of Legal History* 28/2 (1984): 95–134.

Miller, William Ian. *Bloodtaking and Peacemaking: Feud, Law, and Society in Saga Iceland.* Chicago: The University of Chicago Press, 1990.

Miller, William Ian. *Why is Your Axe Bloody?: A Reading of Njáls Saga.* Oxford: Oxford University Press, 2014.

Miller, William Ian. *Hrafnkel or the Ambiguities: Hard Cases, Hard Choices.* Oxford: Oxford University Press, 2017.

Millet, Bella. "Chaucer, Lollius, and the Medieval Theory of Authorship." In *Studies in the Age of Chaucer*. Proceedings, No. 1: *Reconstructing Chaucer*, edited by Paul Strohm and Thomas J. Heffernan (1984): 93–103.

Minnis, Alastair. *Medieval Theory of Authorship: Scholastic Literary Attitudes in the Later Middle Ages.* London: Scholar Press, 1984.

Mol, Johannes A, and Justine Smithuis. "De Friezen als uitverkoren volk. Religieus-patriottische geschiedschrijving in vijftiende-eeuws Friesland." *Jaarboek voor Middeleeuwse Geschiedenis* 11 (2008): 165–204.

Moland, Carolina M. "Født til å Eie: En Kulturvitenskaplig Analyse av Odelsjenter fra Aust-Agder og Telemark." Master thesis. Institutt for kulturstudier og kunsthistorie, seksjon for kulturvitenskap Universitetet i Bergen. University of Bergen: 2005.

Molinari, Maria Vittoria. "Lessico germanico nelle leggi longobarde." *Linguistica e filologia. Quaderni del dipartimento di linguistica e letterature comparate dell'Università di Bergamo* 1 (1995): 5–20.

Moore, Robert I. "Literacy and the Making of Heresy, c. 1000–c.1150." In *Heresy and Literacy, 1000–1530*, edited by Peter Biller and Anne Hudson, 19–37. Cambridge: Cambridge University Press, 1994.

Moreland, John. *Archaeology and Text.* London: Duckworth, 2001.

Morgan, Nigel. *Early Gothic Manuscripts 1190–1250*, 1. London: Harvey Miller, 1986–88.

Morgan, Nigel. "Dating, Style and Groupings." In *Painted Altar Frontals of Norway*, edited by Unn Plahter, Erla B. Hohler, Nigel Morgan, and Anne Wichstrøm, 1:20–38. 3 vols. London: Archtype, 2004.

Morlicchio, Elda. "Dinamiche sociolinguistiche nell'Italia delle 'invasioni barbariche'." In *Archeologia e storia delle migrazioni. Europa, Italia, Mediterraneo fra tarda età romana e alto Medioevo*. Atti del Convegno internazionale di studi, Cimitile–Santa Maria Capua Vetere, 17–18 giugno 2010, edited by Carlo Ebanista and Marcello Rotili, 219–230. Cimitile: Tavolario, 2011.

Moseng, Ole Georg, Erik Opsahl, Gunnar I. Pettersen, and Erling Sandmo. *Norsk Historie 1750–1537*. Oslo: Tano Aschehoug, 2006.

Mostert, Marco. "The Early History of Written Culture in the Northern Netherlands." In *Along the Oral–Written Continuum. Types of Text, Relations and Their Implications*, edited by Slavica Ranković, 449–88. Turnhout: Brepols, 2010.

Mould, Tom. "The Paradox of Traditionalization: Negotiating the Past in Choctaw Prophetic Discourse." *Journal of Folklore Research* 42.3 (2005): 255–94.

Müller, Jörg, and Hans-Georg Hermann. "Urkunden." *Reallexikon der germanischen Altertumskunde* 31 (2006): 545–49.

Murdoch, Brian. "Authority and Authenticity: Comments on the Prologues to the Old Frisian Laws." In *Approaches to Old Frisian Philology*, edited by Rolf H. Bremmer Jr, Thomas S.B. Johnston, and Oebele Vries, 215–43. Amsterdamer Beiträge zur älteren Germanistik 49. Amsterdam: Rodopi, 1998.

Murphy, James J. *Rhetoric in the Middle Ages: A History of Rhetorical Theory from Saint Augustine to the Renaissance*. Berkeley, CA: University of California Press, 1974.

Murray, Alan. *Suicide in the Middle Ages*. Vol. 2: *The Curse on Self-Murder*. Oxford: Oxford University Press, 2000.

Nedrebø, Yngve, Berit Gerland, Jørn Øyrehagen Sunde, and Stig Årdal. *Audun Hugleiksson, Frå Kongens råd til galgen*. Førde: Selja Forlag, 2002.

Nelson, Janet L. "Literacy in Carolingian Government." In *The Uses of Literacy in Early Medieval Europe*, edited by Rosamond McKitterick, 258–96. Cambridge: Cambridge University Press, 1990.

Nelson, Janet L. "Liturgy or Law: Misconceived Alternatives." In *Early Medieval Studies in Memory of Patrick Wormald*, edited by Stephen Baxter, Catherine Karkov, Janet L. Nelson, and David Pelteret, 433–47. London: Routledge, 2009.

Ní Dhonnchadha, Máirín. "An Address to a Student of Law." In *Sages, Saints and Storytellers: Celtic Studies in Honour of Professor James Carney*, edited by Donnchadh Ó Corráin, Liam Breatnach, and Kim McCone, 159–77. Maynooth: An Sagart, 1989.

Nichols, Stephen G. "On the Sociology of Medieval Manuscript Annotation." In *Annotation and Its Texts*, edited by Stephen A. Barney, 43–73. Oxford: Oxford University Press, 1991.

Nichols, Stephen G., and Siegfried Wenzel. "Introduction." In *The Whole Book: Cultural Perspectives on the Medieval Miscellany*, edited by Stephen G. Nichols and Siegfried Wenzel, 2–6. Ann Arbor: University of Michigan Press, 1996.

Nicolaj, Giovanna. "Il documento privato italiano nell'Alto Medioevo." In *Libri e documenti d'Italia: dai Longobardi alla rinascita delle città*. Atti del Convegno dell'Associazione Italiana dei Paleografi e Diplomatisti. Cividale del Friuli (UD), 5–7 ottobre 1994, edited by Cesare Scalon, 153–98. Udine: Arti grafiche friulane, 1996.

Nicolaj, Giovanna. "Fratture e continuità nella documentazione fra tardo antico e alto medioevo. Preliminari di diplomatica e questioni di metodo." In *Morfologie sociali e culturali in Europa fra tarda antichità e alto medioevo, Settimane di studio del centro italiano di studi sull' alto medioevo* 45, edited by CISAM, 963–84. Spoleto: CISAM, 1998.

Nikolov, Angel [Ангел Николов]. *Политическ амисъл в ранносредновековна България* [*Political Thought in Early Medieval Bulgaria*]. Sofia: Paradigma, 2006.

Nikolov, Georgi [Георги Николов]. *Централизъм и регионализъм в ранносредно-*

вековнаБългария [Centralization and Particularism in Early Medieval Bulgaria]. Sofia: Marin Drinov, 2005.

Nostitz-Rieneck, Robert von. "Zur Frage der Existenz eines "Liber Papiensis"." *Historisches Jahrbuch*, 11 (1890): 687–708.

O'Brien, Bruce. "From *Morðor* to *Murdrum*: the Preconquest Origin and Norman Revival of the Murder Fine." *Speculum* 71 (1996): 321–52.

O'Brien, Bruce. "Forgers of Law and Their Readers: The Crafting of English Political Identities between the Norman Conquest and the Magna Carta." *PS: Political Science and Politics* 43 (2010): 467–73.

O'Brien O'Keeffe, Katherine. "Body and Law in Late Anglo-Saxon England." *Anglo Saxon England* 27 (1998): 209–32.

Ó Cathasaigh, Tomás. *The Heroic Biography of Cormac Mac Airt*. Dublin: Dublin Institute for Advanced Studies, 1977.

Ó Cathasaigh, Tomás. *Táin Bó Cúailnge and Early Irish Law*. Dublin: Faculty of Celtic Studies, University College Dublin, 2005.

Ó Coileáin, Seán. "Mag Fuithirbe Revisited." *Éigse* 23 (1989): 16–26.

Ó Corráin, Donnchadh. "Creating the Past: The Early Irish Genealogical Tradition." *Peritia* 12 (1998): 177–208.

Ó Corráin, Donnchadh, Liam Breatnach, and Aidan Breen. "The Laws of the Irish." *Peritia* 3 (1984): 382–438.

Ó Cuív, Brian. *Catalogue of Irish Language Manuscripts in the Bodleian Library at Oxford and Oxford College Libraries*. 2 vols. Dublin: Dublin Institute for Advanced Studies, 2001.

O'Donoghue, Heather. *Skaldic Verse and the Poetics of Saga Narrative*. Oxford: Oxford University Press, 2005.

O'Donovan, John. *The Banquet of Dun na n-Gedh and the Battle of Magh Rath*. Dublin: Irish Archaeological Society, 1842.

O'Neill, Pamela. "Unravelling Time in Early Irish Law." In *Language and Power in the Celtic World: Papers from the Seventh Australian Conference of Celtic Studies, University of Sydney, September 2010*, edited by Anders Ahlqvist and Pamela O'Neill, 323–50. Sydney: University of Sydney, 2011.

Obrist, Barbara. "Wind Diagrams and Medieval Cosmology." *Speculum* 72.1 (1997): 33–84.

Ogris, Walter. "Schenkung." *Handwörterbuch der deutschen Rechtsgeschichte*, 4 (1990): 1382–84.

Oliver, Lisi. *The Body Legal in the Barbarian Law*. Toronto: University of Toronto Press, 2011.

Ong, Walter J. *Orality and Literacy. The Technologizing of the Word*. 3rd ed. London: Routledge, 2002.

Orchard, Andy. "On Editing Wulfstan." In *Early Medieval English Texts and Interpreta-*

tions: Studies Presented to Donald G. Scragg, edited by Elaine Treharne and Susan Rosser, 311–40. Medieval and Renaissance Texts and Studies 252. Tempe, AZ: Arizona Center for Medieval and Renaissance Studies, 2002.

Orchard, Andy. "Re-editing Wulfstan: Where's the Point?" In *Wulfstan, Archbishop of York: The Proceedings of the Second Alcuin Conference*, edited by Matthew Townend, 63–91. Studies in the Early Middle Ages 10. Turnhout: Brepols, 2004.

Orning, Hans Jacob. *Uforutsigbarhet og nærvær: En analyse av norske kongers maktutøvelse i høymiddelalderen*. Oslo: Unipub, 2004.

Orning, Hans Jacob. "Conflict and Social (Dis)order in Norway, c. 1030–1160." In *Disputing Strategies in Medieval Scandinavia*, edited by Kim Esmark, Lars Hermanson, Hans Jacob Orning and Helle Vogt, 45–82 Leiden: Brill, 2013.

Oulion, Rémi. *Scribes et notaires face à la norme dans la Toscane du haut Moyen Âge (VII–XI siècle)*. Clermont-Ferrand: Institute Universitaire Varenne, 2013.

Owen, Morfydd. "Llawysgrif Gyfreithiol Goll." *Bulletin of the Board of Celtic Studies* 22 (1966–68): 338–43.

Paetow, Louis J. *The Arts Course at Medieval Universities with Special Reference to Grammar and Rhetoric*. Champaign, IL: University of Illinois Studies, 1910.

Parker-Pearson, Mike. "The Powerful Dead: Archaeological Relationships Between the Living and the Dead." *Cambridge Archaeological Journal* 3, no. 02 (1993): 203–29.

Parkes, Malcolm B. "The Influence of the Concepts of *Ordinatio* and *Compilatio* on the Development of the Book." In *Medieval Learning and Literature. Essays Presented to Richard William Hunt*, edited by Jonathan James G. Alexander and Margaret T. Gibson, 115–41. Oxford: Clarendon Press, 1976.

Parkes, Malcolm B. *Scribes, Scripts and Readers: Studies in the Communication, Presentation and Dissemination of Medieval Texts*. London: Hambledon Press, 1991.

Parkes, Malcolm B. *Their Hands Before Our Eyes: A Closer Look at Scribes: The Lyell Lectures Delivered in the University of Oxford, 1999*. Oxford: Ashgate, 2008.

Parvanov, Petar. "Medieval Deviant Burials from Bulgaria (7th–14th c.)". Master's thesis, Central European University, 2016.

Parvanov, Petar. "A Tale of Two Graves: Rethinking the Medieval Reuse of Prehistoric Burial Mounds in Madara." *Annual of Medieval Studies at CEU*, 23 (2017): 11–19.

Parvanov, Petar. "The Mass Grave from Devnya and the Judicial Culture in Early Medieval Bulgaria." In *(Re)lecture archéologique de la justice en Europe médiévale et modern*, edited by Matthieu Vivas, 279–294. Bordeaux: Ausonius, 2019.

Patetta, Federica. *Le Ordalie. Studio di Storia del Diritto e Scienza del Diritto Comparato*. Turin: Fratelli Bocca Editori, 1890.

Patetta, Federica. "Nuove ipotesi sulla patria della così detta Lombarda." In *Studi sulle fonti giuridiche medievali*, edited by Guido Astuti, 927–56. Turin: Bottega d'Erasmo, 1967; reprinted from *Festschrift Heinrich Brunner zum siebzigsten Geburtstag dargebracht von Schülern und Verehrern*, 349–78. Weimar: H. Böhlaus Nachfolger, 1910.

Patzold, Steffan. *Episcopus: Wissen über Bischöfe im Frankenreich des späten 8. bis frühen 10. Jahrhunderts*. Ostfildern: Jan Thorbecke Verlag, 2008.

Pearsall, Derek, ed. *New Directions in Later Medieval Manuscript Studies: Essays from the 1998 Harvard Conference*. York: York Medieval Press, 2000.

Peters, Edward. "The Sacred Muses and the Twelve Table: Legal Education and Practice, Latin Philology and Rhetoric, and Roman History." In *Law as Profession and Practice in Medieval Europe. Essays in Honour of James A. Brundage*, edited by Kenneth Pennington and Melodie H. Eichbauer, 137–51. Farnham: Ashgate, 2011.

Petrova, Galabina [ГълабинаПетрова]. "Въпроси на наказателното право в Средновековна България. [Issues of Penal Law in Medieval Bulgaria]." *Правна мисъл* 2 (2002): 3–20.

Petrucci, Armando. "Censimento dei codici dei secoli XI–XII. Istruzioni per la datazione." *Studi Medievali*, s. III, IX (1968): 1115–17.

Petrucci, Armando, and Carlo Romeo. *"Scriptores in Urbibus". Alfabetismo e cultura scritta nell' Italia altomedievale*. Bologna: Il Mulino, 1992.

Petrunova, Boni [Бони Петрунова]. "Некрополите от XIII–XVII в. Като източник за практикуването на обредите против превъплъщаване [Cemeteries from 13th–17th Century as a Source on Practicing Rituals Against Transfiguration after Death]." In *Конфесия и фолклор*, edited by Rossen Malchev and Konstantin Rangochev, 67–76 Sofia: ROD, 1998.

Pisarev, Atanas [Атанас Писарев]. "Църква 18 на хълма Царевец в Търново [Church 18 on the Tsarevets hill]." *Годишник на музеите в Северна България* 6 (1981): 18–37.

Pocock, John G.A. "Texts as Events." In *The Politics of Discourse: The Literature and History of Seventeenth-Century England*, edited by Kevin Sharpe and Steven N. Zwicker, 29–33. London: University of California Press, 1987.

Pohl, Walter. "Memory, Identity and Power in Lombard Italy." In *The Use of the Past in the Early Middle Ages*, edited by Yitzah Hen and Matthew Innes, 9–28. Cambridge: Cambridge University Press, 2000.

Pohl, Walter. "Leges Langobardorum." *Reallexicon Germanischen Altertumskunde* 18 (2001): 208–13.

Pohl, Walter. "Identità etniche nei ducati di Spoleto e Benevento." In *I Longobardi dei Ducati di Spoleto e Benevento*, Atti del XVI Congresso internazionale di Studi sull'alto Medioevo, Spoleto, 20–23 ottobre 2002, Benevento, 24–27 ottobre 2002, edited by CISAM, 79–103. Spoleto: CISAM, 2003.

Pohl, Walter. "La discussa identità etnica dei Longobardi." In *I Longobardi e le Alpi*, Atti della Giornata di Studio "Clusae Longobardorum, i Longobardi e le Alpi," Chiesa di San Michele, 6 marzo 2004, edited by CRISM (Centro di Ricerca sulle Istituzioni e le Società Medievali), 13–24. Susa: Segusium, 2005.

Pohl-Resl, Brigitte. "Ethnische Bezeichnungen und Rechtsbekenntnisse in langobardischen Urkunden." In *Ethnogenese und Überlieferung. Angewandte Methoden der Frühmittelalterforschung*, edited by Karl Brunner and Brigitte Merta, 163–171. Vienna: Veröffentlichungen des Instituts für Österreichische Geschichtsforschung, 1994.

Pohl-Resl, Brigitte. "Legal Practice and Ethnic Identity in Lombard Italy." In *Strategies of Distinction: The Construction of Ethnic Communities 300–800*, edited by Walter Pohl and Helmut Reimitz, 205–19. Leiden: Brill, 1998.

Pokorny, Julius. *Indogermanisches Etymologisches Wörterbuch*. Bern: Francke, 1959.

Polcyn, Marek, and Elzbieta Gajda. "Buried with Sickles: Early Modern Interments from Drawsko, Poland." *Antiquity* 89/348 (2015): 1384–86.

"Political History." In *A History of the County of Middlesex: Volume 2*, edited by William Page, 15–60. London: Victoria County History, 1911. https://www.british-history.ac.uk/vch/middx/vol2/pp15-60.

Pollard, Albert F. "Petrie, (Frederick) Henry (*bap.* 1772, *d.* 1842)." In *Oxford Dictionary of National Biography*, rev. Bernard Nurse. Oxford University Press, 2004, online ed., Jan. 2008. Accessed January 16, 2017. http://www.oxforddnb.com/view/article/22052.

Pollard, Graham. "The *pecia* System in the Medieval Universities." In *Medieval Scribes, Manuscripts and Libraries. Essays Presented to N. R. Ker*, edited by Malcolm B. Parkes and Andrew G. Watson, 145–62. London: Scolar Press, 1978.

Popkonstantinov, Kazimir, and Rossina Kostova. "Minorities and Foreigners in Bulgarian Medieval Towns in the Twelfth to Fourteenth Centuries: Literary and Archaeological Fragments." In *Segregation—Integration—Assimilation: Religious and Ethnic Groups in the Medieval Towns of Central and Eastern Europe*, edited by Derek Keene, Balázs Nagy, and Katalin Szende, 133–49. Farnham: Ashgate, 2009.

Poppe, Erich. "*Grammatica, Grammatic*, Augustine, and the *Táin*." In *Ildánach Ildírech: A Festschrift for Proinsias Mac Cana*, edited by John Carey, John T. Koch, and Pierre-Yves Lambert, 203–10. Andover: Celtic Studies Publications, 1999.

Poppe, Erich. "Latinate Terminology in Auraicept na n-Éces." In *History of Linguistics 1996, Volume 1. Traditions in Linguistics Worldwide*, edited by David Cram, Andrew Robert Linn, and Elke Nowak, 191–201. Amsterdam: John Benjamins Publishing, 1999.

Posner, Richard A. "Medieval Iceland and Modern Scholarship (reviewing William Ian Miller, Bloodtaking and Peacemaking: Feud, Law and Society in Saga Iceland (1990))," *Michigan Law Review* 90 (1992): 1495–1511.

Post, Gaines. *Studies in Medieval Legal Thought. Public Law and the State, 1100–1322*. Princeton NJ: Princeton University Press, 1964.

Powell, Kathryn. "The 'Scipmen' Scribe and Cambridge, Corpus Christi College 383." *The Heroic Age* 14 (2010). http://www.heroicage.org/issues/14/powell.php.

Powicke, F. Maurice. *Stephen Langton: Being the Ford Lectures Delivered in the University of Oxford in Hilary Term 1927*. Oxford: Clarendon Press, 1928.

Qiu, Fangzhe. "Wandering Cows and Obscure Words: a Rimeless Poem from Legal Manuscripts and Beyond." *Studia Celtica Fennica* 10 (2013): 90–111.

Qiu, Fangzhe. "Narratives in Early Irish Law: A Typological Study." In *Medieval Irish Law: Texts and Contexts*, edited by Anders Ahlqvist and Pamela O'Neill, 111–41. Sydney: University of Sydney, 2013.

Qiu, Fangzhe. "Narratives in Early Irish Law Tracts." PhD thesis, University College Cork, 2015.

Qiu, Fangzhe. "Manuscript Contexts of Early Irish Law Tracts: A Case Study on *Uraicecht Becc*." *Proceedings of the Harvard Celtic Colloquium* 35 (2015): 150–71.

Qiu, Fangzhe. "The Ulster Cycle in the Law Tracts." In *Ulidia 4: Proceedings of the Fourth International Conference on the Ulster Cycle of Tales*, edited by Mícheál Ó Mainnín and Gregory Toner, 9–22. Dublin: Four Courts Press, 2017.

Rabin, Andrew. *The Political Writings of Archbishop Wulfstan of York*. Manchester: University Press, 2015.

Radding, Charles M. *The Origins of Medieval Jurisprudence: Pavia and Bologna, 850–1150*. New Haven, CT/London: Yale University Press, 1988.

Radding, Charles M. "*Petre te appellat Martinus*: Eleventh-Century Judicial Procedure as Seen Through the Glosses of Walcausus." In *La Giustizia nell'alto medioevo II (secoli IX–XI), 11–17 aprile 1996, Settimane di studio del centro italiano di studi sull'alto medioevo* 44 (1997), 827–61.

Radding, Charles M. "Legal Theory and Practice in Eleventh-Century Italy." *Law and History Review* 21 (2003): 377–81.

Radding, Charles M. "Reviving Justinian's *Corpus*: The Case of the Code." In *Law Before Gratian: Law in Western Europe c. 500–1100*, edited by Per Andersen, Mia Münster-Swendsen, and Helle Vogt, 35–50. Copenhagen: DJØF Publishing, 2007.

Radding, Charles M. "Law Books." In *The European Book in the Twelfth Century*, edited by Erik Kwakkel, 293–310. Cambridge: Cambridge University Press, 2018.

Radding, Charles M. "Legal Manuscripts in Eleventh-Century Italy: From Royal Edict to Scholarly Compilation." In *Organizing the Written Word: Scripts, Manuscripts and Texts. Proceedings of the First Utrecht Symposium on Medieval Literacy, Utrecht 5–7 June 1997*, edited by Marco Mostert. Turnhout: Brepols, forthcoming.

Radding, Charles, and Antonio Ciaralli. *The Corpus Iuris Civilis in the Middle Ages: Manuscripts and Transmission from the Sixth Century to the Juristic Revival*. Leiden: Brill, 2007.

Rainis, Giulia. "Per la storia della schiavitù femminile nell'Italia longobarda. Prassi contrattuale e quadri legislativi." *Studi Medievali* 48 (2007): 721–52.

Raith, Joseph, ed. *Die Altenglischen Version des Halitgar'schen Bussbuches. Bibliothek der angelsächsischen Prosa XIII*. Hamburg: Henri Grand, 1933.

Ramsay, Nigel. "Law." In *The Cambridge History of the Book in Britain. Volume 2: 1100–1400*, edited by Nigel Morgan and Rodney M. Thomson, 250–90. Cambridge: Cambridge University Press, 2008.

Rashev, Rasho. *Българската езическа култура VII–IX век* [Bulgar Pagan Culture 7th–9th Century]. Sofia: Класика и стил, 2008.

Rees, William. *South Wales and the March, 1284–1415*. Oxford: Oxford University Press, 1924.

Reichel, Oswald J. *The Canon Law of Church Institutions*, vol. 1. London: Society for Promoting Christian Knowledge, 1922.

Reinhard, Ben. "Cotton Nero A.i and the Origins of Wulfstan's *Polity*." *Journal of English and Germanic Philology* 119.2 (2020): 175–89.

Review of *Brut y Tywysogion*, *Archaeologia Cambrensis*, 3rd ser., 25 (1861): 93–103.

Reynolds, Andrew. *Anglo-Saxon Deviant Burial Customs*. Oxford: Oxford University Press, 2009.

Reynolds, Andrew. "Judicial Culture and Social Complexity: A General Model from Anglo-Saxon England." *World Archaeology* 45:5 (2013): 699–713.

Reynolds, Susan. "The Emergence of Professional Law in the Long Twelfth Century." *Law and History Review* 21 (2003): 347–66.

Rhee, Florus van der. *Die germanischen Wörter in den langobardischen Gesetzen*. Rotterdam: Bronder, 1970.

Richards, Mary P. "The Manuscript Contexts of the Old English Law: Tradition and Innovation." In *Studies in Earlier Old English Prose*, edited by Paul E. Szarmach, 171–92. New York: SUNY Press, 1986.

Richardson, Henry G. "Letters of the Oxford *Dictatores*." In *Formularies Which Bear on the History of Oxford c.1204–1420*, edited by Herbert E. Salter, William A. Pantin, and Henry G. Richardson, 2:329–450. 2 vols. Oxford: Clarendon Press, 1942.

Richter, Michael. *The Formation of the Medieval West: Studies in the Oral Culture of the Barbarians*. New York: Saint Martin's, 1994.

Richthofen, Karl von. *Untersuchungen über friesische Rechtsgeschichte*, 3 vols. Berlin: Wilhelm Hertz, 1882–1886.

Rindal, Magnus. "No. 1154 Folio in the Old Royal Collection, Copenhagen." In *King Magnus Håkonsson's Laws of Norway and other legal texts*, edited by Knut Berg and Magnus Rindal, 18–25. Oslo: Selskapet til Utgivelse av gamle Norse håndskrifter, 1983.

Rindal, Magnus. "Dei norske mellomalderloverne. Alder, overlevering, utgåver," in *Skriftlege kjelder til kunnskap om nordisk mellomalder*, 7–20. Oslo: Noregs forskningsråd, 1995.

Rindal, Magnus. "The History of Old Nordic Manuscripts II: Old Norwegian (incl. Faroese)." In *The Nordic Languages: An International Handbook of the History of the North Germanic Languages*, edited by Oskar Bandle, Kurt Braunmüller, Ernst Hakon Jahr, Allan Karker, Hans-Peter Naumann, Ulf Telemann, Lennart Elmevik, and Gun Widmark, 801–08. Berlin: De Gruyter, 2002.

Rio, Alice. *Legal Practice and the Written Word in the Early Middle Ages*. Cambridge: Cambridge University Press, 2009.

Roberts, Sara Elin. "Creu Trefn o Anhrefn: Gwaith copïydd Testun Cyfreithiol." *Cylchgrawn Llyfrgell Genedlaethol Cymru* 32 (2002): 397–420.

Roberts, Sara Elin. "Plaints in Mediaeval Welsh Law." *The Journal of Celtic Studies* 4 (2004): 219–61.

Roberts, Sara Elin. "More Plaints in Medieval Welsh Law." *Studia Celtica* 48 (2014): 171–99.

Robinson, Pamela. "The "Booklet": a Self-Contained Unit in Composite Manuscripts." *Codicologica* 3 (1980): 46–69.

Round, John H. *The Commune of London and Other Studies*. Westminster: Archibald Constable, 1899.

Russell, Paul. "The Sounds of a Silence: The Growth of Cormac's Glossary." *Cambridge Medieval Celtic Studies* 15 (Summer 1988): 1–30.

Russell, Paul. "Scribal (In)Competence in Thirteenth-Century North Wales: The Orthography of the Black Book of Chirk (Peniarth MS. 29)." *National Library of Wales Journal* 29 (1995–6): 129–76.

Russell, Paul. "Laws, Glossaries and Legal Glossaries in Early Ireland." *Zeitschrift für celtische Philologie* 51 (1999): 85–115.

Russell, Paul. "'What was Best of Every Language': The Early History of the Irish Language." In *Prehistoric and Early Ireland*, edited by Dáibhí Ó Cróinín, 405–50. New history of Ireland 1. Oxford: Oxford University Press, 2005.

Russell, Paul. "Quasi: Bridging the Etymological Gap in Early Irish Glossaries." In *A Companion in Linguistics: A Festschrift for Anders Ahlqvist on the Occasion of His Sixtieth Birthday*, edited by Bernadette Smelik, Carmiel Hamans, Rijcklof Hofman, and David Cram, 49–62. Nijmegen: De Keltische Draak, 2005.

Sadourny, Alain. "Les marchands normands en Angleterre au lendemain de la conquête de 1204." *Les Cahiers d'études médiévales de l'Université de Rouen* 1 (1979): 133–44.

Salvesen, Helge. "The Strength of Tradition: A Historiographical Analysis of Research into Norwegian Agrarian History during the Later Middle Ages." *Scandinavian Journal of History* 7 (1982): 75–133.

Sandvik, Gudmund. "Sættargjerda i Tunsberg og kongens jurisdiksjon." In *Samfunn, rett ok rettferdighet. Festskrift til Torstein Eckhoffs 70-årsdag*, edited by Anders Bratholm, Torkel Opsahl, and Magnus Aarbakke, 563–85. Oslo: Tano, 1986.

Sandvik, Guðmund, and Jón Viðar Sigurðsson. "Laws." In *A Companion to Old Norse–Icelandic Literature and Culture*, edited by Rory McTurk, 223–44. Oxford: Blackwell, 2005.

Sayers, Jane. "The Procedure of the Courts of the Judges Delegate." In *Law and Records in Medieval England—Studies on the Medieval Papacy, Monasteries and Records*. London: Variorum Reprints, 1988.

Sayers, Jane. "Marlborough, Thomas of (d. 1236), Historian, Lawyer, and Abbot of Evesham." *Oxford Dictionary of National Biography*. Accessed December 11, 2017. http://www.oxforddnb.com/view/10.1093/ref:odnb/9780198614128.001.0001/odnb-9780198614128-e-18077.

Saxe, Arthur. "Social Dimensions of Mortuary Practices." PhD thesis, University of Michigan. Ann Arbor, University Microfilms Inc., 1970.

Scardigli, Piergiuseppe. "Appunti longobardi." In *Goti e Longobardi. Studi di Filologia Germanica*, 191–246. Rome: Istituto italiano di Studi germanici, 1987. Reprinted in *Filologia e critica. Studi in onore di Vittorio Santoli*, edited by Paolo Chiarini, 91–131. Rome: Bulzoni Editore, 1976.

Scardigli, Piergiuseppe. "All'origine dei longobardismi in italiano." In *Goti e Longobardi. Studi di Filologia Germanica*, 269–93. Rome: Istituto italiano di Studi germanici, 1987. Reprinted in *Sprachliche Interferenz. Festschrift für Werner Betz zum 65. Geburtstag*, edited by Herbert Kolb and Hartmut Lauffer, 335–54. Tübingen: Max Niemeyer Verlag, 1977.

Scardigli, Piergiuseppe. "Le parole longobarde per l'ecdotica dell'Editto di Rotari." In *Goti e Longobardi. Studi di Filologia Germanica*, 303–29. Rome: Istituto italiano di Studi germanici, 1987. Reprinted in *Medioevo e Rinascimento. Annuario del Dipartimento di Studi sul Medioevo e il Rinascimento dell'Università di Firenze* 1 (1987): 53–73.

Scardigli, Piergiuseppe. "Von Langobardischen Königen und Herzögen: Möglichkeiten und Grenzen der Namenkundlichen Betrachtungsweise." In *Die Langobarden: Herrschaft und Identität*, edited by Walter Pohl and Peter Erhart, 446–75. Vienna: Verlag der Österreichischen Akademie der Wissenschaften, 2005.

Schaller, Hans Martin, ed. *Handschriftenverzeichnis zur Briefsammlung des Petrus de Vinea*. Hannover: Hahn, 2002.

Schmale, Franz-Josef. "Der Briefsteller Bernhards von Meung." *Mitteilungen des Instituts für Österreichische Geschichtsforschung* 66 (1958): 1–28.

Schmale, Wolfgang. *Archäologie der Grund- and Menschenrechte in der Frühen Neuzeit. Ein Deutsch–FranzösischesParadigma*. Munich: R. Oldenbourg Verlag, 1997.

Schöll, Rudolf, and Wilhelm Kroll, eds. *Novellae Constitutiones*. Berlin: Weidmann, 1895.

Schupfer, Francesco. *Manuale di storia del diritto italiano*. vol. 1, *Leggi e Scienza*. Città di Castello: S. Lapi, 1904.

Schützeichel, Rudolf. *Althochdeutsches Wörterbuch*. 7. Aufl. Berlin: De Gruyter, 2012.

Schwaibold, Matthias. *Brocardica. 'Dolum per subsequentia purgari'. Eine englische Sammlung von Argumenten des römischen Rechts aus dem 12. Jahrhundert*. Frankfurt: Klostermann, 1985.

Schwarz, Wolfgang. "Die Stätte des Upstalsbooms: die archäologische Wahrnehmung des Upstalsbooms." In *Die Friesische Freiheit des Mittelalters—Leben und Legende*, edited by Hajo van Lengen, 404–21. Aurich: Ostfriesische Landschaft, 2003.

Schwarzmaier, Hans-Martin. *Lucca und das Reich bis zum Ende des 11. Jahrhunderts*. Tübingen: Niemeyer, 1972.

Scovazzi, Marco. *Il diritto islandese nella Landnámabók*. Milan: Giuffrè, 1961.

Seip, Didrik Arup. *Norsk språkhistorie til omkring 1370*. Oslo: Aschehoug, 1955.

Selden, John. *Ad fletam dissertatio historica*. London, 1647.

Senatore, Francesco. "La storiografia cavense dall'Ottocento ad oggi. Storia del Codex Diplomaticus Cavensis." *Rassegna Storica Salernitana* IX/2, n. 18 (1992): 131–60.

Sharpe, Richard. "Dispute Settlement in Medieval Ireland: A Preliminary Inquiry." In *The Settlement of Disputes in Early Medieval Europe*, edited by Wendy Davies and Paul Fouracre, 169–89. Cambridge: Cambridge University Press, 1986.

Siewers, Alfred K. "The Bluest-Greyest-Greenest Eye: Colours of Martyrdom and Colours of the Winds as Iconographic Landscape." *Cambrian Medieval Celtic Studies* 50 (Winter 2005): 31–66.

Silano, Giulio. "Of Sleep and Sleeplessness: The Papacy and the Law, 1150–1300." In *The Religious Roles of the Papacy: Ideals and Realities 1150–1300*, edited by Christopher Ryan, 343–61. Toronto: Pontifical Institute of Medieval Studies, 1989.

Simbolotti, Chiara. "Tradizione giuridica longobarda. Un inedito frammento della Lombarda con glosse (Torino, BNU, F. IV. 1 fr. 11)." *Rivista Internazionale di Diritto Comune* 23 (2012): 223–55.

Simon-Shoshan, Moshe. *Stories of the Law: Narrative Discourse and the Construction of Authority in the Mishnah*. New York: Oxford University Press, 2012.

Simms, Katherine. "The Brehons of Later Medieval Ireland." In *Brehons, Serjeants and Attorneys: Studies in the History of the Irish Legal Profession*, edited by Daire Hogan and William Osborough, 51–75. Dublin: Irish Academic Press, 1990.

Simms, Katherine. "Charles Lynegar, the O Luinín family and the Study of Seanchas." In *A Miracle of Learning: Studies in Manuscripts and Irish Learning: Essays in Honour of William O'Sullivan*, edited by Toby C. Barnard and Dáibhí Ó Cróinín, 266–83. Aldershot: Ashgate Publishing Limited, 1998.

Sipma, Pieter. *Bijdrage tot de kennis van Het Rudolfsboek*. The Hague: Martinus Nijhoff, 1930.

Sivan, Hagith. "The Appropriation of Roman Law in Barbarian Hands: 'Roman-Barbarian' Marriage in Visigothic Gaul and Spain." In *Strategies of Distinction: The Construction of Ethnic Communities, 300–800*, edited by Walter Pohl and Helmut Reimitz, 189–203. Brill: Leiden, 1998.

Sjöblom, Tom. "Before *Geis* Became Magical: A Study of the Evolution of an Early Irish Religious Concept." *Studia Celtica* 32 (1998): 85–94.

Smalley, Beryl, and Stephen Kuttner. "The 'Glossa Ordinaria' to the Gregorian Decretals," *English Historical Review* 60, 236 (1945): 97–105.

Smith, Llinos Beverley. "The Statute of Wales, 1284," *Welsh History Review* 10 (1980): 127–54.

Snook, Ben. *The Anglo-Saxon Chancery: The History, Language and Production of Anglo-Saxon Charters from Alfred to Edgar*. Woodbridge, UK: Boydell & Brewer, 2015.

Somogyi, Péter. "A Kárpát-meden ceisarlóstemetke zésiszo káseredete [Into the Origin of Burials with Sickles in the Carpathian Basin]." *Archaeológiai Értesítő* 109 (1982): 189–202.

Sørlie, Mikjel. *En færøysk-norsk lovbok fra omkring 1310*. Bergen: Universitetsforlaget, 1964.

Spurkland, Terje. *Norwegian Runes and Runic Inscriptions*. Woodbridge, UK: Boydell & Brewer, 2005.

Stacey, Robert K. "Kilkenny, William of (d. 1256), Administrator and Bishop of Ely." *Oxford Dictionary of National Biography*. Accessed December 11, 2017. http://www.oxforddnb.com/view/10.1093/ref:odnb/9780198614128.001.0001/odnb-9780198614128-e-15527.

Stanev, Kamen [Камен Станев]. "Масов гроб 80 от Кюлевча-опит за историческа интерпретация [Mass Grave No. 80 from Kyulevcha—An Attempt for Historical Interpretation]." *История* 5–6 (2008): 58–59.

Staubach, Nikolaus. "Die *Devotio moderna* als Textgemeinschaft." In *Schnittpunkte. Deutsch-Niederländische Literaturbeziehungen im späten Mittelalter*, edited by Angelika Lehmann-Benz, Ulrike Zellmann, and Urban Küsters, 19–40. Münster: Waxmann, 2003.

Stefán Karlsson. "Helgafellsbók í Noregi." *Opuscula* iv (1970): 279–303.

Stefán Karlsson. "Lovskriver i to lande: Codex Hardenbergianus og Codex Belgsdalensis." In *Festskrift til Alfred Jakobsen*, edited by Jan Ragnar Hagland, Jan Terje Faarland, and Jarle Rønhovd, 166–84. Trondheim: Tapir, 1987.

Stefán Karlsson. "Lítið eitt um Lundarbók." In *Eivindarmál. Heiðursrit til Eivind Weyhe á seksti ára degi hansara 25. apríl 2002*, edited by Anfinnur Johansen. Tórshavn: Føroya Fróðskaparfelag, 2002.

Stein, Robert. "Seventeen: The Multiplicity of a Unity in the Low Countries." In *The Ideology of Burgundy: The Promotion of National Consciousness 1364–1565*, edited by Jonathan D.B. D'Arcy and Jan R. Veenstra, 223–62. Leiden: Brill, 2006.

Stephenson, Carl. *Borough and Town: A Study of Urban Origins in England*. Cambridge, MA: Mediaeval Academy of America, 1933.

Stephenson, Paul. *The Byzantine Balkan Frontier. A Political Study of the Northern Balkans, 900–1204*. Cambridge: Cambridge University Press, 2004.

Steuer, Heiko. "Ringgeld: Archeologisches." *Reallexicon Germanischen Altertumskunde* 25 (2003): 16–18.

Stock, Brian. *The Implications of Literacy. Written Language and Models of Interpretation in the Eleventh and Twelfth Centuries*. Princeton: Princeton University Press, 1983.

Stoffella, Marco. "Crisi e trasformazioni delle élites nella Toscana nord-occidentale nel secolo VIII: esempi a confronto." *Reti Medievali Rivista*, 8 (2007): 1–49.

Stoffella, Marco. "Donne e famiglia nella Toscana occidentale (VIII e IX secolo)." *Genesis. Rivista della società italiana delle storiche* IX/1 (2010): 85–106.

Stofnun Árna Magnússonar í íslenskum fræðum. *"Fornritin."* In *Málföng fyrir íslensku.* Accessed November 30, 2017. http://www.malfong.is/?pg=fornritin.

Stoker, David. "William Wotton's Exile and Redemption: an Account of the Genesis and Publication of *Leges Wallicae.*" *Welsh Book Studies* 7 (2006): 7–106.

Stokes, Whitley. "The Irish Ordeals, Cormac's Adventure in the Land of Promise, and the Decision as to Cormac's Sword." In *Irische Texte* 3.1, edited by Ernst Windisch and Whitley Stokes, 183–221. Leipzig: Verlag von S. Hirzel, 1891.

Stokes, Whitley. "The Annals of Tigernach." *Revue Celtique* 17 (1896): 6–33, 116–263, 337–420.

Stokes, Whitley. "The Bodleian *Amra Coluim Chille.*" *Revue Celtique* 20 (1899): 31–55, 132–83, 248–89, 400–37.

Stokes, Whitley. *The Martyrology of Oengus the Culdee: Félire Óengusso Céli Dé.* London: Harrison and Sons, 1905.

Stone, Rachel. *Morality and Masculinity in the Carolingian Empire.* Cambridge: Cambridge University Press, 2012.

Storm, Gustav. *Om Haandskrifter og Oversættelser af Magnus Lagabøters Love.* Christiania: I Commission hos Jacob Dybwad, 1878.

Storm, Gustav. *Norges Gamle Love indtil 1387. Fjerde Bind.* Christiania: Grøndal & Søn, 1885.

Stoyanova, Hristina [Христина Стоянова]. "Обредът "обезвреждане на мъртвите" в езическите некрополи (по данни от района на Плиска и Варна) [The Ritual Against Transfiguration of the Dead in the Pagan Necropoleis (Based on Data from the Area of Pliska and Varna)]." In *Изследвания по българска средновековна археология. Сборник в чест на проф. Рашо Рашев* [Studies in Bulgarian Medieval Archaeology presented to Prof. Rasho Rashev], edited by Pavel Georgiev, 156–66. Sofia: Faber 2007.

Strauch, Dieter. *Mittelalterliches Nordisches Recht bis 1500. Eine Quellenkunde.* Berlin: De Gruyter, 2011.

Stubbs, William. *Seventeen Lectures on the Study of Medieval and Modern History and Kindred Subjects.* Oxford: Clarendon Press, 1886.

Sunde, Jørn Øyrehagen. "Daughters of God and Counsellors of the Judges of Men: Changes in the Legal Culture of the Norwegian Realm in the High Middle Ages." In *New Approaches to Early Law in Scandinavia*, edited by Stefan Brink and Lisa Collinson, 131–83. Turnhout: Brepols, 2014.

Supino Martini, Paola. "Le sottoscrizioni testimoniali lucchesi al documento italiano del secolo VIII: le carte di Lucca." *Bollettino dell'Istituto storico italiano per il medioevo e Archivio muratoriano* 98 (1992): 87–108.

Supino Martini, Paola. "Cultura grafica nella Langobardia maior." In *Visigoti e Longo-*

bardi, edited by Paolo Delogu and Javier Arce, 371–89. Florence: All'insegna del Giglio, 2001.

Svennung, Josef. *Scadinavia und Scandia: Lateinisch-nordische Namenstudien*. Acta Societatis Litterarum Humaniorum Regiae Upsaliensis 44:1. Uppsala: Almqvist & Wiksells, 1963.

Sverrir Tómasson. "The History of Old Nordic Manuscripts I: Old Icelandic." In *The Nordic Languages: An International Handbook of the History of the North Germanic Languages*, edited by Oskar Bandle, Kurt Braunmüller, Ernst Hakon Jahr, Allan Karker, Hans-Peter Naumann, Ulf Telemann, Lennart Elmevik, and Gun Widmark, 793–801. Berlin: De Gruyter, 2002.

Štefan, Ivo, Petra Stránská, and Hana Vondrová. "The Archaeology of Early Medieval Violence: The Mass Grave at Budeč, Czech Republic." *Antiquity* 90 (2016): 759–76.

Tabacco, Giovanni. "Manzoni e la questione longobarda." In *Manzoni e l'idea di letteratura*, Atti del convegno di Torino 5–7 dicembre 1985, edited by Liceo linguistico Cadorna, 47–57. Turin: Tirrenia Stampatori, 1987.

Taranger, Absalon. "The Meaning of the Words Óðal and Skeyting in the Old Laws of Norway." In *Essays in Legal History read before the International Congress of Historical Studies held in London in 1913*, edited by Paul Vinogradoff, 159–73. London: Oxford University Press, 1913.

Tatlock, John S.P. *The Legendary History of Britain: Geoffrey of Monmouth's Historia Regum Britanniae and its Early Vernacular Versions*. Berkeley, CA: University of California Press, 1950.

Thurneysen, Rudolf. "Mittelirische Verslehren." In *Irische Texte* 3.1, edited by Whitley Stokes and Ernst Windisch, 1–182. Leipzig: Verlag von S. Hirzel, 1891.

Tipping, H.A. "Baldock, Ralph (d. 1313), Administrator and Bishop of London." *Oxford Dictionary of National Biography*. Accessed December 11, 2017. http://www.oxforddnb.com/view/10.1093/ref:odnb/9780198614128.001.0001/odnb-9780198614128-e-1154.

Tittle, Charles M. *Control Balance: Toward a General Theory of Deviance*. Boulder, CO: Westview Press, 1995.

Toner, Gregory. "The Ulster Cycle: Historiography or Fiction?" *Cambrian Medieval Celtic Studies* 40 (Winter 2000): 1–20.

Toner, Gregory. "Reconstructing the Earliest Irish Text Tale Lists." *Éigse* 32 (2000): 88–120.

Torfinn Tobiassen. "Tronfølgelov og Privilegiebrev." *Historisk Tidskrift* 43 (1964): 181–273.

Torfinn Tobiassen. "Lagman: Norge." *Kulturhistorisk Leksikon for nordisk middelalder*, edited by Johannes Brønsted et al., 10:153–62. 22 vols. Copenhagen, Gyldendal, 1965.

Tranter, Stephen Norman. *Sturlunga Saga: The Rôle of the Creative Compiler*. Frankfurt: Peter Lang, 1987.

Tria, Luigi. "La disciplina giuridica del matrimonio secondo le consuetudini di terra di Bari." *Iapigia*, anno VII, fasc. IV (1937): 404–15.

Trilling, Renée. "Sovereignty and Social Order." In *The Bishop Reformed: Studies of Episcopal Power and Culture in the Central Middle Ages*, edited by John S. Ott and Anna Trumbore Jones, 58–85. Aldershot: Ashgate, 2007.

Tristram, Hildegard L.C. "Warum Cenn Faelad sein 'Gehirn des Vergessens' verlor—Wort und Schrift in der älteren irischen Literatur." In *Deutsche, Kelten und Iren: 150 Jahre deutsche Keltologie*, 207–48. Hamburg: Buske, 1990.

Tuori, Kaius. *Lawyers and Savages: Ancient History and Legal Realism in the Making of Legal Anthropology*. Abingdon: Routledge, 2015.

Turner, Ralph V. *King John*. London: Longman, 1994.

Ullmann, Walter. "On the Influence of Geoffrey of Monmouth in English History." In *The Church and the Law in the Earlier Middle Ages: Selected Essays*, 257–76. London: Variorum Reprints, 1975.

Vaan, Michiel de. *The Dawn of Dutch. Language Contact in the Western Low Countries before 1200*. Amsterdam: John Benjamins, 2017.

Val de Lièvre, Anton. *Launegild und Wadia: eine Studie aus dem langobardischen Rechte*. Innsbruck: Wagner, 1877.

Valenti, Filippo. "Il documento medioevale. Nozioni di diplomatica generale e di cronologia." In *Scritti e lezioni di archivistica, diplomatica e storia istituzionale*, edited by Daniela Grana, 225–302. Pubblicazioni degli Archivi di Stato, Saggi 57. Città di Castello: Ediprint, 2000.

Vallerani, Massimo. "Scritture e schemi rituali nella giustizia altomedievale." In *Scrivere e leggere nell'alto Medioevo*, edited by CISAM, 97–149. Settimane di studio del centro italiano di studi sull'alto medioevo 59. Spoleto: CISAM, 2012.

Vazharova, Zhivka [Живка Въжарова]. *Славяни и прабългари: по данни на некрополите от VI–XI в. На територията на България* [*Slavs and Protobulgarians Based on Data from the Necropolis from Seventh to Eleventh Century on the Territory of Bulgaria*]. Sofia: БАН, 1976.

Vehse, Otto. *Die amtliche Propaganda in der Staatskunst Friedrichs II*. Munich: Münchner Drucke, 1929.

Villa, Claudio, and Francesco Lo Monaco. "Cultura e scrittura nell'Italia longobarda." In *Die Langobarden. Herrschaft und Identität*, edited by Walter Pohl and Peter Ehrhart, 503–23. Vienna: Verlag der österreichischen Akademie der Wissenschaften, 2005.

Vincent, Nicholas. "Jean sans Terre et les Normands avant 1199: le comte de Mortain à la lumière de ses chartes." In *1204. La Normandie entre Plantagenêts et Capétiens*, edited by Anne-Marie Flambard Héricher, and Véronique Gazeau, 37–56. Turnhout: Brepols, 2007.

Vinogradoff, Paul. "Transfer of Land in Old English Law." *Harvard Law Review* 20 (1907): 532–48.

Vismara, Giulio. "Gian Piero Bognetti storico dei Longobardi." In *L'età longobarda*. 1, edited by Gian Piero Bognetti, vi–xix. Milan: Giuffrè, 1967.

Vismara, Giorgio. *Storia dei patti successori*. Milan: Giuffrè, 1941. Reprint, 1986.

Vòllono, Maria. "Methodik und Probleme bei der Erfoschung des Langobardischen am Beispiel einiger juristischer Fachbegriffe: mundoald, launegild, sculdhais." In *Die Langobarden. Herrschaft und Identität*, edited by Walter Pohl and Peter Ehrhart, 477–502. Vienna: Verlag der österreichischen Akademie der Wissenschaften, 2005.

Vollrath, Hanna. "Gesetzgebung und Schriftlichkeit. Das Beispiel der angelsächsischen Gesetze." *Historisches Jahrbuch* 99 (1979): 28–54.

Vovelle, Michel. *Ideologies and Mentalities*. Translated by Eamon O'Flaherty. Cambridge: Cambridge University Press, 1990.

Vries, Oebele. *Het Heilige Roomse Rijk en de Friese vrijheid*. Leeuwarden: De Tille, 1986.

Vries, Oebele. "*Thet is ac londriucht*. Landrechte und Landrecht im mittelalterlichen Friesland." In *Directions for Old Frisian Philology*, edited by Rolf H. Bremmer Jr, Stephen Laker, and Oebele Vries, 571–87. Amsterdamer Beiträge zur älteren Germanistik 73. Amsterdam: Rodopi, 2014.

Vries, Oebele. "*Frisonica libertas*: Frisian Freedom as an Instance of Medieval Liberty." *Journal of Medieval History* 41 (2015): 229–48.

Wangerin, Laura. "Royal Feuds and the Politics of Sanctity in Anglo-Saxon England and Ottonian Saxony." *Mirabilia* 18 (2014): 78–94.

Webster, Paul. "King John and Rouen: Royal Iteration, Kingship, and the Norman 'Capital', *c.* 1199–*c.* 1204." In *Society and Culture in Medieval Rouen, 911–1300*, edited by Leonie V. Hicks and Elma Brenner, 309–37. Turnhout: Brepols, 2013.

Wehner, Donat, and Katja Grüneberg-Wehner. "Mit Stein im Mund. Ein Fall von Nachzehrerabwehr in der St. Catharinenkirche am Jellenbek, Kr. Rendsburg-Eckernförde?" *Arkæologii Slesvig / Archäologie in Schleswig* 15 (2014): 55–68.

Whitelock, Dorothy. "Archbishop Wulfstan, Homilist and Statesman." *Transactions of the Royal Historical Society* 24 (1942): 25–45.

Whitwell, Robert J. "Libraries of a Civilian and Canonist and of a Common Lawyer." *Law Quarterly Review* 21 (1905): 393–400.

Wickham, Chris. "Economic and Social Institutions in Northern Tuscany in the Eighth Century." In *Istituzioni ecclesiastiche della Toscana medievale*, edited by Chris Wickham, Mauro Ronzani, Yoram Milo, and Amleto Spicciani, 7–34. Galatina: Congedo, 1980.

Wickham, Chris. *Early Medieval Italy*. London: Macmillan Press, 1981.

Wickham, Chris. "Gossip and Resistance Among the Medieval Peasantry." *Past and Present* 160/1 (1998): 3–24.

Wickham, Chris. *Framing the Early Middle Ages. Europe and the Mediterranean: 400–800*. Oxford: Oxford University Press, 2005.

Wigmore, John H. "The Pledge-Idea: A Study in Comparative Legal Ideas." *Harward Law Review* 10, No. 6 (Jan. 25, 1897): 321–50.

Wilcox, Jonathan. "The Wolf on the Shepherds." In *Wulfstan, Archbishop of York Wulfstan, Archbishop of York: The Proceedings of the Second Alcuin Conference*, edited by Matthew Townend, 395–418. Studies in the Early Middle Ages 10. Turnhout: Brepols, 2004.

Wilcox, Jonathan, ed. *Scraped, Stroked and Bound: Materially Engaged Readings of Medieval Manuscripts*. Turnhout: Brepols, 2013.

Wiliam, Aled Rhys. "Y Deddfgronau Cymraeg," *National Library of Wales Journal* 8 (1953): 97–103.

Woolgar, Christopher M., ed. *Testamentary Records of the English and Welsh Episcopate, 1200–1413*, Canterbury and York Society 102. Woodbridge, UK: Boydell & Brewer, 2011.

Worby, Samuel. *Law and Kinship in Thirteenth-Century England*. Woodbridge, UK: Boydell & Brewer, 2010.

Wormald, Patrick. "*Lex Scripta* and *Verbum Regis*: Legislation and Germanic Kingship from Euric to Cnut." In *Early Medieval Kingship*, edited by Peter H. Sawyer and Ian N. Wood, 105–38. Leeds, Leeds University Press, 1977.

Wormald, Patrick. "Quadripartitus." In *Legal Culture in the Early Medieval West: Law as Text, Image and Experience*, 81–114. London: Hambledon Press, 1999.

Wormald, Patrick. "Archbishop Wulfstan and the Holiness of Society." In *Anglo-Saxon History: Basic Readings*, edited by David A.E. Pelteret, 191–224. Basic Readings in Anglo-Saxon England 6. New York: Garland, 2000.

Wormald, Patrick. *The Making of English Law: King Alfred to the Twelfth Century, 1: Legislation and its Limits*. Oxford: Blackwell, 1999. Reprint, 2001.

Wormald, Patrick. "The *Leges Barbarorum*: Law and Ethnicity in the Medieval West." In *Regna and Gentes: The Relationship Between Late Antiquity and Early Medieval Peoples and Kingdoms in the Transformation of the Roman World*, edited by Hans-Werner Goetz, Jörg Jarnut, and Walter Pohl, 21–55. Leiden: Brill, 2003.

Wormald, Patrick. "Archbishop Wulfstan: Eleventh-Century State Builder." In *Wulfstan, Archbishop of York: The Proceedings of the Second Alcuin Conference*, edited by Matthew Townend, 9–27. Studies in the Early Middle Ages 10. Turnhout: Brepols, 2004.

Wretschko, Alfred von, ed. *Der Traktat des Laurentius de Somercote Kanonikus von Chichester über die Vornahme von Bischofswahlen. Enstanden im Jahre 1254*. Weimar: H. Böhlaus, 1907.

Wright, Neil. *History and Literature in Late Antiquity and the Early Medieval West: Studies in Intertextuality*. Aldershot: Ashgate Publishing Limited, 1995.

Zachrisson, Torun. "The Odal and its Manifestation in the Landscape." In *Current Swedish Archaeology*, vol. 2. Edited by Mats Burström and Anders Carlsson, 219–38. Stockholm: The Swedish Archaeological Society, 1994.

Zielinski, Herbert. "Die Charta der Langobarden. Forschungsgeschichte und aktuelle Perspektiven." In *Die Privaturkunden der Karolingerzeit*, edited by Peter Erhart, Karl Heidecker and Berhard Zeller, 47–56. Dietikon/Zürich: Graf, 2009.

Ziemann, Daniel. *Vom Wandervolk zur Großmacht. Die Entstehung Bulgariens im frühen Mittelalter (7. bis 9. Jh.)*. Cologne: Böhlau, 2007.

Ziolkowski, Jan. "Cultures of Authority in the Long Twelfth Century." *Journal of English and Germanic Philology* 108 (2009): 421–48.

Zironi, Alessandro. *Il monastero longobardo di Bobbio. Crocevia di uomini, manoscritti e culture*. Istituzioni e società 3. Spoleto: CISAM, 2004.

Index of Manuscripts

Index of Legal and Regulatory Texts and Commentaries

General Index